T0327613

PRACTICAL FINANCIAL OPTIMIZATION

PRACTICAL FINANCIAL OPTIMIZATION
Decision Making for Financial Engineers

STAVROS A. ZENIOS
University of Cyprus, and
The Wharton Financial Institutions Center

BLACKWELL
Cambridge

BLACKWELL PUBLISHING
350 Main Street, Malden, MA 02148-5020, USA
9600 Garsington Road, Oxford OX4 2DQ, UK
550 Swanston Street, Carlton, Victoria 3053, Australia

The right of Stavros A. Zenios to be identified as Author of this Work has been asserted in accordance with the UK Copyright, Designs, and Patents Act 1988.

First published 2007 by Blackwell Publishing Ltd

1   2007

Library of Congress Cataloging-in-Publication Data

Zenios, Stavros Andrea.
    Practical financial optimization : decision making for financial engineers /
    Stavros A. Zenios.
p. cm.
Includes bibliographical references and index.
ISBN-13: 978-1-4051-3200-8 (hardback)
ISBN-13: 978-1-4051-3201-5 (paperback)
1. Financial engineering. 2. Finance—Mathematical models. 3. Mathematical optimization.
I. Title.

HG176.7.Z46 2007
658.15'5–dc22

2006025668

A catalogue record for this title is available from the British Library.

–

The publisher's policy is to use permanent paper from mills that operate a sustainable forestry policy, and which has been manufactured from pulp processed using acid-free and elementary chlorine-free practices. Furthermore, the publisher ensures that the text paper and cover board used have met acceptable environmental accreditation standards.

For further information on
Blackwell publishing, visit our website:
www.blackwellpublishing.com

FSC
Mixed Sources
Product group from well-managed
forests and other controlled sources
Cert no. SGS-COC-2953
www.fsc.org
© 1996 Forest Stewardship Council

To my wife Nina
and my parents Eleni and Andreas

Contents

Foreword

This volume is both a comprehensive guide to optimization techniques useful in financial decision making and a well-illustrated essay on the relationship between theory and practice. Often in practice the real problem, in complete detail, is beyond optimization. It involves more possible hypotheses about the world we face, and more degrees of freedom in the part of the world we control, than we have time to specify. The practical user of optimization techniques must write down in an explicit formal model a "small world," as Savage called it, which, on the one hand, can be solved by available techniques and, on the other hand, captures the essence of the real problem. The small world of the formal model may seem large, involving many thousands of variables and constraints, but may be dwarfed by the astronomical size of the real problem. Rigorous mathematical arguments can demonstrate that particular computational procedures will solve certain classes of problems. In contrast, there is no such demonstrable procedure for how to formulate the formal model so as to capture the essence of the real problem.

I often use simulation analysis to help decide the details of an optimization analysis to be deployed in a practical setting. For example, a client of mine runs a group of funds, the oldest of which has outperformed its benchmark eight of nine years since inception, as well as substantially outperforming on average. (The funds exploit special properties of a certain class of investments; and they are expected to continue to outperform until too many others exploit the same properties in the same way.) Prior to launch of the original fund we performed a large number of backtests that evaluated how well the contemplated fund would have done if it could have bought and sold at historical prices, taking into account estimated transaction costs and assuming the proposed fund could buy and sell a certain fraction of daily volume. Alternate runs tried out different decision parameters with respect to turnover constraint, upper bounds on the holdings of any asset or certain groups of assets, and certain parameters used in the models of covariance and expected return. Professor Zenios notes the importance of a turnover constraint in practical mean-variance optimization. The aforementioned simulations helped evaluate alternate settings of this constraint along with the settings of other decision parameters. Since the simulation model involved many securities and weekly reoptimization for many years, the combination of simulation with optimization allowed us to capture sufficient details for a practical model without formulating alternative optimization models of astronomical size. While the simulation analysis could not guarantee us the optimal settings of the decision parameters, alternate runs could evaluate alternate combinations of parameter settings, and form part of a search for a good combination.

While the real problem may always be more complex than any model of it we build, that does not necessarily imply that the largest, most complex model will serve us best. Zenios supplies the reader with a spectrum of optimization models, from simple to complex, and sage advice on how to use them.

San Diego, California   Harry M. Markowitz

Preface

> The purpose of the present study is not, as it is in other inquiries, the attainment of theoretical knowledge: we are not conducting this inquiry in order to know what virtue is, but in order to become good, else there would be no advantage in studying it. For that reason, it becomes necessary to examine the problem of actions, and to ask how they are to be performed. For the actions determine what kind of characteristics are developed.
>
> Aristotle, *Nichomachean Ethics*

Optimization is pervasive in finance. More than half a century has passed since quadratic programming was introduced in portfolio selection by Markowitz (1952), and during this period optimization techniques evolved from a theoretical tool of positive analysis to a practical tool for normative analysis. Optimization models are today at the core of decision support systems for financial engineers.

While optimization as a normative model was proposed as early as 1952, it was not until the 1980s that we saw the proliferation of optimization models in financial decision making. The catalysts for this development have been the emergence of financial engineering and the demands for enterprise-wide risk management. The need to integrate multiple interrelated risk factors of the global enterprise brought to the fore the power of optimization models. At the same time, the development of large-scale numerical optimization techniques, advances in optimization models for planning under uncertainty, and the availability of user-friendly modeling languages put optimization tools in the hands of researchers and practitioners with little background in optimization theory. Thus, the synergies between optimization tools and financial decision-making have flourished. And the symbiosis between these two disciplines is becoming more fertile in the current era of business globalization, rapid technological changes, financial innovations, and increased volatility in the financial markets.

This book gives a comprehensive account of optimization models that can be used by financial engineers to support decision making. It starts with classic mean-variance analysis and portfolio immunization, moves on to scenario-based models, and builds towards multi-period dynamic portfolio optimization. As the story unfolds, the relationships between classes of models are revealed. These are the essentials that underlie and outline the broad landscape of financial optimization; upon this basis we proceed to build real-world models and applications. In this way the reader not only acquires solid knowledge of the foundations of financial optimization, but is also exposed to large-scale models that can be grounded on these foundations.

The book is supplemented by the FINLIB library of models in an accompanying book by Consiglio, Nielsen and Zenios (forthcoming). The library contains models implemented in the high-level algebraic modeling language GAMS, complete with real-world data and ready to run on a computer where the modeling language is installed. These models are written in a way that allows users to insert their own data or to modify them to suit their problem's special circumstances.

Throughout, the emphasis is placed on practical models that can be used in normative analysis. Indeed, most of the models are currently used in actual practice. The process of deploying a model in a business environment is crucial in refining the model in ways that serve its ultimate purpose, which is to support decision making. The models in this book have benefited from several years of such refinement. The result is a collection of models well grounded in currently accepted theories of financial economics and enhanced with the 'bells and whistles' required by practitioners.

It is the balance between theoretically correct and elegant models of an approximation to the true problem, and shortcuts in modeling the unadulterated problem, that leads to practical financial optimization. This book does not claim to be the arbiter of where the balance lies. Indeed, some practitioners may find the rigor too abstract. Some academic researchers may find the treatment of some practical issues ad hoc. We yield to both sides – but agree with neither. Our goal is to provide a clear indication of where the line has been drawn. Careful readers will learn enough about the trade-offs to redraw their own lines. The models can be modified to satisfy the aesthetics of the theoretician, or to compromise under the pressures exerted on the practitioner. Either way there are pitfalls. Neither a theoretically correct model applied to the wrong problem, nor a model violating theoretical premises about the correct problem will pass the acid test of reality. The reader will develop skills to avoid the pitfalls, and learn to build models that are grounded on theory and work in practice.

While we chart a large part of the vast landscape of financial optimization, the material we provide here is not exhaustive. Related developments that are not treated in the book are discussed in extensive "Notes and References" sections at the end of each chapter. And although the bibliography we have compiled is extensive we may have missed relevant references or erred in crediting work. We are grateful to readers who bring to our attention such omissions so we can correct them in the future.

The book can be used as a textbook or as a reference book. The intended audience are advanced undergraduate, MBA, MSc or Doctoral students, and practicing financial engineers. A background in finance, equivalent to material covered in basic courses in investments and portfolio theory, is assumed, as is some exposure to optimization acquired through an introductory course in operations research or management science. The introductory material in the book can be used in a one-semester course leading to a Master degree in finance, financial mathematics or financial engineering. It is also well suited to MBA students, especially those with a technical background. Indeed, the seeds for this book lie in my teaching notes for courses I taught to MBA and senior students at the Wharton School of the University of Pennsylvania throughout the 1990s. The ideas were subsequently refined and expanded through material taught at the MSc in Finance programs at University of Cyprus, Executive MBA at the Cyprus International Institute of Management, MSc in Financial Engineering at Athens University of Economics and Business, seminars given at Algorithmics Inc. in London, Vienna and Toronto, and several short courses in London, Athens, Vienna, Milan, and Nicosia.

Readers with a background in finance and operations research will find this book a valuable reference for a wide range of topics. With the exception of the chapters on the applications the chapters are self contained. Thus, for example, the reader interested in multi-period dynamic portfolio optimization models can delve straight into the relevant chapter; he or she need not wade through the earlier material on single-period models.

Practicing financial engineers can also use this material in a cookbook fashion to customize models for their particular environment. While the book is written in a way that permits this cookbook usage, those unversed in the art and science of modeling must proceed with caution. It is easy to make mistakes when jumping straight into the execution of a recipe. Careful reading of the background material and the principles on which a model is built is strongly recommended.

When using the book as a reference, Piet Hein's admonition should be borne in mind:

> To start in a hurry
> and finish in haste
> will minimize worry
> and maximize waste. (*Grooks V*, 1973)

Organization of the book

The material in this book is organized into three main parts: Introduction, Portfolio Optimization Models, and Applications. A fourth part discusses the FINLIB library, and suggests some class projects for students.

Part I: Introduction consists of two chapters that develop the background for financial optimization models. Chapter 1 introduces the basic concepts. It defines enterprise-wide risk management, and outlines the scope of optimization models to support financial engineers in their pursuit of risk management at an enterprise-wide level. Chapter 2 gives a classification of financial risks, and introduces the basics of measuring risks and rewards for the enterprise as a whole. With a solid understanding of financial risks, and in possession of tools for measuring the risks and rewards, we move to the optimization models in Part II.

Part II: Portfolio Optimization Models. This part is the heart of the book, where models for managing the risks are developed. First the classic quadratic programming models for supporting mean-variance analysis are developed in Chapter 3, and then Chapter 4 concentrates on the early fixed-income models for portfolio immunization. Chapter 5 develops scenario optimization, a powerful and flexible tool for risk management at the enterprise-wide level as it overcomes some of the shortcomings of the earlier models. This line of analysis is extended to a dynamic multi-period setting in Chapter 6. The models in these chapters are then applied to the pervasive problem of creating indexed portfolios in Chapter 7. Chapter 8 takes us to a different part of the landscape of financial optimization models; specifically, we advance from the management of risks to the customized design of new financial products with user-specified risk profiles. Finally, Chapter 9 discusses methods for scenario generation, which provide the input data for most of the models discussed in the previous chapters.

Part III: Applications takes us from the modeling of broad classes of stylized problems in Part II, to the modeling of several diverse real-world applications. The models in this part capture policy restrictions, regulatory requirements, business objectives, and similar practical considerations. The models address international asset allocation (Chapter 10), the management of corporate bond portfolios (Chapter 11), asset and liability management for insurance policies with guarantees (Chapter 12), and problems facing individual investors in planning their finances (Chapter 13).

Part IV: Library of Financial Optimization Models describes the FINLIB library containing several of the models described in this book. It is available through the companion volume *Practical Financial Optimization: A library of financial optimization models* by Andrea Consiglio, Søren S. Nielsen and Stavros A. Zenios, Blackwell Publishers (forthcoming). The library is written in the high-level modeling language GAMS – a *General Algebraic Modeling System*. It is envisioned that companion volumes using different modeling environments will be made available in the future. This part also suggests several projects that can be used as classroom assignments for term projects. These proposed projects cover the material in all chapters of the book.

Acknowledgments

Some of the material in this book is based on my own published research, and I wish to express my appreciation to all colleagues and students from whom I have learned a great deal. Their contributions are gratefully acknowledged without implicating them in the final product.

Ron S. Dembo, Harry M. Markowitz, John M. Mulvey, and William T. Ziemba have been a constant source of encouragement and a solid sounding board for ideas, since the first conference on financial optimization I organized in Philadelphia in 1989.

Over the subsequent years I have benefited from interaction with numerous collaborators. They all have had a significant impact on my thinking on this topic, and I thank them in strictly alphabetical order: David Babbel, Andrea Beltratti, Marida Bertocchi, Jorgen Bloomval, Flavio Cocco, Andrea Consiglio, George Constantinides, Rita D'Ecclesia, Michael Dempster, Rosella Giacometti, Ben Golub, Jack Guttentag, Patrick T. Harker, Richard Herring, Martin Holmer, Norbert Jobst, Roy Kouwenberg, Helmut Mausser, Gautam Mitra, Søren S. Nielsen, Stathis Paparoditis, Georg Pflug, Dan Rosen, Anthony Santomero, David Saunders, Jaap Spronk, Nicholas Topaloglou, Hercules Vladimirou, Ton Vorst.

Among my coauthors I would like to especially thank Andrea Consiglio, the late Søren S. Nielsen, and David Saunders, who read drafts of the entire manuscript and offered extensive comments and suggestions.

Ron S. Dembo facilitated my visits to Algorithmics Inc. in Toronto, London, and Vienna as a Marie Curie Fellow of the European Commission throughout 2000. Marida Bertocchi, Georg Pflug, and Gregory Prastacos arranged for extended visits to University of Bergamo, University of Vienna, and Athens University of Economics and Business. These institutions provided not only a stimulating environment, but also the tranquility that was needed to complete significant parts of this work. The manuscript also benefited from the comments of students I taught in the MBA and PhD programs of the Wharton School at the University of Pennsylvania, University of Vienna, Technical University of Vienna, University of Cyprus, and Athens University of Economics and Business. I express my appreciation to these organizations as well as to my former and current institutions, The Wharton School at the University of Pennsylvania, Philadelphia, PA, and the University of Cyprus, Nicosia, Cyprus, for creating an environment wherein international collaborations can be fostered and where long-term undertakings, such as the writing of this book, are encouraged and supported.

This work was funded in part through European Commission contract ICA1-CT-2000-70015 establishing the *HERMES Center of Excellence on Computational Finance and Economics*, and also through research grants from the National Science Foundation (USA), Consiglio Nazionale delle Ricerche (Italy) and the Cyprus Research Promotion Foundation.

Sincere appreciation is due to the Blackwell editors, Seth Ditchick who solicited the publication of this book, George Lobell who gave it the big push, and editorial assistants Laura Stearns and Anna Oxbury who saw this project through. Their professionalism and good humor made the arduous task of book production reasonably enjoyable. Thanks for editing go to Kathy Stephanides; she did a superb job, thus allowing me to take the full credit for any remaining errors.

Family is usually the last to be thanked since family does not contribute scientifically to the scholarly work of an author. But were it not for the insistence of my wife Nina this work would have been buried under my administrative workload as the Rector of the University of Cyprus since 2002. Her support and perseverance, together with the understanding of my daughters Efy and Elena, are as much to be credited for the completion of this work as the scientific contributions of the many excellent collaborators I have had throughout the years. My special thanks go to them, and to our son Denis, who chose to arrive just in time to receive a mention in the book, but not too early to cause delays in its completion.

Nicosia and Philadelphia   Stavros A. Zenios
                                                                                   zenios.stavros@ucy.ac.cy

Text Credits

The author and publisher gratefully acknowledge the permissions granted to reproduce the copyright material in this book. Every effort has been made to trace copyright holders and to obtain their permission for the use of copyright material. The publisher apologizes for any errors or omissions in the above list and would be grateful if notified of any corrections that should be incorporated in future reprints or editions of this book.

Figures 1.2, 1.7 and 1.8 reprinted from D. Rosen and S. A. Zenios (2006), Enterprise-wide asset and liability management, in S. A. Zenios and W. T. Ziemba, editors, *Handbook on Asset and Liability Management, Volume 1, Theory and Methodology*, pp. 1–23, copyright North-Holland, Amsterdam, with permission of Elsevier.

Figure 2.12 reprinted from P. Jorion (1996), *Value at Risk: The New Benchmark for Controlling Market Risk*, copyright Irwin Professional Publishing, New York, with permission of McGraw-Hill Companies.

Figures 7.7 to 7.10 and 11.11 to 11.15 reprinted from N. J. Jobst and S. A. Zenios (2003), Tracking corporate bond indices in an integrated market and credit risk environment, *Quantitative Finance* 3:117–135, with permission of Taylor and Francis, www.tandf.co.uk.

Figures 7.2 to 7.6 reprinted from A. Consiglio and S. A. Zenios (2001), Integrated simulation and optimization models for tracking international fixed income indices, *Mathematical Programming, Series B*, 89:311–339, with permission of Springer Science and Business Media.

Figure 8.5 reprinted from D. F. Babbel and K. B. Staking (May 1991), It pays to practice ALM, *Best's Review* 92(1):1–3, with permission of the A.M. Best Co.

Figures 9.2 and 9.3, and Tables 9.1 to 9.4 reprinted from R. Kouwenberg and S. A. Zenios (2006), Stochastic programming models for asset liability management, in S. A. Zenios and W. T. Ziemba, editors, *Handbook on Asset and Liability Management, Volume 1, Theory and Methodology*, pp. 253–303, copyright North-Holland, Amsterdam, with permission of Elsevier.

Figures 10.5 and 10.6 reprinted from N. Topaloglou, H. Vladimirou, and S. A. Zenios (2002), CVaR models with selective hedging for international asset allocation, *Journal of Banking and Finance* 26:1535–1561, with permission of Elsevier.

Figures 10.1 to 10.4 reprinted from A. Beltratti, A. Laurent, and S. A. Zenios (2004), Scenario modelling of selective hedging strategies, *Journal of Economic Dynamics and Control* 28:955–974, with permission of Elsevier.

Figures 1.6 and 11.3 to 11.9 reprinted from N. J. Jobst and S. A. Zenios (Fall 2001), The tail that wags the dog: Integrating credit risk in asset portfolios, *Journal of Risk Finance*, pp. 31–43, with permission of Emerald Group Publishing Limited.

Figures 12.1 to 12.15 and Tables 12.3 to 12.5 reprinted from A. Consiglio, F. Cocco, and S. A. Zenios (forthcoming), The PROMETEIA model for managing insurance policies with guarantees, in S. A. Zenios and W. T. Ziemba, editors, *Handbook on Asset and Liability Management, Volume 2, Applications*, Handbooks in Finance, pp. 663-705, copyright North-Holland, Amsterdam, with permission of Elsevier.

Figures 13.3 to 13.17 reprinted from A. Consiglio, F. Cocco, and S. A. Zenios (2004), www.personal_asset_allocation. *Interfaces* 34(4):287–302, with permission of the Institute for Operations Research and the Management Sciences, 7240 Parkway Drive, Suite 310, Hanover, Maryland 21076, USA.

Notation

Sets and Indices

$U = \{1, 2, \ldots, n\}$ index set of available financial instruments or asset classes.

$T = \{0, 1, \ldots, \tau, \ldots T\}$ set of time periods, from today (0) until maturity (T). Unless stated otherwise in the text all time periods are of equal duration which is typically taken to be one month.

$\mathcal{K} = \{1, 2, \ldots, \kappa, \ldots, K\}$ index set of risk factors.

$\Sigma_t = \{1, 2, \ldots, S_t\}$ index set of states at period t.

$\Omega = \{1, 2, \ldots, N\}$ index set of scenarios.

i index of instrument or asset class from the set U.

t index of time periods from the set T.

j index of risk factor from the set $\mathcal{K}$.

l index of scenario from the set Ω.

Variables and Parameters

x n-dimensional vector of investments in assets, with elements x_i. The units are in percentages of the total asset value or amounts in face value; the choice of units depends on the model and is made clear in the text.

b_0 n-dimensional vector of initial holdings in assets, with elements b_{0i}.

v_t^+ cash invested in short-term deposits at period t.

v_t^- cash borrowed at short-term rates at period t.

v_0 initial holdings in risk-free asset (cash).

p^l statistical probability assigned to scenario l.

$\tilde{r}$ n-dimensional random vector of asset returns, with elements $\tilde{r}_i$.

r^l n-dimensional vector of asset returns in scenario l, with elements r_i^l.

$\tilde{r}_t$ n-dimensional random vector of asset returns at period t, with elements $\tilde{r}_{ti}$.

r_t^l n-dimensional vector of asset returns at period t in scenario l, with elements r_{ti}^l.

r_{ft} spot rate of return of the risk-free asset at period t.

$\tilde{F}$ n-dimensional random vector of cashflows from assets, with elements $\tilde{F}_i$.

F^l n-dimensional vector of cashflows from assets in scenario l, with elements F_i^l.

$\tilde{F}_t$ n-dimensional random vector of cashflows at period t, with elements $\tilde{F}_{ti}$.

F_t^l n-dimensional vector of cashflows from the assets at period t in scenario l, with elements F_{ti}^l.

$\tilde{P}$ n-dimensional random vector of prices of assets, with elements $\tilde{P}_i$.

P^l n-dimensional vector of prices of assets in scenario l, with elements P_i^l.

$\tilde{P}_t$ n-dimensional random vector of prices at period t, with elements $\tilde{P}_{ti}$.

P_t^l n-dimensional vector of prices of assets at period t in scenario l, with elements P_{ti}^l.

$\tilde{P}_t^a$ n-dimensional random vector of ask prices at period t, with elements $\tilde{P}_{ti}^a$. In order to buy an instrument the buyer has to pay the price asked by traders.

$\tilde{P}_t^b$ n-dimensional random vector of bid prices at period t, with elements $\tilde{P}_{ti}^b$. In order to sell an instrument the owner must accept the price at which traders are bidding.

P_t^{al} n-dimensional vector of ask prices at period t in scenario l, with elements P_{ti}^{al}.

P_t^{bl} n-dimensional vector of bid prices at period t in scenario l, with elements P_{ti}^{bl}.

$\tilde{I}$ random variable of the total return of a benchmark portfolio or a market index.

I^l total return of a benchmark portfolio or a market index in scenario l.

$\tilde{L}_t$ random variable liability due at period t.

L_t^l value of the liability in scenario l.

Q a conformable covariance matrix.

$\sigma_{ii'}$ covariance of random variables indexed by i and i'.

$\rho_{ii'}$ correlation of random variables indexed by i and i'.

$\bar{x}_i$ maximum holdings in asset i.

$\underline{x}_i$ minimum holdings in asset i.

Glossary of Symbols

$\mathcal{E}[\tilde{r}]$ expectation of the random variable or vector $\tilde{r}$ with respect to the statistical probabilities p^l assigned to scenarios $l \in \Omega$.

$\mathcal{E}_{\mathcal{P}}[\tilde{r}]$ or $\mathcal{E}_\lambda[\tilde{r}]$ expectation of the random variable or vector $\tilde{r}$ with respect to the probability distribution $\mathcal{P}$ or the probabilities $\lambda \in \mathcal{P}$.

$\mathcal{U}(a)$ utility function with arguments over the real numbers a.

$\bar{r}$ mean value of a random variable or vector $\tilde{r}$.

$R(x; \tilde{r})$ portfolio return as a function of x with parameters $\tilde{r}$.

$V(x; \tilde{P})$ portfolio value as a function of x with parameters $\tilde{P}$.

$\max[a, b]$ the maximum of a and b.

$\text{Prob}\,(\tilde{r} = r)$ the probability that the random variable argument $\tilde{r}$ takes the certain value r.

I a conformable identity matrix.

$\mathbf{1}$ conformable vector with all components equal to 1.

Abbreviations

ALM Asset and liability management.

APT Arbitrage Pricing Theory.

CAPM Capital Asset Pricing Model.

CBO Collateralized bond obligation.

CEexROE Certainty equivalent excess return on equity.

CEROE Certainty equivalent return on equity.

CLO Collateralized loan obligation.

CRO Chief risk officer.

CVaR Conditional Value-at-Risk.

EWRM Enterprise-wide risk management.

FHA Federal Housing Association.

LTCM Long Term Capital Management.

MAD Mean absolute deviation.

MBS Mortgage-backed security.

OAP Option adjusted premium.

OAS Option adjusted spread.

PSA Public Securities Association.

ROE Return on equity.

SPDA Single premium deferred annuities.

VaR Value-at-Risk.

List of Models

Part I

INTRODUCTION

Chapter 1

An Optimization View of Financial Engineering

> Wisdom consists in being able to distinguish among dangers and make a choice of the least harmful.
>
> Niccolò Machiavelli

1.1 Preview

In this chapter we provide the motivation for using optimization models in financial engineering. We start by introducing enterprise-wide risk management, and we describe the role of financial engineering in the management of risks at an enterprise-wide level. The scope of optimization models in enterprise-wide risk management is then given. These optimization models are the focus of the remaining chapters of the book, and we give here an overview of all the models.

1.2 Optimization in Financial Engineering

Financial engineering blends theoretical finance with computer modeling to support financial decision making in practical settings. It is both an art and a science. As an art it deals with the abstract representation of financial operations; which operation to study, how to go about describing it in the abstract, and how to align the operation at hand with the global economic environment are elements of the art. As a science it applies scientific tools to the study of its objects. The tools are mathematics and the computer. Sometimes the art and the science focus on a single innovative instrument or the investment portfolio of an individual; at other times on the management of the risks of a large enterprise.

Financial engineering is also practical. The art and the science work together, leading to functionality. Civil engineers use the laws of physics and the aesthetics of architecture to build bridges, houses, and office complexes. Financial engineers use the techniques of modern finance to design new securities, synthesize investor portfolios, and build the financial structure of institutions. And like engineers – who routinely use optimization techniques to secure the best possible structural designs for safety, stability, and cost – financial engineers use optimization models to achieve their design goals along the competing dimensions of risk and reward. Regulatory requirements, institutional policies, and investor needs must also be satisfied in efficient trade-offs.

This is a book about the optimization models used to support the decision making of financial engineers. The emphasis is on practical models, and the book is supplemented by a library of financial models – FINLIB – in a companion book by Consiglio, Nielsen and Zenios (forthcoming). The library is implemented in the high-level modeling language GAMS of Brooke, Kendrick and Meeraus (1992). The models come complete with sample real-world data, and are ready to run on a computer where the modeling language is installed. More importantly, however, these models are written in a way that allows users to insert their own data or to modify them to suit their problem's special circumstances.

This is also a book about optimization models in discrete time and not in continuous time. Continuous-time finance laid the foundation for modern portfolio and risk management theories (see Merton 1990). As Paul A. Samuelson put it in his preface to Merton's book, "through continuous time finance what had been complex approximation became beautifully simple truth." In several instances, however, the solution of practical problems requires a return to the approximation with a time-discretization of the continuous model and the subsequent numerical solution of a large-scale optimization problem. Incomplete markets in the presence of liabilities, transaction costs or other market inefficiencies, institutional policy considerations, and complex regulatory requirements also necessitate the use of discrete models. It is the models that address such practical issues that are covered in this book. Figure 1.1 illustrates the interdependencies of these two approaches to optimization models in finance, and shows where discrete time models arise.

The passage of time implies uncertainty about the future, and this plays a key role in financial engineering. The models in this book support optimal decision making in the face of uncertainty. Uncertainty is treated using discrete random variables, that is, random variables that take on values from a countable set. With each value from this set we associate a probability. Random variables will represent, for instance, asset returns, values of the liabilities, timing of events such as a default or a credit rating downgrade. The set of possible values of a discrete random variable together with the associated probabilities is a discrete distribution. We assume, in particular, that as time evolves in discrete steps, the random variables take a value from a finite set of possible values. This set is the sample space, and its elements are indexed by l from an index set Ω. The value taken by a discrete random variable, together with the associated probability is called a *scenario*.

Definition 1.2.1 Scenario. *A scenario is a value of a discrete random variable representing uncertain data together with the associated probability $p^l \geq 0$. Each scenario is indexed by l from a sample set Ω, and the probabilities satisfy $\sum_{l \in \Omega} p^l = 1$.*

Scenarios are a convenient and natural way to represent uncertainty. They can be generated in several ways, for instance, with Monte Carlo simulations, by bootstrapping historical data, or from the opinion of experts. Modern finance gives us numerous models for security pricing, and the simulation of these models provides scenario generation methods.

The use of scenarios in financial optimization models has been gaining popularity only since the late 1990s, and the use of scenario-based models to support financial decision making is still a novelty. At the same time, the use of scenarios for regulatory purposes and margin calculations has become common practice. Perhaps the best-known example is in the use of scenario-based portfolio analysis for the calculation of daily margins by the Chicago Mercantile Exchange. Their methodology, called SPAN (Standard Portfolio Analysis), estimates how a specific derivative security will gain or lose value during a holding period of one trading day under a specific set of market conditions. The market conditions evaluated by SPAN are defined in terms of changes in the price of the underlying instrument, and changes in the volatility of the underlying price. The risk scenarios used by the Chicago Mercantile Exchange are summarized in Table 1.1.

How are optimization models used for decision making in financial engineering? The answer to this question can not be fully appreciated until we describe the process of enterprise-wide risk management, and define the associated risks. We will then understand the role of financial engineering in pursuing enterprise-wide risk management strategies, and the significance of optimization models in supporting financial engineers. (The answer is deferred until Section 1.4.)

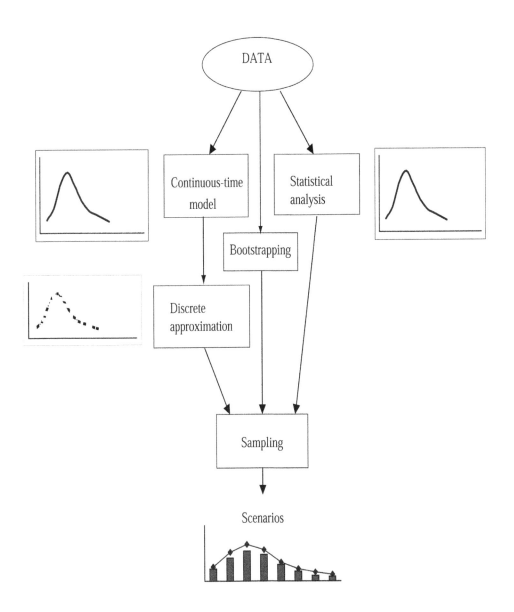

Figure 1.1: Pathways to discrete financial optimization models.

Table 1.1: The scenarios used to estimate maximum losses for a position in interest futures and the calculation of daily margins using the Chicago Mercantile Exchange's SPAN (Standard Portfolio Analysis) methodology.

Scenario	Risk Characteristics
1	Price unchanged; Volatility up.
2	Price unchanged; Volatility down.
3	Price up 1/3 the price range; Volatility up.
4	Price up 1/3 the price range; Volatility down.
5	Price down 1/3 the price range; Volatility up.
6	Price down 1/3 the price range; Volatility down.
7	Price up 2/3 the price range; Volatility up.
8	Price up 2/3 the price range; Volatility down.
9	Price down 2/3 the price range; Volatility up.
10	Price down 2/3 the price range; Volatility down.
11	Price up 3/3 the price range; Volatility up.
12	Price up 3/3 the price range; Volatility down.
13	Price down 3/3 the price range; Volatility up.
14	Price down 3/3 the price range; Volatility down.
15	Extreme scenario: price up 3 times the price range.
16	Extreme scenario: price down 3 times the price range.

As a preview we can say that optimization models in financial engineering are about managing risk by controlling the risk exposure in a way that is commensurate with the prospective rewards. Risk control means one of two things:

1. Limit or totally eliminate specific types of risk; or

2. take an active position in one or more types of risk.

As we will see, financial risks are multidimensional and very few instruments are pure in their risk profile. Modern financial instruments are exposed to more than one risk factor. Examples include instruments such as coupon-bearing bonds denominated in Euro, government bonds in emerging markets, corporate bonds and credit derivatives, Collateralized Loan Obligations (CLO) or Collateralized Bond Obligations (CBO). We will see that risk control for such instruments is a complex task. Investors must specify limits for each type of risk they wish to control, and determine each type of risk in which they take an active position. Liabilities must be paid, performance targets met, and regulatory stipulations adhered to. These requirements can be formulated through systems of equations and inequalities. In addition, corporate policies dictate an objective criterion, a goal, that must be achieved. All these taken together form the building blocks of an optimization model.

The focus of the book is on scenario-based optimization models. The models are carefully formulated step by step and all necessary definitions are provided. Some background in finance is assumed as well as some exposure to operations research at the introductory level. The book can be used by advanced undergraduate students in finance with a quantitative orientation, and by students in operations research, mathematics or computer science who have taken introductory courses in finance and investments. But the book is written primarily for the practicing financial engineer or the researcher who uses optimization models. He or she will find here several essential tools that are robust, flexible, and ready to use.

1.3   Enterprise-Wide Risk Management

Strategy is often conceptualized as the alignment of a firm with its environment. *Enterprise-wide risk management* (EWRM) is the strategy that aligns the firm's business with its uncertain environment in the pursuit of business goals and net zero exposure to the risks (see Definition 1.3.1). Broadly speaking, an organization's goal is to create economic value. Market value added is a generally accepted metric in assessing an organization's performance. However, market value added is difficult to measure and, furthermore, management cannot act directly on this quantity. Some performance metrics that are directly observable are growth and consistency of earnings, stability of cashflows, and the cost of financial distress, and there is some evidence that these metrics are proxies for market value added. However, even though these quantities are easy to measure and monitor, management cannot act directly on these metrics.

The identification of performance measures that are *actionable* – that is, management can act directly on them – remains an open issue for the service industry in general, and financial institutions in particular. It is not clear at the outset which managerial actions will improve consistency and growth of earnings, ensure cashflow stability, and reduce the cost of financial distress. A general framework that links improvements in performance with managerial decisions such as organizational forms, business strategy, process design, human resource management, use of information technology and so on, is not yet available. Such a framework would identify the drivers of performance in financial institutions, thus charting a path for specific managerial actions to improve performance metrics.

While a general framework remains elusive, there is some evidence that enterprise-wide risk management is a driver of performance. A worldwide survey of insurance firms executives, conducted by Tillinghast-Towers Perrin (Miccolis and Shah 2000), shows that a significant percentage (80%) consider EWRM useful in improving earnings growth and consistency, and in achieving other metrics perceived by the executives as indicators of performance such as revenue growth, return on capital, expense control, etc. It is fitting that EWRM today receives attention from both academia and industry, although a stronger case still needs to be made that EWRM is a significant driver of performance with measurable effects on the bottom line.

1.3.1   What is enterprise-wide risk management?

The following definition encompasses the notion of EWRM.

Definition 1.3.1 Enterprise-wide risk management (EWRM). *The strategy that aligns the firm's business with the risk factors of its environment in the pursuit of strategic objectives and neutralizes net exposure to the risks. It consists of the conceptual framework, organizational approaches and tools that integrate market, credit, liquidity, operational and business risks in achieving the organization's objectives.*

We will adopt a specialized vocabulary that reflects applications of enterprise-wide risk management to financial institutions, cognizant that enterprise-wide risk management is applicable to other businesses as well. References to risk imply financial risk, which we define next.

Definition 1.3.2 Financial risk. *The possibility that an unforeseen and unpredictable future event will result in a financial loss.*

As a consequence of the loss, an individual or institution will not meet some specified financial goals. Financial risk is characterized by the magnitude of the loss, its estimated likelihood today, and the *risk factors*, or the potential causes of the event. A classification of financial risk factors is given in Section 2.2. Risk is always in the future; current or past losses do not present a risk as there is no uncertainty about them. Similarly, future events do not pose a risk unless they are unpredictable, for otherwise we could plan for them with perfect foresight. But the unpredictability of the future does not restrict our ability to foresee plausible future events and plan for them. A hiker setting off on the trail cannot predict the weather, but this does not restrict her from noticing that certain cloud formations could bring rain (a plausible event), and thus deciding to carry foul weather gear.

The word "risk" derives from the old Italian word *risicare* which means "to dare." In this sense risk is more a choice than a chance. Risk management is the discipline that provides tools to measure risks, and techniques to help us shape and make rational decisions about them. A survey of risk management techniques used by nonfinancial firms reveals that more than half of the responding firms use derivatives in hedging their financial and other risks. The percentage exceeds 80% for the larger firms in the sample. Risk management is not restricted to financial institutions and, furthermore, the distinction between financial and other types of risk are becoming increasingly blurred. Innovations such as weather derivatives, energy derivatives, catastrophe bonds and the like transform all sorts of risks into financial risks that can be transferred, managed, or hedged. The shift from a generic vocabulary to one focusing on financial institutions adopted in this chapter does not limit the applicability of enterprise-wide risk management in the broader context.

We clarify now the concepts involved in Definition 1.3.1.

Business: A financial institution's business is to provide services for repackaging and selling risks by designing, pricing, capitalizing, funding, and marketing financial products. Financial products are contractual agreements to pay customers contingent cashflows in the future, and they are funded by the assets of the institution.

Objectives: To use the cashflows generated by the business activities, and to leverage debt or equity capital to enhance economic value through growth and consistency of earning, cashflow stability, and reduced costs of financial distress.

Market risks: The risks arising from changes in financial market prices and rates. Definitions 2.2.1–2.2.6 elaborate further on this concept.

Credit risk: The risk of an unkept payment promise when an obligor – counter-party, issuer or borrower – defaults, or when their ability to make future payments comes into question and their quality rating changes; see Definition 2.2.7.

Liquidity risks: The risks that arise when an institution is unable to raise cash to fund its business activities (*funding liquidity*), or cannot execute a transaction at the prevailing market prices due to a temporary lack of appetite for the transaction by other market players (*trading liquidity)*; see Definition 2.2.9.

Operational risks: The risks of potential losses due to human error, fraud, management failure, faulty systems or controls, corrupt data or erroneous models, and legal actions; see Definition 2.2.14.

Business risks: The risks due to volatility of volumes, margins, or costs when engaging in the firm's business; see Definition 2.2.12.

The distinguishing features of EWRM are that it takes a global view of the enterprise, and an integrated view of the risk management process. In order to properly align the firm's business with the risk factors of the environment, EWRM must take a global view of both the enterprise and the risks to which it is exposed. For instance, the credit exposure of a bank to a single counterparty may appear through different lines of business, and a global view is needed if counterparty credit risks are to be identified. Similarly, the risks of an unstable economic environment in a specific country may appear through Treasury activities in the country's bond market or currency exchange contracts; through syndicated loans and lines of credit to corporations operating in the country; or through derivative contracts underwritten by the country's banks. A global view of the firm is essential to identify country-specific risk.

Furthermore, the proper alignment of the firm's business with the risk factors of the environment requires an integrated view of the business processes. As concurrent engineering calls for the integration of engineering design, manufacturing, and marketing of products in a seamless process managed by a product team, similarly, integrated financial product management calls for the integration of the functions involved in designing, pricing, capitalizing, marketing, and funding financial products. These functions are clearly interdependent. The design of a financial product will affect its price and the asset allocation decisions for funding it, much in the same way that the design of an automobile affects the manufacturing process and, eventually, its cost. The interdependencies, and their effects on the return and risk profile of a product, can only be analyzed when considering these functions as an integral part of a process. An additional problem of managing the business portfolio appears when multiple financial products are offered by an institution. Determining the appropriate product mix and allocating the firm's capital should again take an integrated view of the risks and returns of competing lines of business.

In considering the functions that must be integrated in a process, we take first a micro-management perspective focusing only on a single line of business, and then a macro-management perspective focusing on the business portfolio. These concepts are discussed in detail after the example from banking we present next. This example provides a concrete background setting against which we discuss the general principles.

Example: Enterprise-wide view of credit risks in a bank

Credit risk is a central topic in risk management. It is estimated that the total worldwide exposure in credit risky assets – loans, corporate bonds, and credit derivatives – exceeds 30 trillion USD. With a problem of this magnitude it comes as no surprise that substantial efforts have gone into the assessment of obligor creditworthiness, pricing of credit-risky instruments, measurement and control of credit exposure, and analysis of portfolio credit losses.

For banks, in particular, credit risk appears both on the banking book and the trading book, covering various lines of business, diverse products, and customer markets. Figure 1.2 gives an enterprise-wide view of credit risk in banks. In some parts of the business, credit risk is a by-product of the market risk undertaken in the trading book by actively trading bonds, derivatives such as swaps and forwards, and credit derivatives. In other cases, such as in the traditional lending businesses, it arises from actively originating, servicing, and funding corporate loans, or supporting retail-lending operations.

True EWRM solutions for a bank are difficult to develop. The sources of credit risk as seen in Figure 1.2 are remarkably diverse. They come from small and medium business commercial loans, syndicated loans, retail mortgages and credit cards, corporate and sovereign bonds, credit derivatives, and so on. The expertise for managing these diverse risks is developed in different organizational units and credit risk management is traditionally managed in strictly compartmentalized silos. For instance, Commercial Banking manages mortgages, credit cards, and lines of credit, while the Treasury manages corporate bonds and credit derivatives.

When risk is managed in silos the bank does not have an accurate view of its credit risk exposure to a specific borrower through the line of credit extended to the borrower by Commercial Banking, and investments in its corporate bonds by the Treasury. Furthermore, credit risk has been traditionally managed separately from market risk, which has led to the emergence of different cultures within the bank. In today's global financial markets, a compartmentalized approach to risk management is not satisfactory, and banks are compelled to manage the risks in their banking and trading books in a more integrated manner adopting enterprise-wide risk management.

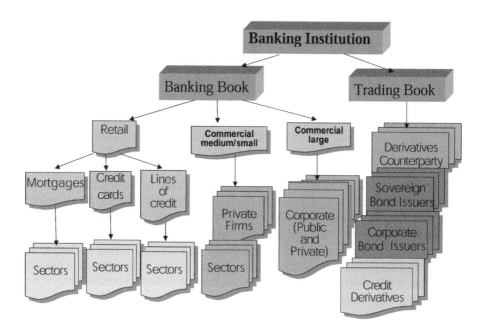

Figure 1.2: Enterprise-wide view of credit risks in a bank.

1.3.2   Enterprise-wide risk management for a single business

The business of a financial institution is to repackage financial risks, to price them, and either to transfer them to other market participants or hold them in a well-diversified portfolio. The means for engaging in this business is the sale of financial products. We consider here an institution that offers a single product. The sale of the product creates contractual obligations to pay customers cashflows in the future. The payments may be contingent on some underlying risk factors, such as an accident – in the case of insurance products; a market movement – in the case of derivative securities; snowfall – in the case of weather derivatives. The firm's financial obligations may stretch well into the future and are uncertain.

In order to align this single line of business with the risk factors of the firm's environment, management engages in the following functions: designing the product, pricing the product in a way that is consistent with its risk profile and the prices of other instruments in the financial markets, and making decisions on asset allocation and asset management to fund the product. These functions correspond to the repackaging of the risks, pricing them, and transferring or diversifying them. These functions are part of the tactical management process (see Figure 1.3) and should be managed in an integrated way.

The three functions are coordinated so that the risk-adjusted return from the process is maximized. The return calculations require prices, while risk adjustments require probability estimates and risk preferences. Probabilities of extreme events, asset prices, and preferences towards risk are the three essential data requirements of risk management. These data requirements apply to the functions of designing, pricing, and funding a product, and should be studied for the integrated process, and not for each function separately. We look at each one of the three functions and discuss how the data requirements apply.

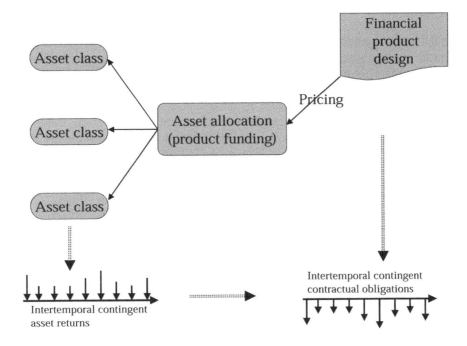

Figure 1.3: The functions of a firm offering a single product (boxes) and their interdependence in an integrated process (arrows).

Designing the product

Modern financial products are very complex. They possess multiple distinct attributes that may be attractive to different investors, but will also affect the price of the product. Consider, for instance, participating insurance policies with guarantees (Chapter 12). This product is characterized by a minimum guaranteed rate of return, a participation rate in the asset portfolio returns with the disbursement of bonuses, and surrender charges. High guaranteed returns are attractive to investors but the product may be expensive to fund. Excessively high guarantees may even lead to bankruptcy, as was the case with Nissan Mutual Life in Japan that failed on a $2.56 billion liability arising from a 4.7% guaranteed investment. Reducing the guaranteed rate and increasing the participation rate make the product less attractive but easier to fund.

The design of financial products remains an art, although extensive research has gone into explaining financial innovation for risk sharing. The probabilities associated with the risk factors underlying the product must be assessed, together with buyers' preferences, in order to arrive at a fair structure for the product and its associated price. Marketing considerations are also important in the design of financial products although not much has been done in this area either.

Pricing the product

Asset pricing is one of the great successes of modern financial economics. The ideas of Black and Scholes (1973) and Merton (1973) have spread with remarkable speed in both academia and industry. At the heart of asset pricing is the replication of complex securities by sophisticated arbitrage-free strategies involving simpler instruments. Naturally, the pricing of a new product is not independent of the design specifications discussed above. Furthermore, risk preferences are also essential for pricing in incomplete markets – such as in evaluating insurance liabilities or pension fund claims as discussed in Section 5.8.

Funding the product

Funding the financial product entails the design of an asset portfolio whose cashflow payments will replicate the contractual obligations of the product into the future and under different contingencies. Therefore, the probabilities of the risk factors, which drive price changes for both the contractual obligations and the asset portfolio, are important. Price changes in the contractual obligations and the assets must be managed following a portfolio strategy, so that assets closely replicate the obligations both across time and across states of the risk factors. Close tracking of the obligations may of course be expensive, and the institution's risk preferences guide the selection of a portfolio that trades off tracking error against excess returns.

1.3.3   Enterprise-wide risk management for a business portfolio

Financial institutions typically support multiple lines of business. In addition to resolving the tactical issues relating to the design, pricing, and funding of each line of business, the firm must deal with the strategic management of a business portfolio of multiple products. The firm's balance sheet can be viewed as a portfolio composed of assets – representing investment portfolios – and liabilities – representing specific products. The difference between asset and liability values is the firm's equity. From a macro-perspective the focus of enterprise-wide risk management is to allocate equity capital among the competing lines of business in a way that is consistent with the risks and potential rewards of the products offered by each one. Maximizing the risk-adjusted return on equity is the strategic objective in this case, which must be tempered by the need to satisfy risk-based capitalization rules and other regulatory requirements.

1.3.4   Integrating design, pricing, funding, and capitalization

The integration of the design, pricing, and funding of each product results in a process that maximizes risk-adjusted return for each product. The risk-adjusted return of a product, however, is not independent from the composition of the overall portfolio, an observation first made by Markowitz with profound implications for the theory of portfolio choice. In particular, if the risks of a product are not perfectly correlated with other risk factors in the portfolio, the overall variance of the portfolio value can be reduced. Therefore, the efficient allocation of equity capital based on the risk-adjusted return of each product must recognize that some lines of business act as natural hedges against each other. This can be achieved only if the management of the business portfolio is integrated with the management of the distinct processes at an enterprise-wide level (see Figure 1.4). The functions of designing, pricing, and funding a product are integrated into a process (see Figure 1.3) and capital allocation is determined among these competing processes (see Figure 1.4). The tactical decisions for the management of a single product provide only marginal estimates of the risk-adjusted return. However, consistency in the management of individual lines of business, by identifying the underlying risk factors and modeling them in a common framework, permits the manager to take a portfolio view when integrating the design, pricing, funding, and capitalization of multiple products.

    This analysis has identified the levers that management can pull in aligning its business with the risk factors of the environment. These are the decisions on the design and pricing of a product, allocation of assets in funding the product, and equity allocation in capitalizing the firm's lines of business. These levers are effective in aligning risk factors only when management takes a global view of the enterprise, and an integrated view of the processes involved. The traditional approach of managing risks in compartmentalized silos is not effective because it gives neither a view of the processes, nor a global view of the enterprise.

    But how are these levers to be managed? How are the design, pricing, funding and equity allocation for products to be executed? The general framework has yet to offer concrete tools to

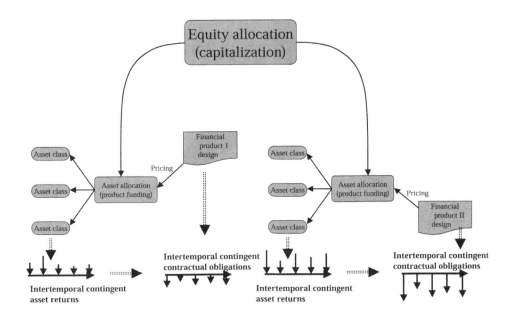

Figure 1.4: Managing a portfolio of products offered by multiple lines of business and their interdependence through integrated processes.

answer these questions and the role of optimization is not yet obvious. To provide more specific answers to these questions we discuss next the essential components that provide management with the tools to support the enterprise-wide risk management framework.

1.3.5   Components of enterprise-wide risk management

Neither academic research nor the experience of end-users and solution providers has produced a definitive description of the components comprising the enterprise-wide risk management framework. It is currently perceived that effective enterprise-wide risk management provides for the following essential components:

1. Risk measurement,
2. risk management,
3. performance measurement, and
4. corporate governance.

These components provide a broad breakdown of EWRM systems. We describe the tasks involved in each one of the four components.

Risk measurement

Risk measurement first identifies the risk factors that arise in the operation of the business and in the environment. Some risks are connected to the core activities of the firm (core exposures) and some to the facilitating activities (peripheral exposures). For instance, actuarial risk is core exposure for an insurer, while credit risk is peripheral exposure in managing the insurer's asset portfolio. For a bank, however, credit risk is the core exposure of its banking book.

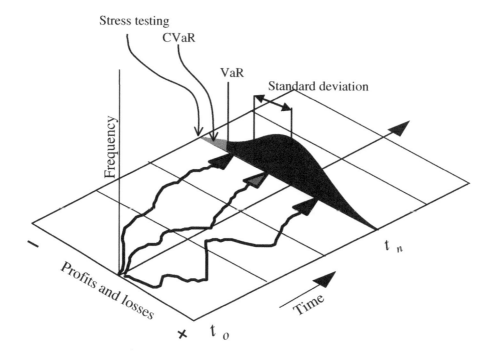

Figure 1.5: Distribution of profits and losses and the estimation of various risk measures.

Risk measurement analyzes how these separate risks interact at the enterprise level and how they influence business performance. The end product of this analysis is a distribution of profits and losses under different future realizations of the risk factors as illustrated in Figure 1.5. From this distribution various risk metrics can be computed. For instance, the classic mean-variance portfolio theory uses the variance of the distribution as a measure of risk (see Chapter 3); Value-at-Risk (VaR) estimates a left percentile as illustrated in the figure (see Definition 2.6.1); and Conditional Value-at-Risk (CVaR) measures the expected value of the losses, conditioned on the losses being in excess of VaR (see Definition 2.6.3). VaR calculations have become an industry standard for risk measurement especially in banking and asset management. Regulators also rely on them as discussed in the Basel Committee on Banking Supervision report, and they are used for assigning risk capital and monitoring risk exposures. Axiomatic characterizations of risk measures that can be used to support EWRM exist in the form of *coherent* risk measures (Definitions 2.7.1). (It is worth pointing out here, however, that the industry standard VaR is not a coherent risk measure.)

For large and complex positions the calculation of risk measures such as VaR or CVaR requires Monte Carlo simulations of the underlying risk factors, and repricing of the positions with changes in the risk factors. When estimating risk exposures for EWRM we need to recognize the multiple interrelated risk factors, and their effect on the firm's portfolio. For instance, Figure 1.6 illustrates how the distribution of returns in a portfolio of credit-risky bonds changes when multiple risk factors are simulated. Similarly, the dynamics of the risk profile should also be recognized. For instance, Figures 11.8 and 11.9 (see Chapter 11) illustrate the changing risk profile of a portfolio of credit-risky bonds for different risk horizons.

Risk analytics support the quantification of the disparate sources of risk recognizing both their interdependencies and their dependence on time. Analytics are also used to quantify business risk, such as, for instance, the contractual obligations to pension fund participants or insurance policyholders, volume changes due to policy surrenders and the like.

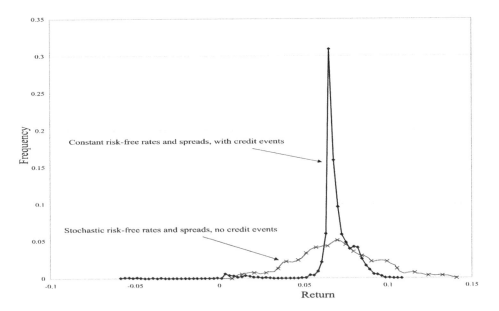

Figure 1.6: A flat-tailed distribution of returns in a portfolio of credit-risky bonds when all relevant risks are incorporated, and the bell-shaped distribution when credit rating migrations or default risks are ignored.

Risk management

The distribution of profits and losses under different future realizations of the risk factors completely specifies the risk profile of a given position or line of business. The risk profiles so identified and measured must be shaped into an overall risk profile for the institution in a way that conforms with management goals. The overall risk profile should not simply be allowed to just happen as the sum of the risk profiles of individual lines of business. Instead it should be shaped to achieve the firm's objectives, while satisfying regulatory restrictions and business policy requirements. In the most basic approach the risk profile can be shaped by controlling the risk of the individual positions by imposing limits. However, enterprise-wide risk management goes beyond this simple form of risk control. It also recognizes that different lines of business may be natural hedges against each other and offer diversification benefits, and hence it uses the financial markets to effectively and efficiently re-allocate specific risks.

In order to support diversification, hedging, and risk transfer a risk management system provides the following functionality:

1. Portfolio compression to represent complex portfolios;
2. risk decomposition to decompose risk by asset and/or risk factors and quantify the contribution of each to an overall portfolio;
3. "what if" analysis to understand how new trades affect portfolio risk;
4. hedging and optimization of complex portfolios.

These components provide the core functionality of a risk management system. We may add to this functionality, systems to understand the nonlinear functions of the instruments' price relations and the effect of non-normal risk factor distributions on portfolio risks. Furthermore, we may use tools to infer the implied views that are implicit in the structure of the held portfolio, the investment policy, or market liquidity.

Analytics that support the decomposition of the risk measures of the previous section, so that risk management can be executed, require approximations of the portfolio sensitivity to the risk factors. Simulation-based tools provide additional insights when the portfolio contains nonlinearities, when the market distributions are not normal or when there are multiple horizons. In particular, simulations are useful when multiple sources of risk interact so that the exposure and loss distributions are generally skewed and far from normal.

Risk transfer strategies are used to lower the cost of undesirable risks and to increase the firm's capacity to originate risks in its core exposure. In the course of doing business, institutions develop risk concentrations in their area of specialization. For instance, a bank may develop large exposures to a foreign currency or large concentrations in a specific industry sector through their loans department. Risk transfer of the portfolio to the secondary markets increases the capacity for risk origination without accumulating highly concentrated risk positions. For instance, the bank may use forward contracts to hedge their currency exposure or credit risk derivatives to balance their industry-specific risk. Derivative securities and insurance products, together with well-diversified portfolios, lower the costs of financial distress, and it is estimated that institutions taking an enterprise-wide approach – bundling together insurance protection with financial risk protection – save 20% to 30% in the cost of risk transfer.

Finally, allocation of equity capital among competing lines of business, taking into account the risk and return profiles of each, creates well-diversified portfolios with reduced risk exposure. Integrated financial product management plays a key role here, and the tasks of risk management are implemented with the use of portfolio optimization models.

Performance measurement

Having estimated through EWRM the risk profile of different lines of business, and having shaped the risk profile of the enterprise, we turn now to the problem of performance measurement. The task is to estimate the contribution of each line of business, or financial product, to the firm's diversified overall risk profile, and provide the feedback loop in the EWRM process. Performance measurement sets goals for line managers when risks are first acquired and evaluates their performance with respect to these goals; it determines local hedges and capital equity allocation, and provides reward incentives. In this way it serves the decentralized management of the enterprise. Performance measurement based on risk measurement and risk management as outlined above ensures firm-wide consistency in the handling of risks.

Managing relations with the firm's stakeholders also requires risk transparency, and this can be achieved through a firm-wide performance measurement system. Regulators need to know that business operations are in compliance with regulatory requirements. Equity analysts and rating agencies need risk information to develop investment and credit opinions. Unless there is full risk transparency the institution may be penalized for its risks, as the stakeholders may see only the risks, but neither the controls nor the natural hedges that may exist among them. Performance measurement ensures that the required transparency is achieved. This information is also of use in the analysis of mergers and acquisitions.

Corporate governance

None of the components of EWRM as outlined above will achieve its tasks without the support of appropriate corporate governance. Guidelines here are scant. For instance, the handbook on financial risk management endorsed by the Global Association of Risk Professionals (Lore and Borodovsky 2000) does not contain any chapters on the topic of corporate governance for enterprise-wide risk management.

Corporate management must ensure that the components needed to execute EWRM strategies are in place, that they function properly, and that they are aligned with each other and with the objective of the enterprise-wide risk management strategy. To do so management must define the institution's risk appetite in terms of loss tolerance, risk-to-capital leverage, and target debt

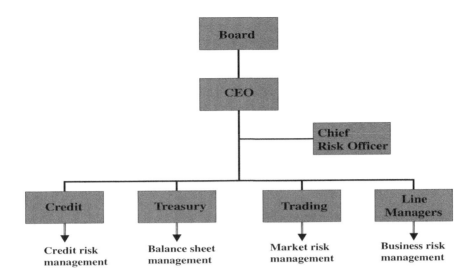

Figure 1.7: Organization structure to support enterprise-wide risk management.

rating. Risk management skills must be available to support the EWRM strategy in the form of both human, technological, and financial resources. An organizational structure that allows the enterprise-wide management of risk should clearly define the roles of risk management at both the enterprise level and by the line managers. Figure 1.7 illustrates the organizational structure of a bank with the addition of a Chief Risk Officer (CRO). A study by Tillinghast-Towers Perrin (Miccolis and Shah 2000) finds that only 20% of the responding institutions have appointed a CRO, with a noticeable difference between North American institutions (8% have appointed a CRO) and institutions in the rest of the world (40% have appointed a CRO). The experience inside and outside the financial services industry documented in the survey shows that creating a CRO function can be an effective step in making enterprise-wide risk management work in practice.

1.3.6   Why enterprise-wide risk management is important

Financial risks come in many forms and quite often are interdependent. EWRM allows an institution to identify the many and disparate sources of risk in its environment, measure their interdependence, and exploit natural hedges that appear in its lines of business. This leads to more efficient capital allocation.

Integration also leads to the design of innovative risk transfer products. For instance, the bundling together of insurance protection with financial risk results in substantial savings in the cost of risk transfer. EWRM also allows the simultaneous management of the business risks and those of the trading book. This results in more efficient use of the financial markets in transferring concentrated business risk, a practice that has been used with success in re-insurance, weather derivatives, and energy contracts. EWRM also allows for more efficient risk transferring internally, since transfer pricing becomes less of a political process among the compartmentalized silos that manage distinct risks, and can be viewed at an integrated enterprise level in conjunction with the firm's external risk factors.

For instance, in the domain of credit risk EWRM facilitates the credit risk transfer pricing between loan origination and portfolio management. The cost of distress from credit losses and credit value volatility is reduced, and liquidity of credit risk instruments is improved, leading to better trading and hedging decisions. Credit risk capital can be allocated more efficiently since various business opportunities are directly comparable.

Overall, EWRM leads to greater risk transparency for both shareholders and regulators. Indeed, some of the motivation for introducing EWRM comes from external pressures from corporate governance bodies and institutional investors. We give some examples. The Bank for International Settlement (BIS) 1988 Capital Accord allows banks to use internal models for determining minimum regulatory capital for market risk of the traded positions. This led to a proliferation of risk measurement systems in banks. The New BIS Capital Accord emerging out of the consultative papers issued by the Basel Committee on Banking Supervision in 2001 extends the use of approved internal models to credit risk, market risk for nontraded positions, and operational risk. The three pillars of sound risk management practices on which the new accord is based are:

1. Regulatory requirements for capital,

2. supervisory review processes, and

3. market discipline imposed by shareholder pressures when risks are properly disclosed.

Risk transparency is key to all three pillars but especially in promoting market discipline, and the significance of EWRM increases within the new BIS Accord.

1.3.7   Asset and liability management

The management of the firm's balance sheet is at the core of enterprise-wide risk management for financial institutions. For nonfinancial institutions, balance sheet management is traditionally viewed as solely an accounting issue, although this is also changing with a shift towards economic value. For financial institutions, however, the balance sheet reflects the risks of the environment from the asset side and most of the business risks from the liability side. The alignment of these risks is the goal of an asset and liability management system (ALM). ALM addresses parts of the problems of EWRM. As such it provides tools for risk measurement and risk management that are applicable to EWRM. ALM has a history that dates back to the seminal contributions of Markowitz in the 1950s for asset allocation, and the subsequent extensions to include liabilities. Tools for ALM are better developed than those for EWRM although they may not be as advanced as needed to support EWRM. In order for ALM to be effective in supporting the broader goals of EWRM it must receive additional information. The interactions between EWRM and ALM are discussed here.

ALM takes a more focused – one could say, restricted – view of risks than EWRM. It focuses on market, credit, and liquidity risk on the asset side. On the liability side it focuses on volatilities of margins and costs. Volatility of sales volumes is not directly part of the ALM function although it is a significant component of business risk. The integration of volatility of sales volumes requires the alignment of the firm's other risks with the marketing environment, which is beyond the scope of ALM. Similarly, the management of operational risk requires an alignment of the business with the operational environment, and again falls outside the scope of ALM.

Managing the financial risks of the balance sheet can be achieved by pulling the levers of EWRM. In particular, asset allocation (funding the products) and equity allocation (capitalization of the products) are the major managerial activities in ALM. The design and pricing of products are usually considered as exogenously given in the context of ALM, although pricing is used as input to the asset allocation phase and in determining hedging positions.

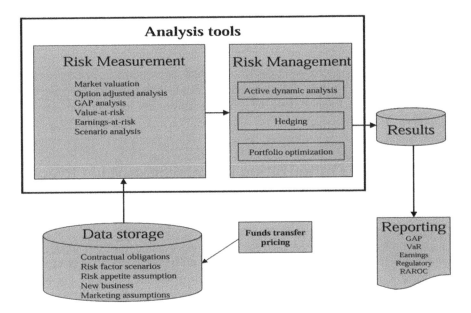

Figure 1.8: Components of an asset and liability management system.

Components of asset and liability management

The basic components of an ALM system are *data storage*, *analysis tools*, and *reporting facilities*. The ALM system is illustrated in Figure 1.8. The goals of the system and its components are to perform tasks such as earnings and balance sheet simulation, sensitivity analysis, current and future valuation, and dynamic balance sheet modeling. These functions provide the necessary input data for management to align the asset and liability sides of the balance sheet through asset allocation or equity capital allocation. The assets and liability sides are properly aligned when the net risk position is neutralized.

Data storage provides data on the contractual obligations, market information such as prices, time series of financial data that can be used to calculate the probabilities of changes in the risk factors, behaviorial assumptions about risk appetite or investor utility, and information about business volumes, customer attrition, and new products. Historical data may be necessary in calibrating other model parameters as well, and they are also provided through data storage.

Analysis tools provide the analytic support for both risk measurement and risk management. Analytics are used to support the quantification of the disparate sources of risk, and facilitate the use of derivative securities and portfolio optimization models to neutralize these risks. ALM analytics are a multi-layer application. At the base level there are some mechanical features such as cashflow generators and duration and convexity mismatch calculations. Next comes the analysis of the economic environment. This typically takes the form of forecasts or simulations of interest rates, exchange rates, and credit spreads. The projected estimates or scenarios for possible future values are used to simulate the balance sheet by repricing the assets and liabilities under the assumed scenarios.

Reporting provides the necessary information to regulators and shareholders, such as earnings-at-risk, value-at-risk, capital adequacy requirement, and so on. It also provides answers to "what if" questions, to support managerial decision making.

Valuation functionality is an important component of ALM analytics, not only for the simulation of the firm's position at the risk horizon, but also for pricing what is on the balance sheet today. For some items on the balance sheet this may be straightforward. For products with embedded options advanced analytics are needed to capture the highly asymmetric value profiles. Mortgage-backed securities and Collateralized Debt Obligations for banks, or participating policies with guarantees for insurers are examples of products whose valuation requires mathematical sophistication.

The simulations can be extended well into the future and the institution's balance sheet can be simulated dynamically across time. Dynamic analysis can be either passive, focusing on the time-evolution of the current balance sheet, or it can be active, and focus on the analysis of explicit institutional ALM strategies.

1.4   The Scope for Optimization in Enterprise-Wide Risk Management

Based on the preceding discussion we can view enterprise-wide risk management as the taking of positions in specific risk attributes so that the risks are aligned. An important problem, however, is that generic risks are not traded in the markets. Rather, we invest in securities that are packages of risk attributes. (A classification of financial risks is given in Chapter 2.) For instance, when we buy the simplest and most secure instrument, a government bond, we are exposed to price fluctuations due to changes in interest rates and exchange rates. Even if we only invest in government bonds of the country where our enterprise operates – an increasingly chimerical task for multinational enterprises operating globally – we are exposed to the risks of the complex changes in the term structure of interest rates. For zero coupon bonds it is only the change of the interest rate, corresponding to the maturity of the bond, that is relevant. For coupon bearing bonds the changes of interest rates with short-, medium- and long-term maturities will affect the price. Thus, several risk factors are present simultaneously.

As pure risk attributes are rarely traded, enterprise-wide risk management is faced with the problem of simultaneously controlling the interaction of many securities and their risk attributes in shaping overall enterprise exposure. The problem is complicated even further when we realize that most investors, institutional or others, face several restrictions in the management of their assets and liabilities. Thus, regulations or firm policy may limit holdings in particular sectors; accounting rules may imply bounds on holdings in securities traded at a discount or premium; the resources allocated internally may favor passive over active portfolio management, and so on. These considerations impose constraints on portfolio compositions.

In this setting, optimization models play an important role in supporting financial engineers to build the blocks of enterprise-wide risk management. Mathematical programming techniques can effectively identify the solution to complex portfolio planning problems with many constraints, and optimization models can find the least costly or the most profitable solution, if one exists, or demonstrate that a target risk profile is unattainable.

The target risk profile could be defined as one where all or some risks are eliminated. Alternatively, a target risk profile may be one where the exposure to some risks is maximized. For instance, if we expect that interest rates will decline we should invest in a long-term coupon bearing bond. Any decline in interest rates will increase the price of the bond, and thus the return of our investment. If instead we invest in a short-term zero coupon bond we benefit less from interest rate decreases. Of course, if interest rates rise the long-term bond will suffer higher price depreciation. An investor who expects rates to fall can take advantage of this change by maximizing his exposure to interest rate risk. Optimization models can be used to synthesize portfolios of securities such that their net risk exposure is zero. Alternatively, they can be used to synthesize portfolios of securities such that the net exposure is zero for some risk attributes, while it is maximized for others.

To recap, two important roles that optimization models play in supporting the decision making of financial engineers are:

- Control or eliminate specific risk attributes; and

- take a position in specific risk attributes.

The role of optimization does not stop here. The types of securities from which portfolios are constructed are not given a priori and their characteristics are not cast in stone. Instead, with the continued deregulation of the markets, increased volatility and synchronization of the global markets, and intensified competition in the finance industry, we have seen a rapid acceleration of financial innovation with the engineering of new products. Securitization and the design of innovative financial products is tantamount to the repackaging of financial risk attributes. This can be made more effective with the use of optimization models to achieve design goals along the competing dimensions of risk and reward. Furthermore, in order to standardize products certain guidelines must normally be obeyed. For instance, when issuing Collateralized Mortgage Obligations (CMOs) one requirement is that the collateral should sustain bond retirements in the extremely unlikely event of full early prepayment of the mortgage loans and in the equally unlikely event of no prepayments at all. Satisfying such guidelines can be achieved effectively with optimization models. In addition, the guidelines are not totally inflexible, but may leave the product issuer some leeway. (For instance, in issuing CMOs a "three-year tranche" is one with maturity between 3.0 and 3.4 years.) The slack provides sufficient reason to optimize profits when several alternative designs satisfy the guidelines. Similarly, with the markets not always at equilibrium certain risk attributes may be relatively cheaper in some securities than others, allowing for constrained profit maximization or cost minimization. Hence, a third important role for optimization models in supporting the decision making of financial engineers is:

- Designing new securities with prespecified risk attributes.

1.4.1   Caveat: What to optimize?

The question of what to optimize is an open-ended question. On the surface this question seems trivial: minimize the costs or maximize the returns. However, modern portfolio theory dictates that the exposure to systematic risks is rewarded in such a way that all securities with the same risk attributes should have the same expected return, if arbitrage is to be avoided and equilibrium preserved.

When an optimization model is used to eliminate the risk attributes, in essence it will eliminate those risk attributes that were explicitly accounted for in the model (systematic risk) and will remain exposed to the risk attributes that were not accounted for (nonsystematic risk). The resulting portfolio will be a known risk-free position, and an unknown position in a nonsystematic risks. The expected return of the risk-free position of the portfolio must be, in equilibrium, the risk-free rate. Therefore, high expected excess return of this portfolio over the risk-free rate implies high exposure to nonsystematic risks, and maximizing the return has the side effect of maximizing the nonsystematic risk. Such risk may also come from data errors, and optimization models have also been called "error maximizers." Hence, a fourth role that optimization models play, inadvertently, in supporting the decision making of financial engineers is:

- Side effects: Maximize the risk exposure to those risks that were not included in the model, or that were included with incorrect or erroneous measurement.

It follows that optimization models cannot be used blindly to support the decision making process of financial engineers. Instead they must be coupled with a careful analysis of the risks that were not included in the modeling process. The financial engineer must be able to formulate clearly stated objectives, understand the economic and institutional constraints, choose a suitable investment universe, accurately identify the risk attributes of the chosen securities, and measure risks and returns. In all these optimization is a tool that facilitates the risk-shaping process. If all risks are monitored, optimization can be used to capitalize on market opportunities and enhance performance by aligning the risk factors of the enterprise. If some risks are not monitored, however, optimization will maximize the exposure to them and misalign the firm's risk exposure. Optimization will make a good financial engineer better, and a bad one worse.

1.5   Overview of Financial Optimization Models

We give now an outline of the book, offering readers a foretaste of the models and analysis that will follow. The ideas discussed above on enterprise-wide risk management, and on the scope for optimization models in supporting the decision making process, are simple and intuitive. The rest of the book develops these ideas into precise and implementable models. This starts in Part I with an introduction to the basic concepts on which the models are grounded, then develops an arsenal of implementable models in Part II, and continues in Part III with a discussion of large-scale applications where the models are used to support financial decision making. A final Part IV describes the FINLIB library of the models described in this book, and suggests potential projects for class assignments.

1.5.1   Basics of risk management

To manage risks we must first understand what risk is, the different types of risk, and how to measure them. In Chapter 2 we give a classification of financial risks, discussing several cases where inadequate understanding of some risk factor(s) had catastrophic consequences.

    We then discuss the methods for quantifying the risks. A distinction is first made between risk measurement for equities, and for fixed-income securities. In the former case tradition wants the use of statistical methods for measuring risk. Several statistical measures are introduced, their appropriateness discussed and their interrelationships are highlighted. In the latter case the risk is measured as a simple function of changes in interest rates, the rate of interest being the primary risk factor in fixed-income securities. Scenario analysis is then introduced for fixed-income securities as the means to bring statistical measures of risk to bear on the study of fixed-income risk. Scenario analysis more accurately captures the complex interactions between interest rates and the risk of fixed-income securities. It also permits an analysis of the multiple risk factors that are present in modern fixed-income securities. As a consequence of the development of scenario analysis we can now use statistical measures of risk for both fixed-income and equities. Having introduced common measures of risk for diverse risk factors we can now embark upon risk measures that are applicable at an enterprise-wide level where the risks are multidimensional. The "industry standard" measure, Value-at-Risk or VaR, is introduced before we give an axiomatic characterization of risk measures that support enterprise-wide risk management. These are the so called *coherent* risk measures. A specific example of a coherent risk measure is Conditional Value-at-Risk or CVaR. This is also introduced, and in later chapters we will see how to optimize this risk using linear programming.

    The measurement of risk is one of the two focal points of risk management. The other one is, of course, the measurement of reward. We discuss the relation between risk and reward and in this way develop measures of performance. The chapter concludes with a classification of the financial optimization models along the axes of time and uncertainty.

1.5.2   Mean-variance portfolio optimization

The seminal developments in financial optimization date back to the work of Markowitz (1952) that developed mean-variance analysis. This laid the foundations for modern portfolio theory, and sparked the proliferation of optimization models for financial planning in the decades that followed. Mean-variance analysis is a point of departure, and in Chapter 3 we develop optimization models to support mean-variance analysis.

We view mean-variance analysis as a normative model that develops recommendations on how investors should behave. In this way it supports the decision making of financial engineers. Constructing efficient portfolios of assets is the most successful application of normative mean-variance analysis, and we start by developing quadratic programming models to support these calculations. We show how to incorporate transaction costs, minimum trading sizes, portfolio turnover, and other issues of concern to the practicing financial engineer. The models are then extended to incorporate liabilities, making an important step towards enterprise-wide risk management.

The calculation of the required input data for mean-variance analysis is a challenging task. This task can be substantially simplified with the use of factor models of security returns. The Capital Asset Pricing Model and Arbitrage Pricing Theory provide the theoretical foundation for factor models of security returns, and we will see how information from arbitrage pricing theory can be used in the formulation of mean-variance optimization models.

Finally, we discuss the sensitivity of mean-variance optimized portfolios to erroneous or noisy data estimates. We discuss the impact of errors in the estimation of expected returns and variances of returns, and discuss some ways to alleviate the problems created by the data estimation errors.

1.5.3   Portfolio models for fixed income

The price of simple fixed-income securities depends in a straightforward manner on the term structure of interest rates. When the timing of a stream of cashflows received from a bond is matched with the stream of liability payments then we have a risk-free portfolio. This simple requirement – matching the cashflows of asset and liability streams – is formulated as a linear program and provides the point of departure for more advanced risk management models.

When cashflows from the asset and liability sides of the balance sheet are not exactly time-matched, the portfolio is exposed to the risk of changing interest rates. We derive the relationship of the price of both sides of the balance sheet to changes in interest rates. If the price changes of assets and liabilities are matched, then the portfolio is immune to changes of the term structure. Models for matching price sensitivities have a history that dates back to the work of Macaulay (1938) and Reddington (1952), and they go under the name of "portfolio immunization." We develop the necessary and sufficient conditions for portfolio immunization, and give linear programming models for structuring immunized portfolios.

These models take a progressively more advanced view of the kind of term structure changes that may shock the value of our assets and liabilities. We start with immunization models that match assets and liabilities under small and parallel shifts of the term structure. We then discuss how the statistical techniques of principal component analysis can be used to study the modes of fluctuation of a term structure. Equipped with an analysis of the factors that affect the term structure we develop factor immunization models; these are linear programs that hedge the portfolio from changes in the factors. This type of analysis is applicable to corporate bonds when the term structure of credit spreads, in addition to the term structure of interest rates, is a risk factor affecting bond prices. Linear programming models for factor immunization of corporate bonds are also developed.

Chapter 4 provides an array of models for fixed-income risk management for some relatively simple, but significant, risk attributes. The simplifying assumptions on the characteristics of interest rate risk lead to simple linear programming formulations. These models are not only instructive, but they are also very useful for applications where the risk attributes satisfy, or almost satisfy, the assumptions.

1.5.4   Scenario optimization

As we move towards more innovative instruments we cannot simplify the complex interactions among multiple risk factors, nor the nonlinear relationships between changes of the risk factors and price movements. The interactions among the risk factors, however, can be captured through Monte Carlo simulations that generate scenarios of security prices. As a result of the nonlinear relationships between prices and risk factors, the distributions of returns generated by the simulations can be highly skewed and have long tails. Such is the case, for instance, in options instruments where the distribution of returns is truncated on one side since the downside of an option is limited.

The nonlinearities that give rise to skewed distributions and long tails are prevalent in modern securities, in both the fixed-income and the equities world. Due to the asymmetric returns we cannot rely on variance as the measure of risk, and the mean-variance optimization models in Chapter 3 serve only as approximations. Similarly, the models in Chapter 4 are approximations for simple changes of interest rates only. In Chapter 5 we develop optimization models that rely on simulated scenarios of prices or returns. These models shape the portfolio risk profile in the presence of multiple risk factors, thus contributing directly to the objective of enterprise-wide risk management in integrating multiple sources of risk. By integrating multiple sources of risk we also reduce the adverse side effect of optimization models, namely the maximization of errors. The burden falls now on the development of accurate simulation models, so that all relevant risk factors are captured in the scenarios before the risk profile is optimized. (The generation of scenarios is discussed in Chapter 9, but for now we assume that scenarios are somehow generated.) We will also see that scenario optimization models can be developed for several risk measures, including measures that are coherent. Including all relevant risk factors and optimizing coherent risk measures are cornerstones of enterprise-wide risk management – although the use of coherent risk measures is not yet the prevalent practice – and the optimization models of this chapter take a big step towards supporting enterprise-wide risk management.

We start with a scenario optimization model for the mean absolute deviation risk metric that, under some assumptions, is equivalent to the variance metric used in Chapter 3. In this way we build the bridge between mean-variance optimization and scenario optimization, while providing a linear programming alternative to the quadratic programming models of Chapter 3. We also develop linear programming models for optimizing a regret function, thus creating a link between scenario optimization and decision theory, and this link is further established when we discuss nonlinear optimization models for expected utility maximization.

A random liability can be incorporated in these models, and this is an important feature of the models in supporting enterprise-wide risk management. The relevant formulations are given for both the mean absolute deviation and the regret optimization models. An interesting by-product of these formulations is the development of a tracking model that will play a central role in structuring index funds in Chapter 7.

We then show how Conditional Value-at-Risk (CVaR) can be optimized using a linear programming formulation. Thus we have models for managing portfolios using coherent measures of risk.

An interesting feature of scenario optimization models is that they can be used not only to shape the risk profile of complex portfolios, but also to infer the cost of portfolio restrictions and compute prices for complex securities. The dual price of linear programming models can be interpreted as market prices when properly normalized against a suitable benchmark. We discuss first a linear programming model that decomposes securities in their downside and upside risk against some benchmark. Typically this benchmark would be the target liability. The dual prices of these models allow us to calculate the prices that make each security neutral with respect to the benchmark, and also to price liquidity risk. The presentation of a general methodology for asset valuation in incomplete markets using linear programming wraps up this chapter.

1.5.5   Dynamic portfolio optimization

The models we have developed in the first chapters are myopic. That is, they optimize a single investment decision that is made "here and now." This decision is made today under the stated assumptions of the model, such as measuring risk using the correlation matrix, or measuring risk using the price derivatives with respect to interest rate changes, or using scenario analysis. In many practical settings, however, portfolio managers rebalance their portfolios over long horizons as more information arrives. In Chapter 6 we develop optimization models for dynamic strategies, those being sequences of buy and sell decisions including borrowing or lending. These models rely on the scenario analysis introduced earlier. However, instead of making a unique decision today that is in some way optimal for all scenarios, they recommend a sequence of decisions that change as the scenarios evolve with time.

One approach to dynamic portfolio optimization is to specify a priori the decision rule applied in rebalancing a portfolio. For instance, a simple rule would be to maintain a constant mix of risk-free and risky assets. The performance of this rule can be analyzed under the assumed scenarios, and the value of the constant could also be optimized. Several popular strategies are discussed in this chapter.

We then develop models for optimizing truly dynamic portfolio strategies. As a first step in this direction we consider an extension of the dedication model of Chapter 4, whereby borrowing and lending decisions are optimized in a dynamic setting. We then proceed to develop models to optimize the rebalancing of the portfolio as new information arrives. A logical requirement in rebalancing is that decisions that depend on the same information up to a time period τ should be indistinguishable from each other, even if these decisions are made in anticipation of different events after τ. For otherwise our models would be endowed with clairvoyance. This requirement is the so-called *non-anticipativity property* of the decision variables. Modeling the arrival of new information without introducing clairvoyance is possible with the use of event trees. Event trees are introduced as generalizations of the linear scenario structures of the previous chapter. Large-scale optimization models can then be formulated to optimize decisions on an event tree. The models have a long tradition in the optimization literature, developed in the 1950s under the term *stochastic programming*. Some general background on stochastic programming is first given, and a generic stochastic programming model for optimizing dynamic portfolio strategies is formulated.

1.5.6   Index funds

A broad problem class where optimization provides indispensable tools is in the management of index funds. Creating portfolios that mimic the performance of some broadly defined market index is an important component of enterprise-wide risk management, in that the risk factors of the environment of an enterprise are reflected in the indices of the markets where the enterprise operates or invests. In Chapter 7 we develop optimization models for tracking market indices. In general terms we can view the target market index as a random liability, generate scenarios of the risk factors affecting the index and the available assets, and apply the scenario optimization models of Chapter 5 or the dynamic optimization models of Chapter 6. We first give some general optimization models that track indices by limiting the downside deviation of the portfolio from the index only and therefore restricting underperformance, or by limiting both downside and upside deviations, thus restricting both under- and overperformance.

An interesting issue arises when tracking composite indices. These are indices of indices, such as those used in monitoring the performance of the global government bond markets that consist of many local markets. In particular, the need to integrate several sources of risk in a common framework manifests itself in this application as well. We develop models for both integrated and nonintegrated (i.e., segmented) optimization of index funds. We then extend the integrated models to the dynamic optimization of index funds using stochastic programming. Finally we discuss the application of these models in the context of international bond portfolio indexation, credit risk indexed portfolios, and indexed portfolios of mortgage-backed securities.

1.5.7 Designing financial products

Up to this point optimization models have been used to shape the risk profile of portfolios. But the risk profile does not have to be defined only by the composition of the portfolio; it can be shaped by the types of instruments that are available to the risk manager in the first place. It is possible that different instruments will better match different risk preferences. The role of the financial engineer is then to design financial products that match the risk preferences. The design of financial products starts by defining the risk profile we expect from a product, and then adjusting some product features (e.g., the coupon rate or maturity) until we achieve the desired risk profile. It is fitting to draw an analogy to the rocket scientist who specifies the drag and lift of a jet wing, and then designs its shape to achieve the required performance at the least cost and with maximum safety.

In Chapter 8 we review financial innovation as a driver that makes product design an essential feature of financial engineering. Several innovative products are described, serving as illustrations of the product features that a financial engineer may control in the design of a product. (These products also appear in several other chapters of this book, where their design will be assumed as exogenously given.) We then describe a general framework for designing financial products. This framework starts with a formulation of the target risk profile, and concludes with an optimization model with the product features as the decision variables and a measure of "fit" to the target profile as the objective function to be maximized. A concrete example is given for the optimal design of the call features of callable bonds.

1.5.8 Scenario generation

The large majority of the optimization models in this book are scenario-based. It is only fitting that some attention is devoted to the discussion of scenarios and scenario generation methods. The literature on this topic is vast, from both a mathematical finance and a financial engineering perspective, and in Chapter 9 we review some basic methods.

The generation of scenarios for enterprise-wide risk management is in part science and in part art. We start the chapter by discussing some essential properties of scenarios. These properties are derived either from the need for scientific validity of the scenarios or for their value in supporting enterprise-wide risk management.

A general framework that sets the stage for concrete scenario generation methods is then presented. The framework is hierarchical, and allows the specification of a cascade of scenario generation models. The cascade allows us to interlink market data and mathematical models in ways that are consistent with empirical observations and with prevalent theories. The framework also allows for expert intervention, at every step of the process, to adjust the results based on expectations and experience.

Specific scenario generation methodologies are then introduced. The generation of scenarios for the liability side of the enterprise takes but little space, since it is a very specialized topic. It depends on the type of business and its liabilities, and some examples are given to highlight the issues involved. We then discuss three methods for the generation of scenarios for asset classes: bootstrapping of historical data, the statistical modeling techniques of the well-known Value-at-Risk approach, and time series analysis.

The models for generating linear scenario structures can be used to construct event trees. However, additional complications arise, as the event trees must satisfy additional theoretical properties, and their size must be carefully controlled – otherwise they grow exponentially in

size with the number of time steps involved and the resulting financial optimization models
become impractical. We discuss how to sample available linear scenarios to fit event trees, and
the construction of arbitrage-free trees.

1.5.9   Applications

Part III of the book develops several large-scale applications of financial optimization models.
The models discussed in Part II refer to general or stylized problems, and while these models
are directly applicable to several types of problem, they are but the building blocks to support
enterprise-wide risk management for large institutions. The chapters of Part III serve two purposes. First, they develop optimization models for several diverse real world applications, capturing policy restrictions, regulatory requirements, business objectives and the like. Second, they
serve as illustrations of how the basic building blocks of Part II are used to support enterprise-
wide risk management in diverse real world settings.

In this part we discuss the modeling of international asset management and management
of credit risk, the management of insurance policies with guarantees and the development of
financial engineering solutions for personal financial planning of individual investors.

Each chapter in this part discusses the problem and the institutional and business settings,
reviews relevant data, develops the optimization models – sometimes several variants of the
model are presented that address different aspects of the problem – and validates the models
with empirical testing. These models are not meant to be turnkey decision support tools for the
applications they discuss. Instead, they introduce the reader to the challenges and rewards that lie
ahead, and they are points of departure for practicing financial engineers to develop meaningful
models to support decision making in the context of their own business setting.

1.6   Postview

This chapter introduced the notion of enterprise-wide risk management and discussed the role
of optimization models in financial engineering for managing a firm's risks. The problems of
enterprise-wide risk management were analyzed first for a model firm offering a single financial
product, and then for firms managing a diverse portfolio of products. Within these contexts
the problems of enterprise-wide risk management were analyzed and the scope for optimization
modeling was revealed.

The chapter concluded with an overview of the subsequent chapters of the book, so that
readers can get a bird's-eye view of all the topics to be addressed.

Readers should make a careful note of the caveat on optimization models given in this chapter.
While optimization models are very flexible tools for financial engineering and enterprise-wide
risk management, they are also potent tools. They can make a good financial engineer better, and
a bad one worse.

Notes and References

The popular books by Bernstein (1996), and Dembo and Freeman (1998) give nonmathematical treatments to the topics of risk, both broadly defined and in the context of financial decision
making. Ross (1989) captures the essence of financial engineering in his presidential address to
the American Finance Association, where he states: "Like engineers who use physics, financial
engineers use the techniques of modern finance to build the equivalent of bridges and airplanes."
Derman (2004) gives a nonmathematical introduction to the role of quantitative methods in finance and risk management.

For further background on the financial terms used in this book readers should refer to the books by Bodie, Kane and Markus (1989), Sharpe, Alexander and Bailey (1998), or Elton and Gruber (1991). Fabozzi (1997) provides a more practical orientation. The science behind the analysis of investments is given by Luenberger (1998), and his treatment of finance concepts is suitable for students of financial optimization. For the seminal treatment of continuous-time finance see Merton (1990). For further reading on optimization refer to introductory books such as Hillier and Lieberman (2001), or Bradley, Hax and Magnanti (1977).

For discussions on the components of enterprise-wide risk management see Lam (1999a), the books by Stulz (2003), and Crouhy, Galai and Mark (2001), the handbook by Lore and Borodovsky (2000), and the collection of papers in Stulz and Apostolik (2004); for some critique see Stulz (1996).

The seminal contribution on the use of optimization models in finance started with Markowitz (1952); see also Markowitz (1991b). The model he suggested for solving portfolio choice problems laid the foundations of modern portfolio theory. See also Perold (1984) for the developments in large-scale application of portfolio optimization.

Several of the research papers that ushered in the era of modern financial optimization models are in the edited books by Zenios (1993a), Ziemba and Mulvey (1998) or Zenios and Ziemba (1992, 2006, forthcoming).

Broader issues relating to the performance of financial institutions, whereby risk management plays only a partial even if very important role, are discussed in Harker and Zenios (2000). On the other hand, risk management techniques used by nonfinancial firms are discussed by Bodnar, Hayt and Marston (1998).

The regulatory views on risk management are founds in the reports by the Basel Committee on Banking Supervision (1996a, b).

The integration of engineering design, manufacturing, and marketing of products in a seamless process is discussed by Hauser and Clausing (1988). From this line of research was later developed the integration of the functions involved in designing, pricing, capitalizing, marketing, and funding financial products by Holmer and Zenios (1995), and Lo (1999). The marketing of financial products is discussed by Wind (1987).

Financial innovation is discussed in the book by Allen and Gale (1994), and a mathematical model for designing financial products for the Federal National Mortgage Association is developed in Consiglio and Zenios (1997, 1999).

The literature on pricing financial claims is vast; for the seminal contributions see Black and Scholes (1973), and Merton (1973). Lo (1999) gives a perspective on pricing in complete markets using replicating strategies, and incorporating risk preferences that are essential in the context of risk management. For pricing in incomplete markets, such as in evaluating insurance liabilities or pension fund claims, see Dembo, Rosen and Saunders (2000).

Our discussion of EWRM is based on Rosen and Zenios (2006). Dembo et al. (2000) present a general framework for analytics to support the risk measurement tasks of EWRM, and Miccolis and Shah (2000) discuss the analytics of EWRM; see also Lo (1999). A collection of tools to support asset and liability management is published by the Kamakura Corporation (1998).

Some discussion on organizational forms to support EWRM is given in Lam (1999b). Relevant is also the work of Santomero (1997), and Santomero and Babbel (1997) who analyze the process of risk management in the distinct institutional settings of banks and insurance firms. Babbel (2001), and Bodnar, Hayt and Marston (1998) discuss the shift of balance sheet management principles from accounting to economic value. A report on the savings in the cost of risk transfer by institutions bundling together insurance protection with financial risk protection is due to Lam (1999a, b).

The decomposition of risk measures into its constituent risk factor components requires approximations of the portfolio sensitivity to the risk factors, and techniques for doing so are discussed in Litterman (1996), and Garman (1996, 1997).

The estimation of the views of market players – such as implied risk aversion, implied volatility, and so on – as implied from the portfolios held or the investment policy or market liquidity is discussed in Dembo and Rosen (2000), Dembo, Merkoulovitch and Rosen (1998), and D'Ecclesia and Zenios (2005); see also Ahuja and Orlin (2001) for the related mathematical model of inverse problems in optimization.

Dynamic simulations to capture the time dependence of fixed-income assets are discussed in Mulvey and Zenios (1994a, b), and Jobst and Zenios (2001, 2005). Perold and Sharpe (1988) analyze some popular dynamic portfolio strategies while Bradley and Crane (1972), and Kusy and Ziemba (1986) introduce models to optimize dynamic multi-period strategies.

Chapter 2

Basics of Risk Management

The modes of causation are many, though when brought under heads they too can be reduced in number. Thus we must inquire what chance and spontaneity are, whether they are the same or different, and how they fit into our division of causes.

Aristotle, Physics

The revolutionary idea that defines the boundary between modern times and the past is the mastery of risk: the notion that the future is more than a whim of the gods and that men and women are not passive before nature.

Peter Bernstein, Against the Gods

2.1 Preview

In this chapter we introduce basic concepts of risk measurement and risk management, and lay the foundations for the development of financial optimization models. We start with a classification of the risk factors that face an enterprise in today's financial markets, and define appropriate risk metrics. We also give measures of reward for performance evaluation. The chapter concludes with a classification of the optimization models used in risk management.

2.2 A Classification of Financial Risks

What is financial risk? It is the uncertainty surrounding the value of assets due to unforeseen and unforecastable future events. The causes of uncertainty are many, and financial risk is multidimensional. In this section we classify the risk factors so that the causes of uncertainty fit into a few categories.

Assume that there is available a universe U of n financial assets from which we can construct a portfolio by investing a fraction of our wealth in each asset. The return of the ith asset is a random variable $\tilde{r}_i$ with expected value $\bar{r}_i$ and variance σ_i^2.

We assume that the random variable may take one of countably many alternative values. For instance, we may have the – admittedly naive – view that the interest rate will take one of two possible values, moving either up or down by 1%. To allow more realistic situations we will assume that a scenario set of possible values of the random variable is available. That is, we assume that the return $\tilde{r}_i$ may take values from the set $\{r_i^l\}_{l \in \Omega}$, where $l \in \Omega$ are indices of plausible scenarios with probability of realization p^l. The expected, or mean, return of asset i is given by

$$\bar{r}_i = \sum_{l \in \Omega} p^l r_i^l. \tag{2.1}$$

Consider now a portfolio of holdings $x = (x_i)_{i=1}^n$ that satisfy the normalization condition $\sum_{i=1}^n x_i = 1$, that is, x_i denotes the proportion of wealth invested in the ith asset. The portfolio return is a random variable given by

$$R(x; \tilde{r}) = \sum_{i=1}^n \tilde{r}_i x_i, \tag{2.2}$$

or, using scenarios, by

$$R(x; r^l) = \sum_{i=1}^n r_i^l x_i. \tag{2.3}$$

It follows from these definitions that the portfolio return is uncertain and therefore risky. It is subjected to the unforeseen and unforecastable changes of the asset returns. Through the specification of a scenario set we know possible values for each asset return, and therefore of portfolio return, but we do not know with certainty which one of the scenarios will be realized in the future. What are the factors that influence the returns of the assets in a portfolio? These are the sources of financial risks. We give here a classification of these risk factors, highlighting the fact that financial risk is multidimensional. Quantitative measures for the risks are given in Sections 2.3 and 2.4.

Definition 2.2.1 Market price risk. *The risk that the market price of the assets will change with time. Depending on the type of asset we distinguish between stock market price risk and fixed-income market price risk.*

Definition 2.2.2 Stock market price risk. *The risk that the price of a stock will change with time due to adverse movements of the stock market as reflected in market index changes.*

According to the Capital Asset Pricing Model (CAPM), Theorem 2.3.1, securities must be priced so that their expected returns at equilibrium are a linear combination of the risk-free return and the market portfolio return. The weight on the market portfolio in this relationship indicates the relative marginal variation of the return of the security with respect to the market portfolio. This weight is known as the *beta* of the security (Definition 2.3.2) and is a measure of the price risk for this particular security when the market portfolio return changes. In more general models using the arbitrage pricing theory (APT), Theorem 3.4.1, the security expected return at equilibrium is a linear combination of several independent risk factors, and the CAPM model uses the return of the market portfolio as a proxy for these factors. Under this hypothesis, stock market price risk is the effect of the market risk factors on the price of the security.

Definition 2.2.3 Fixed-income market price risk. *The risk that the price of a fixed-income security will change with time due to adverse movements of the fixed-income market as reflected in market index changes.*

The predominant risk in fixed-income markets is the risk caused by movements in the overall level of interest rates on straight, default-free securities. When interest rates rise marginally, and uniformly for all maturities, the price of a regular bond will drop. The derivative of the price-yield relationship (Definitions 2.4.8–2.4.10) gives us an estimate of the price drop. This effect is captured in the definition below, which may also apply to other securities, beyond fixed-income, whose price depends, among possibly other factors, on interest rates as well.

Definition 2.2.4 Interest rate risk. *The risk that the price of a security will change with time due to movements of the general level of interest rates.*

Uniform change in the general level of interest rates for all maturities is but one type of interest rate movement, and more complex changes give rise to the following definition of risk.

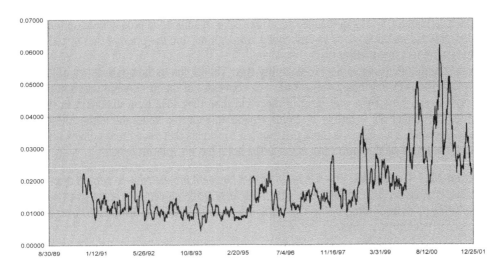

Figure 2.1: Changing volatility of the NASDAQ index during the ten-year period 1991–2001.

Definition 2.2.5 Shape risk. *The risk that the price of a security will change with time due to changes in the shape of the term structure of interest rates.*

To see the effects of shape risk consider two zero coupon bonds with maturities in one and ten years, respectively. Assuming a flat yield curve at 10% the prices of these bonds are 90.91 and 38.55. If interest rates shift by a small amount from the current value of 10%, uniformly across all maturity dates, the long-maturity bond will experience a price change almost ten times as large as the short-maturity bond. (Readers may want to verify the calculations. These statements will become obvious once the notion of duration is introduced in Section 2.4.) Hence, an investor who expects rates to decline will invest in the ten-year bond, which promises the highest return. However, if the term structure of interest rates tilts upwards (this is termed *steepening*) with a decrease in the one-year yield to 9% and increase in the ten-year yield to 11%, the investor will experience a loss of 9.56% relative to investing in the one-year bond. This is the effect of shape risk.

Definition 2.2.6 Volatility risk. *The risk that the price of an asset will change with time due to changes in volatility.*

Figure 2.1 illustrates the significant changes in volatility that may be observed in a market, even during short time periods. We observe from this figure that volatility tripled during the first two quarters of 2000. This example is drawn from the NASDAQ, which has been a very volatile market. (Figure 2.2 shows the performance of this index during the ten-year period from 1991 to 2001.)

Volatility risk is predominant in options. If the underlying asset is worth more than the strike price of a call option on the expiration date then the option is exercised, returning to its holder the difference between the price of the asset and the strike price. But if the price of the asset is less than the strike price then the option expires worthless. The option resembles an insurance policy that is valuable only if there is a chance that something might happen. The higher the price volatility of the underlying asset the more valuable is the option. (This relationship is captured in the Black-Scholes formula for options pricing.) Hence, volatility changes have an impact on the prices of options or securities with embedded options even in an environment that remains unchanged in all other respects. For instance, callable corporate bonds have an embedded call option, mortgage-backed securities have an embedded prepayment option, single-premium deferred annuities have an embedded lapse option, and the price of these fixed-income securities is subject to volatility risk.

Even straight bonds are subject to volatility risk. This is due to the nonlinearity of the price-yield relationship (Definitions 2.4.4–2.4.6). The convexity of the price-yield curve implies that bond prices gain more by a unit drop in the yield than they lose by a unit gain in the yield. Therefore, the higher the volatility of yields around an expected value the higher the expected return of the bond. This effect is more pronounced for bonds that have more convex price-yield curves. If the price-yield relationship is linear the bond has no volatility risk.

Definition 2.2.7 Credit risk. *The risk of an unkept payment promise due to default of an obligor – counterparty, issuer or borrower – or due to adverse price movements of an asset caused by an upgrading or downgrading of the credit quality of an obligor that brings into question their ability to make future payments.*

When a counterparty goes into default the recovery rate, i.e., the fraction of the debt that is recovered, is uncertain. So is the timing of the default, if default ever takes place. As the counterparty's prospects of meeting future obligations change so does his credit quality. If the credit quality deteriorates, investors will demand a higher premium for holding the debt and hence the prices of bonds issued by this counterparty will decline. Such price movements are brought about by changing prospects of meeting future obligations, and by changes in the recovery rates. It is useful to think of these two distinct sources of risk when talking of credit risk; although interrelated, they are distinct.

Definition 2.2.8 Currency risk. *The risk that the price of a security will change with time due to changes in the exchange rates between different currencies.*

Investors with international holding are exposed to the risk of fluctuations in the exchange rates of their base currency vis-à-vis the currencies of countries where they hold assets.

Definition 2.2.9 Liquidity risk. *The risk arising when an institution is unable to raise cash to fund its business activities (funding liquidity), or cannot execute a transaction at the currently quoted market prices due to a temporary lack of appetite for the transaction by other market players (trading liquidity).*

Trading liquidity risk is especially important for actively managed portfolios that may depend on frequent trading. When bid-ask spreads widen, losses will materialize when rebalancing a portfolio. Thus the ability to respond to financial stress is limited and cashflow distress may follow. There exist many and diverse reasons for liquidity drops. For instance, declining interest rates may prompt significant mortgage prepayments with a reduction in the circulating volume of mortgage-backed securities, making it more difficult to match buy with sell orders. Kidder-Peabody experienced significant loss of market value when they quickly liquidated their mortgage-backed securities portfolio. Institutional changes may also cause liquidity problems, as witnessed in the Copenhagen Exchange during the Exchange Reform in Denmark in the early 1990s. Liquidity risk can be catastrophic, as experienced by The Bank of New England in 1990, which faced insolvency due to potential losses and illiquidity in its foreign exchange and interest-rate derivatives. Perhaps the most notorious example of liquidity risk is in the case of Long-Term Capital Management in 1998: when the firm suffered losses of 80%, the need to unwind positions in the trillions of dollars created significant liquidity risks that threatened a global meltdown of the financial markets.

Definition 2.2.10 Sector risk. *The risk of price movements affecting a group of securities that share some common characteristics.*

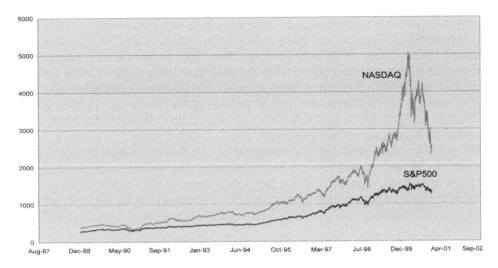

Figure 2.2: The performance of the NASDAQ index compared to the S&P 500 during the first two quarters of 2000 exemplifies sector risk.

Sectors of the economy are affected by different macroeconomic conditions and other factors. For instance, oil price hikes have an immediate impact on the airline industry but affect internet stocks to a lesser degree. Adverse weather conditions affect commodities futures more than precious metals. The dramatic drop of the NASDAQ index in the second quarter of 2000 – the high-tech market lost 30% of its value in just four weeks – that followed its spectacular rise in the late 1990s exemplifies sector risk. Investors who were exposed in this period to the high-tech industries suffered substantial losses, compared to investors in, say, the manufacturing or healthcare industries. This is illustrated in Figure 2.2 where the dramatic rise and drop of the NASDAQ is compared with the S&P 500.

Definition 2.2.11 Residual risk. *The risk of price movements due to firm-specific effects and, in principle, unrelated to the systematic influences given in our list of risks.*

Mergers and acquisitions, or corporate strategy are sources of residual risk. When an industrial segment is undergoing some transformation, then mergers and acquisitions may result in sector risk. The transformation of the US banking industry in the aftermath of interest rate deregulation, in the late seventies and into the nineties, caused both residual and sector risk. During the period 1979 to 1994 the total number of banking organizations in the US dropped from over 12,000 to slightly below 8,000, the number of small banks was reduced almost by half, while the number of employees remained virtually unchanged and the number of automated teller machines increased tenfold. The next definition captures several sources of residual risk.

Definition 2.2.12 Business risk. *The risk due to volatility of volumes, margins, or costs when engaging in the firm's business.*

For firms that are in the business of selling insurance, business risks can be made more precise through the definition that follows. One could define, similarly, the business risks for other enterprises – both financial institutions and other firms. However, insurers have a long tradition in the management of risk, and for their business a widely accepted definition of business risk is currently available.

Definition 2.2.13 Actuarial risk. *The risk associated with the liability side of the balance sheet of insurance firms, and which is due to changes in mortality, casualty or liability exposures.*

In a way actuarial risk is nonfinancial risk. However, several innovative insurance products provide the combination of an insurance policy and an endowment and it may be hard to disentangle the actuarial risk as defined above from the relevant financial risks. For instance, indexed-linked funds provide a bonus to policyholders when the underlying index performs better than some agreed-upon floor. Single premium deferred annuities (SPDA) have an embedded lapse option that is triggered by falling interest rates. Hence, the liability risk of an issuer of SPDAs or index-linked funds is in part due to mortality and in part due to the volatility of the index and the exercise of the lapse option by policyholders.

We add to our definitions two more categories of risk, due to firm-specific events arising from both internal and external sources. Strictly speaking these are not financial risks and one may think of nonfinancial institutions that face similar types of risk. However, the categories below have come to be distinctly identified as significant sources of risk for financial institutions. Hence, recognition of these risks is an essential element of any practical risk management system.

Definition 2.2.14 Operational risk. *The risk of direct or indirect losses resulting from inadequate or failed internal processes, people and systems, and from external events.*

Broadly speaking, operational risk captures all nonfinancial risks, starting from the risks due to a breakdown in risk management operations and moving on to environmental risks. The breakdown of the risk management operations may be due to miscalculation of market prices or the implementation of inadequate hedging strategies, system failures or faulty controls that leave the institution unable to execute its transactions and fulfill its obligations, human error and fraud, or management failures. The use of the wrong models for risk management is one source of operational risks. External, or environmental, risks are due to changing legal, regulatory, and taxation regimes, or due to inappropriate obligor relations.

Operational risks are characterized by low probability events that result in extreme financial losses. Several recent cases of institutions finding themselves in financial distress were due to operational problems. The collapse in 1995 of the venerable British bank, Barings & Co., was due to fraud by the head trader of Barings Futures Singapore (BFS), a Barings subsidiary involved in futures dealing on the Singapore futures exchange, and to management failures on the part of BFS's general manager. Interestingly, the same individual had been both head trader and general manager of BFS since 1992, also indicating faulty controls at Barings & Co. The cumulative losses for Barings & Co. after it went into liquidation were STG 927 million. Daiwa Bank, Morgan Grenfell, and Drexel Burnham are some of the well-known institutions that went into financial distress due to operational risks similar to those faced by Barings & Co. Miscalculation of market prices and hedging strategies, and the use of inappropriate models were responsible for the bankruptcy of Orange County in California and the Metallgesellschaft crisis. The management of operational risk still remains an art more than a science, and the optimization models of this book are not developed with this type of risk in mind.

Finally, to consider catastrophic events and complete the classification of risk we give a complementary definition.

Definition 2.2.15 Systemic risk. *The risk of a widespread collapse or disfunctioning of the financial markets through multiple defaults, widespread disappearance of liquidity, domino effects, etc.*

The attack of September 11, 2001 on the World Trade Center in New York caused systemic risk in all sectors of the insurance industry, including property and casualty, life and health, and reinsurance. Preliminary estimates put insured losses in the range of $30 billion to $58 billion. This is the largest single-event loss in history. It rivals in magnitude the total insured liabilities estimated from environmental claims, which are in the range of $38 to $53 billion arising from several claims worldwide that will be settled over several decades. The previous largest single event was Hurricane Andrew in 1992, which resulted in total insurance claims of $19.7 billion (inflation-adjusted). And as these lines were written Hurricane Katrina added another major catastrophe to the list, with insurance liabilities estimated in the range of $40 to $55 billion. The insurance industry is well capitalized to sustain the losses of such systemic events – US property and casualty insurers have over $300 billion in statutory surplus. However, losses of the magnitude wrought by 9/11 and Katrina stress test reinsurance and other pooling mechanisms that are designed to spread catastrophic losses broadly across the industry, and it is expected that several insurers will face insolvency.

The Long-Term Capital Management crisis, precipitated by the crisis in the Russian Government bond market, also exemplifies systemic risk. With a market exposure in the trillions of dollars, the potential bankruptcy of Long-Term Capital Management threatened the world markets with a global meltdown of the financial markets, and the crisis was averted by a bailout orchestrated by the New York Federal Reserve at a cost of $3.6 billion.

2.3   Risk Measurement for Equities

We now discuss the means available for quantifying the risks through appropriate risk metrics, starting with risk metrics for equities. The systematic risk of equities is predominantly the market risk. Hence, one way to measure the risk of an equity asset is to measure its sensitivity to the changes in the market index. Of course, when the asset in question is the only security that matters – perhaps because it is the only asset in a nondiversified portfolio – what matters is the idiosyncratic risk of the security, as opposed to the systematic risk of the market, and this is measured by the security variance.

Definition 2.3.1 Variance. *The variance of an asset i is given by*

$$\sigma_i^2 = \mathcal{E}\left[(\tilde{r}_i - \bar{r}_i)^2\right]. \tag{2.4}$$

An unbiased estimate of the variance is obtained using scenarios by

$$\hat{\sigma}_i^2 = \frac{1}{1 - \sum_{l \in \Omega}(p^l)^2} \sum_{l \in \Omega} p^l (r_i^l - \bar{r}_i)^2, \tag{2.5}$$

which simplifies to the following well known expression when the scenarios are equiprobable, with $p^l = 1/N$ for all $l \in \Omega$:

$$\hat{\sigma}_i^2 = \frac{N}{N-1} \sum_{l \in \Omega} \frac{1}{N}(r_i^l - \bar{r}_i)^2. \tag{2.6}$$

(The square root of the variance is the standard deviation.)

However, when the security is part of a well-diversified portfolio so that all idiosyncratic risks are diversified away, it is more appropriate to measure the systematic risk through the sensitivity of security price changes to changes in the market index, which is captured by the beta of the security.

Definition 2.3.2 Beta. *The beta of an asset i is defined by*

$$\beta_i = \frac{\sigma_{iM}}{\sigma_M^2}, \tag{2.7}$$

where σ_{iM} is the covariance of the random variable asset rate of return $\tilde{r}_i$ and the market rate of return $\tilde{r}_M$, and σ_M^2 is the variance of the market rate of return.

(For a definition of covariance see Definition 2.3.6.) We will see below that the beta of a security measures the sensitivity of the expected return of the security to changes in a broad market index.

The relationship between security prices and changes in the market index follows from the following theorem, which is fundamental to modern portfolio theory. Before we state the theorem we introduce the notion of an efficient portfolio on which the proof of the theorem rests.

Definition 2.3.3 Efficient portfolio. *A portfolio is efficient if all other (feasible) portfolios have a lower expected return for the same level of risk, or, equivalently, have higher risk for the same level of expected return.*

Theorem 2.3.1 Capital Asset Pricing Model (CAPM). *If the market portfolio, denoted by M, is efficient, the expected return $\bar{r}_i$ of any asset i satisfies*

$$\bar{r}_i = r_f + \beta_i(\bar{r}_M - r_f), \tag{2.8}$$

where r_f is the risk-free rate of return and $\bar{r}_M$ is the expected value of the market rate of return.

It follows that β_i measures the sensitivity of the expected return of the ith security to changes in the market. When the market moves by 1% the expected return of the security will move by $\beta_i\%$.

Proof. The proof of the theorem relies on the fact that efficient portfolios of assets consist of a linear combination of investments in the risk-free rate and the market portfolio. In the diagram of expected return vs. standard deviation of return, efficient portfolios lie on a straight line going through the point of zero standard deviation corresponding to the risk-free rate r_f and to the point with expected rate of return $\bar{r}_M$ and standard deviation σ_M corresponding to the market portfolio. This is called the *capital market line* and is illustrated in Figure 2.3. The equation of this line is

$$\bar{r} = r_f + \frac{\bar{r}_M - r_f}{\sigma_M}\sigma. \tag{2.9}$$

We consider now a portfolio consisting of a portion x_i in asset i and a portion $1 - x_i$ in the market portfolio. The expected rate of return of this portfolio is a function of x_i given by

$$R(x_i; \bar{r}_i) = \bar{r}_i x_i + \bar{r}_M(1 - x_i), \tag{2.10}$$

and the standard deviation of the rate of return is given by

$$\sigma(x_i) = \left[\sigma_i^2 x_i^2 + 2\sigma_{iM} x_i(1 - x_i) + \sigma_M^2(1 - x_i)^2\right]^{1/2}. \tag{2.11}$$

By varying x_i we obtain portfolios with varying expected rates of return and standard deviation of the rate of return. In the diagram of expected return versus standard deviation of return the values obtained by varying x_i trace out a curve (see Figure 2.3). In particular, when $x_i = 0$ the portfolio is the market portfolio, hence the curve goes through the point M of the capital market line. Indeed, the curve must be tangent to the capital market line, for if it were to cross it for some value of x_i that would contradict the fact that efficient portfolios are constructed as a linear combination of the risk-free portfolio and the market portfolio.

We derive the conditions for the curve at $x_i = 0$ to be tangent to the capital market line. The slope of the curve is given by

$$\frac{dR(x_i; \bar{r}_i)}{d\sigma(x_i)} = \frac{\frac{dR(x_i; \bar{r}_i)}{dx_i}}{\frac{d\sigma(x_i)}{dx_i}}. \tag{2.12}$$

From equations (2.10) and (2.11) we calculate the derivatives

$$\frac{dR(x_i; \bar{r}_i)}{dx_i} = \bar{r}_i - \bar{r}_M \tag{2.13}$$

$$\frac{d\sigma(x_i)}{dx_i} = \frac{\sigma_i^2 x_i + \sigma_{iM}(1 - 2x_i) - \sigma_M^2(1 - x_i)}{\sigma(x_i)}. \tag{2.14}$$

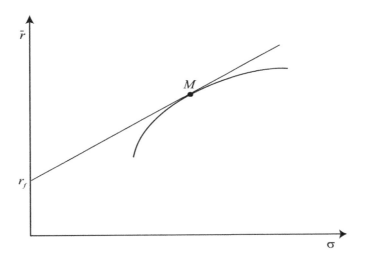

Figure 2.3: The capital market line and the curve of portfolios of holdings $(1-x_i)$ in the risk-free asset and x_i in a single risky asset.

We evaluate these expressions at $x_i = 0$ and substitute in (2.12) to obtain the slope of the curve at the point M as

$$\frac{dR(x_i; \bar{r}_i)}{d\sigma(x_i)}\Big|_{x_i=0} = \frac{(\bar{r}_i - \bar{r}_M)\sigma_M}{\sigma_{iM} - \sigma_M^2}. \tag{2.15}$$

This slope must be equal to the slope of the capital market line (cf. equation 2.9) so that we have

$$\frac{(\bar{r}_i - \bar{r}_M)\sigma_M}{\sigma_{iM} - \sigma_M^2} = \frac{\bar{r}_M - r_f}{\sigma_M}. \tag{2.16}$$

Solving for $\bar{r}_i$ we obtain the capital asset pricing model

$$\bar{r}_i = r_f + \left(\frac{\bar{r}_M - r_f}{\sigma_M^2}\right)\sigma_{iM} = r_f + \beta_i(\bar{r}_M - r_f), \tag{2.17}$$

where $\beta_i = \frac{\sigma_{iM}}{\sigma_M^2}$. ∎

When using optimization models for risk management, one may measure the risk of an equity portfolio either directly – using the moments of the distribution of the asset's return $\tilde{r}_i$ to estimate moments of the portfolio return, or indirectly, using the beta of the assets in the portfolio. The beta of the portfolio is obtained by writing

$$R(x; \bar{r}) = \sum_{i=1}^{n} \bar{r}_i x_i, \tag{2.18}$$

and substituting from CAPM for $\bar{r}_i$ to obtain, after rearranging terms

$$R(x; \bar{r}) = r_f + \sum_{i=1}^{n} \beta_i x_i(r_M - r_f). \tag{2.19}$$

If we view the portfolio as just one more (synthetic) asset, and compare this equation for expected portfolio return with the CAPM model, we obtain the beta of the portfolio as follows.

Definition 2.3.4 Portfolio beta. *The beta of a portfolio of holdings x_i in asset i is given by*

$$\beta_p = \sum_{i=1}^{n} \beta_i x_i. \tag{2.20}$$

The beta of the portfolio measures the sensitivity of portfolio return to changes in the market index. In this respect beta is a measure of risk. A *zero-beta* portfolio is one that remains invariant with changes in the index, while a *beta-neutral* portfolio is one with $\beta_p = 1$ so that portfolio returns change just like the index returns.

The risk of the portfolio return can also be measured directly by its variance, given in the following definition.

Definition 2.3.5 Portfolio variance. *The variance of a portfolio of holdings x_i in asset i is given by*

$$\sigma^2(x) = \mathcal{E}\left[[R(x;\tilde{r}) - R(x;\bar{r})]^2\right] = \sum_{i=1}^{n}\sum_{i'=1}^{n} \sigma_{ii'} x_i x_{i'}, \tag{2.21}$$

where $\sigma_{ii'}$ is the covariance between the returns of assets i and i', and we have $\sigma_{ii} = \sigma_i^2$, the variance of the ith asset. (The square root of the variance is the standard deviation.)

Definition 2.3.6 Covariance. *The covariance between the returns of assets i and i' is given by*

$$\sigma_{ii'} = \mathcal{E}\left[(\tilde{r}_i - \bar{r}_i)(\tilde{r}_{i'} - \bar{r}_{i'})\right]. \tag{2.22}$$

An unbiased estimate of the covariance is obtained using scenarios by

$$\hat{\sigma}_{ii'} = \frac{1}{1 - \sum_{l\in\Omega}(p^l)^2} \sum_{l\in\Omega} p^l(r_i^l - \bar{r}_i)(r_{i'}^l - \bar{r}_{i'}), \tag{2.23}$$

which simplifies to the following well-known expression when the scenarios are equiprobable, with $p^l = 1/N$ for all $l \in \Omega$:

$$\hat{\sigma}_{ii'} = \frac{N}{N-1} \sum_{l\in\Omega} \frac{1}{N}(r_i^l - \bar{r}_i)(r_{i'}^l - \bar{r}_{i'}). \tag{2.24}$$

An estimate of the variance of the ith asset return σ_i^2 is obtained from this definition as $\hat{\sigma}_{ii}$. If Q denotes the $n \times n$ covariance matrix we can write the portfolio variance in matrix notation as

$$\sigma^2(x) = x^\top Q x. \tag{2.25}$$

Note that the variance of the portfolio $\sigma^2(x)$ is a function of the asset holdings $(x_i)_{i=1}^{n}$. It is this dependence of the portfolio variance on x that brings in the optimization models to minimize risk by adjusting the asset allocation.

As a measure of risk, portfolio variance is a symmetric function around the portfolio mean value, as can be seen from Definition 2.3.5. It assumes that investors consider equally undesirable both downside and upside deviations of the portfolio return $R(x;\tilde{r})$ from its mean value $R(x;\bar{r})$. An alternative measure of risk that focuses on downside deviations and ignores upside deviations is the left semi-variance of the portfolio.

Definition 2.3.7 Semi-variance (left).

$$\sigma_-^2(x) = \mathcal{E}\left[(\max[0, R(x;\bar{r}) - R(x;\tilde{r})])^2\right]. \tag{2.26}$$

The argument of the expectation operator has a nonzero value only when the portfolio return is lower than its mean value, and it is zero otherwise. Using scenarios we obtain an estimate for the semi-variance by

$$\hat{\sigma}_-^2(x) = \frac{N}{N-1} \sum_{l \in \Omega} p^l \sum_{i=1}^n \left(\max[0, (\bar{r}_i - r_i^l)x_i] \right)^2.$$ (2.27)

This estimator is biased and a simple and general way to remove its bias is not available; however, it is asymptotically unbiased as the number of scenarios increases. The term $N/(N-1)$ is used to reduce bias; its use is based on empirical observations and for even a modest number of scenarios it can be substituted by one.

Similarly we may define a right semi-variance $\sigma_+^2(x)$ that measures upside deviations of the portfolio return from its mean value by changing the sign of $R(x; \bar{r}) - R(x; \tilde{r})$ in the equation for $\sigma_-^2(x)$.

If the returns of the assets are symmetric it is easy to see that $\sigma_-^2(x) = \sigma_+^2(x) = \frac{1}{2}\sigma^2(x)$ for any x. Furthermore, if the asset returns are multivariate normally distributed then the variance of the portfolio is the only moment we need as a measure of risk.

Variance can be viewed as a quadratic function that penalizes deviations of the portfolio return from the expected return, whereas the semi-variance is a piecewise linear-quadratic function. The left semi-variance, for instance, is a quadratic penalty for portfolio returns lower than the portfolio mean, and is linear and equal to zero when the portfolio returns exceed the mean value. Figure 2.4 illustrates these nonlinear risk measures, as well as a linear measure of risk defined next.

Definition 2.3.8 Mean absolute deviation.

$$w(x) = \mathcal{E}\left[\mid R(x; \tilde{r}) - R(x; \bar{r}) \mid \right].$$ (2.28)

Using scenarios we obtain an estimate for the mean absolute deviation by

$$\hat{w}(x) = \frac{N}{N-1} \sum_{l \in \Omega} p^l \mid \sum_{i=1}^n (r_i^l - \bar{r}_i)x_i \mid.$$ (2.29)

This estimator is also biased without a simple and general way for removing its bias, but it is asymptotically unbiased as the number of scenarios increases.

This risk function assumes that investors consider equally undesirable both downside and upside deviations of the portfolio return $R(x; \tilde{r})$ from its mean value $R(x; \bar{r})$. The penalty value assigned to such deviations is a linear function of the absolute value of the deviation, whereas in the variance model the penalty is a quadratic function of the deviation. It is possible to define a semiabsolute deviation function to consider only downside deviations.

Definition 2.3.9 Left semi-absolute deviation.

$$w_-(x) = \mathcal{E}\left[\max\left[0, R(x; \bar{r}) - R(x; \tilde{r}) \right] \right].$$ (2.30)

Using scenarios we estimate the semi-absolute deviation by

$$\hat{w}_-(x) = \frac{N}{N-1} \sum_{l \in \Omega} p^l \max\left[0, \sum_{i=1}^n (\bar{r}_i - r_i^l)x_i \right].$$ (2.31)

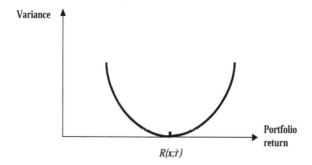

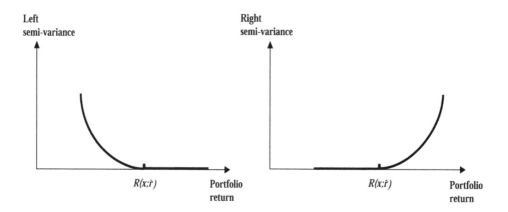

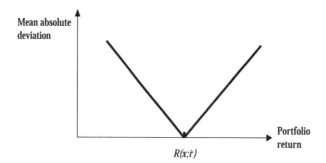

Figure 2.4: The variance, left and right semi-variance, and mean absolute deviation risk functions.

The argument of the expectation operator in $w_-(x)$ has a nonzero value only when the portfolio return is lower than its mean value, and it is zero otherwise. We can define similarly a right semi-absolute deviation $w_+(x)$ by

$$w_+(x) = \mathcal{E}\left[\max\left[0, R(x; \tilde{r}) - R(x; \bar{r})\right]\right], \tag{2.32}$$

and estimate it by

$$\hat{w}_+(x) = \frac{N}{N-1} \sum_{l \in \Omega} p^l \max\left[0, \sum_{i=1}^{n}(r_i^l - \bar{r}_i)x_i\right]. \tag{2.33}$$

It is easy to show (see Section 5.3.2) that the mean absolute deviation and the semi-absolute deviation measures are equivalent. Under some conditions the variance and the mean absolute deviation of a portfolio are also equivalent, as shown in the following theorem.

Theorem 2.3.2 *If asset returns $(\tilde{r}_i)_{i=1}^{n}$ are multivariate normally distributed, then*

$$w(x) = \sqrt{\frac{2}{\pi}}\sigma(x). \tag{2.34}$$

Proof.   Let $\bar{r}_i$ be the mean value of $\tilde{r}_i$, and let $\sigma_{ii'}$ be the covariance between the returns of assets i and i', for all $i, i' \in U$. We know from the properties of multivariate normal distributions that the return of the portfolio $R(x; \tilde{r}) = \sum_{i=1}^{n} \tilde{r}_i x_i$ is a normally distributed random variable with mean $\sum_{i=1}^{n} \bar{r}_i x_i$ and standard deviation

$$\sigma(x) = \sqrt{\sum_{i=1}^{n}\sum_{i'=1}^{n} \sigma_{ii'} x_i x_{i'}}. \tag{2.35}$$

It follows, from the definition of $w(x)$ and the properties of multivariate normal variables, that

$$w(x) = \frac{1}{\sqrt{2\pi}\sigma(x)} \int_{-\infty}^{\infty} |u| \exp\left(-\frac{u^2}{2\sigma^2(x)}\right) du = \sqrt{\frac{2}{\pi}}\sigma(x). \tag{2.36}$$

∎

The question now raised is why introduce another risk measure if it is equivalent to the classic variance measure introduced by Markowitz in the 1950s? In addition to the fact that returns for several modern assets are not normally distributed – and hence the normality assumption underlying mean-variance analysis does not hold – there is also an important practical consideration for the use of absolute deviation measures. The mean absolute deviation model can be formulated (see Definition 2.3.8) using scenario data without the need to estimate a covariance matrix. It can also be cast as a linear programming problem which renders it easier to solve than the quadratic programming problem required to optimize the variance function. Furthermore, models for the minimization of one-sided absolute deviations may be cast as linear programs (see Section 5.3) whereas models optimizing the left or right semi-variance functions require specialized algorithms for the piecewise linear-quadratic penalty function in Definition 2.3.7.

Thus far we have focused solely on some characteristic of the portfolio as a measure of risk. Variance, semi-variance, mean absolute deviation or semi-absolute deviations are functions only of the portfolio composition x and the random variable asset return $\tilde{r}$. However, financial institutions and individuals typically assess the performance of portfolios against some benchmark or an alternative investment opportunity. For instance, an individual may be interested in achieving a certain guaranteed return for the portfolio that will allow her to achieve well-defined goals: pay for the children's college, retire the mortgage debt of a house, make installments on a sailing boat or house appliances. Mutual funds promise returns relative to some volatile market index, while insurance policies may promise some guaranteed rate of return plus bonuses and coverage from actuarial risks. To account for such situations we need a risk measure that is a function of the asset portfolio, the random asset returns, and the target return. *Regret* functions play this role.

The regret risk measure can be viewed as a generalization of mean absolute deviation. Instead of measuring deviations of the portfolio return from its mean value, we consider deviations from some random target $\tilde{g}$, that takes values from the set $\{g^l\}_{l\in\Omega}$. First we define the regret function.

Definition 2.3.10 Regret function. *The difference between the target return random variable $\tilde{g}$ and the portfolio return random variable is the regret given by*

$$G(x; \tilde{r}, \tilde{g}) = R(x; \tilde{r}) - \tilde{g}, \tag{2.37}$$

and for the discrete scenario case by

$$G(x; r^l, g^l) = R(x; r^l) - g^l. \tag{2.38}$$

Note that positive values of the regret function indicate that the target was exceeded by the portfolio and they measure the upside potential of the portfolio. Negative values show that the target was not achieved and they measure the downside risk of the portfolio. The risk measure obtained from the regret function is the expected downside.

Definition 2.3.11 Expected downside. *The expected downside of the portfolio return vis-à-vis the target is given by*

$$G_-(x; \tilde{r}, \tilde{g}) = \mathcal{E}\left[\max\left[0, -G(x; \tilde{r}, \tilde{g})\right]\right]. \tag{2.39}$$

In the discrete scenario case this is estimated by

$$G_-(x; \tilde{r}, \tilde{g}) = \sum_{l\in\Omega} p^l \max\left[0, -G(x; r^l, g^l)\right]. \tag{2.40}$$

Regret functions also appear in decision analysis, where regret is defined as the opportunity loss. This is the loss incurred by not selecting the best alternative. Clearly, a different opportunity loss is realized for each realization of the random variable. Let

$$g^l = \max_x R(x; r^l) \tag{2.41}$$

denote the return of the portfolio with maximal value in scenario l. With this definition the regret function has a target return which is not exogenous, but is computed endogenously. The regret function is then written as

$$G(x; r^l) = R(x; r^l) - \max_x R(x; r^l). \tag{2.42}$$

Note that this is a special case of regret function, and is always nonpositive: regret is zero when the portfolio choice is the best one for a given scenario, otherwise an opportunity loss is realized.

2.4   Risk Measurement for Fixed-Income Securities

The predominant risk in fixed-income securities is the risk associated with changes in the general level of interest rates. In order to develop risk measures for fixed-income securities we will study the relationship between bond prices and interest rates. From this relationship we can then study the sensitivity of prices to changes in the general level of interest rates. Credit risk is also accounted when the analysis of this section is applied to the term structure of the yields of corporate bonds that are exposed to credit risk, instead of the term structure of the risk-free government bonds.

Definition 2.4.1 Spot rate. *The basic rate of interest charged for the risk-free asset (cash) held during a period from $t = 0$ (today) until some time $t = \tau$. We can think of the spot rate as the return on one unit of the risk-free asset during the holding period τ and denote it by $r_{f\tau}$.*

Definition 2.4.2 Term structure of interest rates. *The vector of spot rates for all holding periods $t = 1, 2, \ldots, T$, denoted by $(r_{ft})_{t=1}^{T}$.*

When the only rate of interest is the risk-free rate we will write r_t instead of r_{ft} without ambiguity. In the rest of this chapter r_t denotes the risk-free rate.

Spot rates are usually defined in annualized terms. The length of the time interval from $\tau - 1$ to τ is one year, and one unit of the risk-free asset will grow to $(1 + r_\tau)^\tau$ when held for τ years. If it is assumed that the risk-free rate is compounded m periods per year then the risk-free asset will grow to $(1 + r_\tau/m)^{m\tau}$. Under continuous compounding the growth factor is $e^{r_\tau \tau}$.

Definition 2.4.3 Forward rates. *From the definition of spot rates we can obtain rates of interest for a risk-free asset held from some period t until a later period τ. The forward rate from t to $\tau > t$ is given by*

$$f_{t\tau} = \left[\frac{(1 + r_\tau)^\tau}{(1 + r_t)^t} \right]^{1/(\tau - t)} - 1. \tag{2.43}$$

This definition assumes yearly discrete compounding. It states that the interest earned by holding an asset for t periods at the spot rate r_t and then reinvesting it at the forward rate $f_{t\tau}$ for another $\tau - t$ periods, is equal to the interest earned by holding the asset for τ periods at the spot rate r_τ.

We can now calculate the price of a bond that makes predetermined risk-free payments. These payments could reflect principal and/or coupons. Since the payments are risk free their market price will be the sum of their present values.

Definition 2.4.4 Pricing with continuous compounding. *The price of a bond i that pays risk-free amounts F_{ti} at $t = 1, 2, \ldots, T$, under continuous compounding is given by*

$$P_i = \sum_{t=1}^{T} F_{ti} e^{-r_t t}. \tag{2.44}$$

The definition of spot rates tells us that each amount F_{ti} is worth its present value today $F_{ti} e^{-r_t t}$. The bond is a portfolio of cashflow payments and its price is equal to the total worth of the individual payments.

Definition 2.4.5 Pricing with discrete compounding. *The price of a bond P_i that pays risk-free amounts F_{ti} at $t = 1, 2, \ldots, T$, under discrete yearly compounding is given by*

$$P_i = \sum_{t=1}^{T} \frac{F_{ti}}{(1 + r_t)^t}. \tag{2.45}$$

The price of a bond has been calculated using the term structure of interest rates that applies to the risk-free cashflows for the different holding periods. Equivalently we could estimate the yield-to-maturity of a bond i from the following definition.

Definition 2.4.6 Yield-to-maturity. *The yield-to-maturity of a bond with cashflows F_{ti}, for $t = 1, 2, \ldots, T$, is the discount rate y_i that makes the net present value of the cashflows equal to the current bond price P_{0i}. In the case of continuous compounding it is obtained as the solution of the equation*

$$P_{0i} = \sum_{t=1}^{T} F_{ti} e^{-y_i t}, \tag{2.46}$$

or in the case of discrete compounding, of the equation

$$P_{0i} = \sum_{t=1}^{T} \frac{F_{ti}}{(1+y_i)^t}.$$ (2.47)

Bonds of different maturities may have different yields and we could define a yield curve analogous to the term structure of interest rates. However, the yield curve is arbitrarily using the time-to-maturity as the independent variable. Two bonds with the same maturity, but with different timing of the cashflow payments, will have different yield-to-maturity. Perhaps the average time-to-maturity could serve better as the independent time variable. In order to avoid this ambiguity we will use the term structure of interest rates, instead of the yield curve, when pricing a stream of cashflows arising from holding a bond.

2.4.1 Duration and convexity

We now turn to the measurement of interest rate risk in the price of a bond. The sensitivity of the price equation with changes to the term structure of interest rates provides a risk measure.

Definition 2.4.7 Price derivatives. *Consider a general pricing equation $P_i = \Phi_i(z)$ for bond i, where z is the independent variable subject to unforeseen and unforecastable changes. The sole source of risk for the bond price is the variable z. A first-order estimate of changes in the bond price with changes in z is given by the first derivative*

$$D_i = \frac{\partial \Phi_i(z)}{\partial z}.$$ (2.48)

This definition is ambiguous since z could be the yield or the spot rate. Also, it is not rigorous since z is typically a vector, such as the term structure of interest rates. Hence, we need to specify partial derivatives (i.e., directional derivatives with respect to each one of the components of this vector) or specify in some way simultaneous changes to all components of the vector. We specify further the variable z and its changes and provide rigorous definitions of price derivatives. They all go under the general term duration, a concept that will turn out to be very important in structuring optimal portfolios for fixed-income securities in Chapter 4.

Definition 2.4.8 Dollar duration. *Assuming a flat term structure $r_t = r$, for all $t = 1, 2, \ldots, T$, the dollar duration of bond i is given in discrete time by*

$$D_i^{DOL} = \frac{dP_i}{dr} = -\sum_{t=1}^{T} \frac{tF_{ti}}{(1+r)^{t+1}},$$ (2.49)

or in continuous time by

$$D_i^{DOL} = \frac{dP_i}{dr} = -\sum_{t=1}^{T} tF_{ti}e^{-rt}.$$ (2.50)

Dollar duration is measured in "units of price $\times$ units of time" (e.g., dollar $\times$ years), and it is therefore an absolute measure of price changes. If two bonds have cashflows with identical timing, but the payments of one bond are twice the payments of the other, then it will also have twice its dollar duration. It is preferable to have a relative measure of price sensitivity whereby the timing and relative magnitude of the cashflows are what matter and not their absolute value. Such a measure is given by modified duration.

Definition 2.4.9 Modified duration. *Assuming a flat term structure, $r_t = r$, for all $t = 1, 2, \ldots, T$, the modified duration of bond i with price P_i is given in discrete time by*

$$D_i^{MOD} = -\frac{dP_i}{dr}/P_i = \frac{1}{P_i}\sum_{t=1}^{T}\frac{tF_{ti}}{(1+r)^{t+1}}, \tag{2.51}$$

or in continuous time by

$$D_i^{MOD} = -\frac{dP_i}{dr}/P_i = \frac{1}{P_i}\sum_{t=1}^{T}tF_{ti}e^{-rt}. \tag{2.52}$$

Modified duration is measured in units of time – in our convention this would be in years – and we note that $D_i^{MOD} = -D_i^{DOL}/P_i$.

   Both dollar duration and modified duration assume a flat term structure. It is possible to extend these definitions by assuming a general term structure as given in Definition 2.4.2, and considering a shift of all spot rates by an identical amount Δr. In this way we study bond price sensitivity to parallel shifts of the term structure. The generalization is given by the Fisher-Weil duration which is traditionally defined in continuous compounding. We give definitions below in both continuous and discrete compounding.

Definition 2.4.10 Fisher-Weil duration. *Assume that the term structure $\{r_t\}_{t=1}^{T}$ is subjected to a parallel shift by a small amount Δr to $\{r_t + \Delta r\}_{t=1}^{T}$ so that $dr_t = dr = \Delta r$ for all $t = 1, 2, \ldots, T$. The price of a bond i under the given term structure is P_i, and the price sensitivity to the parallel shift is given by the Fisher-Weil duration in discrete time as*

$$D_i^{FW} = -\frac{dP_i}{dr}/P_i = \frac{1}{P_i}\sum_{t=1}^{T}\frac{tF_{ti}}{(1+r_t)^{t+1}}, \tag{2.53}$$

or in continuous time as

$$D_i^{FW} = -\frac{dP_i}{dr}/P_i = \frac{1}{P_i}\sum_{t=1}^{T}tF_{ti}e^{-r_t t}. \tag{2.54}$$

Note the similarity of the Fisher-Weil duration formulae to the modified duration formulae. Indeed, in the case of flat term structure, i.e., when $r_t = r$ for all $t = 1, 2, \ldots, T$, the Fisher-Weil duration reduces to modified duration.

   Definitions 2.4.8–2.4.10 of duration were given as price derivatives with respect to the term structure of interest rates. The earliest definition of duration was given by the British actuary Frederick R. Macaulay (1938). Macauly's definition is given next, together with a discussion of its relationship to price derivatives.

Definition 2.4.11 Macaulay duration. *Assuming that the yield-to-maturity of a bond i is y_i, the Macaulay duration is given by*

$$D_i^{MAC} = \frac{\sum_{t=1}^{T} t\frac{F_{ti}}{(1+y_i)^t}}{\sum_{t=1}^{T}\frac{F_{ti}}{(1+y_i)^t}}. \tag{2.55}$$

Macaulay duration is measured in units of time. The denominator is the present value of the cashflows of the bond, discounted at the bond yield. The numerator is the weighted sum of the present values of the cashflows F_{ti}, where each cashflow is discounted to $t = 0$ by the bond yield and is weighted by the time when the cashflow was received (see Figure 2.5). It is indeed

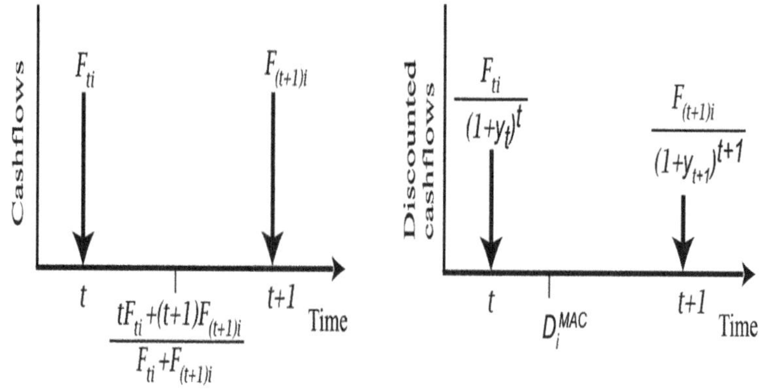

Figure 2.5: Macaulay duration as a time-weighted average of the cashflows for a long and a short bond.

this time-weighted average that first motivated the investigations into duration as a measure of the bond price sensitivity to interest rates. It is obvious that bonds with long maturities are more sensitive to interest rate changes than bonds with short maturities. But does maturity tell the whole story? A "short" bond with several coupon payments at the first few years and principal payment after, say, 10 years will be less sensitive than a "long" bond with coupon payments towards the end of the 10-year horizon. The maturity is the same for both bonds, but not their sensitivity to changes in yield. The "long" bond has greater duration when computed using the Macaulay formula, and this reflects its higher sensitivity.

The Macaulay duration is, within a constant, equal to the derivative of the price-yield equation divided by the bond's price:

$$D_i^{MAC} = -(1 + y_i)\frac{1}{\Phi_i(y_i)}\frac{d\Phi_i(y_i)}{dy_i}. \qquad (2.56)$$

From this equation we obtain the relationship between Macauly duration and the price derivative (Definitions 2.4.8–2.4.10).

Duration can also be interpreted as the slope of the price-yield or price-interest rate curve $P_i = \Phi_i(z)$ at a given point. This slope provides a linear approximation to the curve. A more accurate representation can be obtained through a second-order Taylor series approximation to this curve (see Figure 2.6). If P_i denotes the price computed at z_0 and ΔP_i is the price change when z shifts from z_0 to $z_0 + \Delta z$ we have

$$\Delta P_i \approx \frac{\partial\Phi_i(z)}{\partial z}\Delta z + \frac{1}{2}\frac{\partial^2\Phi_i(z)}{\partial z^2}(\Delta z)^2. \qquad (2.57)$$

The second derivative of the price is the *convexity* of the bond.

Definition 2.4.12 Convexity. *Assume that the term structure $(r_t)_{t=1}^T$ is subjected to a parallel shift by a small amount Δr to $(r_t + \Delta r)_{t=1}^T$ so that $dr_t = dr = \Delta r$ for all $t = 1, 2, \ldots, T$. The price of a bond i under the given term structure is P_i and the convexity of the bond is given in discrete time by*

$$C_i = \frac{d^2 P_i}{dr^2}\bigg/P_i = \frac{1}{P_i}\sum_{t=1}^T \frac{t(t + 1)F_{ti}}{(1 + r_t)^{t+2}}, \qquad (2.58)$$

or in continuous time by

$$C_i = \frac{1}{P_i}\sum_{t=1}^T t^2 F_{ti}e^{-r_t t}. \qquad (2.59)$$

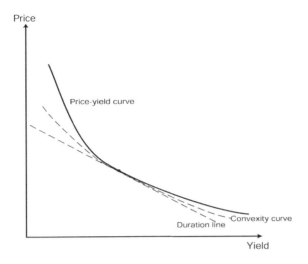

Figure 2.6: The price-yield curve, and duration and convexity as its approximations.

Note that in the case of a flat term structure convexity is equivalent to the first derivative of dollar duration scaled by price

$$C_i = \frac{1}{P_i}\frac{dD_i^{DOL}}{dr}. \tag{2.60}$$

The second-order Taylor series approximation of the price curve changes for small and parallel shifts of the term structure is written in terms of duration and convexity as

$$\Delta P_i \approx -D_i^{FW}P_i\Delta r + \frac{C_iP_i}{2}(\Delta r)^2. \tag{2.61}$$

The measures of risk given above have a clear economic interpretation. They measure the sensitivity of a bond's price to prespecified changes of the term structure, namely to small and parallel shifts. Hence, they measure only fixed-income market price risk (Definition 2.2.3) but not shape risk (Definition 2.2.5). Credit risk can be incorporated if one uses a term structure implied by corporate bonds, instead of the term structure of risk-free rates. Under regulated interest rate regimes – era of the Bretton-Woods agreement or in controlled economies – parallel shifts are all that matter. In the early days following the breakdown of the Bretton-Woods agreement or shortly into interest rate deregulation, most of the changes are still parallel shifts. The popularity of the duration measures throughout the 1970s was well justified. In the 1990s and beyond, the simple duration concepts remain a reasonable approximation, but they are not quite adequate and more advanced risk measures are developed.

2.4.2   Factor analysis of the term structure

Small and parallel shifts are insufficient for describing changes of the term structure in modern fixed-income markets. Figure 2.7 shows that the yields on short- and long-maturity bonds are not perfectly correlated and shape risk is significant. We introduce a method to describe such changes, thus paving the way for general measures of risk that better capture the changes in contemporary fixed-income markets.

Definition 2.4.13 Principal components of the term structure. *Let $\tilde{r} = (\tilde{r}_t)_{t=1}^T$ be the vector of the random variable spot rates, and Q be the $T \times T$ covariance matrix. An eigenvector of Q is a vector $\beta_j = (\beta_{jt})_{t=1}^T$ such that $Q\beta_j = \lambda_j\beta_j$ for some constant λ_j called an eigenvalue of*

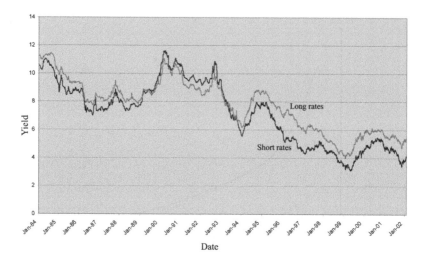

Figure 2.7: The yields of short- and long-maturity bonds are not perfectly correlated, thus giving rise to shape risk.

Q. The random variable $f_j = \sum_{t=1}^{T} \beta_{jt} r_t$ is a principal component of the term structure. The first principal component is the one that corresponds to the largest eigenvalue, the second to the second largest, and so on.

We first illustrate this definition with an example, and then we explain why principal components are useful in measuring risk. Consider the eight yields of Italian treasury bonds (BTP) with maturities between six months and seven years. The correlation matrix of (changes) of the yields is given in Table 2.1. The correlations are higher for bonds with maturities near each other, and they decline for bonds with distant maturities. Yields are correlated, but not perfectly. Figure 2.8 illustrates the eigenvectors corresponding to the three largest eigenvalues, $\lambda_1 = 0.9391, \lambda_2 = 0.0549$, and $\lambda_3 = 0.0042$. These three eigenvectors explain more than 99% of the changes in the yields, as the sum of these eigenvalues is 99.82. Additional insights are obtained from the eigenvector values. For instance, the first eigenvector has almost the same value for all maturities. The yields of different maturities change by almost a parallel shift due to the effects of this eigenvector. Parallel shifts account for 93.91% of the changes in the Italian BTP market, as given by the largest eigenvalue.

Table 2.1: Correlations of the changes in the yields of Italian treasury bonds (BTP) of different maturities over the period 1988–1992.

Time to maturity	6 mos.	1 yr.	2 yrs.	3 yrs.	4 yrs.	5 yrs.	6 yrs.	7 yrs.
6 mos.	1.000							
1 year	0.759	1.000						
2 years	0.387	0.828	1.000					
3 years	0.320	0.694	0.940	1.000				
4 years	0.312	0.571	0.794	0.950	1.000			
5 years	0.306	0.462	0.641	0.852	0.973	1.000		
6 years	0.299	0.380	0.521	0.762	0.926	0.988	1.000	
7 years	0.292	0.322	0.434	0.691	0.882	0.967	0.994	1.000

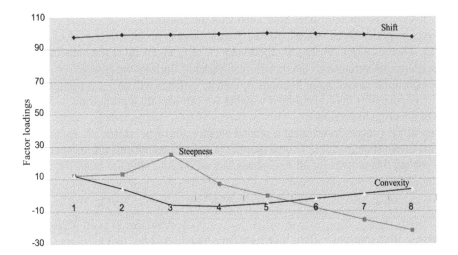

Figure 2.8: The coefficients – factor loadings – corresponding to the three most significant factors of the Italian treasury bonds (BTP) market.

To see why principal components are useful we will show that they can be used to approximate the variance of a portfolio of holdings in the T random variable spot rates. When the number of eigenvectors $j = 1, 2, \ldots, K$, is much smaller than T then this approximation entails significant reduction in the size of the covariance matrix used in estimating the portfolio variance. Even when $K = T$ we do not use all the eigenvectors, but we follow instead some sort of selection rule. Typically, eigenvectors are computed until the principal components explain some arbitrarily large proportion of the variance. For instance, we may want to use only the first κ eigenvectors such that $\sum_{j=1}^{\kappa} \lambda_j$ is greater than 99% of the variance.

Consider now the random variable return of a portfolio

$$R(x; \tilde{r}) = \sum_{t=1}^{T} \tilde{r}_t x_t, \tag{2.62}$$

with holdings x_t in the tth rate such that $\sum_{t=1}^{T} x_t = 1$. We want to approximate the variance of the portfolio $\sigma^2(x) = x^\top Q x$, where Q is the covariance matrix, by using a matrix Q^* of reduced dimension without significant loss of variability. We replace the original variable $\tilde{r}$ by the principal component $\tilde{f}_j = \sum_{t=1}^{T} \beta_{jt} \tilde{r}_t$; this is equivalent to creating a new composite asset j as a portfolio of holdings β_{jt} in the tth rate. The variance of $\tilde{f}_j$ is given by $\sigma_j^2 \doteq \sigma^2(\beta_j) = \beta_j^\top Q \beta_j$. We want to choose β_j such that the variance of $\tilde{f}_j$ is maximized subject to a normalization constraint $\beta_j^\top \beta_j = 1$. If this variance is maximized then so is the sum of the squared correlations of $\tilde{f}_j$ with the random variables $\tilde{r}_t$, and the principal component is a good approximation of the rates. Hence, we must solve for β_j the following quadratic program:

$$\underset{\beta_j}{\text{Maximize}} \quad \beta_j^\top Q \beta_j \tag{2.63}$$

$$\text{subject to} \quad \beta_j^\top \beta_j = 1. \tag{2.64}$$

The first-order optimality conditions (see Appendix A) applied to this problem require that the gradient of the objective function is a weighted function of the gradient of the constraint. Therefore β_j should satisfy

$$Q\beta_j = \lambda_j \beta_j, \tag{2.65}$$

where λ_j is the Lagrange multiplier associated with the constraint.

The vector β_j that satisfies the optimality conditions is an *eigenvector* of Q and λ_j is an *eigenvalue*. Therefore by choosing an eigenvector β_j of Q in obtaining the transformed variable $\tilde{f}_j$ we maximize the variance of the transformed variable. Indeed, we have $\sigma^2(\beta_j) = \lambda_j$. If we construct a portfolio consisting of holdings β_j then its variance will be λ_j. So using only the first principal component as the transformed variable we can explain a proportion $\lambda_1/\sigma^2(x)$ of the variance of the original portfolio.

We repeat the process to estimate a second eigenvector of the matrix $\beta_{j'}$ that is *orthogonal* to β_j. That is, we require $\beta_{j'}^\top \beta_j = 0$ so that the principal components are independent of each other. Repeating this process for all K eigenvectors we obtain a *singular value decomposition* of the matrix

$$Q = B\Lambda B^\top, \tag{2.66}$$

where $B = (\beta_1 \; \beta_2 \; \ldots \; \beta_K)$, $\Lambda = diag(\lambda_1, \lambda_2, \ldots, \lambda_K)$. Note that B is an orthogonal matrix, i.e., its inverse is its transpose, since it follows from equation (2.64) that $BB^\top = I$, where I is a conformable identity matrix. The singular value decomposition (2.66) is a generalization of the eigenvector equation (2.65) from one eigenvector to many.

Consider now the portfolio with holdings β_j in each of the K factors. The variance of the portfolio is given by $\sum_{j=1}^{K} \sigma_j^2$, since the factors are orthogonal. By construction of the eigenvalues this is equal to $\sum_{j=1}^{K} \lambda_j$. If we use $\kappa < K$ factors we will obtain a portfolio with variance given by $\sum_{j=1}^{\kappa} \lambda_j$. A fraction $\sum_{j=\kappa+1}^{K} \lambda_j / \sum_{j=1}^{\kappa} \lambda_j$ of the variance of the original portfolio will not be accounted for.

If we denote by $B_\kappa = (\beta_1 \; \beta_2 \; \ldots \; \beta_\kappa)$ the matrix of the eigenvectors corresponding to the first κ largest eigenvalues, and let $\Lambda_\kappa = diag(\lambda_1, \lambda_2, \ldots, \lambda_\kappa)$, we can approximate the covariance matrix by $\hat{Q} = B_\kappa \Lambda_\kappa B_\kappa^\top$. Using the singular value decomposition of the covariance matrix above we write the variance of a portfolio as

$$\sigma^2(x) = x^\top Q x = x^\top B\Lambda B^\top x, \tag{2.67}$$

and this can be approximated by

$$\sigma^2(x) \approx x^\top \hat{Q} x. \tag{2.68}$$

In practical applications it is customary to work with the correlation instead of the covariance matrix.

In the example with the Italian treasury bonds we can explain up to 99.82% of the 8×8 correlation matrix using only three factors, i.e., $\kappa = 3$. At first glance this may not seem much of a reduction. However, principal component analysis of 360 spot rates of US treasury securities – in monthly steps up to maturity of 30 years – found that three factors were sufficient to explain more than 99% of the variability, and this represents a significant reduction in the dimensionality of the problem. Similarly, empirical analysis has shown that four factors explain 99.6% of the variability in the Danish government bond rates, and three factors explain 98% of the variability in US corporate bond yields.

What does a change in the jth principal component tell us about changes of $\tilde{r}$? If $\tilde{f} = (\tilde{f}_1 \; \tilde{f}_2, \ldots, \tilde{f}_K)$ denotes the vector of the K independent principal components, we have $\tilde{f} = B^\top \tilde{r}$. Since $BB^\top = I$ we have $\tilde{r} = B\tilde{f}$, and the T random rates are expressed as linear combinations of K factors. A unit change in the jth factor will cause a change equal to β_{jt} to rate r_t and the changes of all factors have a cumulative effect on the rates.

Assume that r_t changes by an amount β_{jt} from its current value r_t^0, i.e., $r_t \rightarrow r_t^0 + \beta_{jt}$. Hence, $f_j \rightarrow \sum_{t=1}^{T} \beta_{jt}(r_t^0 + \beta_{jt}) = \sum_{t=1}^{T} \beta_{jt} r_t^0 + \sum_{t=1}^{T} \beta_{jt} \beta_{jt} = f_j^0 + 1$. (The last equality follows from the normalization of the eigenvectors.) Hence, a unit change of the jth factor implies a change by β_{jt} for each spot rate t. Since the factors are independent we may express the total change of r_t by

$$\Delta r_t = \sum_{j=1}^{K} \beta_{jt} \Delta f_j, \tag{2.69}$$

where K is the number of factors identified by the eigenvector analysis. We point out that if we use the first $\kappa < K$ factors in the analysis above then Δr_t will explain only a fraction $\sum_{j=1}^{\kappa} \lambda_j$ of the changes.

Definition 2.4.14 Factor loading. *The coefficient β_{jt} is called factor loading, and it measures the sensitivity of the t-maturity rate r_t to changes of the jth factor.*

Equation (2.69) provides a simple linear model for describing the changes of the term structure. Instead of assuming that the term structure shifts in parallel – as we did in Definitions 2.4.8– 2.4.10 – we can estimate price sensitivities of bonds due to the shifts implied by the eigenvectors. For instance, in Figure 2.8 we observe that the first eigenvector corresponds to almost parallel shifts in the yields of different maturities, the second eigenvector corresponds to a change in the steepness, and the third factor to a change in curvature. It is possible to estimate partial derivatives of bond prices with respect to changes in these factors, which are termed factor durations. The development of factor durations is deferred until Chapter 4 where they are used to develop optimization models for fixed-income portfolios.

2.4.3   Option adjusted analysis

So far we have measured the risk of fixed-income securities by the price sensitivity to small and parallel shifts of the term structure. Furthermore, we assumed that the cashflows received from the securities were interest-rate invariant and, therefore, risk free. Now we relax both of these assumptions and introduce risk measures that are relevant in a world of highly volatile interest rates and for modern fixed-income securities.

Fixed-income securities come today with a variety of options that link their cashflows to some exogenous variables, most notably the interest rate. These options may be explicit or embedded. For instance, callable bonds may be called when interest rates drop. Mortgage-backed securities may experience prepayments when interest rates decline. Corporate bonds may default under adverse economic conditions, in which case the timing of the default and the amount that the debtors recover is uncertain. Owners of insurance endowment products – such as single premium deferred annuities or index-linked funds – may surrender the product to the issuer when interest rates increase. In all these cases the cashflow pattern of the security is contingent on the term structure of interest rates. The relation between the term structure changes and the cashflow pattern could be highly nonlinear and quite complex. For instance, prepayments of mortgages by homeowners depend on the history of interest rates since the loan was assumed, the prevailing rates for 15-year or 30-year fixed or adjustable rate mortgages, and on demographics. Therefore, the risk measures of the previous section that are based on the assumptions of small and parallel shifts of the term structure will grossly underestimate the risk factors.

To address the added complexity we rely on the versatility of scenarios (see Definition 1.2.1). A scenario is the basic description of the evolution of the risk factor over time. It is assumed that the risk factor can be at one of a finite number of states and each one of these states is termed a scenario. Here we define only scenarios of the term structure but we could also define scenarios of the other risk factors defined in Section 2.2. A fixed-income security may be exposed to more than one risk factor and the specification of scenarios for all relevant factors allows us to get an accurate measure of the risk of the security. For instance, the price of a callable corporate bond depends on the exercise of the call option, changes in the term structure of interest rates, and on the credit risk of the issuer.

Scenarios of the term structure cannot be arbitrary. They must satisfy certain properties. For instance, negative spot rates cannot be allowed. The scenarios should also be plausible given the current market observation of the term structure. For instance, prices of risk-free bonds implied from our scenarios should be equal to the observed market prices. The scenarios should also preclude the presence of arbitrage when used to price bonds of different maturities. Other theoretical properties of the term structure should be reflected in the scenarios. More is said on the topic of scenario generation in Chapter 9.

The price of a bond i is now calculated as the expected discounted value of the cashflow payments, with expectations computed over the scenario set. We have

$$P_i = \sum_{l \in \Omega} p^l \sum_{t=1}^{T} \frac{F_{ti}(r^l)}{(1 + r_t^l)^t}. \tag{2.70}$$

The cashflow $F_{ti}(r^l)$ is a function of the term structure which is different for each scenario.

How do we measure the risk in the price of the bond implied by the equation above? One source of risk is due to any options embedded in the cashflow function. Another is the risk that the term structure may shift instantaneously.

Measuring the risk of embedded options

One way to measure the risk due to the embedded options is to estimate the risk premium implied by the security's price. This premium is the surcharge to the yield of risk-free bonds of comparable maturities that the market demands in order to assume the extra risk. The following definition applies.

Definition 2.4.15 Option adjusted spread. *Assume that the term structure of interest rates takes values $r^l = (r_t^l)_{t=1}^{T}$ in scenario l and that a fixed-income security with cashflows given by $F_{ti}(r^l)$ has a market price P_{0i}. The option adjusted spread (OAS) is the surcharge δ_i on the risk-free rate that will bring to equilibrium the observed market price, and is calculated by solving the following equation*

$$P_{0i} = \sum_{l \in \Omega} p^l \sum_{t=1}^{T} \frac{F_{ti}(r^l)}{(1 + r_t^l + \delta_i)^t}. \tag{2.71}$$

Recall that the scenarios must satisfy the property that prices of risk-free bonds computed from equation (2.70) should be equal to the observed market prices. It follows that the OAS for risk-free bonds is zero.

What are the advantages of estimating the OAS as above instead of estimating the yield of the bond by solving the price-yield equation in Definition 2.4.6 for y_i? The OAS takes into account the volatility of the term structure implied in the assumed scenarios. It also captures the sensitivity of the cashflows to changes in the term structure, and in particular the effects of any embedded options that may be exercised under some scenarios (hence the name "option adjusted"). Thus, the OAS of different securities can be meaningfully compared to give an indication of relative differences in expected returns.

The calculation of OAS assumes an average surcharge to the risk-free rate for all time periods until maturity T and the same surcharge is added to the risk-free rate for all scenarios. Both assumptions are flawed. First, we expect the surcharge to decrease as we approach maturity and, second, we expect a surcharge that is proportional to the level of the risk-free rates. The first assumption is difficult to bypass unless we introduce a model of the dynamics of OAS. The second is readily relaxed in the following definition for estimating a proportional risk premium.

Definition 2.4.16 Option adjusted premium. *Assume that the term structure of interest rates takes values $r^l = (r_t^l)_{t=1}^{T}$ in scenario l and that a fixed-income security with cashflows given by*

$F_{ti}(r^l)$ *has a market price P_{0i}. The option adjusted premium (OAP) δ_i is computed by solving the following equation*

$$P_{0i} = \sum_{l \in \Omega} p^l \sum_{t=1}^{T} \frac{F_{ti}(r^l)}{(1 + r_t^l \delta_i)^t}. \tag{2.72}$$

Measuring the risk of term structure shifts

We have assumed scenarios that are plausible given the current term structure of interest rates. Prices of risk-free bonds implied from these scenarios are equal to the observed market prices, and prices of risky fixed-income securities come with a surcharge, OAS or OAP. How do we measure the risk in the price of the bonds when the term structure shifts? For risk-free bonds Definitions 2.4.8–2.4.10 of duration apply. For other fixed-income securities we need to estimate the bonds' price sensitivity taking into account the embedded options by using simulations, and the following definitions apply.

Definition 2.4.17 Option adjusted duration. *The first derivative of the price of a fixed-income security that takes into account the embedded options is estimated numerically as follows:*

Initialization: *Define an index set Ω_0 for the scenarios of the term structure of interest rates. Each scenario $l \in \Omega_0$ occurs with probability p^l such that $\sum_{l \in \Omega_0} p^l = 1$, and the term structure takes the value $r_0^l = (r_{0t}^l)_{t=1}^T$. The scenarios should be plausible given the current term structure of interest rates. That is, the prices of risk-free bonds computed from equation (2.70) should be equal to the observed market prices for an option adjusted premium for risk-free bonds equal to one. Solve equation (2.72) to compute the OAP for security i and denote the solution by $\hat{\delta}_i$.*

Step 1: *Shift the term structure by Δr basis points and define a new index set Ω_+ for scenarios that are plausible under the shifted term structure of interest rates. Each scenario $l \in \Omega_+$ occurs with probability p^l and the term structure takes the value $r_+^l = (r_{+t}^l)_{t=1}^T$.*

Step 2: *Compute the option adjusted price*

$$P_{+i} = \sum_{l \in \Omega_+} p^l \sum_{t=1}^{T} \frac{F_{ti}(r_+^l)}{(1 + r_{+t}^l \hat{\delta}_i)^t}. \tag{2.73}$$

Step 3: *Shift the term structure by $-\Delta r$ basis points and define a new index set Ω_- for scenarios that are plausible under the shifted term structure of interest rates. Each scenario $l \in \Omega_-$ occurs with probability p^l and the term structure takes the value $r_-^l = (r_{-t}^l)_{t=1}^T$.*

Step 4: *Compute the option adjusted price*

$$P_{-i} = \sum_{l \in \Omega_-} p^l \sum_{t=1}^{T} \frac{F_{ti}(r_-^l)}{(1 + r_{-t}^l \hat{\delta}_i)^t}. \tag{2.74}$$

Step 5: *The option adjusted duration of the security is given by*

$$\Delta_i^{OA} = \frac{P_{+i} - P_{-i}}{2\Delta r} \tag{2.75}$$

This equation computes a finite difference approximation of the first derivative of the bond price with respect to small and parallel shifts in the term structure by an amount $\pm \Delta r$.

Definition 2.4.18 Option adjusted convexity. *From the quantities estimated in the calculation of the option adjusted duration we estimate the* option adjusted convexity *as*

$$C_i^{OA} = \frac{P_{+i} - 2P_{0i} + P_{-i}}{(\Delta r)^2}. \tag{2.76}$$

This is a finite difference approximation of the second derivative of the bond price with respect to small and parallel shifts of the term structure.

The second derivative of the bond price is the first derivative of the bond duration. Thus, an equivalent expression for option adjusted convexity is obtained by estimating a finite difference approximation of the first derivative of the option adjusted duration. Let

$$\Delta_{+i}^{OA} = \frac{P_{+i} - P_{0i}}{\Delta r}, \tag{2.77}$$

and

$$\Delta_{-i}^{OA} = \frac{P_{0i} - P_{-i}}{\Delta r}. \tag{2.78}$$

Then the option adjusted convexity can be estimated by

$$C_i^{OA} = \frac{\Delta_{+i}^{OA} - \Delta_{-i}^{OA}}{\Delta r}, \tag{2.79}$$

which is, following some elementary algebra, equivalent to (2.76).

2.5 Scenario Analysis for Fixed-Income Securities

Option adjusted spread, option adjusted premium, and option adjusted duration and convexity are averaging measures of risk. They take the average over all scenarios and report a single quantity: either an average surcharge (option adjusted spread or option adjusted premium), or the first and second derivatives of the price averaged over all scenarios.

In a significant departure from tradition in fixed-income risk management, we have seen in the 1990s an interest in measures of risk that are analogous to those used for equities. Instead of averaging procedures we turn to the study of the scenarios of security returns during the holding period. This approach enjoys several advantages over the averaging measures.

The first advantage of scenario analysis is that it captures correlations among the assets in a portfolio. Negative correlations are particularly useful in reducing risks. In fact the potential for negative correlation may be greater in the fixed-income markets than in the equity market. Many institutional investors are unable to short-sell in equities and most equities display positive correlations with each other. This need not be the case in fixed income. Indeed, several fixed-income securities are designed to offset each other's interest rate risk. The classic example is the split of mortgage-backed securities into IO (interest only) and PO (principal only) products. Their prices move in opposite directions with changes in interest rates and the respective durations, i.e., the slopes of the price-interest rate curves, have opposite signs.

But is duration sufficient to capture the negative correlations? Figure 2.9 illustrates the price sensitivity of a mortgage-backed security and the IO and PO derivatives for several interest rate scenarios ranging from 6.5% to 9.5%. The durations of the derivatives are significantly different for interest rates lower than 7.5% but they are marginally different for rates higher than 9%. Hence, a duration estimated as the average over all scenarios reveals little useful information.

The second advantage of scenario analysis is that it allows us to integrate the risk measurement of equities with the risk measurement of fixed income. Once scenarios of holding period

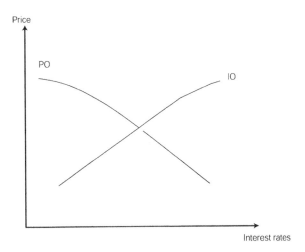

Figure 2.9: Mortgage derivative products with negative correlations: the price sensitivity of IO (interest only) and PO (principal only) mortgage products to interest rates.

returns are generated for a fixed-income security we can compute all the risk measures used for equities in Section 2.3.

As a result of the convergence of risk measures for equities and fixed-income securities, scenario analysis enjoys a third, and most significant, advantage. It allows the development of a general framework for analyzing risks and rewards at an enterprise-wide level, so that EWRM becomes technically feasible. It is possible through scenario analysis to develop holding period returns for a portfolio of assets in response to all relevant risk factors. The correlation of these returns with each other and with the firm's liabilities can then be optimized. Scenario analysis provides the requisite input data for the optimization models described in Chapters 5 to 8, as well as the large-scale applications discussed in Chapters 10 to 13.

The next definition applies to the scenario analysis for fixed-income securities. Figure 2.10 illustrates the concepts used in this definition.

Definition 2.5.1 Holding period return. *Assume that a fixed-income security with cashflows given by $F_{ti}^l \doteq F_{ti}(r^l)$ has a market price P_{0i}. The rate of return of the security during a holding period τ under a scenario l is given by*

$$r_{\tau i}^l = \frac{CF_{\tau i}^l + V_{\tau i}^l}{P_{0i}} - 1, \tag{2.80}$$

where the following parameters are used:

$CF_{\tau i}^l$ *is the future value of the cashflow generated by the security in scenario l during the interval from $t = 0$ to $t = \tau$, and accrued to τ. Denoting the forward rate from t to τ by $f_{t\tau}^l$ (see Definition 2.4.3) we have*

$$CF_{\tau i}^l = \sum_{t=1}^{\tau}(1 + f_{t\tau}^l)F_{ti}^l. \tag{2.81}$$

$V_{\tau i}^l$ *is the market value of the outstanding balance of the security at the end of the holding period in scenario l. It is given by $V_{\tau i}^l = B_{\tau i}^l P_{\tau i}^l$.*

$B_{\tau i}^l$ *is the outstanding face value of the security at the end of the holding period in scenario l. For instance, assuming an original face value of 100 for a risk-free bond then the outstanding*

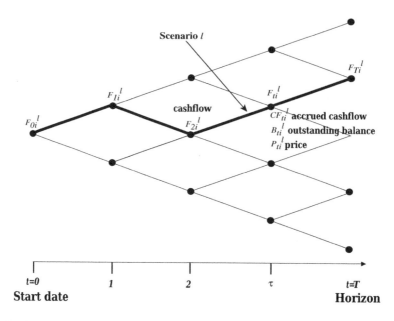

Figure 2.10: The evolution of scenarios as a binomial tree and the quantities used in the calculation of holding period returns.

face value at the end of the horizon is still 100, under all scenarios. If this were a callable bond that under scenario l experienced a partial 25% call or a mortgage-backed security that experienced a 25% prepayment of principal, the outstanding face value would be $B^l_{i\tau} = 75$. The outstanding face value is scenario-dependent. Under scenarios of high interest rates, for instance, no prepayments will be experienced, in which case the outstanding face value will be still 100. For low interest rates prepayments will occur and the outstanding face value will be reduced appropriately.

$P^l_{\tau i}$ is the price per unit face value of the security at the end of the holding period under scenario l. It can be computed as follows. Let $\Omega_{\tau|l}$ be the index set of scenarios that are plausible at τ given that scenario l has been observed during the period from t to τ. The probability of each scenario $l' \in \Omega_{\tau|l}$ is now a conditional probability denoted by $p^{l'|l}$. Then

$$P^l_{\tau i} = \sum_{l' \in \Omega_{\tau|l}} p^{l'|l} \sum_{t=\tau}^{T} \frac{F^{l'}_{ti}}{(1 + f^{l'}_{\tau t})^{(t-\tau)}}. \qquad (2.82)$$

2.6 Enterprise-Wide Risk Measurement

Scenario analysis generates distributions of holding period returns for fixed-income securities that are analogous to the return distributions of equities. Thus it facilitates the use of identical risk measures for both equities and fixed income. We can estimate variance, semi-variance, MAD or regret for the fixed-income portfolio, much as we compute these measures for the equities portfolio. This is a step in the right direction, as multiple sources of risk are measured in a common framework. Focusing solely on one type of risk would simply shift institutional risk exposure from one risk category to others. Risk exposure would be shifted to the risk categories that were less understood and poorly measured. This problem is exacerbated when one uses optimization models, as the optimizer will minimize or eliminate all risks that were included in the model, and unavoidably maximize the exposure to those risks that were not properly modeled.

Using the same risk measure for both equities and fixed income is not enough. What is needed is a methodology to integrate various sources of risk at the enterprise level in a common risk measure so that an aggregate risk exposure is properly measured and controlled. An example of such a measure is Value-at-Risk VaR, which answers the following question: What is the maximum loss with a given confidence level (say $100\alpha\%$) over a given horizon? Its calculation also reveals that with probability $100(1 - \alpha)\%$ the losses will exceed VaR. A formal definition is given below but a word of caution is first in order.

Worst-case losses at a given probability level can be measured for a single position (e.g., VaR in the Euro position of a bank due to adverse movements in the Euro exchange rates), or for a basket of positions (e.g., VaR in the foreign currency position of a bank due to adverse movements in exchange rates) or for a portfolio (e.g., VaR of the international corporate bond portfolio of a bank due to adverse movements in the interest rates, credit spreads and exchange rates). With proper implementation VaR can measure losses at an enterprise-wide level. However, worst-case losses at a given confidence level are not additive. The VaR of a bank due to its currency position and its corporate bond portfolio may be higher than the sum of the VaR due to each position taken separately. The total VaR will be more than the sum of its parts if the sources of risk are independent. For instance, each trader may have risk only at the 4% confidence level but zero risk at the 5% level. The 95% VaR is zero, but the 96% VaR is not! The desk manager will be led to the erroneous conclusion that the total VaR of his desk is zero, while if the traders take independent positions it is likely that there are nonzero risks at the 5% level, and this would especially be the case if the traders' positions are correlated.

Furthermore, VaR measures worst losses at a given level of confidence such as 95%. Losses will not exceed VaR 95% of the time. There is a 5% chance, however, that losses will be even greater. If we have a 1-day time horizon we should expect to suffer losses greater than VaR once every 20 days. The Bank for International Settlement imposes a 10-day horizon on the measurement of VaR for regulatory purposes. Hence, the regulators should expect that institutions under their supervision will suffer losses in excess of the reported VaR once every 200 days. Larger than VaR losses will be observed, on the average, more than once per year. These are shortcomings of VaR when used in EWRM, and are addressed later, after we give the formal definition.

Consider a portfolio with value $V(x; \tilde{P})$. This is a function of the asset holdings in the portfolio x and is parametrized by the random asset prices $\tilde{P}$. If the current value of the portfolio is V_0 then the losses in portfolio value are given by the loss function

$$L(x; \tilde{P}) = V_0 - V(x; \tilde{P}). \tag{2.83}$$

The relationship of the loss function to portfolio returns is easy to establish. We have $V_0 = \sum_{i=1}^{n} P_{0i} x_i$ and $V(x; \tilde{P}) = \sum_{i=1}^{n} \tilde{P}_i x_i$. Hence, the loss function can be written as $L(x; \tilde{P}) = \sum_{i=1}^{n} (P_{0i} - \tilde{P}_i) x_i$. The relationship between the loss function and portfolio returns is given by

$$L(x; \tilde{r}) = -R(x; \tilde{r}) V_0. \tag{2.84}$$

The probability that the loss function does not exceed some threshold value ζ is given, in the discrete scenario setting, by the probability function

$$\Psi(x, \zeta) = \sum_{\{l \in \Omega | L(x; P^l) \leq \zeta\}} p^l. \tag{2.85}$$

The Value-at-Risk of the portfolios is defined as follows:

Definition 2.6.1 Value-at-Risk (VaR). *The Value-at-Risk (VaR) of a portfolio at the α probability level is the left α-percentile of the losses of the portfolio, i.e., the lowest possible value ζ such that the probability of losses less or equal to VaR is greater or equal to $100\alpha\%$. It is given as:*

$$VaR(x; \alpha) \doteq \min \left\{ \zeta \in \mathbb{R} \mid \Psi(x, \zeta) \geq \alpha \right\}. \tag{2.86}$$

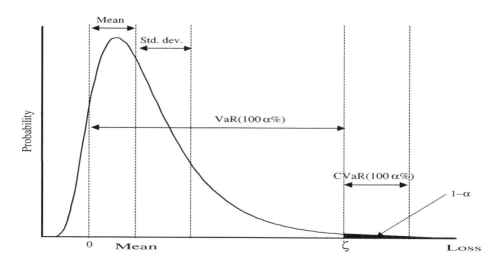

Figure 2.11: Distribution of losses and the quantities used in the definition of VaR and CVaR.

The percentile ζ is the left endpoint of the nonempty interval consisting of the values ζ such that $\Psi(x, \zeta) = \alpha$. Figure 2.11 illustrates the concepts involved in the calculation of VaR. The dependence of VaR on the confidence level α is sometimes made explicit by referring to α-VaR. A typical value for α is .95. For a portfolio with normally distributed values we can calculate the 0.95-VaR as being a value 1.645σ away from the mean.

An equivalent definition of VaR is obtained from the probability function

$$\Psi_+(x, \zeta) = \sum_{\{l \in \Omega \mid L(x; P^l) > \zeta\}} p^l, \tag{2.87}$$

which denotes the probability of losses strictly greater than ζ. The α-VaR is the minimum value of ζ such that the probability of losses in excess of ζ is $100(1-\alpha)\%$. This alternative definition is formalized below.

Definition 2.6.2 Value-at-Risk (alternative definition).

$$VaR(x; \alpha) \doteq \min \left\{ \zeta \in \mathbb{R} \mid \Psi_+(x, \zeta) < 1 - \alpha \right\}. \tag{2.88}$$

We could define similarly a right α-percentile to measure the highest possible losses such that the probability of losses greater than VaR exceeds $100\alpha\%$. For risk measurement it is typically the left percentile we are interested in. However, it might be possible that we are interested in both percentiles. For instance, in portfolios that are structured to track indices the loss function is the difference between the index and the portfolio values, and tracking error should be low in both the upside and the downside.

The VaR measure reveals nothing about the magnitude of the losses outside the given confidence level. Such losses can be catastrophic. The distribution of Long-Term Capital Management monthly returns in Figure 2.12 shows a VaR of -5%. However, a negative 80% return in September 1998 – realized, in part, due to substantial increase in the market volatility from its historically observed values, thus rendering the VaR calculation of -5% obsolete – wiped off a position of $1.85 trillion and threatened a global meltdown of the financial markets. The disruption of the financial markets was averted by a bailout orchestrated by the New York Federal Reserve. Fourteen banks invested $3.6 billion in return for a 90% stake in the firm.

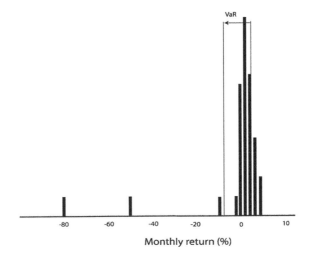

Figure 2.12: The distribution of returns of Long-Term Capital Management position. (Source: Jorion 1996)

A measure of risk that goes beyond the information revealed by VaR is the expected value of the losses that exceed VaR. This quantity is called *expected shortfall, conditional loss* or *conditional Value-at-Risk*. For general distributions the conditional VaR (CVaR) is defined as a weighted average of VaR and the expected losses that are strictly greater than VaR. For discrete distributions, and under a technical condition that the probability of scenarios with losses strictly greater than VaR is exactly equal to $1 - \alpha$, i.e., $\Psi(x, \zeta) = \alpha$, the following definition applies:

Definition 2.6.3 Conditional Value-at-Risk (CVaR). *The Conditional Value-at-Risk (CVaR) of the losses of the portfolio is the expected value of the losses, conditioned on the losses being in excess of VaR.*

$$\text{CVaR}(x; \alpha) = \mathcal{E}[L(x; P^l) \mid L(x; P^l) > \zeta] \tag{2.89}$$

$$= \frac{\sum_{\{l \in \Omega \mid L(x; P^l) > \zeta\}} p^l L(x; P^l)}{\sum_{\{l \in \Omega \mid L(x; P^l) > \zeta\}} p^l} \tag{2.90}$$

$$= \frac{\sum_{\{l \in \Omega \mid L(x; P^l) > \zeta\}} p^l L(x; P^l)}{1 - \alpha}, \tag{2.91}$$

where the last equality follows from the condition $\Psi(x, \zeta) = \alpha$.

The dependence of CVaR on the confidence level α is made explicit by referring to α-CVaR.

It follows from the definitions that CVaR is always greater or equal to VaR. Both VaR and CVaR are functions of the asset allocation vector x and the percentile parameter α. It is natural to seek to minimize these measures by changing the composition of the asset portfolio. VaR is difficult to optimize when calculated using discrete scenarios. The VaR function is nonconvex, nonsmooth and it has multiple local minima. However, CVaR can be minimized using linear programming formulations and Chapter 5 presents the optimization models for CVaR minimization.

2.7   Coherent Risk Measurement

As we said at the outset, financial risk is multidimensional and measuring it with alternative metrics provides insights. All the risk measures given in the previous sections have merit. However, we must inquire about the characteristics of risk measures that make them suitable for decision making in the context of enterprise-wide risk management.

For instance, the variance of a portfolio is not suitable for calculating regulatory capital. Suppose that a supervisor calculates regulatory capital as three standard deviations minus the expected value of the portfolio. If an institution adds to its portfolio a free lottery that pays two dollars with probability 0.5 and zero otherwise, the supervisor will conclude that the expected gain of one dollar does not properly compensate for the increased risk – three standard deviations is three in this case – and will require a margin of two dollars to be added to the regulatory capital. A portfolio that includes this attractive lottery would need more margin than a portfolio without it.

Similarly, VaR suffers as a measure of risk at the enterprise level when it calculates the worst-case losses at a given probability level (say 5%) by adding up the VaR of individual traders. If multiple traders take uncorrelated positions with zero losses at the 5% probability level, the enterprise VaR will appear to be zero. However, if each trader's position has very large losses with probability less than 5% then the firm is likely to be exposed to a nonzero VaR. Two traders writing separately two different put options that are both far out-of-the-money may each have losses with a probability of, say, 4%. Their desk manager, however, may have losses at the 5% level. While no margin may be needed to cover each position separately, some margin is needed to cover both. This examples illustrates that the sum of the VaR of two positions may be less than the VaR of a portfolio of these positions. Thus while it may appear that the total risk exposure – measured by adding up the individual risk exposures – is within acceptable limits, the actual risk exposure of the total position may be unacceptably high. Put another way, by splitting a portfolio into multiple positions one may estimate a much lower risk exposure than what is captured by the VaR of the original portfolio.

Financial institutions facing supervisors with VaR-based formulas for equity requirement could create multiple subsidiaries and thus free regulatory capital. Similarly, an exchange that bases margin requirements on the sum of the variances of individual positions would simply encourage its clients to open multiple accounts. Exchanges do not follow this approach. However, the use of VaR as a measure for supervision is advocated in the Basel Accord of the Bank for International Settlements. This needs careful implementation.

An axiomatic characterization of risk measures that support decision making is given by the following definition.

Definition 2.7.1 Coherent risk measures. *A coherent risk measure φ is a function that assigns numbers $\varphi(\tilde{X}), \varphi(\tilde{Y})$ to two random variables $\tilde{X}, \tilde{Y}$, such that for any pair $\tilde{X}, \tilde{Y}$, independent or not, and for each positive number a and each number b the following relations hold.*

Sub-additivity $\varphi(\tilde{X} + \tilde{Y}) \leq \varphi(\tilde{X}) + \varphi(\tilde{Y})$.

Homogeneity $\varphi(a\tilde{X}) = a\varphi(\tilde{X})$.

Monotonicity $\varphi(\tilde{X}) \leq \varphi(\tilde{Y})$ *if* $\tilde{X} \leq \tilde{Y}$.

Risk-free condition $\varphi(\tilde{X} - b\,r_f) = \varphi(\tilde{X}) - b$.

The random variables are assumed bounded and $\tilde{X} \leq \tilde{Y}$ means that $X^l \leq Y^l$ for almost all $l \in \Omega$. The random variables are defined as losses, so a positive value implies a loss while a negative value implies a net gain. In this respect $\tilde{X} - br_f$ denotes that losses are reduced by investing a positive amount b in the risk-free asset, or increased if b is negative signifying borrowing at the risk-free rate.

Sub-additivity ensures that the risk measure is reasonable when adding two positions. It allows the decentralized calculation of the risk at an enterprise-wide level, since the sum of the risks of individual positions provides an upper bound on the enterprise-wide risk. Sub-additivity and homogeneity imply that the risk measure function is convex. This is consistent with risk aversion on the part of the user of these measures. Monotonicity stipulates that if the losses $\tilde{X}$ are always smaller than $\tilde{Y}$, then $\tilde{Y}$ must be at least as risky as $\tilde{X}$. The risk-free condition requires that the risk of a position is reduced by any amount invested in the risk-free rate. In particular it follows from this condition that $\varphi[\tilde{X} - r_f \varphi(\tilde{X})] = 0$.

A characterization of coherent risk measures can be given in terms of scenarios.

Definition 2.7.2 Generalized scenarios. *Let Ω be the index set of the finitely many states of the random variables and let $\mathcal{P}$ be a set of probability distributions on these states. The states indexed by l in Ω are termed generalized scenarios.*

The scenarios considered in Definition 1.2.1 are generalized scenarios with the set $\mathcal{P}$ being a singleton consisting of a single probability distribution. This is the simple probability distribution with single point support given by the probabilities p^l.

A general definition of risk measures that satisfy the conditions of coherence above can be given in terms of generalized scenarios.

Definition 2.7.3 Coherent risk measures. *A coherent risk measure calculates the expected value of the losses $\tilde{X}$ of a position under all probability distributions belonging to $\mathcal{P}$ and assigns the maximum value of these calculations to $\tilde{X}$ according to the formula*

$$\varphi(\tilde{X}) = \sup \left\{ \mathcal{E}_P[\tilde{X}_+] \mid P \in \mathcal{P} \right\}. \tag{2.92}$$

We define $\tilde{X}_+ = \max[0, \tilde{X}]$ so that the risk measure depends only on possible losses. Negative values of $\tilde{X}$ signify gains and these do not come into play in the risk measure calculation.

How do the risk measures introduced in previous sections stand up to the test of coherence? We have already seen that variance does not satisfy the risk-free property. The same is true for mean absolute deviation. Definition 2.7.3 excludes both variance and mean absolute deviation since these measures incorporate both positive and negative losses. Value-at-Risk violates the sub-additivity property. It is not a coherent risk measure, and its validity for enterprise risk management and for regulatory supervision is questionable.

Conditional Value-at-Risk (CVaR) is a coherent risk measure. CVaR considers all events with probability at least $100\alpha\%$. If we choose $\mathcal{P}$ to be the set of conditional probabilities P on all events such that the losses exceed VaR, then Definition 2.6.3 of CVaR can be written as

$$\text{CVaR}(x; \alpha) = \mathcal{E}[L(x; P^l) \mid L(x; P^l) \geq \zeta] \tag{2.93}$$
$$= \sup \mathcal{E}[L_P(x; P^l) \mid P[L(x; P^l) \geq \zeta] \geq \alpha]. \tag{2.94}$$

This is exactly the definition of a coherent risk measure over generalized scenarios.

Expected downside is also a coherent risk measure. It computes the supremum of the expected value of the losses over the single probability distribution specified by the scenario probabilities p^l. This is the definition of coherent risk measure over generalized scenarios when $\mathcal{P}$ is a singleton.

2.8   Measurement of Reward and Performance Evaluation

Financial decision making involves the weighting of risk against portfolio rewards and optimally trading off one for another. Having studied risk measures we now turn to measures of reward, so that we may address the appropriate trade-off between the two.

A measure of reward, which is already included in the risk measure of variance and mean absolute deviation, is the expected return of the portfolio.

Definition 2.8.1 Expected return. *The expected return of a portfolio with holdings x_i in asset i is given by*

$$R(x; \bar{r}) = \mathcal{E}[R(x; \tilde{r})], \tag{2.95}$$

and in the discrete scenario setting by

$$R(x; \bar{r}) = \sum_{l \in \Omega} p^l \sum_{i=1}^{n} r_i^l x_i. \tag{2.96}$$

From the regret function of Definition 2.3.10 we obtain a measure of reward as the expected upside potential of the portfolio vis-à-vis the random target $\tilde{g}$. This is given by

Definition 2.8.2 Expected upside. *The expected upside potential of a portfolio is given by*

$$G_+(x; \tilde{r}, \tilde{g}) = \mathcal{E}[\max[0, G(x; \tilde{r}, \tilde{g}]] \tag{2.97}$$

and for the discrete scenario case by

$$G_+(x; r^l, g^l) = \sum_{l \in \Omega} p^l \max[0, G(x; r^l, g^l)]. \tag{2.98}$$

2.8.1 Investor choice

How should an investor choose a portfolio that trades off a certain amount of reward for a certain amount of risk? The answer depends on the investor's appetite for risk. The risk measures introduced thus far have been stated without any consideration for investor preferences. We assume that investors prefer upside potential over downside risk, but this trade-off has not been quantified. Financial optimization models are used to generate a set of portfolios that assume the smallest possible risk for a given amount of reward, or, conversely, the higher reward for a given amount of risk. Such portfolios are called *efficient* (see Definition 2.3.3). However, the choice of a specific portfolio from the set of efficient portfolios requires that investors quantify their preferences. To do so we introduce functions that rank risky investments. The role of a ranking function is taken over by the utility functions of economic theory.

Definition 2.8.3 Utility function. *It is a real-valued function $\mathcal{U}$ defined on the real numbers representing possible return or wealth levels.*

Alternative investment opportunities – i.e., risky portfolios $R(x; \tilde{r})$ for different values of the holding vectors x – are ranked according to their expected utility values. Under some conditions on the utility function (see Section 5.6) this ranking establishes investor preferences among the portfolios.

Definition 2.8.4 Preferences. *Portfolio x is preferred over portfolio y if and only if $\mathcal{E}[\mathcal{U}(R(x; \tilde{r}))] \geq \mathcal{E}[\mathcal{U}(R(y; \tilde{r}))]$. If the inequality holds strictly then x is preferred strongly over y.*

Some examples of utility functions used in risk management are given below.

Definition 2.8.5 Quadratic utility function.

$$\mathcal{U}(r) = \bar{r} - \lambda(r - \bar{r})^2, \ \lambda \geq 0. \tag{2.99}$$

Definition 2.8.6 Isoelastic utility function.

$$\mathcal{U}(r) = \frac{1}{\gamma}(1 + r)^\gamma, \ \gamma \leq 1. \tag{2.100}$$

The parameters λ and γ differ from investor to investor and they are a measure of the investor's level of risk tolerance. For $\lambda = 0$ or $\gamma = 1$ we have *risk-neutral* investors with a linear utility function. These investors face uninteresting risk management problems, being interested only in maximizing the expected return of their portfolio. Interesting problems are those facing risk-averse investors. (Risk-seeking investors are of interest too, but more to game theorists than to financial engineers.) The utility function $\mathcal{U}(r) = \frac{1}{\gamma}[(1+r)^{\gamma} - 1]$, which differs from the isoelastic utility function in the above definition by a constant, converges for $\gamma \to 0$ to the logarithmic function.

Definition 2.8.7   Logarithmic utility function.

$$\mathcal{U}(r) = \log(1 + r). \tag{2.101}$$

The logarithmic utility function possesses an interesting property. An investor who ranks investment opportunities, or portfolios, by evaluating their expected logarithmic utility values, and invests in the opportunity with the highest value – that is, who solves an expected logarithmic utility maximization problem – is said to follow a *geometric mean strategy*, also known as the *growth optimal strategy* or the *Kelly criterion*. The term "growth optimal" is due to the following interesting properties of strategies derived by maximizing the expected logarithm of rates of returns:

1. The rate of return of the geometric mean strategy maximizes, asymptotically, the rate of asset growth. That is, no other strategy can reach – asymptotically, in the long run – higher growth rate.

2. The expected time to reach a target level of wealth is asymptotically minimal when following the geometric mean strategy. That is, no other strategy can reach – asymptotically, as the target level of wealth increases – the target in less time.

Expected utility values are useful in ranking and then selecting investments. However, their unit of measurement (sometimes referred to as a *util*) is not standardized across different individuals. A financial engineer will most likely get a blank stare when recommending to a client an investment in a mutual fund of 2.718 *utils*. To communicate the rankings of alternative risky investments it is customary to refer to the certainty equivalent.

Definition 2.8.8   Certainty equivalent. *The certainty equivalent return r_c of an asset with risky return $\tilde{r}$ is the return that satisfies*

$$\mathcal{U}(r_c) = \mathcal{E}[\mathcal{U}(\tilde{r})]. \tag{2.102}$$

That is, the certainty equivalent of the random return $\tilde{r}$ is the sure return r_c that has the same utility value as the expected utility value of the random return.

Investors should be indifferent over the choice between a risky investment with the random return $\tilde{r}$, or a risk-free investment with return equal to the certainly equivalent r_c. Our investor will be relieved to hear that the mutual fund of 2.718 *utils* is the mutual fund selected by other intelligent investors who are willing to accept a certain return of 15.15%. (To put this in mathematical terms, the expected utility of 2.718 *utils* has a certainty equivalent return of 15.15% for investors with a logarithmic utility function.) Utility functions can be used to rank the alternative portfolio and choose the one with the highest ranking. It is also possible to incorporate the utility function in the optimization model and structure a portfolio that optimizes the investor's preferences; see the discussion in Section 5.6.

We give a final piece-wise linear function that can also be used to trade off reward against risk.

Definition 2.8.9 Bi-linear utility function.

$$\mathcal{U}(x; \tilde{r}, \tilde{\rho}) = \text{Reward}(x; \tilde{r}, \tilde{\rho}) - \lambda \,\text{Risk}(x; \tilde{r}, \tilde{\rho}). \tag{2.103}$$

"Reward" and "risk" in the above definition can be any of the reward and risk measures introduced earlier. The parameter λ measures risk aversion. A value $\lambda = 1$ signifies a risk neutral investor that equally values reward and risk. Values greater than one reflect risk-averse investors, while values less than one indicate risk-seeking individuals that value reward more than risk.

2.8.2 Performance evaluation

Utility functions are useful in ranking alternative investments from the point of view of a specific investor. For broader benchmarking we have to specify some generally accepted utility function. In particular, we may use the market's quadratic utility function, which is implicitly assumed in the CAPM model. Hence, we define some performance measures based on the CAPM model, which can be considered as standard, while rankings based on utility functions are custom-made. Standard measures are the Jensen index and the Sharpe ratio.

Definition 2.8.10 Jensen index. *If $\bar{r}_p$ is the average return of a portfolio and $\bar{r}_M$ is the average return of the market portfolio, then the Jensen index is given by*

$$J = (\bar{r}_p - r_f) - \beta_p(\bar{r}_M - r_f), \tag{2.104}$$

where β_p is the portfolio beta.

The Jensen index measures deviations of the average portfolio return from the returns predicted by the CAPM model. Positive values of J reveal a good portfolio, but this inference is made without any consideration of the risk associated with this portfolio. Could it be that other portfolios are better, in the sense that they could achieve equally large positive values of J but with a lower risk? The Sharpe ratio below addresses this issue.

Definition 2.8.11 Sharpe ratio. *Let $\tilde{r}_p$ be the random variable return of the portfolio and let $\tilde{r}_B$ be the random variable return of the benchmark. The differential return is given by $\tilde{d} = \tilde{r}_p - \tilde{r}_B$ and the Sharpe ratio is given by*

$$S = \frac{\bar{d}}{\sigma_d}. \tag{2.105}$$

($\bar{d}$ and σ_d are, respectively, the average and the standard deviation of the differential return.)

Traditionally the benchmark return is taken as the risk-free rate. While it is customary to estimate Sharpe ratios with the risk-free asset taken as the benchmark portfolio, when assessing the performance of a portfolio selection strategy it is more appropriate to use as the benchmark a broadly defined market index with risk characteristics similar to the selected portfolio.

We note that the Sharpe ratio is not time-invariant. The t-period average differential return is t times the single-period return. The t-period standard deviation is $\sqrt{t}$ times the single-period standard deviation. Hence, a Sharpe ratio estimate over t periods will be equal to $\sqrt{t}$ times the single-period estimate.

2.9   Classification of Risk Management Models

We have now completed our description of the two key input parameters of a risk management system: the risks and the rewards. The optimization models in the rest of the book support decision making in determining appropriate risks and rewards, and contribute towards functional risk

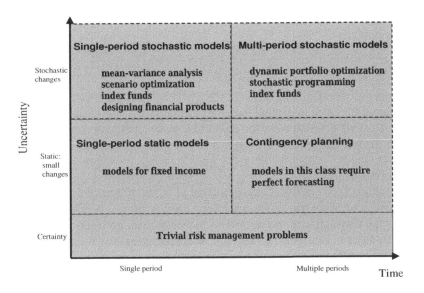

Figure 2.13: Classification of portfolio optimization models in the dimensions of time and uncertainty, and the models of this book.

management. The special characteristics of the instruments or of the institution will be incorporated in the models together with operational considerations. However, a general classification of the risk management models is possible based on how they address risk management problems with respect to the dimensions of time and uncertainty.

The time-axis may consist of a single period from today to the end of the investment horizon. This view is static since no changes are possible after today and before the end of the horizon. Static time models assume that there is only today, $t = 0$, and only one portfolio decision is made. Decisions to be made in the future are not incorporated in the optimization model. The time-axis may also be multi-period, taking a dynamic view of the risk management problems. Dynamic time models recognize that portfolio decisions will be made at future time periods, $t = 1, 2, \ldots, T$, and these decisions are explicitly modeled. This is a more realistic setting since as scenarios evolve and the states are observed it is possible to take remedial action at several discrete points in time from today until the end of the horizon.

Similarly we may view the risk factors as being static or stochastic. Under a static assumption the risk factors – the economy, asset returns, the term structure of interest rates – will remain at their current state and will at most change with only small shifts. Stochastic models assume that risk factors evolve with time according to some probability distribution. Scenarios drawn from this distribution are explicitly incorporated in the model.

Figure 2.13 illustrates a classification of ALM models along the dimensions of time and uncertainty, and places the models of this book in the appropriate class.

Single-period static models

Such models hedge against small changes from the current state of the world. For example, a term structure is input to the model that matches assets and liabilities under this structure. Conditions are then imposed to guarantee that if the term structure shifts somewhat from the current state, the assets and liabilities will move in the same direction and by equal amounts. This is the fundamental principle behind the various immunization models of Chapter 4. A static model does not permit the specification of a random variable to describe changes in the economic environment, the returns of the asset or level of the liabilities, something that is achieved with the models of the next class.

Single-period stochastic models

A stochastic model describes the distribution of the risk factors and ensures that the risks of the enterprise are diversified; when looking at the assets and liabilities side of the balance sheet diversification of the risks is achieved when the asset and liability returns are correlated. This is the idea pioneered by Markowitz (1952, 1991b) with the mean-variance models in his seminal papers for asset allocation, and extended throughout the years to include liabilities and asymmetrically distributed nonnormal returns.

A single-period stochastic model is myopic. That is, it builds a portfolio that will have a well-behaved distribution of the gap between asset and liability returns. However, it does not account for the fact that the portfolio manager is likely to rebalance the portfolio once some surplus is realized or in response to shortfall. Furthermore, as the scenarios evolve across time different portfolios may be more appropriate for capturing the correlations of assets and liabilities, and this is particularly relevant in today's markets with the continuously observed changes in volatility. The single-period model may recommend a conservative strategy if no future remedial actions are possible, while a more aggressive approach may be justified once we explicitly recognize the manager's ability to rebalance the portfolio as new information arrives. While it can be shown that under some conditions myopic policies are optimal in a dynamic setting, they remain restrictive for several important problem classes, especially when there are exogenous liabilities with long time horizons. The limitations of a myopic model are overcome by the multi-period stochastic models discussed below. The models from Chapters 3 and 5, and some of the indexation models from Chapter 7 fit in this category.

Multi-period static models

A multi-period static model will explicitly model portfolio rebalancing decisions at future time periods, but it will assume that the state of the world will shift with small and well-defined changes during this period. A model based on these assumptions is equivalent to a decision maker with perfect foresight. This is an unrealistic setting. Multi-period models that allow for rebalancing in a static world are of practical use when we have perfect forecasting, and can be used for contingency planning.

Multi-period stochastic models

Multi-period stochastic models allow the risk factors to evolve dynamically across time following a stochastic process. Portfolio decisions are revised as time evolves and more information is received about the risk factors. Furthermore, most financial decisions are not irreversible and their reversibility is an option that must be explicitly incorporated in the model. Multi-period stochastic models capture both the stochastic nature of the problem and the fact that the portfolio decisions are reversible. Mathematical models under the general term of stochastic programming with recourse provide the framework for dealing with this broad problem and modeling dynamic strategies (see Chapters 6 and 7, as well as the large-scale applications in Chapters 10 to 13).

2.10   Postview

This chapter introduced the basic concepts that are used throughout the book. It gave first a broad and exhaustive classification of financial risks, and introduced measures for the quantification of risks for both equities and fixed-income securities. However, although these metrics are suitable for measuring a wide range of risk factors that apply in both equities and fixed income, they cannot be applied simultaneously for both types of securities. Hence, they do not allow one to model enterprise risk when both types of financial products are typically present.

Scenario analysis was then introduced as a more flexible means for analyzing the risks, thus allowing us to use common risk measures for both equities and fixed income. Such measures that are well suited for enterprise-wide risk management include: the Value-at-Risk (VaR) measure that is currently considered an industry standard, and the class of coherent risk measures of which a particular instance is the Conditional Value-at-risk (CVaR).

The discussion was completed with the presentation of measures for reward and performance evaluation, so that we can then develop later in this book models that trade off the risks with the rewards of an enterprise.

The chapter concluded with a classification of the optimization models developed in the rest of the book. The classification looks at modeling in the space of the two principal dimensions of risk management modeling: for different time scales and for different forms of uncertainty. Readers can use this classification to understand the relations between different models and their efficacy in dealing with varying levels of complexity of enterprise risk management.

Notes and References

The section on "Notes and References" at the end of Chapter 1 provides general references on financial optimization models.

For modeling the risk of the term structure of interest rates see Platt (1986), Christensen, Fabozzi and LoFaso (1997), and Fabozzi (1997). For credit risk modeling see Duffie and Singleton (2003), and Schönbucher (2003) , and for currency risk see Solnik (1996). For actuarial risks see Doherty (2000), who addresses the problem of integrating insurance risk with capital market risks, and also Embrechts (2000), Correnti (1997), and Babbel and Merrill (1998). Systemic risk is discussed by Rochet and Tirole (1996). The impact of the attacks on the World Trade Center on the insurance industry is analyzed in the report by Tillinghast–Towers Perrin (2001). The RISK books (1998, 2001) provide a collection of papers on operational risk. The modeling of one source of operational risk which is particularly relevant for modelers – i.e., the risk of using the wrong models in different contexts – is discussed in Pierides (1996), Pierides and Zenios (1998), and Consiglio and Zenios (2001b).

The seminal work on variance as a measure of portfolio risk is Markowitz (1952); see also Markowitz (1991b). For a proof of the CAPM see Luenberger (1998), or the seminal papers by Sharpe (1964), Lintner (1965) and Mossin (1966). For a discussion of measures of variability, such as those used in this chapter, see the historical account by David (1998), while the statistical properties of mean absolute deviation are discussed by Bonett and Seier (2003).

The proof of Theorem 2.3 is from Konno and Yamazaki (1991). For additional work on the mean absolute deviation model see Speranza (1993), and Zenios and Kang (1993).

The notion of duration was introduced in Macaulay (1938). For a discussion of the principles behind immunization see Fong and Vasiceck (1984), Granito (1984), Christensen, Fabozzi and LoFaso (1997), Maloney and Yawitz (1986), and de La Grandville (2001). Dahl et al. (1993) give operational optimization models.

The seminal paper on principal component analysis is Hotelling (1933). For applications to the analysis of the term structure of interest rates see Garbade (1986), Reitano (1992), and D' Ecclesia and Zenios (1994).

For option adjusted analysis see Sykes (1989), Hayre (1990), and Babbel and Zenios (1992).

The use of scenarios for portfolio management and financial planning was first discussed by Dembo (1991), Mulvey, Vanderbei and Zenios (1995), and Koskosides and Duarte (1997). See also Dembo et al. (2000) for a general framework for risk management based on scenarios.

Single-period stochastic models for fixed-income portfolio optimization were first suggested by Mulvey and Zenios (1994a, 1994b) and applied at Fannie Mae by Holmer (1994).

Stochastic programming has a history almost as long as linear programming; see Dantzig (1955), and Beale (1955), or Wets (1974). However, it was not until the early seventies – Bradley and Crane (1972) – that its significance for portfolio management was realized and the first application developed for banks by Kusy and Ziemba (1986). With the advances in high-performance computing and large-scale optimization – see, e.g, Kall and Wallace (1994), Birge and Louveaux (1997), or Censor and Zenios (1997) – this approach has been receiving renewed interest from both practitioners and academics; see "Notes and References" at the end of Chapter 6.

The Sharpe measure is discussed in Sharpe (1966, 1975, 1994) and the Jensen measure in Jensen (1969). For a version of the Sharpe ratio that penalizes only downside risk see Ziemba (2005).

The use of a percentile risk measure (such as Value-at-Risk) for regulatory purposes is proposed by the Basel Committee on Banking Supervision (1996a, 1996b, 2001) and the Derivatives Policy Group (1995). Jorion (1996) provides a comprehensive treatment of Value-at-Risk and its use for controling market risk. A probabilistic introduction to this topic is given by Uryasev (2000b). The distribution of returns of Long-Term Capital Management position in Figure 2.12 is also from Jorion (1996).

For coherent risk measures see the papers by Artzner et al. (1997, 1999) and Rockafellar and Uryasev (2000) for the linear programming formulation for CVaR calculations.

A comparison between VaR and CVaR is given by Pflug (2000), and Gaivoronski and Pflug (2005) discuss the optimization of VaR.

Utility theory is discussed in von Neumann and Morgenstern (1953); for its applications in financial decision making see Ingersoll (1987).

The classification of risk management models is due to Zenios (1995). Conditions under which myopic policies are optimal in a dynamic setting were established in Mossin (1968) and Hakansson (1974), and under these conditions single-period and multi-period stochastic models for the same problem will lead to the same solutions.

Part II

PORTFOLIO OPTIMIZATION MODELS

respice finem – Think of the end before you begin.

Chapter 3

Mean-Variance Analysis

> Virtue or excellence is a characteristic involving choice, and it consists in observing
> the mean relative to us, a mean which is defined by a rational principle. It is the
> mean by reference to two vices: the one of excess and the other of deficiency.
>
> Aristotle, *Nichomachean Ethics, Book II*

3.1 Preview

Mean-variance analysis studies the performance of portfolios in the space of reward versus risk in
a single-period context. Reward is measured by the portfolio expected (mean) return, and risk is
measured by the portfolio variance. In this chapter we develop the classic quadratic programming
model to support mean-variance analysis. We discuss variants of the model, addressing limits
on trading size, borrowing, transaction costs, and liabilities. We then develop factor models for
generating the data required in mean-variance analysis, and show how these models can be used
to simplify the quadratic programs. Finally we discuss the sensitivity of mean-variance analysis
to noisy or erroneous input data, and introduce ways to alleviate the potential problems.

3.2 Mean-Variance Optimization

Balancing rewards against risks is at the heart of financial engineering, and the foundations
for this balancing act were laid with the work of Markowitz (1952) on mean-variance analysis. Mean-variance analysis studies the tradeoffs between portfolio reward, as measured by the
portfolio expected (mean) return, and portfolio risk, as measured by its variance. Mean-variance
analysis laid the foundations for modern portfolio theory, and sparked the proliferation of optimization models for financial planning during the last 50 years. While recent optimization
models – covered in subsequent chapters of this book – provide more versatile tools to support
enterprise-wide risk management, mean-variance analysis remains the point of departure and is
widely used in practice.

Mean-variance analysis was proposed both as a positive and as a normative tool. As a positive
tool it supports hypotheses about how the financial markets or investors behave. The Capital
Asset Pricing Model given in Theorem 2.3.1 is the most prominent outcome of positive mean-
variance analysis. As a normative tool mean-variance analysis sets the framework for developing
recommendations on how investors should behave. It is in this latter form that mean-variance
analysis supports the decision making of financial engineers. Constructing efficient portfolios of
assets (Definition 2.3.3) is the most successful application of normative mean-variance analysis,
and in this section we develop the relevant optimization models. In Section 3.3 we extend the

models to incorporate liabilities, and this generalization takes us a step towards enterprise-wide risk management. Section 3.4 develops factor models for estimating the input data of mean-variance analysis, and shows how the optimization models are formulated using factor models. Section 3.5 considers the sensitivity of model recommendations to noisy and erroneous data, and suggests ways to alleviate the problems.

We start by restating Definition 2.3.3 of efficient portfolios in the following equivalent form, which provides a recipe for mean-variance optimization models.

Definition 3.2.1 Efficient portfolio. *A portfolio is efficient if it has maximal expected return given an upper bound on risk or, equivalently, it has minimal risk for a given expected return.*

If we take the variance of a portfolio as a measure of portfolio risk we can formulate quadratic optimization models to construct efficient portfolios.

3.2.1 Canonical formulation

In its most basic form the mean-variance optimization model determines the optimal proportional allocation x_i to the ith asset, where

$$\sum_{i=1}^{n} x_i = 1, \tag{3.1}$$

so that the properties of efficient portfolios are satisfied. There are two equivalent optimization formulations, corresponding to the two equivalent statements about efficient portfolios in the definition above.

Expected return maximization

Recall that the expected return of a portfolio is given by

$$R(x;\bar{r}) = \sum_{i=1}^{n} \bar{r}_i x_i, \tag{3.2}$$

and its variance by

$$\sigma^2(x) = \mathcal{E}\left[[R(x;\tilde{r}) - R(x;\bar{r})]^2\right] = \sum_{i=1}^{n}\sum_{i'=1}^{n} \sigma_{ii'} x_i x_{i'}. \tag{3.3}$$

In matrix notation we write $\sigma^2(x) = x^\top Q x$.

To construct a portfolio with maximal expected return given an upper bound on risk we solve the following model:

Model 3.2.1 Expected return maximization

$$\text{Maximize} \quad R(x;\bar{r}) \tag{3.4}$$

$$\text{subject to} \quad \sigma^2(x) \leq \omega, \tag{3.5}$$

$$\sum_{i=1}^{n} x_i = 1. \tag{3.6}$$

Here ω is an upper bound on risk. The variance of a portfolio is a quadratic function of the vector x, so this program has nonlinear constraints. It is inadvisable to formulate nonlinearly constrained optimization problems, as they may be difficult to solve. We therefore work next with the equivalent definition of efficient portfolios.

Variance minimization

To construct a portfolio of minimal risk for a given expected return we solve the following model.

Model 3.2.2 Variance minimization

$$\text{Minimize} \quad \frac{1}{2}\sigma^2(x) \tag{3.7}$$

$$\text{subject to} \quad R(x; \bar{r}) = \mu, \tag{3.8}$$

$$\sum_{i=1}^{n} x_i = 1. \tag{3.9}$$

Here μ is the target expected return, and the scaling factor $1/2$ in the objective function is introduced to simplify the calculation of derivatives. This is a quadratic program with linear constraints. Models of this form can be solved, even for a large number of variables, using standard optimization software. The model is sometimes stated with μ as a lower bound, in which case the expected return constraint (3.8) takes the form $R(x; \bar{r}) \geq \mu$. At an optimal solution this constraint will be active, i.e., it will hold with equality. Hence, no generality is lost by writing the model above with an equality constraint, although for computer implementation it is best to use the inequality formulation.

We apply now the first-order optimality conditions to the Lagrangian function (see Appendix A) of the quadratic program (3.7)–(3.9), which may be written using vector notation as

$$\text{Minimize} \quad \frac{1}{2}x^\top Q x \tag{3.10}$$

$$\text{subject to} \quad \bar{r}^\top x = \mu, \tag{3.11}$$

$$\mathbf{1}^\top x = 1, \tag{3.12}$$

to express the solution through the system of equations

$$x^* = \pi_\mu^* Q^{-1}\bar{r} + \pi_1^* Q^{-1}\mathbf{1} \tag{3.13}$$

$$\bar{r}^\top x^* = \mu \tag{3.14}$$

$$\mathbf{1}^\top x^* = 1. \tag{3.15}$$

Here π_μ is the Lagrange multiplier for the expected return constraint, and π_1 is the Lagrange multiplier for the normalization constraint. Note that when $\pi_\mu^* = 0$ this implies that the expected return constraint has, marginally, no effect on the optimal solution, and the solution $x^* = \pi_1 Q^{-1}\mathbf{1}$ is, in this case, the minimum variance portfolio.

By varying μ in Model 3.2.2 we can generate several portfolios. If μ is very large the model may be infeasible – this is the case if no asset has an expected return greater or equal to the target. As μ decreases we find portfolios of assets with expected return equal to μ. Figure 3.1 plots the curve obtained by decreasing μ and minimizing variance on the space of expected return versus variance. These portfolios trace a curve called the minimum variance curve. All points on the right of the curve have the same target expected return but higher variance. Points on the left of the curve are infeasible. The largest possible expected return is achieved at point A on the curve. The portfolio corresponding to this point is an undiversified portfolio consisting of holdings only in a single asset, namely the asset with the highest expected return. (Clearly we do not need an optimization model to find this portfolio.) We know from CAPM, however, that the risk of the portfolio will decrease as we lower target returns. Nontrivial solutions of diversified portfolios are obtained as we decrease the expected return.

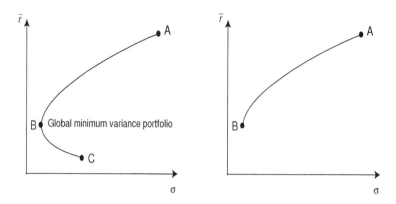

Figure 3.1: The minimum variance curve (left) for portfolios with minimal variance for a given level of expected return. The efficient frontier (right) is the upper portion of the minimum variance curve.

If we force the portfolio to accept very low return we may invest in high-risk assets, moving towards point C on the curve. Of course a reasonable investor would not force very low returns on his or her portfolio. For as long as reduced expected returns lead to lower variance our investor may be content. But she should not force so low a target expected return that variance may have to increase to achieve it. The portfolio with the lowest possible variance is the global minimum variance portfolio, corresponding to point B on the curve. Efficient portfolios are only those corresponding to the upper portion of the minimum variance curve. This portion of the curve is the *efficient frontier.* We point out that a model formulated with a "greater or equal" inequality in place of the equality constraint (3.8) will not generate portfolios lying below point B.

Variance minimization with risk-free asset

If a risk-free asset is available the variance minimization model can be simplified by eliminating the budget constraint. In particular, holdings in the risk-free asset can be used to absorb any residual or can be used to finance purchases through borrowing. If x_f denotes the holdings in the risk-free asset we have $x_f = 1 - \sum_{i=1}^{n} x_i$, and the minimum variance model with a risk-free asset is written as

$$\text{Minimize} \quad \frac{1}{2}\sigma^2(x) \tag{3.16}$$

$$\text{subject to} \quad \sum_{i=1}^{n}(\bar{r}_i - r_f)x_i = \mu - r_f. \tag{3.17}$$

An analytic solution to this model can be obtained by applying the first-order optimality conditions to the Lagrangian function of this quadratic program as

$$x^* = \pi_\mu^* Q^{-1}(\bar{r} - \mathbf{1}r_f) \tag{3.18}$$

$$(\bar{r} - \mathbf{1}r_f)^\top x^* = \mu - r_f \tag{3.19}$$

$$x_f^* = 1 - \sum_{i=1}^{n} x_i^*. \tag{3.20}$$

It can be shown using elementary calculus that the solution to this problem consists of holdings in the risk-free rate and one more portfolio of risky assets. This result is called the *one-fund theorem.*

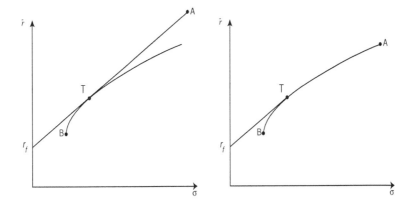

Figure 3.2: The efficient frontier when a risk-free asset is available. When borrowing is allowed at the risk-free rate the frontier extends to infinity (left figure) along the linear segment from r_f to A, while if borrowing is not allowed the frontier is bounded (right figure).

Theorem 3.2.1 One-fund Theorem. *In the presence of a risk-free asset in the set of investment opportunities any efficient portfolio can be constructed as a combination of the risk-free asset and a single risky portfolio T.*

(The portfolio T is known as the *tangency portfolio*.)

The inclusion of a risk-free asset extends the efficient frontier curve with a linear segment as shown in Figure 3.2. It is a reasonable economic assumption that the risk-free rate is lower than the mean rate of return offered by the global minimum variance portfolio, so that the slope of the linear segment is positive. The slope of the line is given by $(\bar{r}_T - r_f)/\sigma_T$. Recall that this is the Sharpe ratio (Definition 2.8.11), and portfolios that lie on the linear segment from r_f to T maximize the Sharpe ratio. Portfolios on the efficient frontier that extends from T to A have lower Sharpe ratios when borrowing is not allowed.

Tracing efficient frontiers

We give now a model, equivalent to those given above, which combines the return maximization with the variance minimization programs to trace the efficient frontier. The model is a multi-objective nonlinear program. The objective function is a weighted combination of risk and reward. For each value of the weight λ in the interval $[0, 1]$ we obtain portfolios that have the minimum risk for the maximum expected return. By varying this parameter we obtain a set of portfolios on the efficient frontier. A set of feasible solutions X in the n-dimensional space $\mathbb{R}^n$ is also introduced and efficient portfolios must belong to this set; the restrictions that specify a feasible set X are discussed later. The model is stated as follows:

Model 3.2.3 Mean-variance efficient portfolios

$$\text{Minimize} \quad \lambda\sigma^2(x) - (1 - \lambda)R(x; \bar{r}) \tag{3.21}$$

$$\text{subject to} \quad \sum_{i=1}^{n} x_i = 1, \tag{3.22}$$

$$x \in X. \tag{3.23}$$

3.2.2   General formulations

Model 3.2.3 is the canonical formulation of mean-variance optimization. The set of feasible solutions X has been left unspecified. For the case where $X = \mathbb{R}^n$, the model above has only one constraint, namely the normalization constraint (3.22). This is the model originally proposed for mean-variance analysis. It is important to understand the assumptions on which this models rests. Some of the assumptions will be relaxed with additional features of the model that are discussed here, while the treatment of other assumptions must wait for the development of models in subsequent chapters.

The explicit assumptions underlying the generation of mean-variance efficient frontiers are the following:

1. Investors consider only the first two moments – mean and variance – of the distribution of returns.

2. Investors choose a portfolio with the lowest possible variance for a given mean return.

3. The investment horizon is one period; this is the *risk horizon* of the model.

The first assumption is relaxed in the scenario optimization models of Chapter 5, where we also allow for investor choices other than the one stipulated in the second assumption. The third assumption will be relaxed in Chapter 6 where we introduce models with multi-period time horizons.

There are some additional assumptions implicit in the canonical model formulations:

1. Investors can sell assets short.

2. The portfolio decisions do not affect market prices and liquidity risk is not present.

3. Investments can be in fractional shares.

4. Investors do not pay transaction costs and taxes.

These assumptions can be relaxed by imposing additional constraints on the canonical model. These constraints also address practical considerations, and render the model useful as a decision support tool. We discuss such constraints next.

No short sales

The variables in Model 3.2.3 are free. When a variable has a negative value in the solution of the model this implies a short sale. To exclude short sales we must add constraints $x_i \geq 0$ for all assets. When short sales are allowed we will have, in general, many nonzero holdings x_i at the solution. When no short sales are allowed many variables are set to zero. It is then desirable to limit the maximum amount invested in any single asset. This is achieved by specifying a vector of upper bounds $\bar{x} = (\bar{x}_i)_{i=1}^n$ on the variables, and the following set of constraints is commonly encountered in practice

$$0 \leq x_i \leq \bar{x}_i, \text{ for all } i \in U. \tag{3.24}$$

Upper bounds on the holdings are imposed in part due to institutional policy considerations, and in part due to the presence of errors in the estimation of returns and covariances. In particular, any errors in the estimation of expected returns will bias the portfolio solution towards those assets for which the expected return was overestimated, and the bounds will limit these biases. This issue is taken up further later, in Section 3.5. Limiting the holding in any single security is also a way to avoid affecting market prices and to create liquidity risk when trading large positions.

General constraints

Policy or regulatory requirements may dictate limits on certain sets of assets. These requirements limit the exposure of a portfolio to one or more risk factors. For instance, insurance companies may face restrictions on their total exposure to corporate bonds or foreign government bonds. With these limits, credit and currency risk, respectively, are controlled. Managers of mutual funds may have stated policies on the total exposure to certain sectors of the economy, such as shares of telecommunications or airline companies. Limiting the total exposure to a group of securities also limits liquidity risk when dealing in thin markets. Such considerations are expressed by linear constraints in the form

$$\sum_{i=1}^{n} a_{ji} x_i \leq b_j, \tag{3.25}$$

for some risk factors $j \in \mathcal{K}$. The coefficients a_{ji} indicate whether the risk factor j has an impact on the return of asset i ($a_{ji} = 1$) or not ($a_{ji} = 0$). The inequalities can also be of the greater-or-equal ($\geq$) type, or they can be equalities.

Sometimes it is argued that ad hoc constraints in the form (3.24) and (3.25) simply prescribe a solution, and defeat the purpose of building a model in the first place. It is certainly true that when many constraints of this form are added the solution will be determined more by the search for a feasible asset allocation, than by trading off risk against expected return. However such constraints, when reflecting corporate policy and regulatory requirements, are essential. We cannot search for efficient portfolios using a mathematical model that ignores policies and regulations. On the other hand, the scope of the model is suspect if it is constrained to generate an efficient frontier with only one or two feasible portfolios.

Risk-free borrowing

While short sales are in general not allowed, borrowing at the risk-free rate is permitted. If we denote by $v^- \geq 0$ the amount borrowed – expressed as a percentage of the initial wealth, which is assumed to be 1 – then Model 3.2.3 can be extended by setting the normalization constraint as

$$\sum_{i=1}^{n} x_i - v^- = 1, \tag{3.26}$$

and setting the expected return of the portfolio by

$$R(x; \bar{r}) = \sum_{i=1}^{n} r_i x_i - r_f v^-. \tag{3.27}$$

The variance term remains unchanged since the borrowing rate is risk-free.

It is also possible to model a situation whereby we borrow at different rates, such as r_{f1} for amounts up to $\bar{v}_1$, and a higher rate r_{f2} for amounts up to $\bar{v}_2$. If we denote the amounts borrowed at the respective rates by v_1^- and v_2^- – again expressed as a percentage of the initial wealth – we can formulate the model with the constraints

$$\sum_{i=1}^{n} x_i - v_1^- - v_2^- = 1, \ v_1^- \leq \bar{v}_1 \text{ and } v_2^- \leq \bar{v}_2, \tag{3.28}$$

and set the expected return of the portfolio by

$$R(x; \bar{r}) = \sum_{i=1}^{n} r_i x_i - r_{f1} v_1^- - r_{f2} v_2^-. \tag{3.29}$$

Since $r_{f2} > r_{f1}$, variable v_2^- will be nonzero only if $v_1^- = \bar{v}_1$. That is, the model will not borrow at the higher rate until the limit on discount borrowing is exhausted.

3.2.3 Trading sizes and transaction costs

Solutions of the canonical model, even with the constraints discussed in the general formulation, may consist of a large number of small positions. Such portfolios are undesirable for two reasons. First, a large number of positions implies larger transaction costs when an existing portfolio is revised. Second, operational costs are also higher due to monitoring requirements when managing large portfolios.

To avoid these shortcomings we restrict the total number of assets in the portfolio to not exceed some limit M. At the same time we can require that any exposure to a given asset must exceed some minimum threshold. This does not mean that every asset must be included in the portfolio. Instead, it implies that if the ith asset is included then the holdings should exceed some minimum level $\underline{x}_i$.

To model these considerations we introduce a binary variable

$$Z_i = \begin{cases} 1, & \text{if asset } i \text{ is included in the portfolio,} \\ 0, & \text{otherwise.} \end{cases} \tag{3.30}$$

The following model ensures that the total number of assets is limited, while any holdings in a given asset exceed the threshold.

Model 3.2.4 Mean-variance efficient portfolios with trading size limits

$$\text{Minimize} \quad \lambda \sigma^2(x) - (1-\lambda)R(x;\bar{r}) \tag{3.31}$$

$$\text{subject to} \quad \sum_{i=1}^{n} x_i = 1, \tag{3.32}$$

$$\sum_{i=1}^{n} Z_i \leq M, \tag{3.33}$$

$$\underline{x}_i Z_i \leq x_i \leq \bar{x}_i Z_i, \quad \text{for all } i \in U, \tag{3.34}$$

$$Z_i \in \{0,1\}, \text{ for all } i \in U. \tag{3.35}$$

Transaction costs

When constructing a portfolio we must pay transaction costs, and these costs must enter the calculation of expected returns. The effective expected return of an investment is the expected return net any costs. However, the cost calculation can be quite involved in practice. A typical cost function is illustrated in Figure 3.3, and we see that it is neither convex nor concave. It is convex for small transactions, reflecting economies of scale since brokerage commissions decrease with transaction size. For larger transactions the cost of illiquidity increases, and the cost function becomes convex.

This function is approximated by a piecewise linear function. Two approximations are also shown in the figure. In the simplest case transaction costs are assumed to be proportional to transaction size. With this approach both brokerage discounts and illiquidity costs are ignored. A more accurate approximation assumes a fixed charge for transactions up to a certain amount, and a linear fee thereafter.

We model now these two approximations. Let c_0 be the flat fee for amounts up to $\bar{x}_i$, and c_1 be the proportional costs (e.g., commissions) for larger transactions. For the case of linearly proportional transaction costs we simply calculate expected return by

$$R(x;\bar{r}) = \sum_{i=1}^{n} (\bar{r}_i - c_1)x_i. \tag{3.36}$$

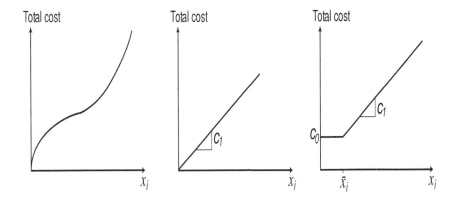

Figure 3.3: Transaction costs function (left) and two piecewise linear approximations: proportionally linear (center) and piecewise linear with fixed charge (right).

For the piecewise approximation we must model the two cost regimes. We let x_i^0 denote transactions up to $\bar{x}_i$, and x_i^1 transactions over this threshold, so that the total allocation to the ith asset is $x_i = x_i^0 + x_i^1$. We introduce a binary variable

$$Z_i = \begin{cases} 1, & \text{if asset } i \text{ is included in the portfolio with a fixed charge } c_0, \\ 0, & \text{otherwise.} \end{cases} \tag{3.37}$$

The expected return of the portfolio is now calculated by

$$R(x;\bar{r}) = \sum_{i=1}^{n} (\bar{r}_i x_i^0 - c_0 Z_i) + \sum_{i=1}^{n} (\bar{r}_i - c_1) x_i^1, \tag{3.38}$$

where the asset decisions are constrained as follows

$$0 \le x_i^0 \le \bar{x}_i Z_i \tag{3.39}$$
$$0 \le x_i^1 \le Z_i. \tag{3.40}$$

When $Z_i = 0$ these inequalities force $x_i^0 = x_i^1 = 0$, and no fixed charge or proportional transaction costs are included in the expected return calculation. When $Z_i = 1$, the first pair of inequalities allows x_i^0 to increase up to $\bar{x}_i$, and a fixed cost c_0 is subtracted from the expected return for each asset included in the portfolio. The second pair of inequalities allows x_i^1 to increase up to 1, and a proportional cost c_1 is subtracted from the expected return per unit invested in asset i over and above $\bar{x}_i$. Since an additional cost c_1 is incurred the optimal solution will keep x_i^1 at zero, unless x_i^0 has reached its upper bound. The following model, with $R(x;\bar{r})$ defined as in (3.38), generates mean-variance efficient portfolios taking into account transaction costs.

Model 3.2.5 Mean-variance efficient portfolios with transaction costs

$$\text{Minimize} \quad \lambda \sigma^2(x) - (1-\lambda) R(x;\bar{r}) \tag{3.41}$$

$$\text{subject to} \quad \sum_{i=1}^{n} (x_i^0 + x_i^1) = 1, \tag{3.42}$$

$$0 \le x_i^0 \le \bar{x}_i Z_i, \quad \text{for all } i \in U, \tag{3.43}$$
$$0 \le x_i^1 \le Z_i, \quad \text{for all } i \in U, \tag{3.44}$$
$$Z_i \in \{0,1\}, \quad \text{for all } i \in U. \tag{3.45}$$

Limits on trading size, and on the maximum number of assets allowed in the portfolio can be imposed along the lines of Model 3.2.4.

3.2.4 Portfolio revision

Most applications of portfolio optimization involve the revision of an existing portfolio $x_0 = (x_{0i})_{i=1}^{n}$. Revisions may be necessary because expectations about future returns and volatilities change, and new cashflows have to be invested. Portfolio revision implies both purchases and sales, and transaction costs must be paid in both cases. The applicable cost function is a symmetric function of asset allocation around x_0. The nonlinearities of the cost function apply both for asset purchases and asset sales, corresponding to asset allocations above and below the current level of holdings x_0, respectively, and the function includes the mirror image of those shown in Figure 3.3.

Trading size restrictions also apply, and in the case of portfolio revision they take the form *zero-or-range*. That is, either no trading takes place, or trading takes place by either selling or purchasing, in which case the new allocations should stay within prespecified ranges. The ranges are given by $\bar{x}_i \leq x_i \leq \bar{\bar{x}}_i$ when increasing the exposure, and by $\underline{x}_i \leq x_i \leq \underline{\underline{x}}_i$ when decreasing the exposure. These restrictions are motivated by the same considerations that imposed upper and lower bounds (cf. equation 3.24) when constructing a portfolio. To model these constraints we introduce two nonnegative variables y_{+i} and y_{-i} to denote, respectively, purchases and sales of the ith asset, so that we have $x_i = x_{0i} + y_{+i} - y_{-i}$. We also introduce two binary variables as follows:

$$Z_{+i} = \begin{cases} 1, & \text{if the exposure to the } i\text{th asset is increased through purchases,} \\ 0, & \text{otherwise.} \end{cases} \tag{3.46}$$

$$Z_{-i} = \begin{cases} 1, & \text{if the exposure to the } i\text{th asset is reduced through sales,} \\ 0, & \text{otherwise.} \end{cases} \tag{3.47}$$

It is easy to see that Model 3.2.6, given below, keeps the asset allocation either at its current value x_{0i} or within the allowable ranges. Note that the model could arbitrarily buy and sell the same security while keeping the desired exposure within the allowable range. In the presence of transaction costs the optimizer will not engage is such frivolous trading, and at most one of the variables y_{+i}, y_{-i} will be nonzero for each security.

Another constraint that is often added when revising an existing portfolio is on *portfolio turnover*. That is, the total change in holdings of assets should not exceed some threshold. Portfolio turnover constraints are added to alleviate a problem typical of the class of single-period models, of which mean-variance optimization is an example. Namely, the large portfolio turnover observed from period to period when mean-variance optimization is used at the start of each new period. Clearly large turnover is undesirable as it increases transaction costs and reduces the marketability of a continuously changing portfolio to clients. The turnover constraint is imposed on the total purchases and it takes the form

$$\sum y_{+i} \leq u. \tag{3.48}$$

It is easy to see that turnover on sales is bounded by the same amount, as the total asset allocation remains equal to one.

We can now summarize the model for generating mean-variance efficient frontiers when revising a portfolio. It is stated as follows:

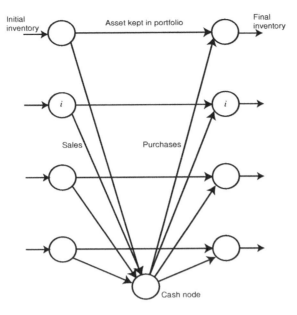

Figure 3.4: Network model for revising a portfolio.

Model 3.2.6 Mean-variance efficient portfolio revision

$$\text{Minimize} \quad \lambda\sigma^2(x) - (1-\lambda)R(x;\bar{r}) \tag{3.49}$$

$$\text{subject to} \quad \sum_{i=1}^{n} x_i = 1, \tag{3.50}$$

$$x_i - y_{+i} + y_{-i} = x_{0i}, \quad \text{for all } i \in U, \tag{3.51}$$

$$0 \le y_{+i} \le Z_{+i}, \quad \text{for all } i \in U, \tag{3.52}$$

$$\bar{x}_i \le x_{0i} + y_{+i} \le \bar{\bar{x}}_i, \quad \text{for all } i \in U, \tag{3.53}$$

$$0 \le y_{-i} \le Z_{-i}, \quad \text{for all } i \in U, \tag{3.54}$$

$$\underline{\underline{x}}_i \le x_{0i} - y_{-i} \le \underline{x}_i, \quad \text{for all } i \in U, \tag{3.55}$$

$$Z_{+i}, Z_{-i} \in \{0,1\}, \quad \text{for all } i \in U. \tag{3.56}$$

Network structure of the portfolio revision problem

The portfolio revision problem can be represented as a problem of flow of funds on a directed network. Figure 3.4 illustrates the problem of portfolio revision. The network representation eases the communication of model features among users, as the mathematical notation can be avoided. Historically it has also been much more efficient to solve large-scale network optimization problems than general linear (or nonlinear) programs and some of the earliest large-scale applications of portfolio optimization were formulated and solved as network problems. However, with the advances in numerical optimization methods, computational considerations ceased to be critical.

Each node on the network represents an algebraic equation which models the principle of conservation of flow, i.e., total flow into a node equals the total flow out of the node. A slightly different interpretation is given for nodes representing conservation of flow for the securities in the portfolio, and for the single node representing conservation of cash. In the former case the algebraic equation stipulates that the inventory of a security is preserved, and is either augmented by purchases or depleted through sales. In the latter case conservation of flow stipulates that the total cash from sales of securities must equal the cash spent in purchasing securities or invested in the risk-free asset.

The arcs of the network represent flow of assets between the nodes. In particular, a security may be transferred to the cash node signifying sales, or transferred to the node corresponding to the same security at the next trading time. This shows that the security was maintained in the portfolio. Similarly, flows from the cash node into the node of a security show purchases. Conservation of flow is not preserved on the arcs. Instead, a multiplier is used to adjust the transferred quantity. When selling a security this multiplier is the price of the security minus any transaction costs. When buying a security the multiplier is one, divided by the price of the security plus transaction costs. When the security stays in the portfolio the multiplier represents gains through price appreciation, depreciation losses, dividends or interest payments.

3.3   Incorporating Liabilities

So far we have been dealing only with assets. The variables of the model determine the allocation to the n asset categories. We now extend the model to include liabilities, and develop mean-variance efficient portfolios of the surplus created when liabilities are subtracted from the assets.

We consider a liability with rate of return given by a random variable $\tilde{\rho}$. The return of the liability is given by the change in the present value of the liability on the risk horizon. For instance, if the present value of the liability today is P_{L0} and the present value at the end of the risk horizon T is given by the random variable $\tilde{P}_{LT}$, then we have

$$\tilde{\rho} = \frac{\tilde{P}_{LT} - P_{L0}}{P_{L0}}. \tag{3.57}$$

The return of the asset minus liabilities in now given by

$$R(x; \tilde{r}, \tilde{\rho}) = \sum_{i=1}^{n} \tilde{r}_i x_i - \tilde{\rho}. \tag{3.58}$$

The expected return of the surplus is given by

$$R(x; \bar{r}, \bar{\rho}) = \sum_{i=1}^{n} \bar{r}_i x_i - \bar{\rho}, \tag{3.59}$$

and the surplus variance by

$$\sigma^2(x) = \mathcal{E}\left[[R(x; \tilde{r}, \tilde{\rho}) - R(x; \bar{r}, \bar{\rho})]^2\right] = \sum_{i=1}^{n}\sum_{i'=1}^{n} \sigma_{ii'} x_i x_{i'} - \sum_{i=1}^{n} \sigma_{iL} x_i + \sigma_L^2. \tag{3.60}$$

Here σ_{iL} denotes the covariance of the return of the ith asset with the return of the liability, and σ_L^2 is the variance of the liability. It is important to note that the covariance of the assets with the liability appears with a negative sign in the expression for surplus variance. Assets that are highly correlated with the liability reduce the portfolio surplus risk, while in portfolios consisting only of assets, highly correlated assets contribute to the overall portfolio risk.

In matrix notation we write the variance of the surplus as $\sigma^2(x) = x^\top Q_A x$, where Q_A is covariance matrix of dimension $(n+1) \times (n+1)$. This matrix is obtained by augmenting the covariance matrix of the assets Q as follows:

$$Q_A = \begin{pmatrix} Q & q_L \\ q_L^\top & \sigma_L^2 \end{pmatrix}. \tag{3.61}$$

The column vector q_L is the vector of covariances of the assets with the liability, i.e., $q_L = (\sigma_{1L}, \sigma_{2L}, \dots, \sigma_{nL})^\top$.

With these definitions of surplus mean and variance we can use any of the models for generating mean-variance efficient portfolios introduced earlier in this chapter.

Index tracking

An interesting application of mean-variance analysis in the presence of liabilities is in tracking market indices. (See Chapter 7 for an introduction to index funds and Chapters 10 and 11 for large-scale applications.) In particular, we may take the liability return to be the return of some broadly defined market index $\tilde{I}$. The model of the previous section can then be used to identify portfolios of assets that are correlated with the index.

3.4   Factor Models of Return

The implementation of mean-variance optimization models requires the estimations of the vectors of means and variances ($2n$ parameters), and the matrix of covariances ($n(n-1)/2$ parameters). The number of parameters could be quite large, even for typical problems of reasonable size. For instance, solving an asset management problem in the S&P500 requires the estimation of 1,000 expected returns and security variances, and 124,750 covariances. It is common practice to specify linear models for a stochastic process that generates security returns, and use these models to calculate the parameters needed for mean-variance analysis.

We discuss here both single- and multi-factor linear models of returns. While a single-factor model is a special case of multi-factor models, we treat them here separately. We do so for expository reasons starting with the simpler models first, but we also follow the historical development of these models whereby single-factor models were introduced first and led to the Capital Asset Pricing Model, whereas multi-factor models were developed later and led to the development of Arbitrage Pricing Theory. There is also a distinguishing feature of single-factor models that is noteworthy. In particular, the factor that drives the return generation process can be taken to be some broad market index. To be more precise, the market index is a good proxy for the factors that drive security returns. In this case the return generation model is also called an index model. For multi-factor models we need to identify the appropriate factors, relying on economic theory and econometric modeling.

3.4.1   Single-factor model

We assume that the security returns are correlated because of their response to some common underlying factor. This factor could be, for example, the changes in the general level of the market as a whole, or a macroeconomic factor such as growth or inflation. We can then estimate the correlations among securities by relating their returns to the changes in the common factor. Taking this common factor to be the return of a market index $\tilde{r}_M$ we can write the following linear model.

Definition 3.4.1 Single-factor model. *The return of the ith security is related to the return of the single-factor $\tilde{r}_M$ through the linear relation*

$$\tilde{r}_i = \alpha_i + \beta_i \tilde{r}_M + \tilde{\epsilon}_i. \tag{3.62}$$

The variance of the factor is given by σ_M^2 and the security-specific residual term $\tilde{\epsilon}_i$ is assumed to be normally distributed with mean 0 and variance $\sigma_{\epsilon i}^2$.

The sensitivity of the security return to the factor is given by β_i which is called the factor loading. We assume, in this model, that the security returns are correlated only through their response to the common factor, and therefore the following assumptions apply:

1. The covariance of the security-specific residual term with the factor is zero, $\text{Cov}(\tilde{\epsilon}_i, \tilde{r}_M) = 0$ for all $i \in U$.
2. The covariance of the residuals is zero, i.e., $\text{Cov}(\tilde{\epsilon}_i, \tilde{\epsilon}_{i'}) = 0$ for all $i \neq i'$, and $i, i' \in U$.

Using the single-factor model we can now derive the parameters needed in the mean-variance optimization model.

Security expected return

The expected return of the ith security is given by

$$\bar{r}_i = \mathcal{E}[\alpha_i + \beta_i \tilde{r}_M + \tilde{\epsilon}_i] \tag{3.63}$$
$$= \alpha_i + \beta_i \bar{r}_M. \tag{3.64}$$

Security variance

The variance of the ith security is given by

$$\sigma_i^2 = \mathcal{E}\left[(\tilde{r}_i - \bar{r}_i)^2\right]. \tag{3.65}$$

Substituting for $\tilde{r}_i$ from the factor model, and for $\bar{r}_i$ from (3.64), we obtain after some rearrangements

$$
\begin{aligned}
\sigma_i^2 &= \mathcal{E}[[\beta_i(\tilde{r}_M - \bar{r}_M) + \tilde{\epsilon}_i]^2] \\
&= \beta_i^2 \mathcal{E}[(\tilde{r}_M - \bar{r}_M)^2] + 2\beta_i \mathcal{E}[(\tilde{r}_M - \bar{r}_M)\tilde{\epsilon}_i] + \mathcal{E}[\tilde{\epsilon}_i^2] \\
&= \beta_i^2 \sigma_M^2 + \sigma_{\epsilon i}^2.
\end{aligned}
\tag{3.66}
$$

(The last equality follows from the fact that the residual term is uncorrelated with the factor so that $\mathcal{E}[(\tilde{r}_M - \bar{r}_M)\tilde{\epsilon}_i] = 0$.) The security variance has been expressed in terms of the factor loadings of the securities, the variance of the factor, and the variance of the security-specific residual term.

Security covariances

The covariance between securities i and i' is given by

$$\sigma_{ii'} = \mathcal{E}[(\tilde{r}_i - \bar{r}_i)(\tilde{r}_{i'} - \bar{r}_{i'})]. \tag{3.67}$$

Substituting for $\tilde{r}_i$ from the factor model, and for $\bar{r}_i$ from (3.64), we obtain

$$
\begin{aligned}
\sigma_{ii'} &= \mathcal{E}[[\beta_i(\tilde{r}_M - \bar{r}_M) + \tilde{\epsilon}_i][\beta_{i'}(\tilde{r}_M - \bar{r}_M) + \tilde{\epsilon}_{i'}]] \tag{3.68} \\
&= \beta_i \beta_{i'} \mathcal{E}[(\tilde{r}_M - \bar{r}_M)^2] \tag{3.69}
\end{aligned}
$$
$$+\beta_i \mathcal{E}[(\tilde{r}_M - \bar{r}_M)\tilde{\epsilon}_i] + \beta_{i'}\mathcal{E}[(\tilde{r}_M - \bar{r}_M)\tilde{\epsilon}_{i'}] + \mathcal{E}[\tilde{\epsilon}_i\tilde{\epsilon}_{i'}]. \tag{3.70}$$

From the assumptions of the single-factor model the last three terms are zero, and we have

$$\sigma_{ii'} = \beta_i \beta_{i'} \sigma_M^2. \tag{3.71}$$

The covariance of the securities has been expressed in terms of the factor loadings of the securities, and the variance of the factor. All security co-movements are driven through their joint response to changes in the common factor.

Mean-variance optimization with single-factor models

We can now combine the results obtained above to write the model for generating efficient port-folios. Using the single-factor model in the estimation of means we write the portfolio expected return as

$$R(x; \bar{r}) = \sum_{i=1}^{n} \alpha_i x_i + \sum_{i=1}^{n} \beta_i \bar{r}_M x_i. \tag{3.72}$$

Similarly, the portfolio variance is written as

$$\sigma^2(x) = \sum_{i=1}^{n} \sum_{i'=1}^{n} \sigma_{ii'} x_i x_{i'} \tag{3.73}$$

$$= \sum_{i=1}^{n} \sigma_i^2 x_i^2 + \sum_{i=1}^{n} \sum_{\substack{i'=1; \\ i' \neq i}}^{n} \sigma_{ii'} x_i x_{i'} \tag{3.74}$$

$$= \sum_{i=1}^{n} \beta_i^2 \sigma_M^2 x_i^2 + \sum_{i=1}^{n} \sigma_{\epsilon i}^2 x_i^2 + \sum_{i=1}^{n} \sum_{\substack{i'=1; \\ i' \neq i}}^{n} \beta_i \beta_{i'} \sigma_M^2 x_i x_{i'}. \tag{3.75}$$

The number of parameters in these expressions is $3n + 2$, which is much less than the number of parameters required when estimating portfolio mean and variance directly using the covariance matrix. These expressions can now be substituted in the quadratic programming model for generating efficient frontiers to obtain the following model.

Model 3.4.1 Mean-variance efficient portfolios with single-factor models

$$\text{Minimize} \quad \lambda \left(\sum_{i=1}^{n} \beta_i^2 \sigma_M^2 x_i^2 + \sum_{i=1}^{n} \sigma_{\epsilon i}^2 x_i^2 + \sum_{i=1}^{n} \sum_{\substack{i'=1; \\ i' \neq i}}^{n} \beta_i \beta_{i'} \sigma_M^2 x_i x_{i'} \right)$$

$$\qquad - (1 - \lambda) \left(\sum_{i=1}^{n} \alpha_i x_i + \sum_{i=1}^{n} \beta_i \bar{r}_m x_i \right) \tag{3.76}$$

$$\text{subject to} \quad \sum_{i=1}^{n} x_i = 1, \tag{3.77}$$

$$x \in X. \tag{3.78}$$

It is common practice to rely on security analysts for the estimation of expected returns $\hat{r}$ and variances $\hat{\sigma}$, and use a factor model to estimate the covariances. Such estimates can be used directly in the objective function of the optimization model which simplifies to:

$$\text{Minimize} \quad \lambda \left(\sum_{i=1}^{n} \hat{\sigma}_i^2 x_i^2 + \sum_{i=1}^{n} \sum_{\substack{i'=1; \\ i' \neq i}}^{n} \beta_i \beta_{i'} \sigma_M^2 x_i x_{i'} \right) - (1 - \lambda) \sum_{i=1}^{n} \hat{r}_i x_i. \tag{3.79}$$

Systematic and nonsystematic risk

Examining the variance equation (3.75) we can draw an interesting conclusion about the effectiveness of mean-variance optimization for risk management and portfolio diversification. We write the portfolio variance (equation 3.75) as

$$\sigma^2(x) = \sum_{i=1}^{n} \sigma_{\epsilon i}^2 x_i^2 + \sum_{i=1}^{n} \sum_{i'=1}^{n} \beta_i \beta_{i'} \sigma_M^2 x_i x_{i'}, \tag{3.80}$$

and by rearranging terms as

$$\sigma^2(x) = \sum_{i=1}^{n} \sigma_{\epsilon i}^2 x_i^2 + \left(\sum_{i=1}^{n} \beta_i x_i \right) \left(\sum_{i'=1}^{n} \beta_{i'} x_{i'} \right) \sigma_M^2 \tag{3.81}$$

$$= \sum_{i=1}^{n} \sigma_{\epsilon i}^2 x_i^2 + \beta_p^2 \sigma_M^2. \tag{3.82}$$

The portfolio beta $\beta_p = \sum_{i=1}^{n} \beta_i x_i$ reflects the sensitivity of portfolio returns to the factor.

Consider now a well-diversified portfolio with holdings $1/n$ in each available security. The first term of the portfolio variance becomes $1/n \sum_{i=1}^{n} \sigma_{\epsilon i}^2/n$, which is $1/n$ times the average residual risk in the investment universe, and it tends to zero as n becomes very large. Hence, with a large number of investments in the portfolio the nonsystematic risk due to firm-specific events can be diversified away.

The second term of the portfolio variance is a function of the average beta of the investment universe, and the variance of the factor. This term cannot be eliminated no matter how many securities we add to the portfolio, assuming that all securities have nonnegative β. For well-diversified portfolios, such as those obtained by solving mean-variance optimization models with $\lambda = 1$, the portfolio risk is dominated by the systematic risk – also known as market risk or nondiversifiable risk – and we have $\sigma(x) \approx \beta_p \sigma_M$.

Single-factor models and the CAPM

The careful reader must have noticed the similarity between the single-factor model in Definition 3.4.1 and the CAPM model of Theorem 2.3.1. In particular, the CAPM gives us the expected return of a security, when the security's random return can be explained using a single factor.

We write the single-factor model as a linear relation between the excess return of the security over the risk-free rate, and the excess return of the market factor over the risk-free rate. Thus we have

$$\tilde{r}_i - r_f = \alpha_i + \beta_i(\tilde{r}_M - r_f) + \tilde{\epsilon}_i. \tag{3.83}$$

(Note that the coefficients α and β will not be the same as those obtained when calibrating Model 3.4.1. Some books use a_i and b_i for the coefficients of the single-factor Model 3.4.1, and α_i, β_i for the excess return model of equation (3.83). If we assume that the residual term is zero we obtain what is known as the *characteristic equation*. Plotting the security excess return against the market excess return, ignoring the residual term, we obtain a straight line with slope β_i that intercepts the vertical axis at α_i. Calculating the expected value of equation (3.83) we obtain

$$\bar{r}_i - r_f = \alpha_i + \beta_i(\bar{r}_M - r_f). \tag{3.84}$$

This is identical to the CAPM except for the constant α_i which, according to the CAPM, should be equal to zero. It is worth pointing out, though, that the CAPM model is derived based on the assumption that the security returns are affected only by the means and the variances.

3.4.2   Multi-factor model

We can extend the analysis of the previous section to include more than one factor in estimating security returns and their covariances. Multi-factor models improve the estimates obtained with a single-factor model. In particular, when a single-factor model results in terms that are correlated with each other, then it is useful to identify the additional common factors that may explain the residual error, or part thereof. When the residual terms are correlated with each other or with the factor – thus violating key assumptions of the single-factor model – this is an indication that the security returns respond to some additional common factor(s) beyond the one included in the single-factor model. Identifying these factors and including them in the model will restore the validity of the assumptions. The extension to multi-factor models is straightforward. However, for the multi-factor models we do not have a simple way to select the factors. For instance, in modeling the US stock market it is customary to use between 3 and 15 factors and these must be carefully selected. We denote these factors by $\tilde{f}_j$, for $j \in \mathcal{K}$, and write the following linear model for security returns.

Definition 3.4.2 Multi-factor model. *The return of the ith security is related to the factors f_j, for $j \in \mathcal{K}$, through the linear relation*

$$\tilde{r}_i = \alpha_i + \sum_{j=1}^{K} \beta_{ij} \tilde{f}_j + \tilde{\epsilon}_i. \tag{3.85}$$

The variance of the jth factor is given by σ_j^2 and the security-specific residual term $\tilde{\epsilon}_i$ is assumed to be normally distributed with mean 0 and variance $\sigma_{\epsilon i}^2$.

We assume, as in the case of the single-factor model, that the security returns are correlated only through their response to the common factors. Hence, the following assumptions apply:

1. The covariance of the security-specific residual term with the factors is zero, that is, $\text{Cov}(\tilde{\epsilon}_i, \tilde{f}_j) = 0$, for all $i \in U, j \in \mathcal{K}$.

2. The covariance of the risk factors is zero, $\text{Cov}(\tilde{f}_j, \tilde{f}_{j'}) = 0$, for all $j \neq j'$ and $j, j' \in \mathcal{K}$.

3. The covariance of the residuals is zero, $\text{Cov}(\tilde{\epsilon}_i, \tilde{\epsilon}_{i'}) = 0$, for all $i \neq i'$ and $i, i' \in U$.

The first assumption will hold by construction of the model if sufficient factors are included. The second assumption can be made to hold by selecting factors that are uncorrelated. It is possible to construct uncorrelated (orthogonal) factors from any set of economically meaningful factors (see "Notes and References" at the end of this chapter for relevant references). The third assumption will hold if sufficient factors are incorporated so that any residual term is, indeed, firm-specific. If the residual terms are correlated this implies that the multi-factor model does not capture all the systematic risk of security returns, and additional factors must be identified and included in the model.

We can now use the multi-factor model to derive the means, variances and covariances needed in the mean-variance optimization model. The calculations are more involved than those carried out for the single-index model, but proceed along the same lines. We skip the derivations and summarize the results.

Security expected return

The expected return of the ith security is given by

$$\bar{r}_i = \alpha_i + \sum_{j=1}^{K} \beta_{ij} \bar{f}_j. \tag{3.86}$$

Security variance

The variance of the ith security is given by

$$\sigma_i^2 = \sum_{j=1}^{K} \beta_{ij}^2 \sigma_j^2 + \sigma_{\epsilon i}^2. \tag{3.87}$$

The security variance is calculated as a function of the security β's, the variance of the factors, and the variance of the security-specific residual terms.

Security covariances

The covariance between securities i and i' is given by

$$\sigma_{ii'} = \sum_{j=1}^{K} \beta_{ij} \beta_{i'j} \sigma_j^2. \tag{3.88}$$

The covariance of the securities is a function of the β's of the securities, and the variance of the factors. All security co-movements are driven by their joint response to changes in the factors.

Mean-variance optimization with multi-factor models

We can now combine the results obtained above to write the model for generating efficient portfolios. Using the multi-factor model we write the portfolio return as

$$R(x; \tilde{r}) = \sum_{i=1}^{n} \alpha_i x_i + \sum_{i=1}^{n} (\sum_{j=1}^{K} \beta_{ij} \tilde{f}_j) x_i + \sum_{i=1}^{n} \tilde{\epsilon}_i x_i. \tag{3.89}$$

The sensitivity of the portfolio to the jth factor is given by the portfolio factor loading

$$\beta_{pj} = \sum_{i=1}^{n} \beta_{ij} x_i, \tag{3.90}$$

and the portfolio return can be written as

$$R(x; \tilde{r}) = \sum_{i=1}^{n} \alpha_i x_i + \sum_{j=1}^{K} \beta_{pj} \tilde{f}_j + \sum_{i=1}^{n} \tilde{\epsilon}_i x_i. \tag{3.91}$$

From this we can write the portfolio expected return as

$$R(x; \bar{r}) = \sum_{i=1}^{n} \alpha_i x_i + \sum_{j=1}^{K} \beta_{pj} \bar{f}_j. \tag{3.92}$$

Similarly, the portfolio variance is written as

$$\sigma^2(x) = \sum_{j=1}^{K} \beta_{pj}^2 \sigma_j^2 + \sum_{i=1}^{n} \sigma_{\epsilon i}^2 x_i^2. \tag{3.93}$$

These expressions can now be used to write out the quadratic programming model for generating efficient frontiers.

Model 3.4.2 Mean-variance efficient portfolios with multi-factor models

---

$$\text{Minimize}_{x \in X} \quad \lambda \left(\sum_{j=1}^{K} \beta_{pj}^2 \sigma_j^2 + \sum_{i=1}^{n} \sigma_{\epsilon i}^2 x_i^2 \right)$$

$$- (1 - \lambda) \left(\sum_{i=1}^{n} \alpha_i x_i + \sum_{j=1}^{K} \beta_{pj} \bar{f}_j \right) \tag{3.94}$$

$$\text{subject to} \quad \sum_{i=1}^{n} x_i = 1, \tag{3.95}$$

$$\beta_{pj} = \sum_{i=1}^{n} \beta_{ij} x_i, \text{ for all } j \in \mathcal{K}. \tag{3.96}$$

As in the case of the single-factor model, security analysts may provide estimates for the security means and variances, and the multi-factor model is then used to estimate only the portfolio variance due to the security covariances.

Multi-factor models and the Arbitrage Pricing Theory

The multi-factor models provide the foundation for the Arbitrage Pricing Theory (APT). This theory essentially describes the law of one price, that is, the fact that two items that are the same cannot sell at different prices. Hence, the expected returns of securities that are affected in the same way by a common set of factors should be identical. But what happens when securities are affected by a common set of factors, but each is affected in different ways? APT gives us a linear relationship between the factor loadings and the expected return of the security. We state the precise relationship in the following theorem, considering the case whereby security returns are described by multi-factor models as given in Definition 3.4.2 but without the security-specific residual terms.

Theorem 3.4.1 Arbitrage Pricing Theory (APT). *Assume that there exist n assets whose returns are governed by K factors, with $K \leq n$ through the linear relation*

$$\tilde{r}_i = \alpha_i + \sum_{j=1}^{K} \beta_{ij} \tilde{f}_j, \text{ for all } i \in U. \tag{3.97}$$

Then there exist constants $\lambda_0, \lambda_1, \ldots, \lambda_K$ such that

$$\bar{r}_i = \lambda_0 + \sum_{j=1}^{\kappa} \beta_{ij} \lambda_j. \tag{3.98}$$

If there is a very large universe of securities we can form well-diversified portfolios, and consider each portfolio as an asset with zero residual term. In this way the theory can be made to work in practice, even when the multi-factor models we fit have residual terms. In general, it is accepted that the universe of all publicly traded stocks in the major stock markets is big enough so that the assumption of the theory is satisfied.

3.5   Are Optimized Portfolios Optimal?

It is worth recognizing a significant pitfall when developing mean-variance efficient portfolios. The input data of a mean-variance optimization model – i.e., the expected asset returns and the

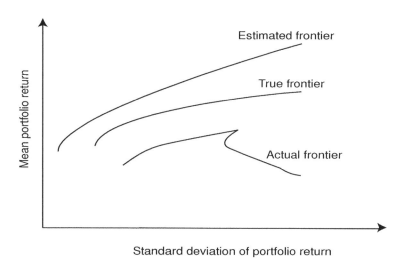

Figure 3.5: Mean-variance frontiers obtained using true and estimated data.

covariance matrix of returns – are subject to estimation error. In the presence of such errors the model will act as an error maximizer, and as a result the portfolios obtained may not be efficient.

Consider a universe of assets from which to select efficient portfolios, with true expected return vector μ^* and covariance matrix Q^*. These true values are not known but are estimated – perhaps from historical data – using estimators, such as the one given in Definition 2.3.6. The mean-variance optimization model is then formulated and solved using the estimated data μ and Q. The true mean and variance of the resulting portfolios will differ from the estimated mean and variance. Depending on the estimation error situations may arise whereby the optimized portfolios are not even efficient. As a consequence, the performance of mean-variance optimized portfolios is an optimistically biased predictor of the actual performance.

Figure 3.5 illustrates the situation. Two different frontiers will be obtained when using the true or the estimated data. However, the true frontier cannot be obtained since we do not know the true data, and the estimated frontier is subject to the estimation error. The actual frontier is the one obtained when we use the portfolios optimized using estimated data, and then calculate for each portfolio its mean and its variance using the true mean and variance, μ^* and Q^*. The resulting frontier, as shown in the figure, is not even efficient.

There are several techniques available for dealing with the problems arising from estimation error. For instance, it may be possible to obtain a confidence region for the efficient frontier based on the error estimates for the input data; related references are given at the end of this chapter.

The problems discussed here are not unique for mean-variance portfolio optimization, but appear in other portfolio models and for different sources of model misspecification. For instance, the data in Section 11.4.1 show the effect of flat tails on portfolios optimized ignoring the tails of the returns, and Figure 11.6 shows that the portfolios obtained using the MAD symmetric risk measure for credit-risky assets are inefficient when evaluated using the more suitable CVaR metric. All these examples highlight the potential adverse side effects of portfolio optimization models, as introduced in Section 1.4.1.

3.6   Postview

This chapter developed the classic mean-variance portfolio optimization models. The canonical formulation of this model was extended to include risk-free assets, leading to the one-fund theorem, and then several practical aspects of mean-variance optimization models were added in order to trace efficient frontiers. Short sales, borrowing, limits on trading size and transaction costs have been modeled, although these extensions require the use of integer variables that complicate the models. The problem of revising efficient portfolios was also introduced, with a graphic network representation. As a final step the models were extended to incorporate liabilities.

The chapter then developed factor models of return that can be used in estimating the data required for the implementation of mean-variance portfolio optimization models. Both single-factor and multi-factor models of security returns were developed, and were used to estimate the mean and variance data required for implementation of the optimization models. The relation of these factor models to the Capital Asset Pricing Model (CAPM) and to the Arbitrage Pricing Theory (APT) was highlighted.

Notes and References

The models in this chapter were introduced in Markowitz (1952), and in a monograph first published in 1959 and reprinted with updates as Markowitz (1991b). Recent reviews of developments in portfolio theory and risk-return analysis are given in Constantinides and Malliaris (1995), and Markowitz and van Dijk (2006). Extensive discussion of mean-variance analysis is given in the book by Elton and Gruber (1991).

The incorporation of transaction costs is discussed in Pogue (1970); Mulvey (1993) compares empirically different models for dealing with transaction costs. Fixed and proportional transaction costs are discussed in Constantinides (1976, 1979) in the context of developing dynamic strategies for cash management, investment, and consumption.

Large-scale mean-variance optimization is discussed in Perold (1984). The network representation of portfolio problems is due to Crum, Klingman and Tavis (1979), and of portfolio revision to Dembo, Mulvey and Zenios (1989); see also Mulvey and Vladimirou (1989, 1992) for network representation of the stochastic programming formulations of Chapter 9. Liabilities were incorporated by Sharpe and Tint (1990), Mulvey (1989), and Mulvey, Armstrong and Rothberg (1995).

The single-factor model was introduced in Sharpe (1963), and extensive discussion on factor models is found in Elton and Gruber (1991), which also treats multi-factor models and discusses both the CAPM and APT; additional references are given in the section on "Notes and References" in Chapter 2. For a practical discussion on the derivation of uncorrelated (orthogonal) factors from a set of correlated factors see Elton and Gruber (1991, ch. 6, Appendix A).

The sensitivity of mean-variance optimized portfolios with respect to errors in the input data was first investigated by Jobson and Korkie (1981). Further contributions on this very important issue were made by Michaud (1989, 1998), Chopra and Ziemba (1993), Broadie (1993) and references therein. The results of Figure 3.5 are based on the work of Broadie that was carried out using simulations.

Chapter 4

Portfolio Models for Fixed Income

> There is no idea, however ancient and absurd, that is not capable of improving our knowledge.
>
> Paul Feyerabend, *Against Method*

4.1 Preview

In this chapter we develop optimization models for fixed-income portfolios when the sources of risk are the level and shape of the term structure of interest rates. Models for structuring portfolios dedicated to matching a stream of cashflows are given first. These are followed by immunization models to protect portfolio returns from changes in the term structure. Additional models for factor immunization protect the portfolio returns from changes in convexity and steepness in addition to parallel shifts. These models are finally extended to immunize portfolios of corporate bonds from simultaneous changes in the term structure of interest rates and credit spreads.

4.2 Portfolio Dedication

Financial intermediaries, as well as nonfinancial institutions, are often faced with liability streams that stretch well into the future. In such cases the cashflows are uncertain and best represented by random variables. Sometimes, however, the streams may be known with certainty: the obligations arising from the sale of a guaranteed investment contract (GIC, see Section 8.3.1) are known with certainty; the liabilities of a defined benefits pension fund are known with the accuracy of mortality rate estimates and since the law of large numbers applies and average mortality rates provide sufficient accuracy so that these parameters may be considered deterministic; nonfinancial institutions planning acquisitions, expansion, or product development also face future cashflow needs that may be known with certainty. One may argue that uncertainty still plays a significant role in all of these cases. Nevertheless, models that deal with only the part of the problem that has certain data are used in practice. It is also instructive to consider portfolio optimization models for the simpler cases, and this is what we achieve in this chapter.

Even managers endowed with perfect information about their liabilities face a nontrivial task in developing an integrative asset and liability management strategy. Insurance companies found this out the hard way in the early 1980s. How should a guaranteed investment contract, for instance, be funded? In the upward sloping yield curve environment of the time, insurers placed the proceeds from GIC sales into 10- to 30-year mortgages or public bond instruments. Industry capitalized on the large spread between the high rate on their long-term assets and the credit rates on the shorter term GIC contracts. But as rates rose dramatically in the early 1980s insurance

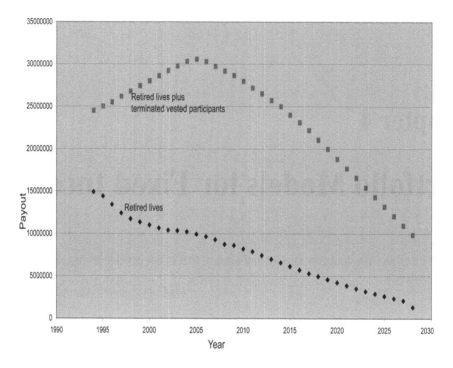

Figure 4.1: Scheduled payout of a pension fund over a 35-year time horizon.

firms saw their liabilities maturing while their assets had 20 years remaining to maturity and were valued at a fraction of their original cost. Similar problems were faced by insurance firms in the 1990s, but this time they were due to the decline in short-term rates to record levels and the firms' sale of products with minimum guaranteed rates of return that, although low, were still above the record low rates. (See the case study on the management of endowments with guarantees in Chapter 12.)

To better understand the issues underlying portfolio dedication we consider the funding of a projected schedule of pension fund payouts for a closed block of retired lives, as shown in Figure 4.1. The total dollar amount of the liabilities is \$276,457,340 and the present value at a 5% actuarial reinvestment rate is \$160,756,160. The pension fund manager wishes to construct a portfolio of bonds to fund these liabilities at a cost lower than \$160,756,160. Is it possible to achieve a return in excess of 5% by investing in a combination of treasury securities and high-quality corporate bonds? Policy considerations impose some constraints on the manager as summarized in Table 4.1. Practical considerations preclude holdings in any security less than one million dollars in par value, and holdings should be in multiples of 100K dollars in par value.

4.2.1 Cashflow matching with perfect foresight

An integrative asset and liability management model will match the cashflows from assets with the liability stream. Figure 4.2 illustrates the mismatching of long-term assets against the liability arising from a guaranteed investment contract and two portfolios with better cashflow matching. We seek a portfolio of minimum cost such that the cashflows from the assets in the portfolio match or exceed the liability at every time period. The following model will give the appropriate portfolio.

Table 4.1: Corporate policies impose constraints on portfolio managers.

	Minimum	Maximum
Quality		
Treasury	20%	100%
Agency	0	100%
AAA	0	100%
AA	0	100%
A	0	50%
BBB and lower	0	0
Sector		
Treasury	20%	100%
Agency	0	100%
Utility	0	30%
Telecom	0	30%
Financial	0	30%
Concentration		
In one issue	0	10%
In one issuer	0	10%

Model 4.2.1 Cashflow matching

$$\text{Minimize} \quad \sum_{i=1}^{n} P_{0i} x_i \tag{4.1}$$

$$\text{subject to} \quad \sum_{i=1}^{n} F_{ti} x_i \geq L_t, \text{ for all } t \in \mathcal{T}, \tag{4.2}$$

$$x \geq 0. \tag{4.3}$$

The model does not allow for borrowing or reinvestment of surplus. Thus interest rate risk is totally avoided. More realistic situations allow borrowing and reinvestment and the model is extended in the next section. But first we give a generalization that allows for negative cashflows in the assets. Such situations arise for investments that require a sequence of up-front payments before returning a positive cashflow. We modify the model to identify the last amount of cash needed to pay for the investments; this amount is denoted by v_0. The following model is a generalized version of the cashflow matching model and it allows negative cashflows.

Model 4.2.2 Cashflow matching (generalized)

$$\text{Minimize} \quad v_0 \tag{4.4}$$

$$\text{subject to} \quad \sum_{i=1}^{n} F_{0i} x_i + v_0 \geq 0, \tag{4.5}$$

$$\sum_{i=1}^{n} F_{ti} x_i \geq L_t, \text{ for all } t \in \mathcal{T}, \tag{4.6}$$

$$x \geq 0. \tag{4.7}$$

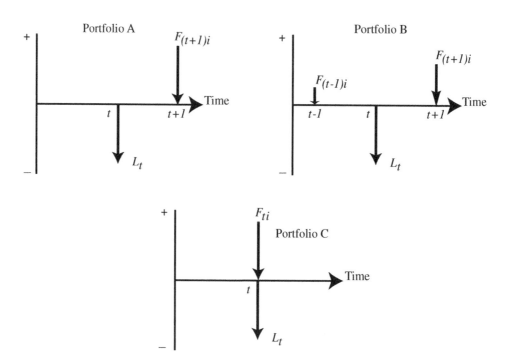

Figure 4.2: A liability L_t and the cashflows from mismatched portfolios A and B, and from a perfectly matched portfolio C.

If all assets have positive cashflows F_{ti} at periods after $t = 0$, then $\sum_{i=1}^{n} F_{0i}x_i$ is the amount we have to pay today in order to receive the future cashflows. This is the cost of the portfolio, and the solution v_0 of the generalized model is the minimum of $\sum_{i=1}^{n} F_{0i}x_i$, which is equal to the price of the portfolio used in the objective function of Model 4.2.1.

4.2.2 Cashflow matching with borrowing and reinvestment

Total cashflow matching can be achieved only if securities with cashflow timing that coincides with the timing of the liability are available. In general, liability payments may be due any day of the month, while bond coupon payments and maturities are typically due every six months. It is possible that no instrument maturing on the date when a liability is due is available. Or better priced bonds may be available, with maturity dates that differ from the liability dates. In such cases it is preferable either to purchase a bond which matures before the liability and reinvest the principal received in short-term money markets, or borrow from the short-term, risk-free markets against bonds that mature after the liability. An asset and liability management strategy that allows some shortfall or surplus around the liability payment date is sometimes referred to as symmetric cash matching. The name is evident from the cashflow stream of portfolio B in Figure 4.2.

We introduce now the vector $v^+ = (v_1^+, v_2^+, \ldots, v_t^+, \ldots v_T^+)$ to denote the variables of cash surplus at each period t that is reinvested in short-term deposits, and the vector $v^- = (v_1^-, v_2^-, \ldots, v_t^-, \ldots v_T^-)$ for shortfall at each period t that is covered by short-term borrowing. We assume a reinvestment rate r_{ft} for cash invested at period t until $t + 1$ and a borrowing rate $r_{ft} + \delta$ for cash borrowed for one period at t. With this additional notation we write the model that determines a least-cost portfolio dedicated to matching the liability stream as follows.

Model 4.2.3 Portfolio dedication

$$\text{Minimize} \quad v_0 \tag{4.8}$$

$$\text{subject to} \quad \sum_{i=1}^{n} F_{0i}x_i + v_0 + v_0^- = v_0^+, \tag{4.9}$$

$$\sum_{i=1}^{n} F_{ti}x_i + (1 + r_{f(t-1)})v_{t-1}^+ + v_t^- =$$
$$L_t + v_t^+ + (1 + r_{f(t-1)} + \delta)v_{t-1}^-, \quad \text{for all } t \in \mathcal{T}, \tag{4.10}$$
$$x, v^+, v^- \geq 0. \tag{4.11}$$

We must also set $v_T^- = 0$ to avoid borrowing at the last time period since the model has no mechanism to repay loans outstanding after T.

4.2.3   Horizon returns

The portfolio dedication Model 4.2.3 is shortsighted in that it ignores the effects of the portfolio policy at the end of the horizon. We have explicitly set the terminal debt to zero, but what happens to the final surplus v_T^+? We can reformulate the model with a view towards horizon returns. To avoid the problem of simultaneously minimizing the initial investment v_0 and maximizing the terminal surplus v_T^+ we assume a given budget $v_0 \doteq b_0$. The following model maximizes the return at the horizon, given a fixed budget and a stream of liabilities that need to be funded.

Model 4.2.4 Portfolio horizon returns

$$\text{Maximize} \quad v_T^+ \tag{4.12}$$

$$\text{subject to} \quad \sum_{i=1}^{n} F_{0i}x_i + b_0 + v_0^- = v_0^+, \tag{4.13}$$

$$\sum_{i=1}^{n} F_{ti}x_i + (1 + r_{f(t-1)})v_{t-1}^+ + v_t^- =$$
$$L_t + v_t^+ + (1 + r_{f(t-1)} + \delta)v_{t-1}^-, \quad \text{for all } t \in \mathcal{T}, \tag{4.14}$$
$$x, v^+, v^- \geq 0. \tag{4.15}$$

We must also set $v_T^- = 0$ to avoid borrowing at the last time period since the model has no mechanism to repay loans outstanding after T.

4.2.4   Lot sizes, transaction costs, and portfolio revision

Several real-world considerations may render the solution of the models impractical. While insights about the appropriate portfolio structures may be gained from the solution of the models as given above, the optimal portfolio may be impractical to purchase. We consider here the issues that arise in practical settings and explain how the models can incorporate them. (See also the discussions in Sections 3.2.2–3.2.4 that address lot size, transaction costs and other related issues in the context of mean-variance analysis.)

Let us first examine the need to obtain portfolios that are easily traded. For instance, a large number of small transactions is expensive when transaction costs are included. It may also be more difficult to execute small transactions. Odd size transactions incur liquidity risk, as traders prefer to deal in even lots. To avoid small transactions and ensure purchases that are multiples of some desirable even-lot sizes we need to add integer variables. If the face value of a bond is \$100 then the constraint $x_i = 1000Y_i$, where Y_i is an integer variable, ensures that all portfolio holdings x_i are in sizes of \$100,000. Y_i denotes the number of lots of size 1000 purchased from asset i.

Some lot sizes may be considered too small to be included in a portfolio. For instance, monitoring a portfolio of several small positions is problematic. Hence, we add constraints in the form

$$\underline{x}_i Z_i \le x_i \le \bar{x}_i Z_i \tag{4.16}$$

where Z_i is a binary – zero or one – variable, $\underline{x}_i$ is the smallest allowable lot size and $\bar{x}_i$ is the largest allowable lot size, which may be a very large number. For $Z_i = 0$ this constraint forces $x_i = 0$, and for $Z_i = 1$ we have $\underline{x}_i \le x_i \le \bar{x}_i$. Hence, portfolio holdings are either zero or within the prescribed range.

With every transaction we incur transaction costs either as brokerage fees or in the form of bid-ask spreads. There is usually a fixed cost associated with each transaction, no matter how small it is, and there is an additional cost which is proportional to the size of the transaction. Every tourist cashing in his or her traveller's check is informed that she will be charged a "commission of 1% with a minimum of \$5." There is a fixed charge of \$5 for transactions up to \$500; for larger transactions the cost is 1%. For purchases in mutual funds there is an entry fee and an additional charge proportional to the amount invested. Figure 3.3 (Chapter 3) illustrates two alternative ways for charging transaction costs.

Variable transaction costs are easy to model (see also the related discussion in Section 3.2.3). Simply subtract the appropriate proportion from the security cashflow F_{0i} to account for the percentage of this cashflow used to cover variable costs. Fixed transaction costs are modeled using the binary variables Z_i. If $Z_i = 0$, no purchase has been made, but if $Z_i = 1$, then we purchase at least $\underline{x}_i$ units at a fixed cost, say c_0. The total fixed cost of the portfolio is given by $c_0 \sum_{i=1}^{n} Z_i$.

Finally, we address models for revising an existing portfolio. A parameter x_{0i} is introduced to denote the initial holdings in asset i. Holdings in the optimized portfolio are denoted by $x_i = x_{0i} + y_{+i} - y_{-i}$, where y_{+i} and y_{-i} denote, respectively, purchases and sales of the ith asset. Transaction costs must be charged on the portfolio changes y_{+i}, y_{-i}, and not on the total exposure x_i, and the discussion of transaction costs above applies. The minimum lot size equation (4.16) applies to the total exposure x_i, although minimum trading sizes may be imposed on y_{+i}, y_{-i}, along the lines discussed in Section 3.2.4.

4.2.5 Diversification

Portfolio managers face constraints imposed by policy considerations (see, e.g., Table 4.1). How are the policies summarized in Table 4.1 incorporated into the optimization model? We consider the portfolio dedication Model 4.2.3, in which v_0 is the total amount invested, and we wish to restrict holdings in securities of different qualities to stay within the limits specified in the table. If, for instance, U_{Tr} denotes the set of treasury securities we add the constraint

$$.2v_0 \le \sum_{i \in U_{Tr}} F_{0i} x_i \le v_0, \tag{4.17}$$

to ensure that at least 20% of the portfolio is invested in treasuries. We impose one such constraint for each subset of securities to reflect the policy considerations by quality, sector, issue or issuer.

4.2.6   Bootstrapping the yield of dedicated portfolios

The optimal solution of the portfolio dedication Model 4.2.3 allows us to bootstrap a yield curve for the liability. The optimal dual price π_t^* (see Appendix A) for the tth constraint in equation (4.10) has the following interpretation: It is the amount by which the optimal solution v_0 will change for one unit of change in the liability at period t. This is then the present value of money we need today in order to pay back a unit of liability at time t, discounted at the rate implied by the portfolio. The yield of liabilities of different maturities is obtained as the solution of the equation

$$\pi_t^* = \frac{1}{(1 + y_t)^t}. \tag{4.18}$$

This notion of yield is consistent with the asset portfolio, and is the yield of the dedicated portfolio at the maturity dates of the liabilities.

4.3   Portfolio Immunization

Portfolio dedication models assume borrowing and reinvestment rates implied by the forward rates from a given term structure. By borrowing to cover shortfalls and reinvesting surpluses at the assumed rates, the cash inflow from the portfolios covers the cash outflow from the liabilities. But what happens to the matching of cashflows if the term structure changes? When the time horizon extends well into the future it is very likely that the assumed rates will change. Immunization is a portfolio strategy that matches the interest rate risk of an asset portfolio against the projected stream of liabilities to achieve zero net market exposure.

We develop the model starting from the cashflow matching Model 4.2.1. The surplus created at period one is given by $v_1^+ = \sum_{i=1}^n F_{1i} x_i - L_1$, and from constraint (4.2) it follows that this quantity is nonnegative. Carrying this surplus from period $t = 1$ to $t = 2$ at the forward reinvestment rate $(1 + f_{12})$ we get the second-period constraint as

$$\sum_{i=1}^n F_{2i} x_i + (1 + f_{12})(\sum_{i=1}^n F_{1i} x_i - L_1) \geq L_2 \tag{4.19}$$

Calculating now the surplus at $t = 2$, carrying it forward to $t = 3$, and repeating this for each period until the end of the horizon T at reinvestment rates $(1 + f_{t,t+1})$, we obtain the following equation

$$\sum_{i=1}^n \left[F_{1i} x_i \prod_{t=1}^{T-1}(1 + f_{t,t+1}) + F_{2i} x_i \prod_{t=2}^{T-1}(1 + f_{t,t+1}) + \ldots + F_{Ti} x_i \right] \geq$$
$$L_1 \prod_{t=1}^{T-1}(1 + f_{t,t+1}) + L_2 \prod_{t=2}^{T-1}(1 + f_{t,t+1}) + \ldots + L_T \tag{4.20}$$

This rather messy expression simply states that the future value of assets at the end of the horizon should be at least equal to the future value of the liabilities. We divide both sides by the constant $\prod_{t=0}^{T-1}(1 + f_{t,t+1})$ to obtain the intuitively appealing relation wherein the present value of the assets should be equal to the present value of the liabilities. If surplus can be reinvested at the assumed rates, then liabilities will be fully funded through the cashflow generated by the assets, or through surplus carried forward from previous periods. This is achieved if the present values of the asset cash inflow and the liability outflow are equal – where in the cashflow of the assets we, of course, include the amount of any asset that matures. Matching the present value of assets and liabilities is the necessary condition for immunization.

Definition 4.3.1 Necessary condition for immunization.

$$\sum_{i=1}^{n} P_i x_i = P_L. \tag{4.21}$$

Under this condition – and assuming reinvestment rates do not change from the assumed values – the portfolio cashflows will match the liability cashflows. We worked out the example only with reinvestment of surplus, but we arrive at the same condition if we allow borrowing as well.

There is no guarantee that the necessary condition will hold when the rates change. For this to happen both sides of equation (4.21) must change by the same amount when the term structure changes. A first order estimate of the change in the present value of a stream of cashflows – either an asset or a liability – with changes in the term structure is measured by the duration (see Definition 2.4.10). Hence, a first-order sufficient condition for portfolio immunization is that the duration of assets and liabilities match.

Definition 4.3.2 First-order condition for immunization.

$$\sum_{i=1}^{n} D_i^{FW} P_i x_i = D_L^{FW} P_L. \tag{4.22}$$

The following model guarantees zero net market exposure against small and parallel shifts only.

Model 4.3.1 Portfolio immunization

$$\text{Maximize} \quad F(x) \tag{4.23}$$

$$\text{subject to} \quad \sum_{i=1}^{n} P_i x_i = P_L, \tag{4.24}$$

$$\sum_{i=1}^{n} D_i^{FW} P_i x_i = D_L^{FW} P_L, \tag{4.25}$$

$$x \geq 0. \tag{4.26}$$

$F(x)$ is the objective function, P_L is the present value of the liabilities, D_i^{FW} is the Fisher-Weil duration of the ith asset, and D_L^{FW} is the Fisher-Weil duration of the liabilities.

The choice of an objective function deserves discussion. The most commonly used objective is to maximize the portfolio yield, which is approximated by

$$y_p \approx \frac{\sum_{i=1}^{n} D_i^{FW} P_i y_i x_i}{\sum_{i=1}^{n} D_i^{FW} P_i x_i}. \tag{4.27}$$

Since the denominator is constant and equal to D_L^{FW} by constraint (4.25) the portfolio immunization model can be solved as a linear program maximizing the linear expression $\sum_{i=1}^{n} D_i^{FW} P_i y_i x_i$.

To see how this basic model can be extended we consider the risk factors that have been controlled, and the risk factors that are still not explicitly handled by the model. Interest rate risk from parallel shifts in the term structure has been controlled through duration matching. However, risks arising from changes in the shape of the term structure have not been controlled, and the portfolio immunization model maximizes the exposure to shape risk. However, there are many ways to construct a duration matched portfolio. Figure 4.3 illustrates three structures: a bullet portfolio with a single payment, a barbell portfolio with two payments at a short and a long horizon, and an even ladder portfolio with several payments spread out evenly across the time horizon.

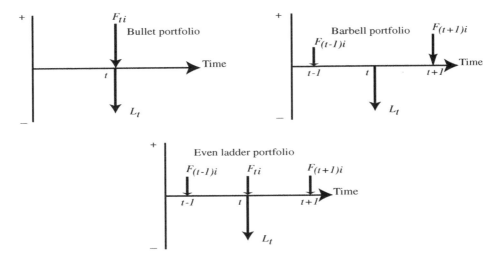

Figure 4.3: Bullet, even ladder, and barbell portfolios immunized against a single liability.

The result of the immunization model as formulated here is a barbell portfolio. Why is this the case? Long bonds are more efficient in maximizing dollar duration times yield – this is the objective function of the model – while a short bond is most efficient in reducing the portfolio duration to its target value. Thus, a barbell portfolio maximizes yield at the lowest possible duration, but the portfolio cashflows will be very dispersed and this implies that the portfolio is highly exposed to shape risk. Consider an immunized portfolio structured to fund a single payment in 10 years. A duration matched portfolio can be put together with a combination of a 15-year bond and cash. If the term structure tilts upwards the asset portfolio will lose money more rapidly than the liability, causing a negative net worth. Of course, a positive net worth will be obtained if the term structure tilts downwards.

Another way to perceive the problem is to recognize that the price-yield relationship is convex and not linear. Hence, while for parallel shifts of the term structure assets and liabilities move in tandem due to the duration matching constraint, for larger changes assets and liabilities will diverge if they have different price-yield relationships. In order to achieve tighter cashflow matching of assets and liabilities we add a second-order necessary condition to ensure that the asset price-yield curve bounds from above the liability price-yield curve. This is achieved by imposing the following convexity constraint on the portfolio, where C_L is the convexity of the liabilities.

Definition 4.3.3 Second-order condition for immunization.

$$\sum_{i=1}^{n} C_i P_i x_i \geq C_L P_L. \tag{4.28}$$

A look at Figure 2.6 (Chapter 2) illustrates why this condition is a second-order condition for immunization: the changes in the liability value due to the nonlinearities of the price-yield relationship are – within the range of validity of the quadratic approximation to the convexity curve – smaller than the changes in the asset side and hence the liabilities will remain funded. Convexity constraints are also a remedy for volatility risk. Large changes in the term structure will cause the first-order necessary condition to break down. However, by forcing the net portfolio convexity to be nonnegative we ensure that the minimum net worth is realized at the current term structure. For bigger changes in the term structure the net worth will only increase.

Convexity constraints are significant when securities with embedded options are included in the portfolio. Such securities may have negative convexity and it is important that the net portfolio convexity remains positive. In this case immunization models are built based on option adjusted duration and option adjusted convexity (see Definitions 2.4.17 and 2.4.18).

The immunization strategy should also consider the dynamics of duration. With time, the duration of both assets and liabilities will change – they converge to zero as we approach maturity – but not necessarily in the same way. The differential effect of time on the duration of assets and liabilities introduces what is often called a *duration drift*. Because of duration drift, immunized portfolios should be periodically revised and this in turn introduces liquidity risk.

4.4 Factor Immunization

Factor immunization is an enhanced immunization technique which explicitly accounts for shape risk. This is achieved by relaxing the assumption that the term structure shifts in parallel, which is implicit in the use of duration for portfolio immunization. We use instead a linear factor model such as the one obtained from the principal component analysis in Section 2.4.2. This model accounts for a significant percentage of the changes in the term structure observed in most practical situations – not simply for the changes that are due to parallel shifts. The independent factors are the principal components of the correlation matrix of the term structure of interest rates (see Definition 2.4.13). We do not necessarily consider all K principal components in the model, but use instead the first κ with the largest eigenvalue until some arbitrary proportion of the variance in the term structure has been explained.

The price sensitivity of bonds to changes in the factors is given in the following definition.

Definition 4.4.1 Factor modified duration. *Recall that the bond price is given by*

$$P_i = \sum_{t=1}^{T} F_{ti} e^{-r_t t}. \tag{4.29}$$

Changes in the term structure of interest rates are expressed as a linear combination of κ independent factors

$$\Delta r_t = \sum_{j=1}^{\kappa} \beta_{jt} \Delta f_j + \epsilon_t. \tag{4.30}$$

ϵ_t *is the error term assumed to be normally distributed with mean 0.*

The change of the bond price with changes of the jth factor is obtained from the total derivative of equation (4.29)

$$\Delta P_i = -\sum_{t=1}^{T} F_{ti} t e^{-r_t t} \Delta r_t. \tag{4.31}$$

Substituting in this expression the factor model (4.30) and ignoring the error term we get

$$\Delta P_i = -\sum_{t=1}^{T} \left(F_{ti} t e^{-r_t t} \sum_{j=1}^{\kappa} \beta_{jt} \Delta f_j \right). \tag{4.32}$$

The factors are independent, and therefore $\partial f_j / \partial f_{j'} = 0$ when $j \neq j'$. Hence, for small – but not necessarily parallel – shifts of the term structure we obtain the sensitivity of the bond price to changes in the jth factor from the above equation by

$$\frac{\partial P_i}{\partial f_j} = -\sum_{t=1}^{T} F_{ti} t \beta_{jt} e^{-r_t t}. \tag{4.33}$$

The factor modified duration of bond i with respect to the factor f_j is defined as the relative price sensitivity as scaled by the bond price:

$$k_{ij} = -\frac{\partial P_i}{\partial f_j} / P_i = \frac{1}{P_i} \sum_{t=1}^{T} F_{ti} t \beta_{jt} e^{-r_t t}. \tag{4.34}$$

The fact that we use only κ principal components explains the error term ϵ_t in equation (4.30) which is absent from equation (2.69) where all K factors are used.

Note that if the term structure shifts only in parallel we have only a single factor with loadings $\beta_{1t} = 1$, for all $t \in \mathcal{T}$, and in this case factor modified duration simplifies to the modified duration given in Definition 2.4.9.

The second-order relative derivative of the bond prices with changes in the factors is the factor modified convexity of the bond.

Definition 4.4.2 Factor modified convexity. *The factor modified convexity of bond i with respect to the jth factor is defined by*

$$C_{ij} = -\frac{\partial^2 P_i}{\partial f_j^2} / P_i. \tag{4.35}$$

The starting point for developing factor immunization models is the necessary condition for immunization that the present value of the assets equals the present value of the liabilities

$$\sum_{i=1}^{n} P_i x_i = P_L. \tag{4.36}$$

We require that this equality holds when factors change. Taking first derivatives with respect to the factors we obtain

$$\sum_{j=1}^{\kappa} \frac{\partial (\sum_{i=1}^{n} P_i x_i)}{\partial f_j} df_j = \sum_{j=1}^{\kappa} \frac{\partial P_L}{\partial f_j} df_j. \tag{4.37}$$

Since by construction the factor changes df_j are independent, the above equation will hold if it holds for each factor. The coefficients of df_j should be equal for all $j = 1, 2, \ldots \kappa$. That is

$$\frac{\partial (\sum_{i=1}^{n} P_i x_i)}{\partial f_j} = \frac{\partial P_L}{\partial f_j}. \tag{4.38}$$

The term $\frac{\partial P_i}{\partial f_j}$ is the negative of the factor modified duration k_{ij} multiplied by the security price P_i, and we have the following first-order conditions for factor immunization against the first $\kappa \leq K$ most significant risk factors.

Definition 4.4.3 First-order conditions for factor immunization.

$$\sum_{i=1}^{n} k_{ij} P_i x_i = k_{Lj} P_L, \text{ for all } j = 1, 2, \ldots, \kappa, \tag{4.39}$$

where k_{Lj} is the factor modified duration of the liability.

Taking second derivatives of (4.36) with respect to the factors – and noting that $\frac{\partial^2 P}{\partial f_j \partial f_{j'}}$ whenever $j \neq j'$ since the factors are independent – we obtain

$$\sum_{j=1}^{\kappa} \frac{\partial^2 (\sum_{i=1}^{n} P_i x_i)}{\partial f_j^2} df_j^2 = \sum_{j=1}^{\kappa} \frac{\partial^2 P_L}{\partial f_j^2} df_j^2. \tag{4.40}$$

We note that the two sides of the equation are the negative of the factor modified convexities multiplied by the prices, and we get the following second-order conditions for factor immunization.

Definition 4.4.4 Second-order conditions for factor immunization.

$$\sum_{i=1}^{n} C_{ij} P_i x_i = C_{Lj} P_L, \quad \text{for all } j = 1, 2, \ldots, \kappa, \tag{4.41}$$

where C_{Lj} *is the factor modified convexity of the liability.*

The following model guarantees zero net market exposure against changes to the factors. If sufficient factors are chosen to account for a large proportion of the variance in the term structure, then the model creates a portfolio which has zero net market exposure under most term structure changes.

Model 4.4.1 Factor immunization

$$\text{Maximize} \quad F(x) \tag{4.42}$$

$$\text{subject to} \quad \sum_{i=1}^{n} P_i x_i = P_L \tag{4.43}$$

$$\sum_{i=1}^{n} k_{ij} P_i x_i = k_{Lj} P_L, \text{ for all } j = 1, 2, \ldots, \kappa, \tag{4.44}$$

$$x \geq 0. \tag{4.45}$$

To this model we can add convexity constraints to obtain a portfolio that satisfies the second-order condition. This constraint is imposed as an inequality

$$\sum_{i=1}^{n} C_{ij} P_i x_i \geq C_{Lj} P_L, \text{ for all } j = 1, 2, \ldots, \kappa. \tag{4.46}$$

The reason we allow for greater factor convexity on assets, rather than the liabilities, is simple. For bonds the factor convexities are uniformly positive. The inequality constraint imposes a non-negative net portfolio convexity with zero net duration at the current rates. If the factors change, the net portfolio value will become positive. Caution is needed in imposing the second-order constraint for instruments with negative convexity, such as callable bonds, mortgages and so on, since the price-yield relationship of such bonds is highly nonlinear and the quadratic approximation obtained by convexity is inadequate. Immunization models for securities with embedded options and negative convexity are based on the option adjusted duration and option adjusted convexity of Definitions 2.4.17 and 2.4.18. Even so, when dealing with complex securities the assumptions on the shifts in the term structure of these models are overly simplistic, and the scenario-based models of Chapter 5 provide much better modeling tools.

4.5   Factor Immunization for Corporate Bonds

The techniques of factor immunization can be extended to hedge against changes in the yields of corporate bonds, in addition to the interest rate and shape risk of the term structure. The analysis of the risks in the corporate bond market is a significant topic in risk management. The attention is well justified given the size of the corporate bond market, its rapid rate of growth, and the large credit risk exposures of major dealers. The outstanding corporate debt in the United States stood at $4.9 trillion as of March 31, 2005. The annual issuance of corporate bonds has been growing rapidly since the eighties. Following the dramatic decline in 1990 we have seen a resurgence of new issues exceeding $600 billion annually over the last several years – although

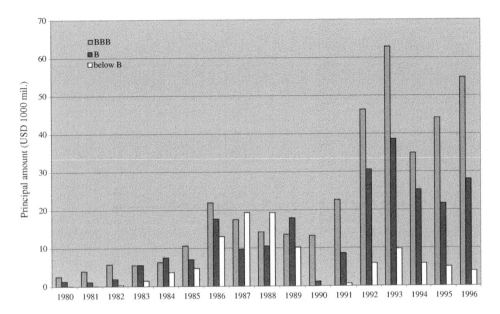

Figure 4.4: The annual issuance of nonconvertible corporate bonds demonstrates a rapid growth of the corporate bond market in the 1990s with a flight to higher quality debt.

we have witnessed a flight-to-quality as evidenced from the data in Figure 4.4. In tandem with the growth of the market we have witnessed large credit risk exposures of major dealers. The average daily corporate trading volume by primary dealers for bonds with maturities greater than one year stood at $23 billion in the first quarter of 2005. The total estimated investment-grade trading volume in the first quarter of 2005 was $685.9 billion and the high-yield trading volume was $266.7 billion.

We could directly apply the factor immunization models of the previous section to analyze the term structure of the yields on corporate bonds. However, in the case of corporate bonds we deal with multiple credit rating classes. The yields are not only correlated across bonds of different maturities, but also across bonds with different credit ratings. Table 4.2 shows the correlations between the yields of bonds of different maturities with credit ratings from AAA to B3. Note, for instance, the high correlation between the yields on AAA and B3 bonds with 10-year maturities, but also the significant correlation between the 10-year AAA and the 6-month B3. These correlations must be accounted for in an effective immunization strategy.

In this section we develop first a model that treats credit rating classes as independent. We will see that this model has some merits. We then develop a model that immunizes against changes in the yields of multiple correlated credit classes.

4.5.1   Factor analysis of corporate yields

To highlight the significance of correlations among credit rating classes, we calibrate first the multi-factor model (see, e.g., equation 2.69) independently for each class. That is, we assume that the correlation coefficients between bonds of different ratings in Table 4.2 are zero. Estimation of the model using corporate bond yield data over the period 1992–1999 results in the factor loadings shown in Figure 4.5. The model is calibrated on the excess returns of the corporate bond yields over the treasury yields of comparable maturities. For comparison, in Figure 4.6 we show the factor loadings for the risk-free US Treasury yields during the same period.

In the case of the AAA class the first factor affects the yield of different maturities by the

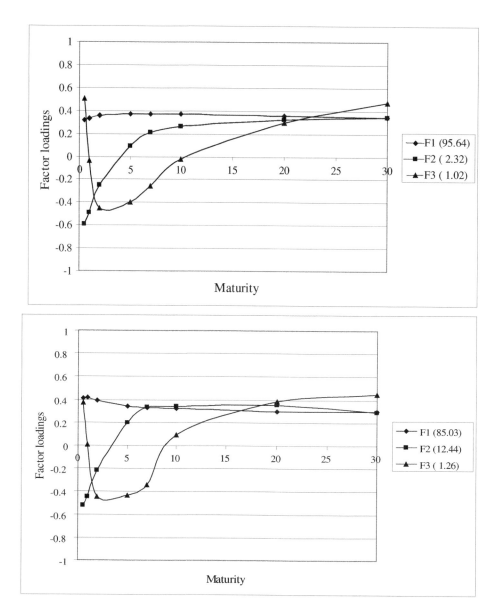

Figure 4.5: Factor loadings for the **AAA** and B3 yield changes assuming uncorrelated rating classes.

Table 4.2: Correlations of weekly yield changes for AAA and B3 bonds of maturities ranging from 6 months to 10 years, during the period March 1992 to July 1999.

	6m AAA	1y AAA	2y AAA	5y AAA	7y AAA	10y AAA	6m B3	1y B3	2y B3	5y B3	7y B3	10y B3
AAA												
6m	1.00											
1y	0.96	1.00										
2y	0.93	0.97	1.00									
5y	0.92	0.94	0.98	1.00								
7y	0.94	0.93	0.97	0.99	1.00							
10y	0.90	0.93	0.96	0.98	0.99	1.00						
B3												
6m	0.62	0.58	0.57	0.55	0.54	0.55	1.00					
1y	0.63	0.64	0.63	0.61	0.60	0.60	0.98	1.00				
2y	0.72	0.73	0.74	0.73	0.72	0.71	0.93	0.96	1.00			
5y	0.82	0.84	0.87	0.88	0.87	0.87	0.75	0.80	0.89	1.00		
7y	0.81	0.83	0.85	0.88	0.88	0.88	0.65	0.71	0.81	0.96	1.00	
10y	0.83	0.85	0.86	0.88	0.88	0.89	0.66	0.70	0.80	0.95	0.96	1.00

same amount and it explains more than 95% of changes in yields as parallel shifts. The second factor, which explains more than 2% of changes, affects short- and long-term yields in opposite directions, and it indicates changes in the steepness of the yield curve. The third factor, which explains more than 1% of changes, affects the curvature for short periods. The same qualitative factors – parallel shifts, steepness and curvature – affect the B3 ratings, although the percentages of the total change explained by each are different.

The multi-factor model can also be calibrated taking into account the correlations among bonds of different credit ratings. This is done by estimating the principal components of the 12×12 matrix in Table 4.2 to obtain the factor loadings shown in Figure 4.7. It is again the case that three factors explain around 98% of the variability in the yields. However, the factor loadings are significantly different from those obtained independently for each credit rating class. For instance, the factor loadings for the second and third factor have opposite signs for the AAA and B3 bonds, and this captures the flight-to-quality observed when investors shift from low to high credit rating bonds.

4.5.2   Factor immunization with uncorrelated credit ratings

Changes in the factors of the yield curve of a rating class affect systematically the bond prices in this particular rating class. It is therefore possible to hedge the impact of factor changes. We start with a model to hedge uncorrelated yield changes across rating classes, and then proceed with a model to deal with the correlations.

Let NC be the number of rating classes, with c denoting the cth credit rating. The parameters in the price equation

$$P_i^c = \sum_{t=1}^{T} F_{ti}^c e^{-r_i^c t} \tag{4.47}$$

are indexed by the credit rating.

A linear factor model for the yield changes in a bond with rating c takes the form

$$\Delta y_t^c = \sum_{j=1}^{\kappa} \beta_{jt}^c df_j^c + \epsilon_t, \tag{4.48}$$

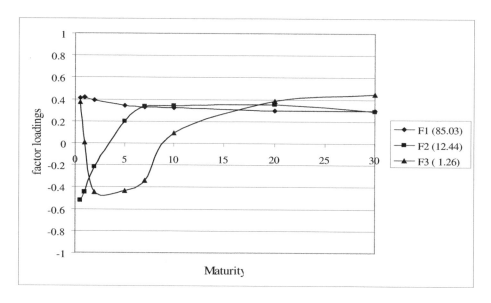

Figure 4.6: Factor loadings for the US Treasury yield changes.

where we assume that κ independent factors explain the yield changes of each class and β_{jt}^c are the corresponding factor loadings. (We assume for simplicity that κ factors are sufficient for all classes. Of course the factors will typically be different for each class, but three to four factors are usually sufficient to explain a significant percentage of yield changes for each class.) The sensitivity of bond prices to factor changes is given by

$$\frac{\partial P_i^c}{\partial f_j^c} = -\sum_{t=1}^{T} F_{ti}^c t \beta_{jt}^c e^{-r_i^c t}. \tag{4.49}$$

The factor modified duration of the bond with respect to the jth factor is the relative price sensitivity

$$k_{ij}^c = -\frac{\partial P_i^c}{\partial f_j^c} / P_i^c = \frac{1}{P_i^c} \sum_{t=1}^{T} F_{ti}^c t \beta_{jt}^c e^{-r_i^c t}. \tag{4.50}$$

Consider now a portfolio of assets with holdings x_i^c in bond i with credit rating c, and we assume for simplicity the same number of bonds in each class, n. The necessary condition for immunization is

$$\sum_{c=1}^{NC} \sum_{i=1}^{n} P_i^c x_i^c = P_L, \tag{4.51}$$

where P_L is the present value of the liabilities. This condition must hold when the factors change. We take derivatives with respect to the factors on both sides of the equation and require that the sensitivities of both sides with respect to each factor f_j^c are equal, to obtain a first-order necessary condition, akin to the one given in Definition 4.4.3.

$$\sum_{i=1}^{n} k_{ij}^c P_i x_i^c = k_{jL}^c P_L, \qquad \text{for all } j = 1, \dots, \kappa, \qquad c = 1, 2 \dots, NC. \tag{4.52}$$

k_{jL}^c is the factor loading for the liabilities with respect to factor j in rating class c.

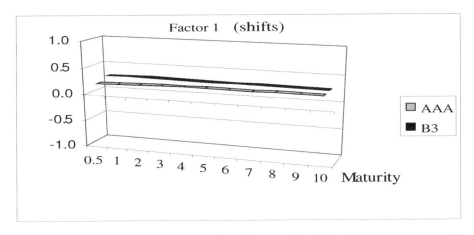

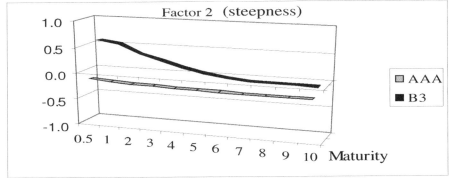

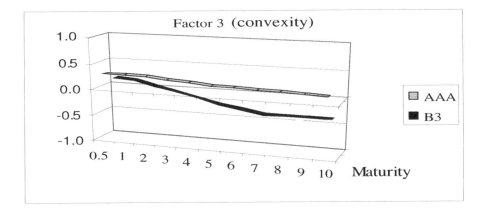

Figure 4.7: Factor loadings for yield changes of the AAA and B3 credit rating classes with correlated changes among rating classes. The three factors explain, respectively, 82%, 12%, and 4% of the variability.

If we assume that the liability has a credit rating, say $c = 1$, then the optimization model is written as follows.

Model 4.5.1 Factor immunization with uncorrelated credit rating classes

$$\text{Minimize} \quad F(x) \tag{4.53}$$

$$\text{subject to} \quad \sum_{c=1}^{NC} \sum_{i=1}^{n} P_i^c x_i^c = P_L, \tag{4.54}$$

$$\sum_{i=1}^{n} k_{ij}^c P_i^c x_i^c = \begin{cases} k_{jL}^1 P_L, & \text{for all } j = 1, \ldots, \kappa, \ c = 1, \\ 0, & \text{for all } j = 1, \ldots, \kappa, \ c = 2, \ldots, NC, \end{cases} \tag{4.55}$$

$$x \geq 0. \tag{4.56}$$

Constraints (4.55) force $x_i^c = 0$ for all i, when $c \neq 1$. Hence bond holdings in assets with ratings different than the target $c = 1$ are excluded. These constraints can be relaxed to allow some exposure to credit risk.

$$\sum_{i=1}^{n} k_{ij}^c P_i^c x_i^c = k_{jL}^1 P_L, \qquad \text{for } c = 1, \tag{4.57}$$

$$\underline{k}^c \leq \sum_{i=1}^{n} k_{ij}^c x_i^c \leq \overline{k}^c, \qquad \text{for all } c = 2, 3, \ldots, NC. \tag{4.58}$$

The user-specified parameters $\underline{k}^c$ and $\overline{k}^c$ limit the credit risk exposure to factors affecting credit rating classes other than the target class for which the risks are being hedged. These are ad hoc constraints and a rigorous model for immunizing a liability against changes in the yields of multiple correlated credit rating classes is given next.

4.5.3   Factor immunization with correlated credit ratings

We relax now the assumption of uncorrelated credit rating classes and obtain a rigorous immunization model. In order to identify the factors affecting co-movements of the yield curves in different rating classes we perform principal component analysis on the full correlation matrix shown in Figure 4.2. The upper left and lower right triangular submatrices are the correlations among the yield changes for securities within the same rating class, while the lower left square submatrix is the correlation matrix of the yields of securities with different ratings. When we assume that rating classes are uncorrelated, as we did in the previous section, the principal component analysis is carried out for each triangular submatrix independently. For the models in this section the principal component analysis is carried out on the full matrix.

The factor analysis of this matrix identifies κ factors that jointly affect yield changes in bonds of different maturities for all classes. If we let k_{ij}^c denote the factor modified duration of bond i with credit rating c to the jth factor, and k_{Lj} denote the liability factor modified duration, we have the following model.

Model 4.5.2 Factor immunization with correlated credit rating classes

Minimize $F(x)$ $\qquad\qquad$ (4.59)

subject to $\displaystyle\sum_{c=1}^{NC}\sum_{i=1}^{n} P_i^c x_i^c = P_L,$ $\qquad\qquad$ (4.60)

$\displaystyle\sum_{i=1}^{n} k_{ij}^c P_i^c x_i^c = k_{Lj} P_L,$ for all $j = 1, 2, \ldots \kappa,\ c = 1, 2, \ldots NC.$

$\qquad\qquad$ (4.61)

$x \geq 0.$ $\qquad\qquad$ (4.62)

4.6 Postview

This chapter developed models for the management of fixed-income portfolios, considering only two types of risk: interest rate and shape risk. It started with portfolio dedication models, where it was assumed that the term structure of interest rates remains fixed and one has to consider the funding of long-term liabilities taking into account the full term structure of interest rates.

It then developed portfolio immunization models that ensured that a dedicated portfolio will finance future liabilities even when interest rates shift up or down uniformly, and the term structure experiences parallel shifts. Important as this model may be it fails when the term structure does not shift in parallel across all maturities, and hence immunized portfolios remain exposed to shape risk. Principal component analysis was then used to identify the factors that cause nonparallel shifts, and to develop factor immunization models to hedge shape risk; such models were developed for both treasury and corporate bonds.

Notes and References

Portfolio immunization was introduced by Reddington (1952); see Macaulay (1938) for the classic analysis of interest rate risk, and Granito (1984), Zipkin (1989), and de La Grandville (2001) for modern treatments. The optimization models for cashflow matching, dedication, and immunization are given in Zenios (1993a). Stochastic dedication is discussed in Hiller and Eckstein (1993).

For factor analysis and factor immunization models see the papers by Garbade (1986), Litterman, Scheinkman and Weiss (1988), Litterman and Iben (1991). A discussion on nonparallel shifts is found in Reitano (1992). Applications of factor immunization to the Danish market are discussed in Dahl (1993) and to the Italian market in D'Ecclesia and Zenios (1994). The credit risk factor analysis is due to Bertocchi, Giacometti and Zenios (2005); see also Keenan (2000) for discussion of the corporate bond market risks. The data on the issuance of corporate debt and the trading volumes are from the May 2005 *Research Quarterly* published by the Bond Market Association, NY; see www.bondmarkets.com.

Chapter 5

Scenario Optimization

No great deed is done by falterers who ask for certainty.

George Eliot

5.1 Preview

Scenario optimization provides powerful and flexible models for risk management in both equities and fixed-income assets, integrating in a common framework several disparate sources of risk. In this chapter we develop models that trade off reward against risk, when both measures are computed from scenario data. The scenarios describing market, credit, liquidity, actuarial, and other types of risk can be quite general. Portfolios of fixed-income, equities and derivative assets can be optimized in the same framework, and liabilities can also be incorporated. The relationships between several models are revealed.

5.2 Basics of Scenario Optimization

In Chapters 1 and 2, we argued that financial risks are multidimensional and must be managed in an integrated fashion. And yet, the two subsequent chapters (3 and 4) took the traditional silo approach and developed optimization models for managing risks for equities and fixed-income securities, respectively. By managing the risks of equities and fixed-income securities independently from each other, it was possible to use some of the simpler risk measures for the respective asset classes, as given in Chapter 2, namely the variance risk measures for equities and the duration and convexity measures for fixed-income.

Having grasped the financial optimization principles for these simpler problem classes, we can now move away from the silo approach and examine optimization models, which address in a meaningful way the need for enterprise-wide risk management. In order to integrate the disparate risk factors we must now use measures of risk that can be consistently applied across multiple asset classes. The scenario-based measures for equities (Section 2.3) and the scenario analysis for fixed-income (Section 2.5) provide precisely the required measures. An optimization can then be applied to optimize the selected risk measures, and trade them off against measures of reward, for a set of user-specified scenarios that encompass all the risk factors relevant for the problem at hand. Scenario optimization refers to optimization models that apply when the uncertain data are represented by a set of discrete scenarios. Several concrete models of this category are discussed next.

5.3   Mean Absolute Deviation Models

We start with a model that trades off the mean absolute deviation measure of risk (see Definition 2.3.8) against the portfolio reward. When asset returns are given by a discrete and finite scenario set the model is formulated as a linear program. Large-scale portfolios can be optimized using linear programming software that is widely available, robust, and efficient. We also know from Theorem 2.3 that when returns are normally distributed the variance and mean absolute deviation risk measures are equal, within a constant. In this case the solution of a mean absolute deviation model is equivalent to the solution of the Markowitz mean-variance model. Identical frontiers are generated by these two models to trade off risk and reward.

We define the optimization model using portfolio values $V(x; \tilde{P})$ instead of portfolio returns $R(x; \tilde{r})$. This allows us to model instruments in the portfolio with zero cost, such as futures. It is also consistent with the commonly used measure of Value-at-Risk which looks at portfolio value as opposed to returns. Note, however, the relationship $V(x; \tilde{P}) = R(x; \tilde{r})V_0$ between value and return, where V_0 is the initial value of the portfolio. A portfolio that consists of positions x_i with current prices P_{0i} has an initial value

$$V_0 = \sum_{i=1}^{n} P_{0i} x_i. \tag{5.1}$$

This is a budget constraint stipulating that the total holdings in the portfolio at current market prices are the initial endowment. The future value of the portfolio is given by

$$V(x; \tilde{P}) = \sum_{i=1}^{n} \tilde{P}_i x_i, \tag{5.2}$$

and its mean value is

$$V(x; \bar{P}) = \sum_{i=1}^{n} \bar{P}_i x_i. \tag{5.3}$$

For now we do not specify the precise time when the future value is realized. In single-period models the investment horizon is a single future time period. This is the risk horizon of the model, and is implicitly assumed to be equal to the time horizon T. A time index t for future prices and returns is needed only for multi-period models of later chapters.

The portfolio value is a linear function of the positions, with coefficients the asset prices. Similarly, portfolio return is a linear function with coefficients the asset returns, $R(x; \tilde{r}) = \sum_{i=1}^{n} \tilde{r}_i x_i$. In the scenario setting we have $V(x; P^l) = \sum_{i=1}^{n} P_i^l x_i$ and $R(x; r^l) = \sum_{i=1}^{n} r_i^l x_i$. It is important to note that the asset allocation vector x is in percentage of total wealth when calculating portfolio return, and in nominal amount when calculating total portfolio value.

Some constraints may be imposed on the asset allocation, in the form $x \in X$, where X denotes the set of feasible solutions. This constraint set is specified by policy and regulatory considerations. Other constraints may include limits on the maximum holdings in each asset, dictated by liquidity considerations, or constraints imposed for diversification or tradeability of the portfolio. Such constraints were discussed in the context of the fixed-income portfolios in Sections 4.2.4–4.2.5. A constraint that is always present in the models of this section is the budget constraint (5.1). The nonnegativity of the variables $x \geq 0$ is subsumed in the general constraint $x \in X$.

The following model trades off the portfolio mean absolute deviation against its expected value. It requires that the expected value of the portfolio at the risk horizon exceed μV_0, parametrized by the target return μ.

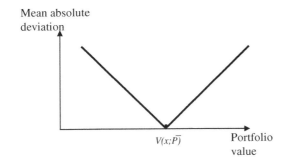

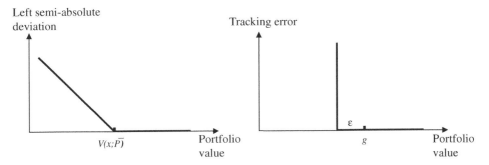

Figure 5.1: The mean absolute deviation function and its variants: the left semi-absolute deviation and function for the tracking model.

$$\text{Minimize} \quad \mathcal{E}\left[\left|V(x;\tilde{P}) - V(x;\bar{P})\right|\right] \tag{5.4}$$

$$\text{subject to} \quad V(x;\tilde{P}) \geq \mu V_0, \tag{5.5}$$

$$\sum_{i=1}^{n} P_{0i} x_i = V_0, \tag{5.6}$$

$$x \in X. \tag{5.7}$$

In the discrete scenario setting we can write model (5.4)–(5.7) as:

$$\text{Minimize} \quad \sum_{l \in \Omega} p^l \left|V(x;P^l) - V(x;\bar{P})\right| \tag{5.8}$$

$$\text{subject to} \quad \sum_{i=1}^{n} \bar{P}_i x_i \geq \mu V_0, \tag{5.9}$$

$$\sum_{i=1}^{n} P_{0i} x_i = V_0, \tag{5.10}$$

$$x \in X, \tag{5.11}$$

whereby the expectation operator in the objective function took the form

$$\sum_{l \in \Omega} p^l \left|V(x;P^l) - V(x;\bar{P})\right|. \tag{5.12}$$

The objective function is piecewise linear with slope 1 when $V(x;P^l) > V(x;\bar{P})$ and slope -1 when $V(x;P^l) < V(x;\bar{P})$ (see Figure 5.1). Viewed along the axis x_i the slope of the

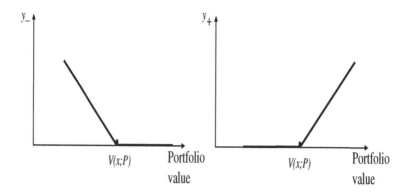

Figure 5.2: The functions $\tilde{y}_+$ and $\tilde{y}_-$ have the same payoff as a European call option and a short position in a European put option, respectively.

objective function is P_i^l when $P_i^l > \bar{P}_i$, and $-P_i^l$ when $P_i^l < \bar{P}_i$. Since this function is not linear the solution of the model is not possible with linear programming. This difficulty can be overcome with a reformulation of the model.

We introduce variables $\tilde{y}_+$ and $\tilde{y}_-$ to measure, respectively, the positive and negative deviations of the portfolio value from its mean, and write the deviation function as

$$V(x; \tilde{P}) - V(x; \bar{P}) = \tilde{y}_+ - \tilde{y}_- \tag{5.13}$$

where

$$\tilde{y}_+ = \max[0, V(x; \tilde{P}) - V(x; \bar{P})], \tag{5.14}$$

$$\tilde{y}_- = \max[0, V(x; \bar{P}) - V(x; \tilde{P})]. \tag{5.15}$$

Figure 5.2 illustrates these two functions. It follows that $\tilde{y}_+$ is nonzero in those scenarios where the portfolio value exceeds its mean value. This variable measures the upside potential of the portfolio in outperforming its mean value. $\tilde{y}_-$ is nonzero when the portfolio value is less than its mean, and it measures the downside risk of the portfolio in underperforming its mean value. In the discrete scenario setting we can express the definitions above through a system of inequalities:

$$y_+^l \geq V(x; P^l) - V(x; \bar{P}),\ y_+^l \geq 0,\ \text{for all } l \in \Omega, \tag{5.16}$$

$$y_-^l \geq V(x; \bar{P}) - V(x; P^l),\ y_-^l \geq 0,\ \text{for all } l \in \Omega. \tag{5.17}$$

The upside potential of the portfolio has the same payoff as a European call option with a strike price equal to the mean value of the portfolio. The maturity of the option is the risk-horizon of the model. Similarly, the downside risk of the portfolio is equivalent to a short position in a European put option.

Now we note that the absolute value $|a|$ of a real number a is the minimum value b, such that $b \geq a$ and $b \geq -a$, and we define an auxiliary variable y^l such that

$$y^l \geq y_+^l,\ \text{and } y^l \geq y_-^l,\ \text{for all } l \in \Omega. \tag{5.18}$$

Hence, the objective function of the mean absolute deviation model can be written as $\sum_{l \in \Omega} p^l y^l$, and using the definitions in equations (5.16) and (5.17) we obtain the term $|V(x; P^l) - V(x; \bar{P})|$ by solving

$$\text{Minimize} \quad y^l \tag{5.19}$$

$$\text{subject to} \quad y^l \geq V(x; P^l) - V(x; \bar{P}), \tag{5.20}$$

$$y^l \geq V(x; \bar{P}) - V(x; P^l), \tag{5.21}$$

$$x \in X. \tag{5.22}$$

Hence, using the auxiliary variable y^l we formulate the mean absolute deviation model above as the following linear program:

Model 5.3.1 Minimization of mean absolute deviation

$$\text{Minimize} \quad \sum_{l \in \Omega} p^l y^l \tag{5.23}$$

$$\text{subject to} \quad \sum_{i=1}^{n} \bar{P}_i x_i \geq \mu V_0, \tag{5.24}$$

$$y^l \geq V(x; P^l) - V(x; \bar{P}), \text{ for all } l \in \Omega, \tag{5.25}$$

$$y^l \geq V(x; \bar{P}) - V(x; P^l), \text{ for all } l \in \Omega, \tag{5.26}$$

$$\sum_{i=1}^{n} P_{0i} x_i = V_0, \tag{5.27}$$

$$x \in X. \tag{5.28}$$

The model is given below in the equivalent formulation for maximizing expected portfolio value with a limit on the risk.

Model 5.3.2 Portfolio optimization with absolute deviation constraints

$$\text{Maximize} \quad \sum_{i=1}^{n} \bar{P}_i x_i \tag{5.29}$$

$$\text{subject to} \quad \sum_{l \in \Omega} p^l y^l \leq \omega, \tag{5.30}$$

$$y^l \geq V(x; P^l) - V(x; \bar{P}), \text{ for all } l \in \Omega, \tag{5.31}$$

$$y^l \geq V(x; \bar{P}) - V(x; P^l), \text{ for all } l \in \Omega, \tag{5.32}$$

$$\sum_{i=1}^{n} P_{0i} x_i = V_0, \tag{5.33}$$

$$x \in X. \tag{5.34}$$

Varying the parameter ω we trace the frontier of mean absolute deviation versus expected value. This is identical to the frontier traced by varying the parameter μ in Model 5.3.1.

5.3.1   Semi-absolute deviation

It is possible to modify the mean absolute deviation models above to differentiate the penalty for upside potential from that for downside risk. Constraints (5.25) set the values of the auxiliary variable y^l equal to the upside potential, corresponding to scenarios in which y^l_+ takes nonnegative values, and y^l_- is zero. Similarly, constraints (5.26) set the values of the auxiliary variable equal to the downside risk corresponding to nonnegative y_-^l and zero y_+^l. Introducing nonnegative parameters λ_u and λ_d, normalized such that $\lambda_u + \lambda_d = 1$, we differentially penalize upside potential from downside risk with the following modification of Model 5.3.1. Figure 5.1 illustrates the semi-absolute deviation function.

Model 5.3.3 Upside potential and downside risk in mean absolute deviation

$$\text{Minimize} \quad \sum_{l \in \Omega} p^l y^l \tag{5.35}$$

$$\text{subject to} \quad \sum_{i=1}^{n} \bar{P}_i x_i \geq \mu V_0, \tag{5.36}$$

$$y^l \geq \lambda_u \left[V(x; P^l) - V(x; \bar{P}) \right], \text{ for all } l \in \Omega, \tag{5.37}$$

$$y^l \geq \lambda_d \left[V(x; \bar{P}) - V(x; P^l) \right], \text{ for all } l \in \Omega, \tag{5.38}$$

$$\sum_{i=1}^{n} P_{0i} x_i = V_0, \tag{5.39}$$

$$x \in X. \tag{5.40}$$

In the limit we may set $\lambda_u = 0$ and $\lambda_d = 1$, in which case we obtain a model with only one half the constraints of Model 5.3.1. This model minimizes the expected downside risk only for a target expected value and places no constraints on the upside potential; it minimizes the left semi-absolute deviation risk measure of Definition 2.3.9. We will see in the next section that the mean absolute deviation and the semi-absolute deviation models are equivalent. Hence, we can solve a simplified version of Model 5.3.3, eliminating either (5.37) or (5.38) by setting, respectively, λ_u or λ_d equal to zero, instead of solving Model 5.3.1.

5.3.2   Equivalence of absolute deviation measures

In this section we show that the mean absolute deviation risk measure is equivalent to both the right and left semi-absolute deviation measures. Consider a random variable $\tilde{r}$ with mean value $\bar{r}$, and let $\text{prob}(\tilde{r} = r) = p(r)$. We have

$$\begin{aligned} \mathcal{E}[\tilde{r} - \bar{r}] &= \int_{-\infty}^{+\infty} (r - \bar{r}) p(r) dr \\ &= \int_{-\infty}^{\bar{r}} (r - \bar{r}) p(r) dr + \int_{\bar{r}}^{+\infty} (r - \bar{r}) p(r) dr. \end{aligned} \tag{5.41}$$

Using the property of random variables that

$$\mathcal{E}[\tilde{r} - \bar{r}] = \mathcal{E}[\tilde{r}] - \bar{r} = 0,$$

we obtain from (5.41)

$$-\int_{-\infty}^{\bar{r}} (r - \bar{r}) p(r) dr = \int_{\bar{r}}^{+\infty} (r - \bar{r}) p(r) dr. \tag{5.42}$$

Consider now the mean absolute deviation function

$$\mathcal{E}[|\,\tilde{r} - \bar{r}\,|] = \int_{-\infty}^{+\infty} |\,r - \bar{r}\,|\, p(r) dr \tag{5.43}$$

$$= \int_{-\infty}^{\bar{r}} -(r - \bar{r}) p(r) dr + \int_{\bar{r}}^{+\infty} (r - \bar{r}) p(r) dr \tag{5.44}$$

$$= 2 \int_{\bar{r}}^{+\infty} (r - \bar{r}) p(r) dr. \tag{5.45}$$

Equation (5.44) follows from (5.43) because of the properties of absolute value functions and the fact that

$$(r - \bar{r}) \leq 0 \text{ for all } r \in (-\infty, \bar{r}),$$
$$(r - \bar{r}) \geq 0 \text{ for all } r \in (\bar{r}, +\infty), \text{ and}$$
$$p(r) \geq 0 \text{ for all } r.$$

Equation (5.45) follows from (5.44) because of (5.42). Similarly, we can show that

$$\mathcal{E}[|\,\tilde{r} - \bar{r}\,|] = -2 \int_{-\infty}^{\bar{r}} (r - \bar{r}) p(r) dr. \tag{5.46}$$

Therefore,

$$\frac{1}{2}\mathcal{E}(|\,\tilde{r} - \bar{r}\,|) = \int_{\bar{r}}^{+\infty} (r - \bar{r}) p(r) dr$$

$$= \int_{-\infty}^{\bar{r}} -(r - \bar{r}) p(r) dr, \tag{5.47}$$

and the semi-absolute deviation (right or left) are equivalent, within a constant, to the mean absolute deviation.

We note that the equivalence of the risk measures holds when the deviations are measured against the mean. When we measure deviations against some exogenous random target, such as a market index, no such equivalence property holds. Measuring deviations against a random target is addressed next.

5.3.3   Tracking model

We start now from the semi-absolute deviation model with only downside risk, i.e., Model 5.3.3 with $\lambda_u = 0$ and $\lambda_d = 1$, but instead of measuring risk using a linear function of the downside deviation, we impose an infinite penalty for any deviations that are more than a user-specified parameter ϵV_0 below the mean. Deviations that are within ϵV_0 below the mean – or greater than the mean – do not contribute to the risk measure (see Figure 5.1). The model maximizes expected return while it restricts the downside deviations to remain within $-\epsilon V_0$ from the target mean value.

Model 5.3.4 Portfolio optimization with limits on maximum downside risk

---

$$\text{Maximize} \quad \sum_{i=1}^{n} \bar{P}_i x_i \tag{5.48}$$

$$V(x; P^l) \geq V(x; \bar{P}) - \epsilon V_0, \text{ for all } l \in \Omega, \tag{5.49}$$

$$\sum_{i=1}^{n} P_{0i} x_i = V_0, \tag{5.50}$$

$$x \in X. \tag{5.51}$$

In this model downside risk is defined with respect to the portfolio mean $V(x; \bar{P})$. The model can be defined with respect to some other target random variable $\tilde{g}$. For instance, $\tilde{g}$ may be set equal to the value of an investment V_0 in some broadly defined market index or alternative investment opportunity – also called the *numeraire* – with growth rate $\tilde{I}$. Or $\tilde{g}$ may be set equal to a fixed value μV_0, in which case the target is the value we want the portfolio to achieve. When adopting an integrated financial product management perspective the target of the portfolio is the liability value.

Assuming that the random target $\tilde{g}$ takes values g^l under scenario $l \in \Omega$, we modify Model 5.3.4 into the following *tracking* model.

Model 5.3.5 Tracking model

$$\text{Maximize} \quad \sum_{i=1}^{n} \bar{P}_i x_i \tag{5.52}$$

$$\text{subject to} \quad V(x; P^l) \geq g^l - \epsilon V_0, \text{ for all } l \in \Omega, \tag{5.53}$$

$$\sum_{i=1}^{n} P_{0i} x_i = V_0, \tag{5.54}$$

$$x \in X. \tag{5.55}$$

The term "tracking" indicates that the portfolio value stays within a margin $-\epsilon V_0$ of the target. Parameter ϵ is user specified with smaller values of ϵ leading to closer tracking but perhaps at the sacrifice of excess returns. The same tracking model can be obtained from the regret models in the next section.

5.4 Regret Models

We now turn to the minimization of the regret function of Definition 2.3.10. As in the rest of this chapter, the model is defined using portfolio values $V(x; \tilde{P})$ instead of portfolio returns $R(x; \tilde{r})$. Letting $\tilde{g}$ be the random target value for the portfolio, we write the regret function as

$$G(x; \tilde{P}, \tilde{g}) = V(x; \tilde{P}) - \tilde{g}. \tag{5.56}$$

The regret function takes positive values when the portfolio outperforms the target and negative values when the portfolio underperforms. In the former case we have gains, and in the latter case losses, with both gains and losses measured vis-à-vis a target which serves as the benchmark.

Following the development of the previous section we introduce variables $\tilde{y}_+$ and $\tilde{y}_-$ to measure, respectively, the positive and negative deviations of the portfolio value from the target, and write the regret function as

$$V(x; \tilde{P}) - \tilde{g} = \tilde{y}_+ - \tilde{y}_-, \tag{5.57}$$

where

$$\tilde{y}_+ = \max[0, V(x; \tilde{P}) - \tilde{g}], \tag{5.58}$$

$$\tilde{y}_- = \max[0, \tilde{g} - V(x; \tilde{P})]. \tag{5.59}$$

It follows that $\tilde{y}_+$ is nonzero in those scenarios when the portfolio value exceeds the target. This variable measures the upside regret when the portfolio outperforms the target. $\tilde{y}_-$ is nonzero when the portfolio value is less than the target, and it measures the downside regret. In the discrete scenario setting we can express the definitions above as systems of inequalities

$$y_+^l \geq V(x; P^l) - g^l, \ y_+^l \geq 0, \text{ for all } l \in \Omega, \tag{5.60}$$

$$y_-^l \geq V(x; g^l) - V(x; P^l), \ y_-^l \geq 0, \ \text{for all } l \in \Omega. \tag{5.61}$$

It is customary to think of downside regret as the measure of risk, and of upside regret as a measure of the portfolio reward. In Section 5.7 we develop models that trace an efficient frontier of risk versus reward using the downside and upside regret, respectively.

The probability that regret does not exceed a threshold value ζ is given by

$$\Psi(x; \zeta) = \sum_{\{l \in \Omega | G(x; P^l, g^l) \leq \zeta\}} p^l. \tag{5.62}$$

The perfect regret has a probability distribution function given by

$$\Psi(x^*; \zeta) = \begin{cases} 0 \text{ if } \zeta < 0 \\ 1 \text{ if } \zeta \geq 0. \end{cases} \tag{5.63}$$

It follows that $\Psi(x; \zeta) \leq \Psi(x^*; \zeta)$ and the distribution of perfect regret provides a useful criterion for comparing portfolios.

Consider now the minimization of expected downside regret, with the requirement that the expected value of the portfolio exceeds μV_0, and imposing constraints such as those used when minimizing the mean absolute deviation risk function. We have the following model that trades off the risk measure of expected downside regret against expected value.

$$\text{Minimize} \quad \mathcal{E}[\tilde{y}_-] \tag{5.64}$$

$$\text{subject to} \quad \mathcal{E}[V(x; \bar{P})] \geq \mu V_0, \tag{5.65}$$

$$\sum_{i=1}^{n} P_{0i} x_i = V_0, \tag{5.66}$$

$$x \in X. \tag{5.67}$$

In the discrete scenario setting we use the definition for y_-^l in equation (5.61) and formulate the regret minimization problem as the following linear program.

Model 5.4.1 Minimization of expected downside regret

$$\text{Minimize} \quad \sum_{l \in \Omega} p^l y_-^l \tag{5.68}$$

$$\text{subject to} \quad \sum_{i=1}^{n} \bar{P}_i x_i \geq \mu V_0, \tag{5.69}$$

$$y_-^l \geq g^l - V(x; P^l), \quad \text{for all } l \in \Omega, \tag{5.70}$$

$$y_-^l \geq 0, \quad\quad\quad\quad \text{for all } l \in \Omega, \tag{5.71}$$

$$\sum_{i=1}^{n} P_{0i} x_i = V_0, \tag{5.72}$$

$$x \in X. \tag{5.73}$$

Note the similarity between the mean absolute deviation Model 5.3.3 and the regret minimization model. More specifically, if we set $\lambda_0 = 0$ and $\lambda_d = 1$ in Model 5.3.3 we obtain Model 5.4.1 when the random target is set equal to the portfolio expected value, i.e., $g^l = V(x; \bar{P})$, for all scenarios. The regret model, however, is modeled with an exogenously given target, whereas for the mean absolute deviation model the target is endogenous, depending on the portfolio.

5.4.1 ϵ-regret models

Let us now relax the notion of downside regret to measure only those losses that exceed some threshold ϵV_0. When the portfolio value underperforms the target by an amount less than a nonnegative value ϵV_0 we consider downside regret as zero. For example, we may consider any underperformance that does not exceed 1% of the initial capital V_0 as acceptable. To model this setting we introduce the ϵ-regret function.

Definition 5.4.1 ϵ-regret function. *The difference between the target random variable $\tilde{g}$ shifted by $-\epsilon V_0$, and the portfolio value random variable is the ϵ-regret given by*

$$G_\epsilon(x; \tilde{P}, \tilde{g}) = V(x; \tilde{P}) - (\tilde{g} - \epsilon V_0), \tag{5.74}$$

and for the discrete scenario case by

$$G_\epsilon(x; P^l, g^l) = V(x; P^l) - (g^l - \epsilon V_0). \tag{5.75}$$

Positive values indicate that the portfolio value outperforms the target or it underperforms by no more than ϵV_0. Negative values indicate that the portfolio underperforms the target by more than ϵV_0. The perfect ϵ-regret has a probability distribution function given by

$$\Psi_\epsilon(x^*; \zeta) = \begin{cases} 0 \text{ if } \zeta < -\epsilon V_0 \\ 1 \text{ if } \zeta \geq -\epsilon V_0. \end{cases} \tag{5.76}$$

The linear programming model for minimizing downside ϵ-regret is defined, similarly to Model 5.4.1, as follows.

Model 5.4.2 Minimization of expected downside ϵ-regret

$$\text{Minimize} \quad \sum_{l \in \Omega} p^l y_-^l \tag{5.77}$$

$$\text{subject to} \quad \sum_{i=1}^{n} \bar{P}_i x_i \geq \mu V_0, \tag{5.78}$$

$$y_-^l \geq (g^l - \epsilon V_0) - V(x; P^l), \text{ for all } l \in \Omega, \tag{5.79}$$

$$y_-^l \geq 0, \qquad\qquad\qquad \text{for all } l \in \Omega, \tag{5.80}$$

$$\sum_{i=1}^{n} P_{0i} x_i = V_0, \tag{5.81}$$

$$x \in X. \tag{5.82}$$

The ϵ-regret model can be written in equivalent formulations that maximize expected value with constraints on the downside regret, as follows.

Model 5.4.3 Portfolio optimization with ϵ-regret constraints

$$\text{Maximize} \quad \sum_{i=1}^{n} \bar{P}_i x_i \tag{5.83}$$

$$\text{subject to} \quad \sum_{l \in \Omega} p^l y_-^l \leq \omega, \tag{5.84}$$

$$y_-^l \geq (g^l - \epsilon V_0) - V(x; P^l), \quad \text{for all } l \in \Omega, \tag{5.85}$$

$$y_-^l \geq 0, \qquad\qquad\qquad \text{for all } l \in \Omega, \tag{5.86}$$

$$\sum_{i=1}^{n} P_{0i} x_i = V_0, \tag{5.87}$$

$$x \in X. \tag{5.88}$$

We can now note an equivalence between the tracking Model 5.3.5 and ϵ-regret optimization. In particular, if we set $\omega = 0$ in Model 5.4.3 we restrict the downside ϵ-regret to zero for all scenarios. In this case $y_-^l = 0$, and substituting for $y_-^l = 0$ in (5.85)–(5.86) we get (5.53). Hence, the tracking model can be obtained as a special case of optimization with ϵ-regret constraints.

5.5   Conditional Value-at-Risk Models

Consider now the minimization of Conditional Value-at-Risk (CVaR). In Definition 2.6.3 CVaR was given as the expected value of the losses, conditioned on the losses being in excess of VaR. Recall from equation (2.83) that the losses in portfolio value are given by the loss function

$$L(x; \tilde{P}) = V_0 - V(x; \tilde{P}). \tag{5.89}$$

Here we should note that positive values of the loss function correspond to downside risk, while negative values of the loss function correspond to gains, and they measure upside potential. This convention is at odds with the convention of using negative values to measure downside risk in the mean absolute deviation models, the regret models, and the put/call efficient frontier models. This difference in notation is historical, as the literature on CVaR has its roots in the calculation of expected shortfall in insurance, where losses are the focus in insurance risk studies and are by convention positive. The literature on mean absolute deviation, regret, and related models has its origins in asset management, where gains are the focus of study, and are by convention positive.

If ζ is the VaR at the $100\alpha\%$ probability level, then the Conditional Value-at-Risk is given by the expression:

$$\text{CVaR}(x; \alpha) = \mathcal{E}[L(x; P^l) \mid L(x; P^l) > \zeta], \tag{5.90}$$

and in the discrete scenario setting we have

$$\text{CVaR}(x; \alpha) \frac{\sum_{\{l \in \Omega \mid L(x; P^l) > \zeta\}} p^l L(x; P^l)}{\sum_{\{l \in \Omega \mid L(x; P^l) > \zeta\}} p^l}. \tag{5.91}$$

Here ζ is the α-VaR, and its value depends on α. Note, also, that the value of ζ also depends on the loss function $L(x; P^l)$ and hence it is a variable, inasmuch as x is a variable whose value determines the distribution of the loss function for different scenarios.

Under a technical condition that the probability of scenarios with losses strictly greater than ζ is exactly equal to $1 - \alpha$, i.e., $\Psi(x; \zeta) = \alpha$ (cf. equation 2.85) we have

$$\text{CVaR}(x; \alpha) = \frac{\sum_{\{l \in \Omega \mid L(x; P^l) \geq \zeta\}} p^l L(x; P^l)}{1 - \alpha}. \tag{5.92}$$

We will see now that this function can be optimized using a linear programming model. The formulation of a linear model is facilitated with the use of auxiliary variables similar to those used in the mean absolute deviation, tracking, and regret models.

Let

$$\tilde{y}_+ = \max\left[0, L(x; \tilde{P}) - \zeta\right]. \tag{5.93}$$

$\tilde{y}_+$ is equal to zero when the losses are less than or equal to the Value-at-Risk, ζ, and it is equal to the excess loss when the losses exceed ζ. In the discrete scenario setting we have

$$y_+^l = \max\left[0, L(x; P^l) - \zeta\right], \text{ for all } l \in \Omega. \tag{5.94}$$

Using this definition of y_+^l we write:

$$
\begin{aligned}
\sum_{l \in \Omega} p^l y_+^l &= \sum_{\{l \in \Omega | L(x; P^l) < \zeta\}} p^l y_+^l + \sum_{\{l \in \Omega | L(x; P^l) \geq \zeta\}} p^l y_+^l \\
&= 0 + \sum_{\{l \in \Omega | L(x; P^l) \geq \zeta\}} p^l \left(L(x; P^l) - \zeta\right) \\
&= \sum_{\{l \in \Omega | L(x; P^l) \geq \zeta\}} p^l L(x; P^l) - \zeta \sum_{\{l \in \Omega | L(x; P^l) \geq \zeta\}} p^l \\
&= \sum_{\{l \in \Omega | L(x; P^l) \geq \zeta\}} p^l L(x; P^l) - \zeta(1 - \alpha),
\end{aligned}
\tag{5.95}
$$

where the first equality is obtained by splitting the summation over $l \in \Omega$ into summations over the subset of scenarios with losses strictly less than ζ and those with losses greater or equal to ζ, the second equality follows from the definition of y_+^l in equation (5.94), the third is obtained by rearranging terms, and the last equality follows from the fact that ζ is the VaR at the $100\alpha\%$ probability level and therefore the sum of the probabilities under the second summation sign is equal to $(1 - \alpha)$.

Dividing both sides of equation (5.95) by $(1 - \alpha)$ and rearranging terms we get

$$\zeta + \frac{\sum_{l \in \Omega} p^l y_+^l}{1 - \alpha} = \frac{\sum_{\{l \in \Omega | L(x; P^l) \geq \zeta\}} p^l L(x; P^l)}{1 - \alpha}. \tag{5.96}$$

The term on the right is $\text{CVaR}(x; \alpha)$ as given in equation (5.92), and it can be optimized using linear programming to minimize the linear function on the left.

We minimize CVaR subject to the condition that the expected value of the portfolio exceeds some target μV_0, and the constraints imposed on the scenario models of previous sections. The model trades off the risk measure CVaR against expected value. It is written as

$$\text{Minimize} \quad \text{CVaR}(x; \alpha) \tag{5.97}$$

$$\text{subject to} \quad \mathcal{E}[V(x; \tilde{P})] \geq \mu V_0, \tag{5.98}$$

$$\sum_{i=1}^{n} P_{0i} x_i = V_0, \tag{5.99}$$

$$x \in X. \tag{5.100}$$

Using the definition of CVaR from (5.96) we write this model as follows.

Model 5.5.1 Minimization of CVaR

$$\text{Minimize} \quad \zeta + \frac{\sum_{l \in \Omega} p^l y_+^l}{1 - \alpha} \tag{5.101}$$

$$\text{subject to} \quad \sum_{i=1}^{n} \bar{P}_i x_i \geq \mu V_0, \tag{5.102}$$

$$y_+^l \geq L(x; P^l) - \zeta, \text{ for all } l \in \Omega, \tag{5.103}$$

$$y_+^l \geq 0, \qquad\qquad \text{for all } l \in \Omega, \tag{5.104}$$

$$\sum_{i=1}^{n} P_{0i} x_i = V_0, \tag{5.105}$$

$$x \in X. \tag{5.106}$$

Note that ζ is a variable of this model, and it is the VaR of the portfolio that is comprised in the asset allocation vector x. The solution of this model gives us the minimum CVaR, and the VaR value ζ^* corresponding to the minimum CVaR portfolio; recall that CVaR$\geq$VaR.

A frontier trading off expected shortfall against expected value can be traced by varying the parameter μ. The frontier can also be traced using a formulation equivalent to Model 5.5.1 that maximizes expected portfolio value subject to a constraint on CVaR.

Model 5.5.2 Portfolio optimization with CVaR constraints

$$\text{Maximize} \quad \sum_{i=1}^{n} \bar{P}_i x_i \tag{5.107}$$

$$\text{subject to} \quad \zeta + \frac{\sum_{l \in \Omega} p^l y_+^l}{1 - \alpha} \leq \omega, \tag{5.108}$$

$$y_+^l \geq L(x; P^l) - \zeta, \text{ for all } l \in \Omega, \tag{5.109}$$

$$y_+^l \geq 0, \qquad\qquad \text{for all } l \in \Omega, \tag{5.110}$$

$$\sum_{i=1}^{n} P_{0i} x_i = V_0, \tag{5.111}$$

$$x \in X. \tag{5.112}$$

When the loss function $L(x; P^l)$ is linear, the CVaR models above are linear programs. This is the case with the loss function (2.83), which in the scenario setting is

$$L(x; P^l) = V_0 - V(x; P^l) \tag{5.113}$$

$$= \sum_{i=1}^{n} (P_{0i} - P_i^l) x_i. \tag{5.114}$$

5.6   Expected Utility Maximization

The scenario optimization models have thus far – following the same line of development as Chapter 2 – optimized a prespecified measure of risk against a prespecified measure of reward to obtain a set of efficient portfolios. With this approach, however, investors are restricted in their choices to specifying a model and setting the target returns, but they are then left with the open problem of selecting a specific portfolio from the efficient frontier. In order to select a particular

portfolio from the set of efficient portfolios we need to incorporate into the optimization model
a measure of the investor's preference, as discussed in Section 2.8.1 on investor choice. The
expected utility maximization model we formulate in this section allows users to optimize according to their own preferences when trading off risk and rewards. More specifically, while the
models of the previous sections trace frontiers of efficient portfolios – from which the user has to
select one – the expected utility maximization model allows the user to select a unique portfolio
that optimizes the user's preferences as expressed through a utility function (see Definition 2.8.3).

We first develop further the concept of a utility function in order to make it useful for portfolio
optimization. Consider the random returns $\tilde{r}_1$ and $\tilde{r}_2$, which take a finite set of values such as
those indexed by a scenario index Ω, i.e., $\tilde{r}_1 = (r_1^l)_{l=1}^N, \tilde{r}_2 = (r_2^l)_{l=1}^N$. Hence, both random
returns are vectors in IR^N. We can describe preferences between these two vectors of returns by
the preordering relation

$$\tilde{r}_1 \succeq \tilde{r}_2,$$

which means that $\tilde{r}_1$ is weakly preferred to $\tilde{r}_2$, or $\tilde{r}_1$ is as good as $\tilde{r}_2$. The related concepts of
strict preference $\succ$ and indifference $\sim$ are induced from this definition. This preordering relation
is assumed to satisfy the following axioms:

Completeness: For every pair $\tilde{r}_1, \tilde{r}_2$ either $\tilde{r}_1 \succeq \tilde{r}_2$ or $\tilde{r}_2 \succeq \tilde{r}_1$.

Reflexivity: For every $\tilde{r}$, we have $\tilde{r} \succeq \tilde{r}$.

Transitivity: If $\tilde{r}_1 \succeq \tilde{r}_2$ and $\tilde{r}_2 \succeq \tilde{r}_3$, then $\tilde{r}_1 \succeq \tilde{r}_3$.

The preordering relation above, however, does not specify a real-valued function from IR^N
into the real numbers that can be used as a utility function with an ordinal property. That is, a
utility function that has the properties

$$\mathcal{U}(\tilde{r}_1) > \mathcal{U}(\tilde{r}_2) \Leftrightarrow \tilde{r}_1 \succeq \tilde{r}_2$$
$$\mathcal{U}(\tilde{r}_1) = \mathcal{U}(\tilde{r}_2) \Leftrightarrow \tilde{r}_1 \sim \tilde{r}_2,$$

will allow us to rank alternative random returns.

Under a continuity assumption on the preordering relation it is possible to show that a continuous ordinal utility function exists for any preordering. We turn now to the definition of such a
utility function, which can be used in a maximization context to implement preference relations
in order to select among portfolios with random returns.

We consider a portfolio that takes values $\tilde{R} = (R^l)_{l=1}^N$ with probability p^l, for $l \in \Omega$. Hence,
the random return of the portfolio is a vector in IR^N. We denote the portfolio, with its possible
values and the associated probabilities by P, and we consider further the set of portfolios, say
P_k, with returns $\tilde{R}_k = (R_k^l)_{l=1}^N$ with probability p^l, for $l \in \Omega$, that could be, for example, the set
of all portfolios that satisfy a set of constraints. We assume that there is a preordering of the set
of portfolios that satisfies the following axioms:

Completeness: For every pair of portfolios P_1 and P_2, either $P_1 \succeq P_2$ or $P_2 \succeq P_1$.

Reflexivity: For every portfolio $P \succeq P$.

Transitivity: If $P_1 \succeq P_2$ and $P_2 \succeq P_3$, then $P_1 \succeq P_3$.

These three axioms have the same meaning as the axioms for the preordering relation, simply
recast in the portfolio context, and lead to ordinal functions. The next three axioms develop the
concept of choice, and lead to the maximization of the expectation of a cardinal utility function,
that is, a function whose numerical value has a precise meaning beyond the ordering (ranking)
of its arguments.

Independence: Let $P_1 = \{(r_1^1, \ldots, r_1^\nu, \ldots, r_1^N), (p^l)_{l=1}^N\}$ and $P_2 = \{(r_1^1, \ldots, r_2^\nu, \ldots, r_1^N),$-
$(p^l)_{l=1}^N\}$. If $r_1^\nu \sim r_2^\nu$, then $P_1 \sim P_2$.

Continuity: If $\tilde{R}_1 \succeq \tilde{R}_2 \succeq \tilde{R}_3$, then there exists a probability π, $0 \leq \pi \leq 1$, such that $\tilde{R}_2 \sim \{(\tilde{R}_1, \tilde{R}_3), (\pi, 1 - \pi)^\top\}$.

Dominance: Let $P_1 = \{(\tilde{R}_1, \tilde{R}_2), (\pi_1, 1 - \pi_1)^\top\}$ and $P_2 = \{(\tilde{R}_1, \tilde{R}_2), (\pi_2, 1 - \pi_2)^\top\}$. If $\tilde{R}_1 \succ \tilde{R}_2$ then $P_1 \succ P_2$ if and only if $\pi_1 > \pi_2$.

It can be shown that, under the above axioms, the decision maker faced with a selection of portfolios will choose the one with the highest expected utility, for a particular cardinal utility function $\mathcal{U}$. The utility functions given as examples in Section 2.8.1 may serve as the cardinal utility functions.

We can therefore now define an expected utility maximization model that will allow us to select from all portfolios the one that satisfies a set of constraints, and furthermore satisfies the preference relation over all other feasible portfolios.

We define the expected utility maximization model using portfolio return, where return is a linear function of the asset allocation vector x and coefficients the asset returns, i.e., $R(x; \tilde{r}) = \sum_{i=1}^{n} \tilde{r}_i x_i$. Recall that the asset allocations x are in percentages of total wealth when calculating portfolio return. In the scenario setting we have $R(x; r^l) = \sum_{i=1}^{n} r_i^l x_i$, and the expected utility maximization model is written as follows.

Model 5.6.1 Expected utility maximization

$$\text{Maximize} \quad \sum_{l \in \Omega} p^l \mathcal{U}(R(x; r^l)) \tag{5.115}$$

$$\text{subject to} \quad R(x; r^l) = \sum_{i=1}^{n} r_i^l x_i, \tag{5.116}$$

$$\sum_{i=1}^{n} x_i = 1, \tag{5.117}$$

$$x \in X. \tag{5.118}$$

5.7   Put/Call Efficient Frontiers

The tracking and regret Models 5.3.5 and 5.4.1 measure risk using a piece-wise linear function of the portfolio deviations from a random target, and trade off risk against portfolio reward, which is given by the expected value of the portfolio. In CVaR models, loss is defined with respect to a constant, such as the initial portfolio value, and in expected utility maximization there is no explicit measure of a reference portfolio. The expected portfolio value is calculated independently of the random target. This view is inconsistent with enterprise-wide risk management, since the reward of the portfolio must be measured vis-à-vis the random target. For instance, if the portfolio value is always equal to a target liability then the portfolio has neither risk nor reward. Reward is manifested when portfolio values exceed the target, and risk is manifested when portfolio values are below the target.

All the models defined earlier can be modified to incorporate a reference portfolio. For instance, the loss function in the CVaR model may be defined with respect to a reference portfolio, and in expected utility maximization we may maximize the expected utility of the excess return of the portfolio with respect to the reference. In this section we formulate a model that explicitly trades off the portfolio downside (risk) against the portfolio upside (reward) taking into account the random target. By explicitly incorporating the liability in measuring both risk and reward the model takes an integrated view of the financial intermediation process.

The upside potential has identical payoffs to a call option on the future portfolio value relative to the target. When the portfolio value is below the target there is zero upside potential, and the call option is out-of-the-money. When the portfolio value exceeds the target the upside potential is precisely the payoff of a call that is in-the-money. Similarly, the downside payoffs are identical to those of a short position in a put option on the future portfolio value relative to the target. The portfolio call value is the expected upside and the put value is the expected downside. Portfolios that achieve the higher call value for a given put value are called *put/call efficient*. Alternatively, we define a portfolio as put/call efficient if it achieves the lowest put value for a given call value. The models in this section generate put/call efficient frontiers.

The deviations of the portfolio value from the random target $\tilde{g}$ are expressed using variables $\tilde{y}_+$ and $\tilde{y}_-$ as

$$V(x; \tilde{P}) - \tilde{g} = \tilde{y}_+ - \tilde{y}_-, \tag{5.119}$$

where

$$\tilde{y}_+ = \max[0, V(x; \tilde{P}) - \tilde{g}], \tag{5.120}$$

$$\tilde{y}_- = \max[0, \tilde{g} - V(x; \tilde{P})]. \tag{5.121}$$

This is the regret function of Section 5.4 from which now we make an interesting observation: $\tilde{y}_+$ measures the upside potential of the portfolio to outperform the target, and $\tilde{y}_-$ measures the downside risk.

We can now separate the upside potential of the portfolio from the downside risk. The following model traces the put/call efficient frontier for put values parametrized by ω.

$$\text{Maximize} \quad \mathcal{E}\left[\tilde{y}_+\right] \tag{5.122}$$

$$\text{subject to} \quad \mathcal{E}[\tilde{y}_-] \leq \omega, \tag{5.123}$$

$$\sum_{i=1}^{n} P_{0i} x_i = V_0, \tag{5.124}$$

$$x \in X. \tag{5.125}$$

We start with a linear programming formulation for this model without any constraints of the form $x \in X$. We will see that the put/call efficient frontier in the unconstrained case is a straight line through the origin with slope at least one. Liquidity constraints will then be added to the model and liquidity premia can be calculated from the optimal solution.

5.7.1   Put/call efficient frontiers without constraints

We formulate a linear program for tracing the efficient frontier in model (5.122)–(5.125). The linear expression for the portfolio value is written explicitly as

$$V(x; P^l) = \sum_{i=1}^{n} P_i^l x_i. \tag{5.126}$$

The budget constraint $\sum_{i=1}^{n} P_{0i} x_i = V_0$ is now eliminated in order to formulate an unconstrained problem, taking also $X = \mathbb{R}^n$. Let I^l be the total return of the benchmark portfolio, also called the *numeraire*. Then our random target is $g^l = V^0 I^l$ and substituting for V^0 from the budget constraint $V^0 = \sum_{i=1}^{n} P_{0i} x_i$ we get

$$g^l = \sum_{i=1}^{n} P_{0i} I^l x_i. \tag{5.127}$$

Hence, equation (5.119) can be expressed in the following discrete form which implicitly includes the budget constraint

$$\sum_{i=1}^{n} P_i^l x_i - \sum_{i=1}^{n} P_{0i} I^l x_i = y_+^l - y_-^l, \text{ for all } l \in \Omega. \tag{5.128}$$

This is a tracking equation that measures the deviations of the portfolio from the benchmark, and model (5.122)–(5.125) is now formulated as follows.

Model 5.7.1 Put/call efficient portfolio

$$\text{Maximize} \quad \sum_{l \in \Omega} p^l y_+^l \tag{5.129}$$

$$\text{subject to} \qquad\qquad\qquad \sum_{l \in \Omega} p^l y_-^l \leq \omega, \tag{5.130}$$

$$y_+^l - y_-^l - \sum_{i=1}^{n} (P_i^l - P_{0i} I^l) x_i = 0, \text{ for all } l \in \Omega, \tag{5.131}$$

$$y_+^l, y_-^l \geq 0, \text{ for all } l \in \Omega. \tag{5.132}$$

We define now the following dual prices for this problem:

π_ω the dual price for the expected downside constraint (5.130),

π^l the dual price for the tracking constraint (5.131) in scenario $l \in \Omega$.

The dual price associated with a constraint measures the change in the objective value per unit change of the right-hand side of the constraint (see Appendix A). The dual price π_ω represents the marginal trade-off between expected upside and expected downside. If the allowable expected downside ω increases by a small amount $\epsilon > 0$, the expected upside will increase by $\pi_\omega \epsilon$. It follows that the slope of the put/call efficient frontier traced by varying ω is a straight line with slope

$$\pi_\omega = \frac{\sum_{l \in \Omega} p^l y_+^l}{\sum_{l \in \Omega} p^l y_-^l}. \tag{5.133}$$

For $\omega = 0$ we have the trivial solution $x = 0$, and the efficient frontier goes through the origin. The efficient frontier is a straight line through the origin with slope π_ω. In the unconstrained case the dual price remains constant as we increase the allowable downside ω. We can trade off unlimited expected upside for unlimited expected downside at a marginal rate π_ω. It will be established next that the slope of the frontier is at least one, which means that a put/call efficient portfolio will generate at least as much upside potential as it has downside risk.

In the constrained case the frontier may become piecewise linear. A new line segment starts when the dual price π_ω changes as ω increases and some of the constraints become inactive. The dual price will decrease with increasing ω, thus producing a concave frontier. This nonincreasing property of dual prices is a standard property of linear programs. In the context of the financial application it has an intuitive explanation. The most attractive securities – those that have the highest upside for a given downside – are used first. The rate of increase of upside potential (call value) per unit of downside risk (put value) diminishes, or it remains constant if no constraint, such as liquidity, restricts the trading of the most attractive security in the portfolio.

A word of caution is needed on the linear programming formulation of the put/call efficient portfolios above. There is no guarantee that only one of the variables y_+^l, y_-^l will be nonzero for each scenario l. For any feasible value of the variables, equation (5.131) will still be satisfied if we add an identical value to both y_+^l and y_-^l, for each scenario l. Indeed, in order to maximize the objective function, the optimal solution will arbitrarily increase y^l_+ while simultaneously increasing y^l_-. However, when the constraint (5.130) is active it is not feasible to increase arbitrarily y^l_-, and as a result y^l_+ and y^l_- will be equal to the maximum values specified by (5.120)–(5.121). A rigorous formulation of the model requires that we add the complimentarity constraints $y^l_+ y^l_- = 0$, for all $l \in \Omega$. These are nonlinear constraints that significantly complicate the model. In practice, since we want to build a dedicated portfolio with the least downside risk, we set ω to small values and the constraint (5.130) is active, avoiding the need to add these nonlinear constraints.

Dual problem for put/call efficient frontiers

Additional insights about the problem are gained from the dual formulation of the primal linear program in Model 5.7.1. When the primal problem has a finite solution it is identical to the solution of the dual, which is formulated using the duality theory from Appendix A as follows:

Model 5.7.2 Dual problem for put/call efficient portfolio

$$\text{Minimize} \quad \omega \pi_\omega \tag{5.134}$$

$$\text{subject to} \quad \sum_{l \in \Omega} (P^l_i - P_{0i} I^l) \pi^l = 0, \quad \text{for all } i \in U, \tag{5.135}$$

$$p^l \pi_\omega - \pi^l \geq 0, \quad \text{for all } l \in \Omega, \tag{5.136}$$

$$\pi^l \geq p^l, \quad \text{for all } l \in \Omega, \tag{5.137}$$

$$\pi_\omega \geq 0. \tag{5.138}$$

From (5.136)–(5.137) we have $p^l \leq \pi^l \leq \pi_\omega p^l$ and it follows that $\pi_\omega \geq 1$. That is, each additional unit of downside results in at least one unit of upside, and the call value of the portfolio is at least as large as its put value. Since the dual price π_ω of the expected downside constraint (5.130) is positive this constraint is always active at optimality. All allowable downside is used, as expected, since the objective function is to maximize the upside potential.

Constraint (5.135) is a tracking constraint in the dual space defined for each security. It is analogous to the tracking constraint (5.131) defined in the primal problem for each scenario. We write the upside and downside, respectively, of each security in scenario l as

$$z^l_{+i} = \max[0, P^l_i - P_{0i} I^l] \tag{5.139}$$

$$z^l_{-i} = \max[0, P_{0i} I^l - P^l_i]. \tag{5.140}$$

These quantities measure, respectively, the upside potential and the downside risk that we assume by investing one unit in a security i instead of selling the security at the current market price P_{0i} and investing the proceeds in the alternative investment provided by the benchmark portfolio. With these definitions we write

$$P^l_i - P_{0i} I^l = z^l_{+i} - z^l_{-i}. \tag{5.141}$$

In the special case where $\pi_\omega = 1$, we get $\pi^l = p^l$. It follows from (5.135) that

$$\sum_{l \in \Omega} (P^l_i - P_{0i} I^l) p^l = 0, \quad \text{for all } i \in U, \tag{5.142}$$

and substituting (5.141) and rearranging we get

$$\frac{\sum_{l \in \Omega} p^l z^l_{+i}}{\sum_{l \in \Omega} p^l z^l_{-i}} = 1, \quad \text{for all } i \in U. \tag{5.143}$$

This relation shows that a unit of upside is achieved for each additional unit of downside. The actual values of x are irrelevant since securities equally trade off expected upside for expected downside.

Scenario probabilities that satisfy $p^l = \pi^l$ are put/call neutral or benchmark neutral. Under these probabilities the securities are neutral in terms of their contribution to the expected upside (call value) and to the expected downside (put value).

Benchmark neutral probabilities

When the solution to the model does not satisfy $\pi_\omega = 1$, it is possible to recover a set of put/call neutral probabilities from the dual prices π^l. We normalize the dual prices by $D_f = \sum_{l \in \Omega} \pi^l$ to obtain

$$\psi^l = \frac{\pi^l}{D_f}. \tag{5.144}$$

D_f is called the risk-free discount factor for reasons that are explained later, in Section 5.8. Now, $\sum_{l \in \Omega} \psi^l = 1$ and the normalized dual prices can be interpreted as probabilities. Scaling equation (5.135) by D_f, substituting in this (5.141), and rearranging we obtain

$$\frac{\sum_{l \in \Omega} \psi^l z^l_{+i}}{\sum_{l \in \Omega} \psi^l z^l_{-i}} = 1, \text{ for all } i \in U. \tag{5.145}$$

Hence, the expected upside of each security computed with probabilities ψ^l is equal to the expected downside. Exactly as we had in the special case of $\pi_\omega = 1$, a unit of expected upside is achieved for each unit of expected downside, when expectations are computed with respect to the probabilities ψ^l. Under these probabilities the securities are put/call neutral. The probabilities obtained by scaling the dual prices of the put/call efficient portfolio model are called put/call neutral or benchmark neutral.

Infinite liquidity benchmark neutral prices

Further insights can be obtained by writing the dual tracking constraint (5.135) as

$$P_{0i} \sum_{l \in \Omega} \pi^l I^l = \sum_{l \in \Omega} \pi^l P^l_i. \tag{5.146}$$

Dividing throughout by D_f and rearranging we get

$$P_{0i} = \frac{\sum_{l \in \Omega} \psi^l P^l_i}{\sum_{l \in \Omega} \psi^l I^l}. \tag{5.147}$$

Under infinite liquidity the price of security i is the expected payoff discounted at the rate $\sum_{l \in \Omega} \psi^l I^l$. This is the infinite liquidity benchmark-neutral price of the security. In the case of a complete market under infinite liquidity the benchmark is the future value of the portfolio and $\tilde{I} = 1$. The equation above gives the risk-neutral price of the security.

5.7.2   Put/call efficient frontiers with finite liquidity

We now develop put/call efficient portfolios in the presence of constraints. In particular, finite liquidity restricts the amount we can invest in a security without affecting its price. Large investments will incur a liquidity premium. The put/call efficient portfolios will allow us to price the liquidity premia. Finite liquidity bounds the maximum amount that can be invested in i by $\bar{x}_i$ and the minimum amount by $\underline{x}_i$.

The bounds can be used to limit the holdings in tranches of a security trading at a given price. For instance, x_i could be holdings in a 10-year corporate bond trading at market price P_{0i} for amounts in the interval $[\underline{x}_i, \bar{x}_i]$, and $x_{i'}$ holdings in the same 10-year corporate that trades at a higher price $P_{i'0}$ for amounts up to $\bar{x}_{i'}$. The higher price reflects a liquidity premium. An investor who finds the 10-year corporate attractive to hold in order to meet the portfolio targets will first buy as much as possible in the cheaper tranche i before purchasing additional amounts in the more expensive tranch i'.

The model for put/call efficient portfolios with finite liquidity is an extension of the unconstrained Model 5.7.1 to include bounds on the holdings.

Model 5.7.3 Put/call efficient portfolio with finite liquidity

$$\text{Maximize} \quad \sum_{l \in \Omega} p^l y^l_+ \tag{5.148}$$

$$\text{subject to} \quad \sum_{l \in \Omega} p^l y^l_- \leq \omega, \tag{5.149}$$

$$y^l_+ - y^l_- - \sum_{i=1}^{n} (P^l_i - P_{0i} I^l) x_i = 0, \quad \text{for all } l \in \Omega, \tag{5.150}$$

$$-x_i \leq -\underline{x}_i, \quad \text{for all } i \in U, \tag{5.151}$$

$$x_i \leq \bar{x}_i, \quad \text{for all } i \in U, \tag{5.152}$$

$$y^l_+, y^l_- \geq 0, \quad \text{for all } l \in \Omega. \tag{5.153}$$

We define now dual prices for the liquidity constraints:

$\underline{\pi}_i$ the dual price for the lower-bound constraints (5.151),

$\bar{\pi}_i$ the dual price for the upper-bound constraints (5.152).

The dual problem is the following linear program.

Model 5.7.4 Dual problem for put/call efficient portfolio with finite liquidity

$$\text{Minimize} \quad \omega \pi_\omega - \sum_{i=1}^{n} \underline{x}_i \underline{\pi}_i + \sum_{i=1}^{n} \bar{x}_i \bar{\pi}_i \tag{5.154}$$

$$\text{subject to} \quad \underline{\pi}_i - \bar{\pi}_i + \sum_{l \in \Omega} (P^l_i - P_{0i} I^l) \pi^l = 0, \quad \text{for all } i \in U, \tag{5.155}$$

$$p^l \pi_\omega - \pi^l \geq 0, \quad \text{for all } l \in \Omega, \tag{5.156}$$

$$\pi^l \geq p^l, \quad \text{for all } l \in \Omega, \tag{5.157}$$

$$\pi_\omega \geq 0 \quad \text{and} \quad \underline{\pi}_i, \bar{\pi}_i \geq 0, \quad \text{for all } i \in U. \tag{5.158}$$

The dual problem always has a feasible solution obtained by setting $\pi^l = p^l$, $\pi_\omega = 1$, and

$$\bar{\pi}_i = \max \left[0, \sum_{l \in \Omega} (P^l_i - P_{0i} I^l) \pi^l \right] \tag{5.159}$$

$$\underline{\pi}_i = \max \left[0, \sum_{l \in \Omega} (P_{0i} I^l - P^l_i) \pi^l \right]. \tag{5.160}$$

The feasibility of the dual implies that the primal solution is bounded. It is therefore not possible to trade infinite expected upside for a given expected downside since the amount traded in the most attractive securities is bounded.

Can we obtain a put/call neutrality condition for the finite liquidity case similar to condition (5.143) for the unconstrained case? Consider the dual constraint

$$\underline{\pi}_i - \bar{\pi}_i + \sum_{l \in \Omega} (P_i^l - P_{0i} I^l) \pi^l = 0, \quad \text{for all } i \in U. \tag{5.161}$$

For the special case of $\pi_\omega = 1$ and substituting in this equation $\pi^l = p^l$ and the definitions of z_{+i}^l and z_{-i}^l we get

$$\sum_{l \in \Omega} p^l z_{+i}^l - \sum_{l \in \Omega} p^l z_{-i}^l = \bar{\pi}_i - \underline{\pi}_i. \tag{5.162}$$

Only securities that have $\bar{\pi}_i = \underline{\pi}_i = 0$ are put/call neutral, trading equal expected upside for equal expected downside. We know from linear programming theory that the dual prices are zero when the corresponding constraints are inactive. Hence, put/call neutral securities are those that trade strictly between their bounds. (In degenerate cases a security may trade at one of its bounds and the corresponding dual price can still be zero.) For securities that are at the bounds – and assuming nondegenerate cases – the corresponding dual price will be nonnegative. The expected upside will increase if the active bound is relaxed and the dual prices for the bounds reflect the cost of liquidity. In particular $\underline{\pi}_i$ reflects a liquidity premium and $\bar{\pi}_i$ a liquidity discount.

Put/call neutral valuation of liquidity

We can now use the analysis of both the constrained and unconstrained models to estimate the cost of liquidity. Normalize the dual prices π^l by $D_f = \sum_{l \in \Omega} \pi^l$ to obtain

$$\psi^l = \frac{\pi^l}{D_f}, \tag{5.163}$$

and scale equation (5.162) by D_f to get

$$\sum_{l \in \Omega} \psi^l z_{+i}^l - \sum_{l \in \Omega} \psi^l z_{-i}^l = \frac{\bar{\pi}_i}{D_f} - \frac{\underline{\pi}_i}{D_f}. \tag{5.164}$$

Let us define the auxiliary variable $z_i^l = z_{+i}^l - z_{-i}^l$, which is the deviation of the security i with respect to the benchmark in scenario l. (To be precise, this is a gain with respect to the benchmark when $z_i^l > 0$, and a loss when $z_i^l < 0$.) The expected deviation of security i under the probabilities ψ^l is then given by

$$\mathcal{E}_\lambda[z_i^l] = \frac{\bar{\pi}_i}{D_f} - \frac{\underline{\pi}_i}{D_f}. \tag{5.165}$$

Securities that trade strictly between their bounds have $\bar{\pi}_i = \underline{\pi}_i = 0$ and their expected deviation is zero. These securities are put/call neutral with respect to the probabilities ψ^l. When a security trades at the upper bound $x_i = \bar{x}_i$ we have $\underline{\pi}_i = 0$, $\bar{\pi}_i \geq 0$ and $\mathcal{E}_\lambda[z_i^l] \geq 0$. (Equality holds in degenerate cases.) The security contributes more to the upside than the downside and, therefore, its current price is at a discount.

We can estimate the liquidity discount as follows. For each security that trades at the upper bound set $\underline{\pi}_i = 0$ in (5.161), scale by D_f and rearrange to get

$$P_{0i} = \frac{\sum_{l \in \Omega} \psi^l P_i^l}{\sum_{l \in \Omega} \psi^l I^l} - \frac{\bar{\pi}_i}{\sum_{l \in \Omega} \pi^l I^l}. \tag{5.166}$$

Recall from equation (5.147) that $\frac{\sum_{l \in \Omega} \psi^l P_i^l}{\sum_{l \in \Omega} p^l I^l}$ is the infinite liquidity price of the security, and therefore the term $\frac{\bar{\pi}_i}{\sum_{l \in \Omega} \pi^l I^l}$ is the liquidity discount.

Similarly we obtain the following pricing equation for for securities trading at their lower bound

$$P_{0i} = \frac{\sum_{l \in \Omega} \psi^l P_i^l}{\sum_{l \in \Omega} \psi^l I^l} + \frac{\pi_i}{\sum_{l \in \Omega} \pi^l I^l}. \tag{5.167}$$

The term $\frac{\pi_i}{\sum_{l \in \Omega} \pi^l I^l}$ is the liquidity premium.

5.8 Asset Valuation using Scenario Optimization

We have seen in the previous section that dual prices from a portfolio optimization model allow us to estimate liquidity premia. In this section we will see that dual prices can be used for the valuation of new securities. Under assumptions of *complete markets*, as defined below, the optimization model and its dual prices are not essential in deriving security prices. However, in incomplete markets there is no unique price for securities, and prices depend on assumptions we make about investor preferences towards risk. In this setting an optimization formulation that trades off the reward from holding a security against its risks is essential. We discuss the use of scenario optimization models for the valuation of securities in both complete and incomplete markets.

Definition 5.8.1 Complete markets. *When the number of independent securities n is equal to the number of states N reached by the scenarios then the market is said to be complete.*

An elementary form of independent securities are the so-called Arrow-Dubreu securities that pay one in state l, and zero in all other states. Arrow-Dubreu securities are indexed by l, denoting the unique dependence of each security's payoff matrix to the states.

An arbitrary security i is characterized by its payoff vector $(P_i^l)_{l=1}^N$ denoting the payment made by this security in each state $l \in \Omega$. P_i^l is known as the *state-* or *scenario-dependent* price, as it is the price of security in state l. In the case of complete markets, the payoff of any arbitrary security can be replicated by a portfolio of Arrow-Dubreu securities. Specifically, it is easy to see that a portfolio consisting of holdings P_i^l in the lth Arrow-Dubreu security for all $l \in \Omega$, will replicate the payoff vector of the security. This observation plays an important role in the valuation of the security: in the absence of arbitrage the ith security should have the same price as the portfolio of Arrow-Dubreu securities. This observation is made precise in the next section, and the absence of arbitrage is the the only requirement for pricing securities in complete markets.

5.8.1 Optimization models of arbitrage

Consider securities $i = 1, 2, \ldots, n$, with market prices P_{0i} and payoff vectors $(P_i^l)_{l=1}^N$. Arbitrageurs act by solving a linear programming model to create portfolios of minimal cost with nonnegative payoff for all possible future states at the end of the horizon. The following single-period stochastic model applies:

$$\text{Minimize} \quad \sum_{i=1}^n P_{0i} x_i \tag{5.168}$$

$$\text{subject to} \quad \sum_{i=1}^n P_i^l x_i \geq 0, \text{ for all } l \in \Omega. \tag{5.169}$$

The decision variable x is unrestricted. The solution of this model determines whether arbitrage exists, or if the prices are at equilibrium. We distinguish the following three cases.

Market equilibrium

Under the market equilibrium condition no arbitrage opportunities are available, and the portfolio x^* created by the model has zero cost today, and neither payoff nor any obligation at any state at the end of the horizon. The solution of the model is bounded, and it satisfies

$$\sum_{i=1}^{n} P_{0i}x_i^* = 0, \tag{5.170}$$

$$\sum_{i=1}^{n} P_i^l x_i^* = 0, \text{ for all } l \in \Omega. \tag{5.171}$$

First-order arbitrage

Under first-order arbitrage it is possible to extract cash from the market today, without creating any future obligations. The portfolio created by the model has an unbounded solution, while the constraints are feasible. The solution of the arbitrageur's problem satisfies:

$$\sum_{i=1}^{n} P_{0i}x_i^* = -\infty, \tag{5.172}$$

$$\sum_{i=1}^{n} P_i^l x_i^* \geq 0, \text{ for all } l \in \Omega. \tag{5.173}$$

Second-order arbitrage

Under second-order arbitrage it is possible to create a portfolio of zero cost today, without any future obligations and with a nonzero probability of positive payoff at some future state. The portfolio created by the model satisfies:

$$\sum_{i=1}^{n} P_{01}x_i^* = 0, \tag{5.174}$$

$$\sum_{i=1}^{n} P_i^l x_i^* > 0, \text{ for some } l \in \Omega. \tag{5.175}$$

In the absence of first-order arbitrage the arbitrageur's linear program is bounded. Hence, its dual problem is feasible (see Appendix A). If π^l denotes the dual variable for the lth equality constraint in (5.169), then feasibility of the dual implies the following system of equations:

$$\sum_{l \in \Omega} P_i^l \pi^l = P_{0i}, \text{ for all } i \in U. \tag{5.176}$$

Furthermore, to eliminate second-order arbitrage the constraints (5.169) must be satisfied with equality. Hence the dual prices must be strictly positive, i.e.,

$$\pi^l > 0, \text{ for all } l \in \Omega. \tag{5.177}$$

Solving the system (5.176)–(5.177) we obtain a set of dual prices that are consistent with the absence of arbitrage. When the number of independent securities n is equal to the number of states N this system has a unique solution. The solution vector $\pi = (\pi^l)_{l=1}^{N}$ that satisfies this system is called the *state price* vector.

The standard interpretation of dual prices of linear programming will allow us to use the state price vector to price securities with arbitrary payoffs. For example if the arbitrageur wishes to receive one extra unit of payment at state l then the objective function will increase by π^l. Hence, the cost of an Arrow-Dubreu security that pays one unit at state l and zero otherwise is π^l.

5.8.2 Valuation in complete markets

In a complete market we can identify as many independent securities as there are states of the economy. Solving then the arbitrageur's linear program, or its dual, we obtain a unique state price vector. This vector gives us the prices of Arrow-Dubreu securities. We can then replicate the state-dependent payoff of any security using a linear combination of Arrow-Dubreu securities, and the security's value is equal to the total price of this replicating portfolio. With this approach we can price securities that generate any arbitrary state-dependent cashflow stream.

For instance, we can estimate the price of a risk-free security that pays one unit in each state. This security must be worth the price of a portfolio holding one of each Arrow-Dubreu security, i.e., $D_f = \sum_{l \in \Omega} \pi^l$. Equivalently, we can calculate the risk-free rate of return associated with the time horizon of the linear program by

$$1 + r_f = \frac{1}{\sum_{l \in \Omega} \pi^l}. \tag{5.178}$$

Note that $D_f = \frac{1}{1 + r_f}$ and this is the *risk-free discount factor*.

Similarly, the price of a security i that pays P_i^l in the lth state is equal to the price of a portfolio holding P_i^l in the lth Arrow-Dubreu security that pays one in the lth state and zero otherwise. Hence, we have the following pricing equation:

$$P_{0i} = \sum_{l \in \Omega} P_i^l \pi^l. \tag{5.179}$$

Risk-neutral valuation

We note that the probabilities of the states, p^l, have not been used in our analysis. The price of an arbitrary payoff can be obtained without the need to know the expected payoff. This, of course, has been a consequence of the assumption about market completeness. Under this assumption the distribution of the payoff is not modeled explicitly, which also means that investors' preferences towards risk are irrelevant.

Our ability to do away with any assumptions on risk preferences leads to what is known as *risk-neutral valuation*. Unfortunately, this is a misnomer. It does not mean that investors are risk neutral, typically they are risk averse. What it means is that valuation can take place in a way that is neutral to investor risk attitudes.

It turns out, however, that we can create a world of probabilities for the states in which investors are indeed risk neutral. We denote these probabilities by ψ^l for each state l. In this hypothetical world investors will discount the expected value of the payoffs for an arbitrary security by the risk-free rate to get the security's price

$$P_{0i} = \frac{1}{1 + r_f} \left(\sum_{l \in \Omega} \psi^l P_i^l \right). \tag{5.180}$$

We can now verify that the above equation is true when ψ^l is given by

$$\psi^l = \frac{\pi^l}{\sum_{l \in \Omega} \pi^l} = \frac{\pi^l}{D_f}, \tag{5.181}$$

by substituting this value of ψ^l in (5.180), and recalling that $D_f = 1/(1 + r_f)$ to obtain

$$D_f \left(\sum_{l \in \Omega} \frac{\pi^l}{D_f} P_i^l \right) = \sum_{l \in \Omega} \pi^l P_i^l = P_{0i}. \tag{5.182}$$

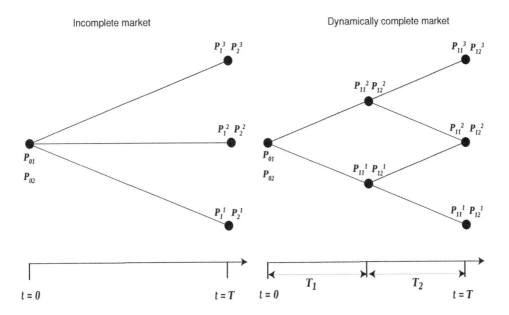

Incomplete market   Dynamically complete market

Figure 5.3: A three-state, single-step model that needs three independent securities to be complete. It can be made dynamically complete when refined into a two-step model with two states at each step.

Here, the last equality follows from (5.179).

In conclusion, the risk-neutral valuation of a security in a complete market is the expected value of its payoff – calculated using the risk-neutral probabilities ψ^l – discounted at the risk-free rate. In the following sections we see how far this analysis can take us when the markets are incomplete.

5.8.3   Valuation in dynamically complete markets

When the number of states exceeds the number of independent securities we cannot use the arguments of the previous section. The arbitrageur's dual program has more variables than constraints and, hence, it does not have a unique solution. The dual prices are not uniquely determined, and it is not possible to determine the price of an arbitrary cashflow using the prices of Arrow-Debreu securities. Something must be done to ensure uniqueness of the Arrow-Debreu prices. Introducing more independent securities or reducing the number of states will work.

In the absence of more independent securities we can reduce the number of states by refining the time step. If, for instance, we have two independent securities but three possible states at the end of the horizon T, we may halve the time step so that two states are possible during the first half of the horizon T_1, and an additional two states are possible from the end of the first half to the end of the horizon T_2. At each time step and for each state we introduce contingent Arrow-Debreu securities associated with each of the possible states at the next time step; the payout of the ith contingent security is denoted by P_{ti}^l. A contingent Arrow-Debreu security is not observed today in the current state, but in a future uncertain state. However, once the future state is realized then the security payoffs are known with certainty and the market is complete during the next time step.

This process is illustrated in Figure 5.3. At each intermediate step there are only two possible states, and the market is complete over each time step as the number of states at each step does not exceed the number of independent securities. The market is *dynamically complete* over the time horizon T as it can be made complete at each time step. (Note that since we have three states at the end of the horizon, the states at T_2 recombine. However, this does not always have to be the case although the number of states of a nonrecombining tree will grow exponentially with the number of time steps. Such growth is computationally intractable.)

5.8.4   Valuation in incomplete markets

We now turn to markets that cannot be made dynamically complete. Such is the case when market imperfections – transaction costs, differential taxation regimes for different investors, portfolio constraints – do not allow us to replicate arbitrary payoff structures. In this setting we will assume some risk preference on the part of the investor, and seek prices that leave the investor indifferent to holding the security or holding a market benchmark. The prices so obtained are not uniquely determined for all investors in the market. But they are *utility invariant* in that the utility value of the investor does not change for the given price. In a sense these are the worst possible prices for an investor, for if the price of a security would decrease the utility function she would then sell the security, while if the price of the security will increase the utility function then she would buy. Utility invariant prices are all called *benchmark neutral* in the sense that the investor is neutral between holding the benchmark or holding the security.

We set up now the utility maximization models that will allow us to obtain utility invariant prices for new securities. We first develop the primal and dual programs for an investor who selects a portfolio from a set of priced securities to maximize a utility function. We then develop the programs for selecting portfolios from a universe of priced securities augmented by a new security whose price is not known. Finally, we develop the conditions on the price of the new security under which its inclusion in the portfolio will not change the utility function, and this will give the utility invariant price.

With the standard notation we have a portfolio of value $V(x; \tilde{P}) = \sum_{i=1}^{n} \tilde{P}_i x_i$, and a benchmark portfolio such as, for instance, a market index, whose value is the random variable $\tilde{g}$. The current prices of the securities are given by $(P_{0i})_{i=1}^{n}$ and the index by V_0. We will consider only portfolios created by an initial endowment V_0, so that the amount V_0 is either used to buy one unit of the benchmark, or to invest in traded securities so that $\sum_{i=1}^{n} P_{0i} x_i \leq V_0$.

We assume that the number of securities n is less than the number of states N, so that the markets are incomplete. Furthermore, portfolio trading constraints in the form

$$\sum_{i=1}^{n} a_{ji} x_i \leq b_j, \text{ for all } j \in \mathcal{K}, \tag{5.183}$$

create market imperfections.

In the discrete scenario setting the state-dependent portfolio value is given by

$$V(x; P^l) = \sum_{i=1}^{n} P_i^l x_i, \tag{5.184}$$

and the benchmark value is given by g^l. The deviations of the portfolio value from the benchmark are expressed using variable y_+^l and y_-^l as

$$V(x; P^l) - g^l = y_+^l - y_-^l, \tag{5.185}$$

where we define

$$y_+^l = \max[0, V(x; P^l) - g^l], \text{ for all } l \in \Omega, \tag{5.186}$$

$$y_-^l = \max[0, g^l - V(x; P^l)], \text{ for all } l \in \Omega. \tag{5.187}$$

With these definitions the risk of the portfolio can be measured using the expected downside $\sum_{l\in\Omega} p^l y_-^l$ (see Definition 2.3.11). The reward of the portfolio can be measured using the expected upside $\sum_{l\in\Omega} p^l y_+^l$ (see Definition 2.8.2). Assuming a bi-linear utility function for our investor (see Definition 2.8.9) we can write the portfolio selection problem as the following linear program.

$$\text{Maximize} \quad \sum_{l\in\Omega} p^l y_+^l - \lambda \sum_{l\in\Omega} p^l y_-^l \tag{5.188}$$

$$\text{subject to} \quad \sum_{i=1}^{n} P_i^l x_i - y_+^l + y_-^l = g^l, \quad \text{for all } l \in \Omega, \tag{5.189}$$

$$\sum_{i=1}^{n} P_{0i} x_i \leq V_0, \tag{5.190}$$

$$\sum_{i=1}^{n} a_{ji} x_i \leq b_j, \quad \text{for all } j \in \mathcal{K}, \tag{5.191}$$

$$y_+^l, y_-^l \geq 0, \quad \text{for all } l \in \Omega. \tag{5.192}$$

To write down the dual of this linear program we associate dual variables π^l, α and θ_j with constraints (5.189), (5.190), and (5.191), respectively. The dual program is now written as follows (see Appendix A):

$$\text{Minimize} \quad \sum_{l\in\Omega} g^l \pi^l + V_0 \alpha + \sum_{j=1}^{K} b_j \theta_j \tag{5.193}$$

$$\text{subject to} \quad \sum_{l\in\Omega} P_i^l \pi^l + P_{0i} \alpha + \sum_{j=1}^{K} a_{ji} \theta_j = 0, \quad \text{for all } i \in U, \tag{5.194}$$

$$-\pi^l \geq p^l, \quad \text{for all } l \in \Omega, \tag{5.195}$$

$$\pi^l \geq -\lambda p^l, \quad \text{for all } l \in \Omega, \tag{5.196}$$

$$\alpha \geq 0, \theta_j \geq 0, \quad \text{for all } j \in \mathcal{K}. \tag{5.197}$$

In the absence of portfolio constraints (5.191) we can drop the term $\sum_{j=1}^{K} a_{ij}\theta_j$ from equation (5.194) and solve for P_{0i} to get

$$P_{0i} = -\frac{\sum_{l\in\Omega} P_i^l \pi^l}{\alpha}. \tag{5.198}$$

Comparing this with the pricing equation for complete markets (5.179) we note that the state price vector in a market with budget constraints is given by

$$\psi^l = \frac{\pi^l}{\alpha}. \tag{5.199}$$

In the absence of the budget constraint the corresponding dual variable α is dropped, and we recover the state price vector for Arrow-Dubreu securities in complete markets.

The effect of the portfolio constraints can be analyzed by solving equation (5.194) for P_{0i} to obtain

$$P_{0i} = -\frac{\sum_{l\in\Omega} P_i^l \pi^l}{\alpha} - \frac{\sum_{j=1}^{K} a_{ij}\theta_j}{\alpha}. \tag{5.200}$$

The first term on the right gives us the price of the security in markets with only budget constraints. The second term is an adjustment factor due to the portfolio trading constraints.

We consider now the pricing of a new security i' with payoff vector $(P_{i'}^l)_{l=1}^N$. This security will be traded in the portfolio if it does not violate the portfolio trading constraints. Indeed, assuming that the constraints will be inactive for this particular security, then the second term in the equation above will be zero, and the price of the new security can be estimated by

$$P_{0i'} = -\sum_{l \in \Omega} P_{i'}^l \psi^l. \tag{5.201}$$

We show next that this price is indeed utility invariant, i.e., investors who are offered the security at this price are indifferent about adding it to their portfolio. If the security is offered at a higher price investors will sell, while if it is offered at a lower price they will buy. In either case the investor's utility will improve, but the investor's trading will affect the price. At the utility invariant price investors will not trade and therefore their actions will not affect the security price. This is an equilibrium price, but it is an equilibrium only for those investors who have a given level of risk aversion denoted by λ. We clarify these statements in the following section.

5.8.5 Utility invariant pricing

We consider the primal problem of arbitrageurs who are offered a security i' with payoff vector $(P_{i'}^l)_{l=1}^N$ at a price $P_{0i'}$, in addition to the usual set of securities U. We denote holdings in the new security by the unrestricted (free) variable $x_{i'}$ and formulate the following linear program:

$$\text{Maximize} \quad \sum_{l \in \Omega} p^l y_+^l - \lambda \sum_{l \in \Omega} p^l y_-^l \tag{5.202}$$

$$\text{subject to} \quad \sum_{i=1}^n P_i^l x_i + P_{i'}^l x_{i'} - y_+^l + y_-^l = g^l, \quad \text{for all } l \in \Omega, \tag{5.203}$$

$$\sum_{i=1}^n P_{0i} x_i + P_{0i'} x_{i'} \leq V_0, \tag{5.204}$$

$$\sum_{i=1}^n a_{ji} x_i \leq b_j, \quad \text{for all } j \in \mathcal{K}, \tag{5.205}$$

$$y_+^l, y_-^l \geq 0, \quad \text{for all } l \in \Omega. \tag{5.206}$$

If the optimal solution to this program is equal to the optimal solution of program (5.188)–(5.192), which was formulated without security i', then the new security plays no role in the arbitrageur's portfolio choice. If this is the case, the investor is indifferent to the new security. Under what conditions, then, are the solutions to (5.202)–(5.206) and (5.188)–(5.192) identical? The answer to this question can be obtained using duality theory.

The dual to the linear program (5.202)–(5.206) is given by:

$$\text{Minimize} \quad \sum_{l \in \Omega} g^l \pi^l + V_0 \alpha + \sum_{j=1}^K b_j \theta_j \tag{5.207}$$

$$\text{subject to} \quad \sum_{l \in \Omega} P_i^l \pi^l + P_{0i} \alpha + \sum_{j=1}^K a_{ji} \theta_j = 0, \quad \text{for all } i \in U, \tag{5.208}$$

$$\sum_{l \in \Omega} P_{i'}^l \pi^l + P_{0i'} \alpha = 0, \quad \text{for all } i \in U, \tag{5.209}$$

$$-\pi^l \geq p^l, \quad \text{for all } l \in \Omega, \tag{5.210}$$

$$\pi^l \geq -\lambda p^l, \quad \text{for all } l \in \Omega, \tag{5.211}$$

$$\alpha, \theta \geq 0. \tag{5.212}$$

The solutions to the primal problem and its dual satisfy the following Kuhn-Tucker optimality conditions (see Appendinx A):

$$\sum_{l\in\Omega} p^l y^l_+ - \lambda \sum_{l\in\Omega} p^l y^l_- = \sum_{l\in\Omega} g^l \pi^l + V_0 \alpha + \sum_{j=1}^K b_j \theta_j \qquad (5.213)$$

$$\sum_{i=1}^n P^l_i x_i + P^l_{i'} x_{i'} - y^l_+ + y^l_- = g^l \qquad (5.214)$$

$$\sum_{i=1}^n P_{0i} x_i + P_{0i'} x_{i'} \leq V_0 \qquad (5.215)$$

$$\sum_{i=1}^n a_{ji} x_i \leq b_j, \text{ for all } j \in \mathcal{K} \qquad (5.216)$$

$$\sum_{l\in\Omega} P^l_i \pi^l + P_{0i} \alpha + \sum_{j=1}^\kappa a_{ij} \theta_j = 0, \text{ for all } i \in U \qquad (5.217)$$

$$\sum_{l\in\Omega} P^l_{i'} \pi^l + P_{0i'} \alpha = 0, \text{ for all } i \in U \qquad (5.218)$$

$$p^l \leq -\pi^l \leq \lambda p^l \qquad (5.219)$$
$$y^l_+, y^l_- \geq 0, \text{ for all } l \in \Omega \qquad (5.220)$$
$$\alpha \geq 0, \theta_j \geq 0, \text{ for all } j \in \mathcal{K}. \qquad (5.221)$$

Similarly, the solutions to the primal problem (5.188)–(5.192) and its dual satisfy the following Kuhn-Tucker conditions:

$$\sum_{l\in\Omega} p^l y^l_+ - \lambda \sum_{l\in\Omega} p^l y^l_- = \sum_{l\in\Omega} g^l \pi^l + V_0 \alpha + \sum_{j=1}^K b_j \theta_j \qquad (5.222)$$

$$\sum_{i=1}^n P^l_i x_i - y^l_+ + y^l_- = g^l \qquad (5.223)$$

$$\sum_{i=1}^n P_{0i} x_i \leq V_0 \qquad (5.224)$$

$$\sum_{j=1}^K a_{ji} x_i \leq b_j, \text{ for } j = 1, 2, \ldots, K \qquad (5.225)$$

$$\sum_{l\in\Omega} P^l_i \pi^l + P_{0i} \alpha + \sum_{j=1}^K a_{ji} \theta_j = 0, \text{ for all } i \in U \qquad (5.226)$$

$$p^l \leq -\pi^l \leq \lambda p^l \qquad (5.227)$$
$$y^l_+, y^l_- \geq 0, \text{ for all } l \in \Omega \qquad (5.228)$$
$$\alpha \geq 0, \theta_j \geq 0, \text{ for } j = 1, 2, \ldots, K. \qquad (5.229)$$

We observe now that a solution x^* that solves (5.222)–(5.229) is also a solution to (5.213)–(5.221) with $x^*_{i'} = 0$ if equation (5.218) is satisfied for any values of α and π^l. In order for this equation to hold we need the following condition, which establishes the utility invariant price of the new security:

$$P_{0i'} = -\frac{\sum_{l\in\Omega} P^l_{i'} \pi^l}{\alpha}. \qquad (5.230)$$

5.9   Postview

This chapter developed portfolio optimization models when the uncertainty of security prices or returns is captured through a set of scenarios. A linear program for minimizing the mean absolute deviation of portfolio returns was given first, followed by tracking models that consider only downside risk against a random target which may represent, for instance, a random liability or a market index. It is worth noting that for scenarios obtained when the asset return follows a multi-variate normal distribution, the mean absolute deviation model is equivalent to the mean-variance portfolio optimization.

We then developed linear programs for minimizing the regret risk measure, and developed a special case for minimizing only downside regret, and a generalization that minimizes downside regret only when losses exceed a threshold. The regret optimization model is a generalization of mean absolute deviation optimization with a random target, and it is further generalized to ϵ-regret optimization from which we obtain the tracking model.

The linear programming model for optimizing the coherent risk measure of conditional Value-at-Risk, and the nonlinear program for expected utility maximization were given next.

Finally the chapter developed the linear programs for generating put/call efficient portfolios, and used duality theory to obtain some interesting results for the optimal portfolios generated from these models. As an outcome of this analysis we can use the linear programming models for the valuation of assets in both complete and incomplete markets.

Notes and References

Scenario optimization in the form presented in this chapter has emerged in the 1990s as a viable approach for risk management with complex financial products. For the early references on scenario optimization see Dembo (1991), Zenios (1993a), Mulvey and Zenios (1994a, b), and for the use of scenario optimization in practice see Dembo et al. (2000). However, these models can be viewed as special and simpler cases of the dynamic stochastic programming models that were introduced for portfolio management much earlier; see the Notes and References of Chapter 6.

For the mean-absolute deviation model see Konno and Yamazaki (1991), and for the semi-absolute deviation and the tracking models see Zenios and Kang (1993), Speranza (1993), and Worzel, Vassiadou-Zeniou and Zenios (1994). For applications to fixed-income securities see Zenios (1993b, 1995). The equivalence of mean absolute deviation models with semi-absolute deviation was established, in a more general form than the one presented here, by Kenyon, Savage and Ball (1999).

The regret minimization model in the framework of scenario optimization for portfolio management was first introduced by Dembo (1991) and further analyzed by Dembo and King (1992), who also introduced ϵ-regret. Dembo (1993) used the regret model to develop portfolio immunization strategies. The ϵ-regret optimization model was developed by Mausser and Rosen (1999), who applied it to study portfolios with credit risk.

For the optimization of conditional Value-at-Risk see Rockafellar and Uryasev (2000), Uryasev (2000a), Palmquist, Uryasev and Krokhmal (1999), Andersson, Mausser, Rosen and Uryasev (2001) and Pflug (2000).

The axiomatic developments of utility theory and its application in financial decision making are given in Ingersoll (1987), based on the work of von Neumann and Morgenstern (1953). The expected utility maximization literature is vast; see Williams (1936), Kelly (1956), Breiman (1960, 1961), Mossin (1968), Samuelson (1971, 1977) Hakansson (1970), McLean, Ziemba and Blazenko (1992), Kallberg and Ziemba (1984), Hakansson and Ziemba (1995).

The put/call efficient frontier model was developed by Dembo and Mausser (2000). Asset valuation using scenario optimization in complete markets is discussed in Aziz (1998b), and in dynamically completed markets in Aziz (1998a). The development is based on earlier work by Ross (1976) and its extensions by Dybvig and Ross (1986), and Prisman (1986). The valuation in incomplete markets is discussed by Aziz (1999, 2000), Dembo, Rosen and Saunders (2000), and Saunders (2001).

Chapter 6

Dynamic Portfolio Optimization with Stochastic Programming

> A dynamic theory would unquestionably be more complete and therefore preferable.
>
> J. von Neumann and O. Morgenstern
> *Theory of Games and Economic Behavior*

6.1 Preview

In this chapter we model the optimization of dynamic trading strategies. Investors dynamically rebalance their portfolio at some discrete trading dates in the future in response to new information. Simple decision rules for portfolio rebalancing are introduced first. Stochastic dedication is then formulated as a simple model for optimizing dynamic strategies of short-term borrowing and lending decisions. Stochastic linear programming is finally presented as a versatile tool for formulating a wide range of financial planning models. Stochastic programming models optimize dynamic strategies of borrowing, lending, and portfolio rebalancing.

6.2 Setting the Stage for Dynamic Models

Many financial decision making problems involve liability streams that extend well into the future. For example, the planning horizon for most insurance products extends beyond a decade; for pension funds it is more than 30 years; and for social security plans it may go up to 50. It is reasonable in such settings to inquire about optimal dynamic strategies that allow portfolio managers to rebalance their portfolio at some discrete trading dates in the future, in response to new information. The discrete time, discrete scenario setting is well suited to the modeling of dynamic strategies.

A dynamic strategy is a sequence of buy and sell decisions, including short-term borrowing and lending. In executing such a strategy the manager has to pay transaction costs, faces both constraints on lines of credit and a spread between the borrowing and lending rates. Constraints may also be imposed on the portfolio composition due to regulatory restrictions or corporate policy considerations.

Portfolio decisions can be made at a finite number of points in time, called *trading dates*, that extend from today, $t = 0$, to $t = T - 1$, the last date before the end of the planning horizon. It is assumed that nothing happens in between trading dates, no portfolio decisions are made, and no coupons or dividends are paid.

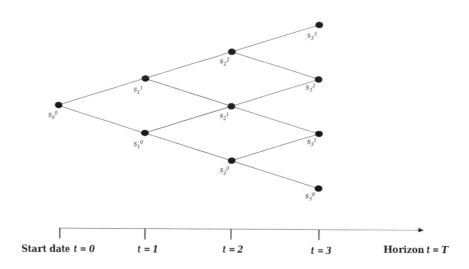

Figure 6.1: Recombining binomial lattice with three trading dates.

Lattice structures

Security prices and liabilities at the initial date $t = 0$ are known but future prices and future liabilities are uncertain. We assume that at each future trading date a finite number of states of the economy is possible. Each state stores the new information that arrives at the corresponding trading date. Each state uniquely determines security prices and the value of the liability. A binomial lattice, such as the one illustrated in Figure 6.1, depicts states of the economy at different trading dates. Nodes in the lattice represent states, and links represent transitions between states with positive probabilities. The term "binomial" indicates that only two transitions are possible during the next time period, when starting from any given state, typically referred to as transition to the up or down state. The term "lattice" indicates that transitions recombine, and an up move followed by a down move leads to the same state as a down move followed by an up. As a result of this property a given state can be reached from more than one states in previous trading dates. States in a lattice are indexed by s, and the index set of possible states at trading date t is denoted by Σ_t.

Linear scenario structures

A path between states from $t = 0$ to T is a sequence $(s0, s1, \ldots, sT) \in \Sigma_0 \times \Sigma_1 \times \ldots \times \Sigma_T$. Such a sequence of states is a scenario and is denoted by l. Not every state in Σ_t can be reached from every state in Σ_{t-1} at the immediately preceding period. For instance, in the binomial lattice of Figure 6.1 we see that s_2^0 can be reached from s_1^0 but not from s_1^1. Given a state s at trading date $t < T$ we denote the set of all states that can occur with positive probability at $t + 1$ by s^+.; these are called the "successor" states of s. Conversely, each state s at $t > 0$ can can be reached from at least one state at $t - 1$, which is called the "predecessor" of s and is denoted by s^-. Starting from a given state at $t - 1$, a scenario l visits only one of the successor states at t, and this state is denoted by $n_t(l)$. For instance, in a scenario l described by the sequence of states $(s0, s1, \ldots, sT)$ we have that $n_0(l) = s0$, $n_1(l) = s1$, $n_2(l) = s2$ and so on. The time subscript of n_t will be dropped when there is no ambiguity.

Figure 6.2 depicts a scenario structure derived from the binomial lattice. Scenarios may have

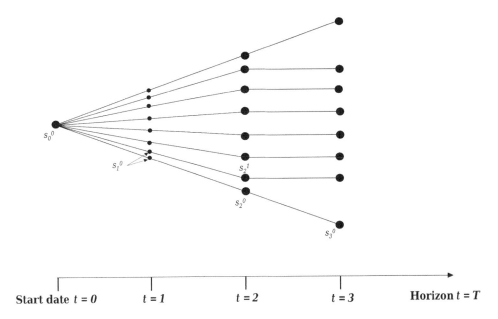

$$\text{Start date } t = 0 \qquad t = 1 \qquad t = 2 \qquad t = 3 \qquad \text{Horizon } t = T$$

Figure 6.2: Linear scenario structure drawn from a binomial lattice with three trading dates.

common states up to a certain trading date in the future. For instance, paths $(s_0^0, s_1^0, s_2^0, s_3^0)$ and $(s_0^0, s_1^0, s_2^1, s_3^1)$ from our example lattice have common states until trading date $t = 1$. However, the information on commonality of states is lost in this scenario tree. The scenarios in Figure 6.2 are independent of each other with the exception of the common initial state s_0^0. The set of scenarios that ignore information on the commonality of states is a *linear scenario tree*, also called "string scenario tree." The scenario optimization models of Chapter 5 are based on linear scenario structures. Only one trading date is allowed (at $t = 0$) in the scenario optimization models and the trading strategies are single-period.

To model dynamic trading strategies on a linear scenario structure we are faced with a dilemma. Either prohibit trading at periods $t > 0$, except for short-term cashflow borrowing to cover shortfalls and lending surplus, or allow trading at periods $t > 0$ which may differ across scenarios even when they have common states. The first choice is clearly restrictive as it does not afford investors the flexibility of rebalancing their portfolio as new information becomes available; they can only react to new information with short-term borrowing or lending. The second choice is a relaxation of the true problem. In reality, trading strategies cannot depend on what will happen in the future, and when two scenarios share the same history up to a date τ then the optimal trading strategy up to this date must be identical for both paths. Decisions that are not identical up to τ violate the logical requirement for absence of clairvoyance.

Event trees

Trading strategies that satisfy the logical requirement for independence from hindsight are called "non-anticipative." To model non-anticipative dynamic strategies we define scenarios on an event tree (see Figure 6.3). Information on the commonality of states is contained in the structure of the event tree, and the states store new information that arrives at the corresponding trading date.

An event tree can be represented formally as a directed graph $\mathcal{G} = (\Sigma, \mathcal{E})$, where nodes Σ denote time and state, and links $\mathcal{E}$ indicate possible transitions between states as time evolves. At time t the states are denoted by $\Sigma_t = \{s_t^\nu \mid \nu - 1, 2, \ldots, S_t\}$, where S_t is the number of possible states at t. Hence, $\Sigma = \bigcup_{t=0}^{T} \Sigma_t$ and $\mathcal{E} \subset \Sigma \times \Sigma$. Elements of $\mathcal{E}$ are denoted by ordered

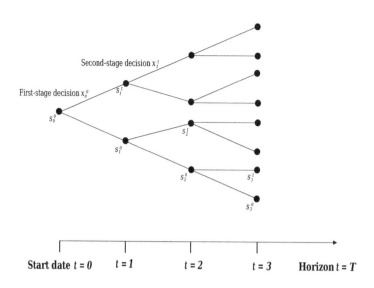

Figure 6.3: Event tree drawn from a binomial lattice with three trading dates.

pairs $(s_t^{\nu(t)}, s_{t+1}^{\nu(t+1)})$ where we explicitly indicate the dependence of the index ν on t. The order of the nodes indicates that state $s_{t+1}^{\nu(t+1)}$ at time $t+1$ can be reached from state $s_t^{\nu(t)}$ at time t. $s_{t+1}^{\nu(t+1)}$ is the successor state and $s_t^{\nu(t)}$ is the predecessor state. That is, $s_t^{\nu(t)+} = s_{t+1}^{\nu(t+1)}$ and $s_{t+1}^{\nu(t+1)-} = s_t^{\nu(t)}$.

An event tree has the following properties: (*i*) $\Sigma_0 = \{s_0^0\}$ is a singleton, and s_0^0 is the unique state known as the *root node*, and it has no predecessor; (*ii*) every state $s_t^{\nu(t)}$ has a unique predecessor from the set of states Σ_{t-1} for all $t = 1, 2, \ldots, T$. Uniqueness of predecessors implies that the graph $\mathcal{G}$ has no cycles.

We can now give a definition of scenarios using the event tree. This is a formalization of Definition 1.2.1, which has been sufficient for the models developed thus far, but is insufficient for developing dynamic models.

Definition 6.2.1 Scenario. *A path of the graph $\mathcal{G} = (\Sigma, \mathcal{E})$ depicting an event tree, denoted by the sequence $\{s_0^{\nu(0)}, s_1^{\nu(1)}, \ldots, s_{\tau_l}^{\nu(\tau_l)}\}$ such that $(s_t^{\nu(t)}, s_{t+1}^{\nu(t+1)}) \in \mathcal{E}$, for all $t = 0, 1, \ldots, \tau_l$, $\tau_l < T$, where τ_l is the last trading date in scenario l, with the associated probability $p^l \geq 0$. Each scenario is indexed by l from a sample set Ω, and the probabilities satisfy $\sum_{l \in \Omega} p^l = 1$.*

The state visited by scenario l at t is denoted by $n_t(l)$, so that $n_t(l) = s_t^{\nu(t)}$ for all $t = 0, 1, \ldots, \tau_l$. We may assume, without loss of generality, that $\tau_l = T$ for all scenarios. However, when dealing with defaultable securities the time to default is a random variable, and the use of scenario-dependent time horizons is essential. This consideration also applies to securities with embedded American type options, which may be exercised at some time before maturity.

The definition of scenarios using event trees clearly shows that some scenarios may have common states up to a given trading date. For instance, in Figure 6.3 we see that four scenarios share common states s_0^0 and s_1^0 up to $t = 1$ while another four share states s_0^0 and s_1^1. A dynamic trading strategy for the first four scenarios may differ at trading dates $t > 1$, but the portfolio rebalancing at $t = 1$ must be the same for these scenarios since they share the same state s_1^1. In the event tree it is clear that states s_2^0 and s_2^1 share the same predecessor, i.e., $s_2^{0-} = s_2^{1-} = s_1^0$.

We are going to consider dynamic strategies using both linear scenario structures and event trees. The decision variables for dynamic strategies on a scenario tree increase linearly with the number of trading dates. The size of dynamic models on event trees grows exponentially with the number of dates. Strategies developed on linear scenarios are easy to compute, but they are simplifications that lead to sub-optimal decisions. Strategies on event trees are computationally challenging to estimate but they lead to optimal decisions.

We consider three distinct approaches for modeling dynamic strategies. Section 6.3 introduces decision rules for the specification of dynamic strategies. Section 6.4 formulates stochastic dedication, which is an extension of the dedication models of Section 4.2. This model optimizes a dynamic strategy of cash borrowing and lending on a linear scenario tree, but without provisions for portfolio rebalancing. Section 6.6 develops models for dynamic strategies on event trees using stochastic programming. These models lead to optimal strategies with portfolio rebalancing.

6.2.1   Notation for dynamic models

In order to develop the dynamic portfolio optimization models we need to introduce variables for portfolio rebalancing at each trading date and for each state. The notation for the dynamic models differs from what has been used in the rest of the book in that random variables are not indexed by scenarios $l \in \Omega$ but, instead, by states $s \in \Sigma_t$. We define variables to represent the buying and selling of securities from the index set U, short-term lending and borrowing at the appropriate rates, and holdings of securities in the portfolio. Investment decisions are in units of face value. The following notation will be used, where time index t takes values over the trading dates $t = 0, 1, \ldots, T$, and state index s from the set Σ_t.

$x_t^s = (x_{ti}^s)_{i \in U}$ face value of assets bought at period t in state s.

$y_t^s = (y_{ti}^s)_{i \in U}$ face value of assets sold at period t in state s.

$z_t^s = (z_{ti}^s)_{i \in U}$ face value of asset inventory at period t in state s.

v_t^{+s} cash invested in short-term deposits at period t in state s.

v_t^{-s} cash borrowed at short-term rates at period t in state s.

The liabilities are specified by:

L_t^s liability due at period t in state s.

We also define some parameters to model the dynamics of assets on the event tree. In particular we need to know, at a given trading date t and state s, the cashflows generated by an asset at the next trading date at successor state s^+.

$\alpha_{ti}^{s^+}$ *amortization factor* for security i, indicating the fraction of outstanding face value of the security at $t + 1$ in the successor states s^+ as a fraction of the outstanding face value at t. This value depends on the successor state s^+ that is reached at $t + 1$ from state s at t. The amortization factor captures the effects of any embedded options, such as prepayments, calls and defaults, or the effect of lapse behavior. For example, a corporate security that is called during the interval has an amortization factor of 0, and an uncalled bond has an amortization factor of 1. A mortgage security that experiences a 10% prepayment and that pays, through scheduled payments, an additional 5% of the outstanding loan has an amortization factor of 0.85.

$F_{ti}^{s^+}$ cashflow generated per unit face value of security i from t to $t + 1$, due to scheduled dividend or coupon payments and exercise of any embedded options. Interest accrued during the time interval from t to $t + 1$ is included in this parameter. The cashflow depends on the successor state s^+ reached at $t + 1$ from state s at t.

$\tilde{P}_{ti}^{as}$ ask price of security i at time t, in state s.

$\tilde{P}_{ti}^{bs}$ bid price of security i at time t, in state s.

$r_{ft}^{s^+}$ rate of return of the risk-free asset held from t to $t + 1$. This value depends on the successor state s^+ reached at $t + 1$ from state s at t.

6.3 Decision Rules for Dynamic Portfolio Strategies

Dynamic portfolio strategies can be specified through simple decision rules. As more information arrives on a linear scenario structure the portfolios are rebalanced according to the decision rules. There is nothing optimal about dynamic strategies based on decision rules, but they are easy to specify and compute, and they work well in certain settings. Decision rules are also intuitively appealing as they are easy to communicate to the portfolio managers and implement in practice. They serve to introduce the issues surrounding the optimization of dynamic strategies, and are often used as benchmarks against which the optimized dynamic strategies are compared.

We consider four decisions rules:

1. Buy-and-hold.
2. Constant mix.
3. Constant proportion.
4. Option-based portfolio insurance.

Each rule is discussed in the context of a simplified portfolio problem of investments in the risk-free asset and a risky market index. We denote by I_{t-1}^s the total return of the market index from the predecessor state s^- at trading date $t - 1$ to state s at t.

6.3.1 Buy-and-hold strategy

A buy-and-hold strategy specifies the proportion of initial wealth x_0 invested in the risk-free rate – assumed for simplicity to offer total return of one – and $1 - x_0$ invested in the risky asset at $t = 0$ with state-dependant total return from $t - 1$ to t denoted by I_{t-1}^s. This portfolio is held to maturity under all scenarios, so there is nothing truly dynamic about this strategy except that the portfolio value varies with the scenarios.

Assuming an initial wealth of V_0 the portfolio takes the value

$$V_{pt}^s = V_0 x_0 + V_0(1 - x_0)I_{t-1}^s \tag{6.1}$$

at trading date t in state s. The *beta* of the buy-and-hold portfolio is $(1 - x_0)$ (see Definition 2.3.2).

The value of the portfolio due to the risk-free investment is given by $V_{ft}^s = V_0 x_0$ and the value of the risky investment is $V_{It}^s = V_0(1 - x_0)I_{t-1}^s$. If the market stays flat ($I_{t-1}^s = 1$) the total portfolio value is preserved at V_0. The portfolio value is guaranteed to at least $V_{ft}^s = V_0 x_0$, which is constant and independent of the state, even if the market collapses with $I_{t-1}^s = 0$ at some future trading date. Figure 6.4 illustrates the changes in value of a buy-and-hold portfolio when the market index fluctuates.

6.3.2 Constant mix strategy

A constant mix strategy specifies that the proportion of the risk-free asset V_{ft}^s and the risky asset V_{It}^s to total portfolio wealth must remain constant at all trading dates t and in all states s. As the market index fluctuates the portfolio must be rebalanced so that the mix of risky and risk-free assets remains constant. More specifically, if the market index declines the portfolio is rebalanced by selling risk-free and buying risky assets, thus maintaining the exposure of the portfolio to the market index. Conversely, if the market index rises, then risky assets are sold to buy the risk-free asset, thus reducing the exposure to the risky index to its original level. This is a truly dynamic strategy as the portfolio is rebalanced in response to market changes.

The initial value of the portfolio is given by $V_0 = V_0 x_0 + V_0 (1 - x_0)$. At some future trading date t, and given a state s, the risk-free and risky parts of the portfolio are given, respectively, by

$$V_{ft}^s = V_{p(t-1)}^{s^-} x_0 \tag{6.2}$$

$$V_{It}^s = V_{p(t-1)}^{s^-}(1 - x_0) I_{t-1}^s, \tag{6.3}$$

where $V_{p(t-1)}^{s^-}$ was the total value of the portfolio at trading date $t-1$ in the predecessor state. The total portfolio value is given by $V_{pt}^s = V_{ft}^s + V_{It}^s$. If the return of the risky index is $I_{t-1}^s = 1$, the proportion of the risky investment V_{It}^s to the total portfolio value V_{pt}^s will remain constant, and equal to $(1 - x_0)$. However, if the market index deviates from 1 the portfolio must be rebalanced so that the risk-free and risky parts of the portfolio are given, respectively, by

$$V_{ft}^s = V_{pt}^s x_0 = \left[V_{p(t-1)}^{s^-} x_0 + V_{p(t-1)}^{s^-}(1 - x_0) I_{t-1}^s \right] x_0 \tag{6.4}$$

$$V_{It}^s = V_{pt}^s (1 - x_0) = \left[V_{p(t-1)}^{s^-} x_0 + V_{p(t-1)}^{s^-}(1 - x_0) I_{t-1}^s \right](1 - x_0). \tag{6.5}$$

It is easy to verify that with this rebalancing the proportion of the risk-free value of the portfolio to the total value remains constant from period $t - 1$ to t.

Example

Changes in the value of the portfolio with changes in the market index are depicted in Figure 6.4 together with the changes of the buy-and-hold strategy. The value of the buy-and-hold portfolio provides an upper bound to the value of the constant mix portfolio. As the constant mix strategy sells risky assets when markets rise, it will achieve lower portfolio value than the buy-and-hold portfolio if the market continues rising. Conversely, as risky assets are bought when the markets decline, the portfolio value will decline more rapidly than the buy-and-hold portfolio if the market declines continously. In particular, the initial investment in the risk-free asset $V_0 x_0$ is not guaranteed, as the portfolio exposure to the risky asset is constantly increased when the market index declines.

Does it make sense to follow a constant mix strategy when it appears from the figure that buy-and-hold dominates? Indeed, in a bullish market one should not sell and in a bearish market one should not buy. However, let us examine what happens to the two strategies when the market reverses its trend. Consider a 10% decline followed by a 10% increase. A buy-and-hold strategy will have a net return of zero. The constant mix portfolio will first suffer a decline of 10% of its risky asset component $(1 - x_0)$. It will then increase the risky asset component to maintain a constant mix and, therefore, the subsequent 10% market increase will benefit the portfolio more than the 10% decline hurt it. The net portfolio return will be positive. Conversely, if a 10% increase is followed by a 10% decline, the constant mix portfolio will again experience a positive net return. The risky component $(1 - x_0)$ will benefit from the 10% increase and the portfolio will then be rebalanced with sales of risky assets. The subsequent 10% decline will adversely affect the portfolio, but less than the benefits it reaped from the increase. When the market reverses its trend, in either direction, the constant mix strategy dominates buy-and-hold.

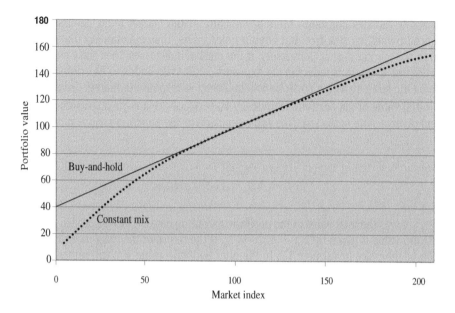

Figure 6.4: Value of portfolios with an initial value $V_0 = 100$ following (i) buy-and-hold, and (ii) constant mix strategies, as the risky market index varies.

6.3.3   Constant proportion strategy

This strategy specifies a fixed proportion of the assets that is invested in the risky asset, and as the asset portfolio value changes the portfolio is rebalanced so that the proportion of risky assets remains constant. Actually, a constant proportion strategy provides for a floor, below which the asset value is not allowed to drop. Hence, if g denotes the floor, this strategy is described by the following relation, which must hold for each time period t and for each state s, where V_{pt}^s denotes the asset portfolio value:

$$V_{It}^s = \mu(V_{pt}^s - \underline{g}). \tag{6.6}$$

Note that a buy-and-hold strategy is a special case of constant proportion, with $\mu = 1$, and the floor equal to the original investment in the risk-free asset. The constant mix strategies are also special cases, with the floor set to zero and varying values of μ.

With a constant proportion strategy, as the asset portfolio declines in value the risky assets are sold, and as the portfolio value increases the exposure to risky assets is increased. The portfolio will do as well as the floor, even in severe market declines, unless the market drops sufficiently fast before the portfolio can be rebalanced. As long as the market drop is less than $1/\mu$ the floor is met. It is worth pointing out that if large numbers of investors – or investors with very large positions – follow this strategy, their actions will exacerbate the decline of a bearish market. Selling risky assets while the market drops increases liquidity risks and puts additional pressures on the market.

6.3.4   Option-based portfolio insurance

This strategy is concerned with meeting a target floor for the portfolio at the end of an investment horizon. This target implies a floor for each previous time period – this being the discounted horizon floor, discounted at the risk-free rate. Option-based portfolio insurance strategies specify a portfolio of risk-free assets and risky assets, so that its payoff matches that of a portfolio composed of risk-free assets and call options. In particular, the risk-free assets are kept equal to the implied floor, while any excess value over the floor is invested in equivalent call options.

6.4   Stochastic Dedication

We consider now a model for optimizing dynamic strategies. The stochastic dedication model developed here optimizes short-term borrowing and lending decisions as new information arrives, but it does not allow for portfolio rebalancing. Portfolio decisions at the starting date $t = 0$ are optimized together with short-term borrowing and lending decisions at future trading dates. Optimization takes place on a linear scenario tree. We can view stochastic dedication as an optimized buy-and-hold portfolio strategy with a dynamic component of borrowing and lending. No portfolio rebalancing decisions are incorporated. The model extends the portfolio dedication models of Section 4.2 to incorporate uncertainty in prices and cashflows through scenarios. Scenarios describe changes that go beyond the parallel shifts of the term structure that were addressed in the dedication model. Thus stochastic dedication extends the applicability of classic portfolio dedication beyond what was achieved with portfolio immunization.

The starting point for developing the model are the necessary conditions for immunization (Definition 4.3.1), which we generalize here for the case when asset and liability values are scenario dependent. Given possible states of the short-term rates $r^s_{ft}, s \in \Sigma_t$ at trading dates $t \in \mathcal{T}$ we define the discount factors

$$d^l_\tau = \prod_{t=0}^{\tau} \frac{1}{1 + r^{n(l)}_{ft}}, \tag{6.7}$$

where $n(l)$ denotes the state visited by path l at period t, as t varies from 0 to τ. (Formally, we denote the visited states by $n_t(l)$ following the discussion in section 6.2, but since there is no ambiguity we drop the subscript t.) The present value of the cashflows of asset i in scenario l is given by

$$P^l_{0i} = \sum_{t=1}^{T} d^l_t F^{n(l)}_{ti}. \tag{6.8}$$

The expected present value of asset i is given by $\bar{P}_{0i} = \sum_{l \in \Omega} p^l P^l_{0i}$ and this is equal to the implied market price P_{0i} with zero option-adjusted spread (Definition 2.4.15).

The present value of the liabilities $L^l = (L^l_t)^T_{t=0}$ in scenario l is similarly given by

$$P^l_L = \sum_{t=1}^{T} d^l_t L^l_t. \tag{6.9}$$

Note that the same discount factors are used for both assets and liabilities. The implicit assumption here is that the short-term borrowing rate for funding shortfalls and the short-term lending rate for investing surplus are the same. This assumption will be relaxed later.

In order for the portfolio to remain dedicated in all scenarios we impose an immunization condition for each scenario as follows:

Definition 6.4.1 Necessary condition for scenario immunization.

$$\sum_{i=1}^{n} P^l_{0i} x_i = P^l_L, \text{ for all } l \in \Omega. \tag{6.10}$$

Under this condition the present value of the portfolio of assets is equal to the present value of the liabilities in all scenarios. Assuming unlimited borrowing and lending at the short-term rates, the portfolio remains dedicated under all scenarios. This condition may be very expensive to satisfy for all scenarios, and most likely it will be impossible to satisfy for all scenarios. Instead of seeking a solution that holds in all scenarios the stochastic dedication model trades off reward when the asset portfolio outperforms the liabilities, against risk when the portfolio underperforms.

The present value of an asset and liability portfolio with asset holdings x_0 at $t = 0$ and liability exposure L^l in scenario l is given by

$$V(x; P^l) = \sum_{i=1}^{n} P_{0i}^l x_{0i} - P_L^l. \tag{6.11}$$

We introduce variables y_+^l and y_-^l to measure, respectively, the positive and negative values of

$$V(x; P^l) = y_+^l - y_-^l \tag{6.12}$$

where

$$y_+^l = \max[0, \sum_{i=1}^{n} P_{0i}^l x_{0i} - P_L^l], \tag{6.13}$$

$$y_-^l = \max[0, P_L^l - \sum_{i=1}^{n} P_{0i}^l x_{0i}]. \tag{6.14}$$

It follows that y_+^l is nonzero in those scenarios when the asset value exceeds the value of the liabilities. This variable measures the upside potential of the portfolio in meeting the target liabilities. y_-^l is nonzero when the asset value is less than the value of the liabilities, and it measures the downside risk of the portfolio in not meeting the target liabilities.

The following model traces the put/call efficient frontier for stochastic portfolio dedication, with an initial budget v_0.

Model 6.4.1 Put/call efficient frontier for stochastic dedication

$$\text{Maximize} \quad \sum_{l \in \Omega} p^l y_+^l \tag{6.15}$$

$$\text{subject to} \quad \sum_{i=1}^{n} P_{0i} x_{0i} \leq v_0 \tag{6.16}$$

$$\sum_{l \in \Omega} p^l y_-^l \leq \omega, \tag{6.17}$$

$$y_+^l - y_-^l - \sum_{i=1}^{n} P_{0i}^l x_{0i} = P_L^l, \text{ for all } l \in \Omega, \tag{6.18}$$

$$y_+, y_- \geq 0. \tag{6.19}$$

As already discussed in the previous chapter, this formulation does not guarantee that only one of the variables y_+^l, y_-^l will be nonzero for each scenario l. For any feasible value of the variables, equation (6.18) will still be satisfied if we add an arbitrary value to both y_+^l and y_-^l, assuming that the same value is added to both variables for each scenario l. Indeed, in order to maximize the objective function, the optimal solution will arbitrarily increase y_+^l while simultaneously increasing y_-^l. However, when the constraint (6.17) is active it is not feasible to increase arbitrarily y_-^l, and as a result y_+^l and y_-^l will be equal to the maximum values specified by

(6.13)–(6.14). A rigorous formulation of the model, with variables as defined in (6.13)–(6.14), requires that we add the complimentarity constraints $y_+^l y_-^l = 0$, for all $l \in \Omega$, but since we typically build a dedicated portfolio with the least downside risk, the constraint (6.17) is active, and there is no need to add these nonlinear complimentarity constraints.

This model is often encountered in practice with an objective function that maximizes the net expected value $\sum_{l \in \Omega} p^l V(x; P^l)$. Note that $\sum_{l \in \Omega} p^l V(x; P^l) = \sum_{l \in \Omega} p^l y_+^l - \sum_{l \in \Omega} p^l y_-^l$, and the resulting model is a special case of our formulation, corresponding to some particular value of the parameter ω. We present the more general model above, using an objective function that separates reward from risk in a way that is consistent with the models in Chapter 5.

Model 6.4.1 discounts both the asset and the liability sides with the same rate and aims for a zero net exposure at $t = 0$. Zero net exposure is achieved for $\omega = 0$, although for this value the model may be infeasible. The model is a version of the put/call models discussed in Chapter 5 that trade off upside potential against downside risk in violating the necessary condition for scenario immunization. In order to satisfy the necessary condition we must introduce borrowing and lending using the short-term rates that apply at different trading dates $t \in \mathcal{T}$, and at different states $s \in \Sigma_t$. Stochastic dedication is achieved following a dynamic strategy of borrowing and lending decisions. These decisions are uniquely determined by the initial portfolio x_0 and the state s at each trading date t.

A stochastic dedication model with borrowing and lending is formulated as follows, and Figure 6.5 illustrates the flow of funds for this model.

Model 6.4.2 Stochastic dedication

$$\text{Minimize} \quad v_0 \tag{6.20}$$

$$\text{subject to} \quad \sum_{i=1}^{n} F_{0i} x_{0i} + v_0 + v_0^{-0} = L_0^0 + v_0^{+0}, \tag{6.21}$$

$$\sum_{i=1}^{n} F_{(t-1)i}^s x_{0i} + (1 + r_{f(t-1)}^s) v_{t-1}^{+s^-} + v_t^{-s} = L_t^s + v_t^{+s} \tag{6.22}$$

$$+ (1 + r_{f(t-1)}^s + \delta) v_{t-1}^{-s^-},$$
$$\text{for all } , \ s \in \Sigma_t,$$

$$x, v^+, v^- \geq 0. \tag{6.23}$$

We must explicitly set $v_T^{-s} = 0$ to avoid borrowing at the last time period since the model has no mechanism to repay loans outstanding after T.

The model closely follows the formulation of the classic portfolio dedication Model 4.2.3. The first equation (6.21) is the cashflow accounting equation at $t = 0$, and equations (6.22) match cashflows from the assets with those of the liabilities at future trading dates and in all states. A closely related formulation maximizes the expected horizon return, analogous to the horizon return portfolio Model 4.2.4. The objective function of the stochastic model for horizon returns is

$$\text{Maximize} \quad \sum_{l \in \Omega} p^l v_T^{+s}. \tag{6.24}$$

6.5   Basic Concepts of Stochastic Programming

We now turn to models for dynamic portfolio strategies, defined and optimized on event trees. The models in this section develop truly dynamic strategies that are optimal and satisfy the logi-

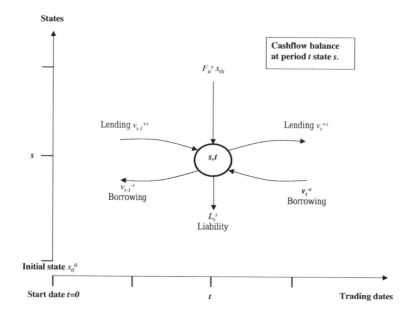

Figure 6.5: Flow of cash in the stochastic dedication model with borrowing and lending at trading date t in state s.

cal non-anticipativity constraints. Portfolio rebalancing is allowed as new information becomes available, and the portfolio decisions do not depend on clairvoyance.

Stochastic programming is the mathematical programming tool that facilitates the optimization of dynamic strategies on event trees. We introduce the basics of stochastic programming and then formulate a canonical model for portfolio management. Appendix B gives some background on probability spaces, which is essential for understanding stochastic programming with continuous random variables. Readers only interested in the resulting large-scale nonlinear programs defined using discrete and finite scenario sets can do without this background.

To develop an understanding of stochastic programming problems we consider first a simple problem of planning under uncertainty, the *newsvendor problem*. We then formulate two special cases of stochastic programs, the *anticipative* and the *adaptive* models. Finally, we combine these two in the most general formulation of the *recourse* model, which is the model suited for most financial applications. Readers without optimization background may want to refer to the books by Birge and Luveaux (1997) or Kall and Wallace (1994) for accessible introductions to stochastic programming. Those readers interested only in the financial applications of stochastic programming may skip the introduction to the basics given here, and proceed to Section 6.6 that formulates stochastic programming models for dynamic portfolio strategies as large-scale linear programs.

6.5.1 The newsvendor problem

On a street corner a young entrepreneur is selling newspapers that she buys from a local distributor each morning. She sells these papers for a profit P_0^+ per unit, and any papers that remain at the end of the day are sold as scrap paper, in which case a net loss P_0^- is realized per unit. The demand for newspapers is a random variable $\tilde{\xi}$ which belongs to a probability space (see Appendix B) with support denoted by $\Xi \doteq \{\tilde{\xi} \in \mathbb{R} \mid 0 \leq \tilde{\xi} < \infty\}$ and probability distribution function $P(\tilde{\xi})$. The problem is to choose the optimal number of papers x that should be bought from the local distributor.

An approach to modeling this situation is to consider a policy x as optimal if it maximizes the expected profit. Profit is a function of the policy and the demand random variable $\tilde{\xi}$. Let $F(x; \tilde{\xi})$ be the profit function:

$$F(x; \tilde{\xi}) \doteq \begin{cases} P_0^+ x & \text{if } x \leq \tilde{\xi}, \\ P_0^+ \tilde{\xi} - P_0^- (x - \tilde{\xi}) & \text{if } x > \tilde{\xi}. \end{cases} \tag{6.25}$$

The expected value of the profit function is the integral with respect to the distribution function

$$\begin{aligned} E\left[F(x; \tilde{\xi})\right] &= \int_{\Xi} F(x; \tilde{\xi}) dP(\tilde{\xi}) \\ &= \int_0^x \left(P_0^+ \tilde{\xi} - P_0^- (x - \tilde{\xi})\right) dP(\tilde{\xi}) + \int_x^\infty P_0^+ x \, dP(\tilde{\xi}), \end{aligned} \tag{6.26}$$

and the mathematical model for the newsvendor problem is the following optimization problem with respect to x,

$$\text{Maximize} \quad E\left[F(x; \tilde{\xi})\right] \tag{6.27}$$

$$\text{subject to} \quad x \geq 0. \tag{6.28}$$

This is a simple example of a problem of planning under uncertainty. It is an *adaptive* model, since decisions adapt as more information becomes available, i.e., as newspapers are sold to customers who arrive during the day. The model has *fixed recourse*, meaning that the reaction to the observed demand is fixed. That is, the number of newspapers sold for a profit is uniquely determined by the number of customers. The same is true for the surplus created at the end of the day, which is sold for scrap at a loss. Other forms of recourse action might have been possible, such as purchasing additional papers at a higher cost later in the day, or returning newspapers before the end of the day, at a value higher than that of scrap paper. This simple, fixed recourse model does not allow for such considerations, and it also assumes that all risk preferences are captured by the expected value of the profit. Higher moments of the distribution of the profit function $F(x; \tilde{\xi})$ are ignored. The next section presents mathematical models for planning under uncertainty in more complicated settings.

6.5.2   Canonical stochastic programming problems

The following problem is the canonical formulation of stochastic programming, where in this section we use the index j to denote m constraints of the model:

$$\text{Minimize} \quad E\left[f_0(x; \tilde{\xi})\right]$$

$$\text{subject to} \quad E\left[f_j(x; \tilde{\xi})\right] = 0, \quad \text{for } j = 1, 2, \ldots, m, \tag{6.29}$$

$$x \in X.$$

The following notation is used: $x \in \mathbb{R}^n$ is the vector of decision variables, $\tilde{\xi}$ is a random vector with support $\Xi \subset \mathbb{R}^N$ and $P \doteq P(\tilde{\xi})$ is a probability distribution function on $\mathbb{R}^N$. Also $f_0 : \mathbb{R}^n \times \Xi \to \mathbb{R} \cup \{+\infty\}$, $f_j : \mathbb{R}^n \times \Xi \to \mathbb{R}$, $j = 1, 2, \ldots, m$, and $X \subset \mathbb{R}^n$ is a closed set. Inequality constraints can be incorporated into this formulation with the use of slack variables.

The expectation functions

$$E[f_j(x; \tilde{\xi})] \doteq \int_{\Xi} f_j(x; \tilde{\xi}) dP(\tilde{\xi}), \tag{6.30}$$

are assumed finite for $j = 1, 2, \ldots, m$, unless the set $\{\tilde{\xi} \mid f_0(x; \tilde{\xi}) = +\infty\}$ has a nonzero probability, in which case $E[f_0(x; \tilde{\xi})] = +\infty$. The feasibility set

$$X \cap \{x \mid E[f_j(x; \tilde{\xi})] = 0, \ j = 1, 2, \ldots, m\} \cap \{x \mid E[f_0(x; \tilde{\xi})] < +\infty\}$$

is assumed to be nonempty.

The model (6.29) is a nonlinear programming problem whose constraints and objective functions are represented by integrals. Much of the theory of stochastic programming is concerned with identifying the properties of these integral functions and devising suitable approximation schemes for their evaluation. The computation of solutions for these nonlinear programs poses serious challenges, since evaluation of the integrals can be an extremely difficult task, especially when the expectation functionals are multidimensional. There are even cases when the integrands are neither differentiable, nor convex nor even continuous. A broad class of stochastic programming models, however, can be formulated as large-scale linear or nonlinear programs with a specially structured constraints matrix. In the next subsections we look at further refinements of the general stochastic programming formulation leading to the large-scale nonlinear programming models.

6.5.3   Anticipative models

Consider the situation where a decision x must be made in an uncertain world where the uncertainty is described by the random vector $\tilde{\xi}$. The decision does not in any way depend on future observations, but prudent planning has to anticipate possible future realizations of the random vector.

In anticipative models feasibility is expressed in terms of *probabilistic* (or *chance*) constraints. For example, a *reliability* level α, where $0 < \alpha \leq 1$, is specified and constraints are expressed in the form

$$P\{\tilde{\xi} \mid g_j(x; \tilde{\xi}) = 0, \ j = 1, 2, \ldots, m\} \geq \alpha, \tag{6.31}$$

where $g_j : \mathbb{R}^n \times \Xi \to \mathbb{R}, \quad j = 1, 2, \ldots, m$. This constraint can be cast in the form of the general model (6.29) by defining f_j as follows

$$f_j(x; \tilde{\xi}) \doteq \begin{cases} \alpha - 1 & \text{if } g_j(x; \tilde{\xi}) = 0, \\ \alpha & \text{otherwise.} \end{cases} \tag{6.32}$$

The objective function may also be of a reliability type, such as $P\{\tilde{\xi} \mid g_0(x; \tilde{\xi}) \leq \gamma\}$, where $g_0 : \mathbb{R}^n \times \Xi \to \mathbb{R} \cup \{+\infty\}$ and γ is a constant.

An anticipative model selects a policy that leads to some desirable characteristics of the constraint and objective functionals under the realizations of the random vector. In the example above it is desirable that the probability of a constraint violation is less than the prespecified threshold value α. The precise value of α depends on the application at hand, the cost of constraint violation, and other similar considerations.

6.5.4   Adaptive models

In an adaptive model observations related to uncertainty become available before a decision x is made, such that optimization takes place in a learning environment. It is understood that observations provide only partial information about the random variables because otherwise the model would simply wait to observe the values of the random variables, and then make a decision x by solving a deterministic mathematical program. In contrast to this situation we have the other extreme where all observations are made after the decision x has been made, and the model becomes anticipative.

Let $\mathcal{A}$ be the collection of all the relevant information that could become available by making an observation. This $\mathcal{A}$ is a subfield of the σ-field (see Appendix B) of all possible events, generated from the support set Ξ of the random vector $\tilde{\xi}$. The decisions x depend on the events that could be observed, and x is termed $\mathcal{A}$-*adapted* or $\mathcal{A}$-*measurable*. Using the conditional expectation with respect to $\mathcal{A}$, $E[\,\cdot\mid\mathcal{A}]$, the adaptive stochastic program can be written as:

$$\text{Minimize}\quad E[f_0(x(\tilde{\xi});\tilde{\xi})\mid\mathcal{A}]$$

$$\text{subject to}\quad E[f_j(x(\tilde{\xi});\tilde{\xi})\mid\mathcal{A}]=0,\quad\text{for all }j=1,2,\ldots,m,\tag{6.33}$$

$$x(\tilde{\xi})\in X,\text{ a.s.}$$

The mapping $x:\Xi\to X$ is such that $x(\tilde{\xi})$ is $\mathcal{A}$-measurable. This problem can be addressed by solving for every $\tilde{\xi}$ the following deterministic programs:

$$\text{Minimize}\quad E[f_0(x;\cdot)\mid\mathcal{A}](\tilde{\xi})\tag{6.34}$$

$$\text{subject to}\quad E[f_j(x;\cdot)\mid\mathcal{A}](\tilde{\xi})=0,\quad\text{for }j=1,2,\ldots,m,\tag{6.35}$$

$$x\in X.\tag{6.36}$$

The two extreme cases (i.e., complete information with $\mathcal{A}=\Sigma$, or no information at all) deserve special mention. The case of no information reduces the model to the form of the anticipative model; when there is complete information, model (6.33) is known as the *distribution model*. The goal in this latter case is to characterize the distribution of the optimal objective function value. The precise values of the objective function and the optimal policy x are determined after realizations of the random vector $\tilde{\xi}$ are observed. The most interesting situations arise when partial information becomes available after some decisions have been made, and models to address such situations are discussed next.

6.5.5   Recourse models

The recourse problem combines the anticipative and adaptive models in a common mathematical framework. The problem seeks a policy that not only anticipates future observations but also takes into account that observations are made about uncertainty as time passes, and thus can adapt by taking *recourse* decisions. For example, a portfolio manager specifies the composition of a portfolio considering both future movements of stock prices (anticipation) and that the portfolio will be rebalanced as prices change (adaptation).

The two-stage version of this model is amenable to formulations as a large-scale deterministic nonlinear program with a special structure of the constraints matrix. To formulate the two-stage stochastic program with recourse we need two vectors for decision variables to distinguish between the anticipative policy and the adaptive policy. The following notation is used.

$x\in\mathrm{IR}^{n_0}$ denotes the vector of first-stage decisions. These decisions are made before the random variables are observed and are anticipative.

$y(\tilde{\xi})\in\mathrm{IR}^{n_1}$ denotes the vector of second-stage decisions. These decisions are made after the random variables have been observed and are adaptive. They are constrained by decisions made at the first stage, and depend on the realization of the random vector $\tilde{\xi}$.

We now formulate the *second-stage problem*. Once a first-stage decision x has been made, some realization of the random vector can be observed. Let $q(y(\tilde{\xi});\tilde{\xi})$ denote the cost function for the second-stage decisions, and let $\{T(\tilde{\xi}),W(\tilde{\xi}),h(\tilde{\xi})\mid\tilde{\xi}\in\Xi\}$ be the model parameters. Those parameters are functions of the random vector $\tilde{\xi}$ and are, therefore, random parameters. T is the *technology matrix* of dimension $n_1\times m_0$. It contains the coefficients that convert the first-stage decision x into resources for the second-stage problem. The term "technology" refers to the fact that it is typically the changes in technology that determine the impact of today's decisions on the future decisions. W is the *recourse matrix* of dimension $n_1 \times m_1$, which imposes constraints on future decisions, and h is the second-stage resource vector of dimension n_1.

The second-stage problem seeks a policy $y(\tilde{\xi})$ that optimizes the cost of the second-stage decision for a given value of the first-stage decision x. We denote the optimal value of the second-stage problem by $\mathcal{Q}(x; \tilde{\xi})$. This value depends on the random parameters and on the value of the first-stage variables x. $\mathcal{Q}(x; \tilde{\xi})$ is the optimal value, for any given ω, of the following nonlinear program:

$$\text{Minimize} \quad q(y(\tilde{\xi}); \tilde{\xi})$$

$$\text{subject to} \quad W(\tilde{\xi})y(\tilde{\xi}) = h(\tilde{\xi}) - T(\tilde{\xi})x, \tag{6.37}$$

$$y(\tilde{\xi}) \geq 0.$$

If this second-stage problem is infeasible then we set $\mathcal{Q}(x; \tilde{\xi}) \doteq +\infty$. The model (6.37) is an *adaptation* model in which $y(\tilde{\xi})$ is the *recourse* decision and $\mathcal{Q}(x; \tilde{\xi})$ is the *recourse cost function*.

The two-stage stochastic program with recourse is an optimization problem in the first-stage variables x, which optimizes the sum of the cost of the first-stage decisions, $f(x)$, and the expected cost of the second-stage decisions. It is written as follows:

$$\text{Minimize} \quad f(x) + E[\mathcal{Q}(x; \tilde{\xi})]$$

$$\text{subject to} \quad Ax = b, \tag{6.38}$$

$$x \geq 0,$$

where A is an $n_0 \times m_0$ matrix of constraint coefficients, and b is an n_0-vector denoting available resources at the first stage.

Combining (6.37) and (6.38) we obtain the following model:

$$\text{Minimize} \quad f(x) + E[\text{Min} \{q(y(\tilde{\xi}); \tilde{\xi}) \mid T(\tilde{\xi})x + W(\tilde{\xi})y(\tilde{\xi}) = h(\tilde{\xi}), y(\tilde{\xi}) \geq 0\}]$$

$$\text{subject to} \quad Ax = b, \tag{6.39}$$

$$x \geq 0.$$

("Min" denotes the minimal function value.)

Let $K_1 \doteq \{x \in \mathbb{R}^{n_o}_+ \mid Ax = b\}$ denote the feasible set for the first-stage problem. Let also $K_2 \doteq \{x \in \mathbb{R}^{n_o} \mid E[\mathcal{Q}(x; \tilde{\xi})] < +\infty\}$ denote the set of *induced constraints*. This is the set of first-stage decisions x for which the second-stage problem is feasible. Problem (6.38) is said to have *complete recourse* if $K_2 = \mathbb{R}^{n_o}$, that is, if the second-stage problem is feasible for any value of x. The problem has *relatively complete recourse* if $K_1 \subseteq K_2$, that is, if the second-stage problem is feasible for any value of the first-stage variables that satisfies the first-stage constraints. *Simple recourse* refers to the case when the resource matrix $W(\tilde{\xi}) = I$ and the recourse constraints take the simple form $Iy_+(\tilde{\xi}) - Iy_-(\tilde{\xi}) = h(\tilde{\xi}) - T(\tilde{\xi})x$, where I is the identity matrix, and the recourse vector $y(\tilde{\xi})$ is written as $y(\tilde{\xi}) = y_+(\tilde{\xi}) - y_-(\tilde{\xi})$, with $y_+(\tilde{\xi}) \geq 0$, $y_-(\tilde{\xi}) \geq 0$ almost surely.

6.5.6 Deterministic equivalent formulation

We consider now the case where the random vector $\tilde{\xi}$ has a discrete and finite distribution, with support $\Xi = \{\xi^1, \xi^2, \ldots, \xi^N\}$. The elements ξ^l of Ξ are scenarios indexed by l from the scenario index set Ω. There is a one-to-one correspondence between the scenarios in Ξ and the scenario index set Ω. Denote by p^l the probability of realization of the lth scenario ξ^l. That is, for every $l \in \Omega$,

$$p^l \doteq \text{Prob}\ (\tilde{\xi} = \xi^l)$$
$$= \text{Prob}\left\{ \left(q(y;\tilde{\xi}), W(\tilde{\xi}), h(\tilde{\xi}), T(\tilde{\xi}) \right) = (q(y;\xi^l), W(\xi^l), h(\xi^l), T(\xi^l)) \right\},$$

where $p^l > 0$ for all $l \in \Omega$, and $\sum_{l \in \Omega} p^l = 1$.

The expected value of the second-stage optimization problem can be expressed as

$$E[Q(x;\tilde{\xi})] = \sum_{l \in \Omega} p^l Q(x;\xi^l). \tag{6.40}$$

For each realization of the random vector $\xi^l, l \in \Omega$, a different second-stage decision $y(\xi^l)$ is made, which is denoted for convenience by y^l. The resulting second-stage problems can then be written as:

$$\text{Minimize}\quad q(y^l;\xi^l)$$
$$\text{subject to}\quad W(\xi^l)y^l = h(\xi^l) - T(\xi^l)x, \tag{6.41}$$
$$y^l \geq 0.$$

Combining now (6.40) and (6.41) we reformulate the stochastic nonlinear program (6.39) in the discrete scenario setting as the following large-scale deterministic equivalent nonlinear program:

$$\text{Minimize}\quad f(x) + \sum_{l \in \Omega} p^l q(y^l;\xi^l) \tag{6.42}$$
$$\text{subject to}\qquad\qquad Ax = b, \tag{6.43}$$
$$T(\xi^l)x + W(\xi^l)y^l = h(\xi^l), \text{ for all } l \in \Omega, \tag{6.44}$$
$$x \geq 0, \tag{6.45}$$
$$y^l \geq 0, \qquad \text{for all } l \in \Omega. \tag{6.46}$$

The constraints (6.43)–(6.46) for this deterministic equivalent program can be combined into a matrix equation with block-angular structure:

$$\begin{pmatrix} A & & & & \\ T(\xi^1) & W(\xi^1) & & & \\ T(\xi^2) & & W(\xi^2) & & \\ \vdots & & & \ddots & \\ T(\xi^N) & & & & W(\xi^N) \end{pmatrix} \begin{pmatrix} x \\ y^1 \\ y^2 \\ \vdots \\ y^N \end{pmatrix} = \begin{pmatrix} b \\ h(\xi^1) \\ h(\xi^2) \\ \vdots \\ h(\xi^N) \end{pmatrix}. \tag{6.47}$$

6.5.7   Split variable formulation

The non-anticipativity requirement that a decision cannot depend on information arriving at later time periods leads to the model above whereby the first-stage decision x is common for all subsequent scenarios. An equivalent formulation, which is intuitively appealing, is to allow for different first-stage decisions x^l for each scenario $l \in \Omega$, but then force these variables to be equal to each other with additional explicit constraints.

We can better understand this new formulation in the context of an event tree. The event tree is split into linear scenarios whenever there is a branching state. Thus multiple split states are created, but the new states corresponding to the same time period and the same state from the

First-stage decisions   Second-stage decisions

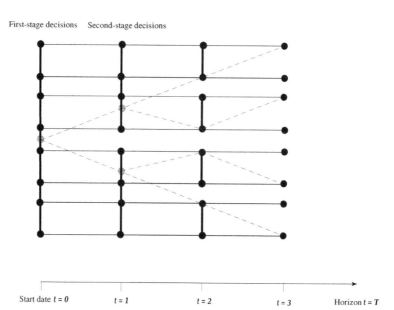

Start date $t = 0$ $t = 1$ $t = 2$ $t = 3$ Horizon $t = T$

Figure 6.6: Splitting an event tree into linear scenarios: dotted lines show the event tree, solid lines show the linear scenarios and thick lines are used to denote the presence of non-anticipativity constraints.

event tree are forced to coincide. Figure 6.6 illustrates the linear scenario structure derived by splitting the event tree of Figure 6.3. The split states that must coincide are connected with thick solid lines.

With the use of the split variables x^l we can define the two-stage stochastic programming model as follows.

$$\text{Minimize} \quad f(x) + \sum_{l \in \Omega} p^l q(y^l; \xi^l) \tag{6.48}$$

$$\text{subject to} \qquad\qquad\qquad Ax = b, \tag{6.49}$$

$$T(\xi^l)x^l + W(\xi^l)y^l = h(\xi^l), \quad \text{for all } l \in \Omega, \tag{6.50}$$

$$x = x^l, \quad \text{for all } l \in \Omega, \tag{6.51}$$

$$x^l, y^l \geq 0, \quad \text{for all } l \in \Omega. \tag{6.52}$$

Constraints (6.51) are the non-anticipativity constraints. They force the split variables to be equal to each other. With these constraints the mathematical program (6.48)–(6.52) is equivalent to (6.42)–(6.46). Note that an alternative formulation of the non-anticipativity constraints would be to set the split variables pairwise equal to each other, and do away with the extra variable x. That is, we could write the objective function term $f(x)$ as $f(x^1)$, write the first-stage constraints as $Ax^1 = b$, and enforce the non-anticipativity conditions by

$$x^1 = x^2, x^2 = x^3, \ldots, x^{N-1} = x^N. \tag{6.53}$$

These are equivalent formulations of the non-anticipativity conditions, and the choice depends on solution algorithms or other structural characteristics of the model.

6.5.8 Multi-stage models

The recourse problem is not restricted to the two-stage formulation. It is possible that observations are made at T different stages and are captured in the information sets $\{A_t\}_{t=1}^{T}$ with

$\mathcal{A}_1 \subset \mathcal{A}_2 \cdots \subset \mathcal{A}_T$. Stages correspond to time instances when some information is revealed and a decision can be made. (Note that, without ambiguity, T is a time index and $T(\tilde{\xi})$ are matrices.)

In the context of an event tree, stages correspond to the trading dates, and information is contained in the states. All information in set $\mathcal{A}_1$ is contained in the states indexed by S_1. Information in set $\mathcal{A}_2$ is contained in the states indexed by S_2, which in turn are the states attainable from S_1. Hence all information in $\mathcal{A}_1$ is also in $\mathcal{A}_2$, and no information is lost. A multi-stage stochastic program with recourse will have a recourse problem at stage τ conditioned on the information provided in the states S_τ, which includes all information provided by the states Σ_t, for $t = 1, 2, \ldots, \tau$. The program also anticipates the information in future states Σ_t, for $t = \tau + 1, \ldots, T$.

Let the random vector $\tilde{\xi}$ have support $\Xi = \Xi_1 \times \Xi_2 \times \cdots \times \Xi_T$, which is the product set of all individual support sets Ξ_t, $t = 1, 2, \ldots, T$. $\tilde{\xi}$ is written componentwise as $\tilde{\xi} = (\tilde{\xi}_1, \ldots, \tilde{\xi}_T)$. Denote the first-stage decision vector by y_0. For each stage $t = 1, 2, \ldots, T$, define the recourse variable vector $y_t(\tilde{\xi}) \in \mathbb{R}^{m_t}$, the random cost function $q_t(y_t(\tilde{\xi}); \tilde{\xi}_t)$, and the random parameters $\{T_t(\tilde{\xi}_t), W_t(\tilde{\xi}_t), h_t(\tilde{\xi}_t) \mid \tilde{\xi}_t \in \Xi_t\}$.

The multi-stage program, which extends the two-stage model (6.39) is formulated as the following nested optimization problem

$$\text{Minimize} \ \ f(y_0) + E\left[\min_{y_1 \in \mathbb{R}_+^{m_1}} q_1(y_1; \tilde{\xi}_1) + \cdots E\left[\min_{y_T \in \mathbb{R}_+^{m_T}} q_T(y_T; \tilde{\xi}_T) \right] \cdots \right]$$

$$\text{subject to} \qquad\qquad\qquad\qquad W_0 y_0 = h_0,$$

$$T_0(\tilde{\xi}) y_0 + W_1 y_1(\tilde{\xi}_1) = h_1(\tilde{\xi}),$$

$$\vdots \qquad\qquad\qquad\qquad\qquad (6.54)$$

$$T_{T-1}(\tilde{\xi}) y_{T-1}(\tilde{\xi}_{T-1}) + W_T(\tilde{\xi}_T) y_T(\tilde{\xi}_T) = h_T(\tilde{\xi}),$$

$$y_0 \geq 0, y_t(\tilde{\xi}_t) \geq 0,$$

$$\text{for all } t \in \mathcal{T}, \text{a.s.}$$

For the case of discrete and finitely distributed probability distributions it is again possible to formulate the multi-stage model into a deterministic equivalent large-scale nonlinear program. Figure 6.7 illustrates the structure of the constraint matrix for the deterministic equivalent formulation of a stochastic programming problem on the eight scenarios generated by the binomial lattice of Figure 6.8. Careful inspection shows that the two constraint matrices depicted in Figure 6.7 are equivalent, the difference between the two being the order in which the scenarios are traversed on the lattice of Figure 6.8. It is possible to formulate the deterministic equivalent linear program following the scenarios using a *depth-first* search strategy on the lattice or a *breadth-first* strategy; in either case all scenarios and eventualities are accounted for, preserving the time-precedence relationships, although the order is different across the multiple states of the lattice.

It is also possible to give a split variable formulation of the multi-stage model, analogous to the formulation of Section 6.5.7.

6.6   Stochastic Programming for Dynamic Portfolio Strategies

We consider now the optimization of dynamic portfolio strategies on an event tree. At each trading date the manager has to assess the market conditions – such as prices and interest rates – that prevail at the current state of the economy. The manager also has to assess the potential fluctuations in interest rates, prices, and cashflows at possible states of the economy at the next

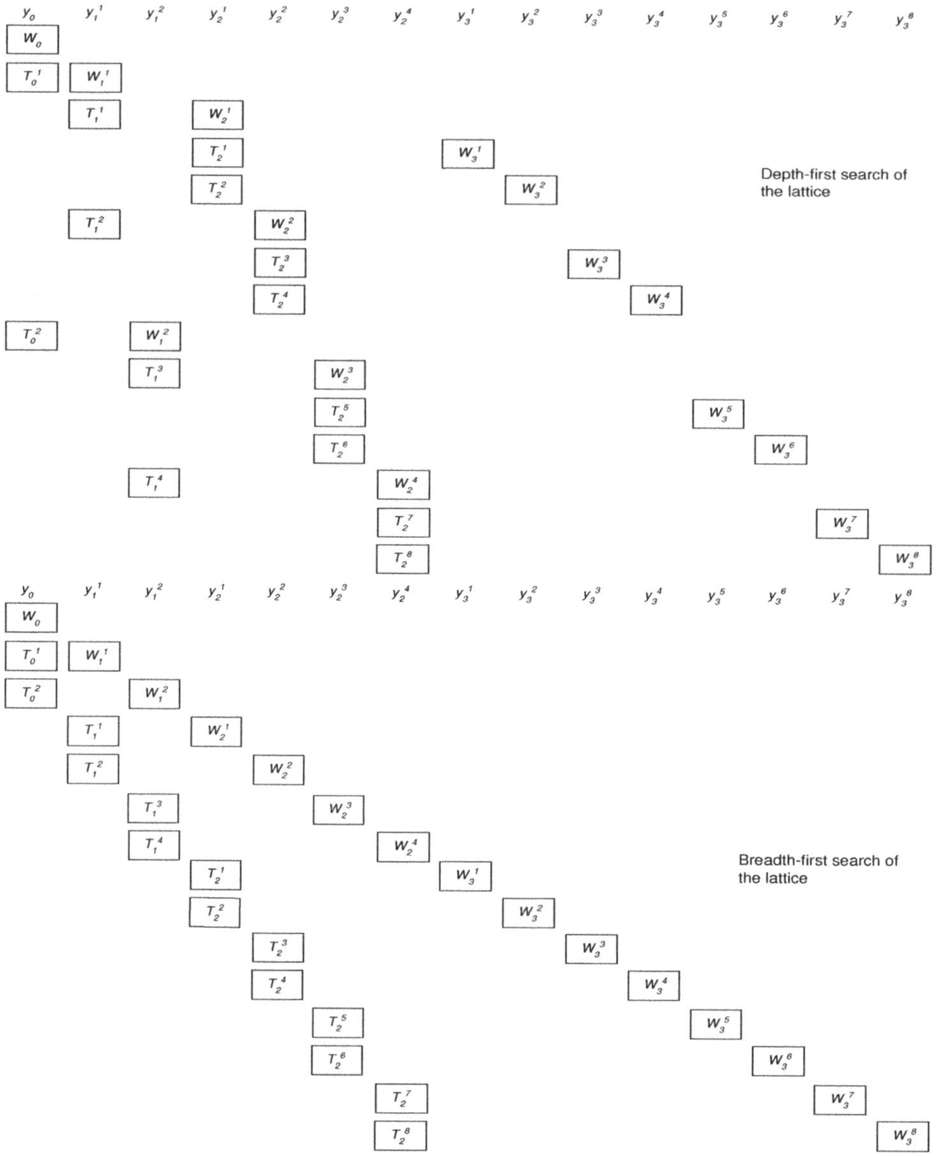

Figure 6.7: Constraint matrix for the deterministic equivalent formulation of a stochastic programming problem; all eight scenarios from Figure 6.8 are searched depth-first (top) and breadth-first (bottom).

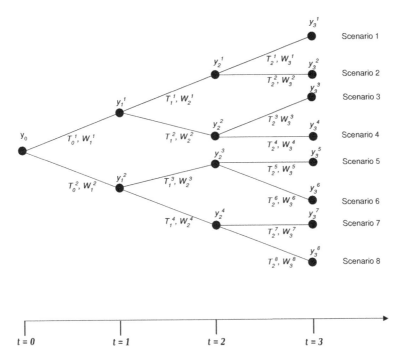

Figure 6.8: The scenarios and the associated constraint matrices for a multi-stage stochastic programming formulation.

trading period. That is, the information at successor states must be evaluated. This information is incorporated into a sequence of transactions in buying or selling securities, and short-term borrowing or lending. At the next trading date the portfolio manager has a seasoned portfolio and, faced with a new set of possible future movements, must incorporate the new information so that transactions can be executed.

The model specifies a sequence of investment decisions at the discrete trading times. Decisions are made at the beginning of each time period. The portfolio manager starts with a given portfolio and a set of scenarios about successor states of the economy which are incorporated into an investment decision. The composition of the current portfolio depends on transactions at the previous decision point and on the scenario realized in the interim. Another set of investment decisions is made, which incorporates both the current status of the portfolio and new information about future scenarios.

A three-stage problem is illustrated in the event tree of Figure 6.3. In the context of a multi-stage formulation introduced earlier the states s_1^0 and s_1^1 are indices of second-stage scenarios from the set Ξ_1, and the states s_2^0, s_2^1 and s_2^2 are indices of the third-stage scenarios from Ξ_2. The scenarios of the stochastic program are the pairs drawn from $\Xi = \Xi_1 \times \Xi_2$.

The stochastic programming model will determine an optimal decision for each state of the event tree, given the information available at that point. As there are multiple succeeding states the optimal decisions will not depend on clairvoyance, but they should anticipate future events.

6.6.1   Model formulation

There are two basic constraints in stochastic programming models for portfolio optimization: one considers cashflow accounting for the riskless asset, i.e., cash; and the other is an inventory balance equation for each security or asset class at all trading dates and for all states. Figure 6.9

illustrates the flow of cash and inventory of asset categories using the notation introduced in Section 6.2.1. Note the differences from the flow of funds illustrated in Figure 6.5 for the stochastic dedication model, where asset sales and purchase decisions were absent and there was no modeling of the asset inventory.

We formulate the components of the model for $t = 0$ and for future trading dates $0 < t < T$. For $t = 0$ we have, in the terminology of stochastic programming, the first-stage problem. Variables for future trading dates are the t-stage variables and they are used to model the recourse problem.

First-stage constraints

At the first stage (i.e., at $t = 0$) all prices are known with certainty. We also know the portfolio composition. For each security or asset class $i \in U$ in the portfolio we have an *inventory balance constraint*:

$$z_{0i}^0 = b_{0i} + x_{0i}^0 - y_{0i}^0, \tag{6.55}$$

where $b_0 = (b_{01}, \ldots, b_{0n})$ denotes the initial inventory in each asset class (that is, the composition of the initial portfolio) and the remaining variables are as shown in Figure 6.9.

The *cashflow balance equation* specifies that the original endowment in the riskless asset, plus any proceeds from liquidating part of the existing portfolio, equal the amount invested in the purchase of new securities, plus the payment of the liabilities, plus the amount invested in the riskless asset, i.e.,

$$\sum_{i=1}^{n} P_{0i}^{b0} y_{0i}^0 + v_0 + v_0^{-0} = \sum_{i=1}^{n} P_{0i}^{a0} x_{0i}^0 + v_0^{+0} + L_0^0. \tag{6.56}$$

Time-staged constraints

Decisions made at future trading dates, $t = 1, 2, \ldots, T$, are conditioned on the state of the economy $s \in \Sigma_t$. Hence, at each time period we have a set of constraints for each state. These decisions also depend on the investment decisions made at the previous trading date $t - 1$ at predecessor state s^-.

Asset inventory balance equations constrain the amount of each security sold or remaining in the portfolio to equal the outstanding amount of face value carried over from the previous trading date, plus any amount purchased at the current trading date. There is one constraint for each security $i \in U$ and for each state $s \in \Sigma_t$:

$$z_{ti}^s = \alpha_{(t-1)i}^s z_{(t-1)i}^{s^-} + x_{ti}^s - y_{ti}^s, \tag{6.57}$$

where α denotes the amortization factors, as introduced in the notation section 6.2.1, and the remaining variables are as shown in Figure 6.9.

Cashflow balance requires that the amount invested in the purchase of new securities and in the riskless asset is equal to the income generated by the existing portfolio during the holding period plus any cash generated from sales and cash reinvested at the previous period at predecessor state s^-, less any liability payments (see the top Figure 6.9). There is one constraint for each state $s \in \Sigma_t$:

$$\sum_{i=1}^{n} F_{(t-1)i}^s z_{(t-1)i}^{s^-} + \sum_{i=1}^{n} P_{ti}^{bs} y_{ti}^s + (1 + r_{f(t-1)}^s) v_{t-1}^{+s^-}$$

$$= L_t^s + \sum_{i=1}^{n} P_{ti}^{as} x_{ti}^s + v_t^{+s}. \tag{6.58}$$

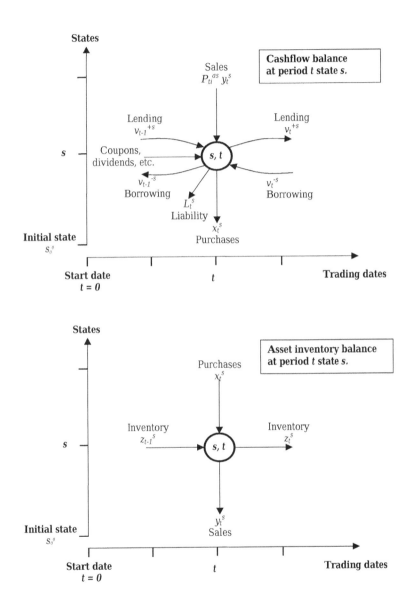

Figure 6.9: Flow of cash and asset inventory in a stochastic programming model for dynamic portfolio strategies at trading date t and in state s.

This constraint considers the investments in the riskless asset at the previous time period and at the predecessor state – variable $v_{t-1}^{+s^-}$ – but does not consider borrowing. Borrowing can be incorporated in this equation by introducing the variable v_t^{-s}. Borrowing will contribute to the cash inflow – left hand side of the equation above – but borrowing from previous time periods must be paid back, with appropriate interest, at subsequent periods. This will increase the cash outflows of the right-hand side of the equation above. The cashflow balance equation with borrowing and reinvestment at each state $s \in \Sigma_t$ is written as follows:

$$\sum_{i=1}^{n} F_{(t-1)i}^s z_{(t-1)i}^{s^-} + \sum_{i=1}^{n} P_{ti}^{bs} y_{ti}^s + (1 + r_{f(t-1)}^s) v_{t-1}^{+s^-} + v_t^{-s}$$

$$= L_t^s + \sum_{i=1}^{n} P_{ti}^{as} x_{ti}^s + v_t^{+s} + (1 + r_{f(t-1)}^s + \delta) v_{t-1}^{s^-}, \qquad (6.59)$$

where δ is the spread between the short-term borrowing and lending rates.

End-of-horizon constraints

At the end of the planning horizon we evaluate the terminal wealth of the portfolio. This will depend on the holdings in different asset classes, including cash, and the state of the economy. It is given by

$$W_T^s = v_T^{+s} + \sum_{i=1}^{n} P_{Ti}^{bs} z_{ti}^s. \qquad (6.60)$$

We also set $v_T^{-s} = 0$ to avoid borrowing at the last time period since the model has no mechanism to repay loans outstanding after the end of the planning horizon.

Modeling other conditions

At each stage of the stochastic program we have formulated two sets of constraints for cashflow and inventory balance. Depending on the application at hand other conditions may need to be modeled as constraints. The general setup with the variables as defined here is usually adequate for formulating additional constraints. We discuss several examples of conditions that appear in practice.

Some applications require multiple cash accounts. For instance, international portfolio management requires different handling of cash in different currencies when exchange rates are hedged. Deposits from different product lines may be held in separate accounts when regulators apply different rules for different sources. This is the case for Japanese saving type insurance policies, which are treated differently than conventional insurance policies. To model these settings we must introduce multiple variables for lending and borrowing, one for each currency or for each account, and formulate multiple cashflow accounting equations.

Other conditions may include limits on the position in a given asset class. Such restrictions were formulated in Section 4.2.5. For instance, the allowable exposure of Italian insurers to corporate bonds or international Government bonds is limited by regulators (see Chapter 12). Investments in *tokkin* funds – subsidiaries set up to invest funds and pay dividend back to the parent company – by Japanese insurers may not exceed a given percentage of the total assets as stipulated by regulators.

Taxes must be computed, distinguishing income return from price return. This requirement can be formulated in the models above using the sales variables (y) to model income return, and the inventory variables (z) to model price return. Finally, leverage restrictions may be imposed by regulators requiring the calculation of the ratio of debt to equity in funding liabilities. The models in Chapter 12 formulate the leverage restrictions imposed on insurance firms. These, and several other conditions, may be added to the basic constraints formulated above.

Objective function

To incorporate risk aversion in the dynamic portfolio strategy we introduce a utility function for terminal wealth. The objective of the portfolio optimization model maximizes the expected utility of terminal wealth

$$\text{Maximize} \sum_{s \in \Sigma_T} p^s \mathcal{U}(W_T^s) \tag{6.61}$$

where p^s is the probability associated with state s in Σ_T, W_T^s denotes terminal wealth given by equation (6.60), and $\mathcal{U}$ denotes the utility function.

The stochastic programming model for optimizing dynamic portfolio strategies is now written as follows.

Model 6.6.1 Stochastic programming for dynamic portfolio strategies

$$\text{Maximize} \quad \sum_{s \in \Sigma_T} p^s \mathcal{U}(W_T^s) \tag{6.62}$$

subject to
$$\sum_{i=1}^{n} P_{0i}^b y_{0i}^0 + v_0 + v_0^{-0} = \sum_{i=1}^{n} P_{0i}^a x_{0i}^0 + v_0^{+0} + L_0^0, \tag{6.63}$$

$$z_{0i}^0 = b_{0i} + x_{0i}^0 - y_{0i}^0,$$
$$\text{for all } i \in U, \tag{6.64}$$

$$z_{ti}^s = \alpha_{(t-1)i}^s z_{(t-1)i}^{s-} + x_{ti}^s - y_{ti}^s,$$
$$\text{for all } t \in \mathcal{T}, s \in \Sigma_t, i \in U, \tag{6.65}$$

$$\sum_{i=1}^{n} F_{(t-1)i}^s z_{(t-1)i}^{s-} + \sum_{i=1}^{n} P_{ti}^{bs} y_{ti}^s + (1 + r_{f(t-1)}^s) v_{t-1}^{+s-} + v_t^{-s}$$

$$= \sum_{i=1}^{n} P_{ti}^{as} x_{ti}^s + v_t^{+s} + (1 + r_{f(t-1)}^s + \delta) v_{t-1}^{s-} + L_t^s,$$

$$\text{for all } t \in \mathcal{T}/\{0\}, s \in \Sigma_t, i \in U, \tag{6.66}$$

$$W_T^s = v_T^{+s} + \sum_{i=1}^{n} P_{Ti}^{bs} z_{ti}^s. \tag{6.67}$$

The objective function used here is not the only one possible, although it is the one in agreement with the discussion in Section 5.6. Other choices may be more appropriate for some applications. We mention some common choices. For defined benefit pension funds, and for fixed liabilities in general, an appropriate objective function is to minimize the expected cost of funding. Sometimes a multicriteria objective function that maximizes terminal wealth net of expected shortfalls may be more appropriate. Return on equity to shareholders as a proxy for shareholder value is also an appropriate function that has been used in modeling portfolio problems of for-profit institutions (see Chapter 12). For index funds the objective function is a measure of deviation of portfolio returns from the target index. Quite often only downside deviations are minimized (see Chapter 7).

In general, creating an objective function for investors over long time horizons is a poorly understood task. First, temporal considerations trading short-term return versus long-term goals must be estimated. Second, uncertainty over extended time periods complicates the decision making process by creating potential regret. Reconciling the choice of an objective function with accepted theories on investor preferences and utility functions is an important step of the modeling process. Any of the measures of risk and reward discussed in earlier chapters can be incorporated into the stochastic programming formulation.

6.7   Comparison of Stochastic Programming with Other Methods

Stochastic programming falls in the general category of multi-period stochastic models for risk management as classified in Section 2.9. How do these models compare with the portfolio optimization methods discussed in Chapters 3 and 5? And how do they compare with alternative risk management models that are not covered in this book?

6.7.1   Mean-variance models and downside risk

The mean-variance framework of Chapter 3 is widely considered as the starting point for models on optimal investment. Intuitively it seems rather odd that variance as a risk measure penalizes positive returns and negative returns equivalently. Of course, it is only important to make a distinction between negative and positive returns if the distribution of the portfolio returns is asymmetric. With the empirically observed skewed distributions of stock returns, and the highly asymmetric return distributions of portfolios with embedded options, the validity of variance as a measure of risk is being questioned. To address this issue, downside-risk measures are needed as a substitute for variance. The criticism of the risk measure in the mean-variance model has been overcome with the alternative risk measures introduced in Sections 2.6 and 2.7. The scenario optimization models of Chapter 5 are not restricted by the assumptions of normality that underlie the mean-variance framework. However, both mean-variance models and the scenario optimization models of previous chapters are myopic, that is, they bundle all future times as a single period and look only one step ahead. A concern that remains unanswered by these models is that they do not allow for the future opportunities to change the investment strategy intertemporally.

6.7.2   Discrete-time, multi-period models

Most asset liability management problems cover a long period of time until the planning horizon, with multiple opportunities to change the investment portfolio. We mention the examples of pension funds and social security that have time horizons of up to 50 years. It is clearly inappropriate to model several decades into the future in one single period without allowing for trading to adjust the investment portfolio.

The single-period restriction of the mean-variance model has been overcome, under some conditions, with the maximization of the expectation of a power utility function of wealth at the end of the horizon (see Section 5.6). A power utility function has the property of constant relative risk aversion and as a result the portfolio weights are equal in each period, regardless of the investor's wealth or time horizon. The investment policies are called myopic as the investor behaves identically to a single-period investor. Under the assumption of intertemporally independent distributed asset returns, without transaction costs, cash infusion, or withdrawals, a sequence of myopic models is optimal for a multi-period investor. When optimizing a logarithmic utility function it is still true that the sequence of myopic models is optimal for multi-period investors even when asset returns are serially correlated and income is stochastic. Several of these assumptions, however, fail in the modern capital markets, especially when dealing with fixed-income and derivative securities. In addition to the ever-prevalent transaction costs, fixed-income securities are subject to defaults, prepayments, surrender options, call provisions and the like. These features result in implicit cash withdrawals from the portfolio. Some of these provisions are also intertemporally dependent. For instance, the exercise of prepayment or a call option is critically dependent on whether the option was exercised in some previous time periods or not. The choice of a logarithmic utility function is also restrictive in that it does not allow the modeling of different levels of risk aversion that may be appropriate for different individuals or institutions.

It is possible to formulate multi-period dynamic programming models for risk management on event trees. Such models lead to interesting insights, as the optimal policies are derived in feedback form. However, the curse of dimensionality – that is, the exponential growth of the size of the problem as stages are added – limits the type of models that can be solved. Models with more than three or four state variables are bound to run into serious computational problems, and it is very difficult to handle transaction costs. An alternative approach is to specify in advance a decision rule for changing the investment strategy dynamically – such as the rules in Section 6.3 – and optimize the parameters of the given rule.

Models with decision rules, such as fixed mix, have several advantages. First, they can handle transaction costs and operational, regulatory or corporate restrictions on the investment policy. Moreover, the optimized rule can be easily interpreted and understood by decision makers. A major problem is that the model is non-unimodal. Multiple local solutions may exist, and global optimization algorithms have to be applied. Recent progress on global optimization notwithstanding, these algorithms can often handle only a small number of decision variables (i.e., coefficients of the decision rules). Finally, we are never sure that a given decision rule is actually optimal for the problem at hand. For example, we do not always know in advance that a fixed mix rule is optimal for a particular problem. It might as well be that another dynamic investment rule is more efficient: for example, we could adjust the asset mix as a function of the ratio of assets to liabilities (funding ratio). If we apply the latter rule, there is still an immense number of different functional forms that we could choose, as the optimal relationship between the asset weights and the funding ratio can be nonlinear. A disadvantage is therefore that we might have to try a large number of different specifications for the decision rule, before we are confident that we have found a rule with relatively good performance.

6.7.3 Continuous-time models

Continuous-time models play an important role in modern finance. The consumption-investment problem can be modeled in a continuous-time framework, where the time step between consecutive trading dates decreases to zero in the limit. In the early models the asset prices were assumed to follow geometric Brownian motions, which correspond to a log-normal return distribution, but increasingly more elaborate stochastic processes are now being used. For the class of power utility functions, myopic investment policies derived as the solution of continuous time models are optimal.

Continuous-time models are of limited practical value for institutional enterprise-wide risk management. The assumptions on the utility function and asset prices are restrictive. More importantly in the context of risk management for large institutions, these models may ignore transaction costs and the trading restrictions that are typically imposed by regulators or dictated by corporate policy. An advantage of the continuous-time framework is that optimal decision rules can be derived for some basic models. Moreover, the impact of transaction costs, trading limits, return predictability, parameter uncertainty and market incompleteness can be analyzed quite accurately in models that focus on one or two of these issues in isolation. However, general models that incorporate all of these issues simultaneously have not been solved yet. Similarly, practical constraints reflecting regulatory restrictions, operational requirements, or corporate policy have not been incorporated. Moreover, an attempt to solve such a general model is very likely to run into computational problems due to the curse of dimensionality.

6.7.4   Stochastic programming

Continuous-time models and discrete-time models solved with dynamic programming and optimal control can provide significant qualitative insights into fundamental issues in investments and risk management, as the optimal decision rules are in feedback form. However, their practical use as a tool for decision making is limited by the many simplifying assumptions that are needed to derive the solutions in a reasonable amount of time. The stochastic programming approach discussed in this chapter can be considered as a practical multi-period extension of the normative mean-variance approach (Chapter 3) and its extensions in scenario optimization (Chapter 5). The advantage of stochastic programming models for multi-period enterprise-wide risk management problems is that important practical issues such as transaction costs, multiple state variables, market incompleteness, taxes and trading limits, regulatory restrictions, and corporate policy requirements can be handled simultaneously within the framework.

Of course this flexibility comes at a price and stochastic programming also has a drawback. The computational effort explodes as the number of decision stages in a multi-stage stochastic programming model increases. While implementing a stochastic programming model for financial optimization, we are therefore often forced to make a trade-off between the number of decision stages in the model and the number of nodes in the event tree that are used to approximate the underlying returns distributions. While setting up stochastic programming models, it is important to keep in mind that a normative model does not necessarily have to include every possible decision moment up to the planning horizon. Capturing the first few opportunities accurately can be good enough to make an informed decision right now.

Stochastic programming can deal simultaneously with all important aspects of an enterprise-wide risk management system. However, even if the model were solvable, too many details would confuse instead of support the decision maker. Like the alternative methodologies discussed in this section, stochastic programming applications to risk management have a strong element of art. Stochastic programming enjoys several advantages over the alternatives, but it is not without shortcomings.

6.8   Postview

This chapter developed models for dynamic portfolio optimization, with emphasis on stochastic programming.

The general setting for modeling dynamic portfolio strategies on lattice structures, linear scenario structures, and event trees was first introduced. The chapter then discussed simple decision rules for dynamic portfolio strategies. These are simple and effective rules, but fall short of optimizing the portfolios. A simple model – stochastic dedication – was then developed to optimize dynamic strategies, but considering only the simplest case of managing borrowing and lending when interest rates are scenario generated, thus extending the portfolio dedication model of Chapter 4.

A basic introduction to stochastic programming was then given, followed by the formulation of stochastic programming models for optimizing dynamic strategies. This is the most general and flexible portfolio optimization model in this book, as it treats stochastic parameters using scenarios; it considers long time horizons; and it models decisions and multiple time periods with both borrowing and lending and portfolio rebalancing as well. A detailed comparison with other portfolio optimization model was then given, thus highlighting the merits of stochastic programming.

Notes and References

The decision rules for dynamic strategies are given in Perold and Sharpe (1988). Maranas et al. (1997) discuss the optimization of one type of decision rule, namely the fixed mix strategy.

Stochastic dedication optimization models were developed by Hiller and Eckstein (1993) and Zenios (1991, 1993b); see also Mulvey and Zenios (1994a, b).

Stochastic programming models were first formulated as mathematical programs in the late 1950s, independently, by G.B. Dantzig and E.M.L. Beale (Dantzig 1955; Beale 1955). Modern textbook treatments of stochastic programming are Kall and Wallace (1994), and Birge and Louveaux (1997), and research literature is given in the handbook chapter by Wets (1989), or the book by Censor and Zenios (1997) which focuses on solution methods.

The early contributions on stochastic programming models for financial applications are collected in the volume by Ziemba and Vickson (1975). The number of publications has risen drastically in the 1990s, probably inspired by the radical increase in efficiency and accessibility of computer systems; see the two volumes by Zenios and Ziemba (2006, forthcoming). Ziemba and Mulvey (1998) categorize the models in three generations: (i) model origins, which deal with the early mathematical formulations; (ii) early models, which deal with real-world applications but are developed and tested in a limited setting, mostly by academic researchers; and (iii) modern models, which deal with a variety of institutional problems, developed as large-scale applications and tested extensively, usually in collaboration with institutional asset and liability managers. From the early models we mention the bond portfolio management model of Bradley and Crane (1972), the bank ALM model of Kusy and Ziemba (1986), the short-term cashflow management model of Kallberg, White and Ziemba (1982), the fixed-income model of Zenios (1991), the asset allocation model of Mulvey and Vladimirou (1989, 1992), and the stochastic dedication model of Hiller and Eckstein (1993).

Under modern models, Ziemba and Mulvey (1998) list around 40 references. We mention a sample that covers a broad range of applications, selecting publications where the industrial component of the model was substantial. The insurance asset and liability management model of Cariño and Ziemba (1998) and Cariño et al. (1998) has been used extensively by the Frank Russell company for consulting ALM managers in insurance and pension funds. Their work with the the Yasuda Fire and Marine Insurance Company (Japan) was a finalist at the Franz Edelman Competition for Management Science Achievements. Similar acclaim was achieved by the Towers Perrin–Tillinghast model of Mulvey, Gould and Morgan (2000) and the PROMETEIA model of Consiglio, Cocco and Zenios (2004) for individual investors. The latter has also been employed by several Italian financial institutions, reaching tens of thousands of investors and received the 2006 EURO Excellence in Practice Award. Stochastic programming models for Dutch pension funds were developed by Dert (1995); for money management with mortgage-backed securities by Golub et al. (1995); and for insurance products by Nielsen and Zenios (1996). A general asset and liability model for insurers was developed by Consigli and Dempster (1998), and an application to the Norwegian insurance industry by Høyland (1998), and Høyland and Wallace (2007). A multi-period model, but without decisions for portfolio revisions, for insurance products with minimum guarantee is discussed in Chapter 12.

Multiple cash accounts in different currencies for modeling hedging decisions is discussed in Consiglio and Zenios (2001a). Modeling of regulatory restrictions for Japanese insurance companies is discussed in Cariño et al. (1998).

The end effects due to the limited number of stages of stochastic programming models in the context of financial applications are studied by Cariño and Ziemba (1998), and Cariño, Myers and Ziemba (1998). Their approach is based on the theoretical foundations laid by Grinold (1977, 1983).

The financial economics literature has lately paid more attention to previously ignored "details" that are very relevant for practitioners in the context of continuous-time models, resorting to numerical techniques if necessary. For example, Brennan, Schwartz and Lagnado (1997) numerically investigate the impact of return predictability on optimal portfolio choice in a continuous-time investment model based on Merton (1969). The optimal portfolio weights reported by Brennan, Schwartz and Lagnado (1997) tend to fluctuate drastically through time, resembling "yoyo-strategies," due to the absence of transaction costs in the model and the lack of uncertainty about the model parameters. Balduzzi and Lynch (1999, 2000) show that transaction costs can indeed stabilize the optimal policy of an optimal control model with return predictability. In practice, transaction costs might not be the only concern, but also uncertainty about the actual value of model parameters such as the mean asset return. Brennan (1998), Barberis (2000), and Xia (2000) study continuous-time investment models under parameter uncertainty, with dynamic learning about parameter values (Brennan 1998), with return predictability (Barberis 2000), and with both learning and predictability (Xia 2000). Another recent development is that optimal portfolio and consumption problems with return predictability can be solved in closed-form, as demonstrated by Kim and Omberg (1996), and Liu (1999). Cairns and Parker (1997), and Rudolf and Ziemba (1998) are good examples of the use of continuous type models for practical financial modeling problems facing large institutions; Kouwenberg and Zenios (2006) provide a survey.

Chapter 7

Index Funds

They also serve who only sit and hold.

Paul A. Samuelson

7.1 Preview

Broadly defined market indices are comprehensive measures of market trends. Passive strategies that manage index funds to mimic market trends are prevalent among portfolio managers. In this chapter we develop optimization models for structuring index funds. We start with a review of the basics of market indices and then discuss two broad model classes for structuring indexed portfolios. Models for creating index funds for international and corporate bond markets help to clarify the issues. The use of multi-period stochastic optimization models is also discussed for this broad problem class, and empirical results with several applications illustrate the uses of the models and establish their efficacy.

7.2 Basics of Market Indices

An index is a single statistic that summarizes the relative changes in a set of variables, such as stock or bond or commodity prices. An index can be broad in scope and include variables based on value, growth rate, or geographical region, or it can take a narrow view of the market and focus on a single economic sector or an industry.

As international institutions change location and invest funds outside their domestic market they need tools to guide investment analysis, asset allocation, and performance measurement in diverse markets. Investors quite often evaluate their portfolio choices with respect to overall market trends. Indices provide comprehensive measures of market trends and are useful benchmarks for portfolio performance. But they can also be used to guide portfolio selection using passive strategies, whereby portfolios are structured to track a market index. There is ample empirical evidence that actively managed portfolios do not outperform the market, and those that do outperform do so inconsistently. This evidence explains the popularity of passive portfolio management strategies. In a study of the performance of 769 all-equity actively managed funds during the period 1983–1989 it was determined that the average fund return was from 200 to 500 basis points below the S&P 500 index. From among those funds that did well in one period only one-fourth continued to do equally well in the next period. One fourth of the best performers would find themselves among the worst performers in the following time period.

Market indices are valuable tools in financial decision making as they monitor performance of broad segments of the market. For instance, the NYSE composite index measures all common

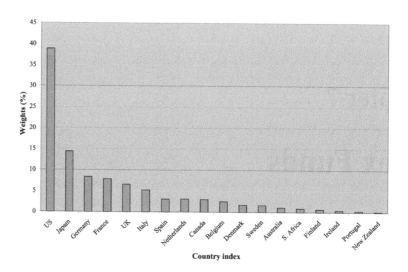

Figure 7.1: Composition of the JP Morgan Government Bond Index (GBI) Broad in September 1997.

stocks listed on the New York Stock Exchange. It has four subgroup indices by sector: industrial, transportation, utility and finance. The index tracks aggregate market trends of NYSE common stocks. However, with more than 3,000 stocks listed on the New York Stock Exchange this index cannot form the basis for a tradeable portfolio. In contrast, the S&P 500 measures the performance of 500 stocks selected by the index committee of Standard & Poor's. The size and the criteria for candidate stocks make this index suitable for trading. It is estimated that more than a trillion dollars in index funds are managed to replicate S&P indices.

Indices are not restricted to the stock markets. Today, bond indices are calculated for government bonds, corporate bonds, asset-backed securities, and so on. For instance, JP Morgan publishes the Government Bond Index (GBI) Broad, which is a widely used benchmark for measuring performance and quantifying risk across international fixed-income bond markets. JP Morgan indices measure the total, principal, and interest returns in 18 government bond markets and are reported in 85 different currencies. The proportional weights of the countries represented in this index are shown in Figure 7.1. Merrill Lynch publishes a Eurodollar index of corporate bonds. The index consists of highly liquid securities so that liquidity risk is eliminated. Currency risk is also eliminated since the securities in the index are dollar denominated.

Indices may be *rules driven* or *discretionary*. In the former case detailed rules govern the choice of securities to form the index. These indices are transparent and predictable in their composition. We emphasize that predictability of composition does not imply predictability of returns. An analyst may expect, based on the publicized rules, that bonds of a certain maturity and coupon rate will be included in the index. But he or she does not know what the return of these securities will be.

The constitution of discretionary indices is determined by a committee. The views of this committee are known, but these are merely views and not detailed rules. For instance, the Standard & Poor's index committee makes its decisions based on trading analysis, liquidity, ownership, fundamental analysis, market capitalization and sector representation. As an example of committee views we mention the committee's announcement of a "pronounced bias" against the addition of tracking stocks in their indices after 1999.

No matter how an index is created, in order to be a meaningful tool for decision support it must have certain characteristics. It is desirable that only traded issues available to investors constitute an index. This provides a realistic measure of market performance and eliminates or reduces liquidity risk. Tradeable portfolios may be created from the securities in the index, were it not for the fact that the index set may be too large. Furthermore, the market or market segments included in the index should not have significant barriers to entry, and expenses for investing in these markets should be predictable and not excessive. The composition of the index should be relatively stable without unnecessary changes to the constituents, and investors should be able to replicate the returns reported by the index using market data. Finally, it is important to choose an index that closely approximates the universe of securities a manager actually invests in – such as large capitalization or small capitalization firms, corporate bonds of a given industrial sector or a given credit rating, or the broad market.

For discretionary indices that are suitable for trading, any addition or deletion from the index has an effect on the market. Analysis of stock prices for the 188 companies that were added in the S&P 500 index during the period 1991 to 2000 showed that significant abnormal returns were realized when the index committee announced that these stocks would be added to the index. Abnormal returns were also realized for the securities added to the S&P MidCap 400 and the S&P SmallCap 600. The effects on stocks added to these two indices were less significant than the effects on stocks added to the S&P 500 stocks, as index fund managers do not follow these indices as closely as the S&P 500.

Once the constituents of the index are determined their weighting must be specified. Securities in the index may be equally weighted, price weighted or cap weighted. Under *equal weighting* each security in the index is given the same weight, which is one divided by the total number of constituent securities. *Price-weighted* indices assume that one share is held in each constituent. As a result the index is more heavily weighted towards the expensive securities. The Dow Jones industrial average is price weighted, because when the index was conceived in 1890 the easiest calculation for assigning weights was to add the prices of the 12 securities in the index and divide by 12. *Cap-weighted* indices assign weights to the securities in proportion to their market capitalization, which is the number of outstanding shares times the price. For instance, Figure 7.1 shows the weights in the JP Morgan international index as the percentage of each country's capitalization in the global government bond market.

The return of an index is a weighted combination of the returns of the constituent securities. Assume that there are K securities in the index with random return vector $\tilde{r} = (\tilde{r}_j)_{j=1}^K$ and normalized weights vector $w = (w_j)_{j=1}^K$, such that $\sum_{j=1}^K w_j = 1$. Note that we assume that the index is not comprised of real securities – which would be denoted by subscript $i \in U$ in our standard notation – but of generic securities that are representative of the risk factors of the index. Hence we use $j \in \mathcal{K}$ to denote the securities in the index. Equity indices are usually represented by real securities, chosen to be representative of some risk factor in the market that is being indexed. For instance, the IBM stock in the S&P 500 may be representative of the risk factors of the computer industry. For fixed-income indices it is usually the case that generic securities that have some characteristics typical of a broad market segment are constructed. The mortgage-backed securities indices consist of generic securities with a given weighted average coupon, and a given weighted average maturity, and are issued by given issuers (e.g., Federal National Mortgage Association, Federal Housing Authority, etc). There may be several traded securities with characteristics similar to the generic securities. The Salomon Brothers index of mortgage-backed securities consists of a couple of hundred generic securities that are representative of the hundreds of thousands of mortgage securities available in the US market.

The return of the index is given by

$$R_I(w; \tilde{r}) = \sum_{j=1}^K w_j \tilde{r}_j, \tag{7.1}$$

and in the discrete scenario setting by

$$R_I(w; r^l) = \sum_{j=1}^{K} w_j r_j^l. \tag{7.2}$$

It is clear from these expressions that the choice of a weighting scheme will make a difference in the index returns. From the viewpoint of the manager of an index fund, however, the weights are given a priori.

How do we structure a portfolio whose growth rate will closely mimic an index? Such a portfolio is called an index fund, and optimization models for structuring index funds are developed next. In some cases funds are managed with the objective of outperforming an index while preserving the key risk characteristics of the index. These funds are called *enhanced index* or *index-plus* funds.

The discussion on indexation models focuses on fixed-income index funds. Indexation of bonds is a much more complex problem than indexation of stocks. There are thousands of bonds with different maturities, coupon rates, issuers or issues, and many of these are completely illiquid. Some indices, such as the indices for the mortgage-backed securities market, may consist of representative or generic bonds. Some of these bonds in actuality may not be issued by any agency, or they may not be actively traded, although bonds with similar characteristics are available. For portfolios of equities it may be the case that the manager of a large fund can invest in all the stocks in the index in proportion to the weights they carry in the index. With this asset allocation the portfolio will perform exactly like the index.

Managers of index funds face significant challenges in matching an index. First, there is the very large number of instruments they must deal with. Second, the purchase or sale of securities by an index fund incurs transaction costs, while the calculation of index returns ignores these costs. Third, indices usually assume that coupon payments during a month are immediately re-invested in the index. (Such indices are called *fully invested*.) An index fund manager, on the other hand, has to identify appropriate asset purchases with the coupon payments, and pay transaction costs for these investments. Finally, managers of large portfolios face liquidity risk in purchasing securities from the market represented by the index. Even if the index does not contain illiquid securities in its composition, the price of actively traded securities may carry a liquidity premium when the manager of a large fund needs to add or drop them from the portfolio. To address the complexities involved in structuring indexed portfolios we turn to optimization models.

7.3   Indexation Models

There are two distinct modeling approaches for creating index funds, which we will call (i) *structural* (ii) and *co-movements based*. In a structural approach the index fund is created so that it contains risk factors similar to those in the index. An approach based on security co-movements creates a portfolio so that its response to the various risk factors is similar to that of the index, although the actual risk contents may differ. The former approach is more mechanistic; it is also called the *cell* approach or the *linear programming* approach. An approach based on co-movements views the target index as a random liability and aims to replicate the response of this liability to the various risk factors when they are aggregated together. An integrative model is used to select securities with returns that mimic the target liability returns under several scenarios. The scenario optimization models in Chapter 5 can then be applied.

7.3.1   A structural model for index funds

We assume that K securities from the universe of securities in which we can invest, or the set of risk factors $\mathcal{K}$ constitute the index, and each carries a normalized weight w_j, $j \in \mathcal{K}$ in the index representation. We need to determine the holdings x_i of securities in the indexed portfolio from the universe U. These holdings are in percentage of total assets. In a structural approach the universe of available securities is classified into cells according to the characteristics that affect returns. A cell may be created for different maturity ranges, sectors, coupon ranges, credit ratings, and features such as call, sinking fund, conversion or other provisions. The weights of bonds in the index that belong to each cell j are readily calculated from the index data as $\sum_{c \in \text{cell } j} w_c$. Since a security in the index may belong to multiple cells – for instance, to the cell of securities with medium maturity, and to the cell of securities of the telecommunications sector – these cell weights must be normalized to add up to one. For simplicity we assume that there are as many cells as securities in the index so that the weight on the kth cell is w_k. An indicator function δ is now introduced as follows:

$$\delta_{ij} = \begin{cases} 1 & \text{if bond } i \text{ belongs to the } j\text{th cell,} \\ 0 & \text{otherwise.} \end{cases} \qquad (7.3)$$

The following linear program creates a portfolio with a structure similar to the index.

Model 7.3.1 Linear program for index funds

$$\text{Maximize} \quad F(x) \qquad (7.4)$$

$$\text{subject to} \quad \sum_{i=1}^{n} \delta_{ij} x_i = w_j, \text{ for all } j \in \mathcal{K}, \qquad (7.5)$$

$$\sum_{i=1}^{n} x_i = 1, \qquad (7.6)$$

$$x \in X. \qquad (7.7)$$

The set X denotes the set of feasible solutions which may be restricted by additional constraints such as diversification constraints, limits on portfolio turnover, the requirement that the duration of the index fund should be equal to the duration of the index, and so on, and it encompasses the nonnegativity constraints $x \geq 0$. For the choice of an objective function $F(x)$ see the discussion following the portfolio immunization Model 4.3.1. In the absence of constraints in a form other than $x \geq 0$ the optimal solution of the model will have $K + 1$ nonzero holdings at optimality, x_i^*, corresponding to the $K+1$ equality constraints in the model. When K is large the resulting index fund consists of a large number of small holdings, thus increasing management costs. A typical practical approach for eliminating this problem is to impose equality constraints for cells with weight w_j greater than some user-specified threshold. Upper and lower bounds on the holdings in any security may also be imposed to limit very small positions that imply higher management costs, and very large positions with significant exposure to security specific risks and perhaps liquidity risk. Section 4.2.4 showed how such constraints can be incorporated.

7.3.2   A model for index funds based on co-movements

A model based on co-movements views both the index return and the returns of securities in the set U as uncertain, conditioned on the scenario set Ω. The tracking error of the portfolio returns against the index is given by

$$R_\epsilon(x; w, \tilde{r}) = R(x; \tilde{r}) - R_I(w; \tilde{r}). \qquad (7.8)$$

In the discrete scenario setting, and using the linear expression for portfolio and index returns, we have

$$R_\epsilon(x; w, r^l) = \sum_{i=1}^{n} r_i^l x_i - R_I(w; r^l). \tag{7.9}$$

We introduce variables y_+^l and y_-^l to measure, respectively, the positive and negative deviations of the portfolio return from the index return (see Section 5.3). The tracking error is written as

$$R_\epsilon(x; w, r^l) = y_+^l - y_-^l \tag{7.10}$$

where

$$y_+^l = \max[0, \sum_{i=1}^{n} r_i^l x_i - R_I(w, r^l)], \tag{7.11}$$

$$y_-^l = \max[0, R_I(w, r^l) - \sum_{i=1}^{n} r_i^l x_i]. \tag{7.12}$$

y_+^l is nonzero in those scenarios when the portfolio outperforms the index and y_-^l is nonzero when the portfolio underperforms the index. With these definitions of y_+^l and y_-^l we may use the scenario optimization models of Chapter 5 to develop index funds. For instance, the tracking Model 5.3.5 is formulated using the notation of this section as follows.

Model 7.3.2 Tracking model for index funds

$$\text{Maximize} \quad \sum_{i=1}^{n} \bar{r}_i x_i \tag{7.13}$$

$$\text{subject to} \quad \sum_{i=1}^{n} r_i^l x_i - R_I(w, r^l) \geq -\epsilon, \text{ for all } l \in \Omega, \tag{7.14}$$

$$\sum_{i=1}^{n} x_i = 1, \tag{7.15}$$

$$x \in X. \tag{7.16}$$

Similarly we can develop models to minimize the expected downside tracking error subject to a target return (see Model 5.4.1), or to trade off upside potential against downside risk (see Model 5.7.1). None of these models is, strictly speaking, a tracking model as they favor upside deviations. A tracking model is obtained as a modification of Model 5.3.5 to limit both upside and downside deviations in the following linear programming form.

Model 7.3.3 Two-sided tracking model for index funds

$$\text{Maximize} \quad \sum_{i=1}^{n} \bar{r}_i x_i \tag{7.17}$$

$$\text{subject to} \quad -\epsilon \leq \sum_{i=1}^{n} r_i^l x_i - R_I(w, r^l) \leq \epsilon, \quad \text{for all } l \in \Omega, \tag{7.18}$$

$$\sum_{i=1}^{n} x_i = 1, \tag{7.19}$$

$$x \in X. \tag{7.20}$$

7.4   Models for International Index Funds

The models in the previous section focus on the problem of picking bonds from a given universe to create an index fund. Quite often indices are composite indices of other indices. There is then a need to determine the broad breakdown of the fund among the constituent indices before picking specific bonds. Such a case arises in the passive management of global portfolios using an indexation strategy. For example, the JP Morgan Government Bond Index Broad (GBI Broad) tracks the trends in the government bond markets in 18 countries. Each one of these countries has its own index, and the GBI Broad is a composite index of these 18 indices. Chapters 10 and 11 discuss the tracking of composite indices of government and corporate bonds. The problem of choosing among broad indices, usually over relatively long horizons, is the strategic asset allocation problem. The tactical asset allocation problem deals with the more immediate task of investing in specific securities so that each index is closely tracked for short time horizons.

When the index of indices refers to a single market the portfolio selection model may be built directly on the universe of the bonds in all sub-indices. When dealing with an international index fund the problem is more complex. The portfolio model must consider exchange rate movements in addition to the trends of the sub-indices. In this section we develop models for tracking global indices. These models can also be used to track composite indices in a local market taking into account the distinctive risk characteristics of each sub-index. The exchange rates will be equal to one in such cases, but other risk factors are introduced to capture the uncertainty of the sub-indices. For instance, an index of corporate bonds may consist of sub-indices for different rating categories or different industrial sectors, and each sub-index has unique credit risk characteristics. Section 7.5 and Chapter 11 describe the application of indexation models to the management of portfolios of corporate bonds. Exchange rate risk is not present – for investors denominated in the base currency – in this application, but credit risk becomes a dominant risk factor.

7.4.1   Creating a global index

Consider a broad international index of K markets, each of which has a large number of available securities in which we can invest. Each market presents its own risk characteristics, and the index summarizing the changes of each market $j \in \mathcal{K}$ consists of securities in a representative sample U_j of securities available in the jth market. The sample is selected from the universe of available bonds Ψ_j and we assume, for simplicity, that all samples are of the same size, n. For each security $i = 1, 2, \ldots, n$, in the representative set $\mathcal{U}_j$ the index specifies its weight w_{ij}. It is usually the case that these weights reflect the capitalization structure of the universe set Ω_j, with bonds that have characteristics identical or similar to the ith bond. The global index assigns proportional weights, γ_j, to each country index based on the market value of each country index. For instance, Figure 7.1 shows the normalized weights γ_j in the 18 countries that compose the GBI Broad.

In practice, the sets Ψ_j may consist of thousands or even hundreds of thousands of bonds differing by issuer, issue data, maturity date, coupon payments, etc. The representative sets U_j consist of a hundred or so representative securities. The process for constructing the global index from the country indices is illustrated in Figure 7.2.

The problem facing an index fund manager is to determine the fraction of the portfolio value invested in each of the K markets, and to pick specific bonds from each market Ψ_j to add to the portfolio. These decisions can be made in two steps. First, the strategic decision in setting the exposure of the portfolio to each market must be made. Then suitable bonds are identified in each market to construct the country-specific portfolio. This portfolio has to track the country-specific index, and these tactical decisions can also be addressed using a tracking model. The time horizons of the two models might differ however. Strategic decisions are usually made with a long time horizon, several months or even years. Bond picking decisions might have short

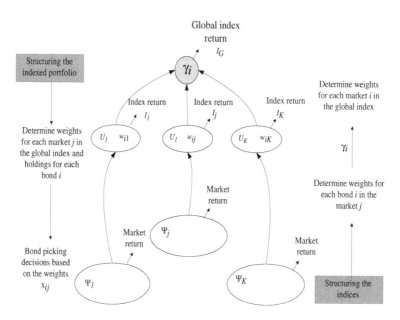

Figure 7.2: A bottom-up process for structuring the market indices and a top-down approach for structuring an indexed portfolio.

horizons, such as weeks or months.

We denote the portfolio weights as a proportion of total assets allocated to the index of each country $j \in \mathcal{K}$, by z_j, and the proportional holdings in bond $i \in U$, in each country by x_{ij}. The strategic asset allocation model determines optimal weights z_j^*, and the bond picking model specifies optimal holdings such that $\sum_{i=1}^n x_{ij}^* = z_j^*$, for all $j \in \mathcal{K}$. An integrated model determines jointly the optimal holdings x_{ij}^* and weights z_i^*. We develop first an integrated model for jointly determining the strategic and tactical decisions, and then develop the optimization models for solving separately the problem of strategic asset allocation among indices, and the tactical problem of bond picking in each market. The modeling process for structuring the indexed portfolios is also illustrated in Figure 7.2.

7.4.2   Integrated indexation models

We use r_{ij}^l to denote the return of the ith bond in the jth currency in scenario l. This is the local return for investors denominated in the jth currency, which is their domestic market. This return will usually differ from the return of the security when viewed by investors denominated in a currency other than j. To get the return for the latter group of investors we scale the local return r_{ij}^l by the exchange rate appreciation or depreciation of the jth market currency against their base currency. The exchange rate appreciation is the ratio of the exchange rate E_j^l of currency j against the base currency in scenario l, to the current exchange rate E_j^0, i.e., $e_j^l = E_j^l / E_j^0$. We can think of e_j^l as the total return of currency j.

The return of the international composite index in the base currency is given by

$$R_I(\gamma; r^l) = \sum_{j=1}^K e_j^l \gamma_j R_j(w; r^l), \tag{7.21}$$

where $R_j(w; r^l) = \sum_{i=1}^n w_{ij} r_{ij}^l$ is the return of the index of the jth market as measured in the local currency, and γ_j are the proportional weights of each country index in the global index.

The return of the portfolio in the base currency is given by

$$R(x; r^l) = \sum_{j=1}^{K} e_j^l R_{pj}(x; r^l), \tag{7.22}$$

where

$$R_{pj}(x; r^l) = \sum_{i=1}^{n} r_{ij}^l x_{ij} \tag{7.23}$$

is the portfolio local return in the jth market.

With this notation we can now define the following tracking model, akin to Model 7.3.3. The model maximizes the expected portfolio return in the base currency while it restricts the tracking error to be within $\pm\epsilon$.

Model 7.4.1 Integrated international indexation model

$$\text{Maximize} \quad \sum_{l\in\Omega} p^l \sum_{j=1}^{K} e_j^l R_{pj}(x; r^l) \tag{7.24}$$

$$\text{subject to} \quad -\epsilon \leq \sum_{j=1}^{K} e_j^l R_{pj}(x; r^l) - R_I(\gamma, r^l) \leq \epsilon,$$

$$\text{for all } l \in \Omega, \tag{7.25}$$

$$\sum_{j=1}^{K} \sum_{i=1}^{n} x_{ij} = 1, \tag{7.26}$$

$$x \in X. \tag{7.27}$$

If the solution of this model is denoted by x^* we can estimate the exposure of the optimal portfolio to the jth currency by $z_j^* = \sum_{i=1}^{n} x_{ij}^*$.

7.4.3 Nonintegrated models

We now develop two models that address separately the strategic asset allocation and the tactical asset allocation (i.e., the bond picking) problem. These models better represent the hierarchical operations of international portfolio managers that usually determine first their currency exposure, and then determine the portfolio holdings in each currency. We will see, however, that the integrated model produces results superior to those of the nonintegrated models.

The strategic asset allocation model

The return of a portfolio with normalized weights z_j in the jth currency takes the following scenario values, when measured with respect to the base currency:

$$R(z; R_{pj}(w; r^l)) = \sum_{j=1}^{K} e_j^l R_{pj}(w; r^l) z_j = \sum_{j=1}^{K} e_j^l \left(\sum_{i=1}^{n} w_{ij} r_{ij}^l \right) z_j. \tag{7.28}$$

Note that at the strategic level the return in each base currency is the index return and not the portfolio return, and hence the use of weights w_{ij} in computing the scenario returns in each market. The strategic asset allocation model determines only the optimal normalized holdings in each market $z^* = (z_j^*)_{j=1}^{K}$ through the following model.

Model 7.4.2 Strategic model for international index funds

$$\text{Maximize} \quad \sum_{l \in \Omega} p^l \sum_{j=1}^{K} e_j^l R_{pj}(w; r^l) z_j \tag{7.29}$$

$$\text{subject to} \quad -\epsilon \leq \sum_{j=1}^{K} e_j^l R_j(w; r^l) z_j - R_I(\gamma; r^l) \leq \epsilon,$$

$$\text{for all } l \in \Omega, \tag{7.30}$$

$$\sum_{j=1}^{K} z_j = 1, \tag{7.31}$$

$$z \geq 0. \tag{7.32}$$

The tactical bond picking model

Having obtained the optimal currency weights $(z_j^*)_{j=1}^{K}$ by solving Model 7.4.2 we can now use the following models to solve the bond picking problem for each constituent index. These models determine the optimal weights $(x_{ij}^*)_{i=1}^{n}$ for bond holdings in each currency $j \in \mathcal{K}$, such that the optimal currency weights are preserved.

Model 7.4.3 Tactical model for international index funds

For each $j = 1, 2, \ldots, K$, solve:

$$\text{Maximize} \quad \sum_{l \in \Omega} p^l R_{pj}(x; r^l) \tag{7.33}$$

$$\text{subject to} \quad -\epsilon \leq R_{pj}(x; r^l) - R_j(w; r^l) \leq \epsilon,$$

$$\text{for all } l \in \Omega, \tag{7.34}$$

$$\sum_{i=1}^{n} x_{ij} = z_j^*, \tag{7.35}$$

$$x \in X. \tag{7.36}$$

From Model 7.4.2, equation (7.31), we have that the weights in the K markets, z_j, add up to one, and it follows from (7.35) that $\sum_{j=1}^{K} \sum_{i=1}^{n} x_{ij}^* = 1$.

7.4.4   Operational model

The models in this section can be formulated in a way that accounts for the cost of transactions in rebalancing a portfolio, and that allows for cash infusion or withdrawal, liquidity and diversification constraints, and other operational considerations. In order to incorporate these practical issues the model variables are expressed not in percentages of total wealth, as was done above, but in face value. This choice of units is necessary in order to model cash infusion or withdrawal. Constraints imposed due to trading liquidity considerations also require the modeling of face values. For instance, allocating the total wealth to a given market may not affect prices if the total portfolio value is small, but it may substantially affect prices for large portfolio values. (This was part of the problem facing Long-Term Capital Management when it had to unwind a very large position under extreme conditions.) We formulate here a model for building international index funds that incorporates operational constraints. The decision variables are redefined in terms of face values, instead of as proportions of total assets, and some additional definitions are introduced:

x_{ij}, face value invested in security i in the jth currency.

y_{ij}, face value sold of security i in the jth currency.

z_{ij}, face value of security i in the jth currency that remains as inventory in the indexed portfolio.

v^+, risk-free investment (i.e., cash) in the base currency.

Various constants and model parameters are also needed:

b_{0ij} face value of initial inventory of security i in the jth currency.

v_0 initial holdings in the risk-free asset (cash) in the base currency.

P^b_{0ij} current bid price of security i in the jth currency.

P^a_{0ij} current ask price of security i in the jth currency.

The difference between bid and ask prices reflects liquidity premia and transaction costs. In a highly liquid market these two prices differ only by the cost of the transaction. For illiquid securities, or for very large transactions, the gap between the bid and ask prices may widen.

With the above definitions we can now develop the model. The initial value of the portfolio is given by

$$V_0 = v_0 + \sum_{j=1}^{K} E_j^0 \sum_{i=1}^{n} P^b_{0ij} b_{0ij}. \tag{7.37}$$

An *inventory balance* equation gives the face value of the inventory in bond i in the jth currency as a function of the investment and sale decisions:

$$z_{ij} = b_{0ij} + x_{ij} - y_{ij}, \text{ for all } i \in U, \text{ and for all } j \in K. \tag{7.38}$$

Similarly, a *cashflow balance* equation gives the amount invested in the risk-free asset (i.e., cash) in the base currency, as a function of the initial available cash v_0; any cash generated from security sales at the given bid prices; and any cash spent for investments at the given ask prices:

$$v^+ = v_0 + \sum_{j=1}^{K} E_j^0 \left(\sum_{i=1}^{n} P^b_{0ij} y_{ij} - \sum_{i=1}^{n} P^a_{0ij} x_{ij} \right). \tag{7.39}$$

With these definitions the value of the portfolio at the end of the holding period in scenario $l \in \Omega$ is given by

$$V_T^l = (1 + r_{fT}^l) v^+ + \sum_{j=1}^{K} E_j^l \sum_{i=1}^{n} (1 + r_{ij}^l) P^b_{0ij} z_{ij}, \tag{7.40}$$

where r_{fT}^l is the risk-free rate of return of the base currency during the holding period T in scenario l.

The rate of return for the portfolio is then given by

$$R^l(x, y, z, v^+; r^l) = \frac{V_T^l - V_0}{V_0}. \tag{7.41}$$

The following model determines an optimal index fund taking into account differences in the bid-ask prices and allowing for risk-free investments in cash.

Model 7.4.4 Operational model for index funds

Maximize $\quad \sum_{l \in \Omega} p^l R^l(x, y, z, v^+; r^l)$ $\hfill$ (7.42)

subject to $\hfill z_{ij} - x_{ij} + y_{ij} = b_{0ij},$

$\hfill \text{for all } i \in U, \ j \in \mathcal{K},$ $\hfill$ (7.43)

$$\sum_{j=1}^{K} E_j^0 \left(\sum_{i=1}^{n} P_{0ij}^a x_{ij} \right) + v^+ - \sum_{j=1}^{K} E_j^0 \left(\sum_{i=1}^{n} P_{0ij}^b y_{ij} \right) = v_0 \qquad (7.44)$$

$\hfill -\epsilon \le R^l(x, y, z; r^l) - R_I(\gamma; r^l) \le \epsilon,$

$\hfill \text{for all } l \in \Omega,$ $\hfill$ (7.45)

$\hfill x, y, z, v^+ \ge 0.$ $\hfill$ (7.46)

Equation (7.43) shows the inventory balance constraints for all securities i in all currencies j. Equation (7.44) is the cashflow balance constraint. Inequalities (7.45) are the tracking constraints restricting the deviations of the indexed portfolio from the target index to be within $\pm\epsilon$. Bounds (7.46) restrict all variables to be nonnegative so that short sales are not allowed.

This model takes into account transaction costs in revising an existing portfolio as reflected in the spread between bid and ask prices. We can also add constraints to restrict holding in any one security to a fraction α of the total value of the portfolio.

$$E_j^0 P_{0ij}^b z_{ij} \le \alpha \left(\sum_{j=1}^{K} E_j^0 \sum_{i=1}^{n} P_{0ij}^b z_{ij} \right), \text{ for all } i \in U, \ j \in \mathcal{K}. \qquad (7.47)$$

Such constraints are useful for diversification purposes. They also serve to limit liquidity risk by prohibiting large positions in any single bond, as for very large funds such positions may carry a liquidity premium.

7.5 Models for Corporate Bond Index Funds

The models in the previous section are also applicable, with some modifications, to problems of tracking corporate bond indices. Currency risk, which is of central concern to international portfolio managers, gives way to credit risk, which is a major source of risk for managers of corporate assets. We discuss here the key components of the models for tracking corporate bond indices.

Managing funds to track a corporate bond index is a challenging task for two reasons. First, the manager has to cope with the diverse sources of risk inherent in the corporate bond market. Second, the number of securities in the index is much larger (over 1,000 for the Merrill Lynch index we consider in Chapter 11) and it is prohibitively expensive to have holdings in all securities in the index.

The major risk factors of corporate bonds are fixed-income market risk (Definition 2.2.3) and credit risk (Definition 2.2.7). In particular, corporate bond prices are affected by the following events:

1. Changes in the term structure of risk-free rates,

2. changes in the term structure of credit spreads,

3. changes in the ratings of the bonds,

4. the likelihood that a bond will go into default,

5. the amount recovered if a bond goes into default.

Scenarios of holding period returns can be generated using Monte Carlo simulation of these risk factors (see Chapter 11), and thus provide the input data for optimization models to track corporate bond indices. The problem is similar to that of managing international index funds, and the models in Section 7.4 serve as the basis for our discussion. First, we note that for investors denominated in the currency of the corporate bond index there is no exchange rate risk. For other investors there is only one exchange risk factor, namely, risk due to exchange rate fluctuations of the index currency against the investor's currency. For simplicity we assume the same currency for the index and the investor.

The corporate bond index is an index of sub-indices. Speicifically, each rating class (AAA, BBB, etc.) is a sub-index of the market. Following Model 7.4.1 we use $j \in \mathcal{K}$, to denote credit rating classes, and the exchange rate appreciation e_j^l is set identically equal to one. The model is then applicable to the management of corporate bond portfolios.

It is common practice for corporate bond portfolio managers – as in the case of international portfolio managers – to separate the strategic from the tactical asset allocation decisions. Strategic asset allocation determines the broad allocation of assets among asset classes such as credit ratings, industrial sectors, or maturity ranges, or any combination of these attributes. Tactical asset allocation will then pick specific bonds from each asset class so that the relevant sub-index is tracked. Models 7.4.2 and 7.4.3 are applicable using, once more, $j \in \mathcal{K}$, to denote the credit rating classes and setting the appropriate exchange rate appreciation. Chapter 11 discusses a case study for the management of corporate bonds using an index fund strategy, and Section 11.5 gives detailed formulations of the models.

7.6   Stochastic Programming for Index Funds

We consider now the optimization of dynamic strategies for index tracking using stochastic programming models. The model is developed on an event tree, assuming multiple trading dates. Multiple states of the index are possible at each trading date. For each state we have available a set of bid and ask prices for all securities in the index – or returns of all sub-indices in a composite index – and the composition of the index. Thus state-dependent values of index returns can be calculated. Following the previous sections of this chapter we develop a model to optimize the portfolio weights so that the portfolio return tracks the index return. However, in the multi-period optimization framework of this section it is possible to rebalance the portfolio at each trading date, conditioned on the observed state. This model reflects more accurately the problem confronting index fund managers, who must rebalance their portfolio as more information arrives with the objective of staying close to the index. We will also see that the stochastic programming models perform better, in ex post testing using out-of-sample data, for several real-world applications.

7.6.1   Notation

In order to develop the dynamic portfolio optimization models we need to introduce variables for portfolio rebalancing at each trading date and for each state. The event tree in Figure 7.3 illustrates three trading dates with multiple states at each trading date after $t = 0$, i.e., today. The security and the index returns are indexed by state $s \in \Sigma_t$ at each trading date t. Note the difference from the indexation models of the previous sections when security and index returns were indexed by scenario $l \in \Omega$, using a linear scenario structure without utilizing any information to arrive at intermediate time periods before the horizon. The time-dependent information about states from $t = 0$ to T is necessary for modeling portfolio rebalancing decisions. An event tree models precisely the arrival of new information.

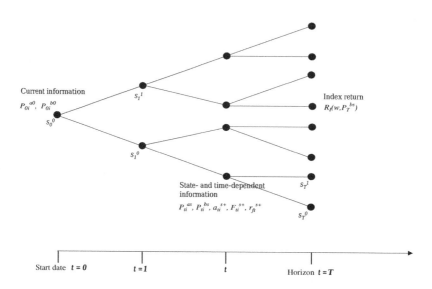

Figure 7.3: Event tree with three trading dates and the random variables used in a stochastic programming model for index funds.

For each trading date and for each state, we define variables to represent the buying and selling of securities, investments in the risk-free asset, and holdings of securities in the indexed portfolio. Investment decisions are in units of face value. The following variables are used:

x_{ti}^s, face value invested in security i at period t in state s.

y_{ti}^s, face value sold of security i at period t in state s.

z_{ti}^s, face value of security i that remains as inventory in the indexed portfolio at period t in state s.

v_t^{+s}, cash invested in the risk-free rate at period t in state s.

We also need to model the dynamics of securities in the index on the event tree. We specifically need to know, at a given trading date t and state s, the bid and ask prices of securities in the index, and the cashflows generated at the next trading date at successor state s^+. (The cashflows may be due to coupon payments, exercise of call options for callable bonds, default for corporate bonds, prepayments for mortgage securities, etc.) The following parameters are used (see also Section 6.2.1 on the notation for dynamic models):

$\alpha_{ti}^{s^+}$ *amortization factor* for security i from state s at period t to the successor state s^+ at period $t+1$.

$F_{ti}^{s^+}$ *cashflow* for security i, indicating cash generated by security i from t to $t+1$ per unit face value, due to scheduled dividend or coupon payments and exercise of any embedded options.

P_{ti}^{as} ask price of security i at period t in state s.

P_{ti}^{bs} bid price of security i at period t in state s.

$r_{ft}^{s^+}$ rate of return of the risk-free asset held from t to $t+1$. This value depends on the successor state s^+ reached at $t+1$ from state s at t.

The initial conditions for the portfolio at $t = 0$ are specified by the parameters:

b_{0i} face value of initial holding of security i.

v_0 initial holdings in the risk-free asset.

7.6.2   Model formulation

The stochastic programming model for index tracking has two basic sets of constraints. One expresses cashflow accounting for the risk-free asset, i.e., cash, and the other is an inventory balance equation for each security in the indexed portfolio at all trading dates and for all states. (See Figure 6.9 illustrating the flow of cash and security inventory in a more general setting of stochastic programming for dynamic portfolio strategies.) We formulate the components of the model for $t = 0$ and for future trading dates $0 < t < T$. In the terminology of stochastic programming we have the first-stage problem at $t = 0$, and the t-stage problem models the recourse decisions.

First-stage constraints

At the first stage (i.e., at $t = 0$) all prices are known with certainty. We also know the portfolio composition, and the portfolio value is calculated by

$$V_0 = v_0 + \sum_{i=1}^{n} P_{0i}^{b0} b_{0i}. \tag{7.48}$$

For each asset class $i \in U$ in the portfolio we have an *inventory balance constraint*

$$z_{0i}^0 = b_{0i} + x_{0i}^0 - y_{0i}^0. \tag{7.49}$$

The *cashflow balance equation* specifies that the original endowment in the riskless asset, plus any proceeds from liquidating part of the existing portfolio, equals the amount invested in the purchase of new securities plus the amount invested in the riskless asset:

$$\sum_{i=1}^{n} P_{0i}^{b0} y_{0i}^0 + v_0 = \sum_{i=1}^{n} P_{0i}^{a0} x_{0i}^0 + v_0^{+0}. \tag{7.50}$$

Time-staged constraints

Decisions made at future trading dates $t = 1, 2, \ldots, T$, are conditioned on the state $s \in \Sigma_t$ at every date. We have a set of constraints for each state at each time period. These decisions also depend on the investment decisions made at the previous trading date $t - 1$ at predecessor state s^-.

Inventory balance equations constrain the amount of each security sold or remaining in the portfolio to be equal to the outstanding amount of face value carried over from the previous trading date, plus any amount purchased at the current trading date. There is one constraint for each security $i \in U$ and for each state $s \in \Sigma_t$:

$$z_{ti}^s = z_{(t-1)i}^{s^-} + x_{ti}^s - y_{ti}^s. \tag{7.51}$$

When dealing with instruments with embedded options – such as callable bonds that may be called, corporate bonds that may default, or mortgage securities that may prepay – we need to introduce amortization factors reflecting the exercise of the options. The asset inventory balance equation takes the form

$$z_{ti}^s = \alpha_{(t-1)i}^s z_{(t-1)i}^{s^-} + x_{ti}^s - y_{ti}^s, \text{ for all } i \in U, \ s \in \Sigma_t. \tag{7.52}$$

Cashflow balance requires that the amount invested in the purchase of new securities and in the risk-free asset is equal to the income generated by the existing portfolio during the holding period, plus any cash generated from sales and cash reinvested at the previous period at predecessor state s^-. There is one constraint for each state $s \in \Sigma_t$

$$\sum_{i=1}^{n} F_{(t-1)i}^{s} z_{(t-1)i}^{s^-} + \sum_{i=1}^{n} P_{ti}^{bs} y_{ti}^{s} + (1 + r_{f(t-1)}^{s}) v_{t-1}^{+s^-}$$

$$= \sum_{i=1}^{n} P_{ti}^{as} x_{ti}^{s} + v_{t}^{+s}. \tag{7.53}$$

End-of-horizon constraints

At the end of the planning horizon we evaluate the value of the portfolio at each state $s \in \Sigma_T$ and restrict its deviations from the corresponding value of the index. The portfolio value will depend on the holdings in different asset classes, including cash, and the state $s \in \Sigma_T$. It is given by

$$V_T^{s}(z, v^+; P_T^{bs}) = v_T^{+s} + \sum_{i=1}^{n} P_{Ti}^{bs} z_{Ti}^{s}. \tag{7.54}$$

Similarly, if we invest an amount V_0 in the index, its value at the end of the horizon will be given by

$$V_I^{s}(w; P_T^{bs}) = V_0(1 + R_I(w; r_T^{s})), \tag{7.55}$$

where $r_T^{s} = (r_{Ti}^{s})_{i=1}^{n}$ is the vector rate of return of the securities, where

$$r_{Ti}^{s} = \frac{P_{Ti}^{bs} - P_{0i}^{b0}}{P_{0i}^{b0}}. \tag{7.56}$$

The rate of return of the portfolio is given by

$$R^{s}(x, y, z, v^+; P_T^{bs}) = \frac{V_T^{s} - V_0}{V_0}, \tag{7.57}$$

and the following model maximizes the expected rate of return of the portfolio, while restricting its value to stay close to the index value.

Model 7.6.1 Stochastic programming for index funds

$$\text{Maximize} \quad \sum_{s \in \Sigma_T} p^s R^s(x, y, z, v^+; P_T^{bs}) \tag{7.58}$$

$$\text{subject to} \qquad z_{0i}^0 = b_{0i} + x_{0i}^0 - y_{0i}^0,$$
$$\text{for all } i \in U, \tag{7.59}$$

$$\sum_{i=1}^n P_{0i}^{b0} y_{0i}^0 + v_0 = v_0^{+0} + \sum_{i=1}^n P_{0i}^{a0} x_{0i}^0, \tag{7.60}$$

$$z_{ti}^s = z_{(t-1)i}^{s^-} + x_{ti}^s - y_{ti}^s,$$
$$\text{for all } t \in T, s \in \Sigma_t, i \in U, \tag{7.61}$$

$$\sum_{i=1}^n F_{(t-1)i}^s z_{(t-1)i}^{s^-} + \sum_{i=1}^n P_{ti}^{bs} y_{ti}^s + (1 + r_{f(t-1)}^s) v_{t-1}^{+s^-}$$

$$= \sum_{i=1}^n P_{ti}^{as} x_{ti}^s + v_t^{+s},$$
$$\text{for all } t \in T, s \in \Sigma_t, i \in U, \tag{7.62}$$

$$-\epsilon \le V_T^s(z, v^+; P_T^{bs}) - V_I^s(w; P_T^{bs}) \le \epsilon,$$
$$\text{for all } s \in \Sigma_T, \tag{7.63}$$

$$x, y, z, v^+ \ge 0. \tag{7.64}$$

Note that the tracking constraint (7.63) is imposed only for the last time period T. The portfolio value will stay within $\pm \epsilon$ of the index value at the end of the horizon, but there is no assurance that it will stay close to the index at other trading dates. This model can be extended by imposing tracking constraints for other trading dates.

7.7 Applications of Indexation Models

The models of the previous sections are now applied to problems of managing indexed funds in diverse settings: (i) tracking an international government bond index; (ii) tracking a corporate bond index; (iii) creating enhanced index funds; (iv) tracking an index of mortgage-backed securities; and (v) tracking an index of callable bonds. The validation of the models is based on the ex post analysis of the performance of portfolios developed using the models. Of course we expect that an "optimal" portfolio will perform well under the scenarios that were input in the modeling process. In this section, however, we study the performance of the indexed portfolios obtained by optimization models using simulated scenarios, under the realized market returns.

These applications serve many purposes: First, through the ex post testing in diverse settings it is demonstrated that the models in this chapter are effective tools for supporting portfolio managers of index funds.

Second, it is shown – in the application to international government bond indexation – that the integrative models generate portfolios that dominate the portfolios obtained using nonintegrated approaches.

Third, it is shown – in the application to corporate bond indexation – that good tracking performance can be achieved by a strategic model that makes asset allocation decisions among sub-indices. However, extra value may be generated with tactical models that address bond picking decisions in an integrated fashion with the tactical asset allocation decision. It is also shown that in the context of tracking government bond indices, small corporate bond holdings can lead to superior risk return characteristics.

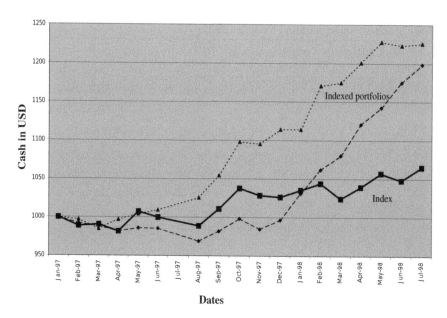

Figure 7.4: Value of a 1,000USD investment in a composite international government bond index and in indexed portfolios.

Fourth, it is shown – in the applications to indexation of mortgage-backed securities and callable bonds – that stochastic programming models generate, ex post, performance superior to the single-period models.

Testing of the models proceeds along the following general lines. Using data available before the starting date of the backtesting period, say the first day of month X, we calibrate appropriate Monte Carlo simulation models, generate scenarios of security returns, exchange rates, and index returns, and run the indexation model under investigation to select a tracking portfolio. We then move our clock a month forward to the 1st of month X+1, at which time we know the precise index return, security returns, and exchange rates. We can therefore determine the performance of our tracking portfolio and the tracking error. This completes one step of the backtest. We then use the data available up to month X+1 to recalibrate the Monte Carlo simulation models, generate new scenarios, and repeat the exercise. The process is repeated until the last month for which we have data. In most cases the experiments are repeated, in monthly steps, over a period of a few years.

7.7.1   Tracking an international government bond index

Using the Salomon Brothers G7 index we create an equally weighted composite index consisting of holdings in three major currencies (USD, DEM, and CHF). A single-sided version of the integrated tracking Model 7.4.1, whereby the right inequality in constraint (7.25) was removed, is backtested in tracking this composite index over the period January 1997 to July 1998. Figure 7.4 shows the asset growth of 1,000 USD invested in January 1997 in the index and in portfolios generated using the models. We observe that the model performs well in tracking the volatile index. Calculating the Sharpe ratios we obtain a value of -0.068 for the index and 0.369 for the indexed portfolios. Figure 7.4 shows the results of a single realization of the random index returns, namely the historical realization during the period of the test. In some sense this is the only realization that matters. But how would the portfolio perform under alternative realizations of the random returns? Figure 7.5 illustrates the tracking error of a typical portfolio under

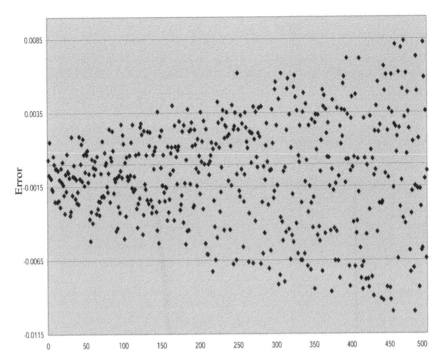

Figure 7.5: Tracking error in annualized basis points of a typical portfolio against the composite index for 500 simulated scenarios of returns and exchange rates.

simulated out-of-sample scenarios. We observe from these simulated data that the tracking error is small, and is limited to 1% (annualized) below the index under worst-case scenarios, while the lead over the index is 2.2% under the most favorable scenario.

To compare the integrated model tested here, to the nonintegrated models of Section 7.4.3, we now develop efficient frontiers – with a mean absolute deviation model – using both the integrated and the nonintegrated models. For the nonintegrated models we first solve the strategic asset allocation model and set the currency exposure to the currency that yields the highest expected return. We then develop the efficient frontiers of portfolios in the three currencies such that the total exposure in each currency is equal to that determined by the strategic asset allocation model. With this hierarchical solution of the models we pick an indexed portfolio that has the highest expected return, which is consistent with the objective function of the integrated tracking model. Figure 7.6 shows the efficient frontiers obtained with both the integrated and the nonintegrated models. Note that integration entails substantial benefits for portfolio managers, by reducing the mean absolute deviation of the portfolio returns while also increasing somewhat the expected return.

A careful inspection of the asset weights, however, reveals that the integrated model generates poorly diversified portfolios. Left without any operational constraints the model would occasionally generate portfolios with holdings up to 99% in bonds in a single currency. When the comparison between the integrated and nonintegrated models is repeated by imposing bounds on the total exposure in a single instrument the efficiency gap of the two models is somewhat reduced. The integrated model with bounds still yields dominating portfolios, and an inspection of the weights shows that the portfolios of the integrated model are now well diversified, similar to the portfolios of the nonintegrated models. In backtesting of the two models we also observe (see Figure 7.6) that the integrated model outperforms the nonintegrated model.

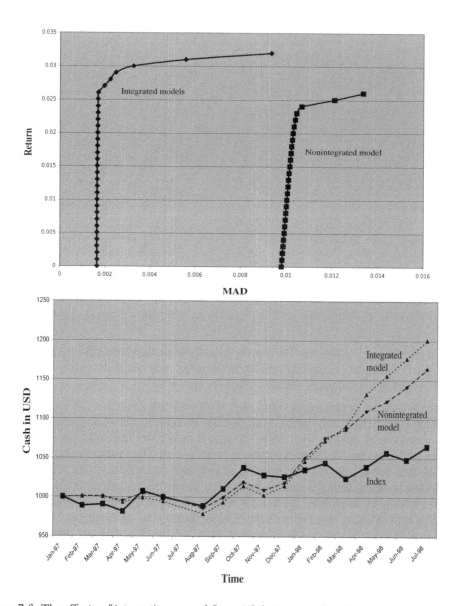

Figure 7.6: The effects of integrating several financial decisions: The efficient frontier generated with the integrated and with the nonintegrated models (top), and value of a 100 USD investment in portfolios generated with the integrated and the nonintegrated models (bottom).

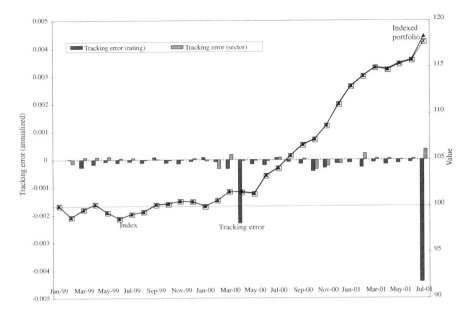

Figure 7.7: Performance of index funds created using broad asset allocation models.

7.7.2   Tracking a corporate bond index

We now apply the models to develop indexed portfolios to track the Merrill Lynch Euro Dollar index of corporate bonds. Similarly to the case of international government bond indexation we study the ex post performance of the model.

We start our experiments on January 31, 1999, and generate three-month holding period return scenarios for all bonds with maturities up to ten years and for each credit rating class using a simulation model calibrated to information available up to end of January only. The tracking model is then used to select a portfolio. Next we move the clock one month forward, at which point (end of February 1999) we know the bond returns and index performance and can therefore calculate the ex post performance of the tracking portfolio. Using the information available up to February 28, 1999, we now repeat the simulation, optimization, and performance analysis. This process is repeated until July 31, 2001. Transaction costs are considered for all trades during the backtesting period. We assume the same transaction cost for all bonds within a rating class: 5 bp for Aaa, 10 bp for Aa, 20 bp for A, and 40 bp for Baa.

We start by creating index funds using a strategic asset allocation model to allocate assets among the sub-indices that comprise the Merrill Lynch Euro Dollar index. (These sub-indices measure the performance of different asset classes of the corporate bond market such as by credit rating category, by industrial sector, by maturity, and for various combinations of these sectors.)

Figure 7.7 shows the value of a 100 USD investment in the index and the portfolio, and the tracking errors of the asset allocation when we define asset classes consisting of securities with the same credit rating. On the same figure we also show the tracking errors when asset classes are defined by industrial sector instead of by rating. Although the portfolio tracks the index very closely, we do not seem to accumulate any extra value. The optimal portfolios have an almost identical structure as the index, and hence the portfolio growth closely follows the index growth.

We apply now the integrated indexation models to create indexed portfolios by picking securities directly from the universe of corporate bonds without any restrictions on tracking the sub-indices. Figure 7.8 shows the growth of 100 USD invested in the index on January 31, 1999 and in the optimal portfolios obtained with the model. The annualized tracking errors for each

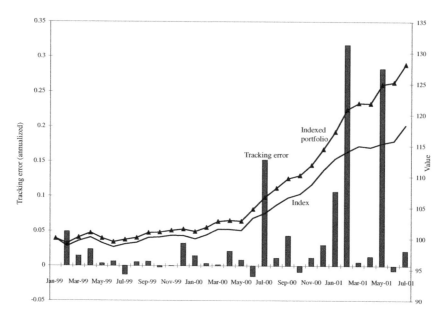

Figure 7.8: Value of a 100 USD investment in the Merrill Lynch Euro Dollar index and in indexed portfolios.

month are also shown. Given the portfolio and index returns during this 30-month period we calculate the historical Sharpe ratio for the tracking portfolio with respect to the index returns as 0.497; this is an encouraging statistic. The tracking errors are small on average and, as expected, the model underperforms by small amounts only in five months. Comparing this with the results shown in Figure 7.7 we observe that an indexed portfolio created using an integrative approach performs better than portfolios that deal with asset allocation and bond picking separately.

7.7.3   Enhanced index funds

We now consider the development of an enhanced index fund to outperform an index, while preserving the key risk characteristics of the index. Specifically, we consider the example of staying within a positive margin from the government bond index by assuming some exposure in the credit risk market. Of course the enhancement in returns results from assuming some extra risks. Perhaps the most significant advance of the integrated models in this chapter is that they allow us to integrate market risk, credit spread, migration, and default risk so that we are now able to take a more holistic view of a manager's portfolio problem. This is demonstrated by creating indexed portfolios of treasury and corporate bonds to track a US Treasury index. We will see that integrating credit-risky bonds in government bond portfolios results in an enhanced index performance.

We focus on the Merrill Lynch US Treasury index. The evolution of the US Treasury index during our backtesting horizon is shown in Figure 7.9. As a first step we track this index by using only US treasury securities. We ignore all bonds with optional payoffs such as callable or putable bonds. A bid-ask spread of 5bp is assumed to capture transaction costs. Figure 7.9 shows the results of the experiment throughout the period. Tracking errors are very small. The historical Sharpe ratio is 0.04 and the model does not pick up extra value from the bond picking. This is expected given the efficiency of the government bond market.

We now expand the universe of bonds to create an enhanced indexed portfolio that also includes the bonds from the Merrill Lynch Euro Dollar index. The broader asset universe offers

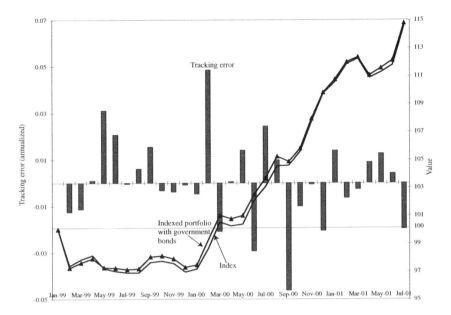

Figure 7.9: Value of a 100 USD investment in the Merrill Lynch US Treasury index and in indexed portfolios constructed using treasury securities only.

additional opportunities which may lead to improved performance, as shown in Figure 7.10, with the ex post analysis of the model. We observe lower and less volatile tracking errors. Including corporate bonds improves the tracking performance, and the Sharpe ratio increases significantly from 0.04 to 0.31. In the optimized portfolio only a small fraction (approximately 5%) is invested in a few corporate bonds (approximately 10). Hence the increased downside risk of corporate bonds is taken into consideration by investing only a small fraction of the value in the risky asset class and, within this class the model invests in a range of corporate bonds in order to minimize the exposure to a single security.

7.7.4   Stochastic programming models for index tracking

In this section we demonstrate, through ex post testing, that stochastic programming models for index funds perform better than the single-period models. The stochastic programming model is expected to perform better than the single-period models when applied on the same, simulated scenarios, since the former model has one more degree of freedom, namely the ability to revise the portfolio before the end of the planning horizon. The tests in this section address the following questions: "Do the stochastic programming models perform well ex post in tracking the market indices?" and "Does a stochastic programming model for tracking an index outperform a single-period model?" The answer to both questions is affirmative, as supported by the empirical results.

In the process we test the indexation models on two additional market indices – an index of mortgage-backed securities and an index of corporate callable bonds. Portfolios generated using the indexation models perform well for these two complex asset classes that contain options (call options for the callable bond market) or embedded options (the option for early repayment of the mortgage loan for the mortgage-backed securities market). The results provide further support to the findings of the previous sections on the effectiveness of the indexation models.

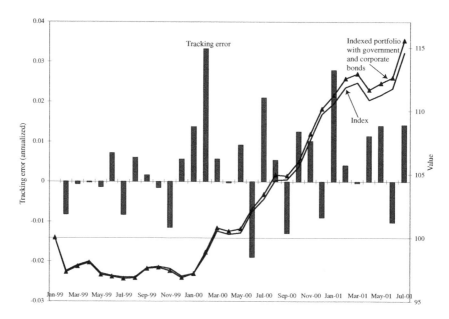

Figure 7.10: Tracking performance of index-plus portfolios that track the Merrill Lynch US Treasury index by investing in both treasury securities and corporate bonds.

Index funds of mortgage-backed securities

Mortgage-backed securities (MBS) are created when mortgages are pooled together and undivided interests or participation in the pool are sold. These securities are described in Section 8.3.5. Understanding the features of MBS is essential in developing scenarios of security returns, although these play no role in the indexation models tested here once the scenarios are somehow generated.

We develop indexed portfolios to track the Salomon Brothers Mortgage index. This index captures the market trends of approximately 300,000 mortgage pools with a market value in excess of $1.5 trillion. This large universe of securities is classified into generic securities characterized by the coupon rate, issuing agency, issuing year, and remaining term. During the period of our backtesting the Salomon Brothers index was comprised of between 118 and 144 generic securities. The indexation models create a portfolio consisting of a small number of generic securities; and then from the available mortgage pool we add securities with characteristics that are identical – or very similar – to the generic securities recommended by the model.

We start our experiments on January 1, 1989, and generate one-month holding period return scenarios for all securities in the index. Security pricing and scenario generation are carried out consistently with the risk-free term structures available on that date, and the model is calibrated to information available up to that day only. The tracking portfolio optimization model is then used to select a portfolio. For any securities that were added or dropped from the portfolio, a transaction fee of 1/16th bp is charged. We then move the clock one month forward, at which point (February 1989) we know the bond returns and index performance and can therefore calculate the ex post performance of the tracking portfolio. Using the updated information available on February 1, 1989, we now repeat the simulation, optimization, and performance analysis. This process is repeated until December 1991.

Figure 7.11 shows the value of a 100 USD investment in the Salomon index during the three-year period 1989–1991, together with the performance of indexed portfolios created using the single-period Model 7.3.2 and a single-sided version of the stochastic programming Model 7.6.1 in which the right inequality of equation (7.63) is relaxed. The tracking errors are small on

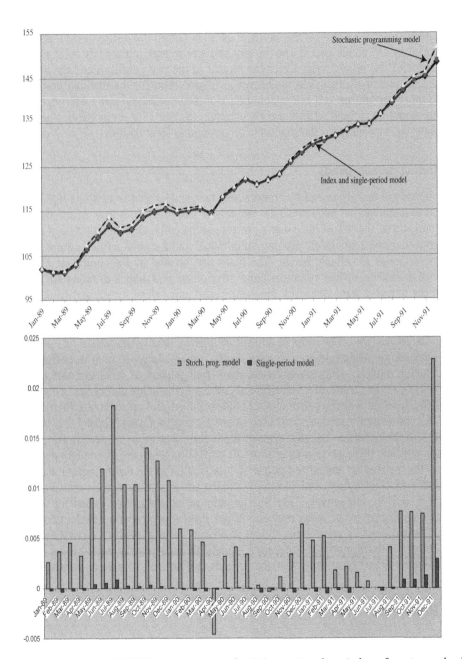

Figure 7.11: Value of a 100 USD investment in the Salomon Brothers index of mortgage-backed securities, and in indexed portfolios developed using a single-period and a stochastic programming model (top), and the tracking errors of the two indexed portfolios developed using a single-period and a stochastic programming model it vis-à-vis the index (bottom).

average for both models, and the stochastic programming model performs better than the single-period model. We observe from this figure that the downside tracking error of the indexed portfolios generated using stochastic programming is less than the tracking error of the indexed portfolios generated by a single-period model.

The index realized an annualized return of 14.05% during the testing period, and the portfolios created by the single-period and the stochastic programming models realized returns of 14.18% and 15.10%, respectively. Given the returns of the two portfolios and the index during this three-year period we calculate the historical Sharpe ratio for the tracking portfolios with respect to the index returns as 0.149 (single-period model portfolios) and 1.071 (stochastic programming model portfolios). These are encouraging statistics for the portfolios generated by both models, but especially for the stochastic programming formulations.

Index funds of callable bonds

Callable bonds are usually issued by corporations or agencies that reserve the right to call the bond prior to maturity (see Section 8.3.2). Holders of these securities face, in addition to fixed-income market risk, the risk of the issuer's exercise of the call option and the risk of default.

We now compare a stochastic programming model and a single-period optimization model in tracking an index of callable bonds. The index was created by selecting a set of 230 securities out of a universe of 600 corporate bonds, excluding junk bonds of rating BBB or lower. Bonds in the universe were issued by financial institutions (18%), credit and banking institutions (17%), telecommunication companies (18%), utilities (17%), department stores (7%), food chains (7%), chemical companies (4%), clothing companies (5%), automobile producers (5%), and other industries (2%). The index of 230 securities was equally weighted.

The backtesting methodology is identical to the methodology we used in testing the mortgage indexation models. Our testing covers the period January 1, 1992 to February 1, 1993. Figure 7.12 shows the growth of a 100 USD investment in the index during the 14-month period of the testing, together with the performance of indexed portfolios created using the single-period Model 7.3.2 and a single-sided version of the stochastic programming Model 7.6.1. We see from this figure that the downside tracking error of the indexed portfolios generated using stochastic programming is less than the tracking error of the portfolios generated by a single-period model.

The index realized an annualized return of 11.63% during the testing period, and the portfolios created by the single-period and the stochastic programming models realized returns of 12.36% and 13.79%, respectively. The Sharpe ratio during the testing period for the tracking portfolios with respect to the index returns is 0.121 for the single-period model portfolios, and 0.589 for the stochastic programming model portfolios. These results are consistent with the results obtained with the mortgage indexation models: the index funds created using a stochastic programming model perform better than index funds created with single-period models.

7.8   Postview

This chapter considered a problem of widespread applicability, namely that of tracking broadly defined market indices. The basics of market indices were first discussed, followed by a classification of indexation models.

It then developed scenario optimization models for tracking international indices of bonds and of corporate bonds. Models that deal with both strategic and tactical decisions were presented, and the chapter formulated a stochastic programming model for structuring index funds.

Finally, the chapter discussed the application of the models to the tracking of both government and corporate bond indices in local and international markets, as well as indices of mortgage-backed securities and callable bonds. The advantages of taking an integrated approach

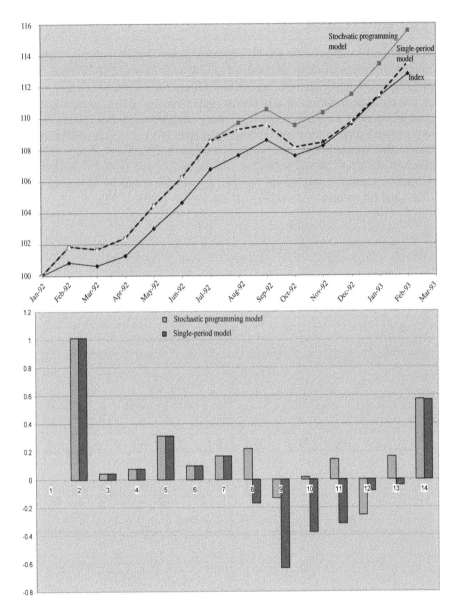

Figure 7.12: Value of a 100 USD investment in the callable bond index, and in indexed portfolios developed using a single-period and a stochastic programming model (top), and tracking error of the two indexed portfolios developed using a single-period and a stochastic programming model vis-à-vis the index (bottom).

to the management of index funds by incorporating multiple sources of risk, were illustrated through numerical simulations. Numerical results illustrated the efficacy and superior performance of the stochastic programming models.

Notes and References

For an introduction to index funds see Mossavar-Rahmani (1997), and the references cited therein. Sources for material on market indices are the web pages of JP Morgan, Standard & Poor's and FTSE (www.jpmorgan.com, www.standardpoor.com, www.ftse.com).

An analysis of the performance of actively managed funds is due to Lakonishok et al. (1992). The effect on prices when a stock is added to an index was studied by Bos (2000).

A review of quantitative approaches for bond indexation is given in Seix and Akhoury (1986). Miller, Krawitt and Wands (1992), and Worzel, Vassiadou-Zeniou and Zenios (1994) discuss the indexation of mortgage-backed securities. International bond portfolio indexation models were developed by Consiglio and Zenios (2001a), for callable bonds by Vassiadou-Zeniou and Zenios (1996), and for corporate bonds by Jobst and Zenios (2001, 2003).

Chapter 8

Designing Financial Products

> We should be just as concerned with "the dog that didn't bark" – that is, the security
> or institution that did not get introduced.
>
> Franklin Allen and Douglas Gale,
> *Financial Innovation and Risk Sharing*

8.1 Preview

In this chapter we introduce the notion of financial innovation and discuss its drivers. Several
innovative financial products are then described. A general framework for the design of new
products is discussed, and optimization models for financial product design are introduced. The
general discussion is followed by a concrete example for designing bonds with embedded call
options.

8.2 Financial Innovation

Financial innovation – the unforecastable and unanticipated changes in financial instruments –
has been occurring for several thousand years. There is evidence that the most primitive type of
a financial arrangement – the loan of goods or money from one person to another – was available
in many early civilizations. Bankers in ancient Greece accepted deposits and lent money, and
they would also issue bankers' acceptances, that is, they would provide written promise to pay
a given amount at a specified date. In modern times financial innovation is even associated with
the printing of paper money as a reaction to the British government's prohibition of the minting
of coins by the North American colonies.

However, it was in the 1980s that financial economics was revolutionized by the many significant and successful innovations in exotic financial instruments like futures, options, synthetic
securities with embedded options, asset-backed securities and collateralized obligations, indexed
instruments, and the like. Indeed, one study reports 58 financial innovations introduced by investment banks during a 10-year period in the mid seventies. The cost of developing these
innovations ranged from $50,000 to $5 million.

The rapid pace of financial innovation has highlighted the need to understand this phenomenon: Why is it happening and what explains the form of present-day securities?

Financial innovation provides opportunities for risk sharing and for intertemporal smoothing
of income. When we live in the financial world of effectively complete markets, any contingent
claim can be synthesized and any risk can be hedged. However, in the real world of the typical
worker or employee, and of nonfinancial companies, their assets are non-diversified and hence

important risks remain unhedged. The income risk of the average worker is not typically insured, and health risk for instance, which is usually insured, is subject to the additional risk of job loss and the subsequent discontinuation of insurance coverage. Large firms can hedge the risks of commodity prices and of exchange rate fluctuations, but many other business risks cannot be shifted. Sector-specific shocks, especially pervasive in high-tech industries and telecommunications today, typically cannot be hedged. Until recently the risk to skiing resort managers from unusually warm weather, or to citrus farmers from unusually cold weather could be insured in part, but not hedged. Then the innovation of weather derivatives came along, and allowed these unlikely partners – farmers and ski resort owners – to share their risks, without ever having to shed their work boots for snow shoes.

As we can glean from this introduction, the types of innovation are many and diverse, to match the motives and the types of innovators. Governments, firms, banks and other intermediaries, as well as exchanges, introduce innovative financial instruments for a variety of reasons. Foremost among the drivers of financial innovation is the desire to complete the markets, in order to hedge some risk that was previously unhedged or to reduce the cost of achieving some degree of insurance. Taxes and government regulations have been characterized as the sand in the oyster that cultivates innovation, since several innovative instruments were introduced as a means to bypass government regulations or to avoid taxes. The need to increase liquidity and to reduce transaction costs has also been a driver for many innovations, as well as the desire to reduce agency costs among different security holders. In these cases the constraints of market participants shape the supply and demand for innovative products, while varying marketing costs shape the features of the innovation. And, finally, financial innovation serves the need to change the price of assets that are being held through asset securitization.

As financial innovations proliferate in variety and complexity, and the rate with which they are introduced accelerates, there is a need to develop a scientific methodology for designing the new products. Financial engineers are called upon to design the specifications of the new products in order to meet end-user requirements for risk sharing and intertemporal smoothing of cash flow. The analogy to engineers who use the laws of physics to design bridges is apt, as financial engineers use the techniques of modern finance to build the financial equivalent of bridges and airplanes. But, as in engineering, a universal methodology is not applicable to the design of all products. However, a general paradigm gradually emerges from the examination of various products and their design parameters.

8.3 Financial Product Novelties

The novelties of the new financial products vary from the trivial and well defined, to the highly complex that are defined through elaborate relations with some underlying uncertain market price(s). At one extreme we have guaranteed investment contracts with guaranteed rates of return and fixed horizons. At the other extreme we have products – mortgage-backed securities and collateralized loan obligations – whose return and time horizon depend on the actions of tens or thousands of individual loan holders, such as the owners of mortgages or personal loans. The features of several such products are defined below.

8.3.1 Guaranteed investment contracts

A guaranteed investment contract (GIC) promises a guaranteed rate of return over a specified period. A single premium GIC with a lump sum payment at maturity replicates the financial pattern of a zero coupon bond. Yet, while a GIC is not a security, it is considered an insurance contract. Insurance companies and banks qualified to issue GICs, also called bank investment contracts (BIC), are exempt from registering them as securities with the Securities and Exchange

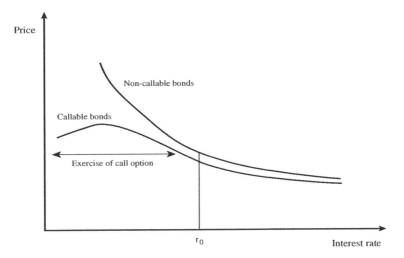

Figure 8.1: The price versus interest rate relationship for callable and non-callable bonds.

Commission. These contracts are typically treated using book value (i.e., amortized cost), and their value remains stable and does not fluctuate with changes in interest rates, as would be the case with zero coupon bonds that are accounted for using market value.

These products are typically backed by the general account of the issuer, or with a separate portfolio of assets owned and managed by the insurance company or the bank. Third-party financial institutions can make arrangements such as "wrapping" the portfolio with a single security or with an immunization strategy that allow for book value treatment. The outstanding market for GICs, as of the end of 2000, was $200 billion.

8.3.2   Callable bonds

Callable bonds allow the issuer to call back the bond from investors by paying them the face value plus a prespecified premium. Corporations, municipalities, utilities, and government agencies issue such bonds, and they are likely to exercise the call provision when interest rates decline sufficiently to make it worth their while to raise funds at the new, lower rates. As a result of the call provision, the cashflow of a callable bond is interest rate sensitive. Callable bonds are the simplest bonds with an embedded option. The value of a callable bond is the value of an equivalent non-callable bond minus the value of the (embedded) call option. The price versus interest rate relationship of a callable bond is bounded from above by the call price, and the difference from the price of the non-callable bond at any given interest rate is the value of the embedded call option. Figure 8.1 illustrates this relationship.

Callable bonds are a major borrowing instrument for issuers with interest rate sensitive assets. The rationale for this choice is simple: the bonds can be called as interest rates drop and assets repay. Agencies like Fannie Mae and Freddie Mac fund their mortgage assets with the issue of callable bonds (see Section 8.3.5). As interest rates drop and mortgages prepay, the bonds are called.

A callable bond is unambiguously specified by the following four parameters, illustrated in Figure 8.2:

Lockout period: The period, following issuance, during which the bond cannot be called.

Redemption price at first call date: The price at which the bond can be called at the first call date. This price is at a premium above par.

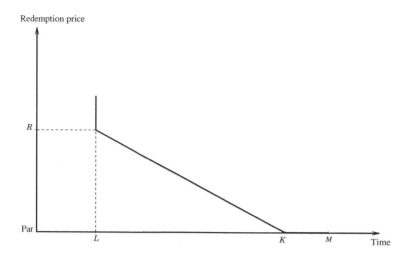

Figure 8.2: The four parameters of the bond design problem: (1) L, lockout period; (2) R, redemption price at first call date; (3) M, time to maturity; and (4) K, time after which the security can be called at par.

Time to maturity: The maturity of the bond, defined as for any fixed-income security.

Schedule of redemption prices: The redemption price at the first call date is at a premium above par. This premium declines as the security approaches maturity. A schedule of redemption prices during the term of the bond is specified by the issuer. We assume, for simplicity, that the redemption prices decline linearly from a starting value of R at the end of the lockout period, to par at some period K. The term during which the security can be called at a premium (i.e., K) is one of the characteristics of the bond. Other schedules of redemption prices – instead of the linear decline – can be easily specified as well. The time parameters are constrained to satisfy the precedence relationship that the lockout period L should be less than K, which in turn must be less than the time to maturity M.

8.3.3   Single premium deferred annuities

An annuity is a contract that promises the holder periodic payments for a specified length of time, which could refer to the holder's lifetime. To purchase the stream of future income the investor makes payments to the issuer either in a single premium or through periodic premia. A popular example of such products is the single premium deferred annuity (SPDA) which has some innovative features that makes it attractive for investors.

The holder of an SPDA makes a single premium payment into an account maintained by the issuer. The issuer accrues interest on this account according to a *crediting rate*. This rate may be adjusted periodically at the discretion of the issuer. When the policyholder reaches retirement age the issuer pays out an annuity – perhaps divided in monthly installments. Thus a constant retirement income stream is guaranteed. Payments can be made either for the lifetime of the policyholder or for a fixed period of time, irrespectively of whether the policyholder passes away or not. Usually the interest income of the account is tax deferred, that is, no taxes are paid until the policyholder starts receiving the annuity.

An SPDA can be viewed as an insurance contract turned upside down. While life insurance is paid in periodic installments, and pays out a fixed amount upon the death of the insured, an SPDA is bought with a single payment, and provides an income stream throughout the policyholder's retirement years. The purchaser of an SPDA expects to live longer than purchasers of insurance, and actuaries use different life expectancy tables to determine the premia. And while a life insurance policy requires the insured to be in good health, there is no such requirement for the purchaser of an SPDA.

The lapse option

The option of the issuer to adjust the crediting rate is offset by the option of the policyholder to *lapse*, that is, to withdraw the balance of the insurance of part thereof, at any time, possibly at a penalty. Hence, the value of an SPDA is equivalent to the value of a fixed-rate bond, minus the option of the issuer to adjust the crediting rate, plus the option of the policyholder to lapse.

Together with the risk of changing interest rates, the lapse option built into the instrument is an additional source of risk for the issuer as, at any time, the holder of an SPDA may withdraw all or part of the assets held in the account. There is typically a penalty – termed *surrender charge* – to be paid in order to exercise the lapse option, although the penalty may not apply for withdrawals of small amounts. For instance, 10% of the total account may be withdrawn at any given year without penalties. The surrender charges are typically adjusted downwards with the age of the account, e.g. starting at 7% for the first year, reduced to 6% for the second year, and so on until some period such as eight years, after which clients can withdraw the full amount without any penalty. In addition, funds withdrawn before the holder reaches a certain age (usually $59\frac{1}{2}$) are taxed, unless the funds are reinvested in other tax-deferred accounts.

The issuer can manage interest rate risk by adjusting the crediting rate. However, drastic reductions in the crediting rate will encourage the exercise of the lapse option, as policyholders will flee to more attractive investments. Hence, proper management of an SPDA line of business requires a good understanding of lapse behavior, noting that the factors that affect lapse are common among the buyers of SPDA and hence, there is a high degree of correlation of lapse activity across different policies.

The following three factors affect lapse behavior, and they are reasonably well understood, at least to the extent that large groups of policyholders behave on the average as rational investors:

Crediting rates. The issuer determines the crediting rate paid to the holders of the instrument. The crediting rate is typically guaranteed for an initial period, after which the rates may be adjusted subject to some minimum requirement (floor) below which the rate may not drop, and perhaps additional limits on the total adjustment that is allowed annually.

Market crediting rates. As already mentioned, holders of an SPDA may cancel the policy without incurring any tax penalties if the assets are reinvested in other tax-deferred assets. Hence, if the market crediting rates – offered by competitors – are higher than the crediting rate offered by a specific SPDA then lapse will accelerate.

Interest rates. If interest rates rise well above the crediting rates, then investors may shift from SPDA policies into risk free assets, even if such a move will incur tax penalties.

These three factors can be incorporated in a model to project the liability of a company that issues SPDA policies.

Modeling lapse

We assume that the issuer will adjust the crediting rates in tandem with the interest rates in order to remain competitive, while the policyholder will lapse driven by the three factors outlined above. All adjustments are conditional on scenarios l from the index set of scenario Ω that captures the uncertainties in prevailing market rates.

The crediting rate (CR_t) is adjusted periodically by a fraction ρ towards the prevailing interest rate r_t. The dynamics of the crediting rate under scenario $l \in \Omega$ can be stated as follows:

$$CR_t^l = CR_{t-1}^l + \rho(r_t^l - CR_{t-1}^l), \text{ for } t = 1, 2, \ldots, T. \tag{8.1}$$

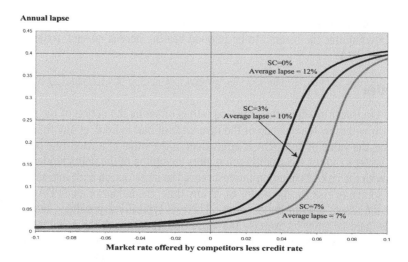

Figure 8.3: The percentage of an SPDA policy that lapses as a function of the differential between the market rate MCR_t and the policy crediting rate CR_t, for different levels of surrender charges (SC).

CR_0 is the contractually specified initial crediting rate, and the time index t typically denotes years. We point out that the short-term, risk-free rate may not be the appropriate rate r_t applicable to this industry, and indeed some applications use the five-year treasury rate as the prevailing interest rate.

The issuer may not be able to adjust the crediting rates for existing products fully up to the prevailing interest rates, i.e., set $\rho = 1$. However, the competition may offer new products much closer to the interest rates, as any premia charged for the sale of the new products can be invested at the prevailing market rates. Hence, the crediting rate of the competition MCR_t is given by the market crediting rate as

$$MCR_t^l = \max \left[\left[MCR_{t-1}^l + \rho_M (r_t^l - MCR_{t-1}^l) \right], r_t^l \right] \text{ for } t = 1, 2, \ldots, T, \qquad (8.2)$$

where ρ_M is an adjustment factor, indicating the rate at which the competition adjusts the crediting rate from its previous value towards some market benchmark rate.

We are now ready to model the lapse behavior, measured as a fraction of the policy that lapses due to the factors outlined above. The following formula incorporates the relevant factors in an equation that estimates the fraction q_t that will lapse at period t:

$$q_t^l = a + b \arctan \left[\mu (MCR_t^l - CR_t^l - SC) - \nu \right]. \qquad (8.3)$$

Here SC denotes the surrender charge and the parameters a, b, μ, ν are estimated to fit the lapse function to empirical data. Figure 8.3 illustrates typical lapse behavior for varying surrender charges.

8.3.4   Asset-backed securities

An important innovation in the financial intermediation process started in the 1980s and continues unabated to date, with the securitization of assets. Through securitization individual, illiquid assets – such as a bank's mortgage loans – are converted into tradeable instruments in the capital markets and may be removed from the balance sheet. In such transactions a portfolio of assets – called the reference portfolio – is transferred from the balance sheet of the originator to a special purpose vehicle (SPV) or special purpose entity (SPE) in the terminology of the Basel Committee on Banking Supervision. The sole purpose of the SPE is to refinance itself by issuing securities on the reference portfolio – hence the term asset-backed securities or ABS – and sell them at a margin, usually to institutional investors.

The motivation for this securitization process is threefold. First, the issuers can reduce their risk beyond what may be possible through diversification, and in particular may reduce business risk by securitizing assets with risk concentration in the primary business of the originator. Second, securitization can improve the quality of the balance sheet by restructuring it through the securitization process to achieve the third, and perhaps most significant, goal of freeing regulatory capital. Specifically, as risky assets are securitized and some are sold off to the capital markets, the risk exposure of the originator is reduced, thus allowing for reduced regulatory capital margins on the one hand, and at the same time freeing capital for purchasing further assets.

The most common asset classes that have undergone securitization are mortgage loans, with the resulting asset-backed securities known as mortgage-backed securities (MBS), discussed in the next section. However, the market has been growing and securitized assets today include Collaterized Bond Obligations (CBO) and Collaterized Loan Obligations (CLO) as significant asset classes. These are classified together under the name Collaterized Debt Obligations (CDO), whereby the reference portfolio consists, respectively, of bonds or loan receivables. Other assets used for securitization purposes include auto loans, credit card receivables, or commercial mortgages and lease receivables.

In the securitization process the asset risk in the reference portfolio is transferred to the investor in return for cashflow payments from the portfolio. The repayment risk is sliced into tranches that are subordinated by seniority. That is, the most senior class has first priority to payments received while the most junior class has the lowest priority and bears the initial losses. When tranches are subordinated they are filled with payments in a cascading effect, so that the most senior classes are touched only if there are highly correlated defaults in the underlying asset pool. For this reason, asset-backed securities bear significant correlation risk. The issued asset-backed securities are typically rated from AAA for the senior tranches, A for the mezzanine class, BB for subordinated, and the most junior class is equity that remains unrated.

Finally, a distinction is made between market value and cashflow asset-backed securities. In the former case, the allocation of payments to the tranches is based on the mark-to-market returns of the reference portfolio. In the latter, the tranches are serviced by the payments of coupons, early repayments of loans, recovery of defaulting loans, and so on, from the reference portfolio.

8.3.5   Mortgage-backed and derivative securities

Mortgage-backed securities (MBS) hold a prominent position in the securities market, and the outstanding mortgage debt in the US currently exceeds $3.5 trillion. Since the 1980s, mortgage debt has been financed in part by the issuance of mortgage-backed securities. More than 25% of the outstanding residential debt had been securitized. These securities are actively traded in the secondary markets, with trading volumes reaching in the trillions of dollars. On top of the mortgage pass-through securities – where all the cashflow from the underlying mortgages, net a service fee, is passed on to the investors – there has been a proliferation of derivative products. Collateralized mortgage obligations (CMO), interest only (IO), and principal only (PO) are some of the derivative instruments.

All these products are quite complex. First, a mortgage-backed security combines features of annuities and options, as the homeowners' ability to prepay represents a call option. Second, this call option is not necessarily exercised optimally, according to the rational behavior prescribed by option pricing theory. For example, a homeowner may sell a property and prepay the mortgage even if the prevailing mortgage rates are higher than the contract rate of her mortgage. Employment changes, births and deaths, divorce, and so on are factors that affect prepayment

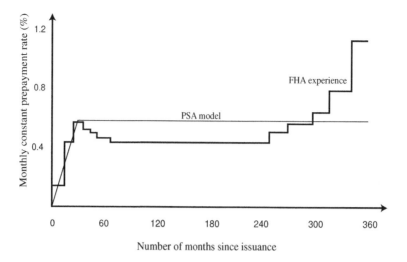

Figure 8.4: The Public Securities Association (PSA) model and historical Federal Housing Administration (FHA) experience of mortgage prepayment rates.

decisions.

To cope with the various sources of uncertainty in modeling MBS – and to capture the complex relationships between the cashflows of an MBS and interest rate paths – analysts resort to Monte Carlo simulation methods. These methods combine models for the evolution of interest rates (see Chapter 9) with models of prepayment for the mortgage pool. Estimating the prepayment rates of a pool is critical input for pricing methodologies, and this is the weak link of models for pricing and managing MBS portfolios.

Standard models for estimating the prepayment of mortgage-backed securities are the Public Securities Association (PSA) model and the Federal Housing Administration (FHA) experience. The PSA model assumes that the prepayment rates increase as a constant rate during the first 30 months of the life of the mortgage until they reach 6%. Then they remain constant. The FHA experience is summarized by a series of annual survival rates for various populations of FHA insured mortgages. Figure 8.4 illustrates both the PSA model and historical FHA experience. A severe limitation of both the PSA and the FHA models is that they are interest rate invariant and assume a very simple aging process for mortgages. Hence, both models are of limited value within the context of pricing models where the evolution of interest rates is modeled explicitly.

The severe limitations of models that assume a fixed time period for the full prepayment of a mortgage (such as a 12-year rule of thumb used in the earlier studies of mortgages) were recognized early on. More specifically, it was recognized that prepayment rates will depend on the age of the mortgages in the pool, the coupon rate, and the currently prevailing mortgage rates in the market. Therefore models are developed that explicitly account for the dynamic nature of prepayment activities taking into account seasonal variations, pure refinancing effects due to competitive pressures from the prevailing mortgage rates, and aging effects.

Prepayment modeling

We consider the aggregate prepayment activity of groups of homeowners whose individual mortgages are pooled together in a somewhat homogeneous MBS. The model discussed here captures the key factors that affect prepayment rates in a common framework. The model, however, focuses on factors that have a similar effect on all outstanding mortgage pools and it ignores, for instance, the geographic locations of the mortgaged properties in the pool and other demographic effects. While we must recognize that pools from different geographic locations will exhibit distinct prepayment behavior, the model predicts prepayments of generic pools. The factors of prepayment that are included are sufficient for explaining historically observed prepayments on generic pools.

The characteristics of a mortgage that are relevant for modeling the prepayment behavior of the mortgage borrower are: (i) the age of the mortgage, call it t; (ii) the month of the year, m; and (iii) the ratio between the mortgage contract rate denoted by C, and the prevailing rate at which the mortgage can be refinanced, r_t. We also recognize that the prepayment activity of a pool will depend on the whole history of C/r_t ratios since its issuance. We use R_t to denote the vector of these ratios for all time periods less than t, i.e., $R_t = (C/r_1, C/r_2, \ldots, C/r_{t-1})$. This ratio captures the economic incentives for homeowners to prepay their mortgages, and it depends on the whole history of market rates since the mortgage loan was originated. Indeed, it is this *path dependence* of prepayments on the complete history of mortgage refinancing rates, since the mortgage was issued that complicates the modeling of prepayment rates.

The model deals with the estimation of the prepayment activity of pools of mortgages, and not of individual mortgages. The formation of a pool, according to the legal specifications adhered to by the issuing agencies, creates MBSs which are not perfectly homogeneous with respect to the aforementioned characteristics. For example, for an MBS with a given pass-through rate, the underlying mortgage rates may be slightly different from each other, as will be their maturities. Since our interest is in dealing with generic MBSs we ignore this heterogeneity. Each pool is treated as a homogeneous collection of mortgages with contract rates equal to the weighted average coupon (WAC) of the pool and with maturity equal to its weighted average maturity (WAM). This treatment of the pools is consistent with practice, and the model loses little realism in this respect. Furthermore, detailed information on the individual mortgages that are in a given pool is usually unavailable.

Other characteristics of a mortgage pool may be relevant to the prepayment activity. Geographic location is particularly relevant in capturing demographic phenomena. Nevertheless, the three pool characteristics mentioned above are sufficient for the representation of the factors that we include in our models. The age of the mortgage t and the vector R_t are essential, as the prepayment rates are not static, but change dynamically with the age of the mortgages in the pool. (Evidence to this effect is seen in the FHA experience curve and is also assumed in the PSA model; see Figure 8.4.) The month of the year m captures seasonal variations, with high prepayment rates in the late summer and early fall, and low prepayment rates during the winter months.

The use of the ratio C/r_t, as an indicator of prepayment rates due to refinancing incentives, is in agreement with the options pricing analysis, as opposed to the alternative differential $C - r_t$ that was used in early modeling attempts. To understand the prepayment process, consider the financial incentives of a homeowner to prepay the mortgage. He or she will do so if the cost of continuing the current payments is greater than the cost of payments of a new mortgage at the current rates (including mortgage origination costs).

The present value of a 30-year mortgage, per unit of monthly payment, is given by

$$V_t = \frac{1 - (1 + r_t)\, t - 360}{r_t}. \tag{8.4}$$

The mortgage balance, per unit of monthly payment, is given by

$$B_t = \frac{1 - (1 + C)\, t - 360}{C}. \tag{8.5}$$

Mortgage owners will exercise the prepayment option if the ratio V_t/B_t exceeds some critical value that reflects the implicit costs of refinancing. The ratio V_t/B_t is well approximated by

C/r_t for a wide range of values of t, and we use this ratio as a proxy for the pure economic incentive to refinance the mortgage.

The model for estimating prepayment brings together four effects that determine the prepayment activities. Each of these effects is in turn determined by the mortgage characteristics introduced above, and the prevailing refinancing rates. These effects and their independent variables are the following:

Seasonality effect, $s(m, C/r_t)$. This factor captures the increase in house sales during the summer and early fall, and the decrease of sales in the winter months. This effect arises primarily due to housing activity, although an argument can be made that refinancing activity is higher following the end of a tax year.

Economic effect $\rho(C/r_t)$. This factor captures the homeowners' decision to refinance their mortgage if the prevailing mortgage rates r_t are lower than the coupon rate of their mortgage.

Seasoning effect, $\sigma(R_t, t, C/r_t)$. Prepayment rates are lower in the early years of the life of the mortgage because homeowners do not take out mortgages with the expectation that they will quickly move. At the same time they may lack the energy and money needed to refinance a new mortgage. As the time from origination lengthens, the probability of a move, leading to prepayment, increases. The rate at which prepayments increase depends on the history of R_t ratios experienced by the pool since its issuance. Premium pools season faster than discount pools.

Burnout effect, $\beta(R_t, t, C/r_t)$. Prepayment activity tends to decrease for older mortgages. The shorter the time to maturity the larger the ratio C/r_t required to generate any level of savings due to refinancing. Furthermore, even if $r_t < C$, not all borrowers will refinance. There are several reasons for this behavior. Some homeowners expect even more favorable opportunities in the future; some are just lethargic; others do not qualify for a new loan. Whatever the reason, with the passage of time those borrowers with the greatest sensitivity to C/r_t will prepay, leaving in the pool those with less sensitivity. The combined result of all these considerations is that prepayment activity tends to slow at the end of the life of the mortgage. However, pools that have been at discount since origination will experience less burnout than those that have been at par or at premium. The last two factors together capture the effect of aging on the prepayment rates.

The following model equation combines these four effects to estimate the constant prepayment rate (CPR), that is, the percentage of the outstanding mortgage balance that will prepay during the next time period for the specific mortgage characteristics:

$$CPR(t, m, R_t) = s(m, C/r_t) \cdot \rho(C/r_t) \cdot \sigma(R_t, t, C/r_t) \cdot \beta(R_t, t, C/r_t) \cdot \epsilon. \qquad (8.6)$$

Here ϵ is used to denote the error in the model which is assumed to be normally distributed with mean one.

The prepayment model is highly nonlinear. The four effects depend on one or more of the independent variables, and most of them depend on the same variable, but not necessarily in the same way. Optimization models can be used to filter out the four factors based on historical observations. Historical data tabulate the outstanding balance for each observed pool for each month since its issuance, or since the beginning of the observation period. The observed outstanding mortgage balance, and the scheduled outstanding balance – if prepayments were not exercised – can be combined to estimate the monthly mortality rate of the mortgage. Hence, a series of constant prepayment rates are observed under known values of the independent variables. This series provides the information for the calibration of our prepayment model. Details on calibration procedures can be found in the references.

8.4   A Framework for Financial Product Design

We consider now the problem of designing financial products, that is, of specifying the characteristics of a specific product so that its risk – return profile meets some user-prescribed criteria. Of course the problem of designing innovative products for an institution is a highly complex problem that requires a multidisciplinary approach from options pricing and product positioning, marketing of new products, and organizational process management. We do not attempt to capture all such aspects in a single model. However, significant asset decisions are integrated in the developed model, together with decisions on leverage and the specification of product characteristics.

We consider an institution operating in an uncertain world, and we capture uncertainty in our customary way, using a discrete set of scenarios indexed by the set Ω. The institution holds a portfolio of assets, and we use r_A^l to denote one plus the rate of return of this portfolio under scenario $l \in \Omega$, during some holding period of interest, i.e., the risk horizon. It is assumed here that the portfolio of assets is given a priori, and scenarios of holding period returns for this portfolio can be computed using standard pricing models, such as those described in Chapter 9. The institution funds these assets through the issue of debt (D) and the investment of shareholders' equity (E).

Debt is issued in the form of a portfolio of financial products, and the yield on this debt is denoted by R_L^l. We assume that the yield on the debt during the holding period can be calculated using the pricing models, but we do not assume that the debt structure is given a priori. Indeed, determining the debt structure is a key aspect of the institution's problem.

The position of the institution at the end of the holding period is given by the terminal wealth

$$WT^l = (D + E)r_A^l - R_L^l. \tag{8.7}$$

The return to shareholders is given by the *return on equity* (ROE)

$$\text{ROE}^l \doteq \frac{WT^l}{E} = \frac{(D + E)r_A^l - R_L^l}{E}. \tag{8.8}$$

This equation reveals the important relation between financial leverage (i.e., the debt to equity ratio) and return on equity. For scenarios under which the return on assets exceeds the interest rate on debt, then financial leverage will increase the return on equity. When the return on assets falls below the cost of debt, then financial leverage will decrease the return on equity.

As the expected return on assets exceeds the required yield on debt it follows that financial leverage has two effects on the return on equity. It increases the expected return on equity, while at the same time it increases the variability of this return. Therefore, depending on the shareholders' aversion towards risk, there is an optimal level of financial leverage. An empirical illustration of this effect for property and casualty insurance firms in the United States is shown in Figure 8.5. We observe from these empirical data that there is an optimal level of financial leverage, around four, for this particular industry segment. We also observe that the market rewards firms with lower duration of the asset minus liability surplus. Firms that engage in effective asset-liability management strategies, which reduce their interest rate exposure, achieve higher market rewards. It is worth pointing out that the average leverage of companies in the sample is around 3.5, very close to optimal, while the average duration surplus is around 12 to 13, close to the saddle point. Financial leverage is under regulatory control, and the empirical evidence suggests that the regulatory process has converged to a point that is best for the market. The situation is not as encouraging for the asset-liability management dimension. We observe large duration gaps, which speak in favor of the need for integrated financial product management, as advocated throughout this book.

In order to determine the optimal level of leverage, however, we need to determine the cost of debt under different scenarios $l \in \Omega$. (Recall that in our setting the value of the other parameter

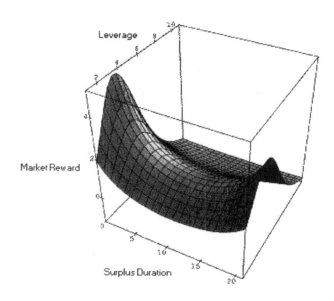

Figure 8.5: Market reward for different levels of leverage and for different values of duration of the gap between assets and liabilities, for a large sample of property-casualty insurance companies. (Reprinted from Babbel and Staking, 1991, with permission of the A.M. Best Co.)

that appears in the ROE calculation, i.e., the return on the asset portfolio r_A^l, is exogenous to the institution's decisions.) The cost of debt is determined by the amount of debt raised through issues in different financial products. Hence, the institution has to determine simultaneously the structure of its debt (i.e., the amount issued in each product) and the optimal level of financial leverage. A model that answers this question is developed in the next section.

However, there is an additional level of flexibility for our institution. The return on the debt is a function of the yield of each particular product. Herein lies the opportunity for financial innovation and the design of new products. Since the institution is issuing the products, their yield can be adjusted with the judicious setting of some design parameters.

In conclusion, the problem of maximizing the return on equity can be broken down into three interrelated decisions: (i) design the financial products to be used to issue debt; (ii) specify the amount issued in each product; (iii) determine the optimal level of financial leverage. The design of a product deals with the micro-management of a single line of business as discussed in Section 1.3.2, while the allocation of equity among the designed products deals with the macro-management of a portfolio of products discussed in Sections 1.3.3 and 1.3.4. As argued in Chapter 1 these decisions have to be made in an integrated fashion, taking into account the uncertain environment and the shareholders' risk aversion, and this is the aim of the framework for product design developed here.

8.4.1   Risk aversion and certainty equivalent return

We have thus far considered the problem of specifying a policy – which consists of the product design parameters, the structure of the debt, and the amount of leverage – but have not yet specified a measure to characterize a "good" policy. We do so in this section, thereby clarifying the notion of quality of the product design. Specifically, a given product design is considered to be of high quality if it maximizes our measure of a "good" policy.

To compare alternative policies we need to incorporate the decision maker's risk aversion for different levels of ROE^l. If we let $\mathcal{U}$ denote the utility function of the decision maker then, following Definition 2.8.4, we search for policies that maximize the expected utility $\sum_{l \in \Omega} p^l \mathcal{U}(\text{ROE}^l)$.

With each policy we associate its *certainty equivalent return on equity* (CEROE; see Definition 2.8.8) given by

$$\mathcal{U}(\text{CEROE}) = \sum_{l \in \Omega} p^l \mathcal{U}(\text{ROE}^l). \tag{8.9}$$

Assuming nondecreasing utility functions we can rank policies by their CEROE, and the one with the highest value of CEROE is the best policy. A set of products are then considered to be of high quality if they allow the institution to decide a debt structure and the optimal leverage with a large value of CEROE.

The discussion focuses on the ranking of designs using a utility function of ROE at the end of some planning horizon. There is no guarantee that the designed products will have large utility values of ROE at earlier, intermediate periods. The problem of temporal utility assessment is important when consumption of wealth at each point of the planning horizon is under consideration, and it is a difficult problem. We do not address this problem here as consumption of wealth is not a consideration when an institution is issuing debt in order to hold some asset.

We also note that an alternative objective for choosing a "good" policy is to specify a design that limits the value-at-risk (VaR) or the conditional value-at-risk (CVaR) of the decision maker's surplus, where surplus is defined as the market value of assets minus market value of liabilities. Both VaR and CVaR are popular measures of risk, and designs that result in low VaR or CVaR of surplus can be considered designs of high quality. However, these measures tell us nothing about the decision maker's views on losses. In this respect we consider the analysis with expected utility maximization as more complete, in that it includes the decision maker's utility function. We point out, however, that the models could be adapted to generate policies that minimize VaR or CVaR.

8.4.2   Model formulation

We formulate a hierarchy of optimization models that address the issues of product design in an integrated fashion. First, for a given universe of products and their associated returns the institution can decide the optimal mix of products to be issued and the optimal leverage. A nonlinear program can be formulated to resolve these two decisions. Then, new products can be introduced, and those redefine the input data to the nonlinear optimization program. The goal is to find the design of products that, together with an appropriate product mix and an appropriate financial leverage, yield the overall highest CEROE. This is then the design of the best quality.

We point out that the model assumes asymmetric information: the institution issues its own debt which is priced at the prevailing market rates, while the amount of debt does not affect either the market rates or the cost of equity of the institution. Were we to impose market equilibrium conditions – whereby the market rates adjust in response to the new debt issued, and the institution's cost of equity increases as increasing debt raises credit risk – we would obtain the indifference between debt and equity implied by the well-known Modigliani-Miller theorem. For application of the model in a real-world setting we would need to determine whether the magnitude of the issued debt would affect the cost of equity or market rates, and model such effects appropriately.

Notation

First we introduce some notation:

x^i denotes the vector of *design parameters* for product $i \in U$. For example, if the product is a callable bond the design parameters could be the lockout period and the schedule of redemption prices before maturity. We assume that ν parameters are needed to characterize each product, so that x^i is a vector in $\mathbb{R}^\nu$.

$x = ((x^1)^\top, (x^2)^\top, \ldots, (x^n)^\top)^\top$ is the concatenated vector of design parameters for all products in U. x is a vector in $\mathbb{R}^{\nu n}$.

$r_i^l(x^i)$ denotes 1 plus the rate of return of the ith product. The return of each product depends on the design parameters x^i and on the scenario $l \in \Omega$.

$y = (y_i)_{i=1}^n$ is the vector denoting the amount (in face value) of debt issued in each product $i \in U$. This vector specifies the debt structure.

$P = (P_i)_{i=1}^n$ denotes the price per unit face value of each product in U.

With this notation we can express the yield on the liability portfolio due to the debt issued by

$$R_L^l(y, x) = \sum_{i=1}^n y_i r_i^l(x^i), \text{ for all } l \in \Omega. \tag{8.10}$$

The return on equity (equation 8.8) can now be written in a way that reflects its dependence on the policy of our institution

$$\text{ROE}^l(y, x, D/E) = \frac{(D + E)r_A^l - R_L^l(y, x)}{E}. \tag{8.11}$$

The calculation of return on equity involves the evaluation of the nonlinear equation (8.10) in y and x. Furthermore, the values of $r_i^l(x^i)$ as a function of the design parameters x^i for each scenario $l \in \Omega$ are not available analytically, but are obtained through a Monte Carlo simulation procedure of the underlying market rates (see Chapter 9).

The optimization models

A hierarchy of models is now developed to address the problem of issuing new products as outlined above. The first model assumes that a universe of designed products is given and determines the optimal debt structure (y) and the optimal level of financial leverage (E). The second model expands the universe of available products by designing new products, thereby expanding the feasible region of the first optimization model and so improving the solution. The two models are used hierarchically and their joint solution solves in an integrated fashion both the problem of debt structure and that of financial leverage.

Debt structure and optimal leverage

For a given value of the design parameter vector $x \doteq \hat{x}$ the returns $r_i^l(\hat{x}^i)$ can be estimated using Monte Carlo simulation procedures. The following optimization program determines the optimal leverage and the debt structure.

Model 8.4.1 Financial product design: debt structure and optimal leverage

$$\text{Maximize} \quad \sum_{l \in \Omega} p^l \mathcal{U}\left(\text{ROE}^l(y, \hat{x}, D/E)\right) \tag{8.12}$$

subject to $\quad$ (8.10) and (8.11), $\tag{8.13}$

$$\sum_{i=1}^n \pi_i y_i = D, \tag{8.14}$$

$$D + E = 100, \tag{8.15}$$

$$(D + E)r_A^l - \sum_{i=1}^n y_i r_i^l(\hat{x}^i) \geq 0, \quad \text{for all } l \in \Omega. \tag{8.16}$$

The last inequality, taken together with the nonnegativity of E, ensures that return on equity remains nonnegative under all scenarios, and hence it guarantees the solvency of the institution for any debt structure and leverage obtained by the model. Changing the objective function (8.12) to minimize E we may calculate the minimum equity required to ensure solvency under extreme-case scenarios.

The model maximizes the expected utility of ROE over a target holding period. No decisions to rebalance the portfolio are made during this period, and any cashflows generated by the assets or liabilities are invested in the riskless rates and are captured in the calculations of holding period returns.

Several issues deserve further elaboration at this point, as they are relevant for the implementation of the model. First, it must be recognized that the universe of scenarios should encompass all events that are relevant to the institution and against which the institution wants to protect itself, such as interest rate and credit risk. An insurance firm, for instance, may wish to also consider events such as large earthquakes and hurricanes that are independent of interest rate and other market risks. Second, the choice of a utility function could pose a problem since shareholders are a diverse group, and a single utility function may not be appropriate. The specification of the objective function should reflect such considerations, either by aggregating the diverse groups in a single (average) risk preference category, or by allowing for trade-offs between alternative utility functions. Finally, we point out that the debt leverage decision and the equity mix decision are connected. While in our work we assume that the equity mix is exogenous and given by a single variable E, it could also be computed as the value of an equity portfolio with stochastic returns, E^l. The optimization model can incorporate the appropriate equation for the definition of E^l, although we would then need to develop Monte Carlo simulation models that correlate the return of the equity portfolio with the return of the issued debt. It is important to note that the integrated framework developed here can assist in the analysis of these macro-decisions faced by the institution.

The issues raised above may be relevant for different institutions and must be carefully addressed before the model is implemented. It is important to recognize the limitations of the model as proposed here, but also to understand that these important extensions can be accommodated.

Optimal design of products

Let CEROE (x) denote the certainty equivalent of the optimal value of Model 8.4.1 that specifies the optimal debt structure and leverage, when the vector of design parameter $\hat{x}$ takes any value x. That is, if v^* denotes the optimal objective function value of Model 8.4.1 when $x = \hat{x}$, then CEROE $(\hat{x}) = \mathcal{U}^{-1}(v^*)$. The optimal design parameters of the financial products can now be obtained as the decision variables of the following program.

Model 8.4.2 Financial product design: product specification

$$\text{Maximize} \quad \text{CEROE}\,(x) \tag{8.17}$$

$$\text{subject to} \quad x \in X. \tag{8.18}$$

Here X denotes some constraints on the design parameters (for instance, maximum allowable maturity). Note that this is a global optimization program, since the function CEROE (x), which is obtained by solving Model 8.4.1 is not necessarily unimodal in x. This problem can be solved using techniques from global optimization, bearing in mind that the objective function is not available analytically, but is obtained as the solution to an optimization program.

A systematic procedure for solving this hierarchy of optimization models is summarized as follows:

Initialization. Parametrize by a vector x the design characteristics of the financial products and assume some initial values $\hat{x}$. The specification of the holding period, generation of the index set of scenarios Ω, and estimation of the holding period returns for the target asset are determined during the initialization step.

Step 1. Generate holding period returns for the target product designs, using the same scenarios and holding period used to estimate the returns of the target asset. Scenarios of holding period returns are generated using appropriate Monte Carlo simulation procedures (see Chapter 9).

Step 2. Solve Model 8.4.1 to obtain the optimal debt structure and leverage. The optimal objective value of this program defines the CEROE for the product design simulated in Step 1. If some termination criteria are satisfied, stop. Otherwise proceed with Step 3.

Step 3. Adjust the design parameters x of the financial products and return to Step 1.

This iterative procedure seeks product designs x that allow the institution to specify an optimal debt structure and optimal leverage with the highest possible CEROE. Of particular interest is the specification of the rules for adjusting the design parameters in Step 3, in order to maximize the CEROE obtained in Step 2. The rules should take into account the fact that there exist multiple locally optimal solutions to the product design problem. It may be possible to find a design that is optimal only in a neighborhood of the initial design parameters. Heuristic algorithms such as tabu search or simulated annealing, which search for a globally optimal solution from among the local maxima, are discussed in the references.

8.5 Optimal Design of Callable Bonds

As an example of product design we consider now, in some detail, the problem of designing the parameters of a callable bond. We simplify the problem by considering a single bond, as opposed to a portfolio of bonds discussed in the previous section.

The distribution of returns of the issued liability is given as a function of the four design parameters of the callable bond, i.e., the lockout period (L), the redemption price at the first call date (R), the maturity (M) and the schedule of redemption prices (K). In the discrete scenario setting we write

$$R_L^l = \Phi(L, R, M, K), \text{ for all } l \in \Omega. \tag{8.19}$$

where the function Φ is not available explicitly, but is obtained from a simulation procedure that generates holding period returns for a given setting of the bond parameters L, R, M, K for the interest rate scenarios $l \in \Omega$.

The institution will raise D units of funds by issuing callable bonds at par prices and invest an additional E units of equity to purchase assets with return given by r_A^l. We assume that the total amount of debt and equity adds up to 100 – that is, we normalize the debt and equity issue. The return on equity equation (8.8) can be written as

$$ROE^l = 100 \frac{r_A^l - \Phi(L, R, M, K)}{E}. \tag{8.20}$$

Introducing once more a utility function we can write the optimization model that maximizes the expected utility of return on equity to obtain the optimal design parameters as follows:

$$\underset{L,R,M,K}{\text{Maximize}} \quad \sum_{l \in \Omega} p^l \mathcal{U}(ROE^l) \tag{8.21}$$

$$\text{subject to} \quad 0 \le L \le K \le M. \tag{8.22}$$

One parameter missing from the design model above is the coupon rate C. This parameter is set in such a way as to price the issued bond at par (i.e., 100). For a given setting of the

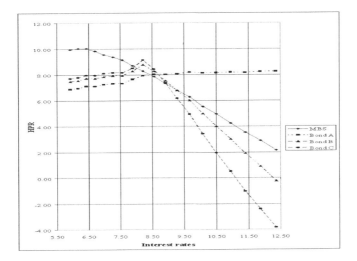

Figure 8.6: Holding period returns of a mortgage-backed security (MBS) and three alternative callable bonds, under different interest rate scenarios. The horizontal axis denotes the geometric mean of the term structure of interest rates during the holding period (36 months); the vertical axis denotes holding period returns. Bonds B and C are preferable liabilities to hold against the mortgage asset, as opposed to bond A which has a much higher rate of return than the asset for all interest rates above 8.5%.

parameters L, R, M, K the coupon rate C is first estimated so that the bond price – estimated from the postulated scenarios $l \in \Omega$ using, for instance, pricing equation (2.70) – is at par. To do so we need an iterative procedure: (i) estimate the cashflows of the bond, denoted by $F_{ti}(r^l)$ in equation (2.70), for a given coupon rate; (ii) estimate the price P_i; (iii) if the price is not 100 change the coupon rate and repeat. Any standard algorithm for solving nonlinear equations can be applied to execute this iterative procedure.

This model is used to design callable bonds to finance a portfolio of mortgage assets – this is the problem faced by institutions issuing mortgage-backed securities, such as the Federal National Mortgage Association. The issue of a callable bond allows the institution to call its debt when mortgages prepay as interest rates drop.

We applied the model to design a portfolio of callable bonds to fund a characteristic mortgage asset. The target asset is a mortgage-backed security with weighted average coupon 9.5% and weighted average maturity of 360 months. The holding period is taken to be 36 months. Figure 8.6 illustrates the holding period return of the asset under different interest rate scenarios. The same figure illustrates the returns of three different callable bonds under the same scenarios.

It is clear that bonds B and C are preferable to bond A, but the choice between B and C is not obvious, nor it is easy to see how one could combine these securities to get a portfolio of bonds that tracks the asset return more closely.

Figure 8.7 illustrates the tracking error of the yield on the issued bonds against the institution's mortgage assets, under different interest rate scenarios. This calculation illustrates the tight correlation between the return of the given assets and the return of the designed bond for a wide range of interest rate scenarios. We observe from this figure that the debt structures corresponding to issues in a single bond have, potentially, higher tracking error than the debt structure consisting of issues in a portfolio of bonds. The overall tracking error is quite small (even in the single-bond issues), providing an indication of the efficacy of the developed models in designing products according to the prespecified target, even when the target is scenario dependent and, hence, uncertain. The model was implemented using a logarithmic utility function.

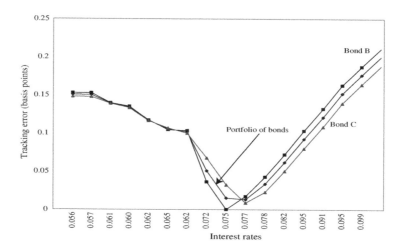

Figure 8.7: Tracking error between the mortgage assets and the issued debt of callable bonds under different interest rate scenarios. The horizontal axis denotes the geometric mean of the term structure of interest rates during the holding period (36 months).

Finally we use callable bonds with the same duration as the target asset as a benchmark, against which we compare our results. We evaluate the CEROE obtained when debt is raised by issuing a single bond that has the same option-adjusted duration as our target assets. The CEROE of the duration matched bond is 1.3313, which is much less than the CEROE of 1.647 obtained when raising debt with the portfolio of bonds designed with the models in this chapter.

8.6 Postview

This chapter introduced a general framework for the design of financial products. First the notion of financial innovation was discussed, followed by several examples of modern financial innovations, such as callable bonds, single premium deferred annuities, and mortgage securities.

The chapter then developed the modeling framework for designing financial products, formulated a specific model, and gave an example from the design of callable bonds.

Notes and References

Financial innovation is treated in Allen and Gale (1994), while issues relating to product positioning and the marketing of financial products are discussed by Wind (1987) and Green and Krieger (1991). Tufano (1989) refers to a database of 58 financial innovations introduced between 1974 and 1986 by investment banks. Miller (1986), Merton (1988), and Ross (1989), provide complementary arguments on the drivers of financial innovation. Miller makes the case for taxes and regulations; Merton makes the case for transaction costs; and Ross analyzes the role of financial institutions and of marketing. Holmer and Zenios (1995) suggest the framework for designing financial products.

Single premium deferred annuities and their pricing are discussed in Asay, Bouyoucos and Marciano (1993), and the development of risk management models for portfolios of these products is discussed in Nielsen and Zenios (1996).

For asset-backed securities see Jobst (2003), Fabozzi and Goodman (2001), and Kendall (1996).

Mortgage-backed securities are discussed in Fabozzi (1989), and prepayment models by Richard and Roll (1989), and Kang and Zenios (1992). Kang and Zenios in particular give details of both their models and the calibration process. The literature on this topic is extensive and additional references can be found in these publications. One of the earlier successful attempts to model explicitly the effect of interest rates and other factors on prepayment is due to Curley and Guttentag (1974), followed by the dissertation of Peters (1979) where she identified more than a dozen explanatory variables that influence the prepayment behavior of different types of mortgages. Navratil (1985), and Green and Shoven (1986) use, respectively, a logistic model and a proportional hazards model to estimate the effect of variations in interest rates on prepayments. Jacob, Lord and Tilley (1987) discuss a prepayment model used in generalized pricing; Boyle (1989) discusses the valuation of Canadian mortgage-backed securities; and Zenios (1993c) discusses Monte Carlo simulation methods for the valuation of these complex securities.

For a discussion on the Modigliani-Miller theorem see Ingersoll (1987).

The market reward for different levels of leverage and for different values of duration of the gap between assets and liabilities was studied empirically for a large sample of property-casualty insurance companies by Babbel and Staking (1991).

The models for designing callable bonds and portfolios of callable bonds are from Consiglio and Zenios (1997, 1999); the empirical results reported in this chapter are from Consiglio and Zenios (1999).

A tabu search heuristic algorithm for solving the global optimization problems arising in the design of callable bonds is described in the Appendix of Consiglio and Zenios (1997). For general references on tabu search see Glover (1986), and Glover and Laguna (1997); for simulated annealing see Kirkpatrick et al. (1983).

Chapter 9

Scenario Generation

> The very notion of accuracy and the acceptability of a measurement, observation, description, count, is inseparably tied to the use to which it is to be put.
>
> Oscar Morgenstern, *On the Accuracy of Economic Observations*

9.1   Preview

In this chapter we discuss the generation of forward-looking scenarios describing uncertainty in the states of an economy and in the financial markets. Disparate sources of risk are integrated in a common framework, and time information is also incorporated. These scenario generation methods provide the data needed to implement the optimization models discussed in previous chapters. Scenarios and their properties are discussed first, followed by a general framework for building scenario generation models for both assets and liabilities. Three scenario generation methods are then introduced, using either historical data or mathematical models. These methods are suitable for the generation of scenarios for single-period optimization models. The chapter concludes with methods for constructing event trees for multi-period, dynamic, portfolio optimization models.

9.2   Scenarios and their Properties

The models in this book address optimal decision making in the face of uncertainty. Uncertainty is treated using discrete random variables together with the associated probabilities. As time evolves in discrete steps, the random variables take one of a finite set of values. This set is the sample space, and its elements are indexed by l from an index set Ω. The value taken by a discrete random variable, together with the associated probability is a scenario, as introduced in Definitions 1.2.1 and 6.2.1. The scenarios, indexed by l from a set Ω, have a probability $p^l \geq 0$ associated with them such that $\sum_{l \in \Omega} p^l = 1$.

Scenarios describe the evolution of a random variable over time; they are not forecasts of the random variable. A forecast is a prediction that the random variable will take on a specific value, that is, a single scenario will occur. Being right about which scenario will occur is crucial but difficult to achieve. There are even arguments that financial forecasting is impossible: if we could predict with certainty the value of a financial quantity, this prediction would encourage trading behavior, which would in turn cause a change in the value. Scenarios do not forecast, but aim to identify possible future events indexed by a set Ω. They also prescribe a likelihood to each one of these events, i.e., the probabilities p^l for all $l \in \Omega$. Scenarios give an accurate description of the future in the form of plausible events. We may not know which event will occur, but we know plausible events and the likelihood that each will occur.

In the context of the financial applications, scenarios describe the evolution of random variables related to the relevant financial and economic quantities, such as commodity prices, asset or index returns, macroeconomic indicators such as price and wage inflation, or economic growth. We will identify the underlying sources of uncertainty, i.e., the risk factors, and develop scenarios describing the random nature of these factors. All other quantities can be derived from these basic random variables. The risk factors of Section 2.2 are the basic random variables for financial applications, and we will use scenarios to study the evolution of the risk factors over time.

We could use scenarios to study directly the evolution of financial instruments or of portfolios over time, instead of studying the underlying risk factors. This approach is inappropriate for enterprise risk management, as it would make the study of portfolio risk, and therefore of enterprise risk, opaque. That is, we would have no information on the sources of uncertainty for the prices of the instruments in a portfolio, or for multiple portfolios.

Working with scenarios of the risk factors has several advantages for enterprise risk management. Risk factor scenarios allow us to integrate disparate sources of risk by generating plausible values for each one. Since most financial instruments or asset classes are exposed to multiple sources of risk their integration is essential, and the correlations between the risk factors must be captured. With the use of scenarios risk management becomes transparent, as the uncertainty of a portfolio value or the enterprise-wide risk can be attributed to specific factors.

There are also some computational advantages to using scenarios. For instance, given scenarios of multiple risk factors we can generate scenarios of portfolio values from the risk factor values and the exposure of the portfolio assets to these factors. New portfolios or instruments can be analyzed jointly with our existing portfolios since correlations are captured though the common factors. There is no need to recalculate joint scenarios for both existing and new instruments since the prices of the new instruments can be derived conditional on values of the risk factors.

Scenarios are defined over a single time horizon or for multiple future time periods. The models of Chapter 5 deal with a single time period, and scenarios describe plausible values of the risk factors at the end of the horizon T. In the models of Chapter 6 we have multiple trading dates. Scenarios should describe plausible values of the risk factors at the next trading date, conditioned on the prevailing state at the current trading date. To accommodate multi-period dynamic optimization we study scenarios using event trees that capture the intertemporal evolution of the risk factors.

9.2.1 Scenario definition

A formal definition of scenarios was first given in the context of the dynamic portfolio optimization models in Section 6.2 (see Definitions 1.2.1 and 6.2.1). The definition makes use of event trees. An event tree is represented formally as a graph $\mathcal{G} = (\Sigma, \mathcal{E})$ where nodes Σ denote time and state, and links $\mathcal{E}$ indicate possible transitions among states as time evolves. At time t the states are denoted by the set $\Sigma_t = \{s_t^\nu \mid \nu = 1, 2, \ldots, S_t\}$, and there are S_t possible states at time t. Hence, $\Sigma = \bigcup_{t=0}^{T} \Sigma_t$ and $\mathcal{E} \subset \Sigma \times \Sigma$.

The elements of $\mathcal{E}$ are denoted by ordered pairs $(s_t^{\nu(t)}, s_{t+1}^{\nu(t+1)})$ where we explicitly indicate the dependence of the index ν on t. The order of the nodes indicates that state $s_{t+1}^{\nu(t+1)}$ at time $t + 1$ can be reached from state $s_t^{\nu(t)}$ at time t. $s_{t+1}^{\nu(t+1)}$ is the successor state and $s_t^{\nu(t)}$ is the predecessor state. That is, using the superscript $+$ to denote successor states, and superscript $-$ to denote predecessors, we have $\left(s_t^{\nu(t)}\right)^+ = s_{t+1}^{\nu(t+1)}$ and $\left(s_{t+1}^{\nu(t+1)}\right)^- = s_t^{\nu(t)}$.

An event tree has the following properties:

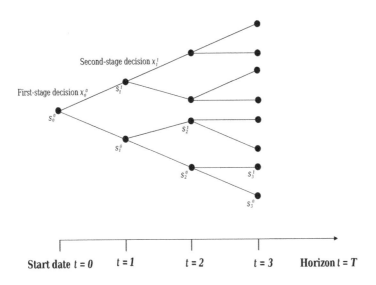

Figure 9.1: Event tree with three trading dates.

1. $\Sigma_0 = \{s_0^0\}$ is a singleton, and s_0^0 is the unique state known as the *root node*, and it has no predecessor.

2. Every non-root state $s_t^{\nu(t)}$ has a unique predecessor from the set of states Σ_{t-1} for all $t = 1, 2, \ldots, T$. Uniqueness of predecessors implies that the graph $\mathcal{G}$ has no cycles.

A formal definition of scenarios using event trees was given in Definition 6.2.1 as paths of the graph $\mathcal{G} = (\Sigma, \mathcal{E})$ denoted by the sequence $\{s_0^{\nu(0)}, s_1^{\nu(1)}, \ldots, s_{\tau_l}^{\nu(\tau_l)}\}$ such that $(s_t^{\nu(t)}, s_{t+1}^{\nu(t+1)}) \in \mathcal{E}$, for all $t = 0, 1, \ldots, \tau_l$, and $\tau_l \le T$, together with their associated probabilities. Scenarios are indexed from a set Ω with a scenario index l, and the probabilities satisfy $\sum_{l \in \Omega} p^l = 1$. The state visited by scenario l at t is denoted by $n_t(l)$, so that $n_t(l) = s_t^{\nu(t)}$.

The definition of scenarios using event trees clearly shows that some scenarios may have common states up to a given trading date. For instance in Figure 9.1 we see that four scenarios share common states s_0^0 and s_1^0 up to $t = 1$, while another four share state s_0^0 and s_1^1. A dynamic trading strategy for the first four scenarios may differ at trading dates $t > 1$, but the portfolio rebalancing at $t = 1$ must be the same for these scenarios since they share the same state s_1^1. In the event tree it is clear that states s_2^0 and s_2^1 share the same predecessor, i.e., $(s_2^0)^- = (s_2^1)^- = s_1^0$.

9.2.2   Scenario properties

In order to be useful for financial planning, scenarios should posses the following properties.

Correctness. Scenarios should conform with the prevalent theories that model the underlying random variable. For instance, term structures should exhibit mean reversion, and intertemporal volatility of the random variables should be persistent. Scenarios should be derived from a "correct" theoretical model of the random variable – to the extent that prevalent theoretical models are considered correct. Scenarios that satisfy this property must also cover all relevant past history, as it is plausible that any events observed in the past may also occur in the future. Furthermore, scenarios should account for events that were not observed in the past but which are plausible under current market conditions. Scenarios derived from correct theoretical models and properly calibrated using all available historical data will account for past observations, and will also foresee possible events that were not observed in the past.

Accuracy. Scenarios should accurately approximate the theoretical model from which they are derived. As scenarios are discretizations of some, often continuous, probability distribution function, it is unavoidable that some errors will be introduced in the discretization process. Accuracy is ensured when, for instance, the first and higher moments of the scenarios match those of the underlying theoretical distribution. A large number of scenarios may be necessary, using a fine discretization grid, to achieve the accuracy considered acceptable for the application at hand.

Consistency. Scenarios that model more than one variable should ensure that the values of these variables are internally consistent. The generation of event trees with multiple bonds or derivatives requires special attention. The prices of bonds with different maturities are often driven by a small number of underlying risk factors such as the short-term interest rate, a long-term yield, and the credit spread. Because of the close relationship between bond prices and interest rates, the price movements of bonds of a similar type, but with different maturities, should be consistent. For instance, arbitrage opportunities (see Definition 9.5.1) between the short and long rates should be avoided in term structure models. Similarly, arbitrage opportunities should not be present in scenarios of multiple exchange rates.

The scenarios should also possess some practical properties that are desirable but not necessary. For instance, scenarios should be acceptable to the user, and if need be, modified to gain the user's acceptance. Other practical considerations include ease of calibration and understanding, expandability to accommodate new demands, modularity and ease of computation.

9.3 A Framework for Scenario Generation

Successful applications of financial optimization models hinge on the availability of scenarios that are correct, accurate, and consistent for both assets and liabilities. Obtaining such scenarios is a challenging task. As a first step, a return-generating process for relevant economic factors and asset classes must be specified. This task can be quite complicated; as we have seen in Chapters 1 and 2 many economic factors can affect the assets and liabilities of a large firm, pension fund, or financial institution. Secondly, the liability values have to be estimated with appropriate rules taking into account actuarial risks, pension or social security fund provisions, and other factors that are relevant to the institution's line of business.

Hierarchy of simulation models

The complexity of the financial markets, the interrelationships among risk factors, and their strong dependence on macroeconomic conditions necessitate the development of a hierarchy of models. Market data and mathematical models are interlinked in ways that are consistent with empirical observations and with prevalent theories, while experts may intervene to adjust the results based on their expectations.

A hierarchy of models is illustrated in Figure 9.2 and it provides the framework for scenario generation. At the first level of the hierarchy we model macroeconomic variables. Those drive the financial markets and the liabilities. For instance, price and wage inflation define the benefits of pension funds or the social security system, but they also affect stock dividend growth and stock returns. The second level of analysis deals with the basics of the financial markets and the modeling of yield curves, credit spreads, exchange rates, and dividends. These variables are used to determine the performance – price or return – of asset classes, but they may also determine the liabilities. For instance, the short rates on the yield curve determine the return on cash, but

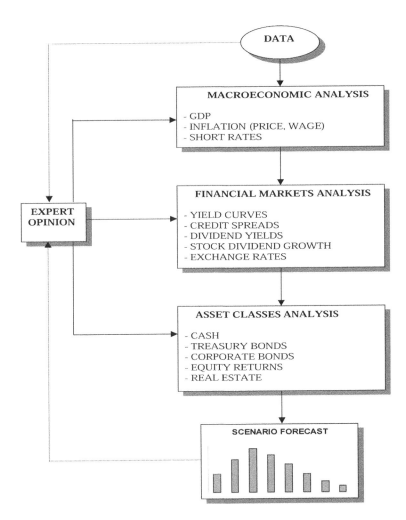

Figure 9.2: Hierarchy of simulation models for the generation of scenarios for asset and liability management.

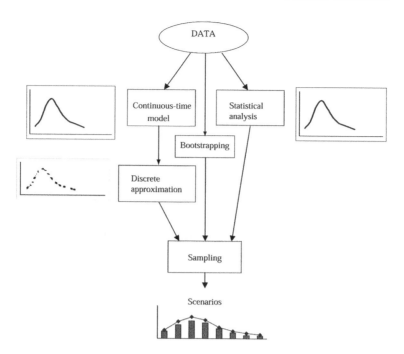

Figure 9.3: Scenario generation methodologies: Bootstrapping of historical data, statistical analysis of data, and discrete approximations of continuous-time models.

also set the discount rate applied in the pricing of liabilities with actuarial methods. Similarly, the long rates determine the returns of long maturity bonds, but also affect the lapse behavior of insurance contract policyholders or mortgage refinancing by a bank's borrowers. The third level of the hierarchy uses the information about the financial markets to determine prices and returns of all relevant asset classes. The hierarchy of models is completed with a feedback mechanism that allows for expert intervention.

Scenario generation methodologies

At each level of the hierarchy we may adopt different methodologies for generating scenarios. These choices are illustrated in Figure 9.3. One approach samples historical data through boot-strapping to develop scenarios for the random variable of interest. A second approach develops statistical models to fit the observed data and then samples the fitted probability distributions. A third approach develops continuous-time theoretical models with parameters estimated to fit the historical data. These models are then discretized and their performance is simulated to generate scenarios. Sampling is a data-based method for scenario generation, while statistical analysis and discretizations of continuous-time models are model-based methods. These three methods are further discussed in Section 9.4.

The hierarchy of models and the methodological choices illustrated in the two figures (9.2 and 9.3) provide a comprehensive framework for scenario generation for financial optimization models. They also allow for the generation of scenarios that satisfy the properties of correctness, accuracy, and consistency.

Bootstrapping methods are correct in describing historical data, but they are not able to generate scenarios that have not been observed in the past, even if they are plausible given current conditions. Since these scenarios have been observed in practice they also satisfy consistency requirements and, given large enough samples, they are also accurate.

Statistical modeling is correct to the extent that the fitted probability distributions satisfy the necessary theoretical properties. For instance, a normal distribution for modeling exchange rates is incorrect as exchange rates cannot become negative. A lognormal distribution has better theoretical properties for modeling exchange rates. Normality may be a good approximation for stock returns when estimating means and variances for the models in Chapter 3. However, the fat tails of stock returns are important for capturing the extreme events needed in the calculation of the VaR or CVaR risk measures (Definitions 2.6.1 and 2.6.3). Accuracy requires careful sampling of large scenario sets using variance reduction techniques. Consistency may be more difficult to satisfy as it requires imposing restrictions on the sampled scenario.

Continuous-time models that are both theoretically correct and consistent can be developed. Accuracy, however, may be sacrificed in the discretization step. Coarse discretizations introduce errors, while finer discretizations will create a very large scenario universe. Sampling this scenario universe introduces additional inaccuracies, and inconsistencies may also arise when small sample sizes are used.

Event trees

In order to solve multi-stage dynamic models the distributions underlying the scenario generation process have to be discretized with a small number of nodes in an event tree. Otherwise the computational effort needed for solving the model would explode. Clearly, a small number of nodes for describing the return distribution might lead to approximation error. An important issue is to limit the approximation error in the event tree to avoid biases in the optimal solutions of the model. Moreover, event trees for models with options and derivative securities require special attention to preclude arbitrage opportunities and preserve the consistency of the scenario generation method. These issues are addressed in Section 9.5

9.3.1   Scenarios for the liabilities

An enterprise-wide risk management model requires a projection of the future value of the liabilities. The liabilities typically represent future obligatory payments by the financial institution or firm. Examples include liabilities resulting from bank deposits, pension fund or social security obligations due to future benefit payments, and liabilities resulting from the sale of insurance contracts. Each firm and financial institution typically has its own unique set of liabilities. Hence we cannot provide a general recipe for calculating the value of the liabilities. For pension funds and insurance companies actuarial methods can be very important, while other financial institutions might require financial economic valuation models.

The liabilities of pension funds and insurance companies usually consist of a large number of individual contracts, and the development of the total liability value is influenced by multiple sources of uncertainty. As this setting frustrates mathematical analysis, simulation is an important approach for risk management applications with a complex liability structure. A simulation model must be able to capture the complex interactions between the state of the economy, the financial markets, asset prices, and the value of the liabilities. We mention a few examples to illustrate the interactions: the liabilities of defined benefits pension funds are driven by inflation; the liabilities created by insurance investment products may depend on the yield curve as high long-term yields may encourage policyholders to surrender their policies before maturity; the liabilities of multinational corporations depend on exchange rates. The hierarchy of simulation models in Figure 9.2 generates sufficient information to capture these interactions.

User intervention is an important part of the process as some effects cannot be captured by simulation models. These are sometimes called "Gorbachev effects" in reference to changes brought about by events that could not be anticipated in any simulation model, such as those initiated by the Soviet leader Mikhail Gorbachev in the 1980s that brought about the unexpected fall of the Soviet Union.

We discuss briefly two examples of liability models. Simulation systems for pension funds first simulate the future status of a large group of fund participants, according to assumed mortality rates, retirement rates, job termination rates, and career promotion probabilities. As a second step, values of the future wage growth are simulated, as this is an important factor for determining the pension payments in the long run. Combining the simulated status of the individual participants with the simulated wage growth we generate the future liabilities under the scenarios. The value of these liabilities at some planning horizon τ is calculated as the discounted expected value of the pension payments for periods past τ. Established actuarial rules apply for the valuation once the economic and financial scenarios have been generated, and the formula used in Definition 2.5.1 for the calculation of holding period returns applies. Accurate projections of the future liabilities are then needed for periods past the planning horizon.

A different approach is taken by financial institutions such as banks and money management firms, which deal primarily with assets and liabilities that are highly influenced by changes in interest rates. The same is true for some investment products offered by insurers. The nature of their business gives rise to another important class of risk management problems where the main source of risk is the volatility of the asset classes. The liabilities of defined contribution pension plans – i.e., pension plans whereby the benefits are linked directly to the pensioner's contributions – are also mainly affected by interest rate changes, as fixed future payments are discounted at the current market interest rate. For this class of problems the scenario generation methods focus on the simulation of the financial markets, including the risk-free rates, credit spreads, liquidity premia, prepayment, and lapse. Defined benefits pension funds and social security on the other hand – whereby the benefits are independent of prior contributions by the pensioners – fall under the class of models described in the previous paragraph as the benefits depend, through some regulatory formula, on economic indicators such as inflation or wage growth.

9.3.2   Scenarios of economic factors and asset returns

We now turn to scenario generation for asset returns. Enterprise-wide risk management requires simulation systems that integrate the asset prices with the liability values. This integration is crucial as the assets and liabilities are often affected by common underlying economic factors. For example, in pension fund simulations wage growth and inflation are crucial factors for the value of the liabilities, but these factors are also associated with the long-run returns on stocks and bonds. In fixed-income applications for money management, the short-term interest rate drives the returns on both assets and liabilities. Integration of assets with liabilities is critical for successful risk management applications at an enterprise-wide level. This integration starts with consistent simulations of future scenarios for both sides of the balance sheet. As mentioned above, the liabilities are often unique and different in each application, so we concentrate on generating scenarios for economic factors and asset returns. Values of the liabilities may be added to the economic scenarios with a consistent method following actuarial practices or standard financial valuation tools.

Scenario generation methods for different asset classes have different characteristics. As in the case of liabilities, a general recipe for calculating asset returns is not possible, although some methods are applicable to broad asset classes. We discuss here some examples to illustrate the issues.

Methods for generating price scenarios for fixed-income and interest-rate derivatives require first the generation of short-term interest rates. For instance, a suitable model can be calibrated for short-term rates in such a way that the prices of treasury bonds computed with this model are consistent with observed market prices. At a minimum the interest rates generated from the model can price accurately, in a risk-neutral world, the default-free treasury bonds. The prices of other relevant interest rate dependent securities – such as mortgage-backed securities, single-premium deferred annuities or callable bonds – can be estimated from the same model by applying financial valuation rules and simulations for other risk factors such as prepayments, lapse, or exercise of call options. The prices of these securities are now consistent with the prices of risk-free treasury bonds and the additional risk factors for each new security. Finally, consistent scenarios of interest rates and fixed-income security prices can be constructed from simulations of the model. This methodology generates price scenarios under the risk-neutral probability measure. For short horizons the risk-neutral and the objective measures are indistinguishable and the scenario generation is valid. For long horizons the methodology breaks down – except for problems involving index replication when the probabilities are not used in the optimization models – and a risk premium must be estimated and incorporated in the valuation stage.

For corporate bonds and credit derivatives we need to model together the short-term rates and the credit spreads. Once again appropriate models can be calibrated to jointly represent these two risk factors, for example, multinomial lattices that provide discrete approximations to continuous models and are extensively used in practice. Such models are calibrated so that the interest rates and credit spreads from these lattices correctly price corporate bonds of different maturities and different rating classes. The prices of credit derivatives can be computed from the model by simulating other risk factors – such as default and recovery rates, or migration among rating classes – and applying financial valuation rules. Scenarios of security prices can be generated by simulating interest rates, credit spreads, migration or default events, and recovery rates from these models.

In the case of discrete lattice-based models an important distinction must be made between *state-dependent* and *path-dependent* securities. In the former case the price of a security is uniquely determined at each state of the lattice. In the latter case the prices depend on the path that leads to a given state. While the number of states is a polynomial function of the number of steps, the number of paths grows exponentially. For instance, a 360-step binomial lattice of monthly steps over 30 years has $360^2/2$ states but 2^{360} paths.

The generation of scenarios for the equities markets requires yet a different approach. Stock returns are due to dividend growth and capital appreciation. Dividend growth is linked to macroeconomic variables such as price and wage inflation, while both dividend growth and capital appreciation are linked to short rates. The linkages can be modeled either with the use of continuous-time models or with statistical analysis of time series. The linkage is usually studied first at an aggregate level whereby a stock index is linked to the marcoeconomic and financial variables of the country. Dividend yields and capital appreciation are then linked to the return of a major stock index. The prices of specific stocks or of stock market sub-indices – technology stocks, large capitalization stocks – can be derived from a CAPM model that relates stock prices to the level of an index. This hierarchical approach links the returns of equities to macroeconomic variables.

9.4   Scenario Generation Methodologies

Methodologies for scenario generation at any level of the simulation hierarchy, and for either assets or liabilities, were highlighted in Figure 9.3. We discuss here three specific approaches taking market data as the point of departure.

One approach directly samples historical data (bootstrapping), assuming that historical observations are events that provide a representative set of likely future events. This is the approach sometimes followed in solving aggregate asset allocation problems in the context of enterprise-wide risk management. Since all scenarios consist of combinations of market data that have been observed in practice, they are both correct and consistent. These scenarios could also be sufficiently accurate For large samples. However, this approach does not provide any causal relationships among the different levels of the modeling hierarchy. Hence, it leaves little room for expert intervention. For instance, experts may have views on the macroeconomy (e.g., inflation rates) but in the absence of a model that relates the macroeconomic variables to financial markets and asset classes performance they are unable to adjust the scenarios of asset returns.

A second approach models historical data using statistical analysis. A probability distribution is fitted to the data, and sample scenarios are then drawn from this distribution. This is the approach typically followed in the RiskMetrics methodology for estimating Value-at-Risk. There is no causal relationship among the variables in the hierarchy of models. However, the variables are related through the choice of the theoretical distributions and the calibrated coefficients. For instance, if a multivariate normal distribution is calibrated for multiple risk factors the correlations among them will be properly modeled. The scenarios generated with this method will be correct, if distributions with the appropriate theoretical properties are selected. Accuracy can be ensured if the chosen distribution is accurately fitted to available data. Consistency is more difficult to achieve, as it requires the estimation of multivariate distributions with consistency constraints. Time series analysis with vector autoregressive modeling is also applied, and this allows the joint calibration of economic factors and asset returns. The properties of correctness and accuracy can be satisfied, but to achieve consistency special methods are needed for constructing the sample space.

Statistical modeling allows for user intervention. Users intervene with Bayesian updates of the parameters of the estimated probability distributions. This practice is prone to introducing errors, and errors may also be introduced at the sampling stage.

The third approach to scenario generation is to develop continuous-time models and discrete approximations of these models. These models are calibrated using market data, and samples drawn from these models provide the scenarios. This is the approach typically followed in pricing interest rate contingent claims. The continuous-time models and their discrete approximations satisfy the properties of correctness, accuracy, and consistency. However, errors may be introduced at the sampling stage. For instance, the discrete model may have a lognormal distribution with market-driven means and variances, but the sample of scenarios may not follow a lognormal distribution, or its mean and variance may be biased.

9.4.1 Bootstrapping historical data

The simplest approach for generating scenarios using only the available data without any mathematical modeling is to bootstrap a set of historical records. Each scenario is a sample of returns of the assets obtained by sampling returns that were observed in the past. Dates from the available historical records are selected randomly, and for each date in the sample we read the returns of all asset classes realized during the previous month. These samples are scenarios of monthly returns. To generate scenarios of returns for a long horizon – say 10 years – we sample 120 monthly returns from different points in time. The compounded return of the sampled series is one scenario of the 10-year return. The process is repeated to generate the desired number of scenarios for the 10-year period. With this approach the correlations among asset classes are preserved.

9.4.2 Statistical modeling: the Value-at-Risk approach

The standard RiskMetrics methodology of JP Morgan uses statistical analysis of historical data in estimating expected returns, volatilities, and correlation matrices. These are then used to measure risk exposure of a position through the Value-at-Risk methodology. A standing assumption in RiskMetrics and the estimation of VaR is that returns follow a multivariate lognormal distribution. Hence, the three sets of parameters – expected returns, volatilities, and correlations – are sufficient in describing the return distributions.

We denote the random variables by the K-dimensional random vector $\tilde{\omega}$. The dimension of $\tilde{\omega}$ is equal to the number of risk factors we want to model. The probability density function of $\tilde{\omega}$ is given by

$$f(\tilde{\omega}) = (2\pi)^{-K/2} \mid Q \mid^{-1/2} \exp\left[-\frac{1}{2}(\tilde{\omega} - \bar{\omega})^{\top} Q^{-1}(\tilde{\omega} - \bar{\omega})\right],$$ (9.1)

where $\bar{\omega}$ is the expected value of $\tilde{\omega}$ and Q is the covariance matrix.

The covariance matrix Q and the expected values $\bar{\omega}$ of all random variables involved in the model can be calculated from historical data. For instance, the expected value can be estimated by the mean. Assuming a sample of size N of historical observations ω^l, and assuming that all historical events are equally probable, we have

$$\bar{\omega} = \frac{1}{N} \sum_{l=1}^{N} \tilde{\omega}^l.$$ (9.2)

Similarly, the covariance between factors j and j' is estimated using the historical observations by

$$\rho_{jj'} = \frac{N}{N-1} \sum_{l=1}^{N} \frac{1}{N}(\omega_j^l - \bar{\omega}_j)(\omega_{j'}^l - \bar{\omega}_{j'}),$$ (9.3)

and we have $\rho_{jj} = \sigma_j^2$.

Once the multivariate normal distribution is calibrated we can use it in Monte Carlo simulations.

Conditional sampling of multivariate normal distributions

We can generate scenarios of some of the random variables conditioned on values of the remaining variables. Users may have views on some of the variables, or a more detailed model from the cascade of simulation models in Figure 9.2 may be used to estimate a subset of the variables. This information can be incorporated when sampling the multivariate distribution.

The multivariate normal variable $\tilde{\omega}$ is partitioned into two subvectors $\tilde{\omega}_1$ and $\tilde{\omega}_2$, where $\tilde{\omega}_1$ is the vector of dimension κ_1 of random variables for which some additional information is available and $\tilde{\omega}_2$ is the vector of dimension $\kappa_2 = K - \kappa_1$ of the remaining variables. The expected value vector and covariance matrix are partitioned similarly as

$$\bar{\omega} = \begin{pmatrix} \bar{\omega}_1 \\ \bar{\omega}_2 \end{pmatrix} \text{ and } Q = \begin{pmatrix} Q_{11} & Q_{12} \\ Q_{21} & Q_{22} \end{pmatrix}.$$ (9.4)

The marginal probability density function of $\tilde{\omega}_2$ given $\tilde{\omega}_1 = \omega_1^*$ is

$$f(\tilde{\omega}_2 \mid \tilde{\omega}_1 = \omega_1^*) =$$
$$(2\pi)^{-\kappa_2/2} \mid Q_{22.1} \mid^{-1/2} \exp\left[-\frac{1}{2}(\tilde{\omega}_2 - \bar{\omega}_{2.1})^{\top} Q_{22.1}^{-1}(\tilde{\omega}_2 - \bar{\omega}_{2.1})\right],$$ (9.5)

where the conditional expected value and covariance matrix are given by

$$\bar{\omega}_{2.1}(\omega_1^*) = (\bar{\omega}_2 - Q_{21} Q_{11}^{-1} \mu_1) + Q_{21} Q_{11}^{-1} \omega_1^*,$$ (9.6)

and

$$Q_{22.1} = Q_{22} - Q_{21} Q_{11}^{-1} Q_{12},$$ (9.7)

respectively. Scenarios of $\tilde{\omega}_2$ for t periods conditioned on values of $\tilde{\omega}_1$ given by ω_1^* can be generated from the multivariate normal variables from (9.5) through the expression

$$\tilde{\omega}_{2i}^t = \omega_{2i}^0 e^{\sigma_i \sqrt{t} \tilde{\omega}_{2i}},$$ (9.8)

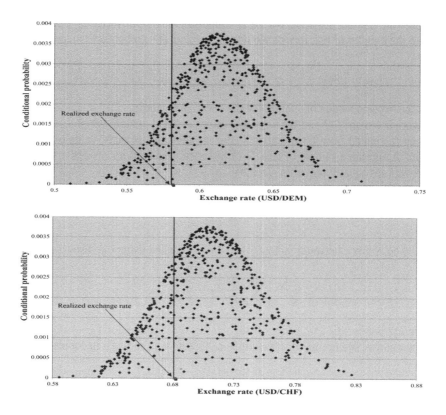

Figure 9.4: Exchange rate scenarios and their conditional probabilities for the deutchmark (DEM) and Swiss franc (CHF) against the USD.

where ω_{2i}^0 is today's value and σ_i is the single-period volatility of the ith component of the random variable $\tilde{\omega}_2$.

This method is used in Chapter 10 to generate exchange rate scenarios, conditioned on scenarios of interest rates. These joint scenarios of interest and exchange rates are used in the management of international bond portfolios. Figure 9.4 illustrates the conditional probabilities for several exchange rate scenarios. On the same figure we plot the exchange rate that was realized ex post on the date for which the scenarios were estimated. Note that the same exchange rate value may be obtained for various scenarios of interest rates and samples drawn from equation (9.5); the figure plots several points with the same exchange rate value but different conditional probabilities.

9.4.3   Statistical modeling: time series analysis

Time series models relate the value of variables at given points in time to the values of these variables at previous time periods. Is this methodological approach appropriate for the hierarchy of scenario generation models? Causal effects between variables are not captured, but correlations between them are. Time series analysis is particularly suitable for solving aggregate asset allocation problems when the correlations among asset classes are very important. When time series analysis is extended to model the correlations with some macroeconomic variables such as the short rates, or the financial markets such as yield curves, the resulting simulation models can also be used to describe the evolution of liabilities.

Time series analysis

Vector autoregressive models (VAR and not VaR which stands for Value-at-Risk) are used extensively in economic modeling. Assume that some variable I_j can be explained in part by its past values. Such a relationship can be described by the following autoregressive model with autocorrelations up to order τ_0:

$$I_{j\tau} = \alpha_0 + \sum_{t=1}^{\tau_0} \alpha_t I_{j(\tau-t)} + \epsilon_\tau. \tag{9.9}$$

$\{\alpha_t\}_{t=0}^{\tau_0}$ are parameters of the model and the error term is assumed to be normally distributed with mean zero, $\epsilon_\tau \sim N(0, \sigma^2)$. It is interesting to gain some insights into the behavior of this model for generating scenarios of $I_{j\tau}$ as $\tau \to \infty$. For instance, if $\tau_0 = 1$ the model takes the form $I_{j\tau} = \alpha_0 + \alpha_1 I_{j(\tau-1)} + \epsilon_t$. If $|\alpha_1| > 1$ the process does not converge even for $\tau \to \infty$. For $|\alpha_1| < 1$ we obtain a mean-reverting process that converges to $\alpha_0/(1 - \alpha_1)$. The larger the deviation from a long-term average the stronger is the tendency toward the average at the next step.

   If instead of modeling the random variable directly we model its logarithm, then, due to the normality assumption of the error terms, we obtain a lognormal distribution of the variable. Hence, vector autoregressive models can be correct in modeling risk factors that follow normal or lognormal processes. The generation of scenarios from a VAR process may introduce sampling error, and the accuracy of scenario generation methods from VAR models hinges on the use of variance reduction techniques and the use of large samples. As normality of errors is assumed, a simple antithetic sampling may work well.

   Ensuring consistency of the scenarios is nontrivial when extending VAR to the multivariate case, modeling simultaneously multiple time series as discussed below. Scenarios sampled without restrictions from a multivariate VAR model may not be consistent except in matching the observed auto- and cross-correlations.

Multivariate time series analysis

A multivariate VAR model on the time series of K risk factors takes the form

$$I_\tau = \bar{I} + V(I_{\tau-1} - \bar{I}) + \epsilon_\tau, \tag{9.10}$$

where I_τ is the K-dimensional vector of the risk factors with a long-term expected value $\bar{I}$; V is a $K \times K$ matrix of coefficients; and $\epsilon_t \sim N(0, Q)$ is the vector of error terms. This model allows for autocorrelation and cross-correlation of the first order. However, it is not a full hierarchical model as given in Section 9.3. Autocorrelations and cross-correlations are captured but no causal effects among the variables are identified.

   To illustrate the calibration process of a scenario generation system for economic factor values and asset returns, we consider a simulation system for modeling financial assets used for long-term strategic planning by pension fund managers. The model considers only a small set of broad asset classes as possible investments: deposits, bonds, real estate, and stocks. Apart from the returns on these assets, each scenario should contain information about future wage growth in order to calculate the future values of the pension liabilities. The vector autoregressive model of the time series of asset returns and of wage growth is as follows:

$$R_t = c + V h_{t-1} + \epsilon_t, \ \epsilon_t \sim N(0, Q), \ t = 1, 2, \ldots, T, \tag{9.11}$$

$$R_{it} = \ln(1 + r_{it}), \ \text{for all } i \in U, \ t = 1, 2, \ldots, T, \tag{9.12}$$

where n is the number of asset time series; r_{it} is the discrete rate of change of variable i in year t; R_t is an n-dimensional vector of continuously compounded rates; c is the n-dimensional vector

Table 9.1: Statistics of time series for asset returns in the Netherlands for the period 1956–1994.[1]

	mean	standard deviation	skewness	kurtosis
wages	0.061	0.044	0.434	2.169
deposits	0.055	0.025	0.286	2.430
bonds	0.061	0.063	0.247	3.131
real estate	0.081	0.112	-0.492	7.027
stocks	0.102	0.170	0.096	2.492

[1] Wages represent the rate of change of the general wage level in the Netherlands. The time series for deposits is based on the average of the 3-month borrowing rate for government agencies. In each year a premium of 0.5% has been subtracted, because the pension fund will have to lend cash to commercial banks. The asset class of bonds represents the total return of a roll-over investment in long-term Dutch government bonds. Real estate consists of total returns of the property fund Rodamco. Stocks are the total return of the internationally diversified mutual fund Robeco.

Table 9.2: Correlations of asset classes, annually 1956–1994.

	wages	deposits	bonds	real estate	stocks
wages	1				
deposits	-0.059	1			
bonds	-0.127	0.259	1		
real estate	0.162	-0.053	0.360	1	
stocks	-0.296	-0.157	0.379	0.326	1

of coefficients; V is an $n \times n$ matrix of coefficients; ϵ_t is the n-dimensional vector of error terms; and Q is the $n \times n$ covariance matrix. The coefficients of the model were estimated using annual observations of the total asset returns and the general wage increase in the Netherlands from 1956 to 1994 (see "Notes and References" at the end of this chapter for related references on this application). Table 9.1 displays descriptive statistics of the time series and Table 9.2 displays the correlation matrix.

The specification of the VAR model should be chosen carefully. Although some intertemporal relationships between the returns might be weakly significant based on historical data, that does not imply that these relationships are also useful for generating scenarios for a financial optimization model with long time horizons. To avoid any problems with unstable and spurious predictability of returns, we do not use lagged variables to explain the returns of bonds, real estate, and stocks in the VAR model (Table 9.3). The time series of the return on deposits and the increase in the wage level, on the other hand, are known to have some memory, so we model them using a first-order autoregressive process.

There are many methods for estimating VAR models (see references at the end of this chapter). Table 9.3 shows the estimated coefficients, while Table 9.4 displays the estimated correlation matrix of the residuals. We would like to point out that the average return on bonds is rather low in our sample of data, due to two outliers in 1956 and 1957. To generate plausible future bond returns we increase the coefficient of the bond returns in the VAR model by 1%. For the purpose of generating scenarios we can adjust the coefficients based on subjective expectations, as historical data is not necessarily representative for the future. User intervention may be required, as illustrated in Figure 9.2.

Table 9.3: Coefficients of the Vector Autoregressive (VAR) model for asset returns in the Dutch markets[1]

$\ln(1 + wages_t)$	=	0.018 (2.058)	+	$0.693 \ln(1 + wages_{t-1}) + \epsilon_{1t}$ (5.789)	$\sigma_1 = 0.030$
$\ln(1 + deposits_t)$	=	0.020 (2.865)	+	$0.644 \ln(1 + deposits_{t-1}) + \epsilon_{2t}$ (5.448)	$\sigma_2 = 0.017$
$\ln(1 + bonds_t)$	=	0.058 (6.241)	+	ϵ_{3t}	$\sigma_3 = 0.060$
$\ln(1 + realestate_t)$	=	0.072 (4.146)	+	ϵ_{4t}	$\sigma_4 = 0.112$
$\ln(1 + stocks_t)$	=	0.086 (3.454)	+	ϵ_{5t}	$\sigma_5 = 0.159$

[1] Estimated with iterative weighted least squares using annual data for the period 1956-1994, t-statistics in parenthesis. σ_i denotes the mean square error (standard deviation of the residuals) for each asset return equation $i = 1, 2, \ldots, 5$.

Table 9.4: Residual correlations of VAR model.

	wages	deposits	bonds	real estate	stocks
wages	1				
deposits	0.227	1			
bonds	-0.152	-0.268	1		
real estate	-0.008	-0.179	0.343	1	
stocks	-0.389	-0.516	0.383	0.331	1

Finally, scenarios of asset returns for a financial planning model can be constructed by sampling from the error distribution of the VAR model, given the estimated – and possibly user-adjusted – coefficients of Table 9.3. After the VAR model has been used to generate scenarios of asset returns and wage growth, the liability values can be added to each scenario in a consistent manner by applying appropriate actuarial rules or financial valuation principles.

9.4.4   Discrete lattice approximations of continuous models

Consider the value of some financial asset V as a stochastic process that solves the stochastic differential equation

$$dV_t = \mu(V_t, t)dt + \sigma(V_t, t)dZ. \tag{9.13}$$

In the equation above Z is a standard Wiener process; μ and σ are given functions of V_t and t. An important special case of (9.13) considers the financial asset to be the logarithm of the short-term rate that solves the stochastic differential equation

$$d\ln(r) = \left[\theta(t) + \frac{d\sigma(t)/dt}{\sigma(t)} \ln(r) \right] dt + \sigma(t)dZ. \tag{9.14}$$

It is possible to construct a binomial lattice that is equivalent – as the discretization step tends to zero – to the above model. The short-term rate at period $t = 0, 1, \ldots, T$, and at the state $s_t^{\nu(t)}$ of the binomial lattice is given by

$$r_t^{\nu(t)} = r_t^0 (k_t)^{\nu(t)}, \tag{9.15}$$

where $\{r_t^0\}_{t=0}^T$ and $\{k_t\}_{t=0}^T$ are parameters of the binomial lattice. These parameters are estimated so that the discretized model matches the spot rates and the volatilities of all rates at time

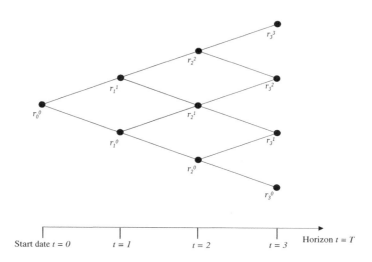

Figure 9.5: Binomial lattice of short-term rates.

zero (i.e., the term structure of interest rates and the rate volatilities are input data). All states of the lattice are assumed equiprobable.

A scenario of short-term interest rates $r^l = \{r_t^{n(l)}\}_{t=0}^\tau$ is a path of rates at different states of the lattice as time passes from today to τ. The state visited by l at time period t is denoted $n_t(l)$ (the time index t on n is dropped from $r_t^{n_t(l)}$ without ambiguity). The scenario can be represented by a sequence of zero-one digits $\{\delta_1^l, \delta_2^l, ..., \delta_\tau^l\}$, where a 0 digit at the tth position corresponds to a down movement on the lattice, and 1 corresponds to an up movement. The state $n_\tau(l)$ reached by this sequence of up and down movements at τ is given by $s_\tau^{\nu(\tau)}$ where $\nu(\tau) = \sum_{l=1}^\tau \delta_t^l$. The corresponding short rate at time τ conditioned on the scenario l is given by $r_\tau^{\nu(\tau)} = r_t^0(k_t)^{\nu(\tau)}$. The probability of each value 0 or 1 is 0.5, and the probability of each scenario of time horizon τ is given by $1/2^{(\tau-1)}$. Figure 9.5 illustrates the binomial lattice.

When there is more than one underlying asset the process is a multidimensional stochastic differential equation. For instance, a two-factor model of short-term, risk-free rates, r_f and credit spreads h, respectively, solves the system of equations:

$$dr_f = r_f \mu_f(t)dt + r_f \sigma_f dZ_f, \tag{9.16}$$
$$dh = h\mu_h(t)dt + h\sigma_h dZ_h. \tag{9.17}$$

A discrete approximation to these processes requires at a minimum a trinomial lattice. The parameters of the lattice are estimated so that the means and variances of the two rates match the current empirically observed rates and their volatilities. Furthermore, the correlation of the two rates should match the current estimate of the correlation matrix. The literature on calibrating lattices is vast and references are given at the end of the chapter.

Figure 9.6 illustrates scenarios of short rates obtained from a binomial and a trinomial lattice, respectively. It is worth noting that while both models were calibrated on the same market data and the scenarios have the same mean and the same variance – within the level of accuracy introduced by the sampling errors – their higher moments are substantially different. The scenarios obtained from a trinomial lattice have much higher extreme values than those generated by the binomial lattice. While for pricing simple bonds these differences are not important, the calcu-

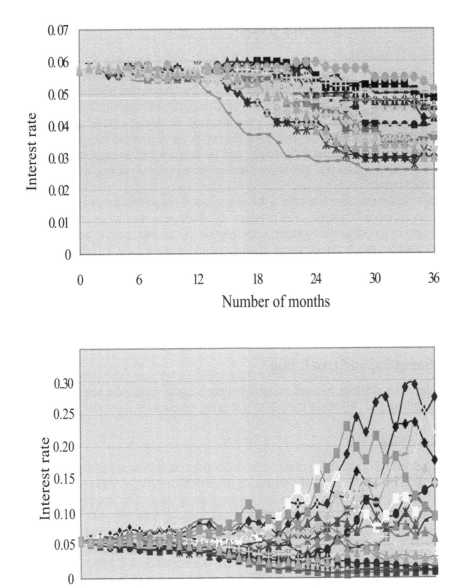

Figure 9.6: Scenarios of short-term interest rates generated using a binomial lattice (top) and a trinomial lattice (bottom), using a downward sloping term structure as input data. For the input data used in the calibration, the binomial lattice generates future term structures that are all downward sloping, while a trinomial lattice generates upward sloping structures as well.

lations of Value-at-Risk and the pricing of bonds with embedded options will differ significantly depending on the model we use.

9.5 Constructing Event Trees

We now turn to the calibration of event trees for multi-period dynamic portfolio optimization. These trees are needed for the implementation of the stochastic programming models of Section 6.6. The return distribution underlying the scenario generation methods discussed in the previous sections must be discretized with a small number of nodes in the event tree, otherwise the computational effort for solving a multi-period, multi-stage model can easily explode. Clearly, a small number of nodes describing the return distribution at every stage of the event tree might lead to some approximation error, and the scenarios of an event tree will not satisfy the required accuracy property. The approximation error in the event tree will bias the optimal solutions of the model.

Another requirement for scenarios used in stochastic programming portfolio models is the pervasive no-arbitrage condition. The presence of arbitrage opportunities in an event tree will bias the results of the optimization model. The solution will develop trading strategies that exploit profit opportunities due to the existence of arbitrage in the event tree, but which are unlikely to materialize in the real world. Event trees that do not satisfy this property are incorrect, even if the scenario generation method from which the event tree was constructed did satisfy the property of correctness.

The construction of event trees that are both correct and accurate is the topic of this section. Consistency is also addressed.

9.5.1 Sampling and tree fitting

We consider three different methods to construct event trees: (i) random sampling; (ii) adjusted random sampling; and (iii) fitting the tree to match the moments of the underlying distribution.

Random sampling

As a first method for constructing event trees we consider random sampling from the error distribution of the VAR model. Given the estimated coefficients and the estimated covariance matrix of the VAR model, we can draw one random vector of yearly returns for bonds, real estate, stocks, deposits, and wage growth. If we would like to construct an event tree with 10 nodes after one year (we assume that the duration of each stage is one year), we can simply repeat this procedure 10 times, sampling independent vectors of returns for each node. The nodes at stage two in the event tree can also be sampled randomly; however, the conditional distribution from stage one to stage two depends on the outcomes at the first stage. For example, wage growth follows an autoregressive process, so the expected wage growth from year one to year two depends on the realized wage growth rate in the previous period. The sampled wage growth data at stage one will be input to the right-hand side of the wage equation (Table 9.3) when sampling error terms at stage two.

Similarly we could construct an event tree using the RiskMetrics Value-at-Risk approach for scenario generation. At each state of the event tree we simulate conditional distributions from equation (9.5).

Consider now a four-stage event tree that branches out to 10 states in stage two; 8 states from each state at stage three; 6 states at the next stage and 2 states at the final stage. This event tree has $10 \times 8 \times 6 = 960$ states at the end of the horizon and presents a reasonably sized model. However, at each time period there are from 10 to two states of the world to represent the underlying conditional distribution of all asset classes of interests. Even for broad strategic asset allocation problems that deal with only a few asset classes, the event tree is very sparse. For instance, with the five asset classes considered in the example of Table 9.3 it is likely that the mean and covariance matrix will be specified incorrectly in most nodes of the tree. As a result the optimizer chooses an investment strategy that has the best return and downside risk characteristics, but based on an erroneous approximation of the return distribution.

The random sampling procedure for constructing a sparse multi-period event tree leads to unstable investment strategies. An obvious way to deal with this problem is to increase the number of nodes in the randomly sampled event tree, in order to reduce the approximation error relative to the scenario generation model. However, the stochastic program might become computationally intractable if we increase the number of nodes at each stage, due to the exponential growth rate of the tree. Alternatively, the switching of asset weights might be bounded by adding constraints to the model. Although we might get a more stable solution in this case, the underlying problem remains the same: the optimal decisions are based on an erroneous representation of the return distributions in the event tree. What is needed is a method to reduce the error. A first approach in doing so is discussed next.

Adjusted random sampling

An adjusted random sampling technique for constructing event trees can resolve some of the problems of the random sampling method. First, assuming an even number of nodes, we apply simple variance reduction techniques, such as *antithetic sampling*, to fit every odd moment of the underlying distribution. Consider, for example, the generation of scenarios from a binomial lattice. If there are 10 succeeding nodes at each stage of the event tree, then we sample first randomly five paths from the lattice. The remaining scenarios are constructed from these five scenarios by simply switching an up movement with a down movement and vice versa, so for each randomly selected scenario we also sample its mirror image.

Similarly, we may sample five vectors of error terms from the VAR model, and the error terms for the five remaining samples are identical but with opposite signs. As a result we match every odd moment of the underlying error distributions. Note that the errors sampled from a VAR model have a mean of zero, whereas the samples from the lattice will have the mean specified as an input parameter in calibrating the lattice.

As a second step we rescale the sampled values to fit the variance. This can be achieved by multiplying the set of sampled returns for each particular asset class by an amount proportional to their distance from the mean. In this way the samples are shifted away from their mean value, thus changing the variance until the target value is achieved.

Investment strategies optimized on an event tree generated by adjusted random sampling are subject to less asset mix switching than that observed with the randomly sampled event trees. The heavy trading activity in the optimal solution obtained using unadjusted random sampling probably results from errors in the mean returns, to which portfolio optimization models are very sensitive. Estimation errors in the mean value can have an effect on the optimal portfolio cash-equivalent value, which may be an order of magnitude larger than the error introduced from misspecification of the variances, which in turn is twice as significant as errors in the estimation of covariance matrices. Using adjusted random sampling to match the mean and the variance substantially reduces useless trading.

Fitting the mean and the covariance matrix

A third method for constructing event trees is to estimate returns that match the first few moments of the underlying return distributions. This can be achieved by solving a nonlinear optimization model. The decision variables in the optimization model are the returns and the probabilities of the event tree, while the objective function and the constraints enforce the desired statistical properties. The probabilities and returns in all nodes of the event tree can be estimated simultaneously. However, with this approach it might take longer to construct a desirable event tree than to solve the stochastic programming model itself. The tree fitting problem can be simplified by applying the method at each stage recursively. This requires the assumption that the return distributions are not path-dependent. This assumption is valid for long-term asset and liability management with broad asset classes, but fails when modeling money management problems with path-dependent securities.

To illustrate the concepts, we write down the tree fitting equations to estimate a set of perturbations that will fit the mean and the residual covariance matrix of the VAR process. The probabilities are assumed uniform in order to ease comparison with random sampling. Let $i = 1, 2, \ldots, n$, denote the random time series that are modeled by the VAR process. In our example these are the returns on stocks, bonds, deposits, real estate and the wage growth rate. Suppose that a total of M succeeding nodes at stage $t+1$ are available to describe the conditional distribution of these random variables in a particular node at stage t. We define the perturbation ϵ_{ti}^l as the realization in node l for the ith element of the vector ϵ_t.

We discuss the tree fitting methods for scenarios generated by the VAR model. The method is equally applicable to scenarios bootstrapped from historical data, those generated by lattice models, and those designed with the RiskMetrics methodology.

A tree fitting model that matches the mean of zero and the estimated covariance of VAR model (9.11)–(9.12) estimates the perturbations by solving equations (9.18) and (9.19). Equation (9.18) specifies that the average of the perturbations should be zero, while equation (9.19) states that they should have a covariance matrix equal to Q:

$$\frac{1}{N} \sum_{l=1}^{N} \epsilon_{ti}^l = 0, \text{ for all } i \in U, \tag{9.18}$$

$$\frac{1}{N-1} \sum_{l=1}^{N} \epsilon_{ti}^l \epsilon_{ti'}^l = Q_{ii'}, \text{ for all } i \in U, \ i' \in U. \tag{9.19}$$

Obtaining a solution of the nonlinear system (9.18)–(9.19) can be difficult, especially when higher order moments like skewness and kurtosis are also included as additional restrictions. Instead of solving a system of nonlinear equations we may solve instead a nonlinear optimization model that penalizes deviations from the desired moments in the objective function. Good starting points for this optimization can be obtained using the adjusted random sampling method of the previous subsection, which is computationally very efficient. After solving the nonlinear fitting model, we can substitute the optimal set of perturbations in the estimated equations of the VAR model to generate conditional return distributions. By applying this procedure recursively, from node to node and from stage to stage, we generate an event tree that fits the time varying conditional expectation and the covariance matrix of the underlying return distributions.

9.5.2 Arbitrage-free event trees

We now turn to the no-arbitrage requirement for event trees. We review first the issues in the context of stochastic programming and then discuss the construction of arbitrage-free event trees. The generation of event trees with multiple bonds or derivatives requires special attention. The prices of bonds with different maturities are often driven by a small number of underlying factors such as the short-term interest rate, a long-term yield and the credit spread. Because of the close relationship between bond prices and interest rates, the price movements of bonds of a similar type, but with different maturities, are often strongly associated. The price changes of derivative securities with a single underlying value, e.g., a stock index, are also often closely related.

An important concept for bond and option valuation is the construction of so-called replicating strategies. For example, consider a portfolio consisting of one stock with price S and a

European put option on this stock with price p, exercise price X and maturity T. We assume that the stock does not pay dividends and that the riskless interest rate for a maturity of T is equal to r. It is straightforward to verify that the value of the first portfolio at time T can be replicated by a strategy that invests $exp(-rT)X$ at the riskless interest rate and holds a European call on the stock with price c, exercise price X and maturity T. Because both portfolios eventually deliver the same payoff at time T, their prices should also be equal at all times t, with $0 \leq t < T$. It follows that the option prices should satisfy the following relation, called put-call parity:

$$p + S = exp(-r(T - t))X + c. \tag{9.20}$$

If the prices of European call and put options with equal strike prices do not satisfy the put-call parity relationship within the range of transaction costs, then there is an arbitrage opportunity available. We could make a riskless profit by selling the overvalued option, while replicating its payoff with a portfolio containing the cheap option. One of the fundamental assumptions in the theory of finance is that arbitrage opportunities are not available: some investors will recognize these opportunities and their trading will immediately eliminate them. The absence of arbitrage and the concept of replicating strategies are at the heart of modern derivative pricing methods.

The absence of arbitrage opportunities is an important property for event trees of asset returns that are used as input for stochastic programming models. If there is an arbitrage opportunity in the event tree, then the optimal solution of the stochastic programming model will exploit it. An arbitrage strategy creates profits without taking risk, and hence it will increase the objective value of nearly any financial planning model. An important question is whether the arbitrage opportunities in the event tree are also available on the actual financial market. It is prudent for long-term risk management applications to generate scenarios that do not allow for arbitrage. If arbitrage does arise in practice the arbitrageurs will exploit it, quickly aligning the real-world with our event tree.

A potential problem for stochastic programming models in risk management is the presence of arbitrage opportunities in the event tree that are due to approximation errors. Arbitrage opportunities might arise because the underlying return distributions are sometimes approximated poorly with a small number of nodes in the event tree. If the application only involves broad asset classes such as a stock index, a bond index, and a real estate index, then arbitrage opportunities might not appear very often because of errors in the event tree. Arbitrage-free scenarios are generated by lattice-based models when the lattice is calibrated to incorporate simultaneously several relevant risk factors. However, applications that involve options, multiple bonds, or other interest rate derivative securities can be quite vulnerable to these problems. For example, the prices of European call and put options with equal strike prices should satisfy put-call parity in each node of the event tree. If this relationship is violated because of approximation error, then the event tree contains a source of spurious profits. The problem is particulary relevant when one needs both asset returns and economic scenarios for the liabilities. In such cases the cascade of scenario generation modules in Figure 9.2 must be arbitrage-free.

Before we introduce scenario generation methods for arbitrage-free event trees we introduce the no-arbitrage theorem from financial economics. First we define arbitrage.

Definition 9.5.1 Arbitrage. *Arbitrage exists when it is possible to create a portfolio with a negative price that provides a nonnegative payoff.*

Suppose that n primitive securities are traded in a one-period model. The initial asset prices are denoted by P_{0i} and the final asset prices and payoffs are P_{1i}^l and F_{1i}^l, respectively, for $i = 1, 2, \ldots, n$, and $l \in \Omega$, where Ω is a scenario set denoting nodes on our event tree. The following conditions are both necessary and sufficient for the absence of arbitrage opportunities:[1]

---

[1]We assume that all initial asset prices are strictly positive. Moreover, at least one primitive asset should have a set of strictly positive prices at time 1.

Theorem 9.5.1 *There are no arbitrage opportunities if and only if there exists a strictly positive probability measure $\pi^l > 0$, such that*

$$\sum_{l \in \Omega} \pi^l \frac{P^l_{1i} + F^l_{1i}}{P_{0i}} = \sum_{l \in \Omega} \pi^l \frac{P^l_{11} + F^l_{11}}{P_{10}}, \quad \text{for all } i \in U. \tag{9.21}$$

If we take the base security $i = 1$ to be the one-period riskless bond, providing a continuously compounded return of r_f, then condition (9.21) reduces to

$$P_{0i} = e^{-r_f} \sum_{l \in \Omega} \pi^l (P^l_{1i} + F^l_{1i}), \quad \text{for all } i \in U. \tag{9.22}$$

It is clear that given a set of n primitive assets, at least n states are needed in the set Ω to satisfy the no-arbitrage condition if we would also like to avoid linearly dependent asset returns. For the event tree of a stochastic programming model this means that we need at least n succeeding states in every node of the event tree in order to represent the conditional return distribution of the assets $i = 1, 2, \dots, n$, from one period to the next. Otherwise we either introduce a money machine or the asset returns become linearly dependent.

In practice, round-off errors might cause the system (9.22) to be infeasible, even if arbitrage profits are economically insignificant due to transaction costs. A version of the no-arbitrage conditions that takes bid-ask spreads into account and is easier to apply is given in the following theorem.

Theorem 9.5.2 *Suppose that assets are bought at time zero at the ask price P^a_{0i} and sold at the bid price P^b_{0i}, with $P^a_{0i} > P^b_{0i}$. Security $i = 1$ is a riskless bond, with rate r. There are no arbitrage opportunities if and only if there exists a strictly positive probability measure $\pi^l > 0$, such that*

$$P^b_{0i} \le e^{-r_f} \sum_{l \in \Omega} \pi^l (P^l_{1i} + F^l_{1i}) \le P^a_{0i}, \quad \text{for all } i \in U. \tag{9.23}$$

Once an event tree with asset prices has been constructed, we can check for arbitrage opportunities by solving equation (9.22) or (9.23) in each node of the event tree. If we can find a set of strictly positive probabilities π^l for each node then the event tree does not contain arbitrage opportunities. In case the system is infeasible, it is unwise to solve a stochastic programming model with this event tree as input, as this might lead to unbounded and biased solutions.

It is possible to enforce the absence of arbitrage opportunities while constructing an event tree for asset returns. The first approach is to add the no-arbitrage condition (9.23) as a constraint to the tree fitting model (9.18)–(9.19). The tree fitting model has risk-neutral probabilities π^l as additional decision variables, which are required to be strictly positive. If we cannot find a feasible solution for the tree fitting problem, then arbitrage opportunities are inevitable. In this case we could eliminate arbitrage by reducing the number of moment matching constraints in the tree fitting model or by increasing the number of nodes in the event tree. This entails a trade-off between model accuracy and computational complexity.

A second approach is to start with a very fine-grained event tree of asset prices without arbitrage opportunities, and then to reduce it to a smaller tree through aggregation of nodes while preserving the property of no-arbitrage. A good application of this approach is to bond portfolio management, where bond prices are calculated with a one-factor model for the term structure of the interest rates. Bond prices are first generated with a binomial lattice for the one-factor interest rate model: the lattice is consistent with the initial bond prices on the market and contains no arbitrage opportunities. However, the lattice is not suitable as input for a stochastic programming model, as it requires many small time steps in order to calculate prices of bonds and other interest rate dependent securities accurately. The problem arises as each possible path on the recombining interest rate lattice from the initial period to the planning horizon becomes a unique scenario in the non-recombining event tree for the stochastic programming model. Aggregation methods are essential to reduce the recombining lattice to a much smaller event tree with fewer trading dates, while preserving the property of no-arbitrage.

An aggregation method starts with a full-blown, non-recombining event tree consisting of all possible interest rate scenarios. Recursively, a combination of nodes at a particular time period can be replaced by one aggregated node, while preserving the no-arbitrage property. If a node has only one particular successor remaining at the next time period, then the intermediate period can be eliminated.

A similar approach can be applied to create arbitrage-free scenarios from a grid used in options pricing. First a three-dimensional, fine-grained grid of time versus stock price and volatility is constructed to calculate option prices. Second, the points on the grid are partitioned into groups at a small number of trading dates, corresponding to the decision stages in the stochastic programming model. Each group of points on the grid is represented by a single aggregated node in the event tree of the stochastic programming model. If the prices in each aggregated node are calculated as a conditional expectation under the risk-neutral measure of the prices in the corresponding partition on the grid, then the aggregated event tree will not contain arbitrage opportunities.

Although the absence of arbitrage opportunities is important for financial stochastic programs with derivative securities, one should keep in mind that it is only a minimal requirement for the event tree. The fact that the stochastic program cannot generate riskless profits from arbitrage opportunities does not imply that the event tree is also a good approximation of the underlying return process. We still have to take care that the conditional return distributions of the assets and the liabilities are accurately represented in each node of the event tree. To avoid computational problems that arise if the tree becomes too big we could reduce the number of stages in the stochastic program. In this way more nodes are available to describe the return distributions accurately. It is also important to include more nodes for the earlier stages, while larger errors in the later stages will have a small effect on the first-stage decisions which are the decisions implemented today by the decision makers.

9.6   Postview

This chapter introduced methods for scenario generation. As scenario data are key input data for most of the optimization models of this book, this chapter addressed the key issue of obtaining model data needed for practical implementation of financial optimization models.

The chapter started with a general overview of scenarios and the properties imposed upon them. It then proposed a general framework for generating scenarios. This framework is hierarchical and specific methodologies were presented for implementing the various levels of the hierarchy. These methodologies include the bootstrapping of historical data, the statistical analysis employed in typical Value-at-Risk calculations, and time series analysis.

The chapter concluded with a discussion on constructing event trees that are needed for the implementation of stochastic programming models, paying particular attention to the generation of arbitrage-free event trees that match prescribed statistics, such as the mean and the covariance.

Notes and References

The development of sophisticated multi-period simulation models for asset liability management was reported in the early eighties by Goldstein and Markowitz (1982), Kingsland (1982), and Winklevoss (1982). Some of the contemporary simulation systems that have been proposed in the literature to handle the complicated task of scenario generation for enterprise-wide risk management are due to Mulvey and Zenios (1994a), Mulvey (1996), Boender (1997), Cariño et al. (1998), Mulvey and Thorlacius (1998), Koskosides and Duarte (1997), and Zenios (1991, 1995). See also Bunn and Salo (1993) for the use of scenarios in operations research modeling.

Model-based scenario generation methods for asset returns are popular in the insurance industry – e.g., the Wilkie (1995) model, or the Towers Perrin model (Mulvey and Thorlacius 1998). A general framework for scenario generation models that includes the use of expert opinion or "scenario proxies" in addition to mathematical models and simulation, is discussed in Dembo et al. (2000).

A method for analyzing expert interventions in scenario generation is the Martingale Model of Forecast Evolution (MMFE) of Heath and Jackson (1994).

The simulation of insurance liabilities is discussed in Embrechts (2000). Simulation models try to replicate the composition and development of the liability structure as closely as possible in order to increase the accuracy of liability estimates. Macroeconomic variables and actuarial predictions drive the liability side. Boender (1997) developed models for the simulation of liabilities of Dutch pension funds, from which the data for the calibrated vector autoregressive models given in the tables of this chapter are taken.

Perhaps the most complete instantiation of the framework illustrated in Figure 9.2 is the scenario generation system developed by the company Towers Perrin for pension management problems (Mulvey 1996). The economic forecasting system consists of a linked set of modules that generate scenarios for different economic factors and asset returns. At the highest level of the system, the Treasury yield curve is modeled by a two-factor model based on Brennan and Schwartz (1982). Other models could have been used here as well, perhaps accounting for market shocks. Based on the scenarios for the short and consol rates, other modules generate forecasts of the price inflation, bond returns, and the dividend yield on stocks. After the return on a major stock index (e.g., the S&P 500) has been generated conditional on the dividend yield, the return on corporate bonds and small cap stocks are derived at the lowest level of the system. The hierarchical design of a scenario generation system limits the number of coefficients that have to be estimated with the available data and leads to consistent forecasts for the returns on a large number of assets.

Other models generating asset returns are described in Brennan, Schwartz and Lagnado (1997) for strategic asset allocation; Cariño et al. (1998) for an insurance company; and Consiglio, Cocco and Zenios (forthcoming) for minimum guarantee products, amongst others.

Once the model for generating scenarios has been specified, the coefficients have to be calibrated. For example, the Towers Perrin system consists of a number of diffusions for the key economic factors such as the interest rate and the dividend yield. The coefficients of these diffusions have to be estimated: one can apply a pragmatic approach that matches historical summary statistics and expert opinions (Høyland and Wallace 2001; Mulvey, Gould and Morgan 2000), or traditional econometric methods for discrete-time models (Green 1990; Hamilton 1994) and for continuous-time models (Duffie and Singleton 1993; Hansen and Scheinkman 1995).

Lattice models require the calibration of a lattice that matches the current yield curve of treasury bills and bonds. Proper calibration ensures that the coefficients of a model are consistent with historical data or current prices (Black, Derman and Toy 1990; Hull and White 1990; Hull 2000, Heath, Jarrow and Morton 1992). As scenarios are projections of the future, the users of risk management models can of course adjust the estimated coefficients to incorporate their own views about the economy and the asset markets (Koskosides and Duarte 1997). Sometimes stress scenarios are incorporated in response to requirements by the supervisory authorities or to satisfy corporate safeguards.

Black, Derman and Toy (1990) suggested a procedure for constructing a binomial lattice for short-term interest rates. Nielsen and Ronn (1997), following earlier work by Brennan and Schwartz (1982), consider the two-factor model of short- and long-term rates and propose a trinomial lattice approximation. The scenarios of Figure 9.6 were obtained from a binomial and a trinomial lattice, respectively, due to Black, Derman and Toy (1990), and Nielsen and Ronn (1997).

High-performance computations may be needed for the simulation of path-dependent securities from lattice models (Cagan, Carriero and Zenios 1993).

Bootstraping of historical data for VAR calculation is discussed, for example, by Duffie and Pan (1997), and Jorion (1996).

Extensive discussion on the Value-at-Risk methodology is presented in the book by Jorion (1996). For multivariate normal random variables and their properties see, e.g., Jobson (1992); for Monte Carlo simulations see, e.g., Benninga (1989), or the scenario generation procedures based on principal component analysis discussed in Jamshidian and Zhu (1997). Consiglio and Zenios (2001a) use the RiskMetrics methodology in conjunction with the discrete lattice models to generate joint scenarios of term structure and exchange rates.

Vector autoregressive models for economic modeling are discussed, for example, in Sims (1980). The use of VAR models for the generation of scenarios for asset and liability modeling has been advocated by Dert (1995). The development of VAR models for Dutch pension funds is given in Boender (1997). Calibration of VAR models is discussed, for example, in Judge et al. (1988).

The estimation of scenarios of holding period returns based on discretized interest rate models was first suggested by Zenios (1993a) for the management of mortgage portfolios, and was subsequently used by Golub et al. (1995) for money management; Mulvey and Zenios (1994a, b) for high-yield bonds; Dupačová and Bertocchi (2001) for government bonds; and Consiglio and Zenios (2001a) for international bond portfolios. Problems arising when using the wrong interest rate model in these applications have been discussed by Pierides and Zenios (1998). Lattice models for scenario generation that integrate interest rate and credit risk are given in Jobst and Zenios (2005).

Research on the important issues of building event trees is discussed in Cariño et al. (1998), Klaassen (1997, 1998, 2002), Kouwenberg (2001), Høyland and Wallace (2001), and Gondzio, Kouwenberg and Vorst (2003). The generation of event trees that match the moments of an underlying distribution are discussed in Høyland and Wallace (2001); see also Klaassen (2002), and Høyland, Kaut and Wallace (2003). Cariño, Myers and Ziemba (1998) introduce a clustering algorithm that reduces a large random sample of asset and liability returns to a small number of representative nodes, while preserving important statistical properties such as the mean and the standard deviation of the larger sample. This is an idea similar to the adjusted random sampling method we discussed above. Pflug and Świetanowski (1998) derive promising theoretical results for optimal scenario generation for multi-period financial optimization. Shtilman and Zenios (1993) derive theoretical results for the optimal sampling from lattice models, while importance sampling from lattices is discussed by Nielsen (1997).

Theorem 9.5.1 is due to Harrison and Kreps (1979), and Theorem 9.5.2 is due to Naik (1995). Klaassen (1997) was the first to address the issue of arbitrage in event trees for stochastic programming. The lattice aggregation method is discussed in Klaassen (1998, 2002).

The grid aggregation method was proposed by Gondzio, Kouwenberg and Vorst (2003). They apply their method to an option hedging problem with two sources of uncertainty: the stock price and stochastic volatility.

Kallberg and Ziemba (1981, 1984), and Chopra and Ziemba (1993) have shown that estimation errors in the mean value can have an effect on the optimal portfolio cash-equivalent value which is an order of magnitude larger than the error introduced from misspecification of the variances, which in turn is twice as significant as errors in the estimation of covariance matrices.

It is still difficult to conclude much about the quality of the optimal solutions from a stochastic programming model when using different event trees. Testing of stochastic programming models requires extensive out-of-sample simulations (Dupačová, Bertocchi and Morrigia 1998) and rolling horizon dynamic games (Golub et al. 1995). A rolling horizon simulation was used by Kouwenberg (2001) to investigate the issue of scenario generation comparing the three different methods for constructing event trees discussed in this section. The results of repeated experiments for a five-period pension fund model based on an event tree that branches out to $10 \times 6 \times 6 \times 4 \times 4$ states in the five time stages, confirm that random sampling leads to poor results. Adjusted random sampling significantly improves the performance of the model. Tree fitting is only slightly better for the particular application investigated by Kouwenberg.

Part III

APPLICATIONS

Selecting a model becomes a question of finding one that is rich enough to represent most of the risks your product faces, efficient enough to run on a computer in a tolerable amount of time, and simple enough so that programming it is not too complex and burdensome a task.

Emanuel Derman, *My Life as a Quant: Reflections on Physics and Finance*, 2004

Chapter 10

International Asset Allocation

10.1 Preview

Portfolio managers in the international markets must address jointly the market price risk in each market and the currency risk across markets. International asset allocation diversifies market risk, but increases the exposure to currency risks. In this chapter we develop models for integrating the asset allocation decisions with appropriate hedging strategies, thus managing market and credit risk in an integrated fashion. The effectiveness of the models is investigated empirically in different settings. Results show that the optimal hedging strategies depend on the investors' perspective, i.e., asset classes and currency denomination. The models, however, are general and can generate a range of optimal strategies: from complete to partial hedging or selective hedging.

10.2 The Risks of International Asset Portfolios

Does international diversification pay? This question has been answered affirmatively since the 1960s. International markets seemed sufficiently uncorrelated at that time, so that portfolio risks could be reduced by a well-diversified international portfolio, even when accounting for the currency risk exposure. This observation held true for both the equities and fixed-income markets.

Today, however, a black-or-white answer to this question is no longer acceptable, since many interrelated factors need to be considered. For instance, the volatilities of the fixed-income markets – especially bond markets – are typically lower than the volatilities of exchange rates, and hence the currency risk of an international portfolio might offset any benefits from diversification for bond investors. Even in the equities markets it has been argued that multiple acquisitions in a foreign country will not significantly improve the efficiency of a portfolio when accounting for the added currency risk,

The globalization of the financial markets only exacerbates the difficulties facing international portfolio managers. For instance, reductions in capital controls, technological advances in dissemination of information, and increased computing power for tracking portfolios and forecasting market trends led to an explosive growth of international bond trading over the last two decades. On the other hand, the very same developments have led to increased synchronization of market returns. Table 10.1 summarizes the correlation coefficients between US and foreign bond market (domestic) returns for two different time periods. In all cases, except Canada, correlations increased with time, thus eroding any benefits from international diversification. However, when we account for currency volatilities, and calculate correlation coefficients with market returns converted to the home currency of the investor we observe that the degree of correlation remained constant or even declined. Hence, benefits can still be reaped from diversification, but

Table 10.1: Correlation coefficients between US and other international bond markets computed using returns in the home currency and returns as viewed from a US dollar-based investor.

Market	Returns in home currency		Returns in USD
	1978–1995	1990–1995	1990–1995
Australia	.32	.68	.42
Canada	.71	.51	.49
France	.34	.49	.38
Germany	.50	.51	.33
Japan	.38	.43	.26
Netherlands	.52	.53	.35
Switzerland	.36	.46	.26
UK	.39	.49	.39
International index	.59	.64	.44

to a large extent those are due to exchange rate movements.

Another important question is now raised: Should currency risk be hedged? The answer is intuitively deceptively simple. If currency risk is completely hedged, then international market returns are highly correlated and diversification may not pay. If currency risk is not hedged, then the lowered correlation of market returns may lead to improved portfolio efficiency. To hedge or not to hedge now becomes the question, and the answer is "it depends."

10.3 Hedging Strategies

There are alternative views as to the optimal course of action for international portfolio managers, when the issue is the management of currency risk. The analysis varies depending on the portfolio strategy used – making a distinction between static (passive) and dynamic (active) strategies – the base currency, the portfolio structure, and the hedging policy.

There are three major strategies when it comes to currency hedging: *unitary*, *partial*, and *selective hedging*. Unitary hedging means that there is either complete or no hedging of the exchange rate risk connected with all the assets denominated in foreign currency. Partial hedging specifies a hedge ratio that determines the fraction of the portfolio that is hedged. When the value of this ratio is zero or one it leads, respectively, to unhedged or hedged portfolios, the two examples of unitary strategies. In partial hedging the hedge ratio is uniform across assets. Selective hedging allows the hedge ratio to change across currencies, and to take any value between zero and one. That is, the portfolio manager may be fully hedged in some markets, remain unhedged in others, and specify different hedge ratios for the rest. Selective hedging is the most general approach, and it requires optimization models to determine the hedge decisions for the different currency exposures.

In early studies of international currency management it was perceived that complete hedging was optimal due to the low impact of currency hedging on expected returns and the substantial reduction in volatility for international diversification. The state of the markets in the 1980s led to the idea that hedging could be a "free lunch." Indeed, in a mean-variance world complete hedging is optimal under some mild conditions. That is, when uncovered interest rate parity holds and there is no covariance between the rate of change in the exchange rate and the rates of return for the various assets denominated in foreign currency, it can be shown that complete hedging is optimal. The first condition implies equality between the expected return from unhedged and hedged assets; the second implies that exchange rate fluctuations strictly increase the volatility of the portfolio, and as a consequence hedging will decrease volatility at no expected penalty.

This line of thinking was overturned in the late 1990s when new empirical evidence – using more recent data – found that average unhedged returns are very close to average fully hedged returns, for indices of both stocks and bonds, and that the standard deviation of hedged returns is marginally lower – about 3 to 4 percentage points in most cases – than the standard deviation of unhedged returns in the case of stock indices. Evidence also suggested that the standard deviation of hedged returns is significantly lower – about 8 to 10 percentage points in most cases – than the standard deviation of unhedged returns in the case of bond indices. These findings advanced the position that to find the "right" answer to the currency hedging question would require a specification of the objective function of the investor, including the time horizon and the amount of risk that could be accepted in the short run, together with an analysis of the various covariances.

Additional empirical evidence shows that the signs of covariances between exchange rates and domestic returns have historically been different across base currencies. For example, complete hedging was optimal for a US investor for the period 1980–1989, while selective hedging was optimal for a non-US investor over the same period. For example, a US investor looking for the minimum variance bond portfolio should have been 100% invested in foreign bonds with complete hedging, while a German or Japanese investor should have been largely invested in domestic bonds with no hedging. A British investor should have allocated one-third of his assets to domestic bonds and should have hedged three-quarters of the foreign investment.

Therefore the optimal hedging strategy is dependent on the currency of denomination of the investor and on the composition of the optimal portfolio, challenging the validity of a hedging strategy based on a universal hedge ratio that is optimal for all investors.

The importance of the static single-period analysis for deriving implications for strategic asset allocation using mean-variance optimization is called into question by further empirical studies on the temporal stability of the efficient frontiers. While it is widely accepted that international diversification is highly beneficial to portfolio returns, it is accepted that the optimal hedging strategy is highly time-dependent. Efficient frontiers are unstable across portfolios and across periods. For a US investor, for instance, investing in stocks and bonds from seven industrialized countries over the period 1980 to 1996, hedging was the best policy for equities over the period 1980–1985, while no hedging was optimal over the periods 1986–1990, 1991–1996, and the overall period 1986–1996. In contrast, the two policies are complementary when the investor acquired bond portfolios, as the hedged frontier usually covers a risk-return space that is not covered by the unhedged frontier. The optimal policy is therefore a function of the investor's degree of risk aversion. A conservative investor should hedge while an aggressive investor should not. However, such empirical analysis considers only unitary hedging instead of the more flexible selective hedging.

The overarching conclusion of the current state of knowledge on international asset allocation is that international diversification pays; that currency hedging is a valid strategy for international investors; and that the hedging strategies are sensitive to the time horizon, the currency of the investor, and the correlations of the asset classes and of the currency returns. As a result there is need for quantitative models that will guide investors in choosing the optimal hedging strategy for each problem instance.

10.4   Statistical Characteristics of International Data

The complexities of the international asset allocation problem are highlighted through analysis of the statistical characteristics of historical data. We consider both stock and bond indices of short term (1–3 years) and long term (7–10 years) maturity, in the United States (US), United

Kingdom (UK), Germany (GR) and Japan (JP). The following time series are analyzed over the period from April 1988 through May 2001:

USS	US stock index
UKS	UK stock index
GRS	German stock index
JPS	Japanese stock index
US1	US government bond index with 1 to 3 years maturity
US7	US government bond index with 7 to 10 years maturity
UK1	UK government bond index with 1 to 3 years maturity
UK7	UK government bond index with 7 to 10 years maturity
GR1	German government bond index with 1 to 3 years maturity
GR7	German government bond index with 7 to 10 years maturity
JP1	Japanese government bond index with 1 to 3 years maturity
JP7	Japanese government bond index with 7 to 10 years maturity

The statistical characteristics of the time series covering the 10-year period 1990–2000 are summarized in Table 10.2, where it is shown that both the domestic returns of the indices and the proportional changes of exchange rates exhibit skewed distributions and large variance. Statistical tests on these data indicate that normality and lognormality hypotheses cannot be accepted for the majority. (A Jarque-Bera test is used for normality.)

This analysis leads us to consider models with symmetric penalty functions (such as MAD in Section 5.3) in the development of hedging models, and also to investigate the performance of models with asymmetric risk measures (such as CVaR in Section 5.5).

10.5   Model for Selective Hedging

A scenario optimization model is now developed to address jointly the asset allocation and the hedging strategy. The model allows for selective hedging and, of course, unitary hedging, which may be obtained as a result of solving the model for a given set of parameters.

In order to apply the models of Chapter 5 we need to introduce some additional notation to differentiate between unhedged and hedged positions. The index set of scenarios Ω denotes scenarios of returns in the domestic currency of each asset (denoted by r_i^l below) and currency return against a fixed base currency (denoted by e_i^l, where $e_{i_0} = 1$ and i_0 denotes the base currency).

The following notation applies to the model in this section and supersedes, where applicable, the more general notation used elsewhere:

$U = \{1, 2, \ldots, n\}$, index set of available markets.

$U_u = \{1, 2, \ldots, n\}$, index set of available unhedged markets.

$U_h = \{1, 2, \ldots, n\}$, index set of available hedged markets.

$u_i, i \in U_u$, position in unhedged market i in percentage of total wealth.

$h_i, i \in U_h$, position in hedged market i in percentage of total wealth.

r_i^l, domestic currency return of asset i under scenario l in local currency.

e_i^l, currency return of asset i under scenario l against the base currency.

f_i, forward return of asset i against the base currency.

For simplicity we have assumed that we hold both unhedged and hedged positions in the same markets. Hence, there is one-to-one correspondence of the elements in index sets U, U_u, U_h. For instance, if the first element of U denotes, say, the US stock market, then the first element of U_u

Table 10.2: Statistical characteristics of historical monthly data for domestic returns of assets (top) and proportional changes of spot exchange rates (bottom) over the 10-year period 1990–2000. The Jarque-Bera statistic has an $\mathcal{X}^2$ distribution with two degrees of freedom. Its critical values at the 5% and 1% confidence levels are 5.991 and 9.210, respectively. Therefore, the normality hypothesis is rejected when the Jarque-Bera statistic has a higher value than the corresponding critical value at the respective confidence level.

Asset class return	Mean	Standard deviation	Skewness	Kurtosis	Jarque-Bera statistic
USS	1.519%	3.900%	-0.465	4.271	11.769
UKS	1.164%	4.166%	-0.233	3.285	1.391
GRS	1.213%	5.773%	-0.511	4.503	15.738
JPS	-0.133%	6.336%	0.022	3.609	1.546
US1	0.537%	0.473%	-0.144	2.801	0.727
US7	0.688%	1.646%	-0.047	3.276	0.299
UK1	0.723%	0.710%	1.330	7.209	121.156
UK7	0.913%	1.932%	0.108	3.482	1.157
GR1	0.537%	0.458%	0.655	5.319	34.052
GR7	0.670%	1.390%	-0.863	4.482	25.421
JP1	0.327%	0.522%	0.492	4.147	10.891
JP7	0.608%	1.731%	-0.514	5.149	27.039
Exchange rate	Mean	Standard deviation	Skewness	Kurtosis	Jarque-Bera statistic
US to UK	-0.074%	0.081%	-1.084	6.790	189.330
US to GR	-0.167%	0.088%	-0.398	3.908	18.842
US to JP	0.303%	0.133%	1.123	6.904	35.966

also denotes the US stock market as perceived from the vantage point of an unhedged investor, and the first element of U_h denotes the US stock market from the point of view of a hedged investor.

With the above notation we can specify the overall exposure in each market, in both unhedged and hedged positions, by

$$x_i = u_i + h_i, \text{ for all } i \in U. \tag{10.1}$$

The scenario-dependent return for each asset depends on whether the position is hedged or unhedged, and it is denoted by ξ_i^l for each market i and under scenario $l \in \Omega$. For unhedged positions the return is given by

$$\xi_i^l = r_i^l + e_i^l, \text{ for all } i \in U, \text{ for all } l \in \Omega, \tag{10.2}$$

and for hedged positions the return is given by

$$\xi_i^l = r_i^l + f_i, \text{ for all } i \in U, \text{ for all } l \in \Omega, \tag{10.3}$$

where the forward rate is scenario-independent and is given by $f_i = \ln \left(\frac{1+r_{i_0}}{1+r_i} \right)$, and r_{i_0} and r_i denote, respectively, the interest rate in the domestic market i_0 and the foreign market i, and are known at the time of the construction of the portfolio. We also specify a target expected return μ for the portfolio, and by varying this target we generate the efficient frontiers.

With this notation the mean-absolute deviation portfolio selection model for international asset allocation can now be written as follows:

Model 10.5.1 Scenario optimization for selective hedging

$$\text{Minimize} \quad \sum_{l \in \Omega} p^l \left| \sum_{i=1}^{n} \xi_i^l x_i - \left(\sum_{l \in \Omega} p^l \sum_{i=1}^{n} \xi_i^l x_i \right) \right| \tag{10.4}$$

$$\text{subject to} \quad \sum_{l \in \Omega} p^l \sum_{i=1}^{n} \xi_i^l x_i \geq \mu, \tag{10.5}$$

$$\sum_{i=1}^{n} x_i = 1, \tag{10.6}$$

$$x_i \geq 0, \text{ for all } i \in U. \tag{10.7}$$

The optimization structure is quite general and will produce hedge ratios which differ across assets denominated in different currencies. The special case of complete hedging is obtained from the solution of the model when $u_i = 0$ for all markets. Completely unhedged portfolios are obtained when $h_i = 0$ for all markets. A partial hedging strategy is obtained when the hedge ratio h_i/u_i has the same value for all markets. The scenario optimization model developed here encompasses most of the empirical analysis that has been reviewed in the previous section.

Since the model is based on scenarios it may use all the available historical data or it may use various subsets of observations. For long-term strategic decisions the investor may want to base the portfolio optimization on long time series. However, when investors make sequential decisions at different points in time, they may pursue tactical portfolios that deviate from the strategic portfolio in order to exploit perceived over- and under-valuation of assets. Hence, they may implement a tactical dynamic asset allocation by continuously reestimating the efficient frontier using the most recent data, and changing the asset allocation accordingly.

We use the simplest approach for generating scenarios relying on the available data without any mathematical modeling by bootstraping a set of historical records (see Section 9.4). Each scenario is a sample of returns of the assets obtained by sampling returns that were observed in the past. Dates from the available historical records are selected randomly, and for each date in the sample we read the returns of all asset classes realized during the previous month. Thus we generate scenarios of monthly returns. To generate scenarios of returns for some horizon – say one year – we sample 12 monthly returns from different points in time. The compounded return of the sampled series is one scenario of the one-year return. The process is repeated to generate the desired number of scenarios for the 10-year period used in this application.

10.6   Asset Allocation

The model is applied to develop efficient frontiers using unhedged and hedged positions in both stocks and bonds. We consider an investment universe consisting of two assets in five different markets – United States, Japan, United Kingdom, Europe (which is proxied by the German bond market and the DJ Euro Stoxx 50 for stocks) and Switzerland.

The period considered covers January 1985 to May 1998 and data are on a monthly basis. As a proxy for the bonds we use the Salomon Brothers World Government Bond Index, all maturities, while for the stocks we use the local currency Morgan Stanley MSCI Index, with dividends reinvested. The returns of the hedged markets are computed using the one-month euro-interest rate. Scenarios are generated from the historical data, so there are 156 scenarios derived from all the months in the sample.

Several efficient frontiers are generated, from the point of view of both a US dollar-based investor and a Swiss franc-based investor. For the US dollar we also consider the two subperiods 1985–1991 and 1992–1998.

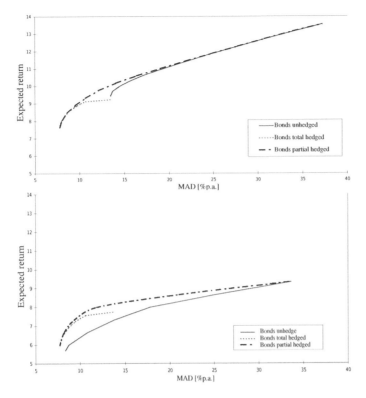

Figure 10.1: Efficient frontiers for bond portfolios, base currency US dollar (top) and Swiss franc (bottom), for the period 1985–1998.

10.6.1 Asset allocation in treasuries

Figure 10.1 shows the efficient frontiers for bonds-only portfolios for investors based in US dollars and Swiss francs, respectively, for the sample period 1985–1998. We observe that low levels of risk can be achieved only through hedging for the US dollar investor, while a Swiss franc-based investor can also achieve low levels of risk without hedging, although this strategy is inefficient in that even higher expected returns can be achieved for the same level of risk with hedged portfolios. This is an indication of the relevance of the currency of denomination. Certain trade-offs between risk and return can be achieved in some cases with hedging alone, but the amount of hedging depends on the currency of the investor.

Secondly, we observe that selective hedging envelops the hedged and unhedged efficient frontiers. Selective hedging coincides with full hedging for low volatility portfolios and with no hedging for higher levels of volatility. The picture looks different for a Swiss investor, where the gains from selective hedging are more evident for a large set of portfolios. This suggests that the value added by selective hedging with respect to a no-hedging or a complete hedging strategy again depends on the reference currency.

We now examine the impact of various hedging strategies across time, depending on the volatilities and correlation of the markets. Figure 10.2 shows the efficient frontiers for both unhedged and hedged portfolios for a US dollar investor, for the periods 1985–1991 and 1992–1998. As in the case of the overall period 1985–1998, low-risk portfolios can only be obtained by complete hedging. It is interesting to notice the downward shift of the unhedged frontier from the first subperiod to the second, and the upward shift of the completely hedged frontier.

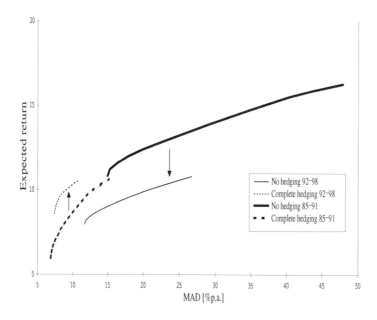

Figure 10.2: Efficient frontiers for bond portfolios for various subperiods, with the USD as the base currency.

10.6.2   Asset allocation in equities

We now apply the model for the evaluation of hedging strategies for equities portfolios. Figure 10.3 shows the efficient frontiers for stock-only investors in US dollars and Swiss francs. For the US investor the unhedged portfolios dominate the hedged portfolios and coincide with selective hedging everywhere, except for a small range of low-risk portfolios. From the Swiss investor's perspective things are different. In this case complete hedging is optimal and coincides with selective hedging. This confirms, once again, the importance of the base currency in the hedging decision. In this particular application the selective hedging model is mainly useful for determining which of the two unitary policies is optimal.

10.6.3   Asset allocation in treasuries and equities

The overall performance of the optimization models is best illustrated when applied to the full set of treasury and equity securities. The results are illustrated in Figure 10.4, where the superiority of selective hedging strategies is further highlighted.

The main results of the analysis in this section can be summarized as follows. First, hedged bond portfolios cover only a small region of the global risk-return trade-off, limiting in an important way the choices of a bond investor. Second, selective hedging improves only marginally upon complete or no hedging for the extreme cases, and an investor does best by choosing the hedging policy most suited to his risk aversion. That is, highly risk-averse investors should pick hedged, low volatility portfolios, while other investors should pick unhedged, high volatility portfolios. An optimization model serves in selecting intermediate positions. Third, the efficient frontier is unstable across time periods. Fourth, efficient frontiers for stocks are rather flat, and the results offered by selective hedging are very close to those obtained with either complete hedging or no hedging, even though the optimal policy varies with the currency of denomination.

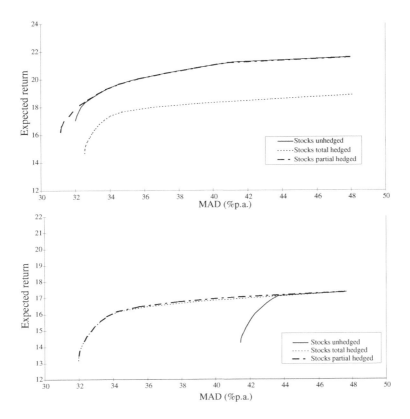

Figure 10.3: Efficient frontiers for stock portfolios – base currency US dollar (top) and Swiss franc (bottom) – for the period 1985-1998.

10.7   Risk Measure for International Asset Allocation

It has already been highlighted that the statistical characteristics of the international asset returns exhibit skewness and kurtosis (see Section 10.4). As a result, a risk measure that deals with symmetric distributions of returns does not adequately manage the risks of international investors. In this section we analyze the effect of the choice of risk measure on the performance of the portfolio optimization models. First, we generate efficient frontiers for portfolios of stocks and bonds, using data over the period until 2000, modifying Model 10.5.1 to use the CVaR risk measure instead of MAD as the objective function.

Figure 10.5 shows the frontiers constructed with both the CVaR and MAD models, using all three alternative hedging policies. Irrespective of the risk measure used, the results indicate that at the low-risk end of the spectrum completely hedged portfolios are preferable to unhedged portfolios as they yield dominant risk-return profiles over the overlapping range of their efficient frontiers. However, completely hedged portfolios can reach only a limited range of expected return. The efficient frontiers of the no-hedging strategy extend into a range of higher expected returns (and risk) than are attainable by complete hedging. Hence, more aggressive return targets are reached only with riskier unhedged investments.

Selective hedging is the superior strategy as it leads to efficient frontiers that envelop those generated by the unitary hedging strategies. This observation holds for both optimization models, and the CVaR as well as the MAD models lead to consistent assessments regarding the appropriate choice of hedging strategy at any level of target return.

The above tests are static. Under static testing the portfolios generated by the two models

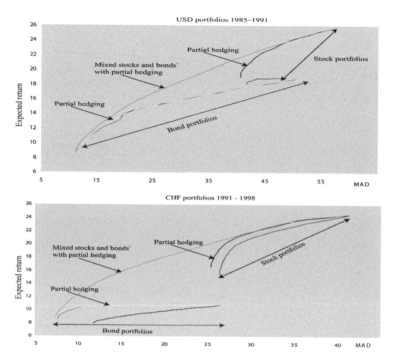

Figure 10.4: Efficient frontiers for different hedging strategies for mixed portfolios of stocks and bonds for the period 1985–1991 (top) and 1991–1998 (bottom) with base currency US dollar (top) and Swiss franc (bottom).

exhibit practically the same behavior, and the two models yield almost indistinguishable frontiers for the asset selection problem: i.e., the frontier of CVaR versus expected return for the MAD-optimized portfolios is almost indistinguishable from the efficient frontier generated using the CVaR optimization model. Conversely, the frontier of MAD versus expected return for the CVaR-optimized portfolios is almost identical to the efficient frontier generated by the MAD model. However, a definitive comparison between the CVaR and the MAD models requires their assessment under dynamic testing.

Backtesting experiments are now carried out on a rolling horizon basis, for the period from April 1998 to April 2001. At each month τ, the historical data from the previous 10 years (i.e., 120 monthly observations) are used to generate scenarios. The resulting optimization model is then solved to obtain an optimal portfolio. The clock is then advanced by one month to $\tau + 1$ and the realized return of the portfolio is determined from the actual market values of the assets and the observed exchange rates that are available from the historical data. The same procedure is then repeated for the next time period and the ex post realized returns are compounded. Backtesting experiments are carried out for both the CVaR and the MAD models using various values of target monthly return.

The results for the CVaR model are depicted in Figure 10.6. The MAD model generates portfolios with growth paths similar to those of the CVaR model. However, as illustrated in Figure 10.7, its ex post performance is worse than that of the CVaR model. The CVaR model consistently outperforms the MAD model, especially for the low-risk strategies. As the value of the target return parameter is increased the two models behave more similarly. This is due to the fact that for more aggressive strategies the requested target return level becomes the governing factor over the minimization of the respective risk measure, so that using MAD that does not fully capture the asymmetries of the return distributions becomes irrelevant.

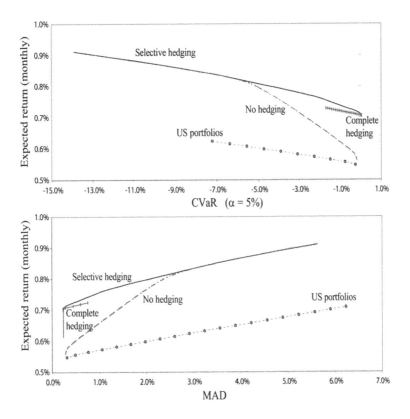

Figure 10.5: Efficient frontiers of CVaR (top) and MAD (bottom) optimization models for US and internationally diversified portfolios of stocks and bonds with alternative hedging strategies.

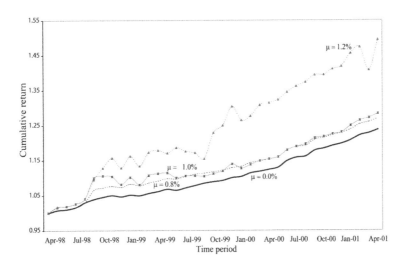

Figure 10.6: Ex post realized returns with the selective hedging CVaR model ($\alpha = 5\%$) for different target expected return (μ).

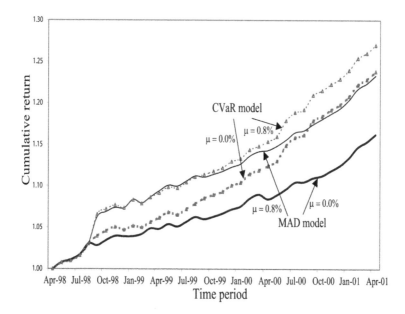

Figure 10.7: Ex post realized return paths with the selective hedging CVaR and MAD models for target expected return 0.0% and 0.8%.

The superiority of the CVaR model over the MAD model for international asset allocation is evident in Figure 10.8. This figure depicts the geometric mean against the standard deviation of ex post realized monthly returns over the 37-month test period for all simulation experiments. Clearly, the CVaR model outperforms the MAD model at all levels of target expected return by generating steeper and more stable growth paths (i.e., higher returns with lower volatility). The difference in the performance of the two models is gradually reduced with increasing values of the target return. On the same graph we also plot the ex post performance of individual assets over the same test period. Both optimization models outperform all individual assets, with the CVaR model being the most successful in realizing effective growth performance while limiting risk.

10.8   Postview

This chapter developed models for asset allocation in the global financial markets. The risks of international asset portfolios are first discussed and the basic hedging strategies are reviewed. Statistical analysis of international data reveals that rates of return do not satisfy normality assumptions and, hence, asymmetric risk measures must be used.

The chapter went on to develop models for international asset allocation using first a mean-absolute deviation model that allows currency hedging using a flexible strategy – selective hedging – and several efficient frontiers were traced. Conditional Value-at-Risk models were then developed and implemented, and the results were compared with those obtained using mean absolute deviation.

The overall conclusions are that selective hedging is effective for hedging currency risk; MAD and CVaR models are practically indistinguishable from each other for static portfolios; when used in a dynamic setting the CVaR optimized portfolios produce superior results to the MAD optimized portfolios.

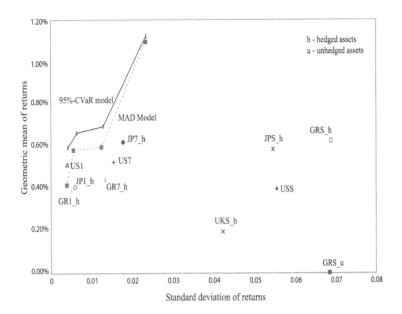

Figure 10.8: Comparative ex post performance – in terms of the realized geometric mean and standard deviation of monthly returns – of individual assets, and international portfolios selected by the CVaR and MAD models over the period April 1998 to April 2001.

Notes and References

The book by Solnik (1996) provides a comprehensive treatment of international portfolio management. Extensive empirical work on international asset management is found in Grubel (1968), Jorion (1989), Solnik, Bourcelle and Le Fur (1996), and Michaud et al. (1996). Table 10.1 is from Fabozzi (1997, ch. 54). For analysis on the predictability of currency returns and volatilities see the works by Solnik, Bourcelle and Le Fur (1996), Glen and Jorion (1993), Fishwick (1994), and Bansal (1997).

More recent work that questions the validity of international diversification, unless it is linked with currency hedging is reported in Perold and Schulman (1988), Kaplanis and Schaefer (1991), Ziobrowski and Ziobrowski (1995). Perold and Schulman (1988) advocated the idea of "free lunch." The validity of a universal hedge ratio was advocated by Black (1990), although the validity of his assumptions for the market data were questioned in the analysis of Filatov and Rappoport (1992) who suggested that complete hedging is dominated by selective hedging. The analysis of efficient frontiers for different time periods is due to Abken and Shrikhande (1997). Glen and Jorion (1993) consider dynamic hedging strategies and report on extensive empirical analysis.

The optimization models discussed in this chapter are based on the three papers by Beltratti, Consiglio and Zenios (1999), Consiglio and Zenios (2001a), and Beltratti, Laurent and Zenios (2004). The first paper develops the general framework, the second develops and tests the indexation models, and the third develops and tests various hedging strategies and introduces selective hedging. The suitability of the conditional Value-at-Risk (CVaR) risk measure for international portfolio management was proposed in Topaloglou, Vladimirou and Zenios (2002), from where the empirical analysis of market data and the dynamic testing of hedging strategies are obtained. Optimization models for incorporating derivatives for currency hedging in international portfolios are discussed in Topaloglou, Vladimirou and Zenios (2004).

Chapter 11

Corporate Bond Portfolios

With *Norbert Jobst*[1]

11.1   Preview

The corporate bond market is one of the largest and fastest growing segments of fixed income securities. Investors in corporate bonds must deal with the credit risk inherent in these securities, and their derivative products. In this chapter we discuss the integration of corporate bonds in asset portfolios. As a first step we integrate credit risk with market risk, and this requires advanced scenario generation methods and the use of suitable risk metrics. CVaR optimization models are well suited to this application. As a second step we manage the corporate bond assets using an indexation strategy, and apply index fund models from previous chapters. Empirical results with a large-scale application illustrate the effectiveness of the financial optimization models. We also test the sensitivity of the results to the assumptions made about the data or about the models.

11.2   Credit Risk Securities

The corporate bond market has been receiving increased attention recently. The rapid growth in the number of new issues since the early 1990s (Figure 4.4) coupled with the low yields and reduced liquidity in the government bond markets of the late 1990s and early 2000s have attracted investors to corporate products. The credit derivatives market has also burgeoned during the last decade, with the total outstanding amount of interest rate swaps for AA risk standing at over $43 trillion dollars, about eight times as much as the US government bond market. As of the end of 1995 the top dealers had credit risk assets in excess of $5 billion each: Mitsubishi Bank led with $33 billion, followed by Citicorp at $32 billion, and Chase Manhattan at $26 billion. Credit derivative make large and important risks tradeable, and are making an impact on the practice of fixed-income portfolio and risk management. For instance, some European telecommunication companies currently issue their bonds with embedded credit derivatives protection: the coupon rate is adjusted automatically upwards if the issuing corporation is downgraded by the rating agencies.

   The growing market of credit risk securities, and dissatisfaction with the standardized risk-based capital requirements of the regulatory accords set out by the Bank for International Settlement have prompted an interest in methodologies to integrate market and credit risk. The traditional approaches to managing market risk are based on strong assumptions such as the normality of the return distribution. Although these methods became the industry standard in the RiskMetrics methodology and are widely accepted for a number of applications, they are inadequate for credit risk management as a number of assumptions break down. The distribution of

---

[1]   Standard & Poors, Structured Finance Ratings, London, UK.

losses due to credit events can be described as a large chance of small earnings and a very small probability of large losses. They are non-normal and heavily skewed. The causes of these losses are many and complex in nature and can be captured only with Monte Carlo simulation methods. It remains, however, common practice in risk management to treat credit and market risk separately. Sometimes market risk is even ignored to reach analytic tractability in the calculation of Value-at-Risk and other risk metrics.

Tools such as CREDITRISK$^+$ from Credit Suisse Financial Products, CreditMetrics from JP Morgan, Credit Portfolio View from McKinsey & Co or KMV's Portfolio Manager allow risk managers to gain insights about the credit risk of their portfolios, but a number of important aspects are missing. CREDITRISK$^+$, for example, only assesses the risk due to default losses. Market information such as credit rating changes and the term structure of credit spreads is not taken into account. The default event is modeled using historical default rates. This system enable users to calculate the loss distribution analytically, but the approach is inappropriate for valuation problems when consistency with market prices is essential. CreditMetrics is a typical "mark-to-market" model. It allows users to calculate the present value of a portfolio of credit risk assets dependent on credit risk only, but market risk is not incorporated explicitly. As a result, no other risks apart from credit risk can be assessed for their impact on the valuation of the portfolio, and prices calculated in CreditMetrics may not be consistent with quoted market prices.

Figure 11.1 illustrates the distribution of returns on a portfolio of credit risk bonds obtained when simulating either market or credit risk, but not both, using models similar to those discussed above. The figure illustrates the significant effects of the risk factors on the portfolio returns. If we assume that risk-free rates and credit spreads remain constant, while the bond quality rating changes, we obtain a highly skewed distribution. These simulations reveal the flat lower tails of the return distributions of corporate bonds due to the low probability but high impact events of quality rating migrations and default. If we assume that the bonds remain in their current quality ratings but the risk-free rates and spreads change we obtain a symmetric distribution.

Clearly neither of the two distributions shown in this figure is adequate for enterprise risk management; the correct distribution of returns is a mixture of the two. Simulation models are first needed to integrate market and credit risk in a common framework. Section 11.3 discusses appropriate scenario generation methods and paves the way for the portfolio optimization models for credit risk. The choice of a risk metric that is suitable for credit risk instruments is discussed in Section 11.4, and Section 11.6 develops indexed corporate bond portfolios, and backtests the models in tracking the Merrill Lynch Euro Dollar Corporate Bond index, while the funding of fixed liabilities with corporate bonds is addressed in Section 11.7.

11.3   Integrating Market and Credit Risk

The major risk factors for corporate bonds are fixed-income market risk (Definition 2.2.3) and credit risk (Definition 2.2.7). As mentioned in previous chapters the prices of corporate bonds are affected by the following events:

1. Changes in the term structure of risk-free rates.

2. Changes in the term structure of credit spreads.

3. Changes in the rating of the bond.

4. The likelihood that a bond will go into default.

5. The amount recovered if a bond goes into default.

In order to generate scenarios of returns on credit risk securities we must simulate these risk factors taking into account their correlations. The scenario properties discussed in Section 9.2

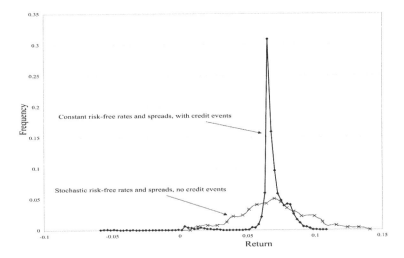

Figure 11.1: Distribution of returns of a portfolio of credit risk bonds for: (i) constant interest rates and credit spreads with credit rating migrations and default (thick line); (ii) stochastic interest rates and credit spreads without credit rating migrations or default (thin line).

must be satisfied, otherwise the optimization models built on the resulting scenarios will inadvertently expose the portfolios to large risks that were unaccounted for.

To generate scenarios that can be used for risk management of credit risk securities, the portfolio simulator must possess the following features:

Integrate disparate sources of risk. The dynamics of the state variables must be flexible enough to capture multiple risks and match empirical observations. For example, all bonds must be priced and evaluated in a unified non-arbitrage framework, consistent with today's term structure of both risk-free interest rates and credit spreads.

Capture correlations between disparate risk factors. Empirical observations show a significant correlation between credit spreads and interest rates. Empirical results also show significant correlations between defaults and migrations, especially among securities issued by corporations in the same industrial sector. When dealing with portfolios of credit risk securities it is critical that the simulation model capture the correlations between these risk factors.

Risk-neutral pricing and real probabilities of extreme events. An important consideration when extending pricing models for simulation and risk management purposes is the difference between the risk-neutral probability measure used for arbitrage-free pricing, and the real, observed, probability measure used to estimate risk. This point is particularly important in the context of corporate bond management, and it may not be of similar significance in the context of interest rate risk. When considering only interest rate risk, the risk horizons are likely to be much shorter than for problems involving credit risk. Typically the horizon for market risk is around a few days, whereas credit risk problems consider horizons longer than a year. For short horizons it is a good first approximation to assume that the risk-neutral probability measure and the observed measure are indistinguishable. For longer horizons a risk premium must be estimated and used to adjust the risk-neutral probabilities.

Although consistency of prices with observed data can be achieved under a risk-neutral probability measure, assessing a portfolio at a future point in time should be done under the real, objective measure. The valuation requires future security prices at the risk horizon τ. Those are calculated in a risk-neutral framework depending on the realization of some state variables such as interest rates or credit spreads at time τ. It is necessary to simulate the state variable until τ

under the objective measure, whereas the pricing at time τ is based on the risk-neutral dynamics of the state variables for times $\tau \leq t \leq T$.

Computational tractability. Finally, because of the complex nature of credit risk, analytic results are rare and simulation remains the only way to estimate risk measures. The computational complexity must be reduced for practical considerations by making simplifying assumptions about the state variables such as quality rating, interest rate, default intensity, recovery rate, etc., that drive security prices. The specification of the dynamics of these variables is important as, for example, assuming a simple stochastic process like the Gaussian process for the short rate will lead to closed-form solutions for some securities but will also imply that the short rate may become negative. As a result, the requirement of consistency with empirical observations and theory may be violated. On the other hand, closed-form solutions may be necessary if large portfolios are to be simulated, and therefore the assumption may be acceptable. It should also be possible to calibrate the models using data that are readily available in the market.

11.3.1   Scenario generation for corporate bonds

A scenario generator for credit risk portfolios is built by extending some pricing models that are standard in the literature. We briefly discuss here pricing models and show how to combine them to develop a portfolio simulator.

Pricing models for credit risk securities fall into two categories: (i) structural models, and (ii) intensity models, although hybrid models also exist. Structural models are based on the assumption that default time is driven by an underlying stochastic process describing the value of the firm. Default occurs when the process hits a certain boundary, and the value of the defaultable claim is then derived using options pricing theory.

Intensity models are based on the idea that default happens contingent on the arrival of some "hazard," and the timing of this event takes bondholders by surprise. This approach does not define the default event based on the firm's value, but derives instead the probability of the event as the instantaneous likelihood of default, called "hazard rate." Hazard rate is a measure of the propensity of default per unit of time. Usually the time of default is modeled as the first jump in a point process with a given intensity (hazard rate). The point process often employed in practice is a Poisson process with intensity λ, or a generalization assuming λ to be random and conditional on the path. The probability of a jump in a point process with an intensity is approximately proportional to the length of the time interval (for small intervals), and this is one of the main reasons for using these processes.

A special case of intensity models are rating-based models where the stochastic intensity is modeled, in its simplest way, as a finite state space Markov chain (see Appendix C) representing the credit rating; default is the absorbing state of the Markov chain.

We consider a simulation framework that incorporates elements of both rating-based models and stochastic intensity models. In particular we will perturb any model assumption on recovery rates, spreads, and rating migration, in addition to default events, to extend the state space and generate scenarios.

11.3.2   The simulation framework

We first generate interest rate and credit spread scenarios. These are called economic scenarios as they apply to all securities in a given rating class. Securities are then priced conditional on the economic scenario according to an intensity-based pricing model, simulating each security's rating and default scenarios through time. These additional simulations generate *rating scenarios* that are idiosyncratic for each security or rating class. In the event of default the recovery payment is also simulated. We describe in this section the economic dynamics, the pricing equations, the portfolio valuation formulae, and the dynamics of migration and default.

The dynamics of the economic variables

Generally the default-free spot rate r_{ft} is modeled by the stochastic differential equation

$$dr_{ft} = \hat{\mu}_f(r_{ft}, t)\, dt + \sigma_f(r_{ft}, t)\, d\hat{W}_{ft} \tag{11.1}$$

where $\hat{W}_{ft}$ is the standard Wiener process under the real probability measure $\mathcal{P}$. This process is useful for scenario generation, but for pricing purposes we need to consider the process under the risk-neutral probability measure $\mathcal{Q}$. The risk-neutral dynamics are obtained by introducing a market price of risk $\gamma_f(t)$ with

$$\hat{\mu}_f(r_{ft}, t) = \mu_f(r_{ft}, t) + \gamma_f(t)\sigma_f(r_{ft}, t).$$

The risk-neutral process is then

$$dr_{ft} = \mu_f(r_{ft}, t)\, dt + \sigma_f(r_{ft}, t)\, dW_{ft} \tag{11.2}$$

with $dW_{ft} = \gamma_f(t)dt + d\hat{W}_{ft}$ under $\mathcal{Q}$.

In addition to the process for the spot rate r_{ft} we model the credit spread according to a stochastic intensity model. A different credit spread is considered for each rating class $j = 1, \ldots, K - 1$, where 1 denotes the highest rating (AAA), $K - 1$ denotes the lowest rating (CCC) and K denotes the default state. (Alternatively one could model a process for each individual bond, which may be difficult due to data availability, or according to a different level of aggregation. For example, a spread process for each industrial sector and rating combination could be considered.) The corresponding spread processes are denoted by h_{jt} and are assumed to follow

$$dh_{jt} = \hat{\mu}_j(h_{jt}, t)\, dt + \sigma_j(h_{jt}, t)\, d\hat{W}_{jt} \tag{11.3}$$

under the real probability measure. Again, the risk neutral-process can be obtained by introducing the market price of risk.

The correlation between the processes for the risk-free rate and the spreads is captured by correlating the processes for the Brownian motion, i.e.,

$$d\hat{W}_{jt}\, d\hat{W}_{j't} = \rho_{jj'}dt \tag{11.4}$$

where $j, j' \in \{r_{ft}, 1, \ldots, K - 1\}$, and $\rho_{jj'}$ is the correlation of the two processes.

Pricing formulae

Given the specifications of the risk-free rate and the spread process a number of valuation tools are available for risky zero-coupon bonds. Some of the relevant formulae are given next. Their differences stem mainly from different assumptions about the recovery amount in the case of default. We give here formulae for the price at time τ of a zero coupon bond with face value of 1 and maturity T, and then use these prices to price portfolios of coupon bearing bonds. (We drop the dependence of the spread process on j and write h_t instead of h_{jt}, and denote prices by v instead of v_j. It is understood that we are using the spread process corresponding to the credit rating j of the bond we are pricing.)

Zero-Recovery (ZR). The bondholder receives nothing in the event of default. For most practical problems zero recovery is unrealistic. The price of a defaultable zero coupon bond at time τ with maturity T is given as

$$v^{ZR}(\tau, T) = \mathcal{E}_{\mathcal{Q}}\left(e^{-\int_\tau^T (r_{ft} + h_t)dt}\right), \tag{11.5}$$

where the bond face value of 1 is discounted with a risk adjusted short rate $r_{ft} + h_t$, and E_τ^Q denotes expectations under the risk-neutral probability measure, computed at time τ.

Recovery of Treasury (RT). In the event of default the bondholder receives an exogenously specified fraction γ of the value of an equivalent default-free bond. The price is given as

$$v^{RT}(\tau, T) = \gamma p(\tau, T) + (1 - \gamma) \, v^{ZR}(\tau, T) \tag{11.6}$$

where $p(\tau, T)$ denotes the price at time τ of an equivalent risk-free zero coupon bond with maturity T.

Recovery of Face Value (RFV). The creditor receives a fraction $1 - \gamma$ (possibly random) of face value immediately upon default. The price is given as

$$v^{RFV}(\tau, T) = \mathcal{E}_Q \left[e^{- \int_\tau^T (r_{ft} + h_t) dt} + \int_\tau^T (1 - \gamma) h_t e^{- \int_\tau^t (r_{fu} + h_u) du} dt \right] \tag{11.7}$$

Recovery of Market Value (RMV). The default payoff is specified as a fraction $1 - \gamma$ (possibly random) of the pre-default value of the risky bond. The price is obtained as

$$v^{RMV}(\tau, T) = \mathcal{E}_Q \left[e^{- \int_\tau^T (r_{ft} + h_t \gamma) dt} \right]. \tag{11.8}$$

Portfolio valuation and scenarios

The present value of the portfolio is now given as

$$V_0 = \sum_{i=1}^n P_i^j(0, T) x_i \tag{11.9}$$

where x_i denotes the holdings of bond i in the portfolio, $P_i^j(0, T)$ denotes the current price of bond i with maturity T and current rating $j \in \{1, \ldots, K - 1\}$. We assume, without loss of generality, that all bonds have the same maturity T. The bond price is given as

$$P_i^j(0, T) = \sum_{t=1}^T F_{ti} v_j(0, T) \tag{11.10}$$

where F_{ti} denotes the coupon payment from bond i at period t (this amount also includes principal payment at maturity T). The zero coupon bond price $v_j(0, T)$ is given by applying the pricing formula of choice from (11.5)–(11.8). The spread process applied in the pricing equation is the process h_{jt} from equation (11.3) corresponding to the credit rating of bond i. Therefore, this price is a function of the current rating, which is observable, and the future evolution of interest rates and credit spreads under the risk-neutral probability measure Q.

The value of the portfolio at a risk horizon τ, which is needed for scenario generation purposes, is given as

$$V_\tau = \sum_{i=1}^n P_i^{j_\tau}(\tau, T) x_i \tag{11.11}$$

where $\tau \leq T$. $P_i^{j_\tau}(\tau, T)$ denotes the price of bond i at time τ, given that the bond will be rated j_τ at that time, and is computed by

$$P_i^{j_\tau}(\tau, T) = \sum_{t=\tau}^T F_{ti} v_{j_\tau}(t, T). \tag{11.12}$$

The corresponding zero coupon bond price $v_{j_\tau}(\tau, T)$ depends on the evolution of r_{ft} and h_{jt} under the risk-neutral probability Q after τ and until maturity T, conditioned on the level of interest rates and credit spreads at the risk horizon τ, and the credit rating j_τ of the ith bond at τ. This price is given according to the underlying pricing model (11.5)–(11.8).

Rating migrations and defaults

The future credit rating j_τ of the ith bond is simulated according to the actual migration process under $\mathcal{P}$. Defaults are modeled when the process hits the absorbing state K. When simulating a portfolio of assets, we should also consider correlations between the migrations and defaults of different bonds.

Ignoring correlations, we simulate the rating transitions according to a transition matrix describing the Markov chain of migrations among different rating categories and into the default state under the real probability measure $\mathcal{P}$. Table 11.1 shows a typical transition matrix obtained by counting historical transitions of bond ratings; default is modeled as an absorbing state of the Markov chain and once a bond is in default it does not reenter the market. We note some inconsistencies in the transition matrix given in the table. For instance, it appears that more AAA bonds migrate to BB than do AA bonds. This is just an artifact of the calibration period when more AAA bonds migrated, while in the long run more AA bonds migrate into BB. A matrix such as the one shown here must be adjusted for consistency before it can be used for risk management simulations.

Table 11.1: One-year transition matrix as published by Standard and Poors, after adjustments to remove the non-rated category. (Source: Standard & Poors *CreditWeek* April 15, 1996)

	AAA	AA	A	BBB	BB	B	CCC	Default
AAA	.9081	.0833	.0682	.0006	.0012	.0000	.0000	.0000
AA	.0070	.9065	.0779	.0064	.0006	.0014	.0002	.0000
A	.0009	.0227	.9105	.0552	.0074	.0026	.0001	.0006
BBB	.0002	.0033	.0595	.8693	.0530	.0117	.0012	.0018
BB	.0003	.0014	.0067	.0773	.8053	.0884	.0010	.0106
B	.0000	.0011	.0024	.0043	.0648	.8346	.0407	.0520
CCC	.0000	.0000	.0022	.0130	.0238	.1124	.6486	.1979
Default	.0000	.0000	.0000	.0000	.0000	.0000	.0000	1.0000

If the migration process hits the default state, we must generate the amount recovered assuming one of the models introduced earlier. Note, however, that whereas in the context of pricing the expected recovery rate is sufficient, uncertainty in recovery rates is important in a simulation context, and in particular for modeling credit derivatives such as collateralized loan and bond obligations.

An overview of the simulation framework

The modules discussed above are now pieced together to build a portfolio simulator. The simulator takes as input term structures on default-free and defaultable bonds of different ratings, and generates the economic scenarios. In addition, it generates rating and default scenarios according to the rating transition probabilities. If the ith bond is in rating j_τ at time τ, we obtain its price according to the evolution of the state variables under the risk-neutral measure Q from time τ until T, conditioned on the realization of the economic scenarios until τ.

Figure 11.2 illustrates the simulator that proceeds along the following steps:

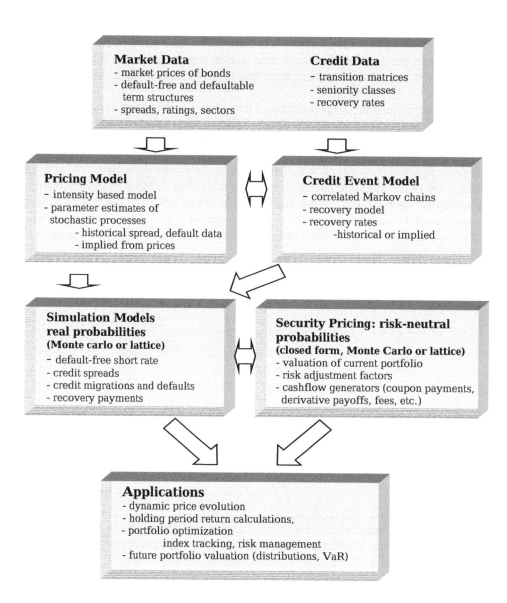

Figure 11.2: The simulation framework for credit risk securities.

Step 1. Simulate under the real probability measure economic scenarios denoted by the set $\Omega_e = \{1, 2, \ldots, N_e\}$ of the default-free short rate r_{ft} and the credit spread h_{jt} for $0 \leq t \leq \tau$, and for each rating $j = 1, \ldots, K - 1$. We denote these outcomes as r_{ft}^l and h_{jt}^l, respectively, where l is the scenario index from the set Ω_e.

Step 2. Simulate a set of credit rating scenarios $\Omega_c = \{1, 2, \ldots, N_c\}$, that is, sample ratings j_τ for each bond $i \in U$, at time τ, according to a Markov model. We denote the credit rating of each bond under scenario $l \in \Omega_c$ by j_τ^l.

Step 3. Calculate the price $P_i^{j_\tau l}(\tau, T)$ of bond i for each rating scenario in Ω_c and each economic scenario in Ω_e. We therefore obtain $N_e N_c$ scenarios where $l \in \Omega_c \times \Omega_e$. The prices are calculated using (11.12) according to the underlying pricing model (11.5)–(11.8). This calculation may require – if no closed-form solutions are available – the simulation of the dynamics of interest rates r_{ft} and credit spreads h_{jt} under the risk-neutral measure for $\tau \leq t \leq T$ and for each rating $j_\tau = 1, 2, \ldots, K - 1$, conditional on the economic scenarios observed until τ.

Step 4. The simulation can be used to value a portfolio at a future point in time (i.e., calculation of V_τ^l for every scenario l), and can then use this information to compute the risk measures needed in scenario optimization models. It can also be used to model the price dynamics by simulating for different risk horizons τ, and to generate scenario trees for stochastic portfolio optimization models.

11.4   Optimizing the Right Risk Metric

We use the simulation models to generate the distribution of returns for a portfolio of predetermined holdings in investment-grade bonds. Figure 11.3 summarizes the results when integrating market and credit spread risk, and then adding the credit events, such as rating migrations and defaults. There is an interesting observation in these figures: when credit events are accurately simulated, the distribution of returns becomes skewed and has a flat tail on the downside risk. This is, of course, expected, since credit events are low probability but high impact events.

However, when comparing the two distributions using VaR at the 0.95 percentile we do not notice any differences in the tails. The 0.95-VaR of the two distributions shown in the figure are positive and very close to each other. However, the 0.99-VaR have opposite signs and differ by an order of magnitude. There are no losses at the .95 probability level, even when credit events are properly simulated. At the 0.99 probability level, however, we observe losses of -1.7% when credit events are simulated. This leads to an important observation:

> Without adequate accuracy of the scenario generation method some important risk features of the distribution of credit risk portfolios will be missed.

This observation has ramifications when choosing an appropriate risk metric for portfolio optimization. We turn to the choice of a suitable risk metric next.

11.4.1   Tail effects on efficient frontiers

We study now the efficient frontiers generated when trading expected return against risk in credit risk portfolios. We will see that ignoring the tails has a significant effect on the efficient frontiers. We simulate first the distribution of returns of 17 investment-grade bonds (rated Baa on Moody's scale) without credit rating migration and defaults, and generate frontiers of expected return versus mean absolute deviation using Model 5.3.1. The efficient frontier is shown by the thin solid line in Figure 11.4. On the same figure we re-draw (dotted line) the frontier by calculating the expected return and the mean absolute deviation of the portfolios, using distributions of

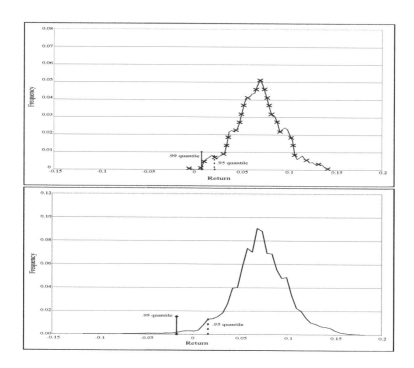

Figure 11.3: Distribution of returns on a portfolio of investment-grade corporate bonds during an eight-month risk horizon for stochastic risk-free rates and credit spreads. Top figure: without credit rating migrations or defaults. Bottom figure: with credit rating migrations and defaults.

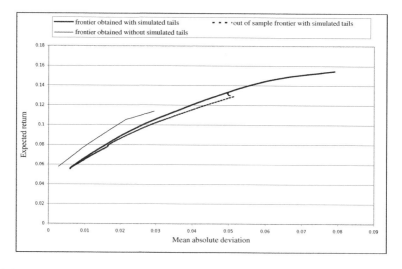

Figure 11.4: Frontier generated using mean absolute deviation (MAD) portfolio optimization without simulating the tails due to credit events (thin solid line), and its out-of-sample performance when credit events are included (dotted line). The frontier traced using a MAD model and simulated data of credit events is also shown (thick solid line).

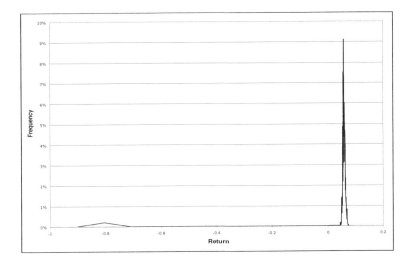

Figure 11.5: Distribution of returns for the minimum risk portfolio obtained using the MAD model. Note the small probability of negative returns worse than -80%.

returns with credit rating migrations and defaults. Thus we perform a sensitivity analysis of the frontier using out-of-sample tail scenarios that were not included in the set of scenarios for the optimization model. We see that tails distort the risk-return frontiers, rendering seemingly efficient portfolios into inefficient ones. There is nothing efficient about the optimized portfolios obtained by ignoring the tails once the tails are properly accounted for.

Running the MAD model using the distribution with credit events we obtain a frontier which is very close to the out-of-sample frontier and which eliminates the inefficient portfolios. This frontier is shown by the thick solid line on Figure 11.4. Does this imply that it is sufficient to accurately simulate the tails and then develop portfolios that optimally trade expected return against risk? To do so is necessary but not sufficient, as the risk measure used should accurately account for the tails as well. The distribution of returns on the minimum risk portfolio obtained using the MAD model on the tailed distribution is shown in Figure 11.5. We note a small probability of losses in excess of 80% of the portfolio value. These losses are likely to be catastrophic, and when they occur they will most likely – due to bankruptcy – block the portfolio's growth to its long-term expected return. The long-term expected return of the minimum risk portfolio obtained using MAD is 5.5%, but this return will be realized only if the portfolio is not ruined in the short-term.

What then should be done in order to correctly account for the tail effects? The answer lies in selecting a risk metric that appropriately penalizes extreme events, and then optimizing the portfolio composition with respect to this metric of risk. We will see in the next section that conditional Value-at-Risk (Definition 2.6.3) provides a risk metric suitable for integrating credit risk in asset portfolios.

11.4.2   Conditional Value-at-Risk efficient frontiers

We trace the efficient frontier trading off expected shortfall against expected portfolio value using Model 5.5.1. We develop CVaR efficient frontiers at the 0.99 and 0.95 probability levels (see Figure 11.6). On the same figures we plot the trade-offs between CVaR and expected return of the optimal portfolios obtained above using the MAD model. That is, we take the portfolios of the efficient frontier of Figure 11.4 and calculate their CVaR. We observe from the two frontiers of Figure 11.6 that the MAD optimized portfolios are inefficient when using a risk metric that

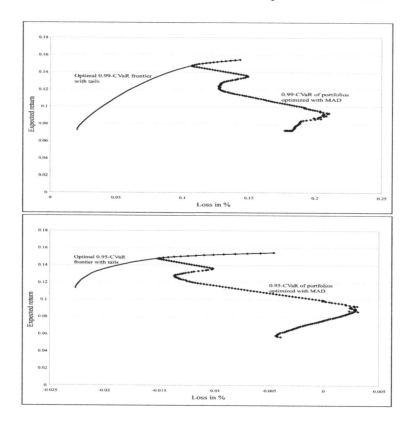

Figure 11.6: Frontier generated using a CVaR portfolio optimization with credit event simulations (solid line), and the CVaR of efficient portfolios optimized with the MAD model (dotted line). Top figure: CVaR estimated at the 0.99 probability level. Bottom figure: CVaR estimated at the 0.95 probability level.

accurately accounts for the tails of the portfolios. It is not sufficient to capture the tails in the simulation phase, as was done in Figure 11.4; we must also optimize the appropriate risk metric, as is done in Figure 11.6.

In other words, to avoid distortions in the efficient frontier due to the tail events we need to optimize a risk metric that appropriately penalizes the tails. CVaR provides such a risk metric. Note, however, in Figure 11.6 (bottom), that the distortions of the frontiers calculated at the 0.95 probability level are barely noticeable for a wide range of target expected returns, while the differences are distinct for a wider range of target returns at the 0.99 probability level. This observation reemphasizes the fact that tail effects can be captured only sufficiently accurate models.

The risk profile of a portfolio is shaped by the effectiveness with which the tails are modeled. Using the CVaR risk metric for optimizing the portfolio structure substantially reduces the tails. Figure 11.7 shows the distribution of returns on the minimum risk portfolio obtained when minimizing CVaR at probability levels 0.95 and 0.99. The tail extends up to almost -40% when minimizing CVaR at the 0.95 probability level, but shrinks to -10% when minimizing CVaR at the 0.99 probability level. These losses are substantially lower than the losses resulting from returns of -80%, realized when minimizing mean absolute deviation (Figure 11.5).

The choice of a risk metric has an effect on the upside potential of the portfolio as well. Notice from the distributions in Figures 11.5 and 11.7 that the upside potential is reduced as the tails are shrunk. We have the usual trade-offs between upside potential and downside risk. However, in the context of credit risk securities the downside risk is hidden in the tail and not in

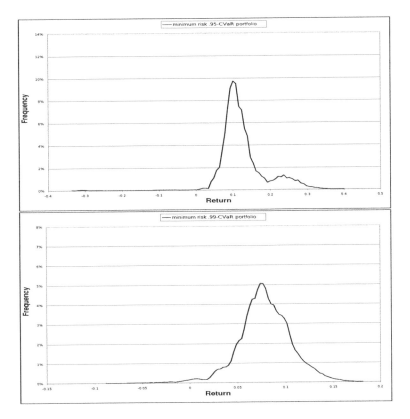

Figure 11.7: Distribution of returns for the minimum risk portfolio obtained using the CVaR model at the 0.95 (top) and 0.99 (bottom) probability levels. Note that the flat tail of negative returns worse than -80% – pronounced in Figure 11.5 when using a MAD optimization – has been significantly reduced, especially at the higher accuracy of 0.99 probability.

the variance or the mean absolute deviation.

The significance of choosing the appropriate risk metric is highlighted even further when we look at long-term performance. Optimization of portfolio performance for the long run ignores the short-term effects. This has been the case in myopic single-period optimization models. Ignoring the short term effects can be catastrophic in the presence of fat tails. In particular, the long-term (expected) potential of a portfolio strategy may never be realized if an extreme event in the short run results in bankruptcy. Long-Term Capital Management is a case in point. When LTCM suffered losses of 80% in September 1998 the New York Federal Reserve orchestrated a bailout, and 14 banks joined forces to acquire a 90% stake in the firm. The fund eventually recovered its losses and posted positive returns, but the original stakeholders were no longer there.

We look at the short-term effects of the tails on portfolios obtained with the MAD and the 0.99-CVaR optimization models. We take the minimum risk portfolio from these models at a 12-month risk horizon, and using out-of-sample scenarios simulate the distributions of returns at months three, six and twelve. The results for the portfolio obtained by the MAD model are shown in Figure 11.8, and for the CVaR model in Figure 11.9.

The expected return of the MAD optimized portfolio over the 12-month period is 5.5%. The worst-case losses are on the order of -2% in the first three months, but jump to -80% at months six and twelve. The probability of these losses also increases with time – from 0.17% at month six, to 0.34% at month twelve. Although the probabilities are small, these losses are potentially

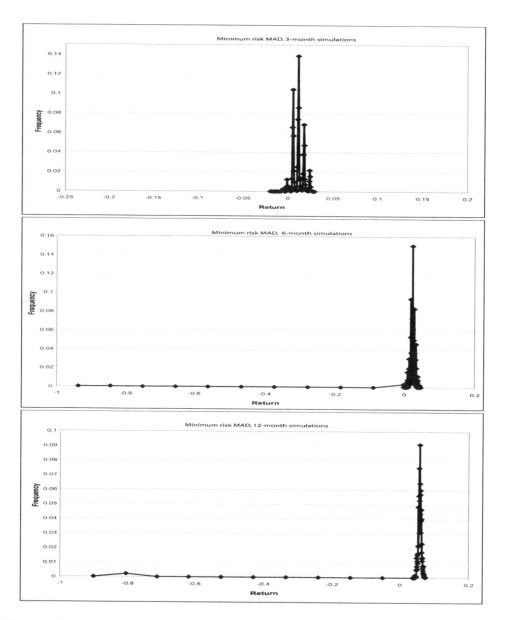

Figure 11.8: Distribution of returns at different time horizons for the minimum risk MAD optimized portfolio across time, using out-of-sample scenarios. Catastrophic losses of up to -80% are probable after the first three months.

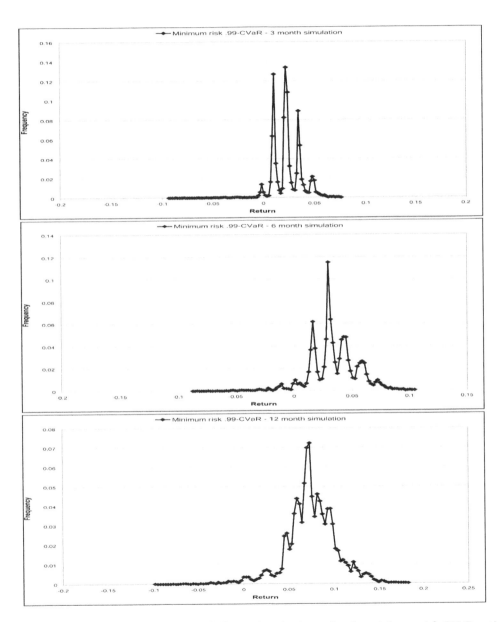

Figure 11.9: Distribution of returns at different time horizons for the minimum risk CVaR optimized portfolio, using out-of-sample scenarios. Worst-case returns are limited to around -10% throughout.

catastrophic. The expected return of the MAD optimized portfolio increases with time, but so does the probability that a catastrophic event will prevent the portfolio path from attaining the long-run average.

The expected return of the CVaR optimized portfolio over the 12-month period is 7.2% (Figure 11.9). The worst-case losses of this portfolio remain at around 10% throughout this time period. The probability of losses increases marginally from month three to month twelve. In any event these losses are not catastrophic, and the long-term expected return can be achieved. Not only does the CVaR optimized portfolio have higher expected return than the MAD optimized portfolio in the long run, it also has a better downside risk profile in the short run.

The impact of the tails appears to be devastating for the MAD portfolio. Of course there is an underlying assumption here that investors will not rebalance their portfolio. Recall that the intensity models assume that credit events are typically unpredictable, and under this class of simulation models investors will not be able to rebalance prior to a credit event. However, there is evidence that credit events may be in part predictable, for example from equity returns, and such information can be included in a pricing framework. This implies that investors would use these signals and reduce their exposure in anticipation of adverse events. The multi-period optimization models of Chapter 6 can be used to further improve the performance of the models introduced here.

11.5 Index Funds for Corporate Bond Portfolios

The previous section developed well-diversified portfolios of credit risk securities, taking into account the multifarious risk factors and their complex interactions. We now proceed to address the problem of creating a diversified portfolio with a well-defined performance measure. Specifically, we will formulate optimization models to achieve good tracking performance of the credit risk portfolio vis-à-vis an appropriate index. Development of the models follows the discussion on index funds from Chapter 7.

From a strategic point of view the portfolio manager is interested in determining the allocation among general asset classes. An asset class may consist of all bonds with a certain rating, bonds in a certain industrial sector, or with a given maturity range, or any combination of these characteristics. Tactical bond picking decisions follow the broad asset allocation, and credit analysts bring in expert knowledge to select the bonds of specific companies at that point. For very large indices, such as the corporate bond index we consider here, the asset allocation decision may be used to reduce the problem size. The subsequent bond picking problems may also be solved via optimization models on the reduced set.

Models for index funds were developed in Chapter 7, and based on that discussion we now develop indexation models for corporate bonds. We develop two models to address separately the strategic asset allocation and the tactical bond picking problem. These models reflect the hierarchical operations of portfolio managers, who usually determine first a broad asset allocation, and then the specific portfolio holdings. An integrated model is subsequently developed that jointly determines the asset allocation and the bond picking decisions. We will see from the empirical results that the integrated model produces better results than the nonintegrated models.

11.5.1   Indexation by strategic asset allocation

In the strategic model we seek the optimal asset allocation among broad asset classes. The asset classes can be a credit rating, an industrial sector, a maturity range, or a combination of these attributes. We assume that there are K asset classes with some unique risk characteristics in the broad index. We denote these classes by a subscript j, and the set of securities in each class by U_j. We assume for simplicity that all asset classes are of the same size, m. Each security i in the set U_j carries a weight w_{ij} in the broad index. The proportional weights of each asset class in the index are given by $\gamma_j = \sum_{i=1}^{n} w_{ij}$.

We denote the portfolio weights – as a proportion of total assets – allocated to the jth asset class by z_j, and the proportional holdings in bond i in the jth asset class by x_{ij}. The strategic asset allocation model determines optimal weights z_j^*, and the bond picking model specifies optimal holdings x_{ij}^* such that $\sum_{i=1}^{n} x_{ij}^* = z_j^*$, for all $j \in \mathcal{K}$. An integrated model will determine jointly the optimal holdings x_{ij}^* and weights z_i^*.

With this notation the return of the broad index is given by

$$R_I(\gamma, r^l) = \sum_{j=1}^{K} \gamma_j R_j(w, r^l), \tag{11.13}$$

where $R_j(w, r^l) = \sum_{i=1}^{n} w_{ij} r_{ij}^l$ is the return of the sub-index of the jth asset class. We also use $R_{pj}(x, r^l) = \sum_{i=1}^{n} r_{ij}^l x_{ij}$ to denote the return on the sub-portfolio of holdings in the jth asset class, so that the return on the overall portfolio is given by

$$R(z, x; r^l) = \sum_{j=1}^{K} z_j R_{pj}(x; r^l). \tag{11.14}$$

The strategic asset allocation for indexed funds of corporate bonds now follows along the lines of Model 7.4.2:

Model 11.5.1 Strategic model for corporate indexed funds

$$\underset{z \in X}{\text{Maximize}} \quad \sum_{l \in \Omega} p^l R(z, x; r^l) \tag{11.15}$$

$$\text{subject to} \quad -\epsilon \leq \sum_{j=1}^{K} R_j(w, r^l) z_j - R_I(\gamma, r^l) \leq \epsilon,$$

$$\text{for all } l \in \Omega, \tag{11.16}$$

$$\sum_{j=1}^{K} z_j = 1, \tag{11.17}$$

$$z \geq 0. \tag{11.18}$$

11.5.2   Tactical bond picking model

The portfolios of the previous section are not tradeable as they consist of investments in broad asset classes and not in individual securities. Bond analysts can use the recommendations of the model and select specific bonds from each asset class to create a tradeable portfolio. If the selected bonds perform exactly as the class average, then tracking performance such as that illustrated in Figure 11.14 will be realized. If the performance of the selected bonds deviates from the average then the resulting portfolio performance will also deviate from the index.

In a hierarchical approach a portfolio manager can use an indexation model to pick bonds from each asset class, while restricting the total asset allocation in each class j to some target value $\hat{z}_j$. The following linear programming models, based on Model 7.4.3, can be used:

Model 11.5.2 Tactical model for corporate indexed funds

For each $j \in \mathcal{K}$, solve:

$$\underset{x \in X}{\text{Maximize}} \quad \sum_{l \in \Omega} p^l R_{pj}(x; r^l) \tag{11.19}$$

$$\text{subject to} \quad -\epsilon \leq R_{pj}(x; r^l) - R_j(w, r^l) \leq \epsilon,$$
$$\text{for all } l \in \Omega, \tag{11.20}$$

$$\sum_{i=1}^{n} x_{ij} = \hat{z}_j, \tag{11.21}$$

$$x \in X. \tag{11.22}$$

The target value can be set either based on the optimal asset allocation derived from the solution of the strategic model, $\hat{z}_j = z_j^*$, or based on the actual composition of the index $\hat{z}_j = \gamma_j$. It is also possible to leave the target value unconstrained, i.e., $\hat{z}_j$ being a nonnegative variable, in which case the model jointly optimizes the asset allocation and the bond picking decisions.

11.6   Tracking the Merrill Lynch Euro Dollar Corporate Bond Index

The models are applied to track the Merrill Lynch Euro Dollar index, which consists of highly liquid securities so that liquidity risk is eliminated. The index experienced significant growth, both in terms of volume and in terms of returns, over the last several years. In January 1997 there were 450 securities in the index; the number increased to 665 by March 2000, and was over 1000 by August of the same year. All bonds in the index are investment-grade quality, rated Baa or higher in Moody's scale, and in January 1999 approximately 84% of the index value was in bonds rated Aa or higher. The growth of a \$100 investment in the Merrill Lynch Euro Dollar index over an 18-month period starting in January 1999 is illustrated in Figure 11.10. While the growth has been modest – reflecting rising yields and widening credit spreads during this period – the index fares well compared to other fixed-income indices, as summarized in Table 11.2.

The models were evaluated by backtesting the performance of the indexed portfolios during the period January 1999 to June 2001 (see Section 7.7 for discussion of the testing methodology). The performance of the indexed portfolios will depend on many factors, and in this section we test the sensitivity of the portfolio performance on the risk factors of corporate bonds, and on the modeling choices. We will see that overall portfolio performance during the backtesting period is quite good, but care must be exercised when some risk factors are ignored. In particular, the portfolio will perform well if the risks that are ignored do not materialize during the testing period. A careful examination of the portfolio composition, however, would reveal that catastrophic losses could have been realized if these risks did occur.

Table 11.2: Performance of some global bond indices during the period January 1999–June 2000.

Index	Total Return	Price Return
Merrill Lynch Euro Dollar	2.778	-5.939
AAA Agency	1.882	-6.560
Domestic Corp.	-0.807	-10.284
US Treasury	2.099	-6.633

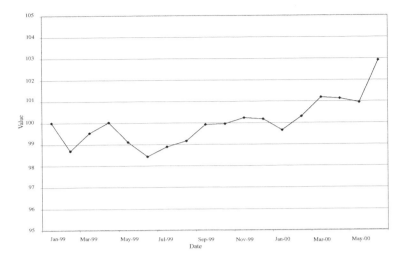

Figure 11.10: Performance of the Merrill Lynch Euro Dollar index during the period from January 1999 to July 2000.

11.6.1   Sensitivity to alternative risk factors

We study first the effect of the following risk factors on performance:

1. Changes in the term structure of risk-free rates and credit spreads;
2. changes in the rating of the bond, including default events; and
3. the amount recovered if a bond goes into default.

We consider as a base model for comparison the one tested in Figure 7.8. Those results were obtained by simulating economic scenarios and credit events, but in the case of default we assumed zero recovery. The impact of alternative recovery assumptions on the indexed portfolios is investigated next.

Alternative recovery assumptions

In practice when a bond defaults some amount may be recovered by the bondholders, and the zero recovery assumption is clearly unrealistic. Table 11.3 summarizes the average price after default by pre-default bond rating. (We note some inconsistencies in the recovery rates reported in this table: slightly less is recovered when an Aa bond goes into default than when an A bond does. This inconsistency is analogous to the problem we noted in Table 11.1.) We backtest the indexation model, using the same scenarios of interest rates, credit spreads, rating migration, and default used in the base model, but making different assumptions about recovery rates in the case of default.

Figure 11.11 (top) shows the performance of the indexed portfolios obtained by assuming that when a bond goes into default its price drops to the historical average. The same figure (bottom) shows the results when a random recovery price is assumed generated by sampling uniformly from the interval $[0, 100]$. These figures are similar to that obtained using the base model with zero recovery rates. The Sharpe ratio, computed with respect to the index, is 0.530 during the testing period under the assumption of historical recovery rates, and 0.538 for random recovery rates. These ratios are significantly higher than the Sharpe ratio of 0.497 achieved with the base model of Figure 7.8.

The models with nonzero recovery rates choose more aggressive portfolios than the base model. This is expected due to the smaller losses anticipated in the case of default. As a result,

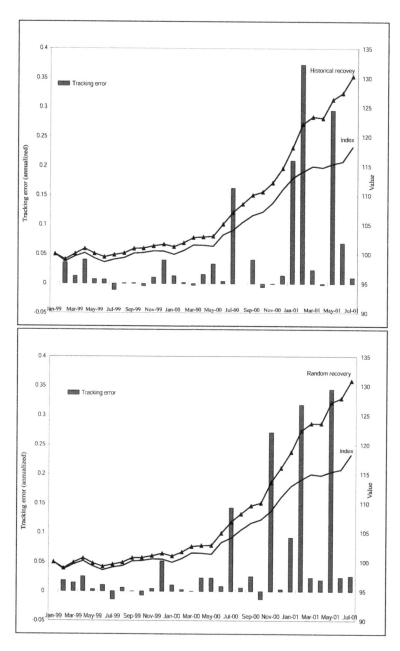

Figure 11.11: Performance of the tracking portfolios built with different recovery models versus the index: using historical recovery rates (top), and using random recovery rates (bottom). Bars denote tracking errors.

Table 11.3: Average price after default for different pre-default bond ratings during the period 1971–1998.

Pre-default ratings (Moody's scale)	Average price in default
Aaa	68.34
Aa	59.09
A	60.63
Baa	49.05
Ba	39.25
B	37.89
Caa-C	38.23

both the value of the portfolio at the end of the period and the Sharpe ratios improve when the models accurately evaluate recovery rates. On the other hand, defaults or downgrading would lead to extreme losses, and credit risk portfolio managers are also concerned about exposure to a single issuer in the portfolios; this is known as name concentration. They want portfolios that are diversified with respect to the number of bonds. An analysis of the portfolios obtained with different assumptions on recovery rates found no significant differences. The portfolios obtained with all three models consist of approximately 40 to 100 bonds throughout the backtesting period.

Impact of economic scenarios

We now assume that the economic environment – interest rates and credit spreads – remains unchanged and we generate only scenarios of rating migrations and default. Of course, assuming zero volatility of interest rates and credit spreads is an oversimplification for fixed-income portfolio management. However, the separation of market and credit risk is still practiced and many models focus on rating and default events, assuming fixed interest rates. We examine here the impact of these assumptions on indexed portfolios. The results are shown in Figure 11.12, and we observe that, in comparison to the results earlier in this section and of the base model summarized in Figure 7.8, ignoring uncertainty in interest rates and spreads has a significant impact on the performance of the tracking portfolio. The Sharpe ratio drops to -0.23. Comparing this with the Sharpe ratios of 0.497 to 0.538 obtained with the indexed portfolios earlier in this section provides strong support for the drive towards integration of market and credit risk, and in favor of enterprise-wide risk management.

Impact of rating and default scenarios

We now remove the effects of rating and default scenarios, and consider only economic scenarios. When ignoring credit quality downgrading and defaults the optimizer will select risky portfolios, investing heavily in low quality bonds or bonds that appear cheap. The potential downside risk is ignored and the optimizer chooses low quality bonds that offer, on average, higher yields. Figure 11.13 shows the backtesting performance when we carry out the simulations assuming that all bonds stay in their current rating class, so that only economic scenarios are generated. We sample exactly the same economic scenarios used in the base model, but, unlike the base model, we price all bonds according to their initial credit rating. We observe from this figure that indexed portfolios obtained when ignoring migrations and defaults perform well, with a Sharpe ratio of .56. The model appears to pick the right bonds in a stochastic interest rate and spread environment, even when the downside risk of default is ignored. However, a closer look at

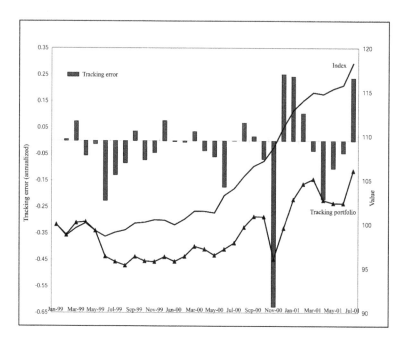

Figure 11.12: Performance of the tracking model versus the index and corresponding tracking errors when the scenario generation does not include uncertainty in interest rates and credit spreads.

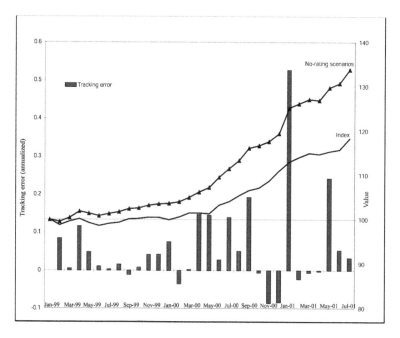

Figure 11.13: Performance of the tracking model versus the index and corresponding tracking errors. The scenario generation does not include rating and default simulations.

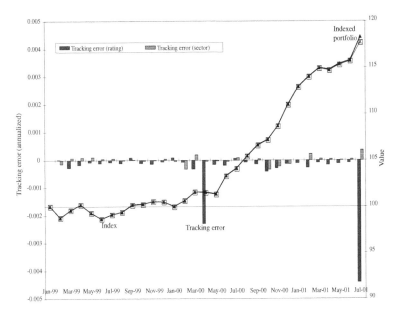

Figure 11.14: Performance of index funds created using broad asset allocation models.

the portfolio holdings reveals a disturbing observation: there is high concentration in individual bonds. All portfolios throughout the backtesting period consist of only four to ten bonds. This size is an order of magnitude smaller than the size of the portfolios obtained when rating and default scenarios were included. The portfolios obtained when ignoring credit events are poorly diversified, and will suffer substantial losses if there is a rating downgrade or a default. As these are low probability events they did not occur for any one of the bonds in the portfolio during the 30-month backtesting period. As a result the performance of the portfolio is deceptively good. Managers who rely on the backtesting results of Figure 11.13, and use only economic scenarios, are in for a big surprise during economic downturns when defaults and downgrades are on the rise. This example highlights the side effects of portfolio optimization discussed in Section 1.4.1.

11.6.2   Sensitivity to model choices

We examine here the sensitivity of indexed funds to the type of modeling that is employed: strategic, tactical, or integrated.

Indexation by strategic asset allocation

We run the strategic asset allocation Model 11.5.1, defining first asset classes consisting of bonds in the Merrill Lynch index with the same credit rating. Figure 11.14 shows the tracking errors of the asset allocation obtained with the strategic model against the index. In the same figure we also show the tracking error obtained when we run the model defining asset classes of bonds in the same industrial sector rather than of the same rating. In both cases the portfolios track the index closely, but no extra value is created. Closer examination of the optimal portfolios shows that their composition is almost identical to the Merrill Lynch index. Similar results are obtained when the strategic asset allocation model is solved, using asset classes defined by rating and maturity – maturities are grouped in buckets of 1–3, 3–5, 5–7 and 7–10 years – by rating and industrial sector, by rating and maturity, and by industrial sector and maturity.

Table 11.4: Sharpe ratios of indexed portfolios obtained under different assumptions on the risk factors, and for alternative model structures when constraints are imposed on the tactical bond picking model.

Risk factor assumptions	Sharpe ratio
zero recovery	.497
random recovery	.538
historical recovery	.530
no rating migration	.560
no economic scenarios	-.230

Constraints on the tactical model	Sharpe ratio
by index rating	.541
by index rating and maturity	.644
by optimal rating	.572
by optimal rating and maturity	.677

Tactical bond picking with constraints based on the index composition

We now create indexed portfolios using the tactical Model 11.5.2, and constraining the holdings in each asset class to match the actual exposure of the index to the asset classes. First we match the holdings by rating category, and then we match the holdings by maturity dates. In all simulations we assume random recovery in the case of default.

Figure 11.15 shows the ex post performance of portfolios constructed with this model. Constraining the asset allocation by credit rating category leads to performance similar to the unconstrained model with a Sharpe ratio of 0.541. Constraining the asset allocation by rating and maturity improves tracking performance with a Sharpe ratio of 0.644.

Tactical bond picking with constraints based on the optimal asset allocation

We repeat the exercise with the tactical model restricting the total holdings in each asset class to equal the optimal solution of the strategic asset allocation models. The results are almost identical to those obtained when we impose constraints based on the actual composition of the index. This is expected, as the strategic asset allocation results in allocations that are very close to the actual composition of the index. There is a slight increase in the Sharpe ratio from 0.541 to 0.572 when using the optimal weights as opposed to the index weights. Similarly, constraining the tactical model by credit rating and maturity class produces a Sharpe ratio of 0.677 instead of 0.644, which was obtained when constraining the tactical model using the actual index weights. The optimized asset allocation adds value only marginally.

Summary of results

A summary of the results for backtesting the models using different assumptions – either on the simulation of the risk factors or on the use of the models – is given in Table 11.4.

The most important risk factors are interest rates and credit spreads. However, ignoring downgrading and default risk has a significant impact on the portfolio composition and very few securities are included in the portfolio. This places large bets on single names which is a very risky strategy. If default occurs the actual portfolio will suffer large investment losses.

The tactical models generate portfolios with better tracking performance than the strategic models. This observation is true irrespective of how the tactical models are constrained. How-

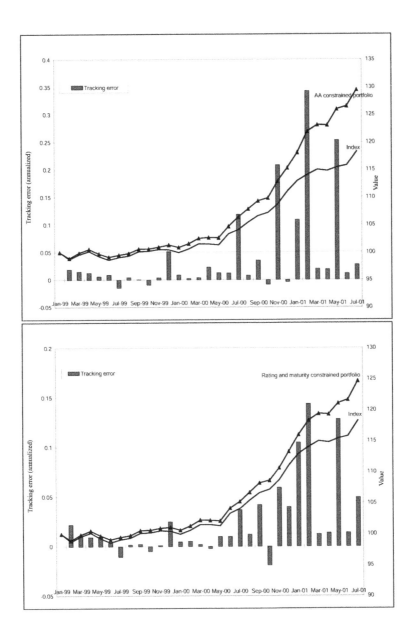

Figure 11.15: Performance of index funds created using a tactical model and constraining the holdings by credit rating category (top), and by rating and maturity (bottom).

ever, it appears that imposing constraints by quality rating and maturity works best. It makes little difference whether we restrict the asset class exposure to be identical to that of the index, or if we use the asset allocation decisions from the strategic model.

As a final building block in the management of corporate bond portfolios we bring up the need to integrate credit risk into government bond portfolios. This issue has already been addressed in Section 7.7.3. Significant improvement in the performance of a government bond portfolio can be realized, with the use of an integrative model, as illustrated in Figure 7.10.

11.7   Funding Liabilities with Corporate Bonds

We consider now the problem of funding a fixed liability using credit risk assets of corporate bonds. Such problems appear in portfolio dedication and portfolio immunization for pension funds, and in numerous business settings (see Chapter 4). As discussed earlier these problems have traditionally been tackled using government bonds alone in order to avoid the risks associated with default. In this section we show that the simulation models developed in this chapter, together with the stochastic programming models of Chapter 6, allow us to use corporate bonds to address these important financial planning problems.

We set up an example whereby an initial endowment of 10,000 EUR must be invested over an 18-month horizon in order to achieve a target annualized return of 5% while paying a fixed liability of 2,000 EUR at month 12. An asset universe of AAA, AA, A, and BBB rated bonds of different maturities were used to construct an optimal portfolio. The optimality criterion was to minimize the CVaR against the target 5% return at the 99% confidence level.

As a benchmark we solve a single-period CVaR optimization model without any constraints for funding the target liability. Figure 11.16 illustrates the portfolio terminal wealth for the generated scenarios and the cash (reserve) account created through coupon payments, bonds maturing, or cash investment from the beginning. Note that at month 12 the cash account has reached a level of 1,200 EUR, which is significantly below the target. The portfolio expected return over the 18-month period is 15.2%. This figure can be used to benchmark the results of the following two experiments.

We then solve a single-period model that imposes CVaR constraints on the target liability. That is, we aim to accumulate sufficient cash reserves to finance the liability. Figure 11.17 illustrates the portfolio terminal wealth and the cash (reserve) account created through coupon payments and bond maturing. Note that at month 12 the cash account has reached the target level of 2,000 EUR. However, this was possible through substantial investments in cash at the start of the planning period, and as a result the expected return over the 18-month horizon is reduced to 13%, indicating a significant cost in expected return in order to finance the liability.

Finally, we solve a two-stage model that imposes CVaR constraints on the target liability and allows us to rebalance the portfolio and sell bonds at period 12 in order to satisfy the risk constraints. Figure 11.18 illustrates the portfolio terminal wealth and the cash (reserve) account created through coupon payments and bond maturing. Note that at month 12 the cash account is only 700 (a substantial reduction from the previous experiment); however, with proper rebalancing we can still meet the liabilities. Note that some cash remains after the portfolio is rebalanced, and the amount of cash depends on the senarios – hence the multiple data points for each time period after month 12. The expected return over the 18-month horizon is increased to 15.9%, thus indicating that superior returns can be achieved while funding the liability when we use a stochastic programming model that allows us to model the complex dynamics of the problem.

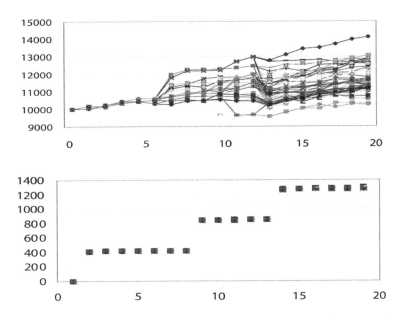

Figure 11.16: Terminal wealth under different scenarios (top) and cash reserve (bottom) for a portfolio optimized using single-period optimization without risk constraints in funding the target liability. The expected return is 15.2%.

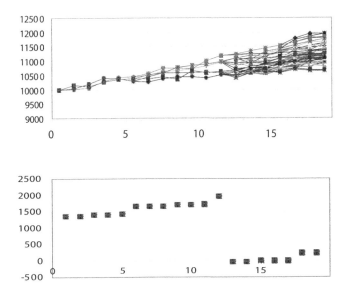

Figure 11.17: Terminal wealth under different scenarios (top) and cash reserve (bottom) for a portfolio optimized using single-period optimization with risk constraints in funding the target liability. At month 12 there is sufficient cash at hand to finance the liability, primarily through cash investment at the start of the planning period. The expected return is 13%.

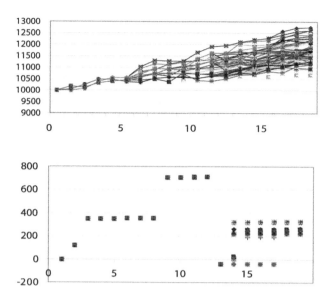

Figure 11.18: Terminal wealth (top) and cash reserve (bottom) for a portfolio optimized using the two-stage model, with risk constraints in funding the target liability. Cash at month 12 is below the target liability, but portfolio rebalancing covers the shortfall. The expected return is 15.9%. (Note that after month 12 there are different levels of cash for each remaining time period depending on the scenario realized until this month, as a result of the different rebalancing strategies followed for different first-stage scenarios.)

11.8 Postview

This chapter developed both simulation and optimization models for structuring portfolios with assets such as corporate bonds whereby credit risk is a predominant risk factor. Simulation models were first developed to integrate credit risk with the fixed-income market risk, paying particular attention to the modeling of defaults and recovery rates.

It was then shown that the choice of risk metric is very important when managing credit risk portfolios, since the distributions of holding period returns of such assets exhibit flat tails. The CVaR models were shown to be suitable for this problem class.

The chapter then went on to develop integrative models for tracking corporate bond indices, and a two-stage stochastic programming model for financing a fixed liability stream with a portfolio of corporate bonds.

Notes and References

The optimization models discussed in this chapter are based on the articles by Jobst and Zenios (2001, 2003, 2005). The first article illustrates the importance of flat tails in the management of corporate bond portfolios and introduces CVaR models for this problem, and the second develops and tests the indexation strategies. The simulation models are discussed by Jobst and Zenios (2005). Jobst, Mitra and Zenios (2006) develop stochastic programming models for funding fixed liabilities with credit risk assets. Related work using optimization models for the management of credit risk can be found in Mausser and Rosen (1999), and Andersson et al. (2001).

For treatment of credit risk and the management of corporate bond portfolios see Saunders (1999), Duffie and Singleton (2003), Schönbucher (2000), or the more applied publications such as JP Morgan's CreditMetrics (1997), Wilson (1997a, b), Kaelhofer (1996). For the pricing of credit risk assets and derivative securities see Jarrow and Turnbull (1995), Lando (1998), Duffie and Singleton (1999), and Schönbucher (2000). For background on stochastic processes see Bhat (1972), or Brémaud (1981).

Structural models date back to Black and Scholes (1973), and Merton (1974). An overview of both structural and intensity based models can be found in Lando (1998), Jarrow (1998), and Schönbucher (2000). Correlated migrations and defaults have been studied by Lando (2004), and Kijima et al. (2000), among others.

Two models closely related to the models proposed here are due to Kijima et al. (2000), and Kijima and Muromachi (2000). The first paper extends the work of Jarrow, Lando and Turnbull. Lando (1998) extends the Jarrow, Lando and Turnbull model in this direction in the context of pricing a single security by introducing stochastically varying transition intensities. This also implies uncertainty in spread movements. The estimation of the dynamics of the underlying diffusion processes from risky bond prices alone is almost impossible and bond option prices are required (see Arvanites et al. 2001).

Kijima and Muromachi (2000) develop another risk management model based on a stochastic default intensity model (the "Recovery of Treasury model") introduced by Jarrow and Turnbull (1995). The model incorporates stochastic interest rate and default intensity processes in a theoretically consistent way and allows one to assess the relative importance of interest rates and default processes in an integrated framework. Defaults are sampled from the intensity processes under the real probability measure. However, rating migrations are not captured, which may affect results especially if a portfolio of investment-grade bonds is considered.

Zero recovery assumptions are used in Litterman and Iben (1991). Valuation under the recovery of market value assumption is due to Duffie and Singleton (1999), and has gained acceptance as it gives a nice representation of the credit spread process $s_t = L\lambda_t$. Many numerical studies on risky security and swap pricing are based on this model; see, for example, Nielsen and Ronn (1997).

Depending on the form of the stochastic processes and the correlation structure, closed-form solutions may be obtained for some models and various securities, see Kijima (2000).

The impact of the flat tail outcomes of credit risk assets was used by Stulz (1996) to explain the discrepancy between the corporate use of derivative securities advocated by theory, and their actual use in practice as revealed by the Wharton surveys (see Bodnar et al. 1998 for the survey results). Ignoring the flat tails is a common limitation when applying mean-variance or MAD models to optimize non-normal distributions; Leland (1999) shows similar problems with Sharpe ratios.

Incorporating information about forthcoming defaults in a reduced-form pricing framework is discussed by Schönbucher and Schubert (2001).

Bucay and Rosen (1999) study the impact of alternative transition matrices on the portfolio composition. The data in Table 11.3 are due to Altman, Cooke and Kishore (1999). Jobst and Zenios (2001), and Kiesel, Perraudin and Taylor (2001) show that interest rate and spread risk are crucially important, not only for Value-at-Risk analysis but also for portfolio management.

Chapter 12

Insurance Policies with Guarantees

With *Andrea Consiglio*,[1] *Flavio Cocco*,[2] and *David Saunders*[3]

12.1 Preview

Insurance products have become increasingly more innovative in order to face competitive pressures. Insurance policies today come with guarantees on the minimum rate of return, bonus provisions, and surrender options – features that make the new policies much more complex to price and fund than traditional insurance products. In this chapter we discuss the development of scenario-based optimization models for asset and liability management of participating policies with guarantees and bonus provisions offered by Italian and UK insurers. The developed models are applied to the analysis of policies offered by both Italian and UK insurance firms. Numerical investigations with the models provide significant insights on these policies.

12.2 Participating Policies with Guarantees

The last decade brought about a phenomenal increase of consumer sophistication in terms of the financial products they buy. This trend is universal among developed economies, from the advanced and traditionally liberal economies of North America, to the increasingly deregulated economies of the European Union and pre-accession States, and the post-Communist countries.

The numbers are telling: In the 1980s almost 40% of US consumer financial assets were in bank deposits. By 1996 bank deposits accounted for less than 20% of consumers' financial assets, with mutual funds and insurance and pension funds absorbing the difference. Similar trends are observed in Italy. The traded financial assets of Italian households more than doubled in the 5-year period from 1997 to 2002, and the bulk of the increase was absorbed by mutual funds and asset management (see Table 12.1).

The increase in traded financial assets comes with increased diversification of the Italian household portfolio, similar to the situation in the US a decade earlier. Figure 12.1 shows a strong growth in mutual funds and equity shares at the expense of liquid assets and bonds. Today one-third of the total revenues of the Italian banking industry is derived from asset management services.

These statistics reveal the outcome of changing behavior on the part of consumers. What are the specific characteristics, however, that bring about this new pattern of investment? First, the traditional distinction between delegation of asset management to a pension fund board or an insurance firm by the majority of consumers, and autonomy in the management of assets by

---

[1] Faculty of Economics, University of Palermo, Palermo, Italy.
[2] Prometeia S.r.l., Bologna, Italy.
[3] Department of Statistics and Actuarial Science, University of Waterloo, Ontario, Canada.

Table 12.1: Traded financial assets by Italian households during 1997–2002 in billions of ITL.

	1997	1998	1999	2000	2001	2002
Household total	944.853	1427.999	1781.996	2124.102	2488.154	2877.773
Mutual funds	368.432	720.823	920.304	1077.360	1237.964	1386.519
Asset Management	375.465	542.205	673.500	781.300	880.450	956.970
Insurance	165.000	202.300	257.400	329.600	433.400	574.000
% of household assets	23.6	31.4	34.6	38.3	41.9	44.8

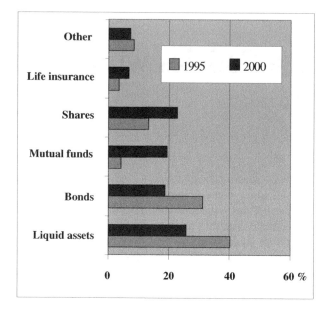

Figure 12.1: The evolution of Italian household portfolios.

wealthy investors no longer appears to be valid. Both attitudes are present in the behaviorial patterns of private savers.

Second, the trend in behaviorial profiles is towards higher levels of autonomy, and there is an increased propensity towards innovative instruments as manifested in the data of Figure 12.1. For instance, the group of Italian households classified as "innovators" grew steadily from 6.7% in 1991 to 22.6% by 2001. Each percentage point increase added a further 200,000 households to this category. Today this segment numbers 4.3 million Italian households. Households in this category adopt a very professional approach to questions of finance. They are able – or at least they feel so – to manage their financial affairs, and they rely on integrated delivery channels such as using on-line information and conducting business by phone.

Third, an analysis of the influence of quantitative variables on the savings habits of households shows that awareness of financial indicators, and in particular the performance of managed asset returns, is influencing household behavior. Investors in older age groups are more aware of such indicators than the younger generations. The trend seems to be towards increased diversification of assets under management, with the investors' favorites being insurance and portfolio management. However, as the worldwide bull markets stall so does the projection of a continued bias towards portfolio management.

In this environment some of the traditional institutions serving the individual's asset management needs, such as insurance firms, have come under increasing pressure. The statistics of Table 12.1 reveal that assets invested in life and general insurance increased by 99% in the period of interest while assets in mutual funds increased by 190%, and those under asset management by 110%. Insurance companies trail the competition in claiming a share of the household's wallet.

In the immediate future Italian households are expected to increase their traded assets by 200%, with insurance policies increasing their share by 250%, mutual funds by 280%, and asset managers by 150%. The main competitive weapon in the arsenal of insurance firms are innovative policies that offer both traditional insurance and participation in the company's profits. These policies combine features of traditional insurance from actuarial risks and of investment vehicles such as mutual funds.

Insurance products with minimum guaranteed rate of return and bonus provisions today play a key role in the insurers' business portfolio. Such products were first offered by insurance companies in the inflationary seventies: in order to compete with the high yields of treasury bonds of that time, insurance policies were enhanced with both a minimum guaranteed rate of return and a bonus provision when asset fund returns exceeded the minimum guarantee. The right to surrender the product at any time before maturity is also often given to policyholders. Such policies, known as unit-linked or index-linked, are prevalent among continental European insurance companies, but they are also encountered in the UK, United States, and Canada. In the low-inflation 1990s insurance companies still could not abandon these products due to the competitive pressures outlined above.

With the historically low interest rates currently prevailing the management of such policies is becoming more challenging. Reliance on fixed-income assets is unlikely to yield the guaranteed rate of return. For instance, Italian guaranteed rates after 1998 are at 3%. The difference between the guaranteed rate and the 10-year yield is only 1%, which is inadequate for covering the firm's costs. In Germany the guaranteed rates after 1998 are at 3.5%, differing from the 10-year yield only by 0.5%. Danish products offered guarantees of 3% until 1999, which were reduced to 2% afterwards. In Japan, Nissan Mutual Life failed on a $2.56 billion liability arising from a 4.7% guaranteed policy.

In this chapter we develop an asset and liability management model for participating insurance policies with guarantees. The model uses scenario optimization and expected utility models to integrate the insurer's asset allocation problem with that of designing competitive policies. The competing interests of shareholders, policyholders, and regulators are cast in a common framework so that efficient trade-offs can be reached. In this chapter we discuss the model and illustrate its performance. In particular it is shown that traditional methods are inadequate and innovative models are needed to address the complexities of these products. The resulting model allows the insurer to address asset allocation issues both locally and internationally in a way that is consistent with the offering of competitive products and the shareholders' interests, while satisfying the regulators. Section 12.3 discusses the Italian insurance industry and describes the characteristics of modern insurance products. Section 12.4 describes the model and Section 12.5 reports on model performance from the perspective of the shareholders, the policyholders, and the regulators.

12.3   The Italian Insurance Industry

The Italian insurance industry is regulated and supervised by ISVAP, Istituto per la Vigilanza sulle Assicurazioni, established by law in 1982. The supervisory framework aims at the stability of the market of insurance undertakings, and at the solvency and efficiency of insurance market participants. ISVAP ensures that the technical, financial, and accounting management of institutions under its supervision comply with the laws, regulations, and administrative provisions in force.

In the performance of its duties ISVAP may require insurance undertakings to disclose data, management practices, and other related information. This supervision monitors the firm's financial position, ensuring that there are sufficient solvency margins and technical provisions so that adequate assets are available to cover the entire business.

Table 12.2: The structure of portfolios of Italian life insurers in percentage of total assets held in the major asset categories. (Source: ISVAP, the regulatory board for Italian insurers.)

Year	Titoli di Stato (Gov. bonds)	Azioni (Stocks)	Obligazzioni (Bonds)	Titoli in valuta (Internat. investment)
1995	65.2	7.8	14.8	11.4
1996	65.2	7.6	13.6	13.2
1997	60.2	9.1	14.7	15.0
1998	55.2	10.0	16.6	16.4

The development of the Italian legal framework over the last 20 years – the ISVAP web page lists 51 regulatory provisions – led supervisors to devote increasing attention to data processing and real-time analysis of data. With solid preventive supervision in place ISVAP can intervene in a timely fashion in any risky situation. The availability of sophisticated safeguards, and the increased financial activity of the last decade driven by the changing nature of the Italian consumer described above, have resulted in the creation of numerous and complex groups of insurance undertakings. These undertakings offer more innovative products in response to market pressures, and they also take a more active role in the management of their assets and market risks in delivering quality products to clients. The average composition of the portfolios for life insurance, for instance, has been evolving towards more aggressive positions with increasing holdings in equity and high-quality corporate bonds as shown in Table 12.2. During the same period the industry has been promoting novel insurance policies with guarantees and participation in the profits.

12.3.1 Guaranteed products with bonus provisions

Financial products with guarantees on the minimum rate of return come in two distinct flavors: maturity guarantees and multi-period guarantees. In the former case the guarantee applies only at maturity of the contract, and returns above the guarantee at some time periods before maturity offset shortfalls at other periods. In the latter case the time to maturity is divided into subperiods – quarterly or biannually – and the guarantee applies at the end of each period. Hence, excess returns in one subperiod cannot be used to finance shortfalls in other subperiods. Such guaranteed products appear in insurance policies, guaranteed investment contracts, and some pension plans.

Policyholders participate in the firm's profits, receiving a bonus whenever the return on the firm's portfolio exceeds the guarantee, creating a surplus for the firm. Bonuses may be distributed only at maturity, at multiple periods until maturity, or using a combination of distribution plans. Another important distinction is made according to the bonus distribution mechanism. In particular, some products distribute bonuses using a smoothing formula such as the average portfolio value or portfolio return over some time period, while others distribute a prespecified fraction of the portfolio return or portfolio value net any liabilities. The earlier unit-linked policies would pay a benefit – upon death or maturity – which was the greater of the guaranteed amount and the value of the insurer's reference portfolio. These were simple maturity guarantees with bonus paid at maturity as well.

At the other extreme of complexity we have the modern UK insurance policies. In particular, legislation in the UK requires that companies structure their bonus policies in order to match "policyholders' reasonable expectations" (known as PRE), and to also meet the goal of "treating customers fairly" (the newer terminology). The notion of PRE came under fire in the UK in the early 2000s in a number of high profile court cases. These policies declare at each subperiod a fraction of the surplus, estimated using a smoothing function, as *reversionary* bonus, which is then guaranteed. The remaining surplus is managed as an *investment reserve*, and is returned to customers as terminal bonus if it is positive at maturity or upon death. These policies are

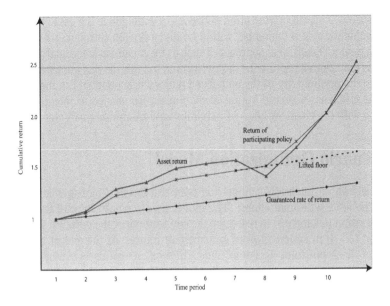

Figure 12.2: Typical returns of the asset portfolio and a participating policy with multi-period guaranteed return of 3% and participation rate 85%. The guarantee applies to a liability that is lifted every time a bonus is paid, as illustrated at period seven. The asset portfolio experienced substantial losses at period seven while the liability grew at the 3% guaranteed rate. Subsequent superior returns of the assets allowed the firm to recover its losses by the tenth period and achieve a positive net return at maturity.

multi-period guarantees with bonuses paid in part at intermediate times and in part at maturity.

The model described here considers multi-period guarantees with bonuses that are paid at each subperiod and are subsequently guaranteed. The bonus is contractually determined as a fraction of the portfolio excess return above the guaranteed rate during each subperiod. The guaranteed rate is also contractually specified. To illustrate the nature of this product we graph in Figure 12.2 the growth of a liability with 85% participation in a given portfolio while it guarantees a return of at least 3% in each period. The liability is *lifted* every time a bonus is paid and the minimum guarantee applies to the increased liability: what is given cannot be taken away. This feature creates a complex nonlinear interaction between the rate of return of the portfolio and the total return of the liability.

12.3.2   Current asset and liability management practices

The shift from actuarial to financial pricing of insurance liabilities and widely perceived problems (highlighted by the Nissan bankruptcy case) brought about an interest in applying the theory of financial asset pricing to the analysis of insurance policies with guarantees and bonus provisions. Single-period guarantees have payoffs that resemble those of a European-type option, as the policyholder receives at maturity the maximum between the guaranteed amount and the value of the bonus. Multi-period guarantees may have features, such as surrender options, that make their payoffs identical to American type options. Hence, option pricing could be applied to the pricing of these policies.

Options pricing requires the specification of the volatility of the underlying asset. Hence, in pricing the option embedded in these novel policies one must assume that the asset side is given a priori as a well-diversified portfolio which evolves according to some stochastic process. An integrative approach using scenario optimization allows us to endogenize the asset.

However, the combination of a guarantee with a bonus provision introduces nonlinearities which complicate the model. Traditional approaches such as the mean-variance analysis of Chapter 3 are inadequate as they cannot capture the highly asymmetric returns that are characteristic of these products. When the nonlinearity of the embedded options is accounted for, mean-variance portfolios cease to be efficient. Scenario optimization models are needed to integrate the asset management problem with the characteristics of liabilities with minimum guarantee.

12.4   The Scenario Optimization Model

We develop in this section an integrative model for asset and liability management for multi-period participating policies with guarantees. The model uses scenario optimization with expected utility maximization (Chapter 5) to represent the key features of the policies. All portfolio decisions are made at $t = 0$ in anticipation of an uncertain future. At the end of the planning horizon the impact of these portfolio decisions under different scenarios is evaluated and risk aversion is introduced through a utility function. Portfolio decisions optimize the expected utility over the specified horizon.

12.4.1   Features of the model

In the model we consider three accounts: (i) a liability account that grows according to the contractual guaranteed rate and bonus provision; (ii) an asset account that grows according to the portfolio returns, net any payments due to death or policy surrenders; and (iii) a shortfall account that monitors lags of the portfolio return against the guarantee. In the base model shortfall is funded by equity but later we introduce alternative reserving methods.

The multi-period dynamics of these accounts are conditioned on discrete scenarios of realized asset returns and the composition of the asset portfolio. Within this framework a regulatory constraint on leverage is imposed. At maturity the difference between the asset and the liability accounts is the surplus realized by the firm after it has fulfilled its contractual obligations. In the policies considered here this surplus remains with the shareholders. This surplus is a random variable, and a utility function is introduced to incorporate risk aversion.

12.4.2   Notation

We define the parameters and variables used in developing the model. Time takes values over the dates $t = 0, 2, \ldots, T$, and scenarios are indexed by l from the set Ω. The data of the problem are as follows:

   r_{ti}^l rate of return of asset i at period t in scenario l.

   r_{ft}^l risk-free rate during the period $t - 1$ to t in scenario l.

   g minimum guaranteed rate of return.

   β participation rate indicating the percentage of portfolio return paid to policyholders.

   ρ regulatory equity to debt ratio.

   Λ_t^l rate of abandon of the policy due to lapse or death at period t, scenario l.

The variables of the model are defined as follows:

   x_i percentage of initial capital invested in the ith asset, for all $i \in U$.

   y_{At}^l expenses due to lapse or death at time t in scenario l.

   z_t^l shortfall below the guaranteed rate at time t in scenario l.

A_t^l asset value at time t in scenario l.

E_t^l total equity at time t in scenario l.

L_t^l liability value at time t in scenario l.

R_{pt}^l portfolio rate of return during the period $t - 1$ to t in scenario l.

y_{+t}^l excess return over g at time t in scenario l.

y_{-t}^l shortfall return under g at time t in scenario l.

12.4.3 Variable dynamics and constraints

We invest the premium collected (L_0) and the equity required by the regulators ($E_0 = \rho L_0$) in the asset portfolio. Our initial endowment $A_0 = L_0(1 + \rho)$ is allocated to assets in proportion x_i such that $\sum_{i \in U} x_i = 1$, and the dynamics of the portfolio return are given by

$$R_{pt}^l = \sum_{i \in U} x_i r_{ti}^l, \text{ for } t = 1, 2, \ldots, T, \text{ and for all } l \in \Omega. \tag{12.1}$$

The investment variables are nonnegative so that short sales are not allowed.

We now turn to the modeling of the liability account. Liabilities will grow at a rate which is at least equal to the guarantee. Excess returns over g are returned to the policyholders according to the participation rate β. The dynamics of the liability account are given by

$$L_t^l = (1 - \Lambda_t^l)L_{t-1}^l(1 + \max\left[\beta R_{pt}^l, g\right]), \text{ for } t = 1, 2, \ldots T, \text{ and for all } l \in \Omega. \tag{12.2}$$

The $\max$ operator introduces a discontinuity in the model. To circumvent this difficulty we introduce variables y_{+t}^l and y_{-t}^l to measure the portfolio excess return over the guaranteed rate, and the shortfall below the guarantee, respectively. They satisfy

$$\beta R_{pt}^l - g = y_{+t}^l - y_{-t}^l, \text{ for } t = 1, 2, \ldots, T, \text{ and for all } l \in \Omega, \tag{12.3}$$

$$y_{+t}^l \geq 0, \; y_{-t}^l \geq 0, \; y_{+t}^l \cdot y_{-t}^l = 0, \text{ for } t = 1, 2, \ldots, T, \text{ and for all } l \in \Omega. \tag{12.4}$$

Only one of these variables can be nonzero at any given time and in a given scenario.

The dynamics for the value of the liability are rewritten as

$$L_t^l = (1 - \Lambda_t^l)L_{t-1}^l(1 + g + y_{+t}^l), \text{ for } t = 1, 2, \ldots, T, \text{ and for all } l \in \Omega. \tag{12.5}$$

Liabilities grow at least at the rate of g. Any excess return is added to the liabilities and the guarantee applies to the lifted liabilities.

At each period the insurance company makes payments due to policyholders abandoning their policies because of death or lapse. Payments are equal to the value of the liability times the rate of abandonment, i.e.,

$$y_{At}^l = \Lambda_t^l L_{t-1}^l(1 + g + y_{+t}^l), \text{ for } t = 1, 2, \ldots, T, \text{ and for all } l \in \Omega. \tag{12.6}$$

Whenever the portfolio return is below the guaranteed rate we need to infuse cash into the asset portfolio in order to meet the final liabilities. The shortfall account is modeled by the dynamics

$$z_t^l = y_{-t}^l L_{t-1}^l, \text{ for } t = 1, 2, \ldots, T, \text{ and for all } l \in \Omega. \tag{12.7}$$

In the base model shortfalls are funded through equity. We assume that equity is reinvested at the risk-free rate and is returned to the shareholders at the end of the planning horizon. (This is not all the shareholders get; they also receive dividends.) The dynamics of the equity are given by

$$E_t^l = E_{t-1}^l(1 + r_{ft}^l) + z_t^l, \text{ for } t = 1, 2, \ldots, T, \text{ and for all } l \in \Omega. \tag{12.8}$$

By assuming the risk-free rate as the alternative rate at which the shareholders could invest their money we analyze the excess return offered to shareholders by the participating contract modeled here, over the benchmark risk-free investment. In principle one could use the firm's internal rate of return as the alternative rate, and analyze the excess return offered by the policy modeled here over the firm's other lines of business. In this setting, however, the problem would not be to optimize the asset allocation to maximize shareholder value, since this would already be endogenous in the internal rate of return calculations. Instead, we could determine the most attractive features for the policyholders – g and β – that will make the firm indifferent to either offering the new policy or maintaining its current line of business. This approach deserves further investigation. For the purpose of optimizing alternative policies for the shareholders, while satisfying the contractual obligations to the policyholders, the estimation of excess return over the risk-free rate is a reasonable benchmark. In Section 12.5.3 we consider other alternatives for funding the shortfalls through long-term debt or short-term borrowing.

We now have the components needed to model the asset dynamics, taking into account the cash infusion that funds shortfalls, z_t^l, and the outflows due to actuarial events y_{At}^l, i.e.,

$$A_t^l = A_{t-1}^l(1 + R_{Pt}^l) + z_t^l - y_{At}^l, \text{ for } t = 1, 2, \ldots, T, \text{ and for all } l \in \Omega. \tag{12.9}$$

In order to satisfy the regulatory constraint the ratio between the equity value and liabilities must exceed ρ. That is,

$$\frac{V_{ET}^l}{L_T^l} \geq \rho, \text{ for all } l \in \Omega, \tag{12.10}$$

where V_{ET}^l is the value of equity at the end of the planning horizon T. If the company sells only a single policy the value of its equity will be equal to the final asset value – which includes the equity needed to fund shortfall – minus the final liability due to the policyholders, and we have

$$V_{ET}^l = A_T^l - L_T^l. \tag{12.11}$$

Having described the assets and liability accounts in a way that the key features of the policy – guaranteed rate and bonus provisions – are accounted for, we turn to the choice of an appropriate objective function. We model the goal of a for-profit institution to maximize the return on its equity, and, more precisely in this case, to maximize any excess return on equity after all liabilities are paid. Since return on equity is scenario dependent we maximize the expected value of the utility of excess return. This expected value is converted into a certainty equivalent for easy reference. The objective function of the model is to compute the maximal Certainty Equivalent Excess Return on Equity (CEexROE) given by

$$\text{CEexROE} \doteq \mathcal{U}^{-1} \left[\underset{x}{\text{Max}} \sum_{l \in \Omega} p^l \mathcal{U} \left(\frac{A_T^l - L_T^l}{E_T^l} \right) \right], \tag{12.12}$$

where $\mathcal{U}(\cdot)$ denotes the decision maker's utility function and $A_T^l - L_T^l$ is the shareholder's reward in scenario l. We assume a power utility function with constant relative risk aversion of the form

$$\mathcal{U}(V) = \frac{1}{\gamma} V^\gamma, \tag{12.13}$$

where $V \geq 0$, and $\gamma < 1$. In the base model we assume $\gamma = 0$, in which case the utility function is the logarithm corresponding to growth-optimal policies for the firm. In Section 12.5.5 we study the effect of changing the risk aversion parameter.

As a by-product of our model we calculate the cost of funding the guaranteed product. Every time the portfolio return drops below the guaranteed rate, we counterbalance the erosion of our assets by infusing cash. This cost can be either charged to the policyholders as soon as they enter the insurance contract, or covered through shareholder's equity or by issuing debt. These choices entail a trade-off between the return to shareholders and return to policyholders. We study this trade-off in the next section.

The cost of the guarantee is the expected present value of reserves required to fund shortfalls due to portfolio performances below the guarantee. The dynamic variable E_t^l models precisely the total funds required up to time t, valued at the risk – free rate. However, E_t^l also includes the initial amount of equity required by the regulators. This is not a cost and it must be deducted from E_t^l. Thus, the cost of the guarantee is given as the expected present value of the final equity E_T^l adjusted by the regulatory equity, that is,

$$\bar{O}_G = \sum_{l \in \Omega} p^l \left[\frac{E_T^l}{\prod_{t=1}^{T}(1 + r_{ft}^l)} - \rho L_0 \right]. \tag{12.14}$$

$\bar{O}_G$ is the expected present value of the reserves required to fund this product. This can be interpreted as the cost to be paid by shareholders in order to benefit from the upside potential of the surplus. A more precise interpretation of $\bar{O}_G$ is as the *expected downside risk* of the policy. This is not the risk-neutral price of the participating policies with guarantees that would be obtained under an assumption of complete markets for trading the liabilities arising from such contracts; this is the question addressed through an options pricing approach elsewhere in the literature.

12.4.4   Linearly constrained optimization model

The model defined in the previous section is a nonlinearly constrained optimization model and is computationally intractable for large-scale applications. However, the nonlinear constraints (12.5)–(12.9) are definitional constraints which determine the value of the respective variables at the end of the horizon. We can solve these dynamic equations analytically to obtain end-of-horizon expressions for A_T^l, L_T^l, and E_T^l. These expressions are substituted in the objective function to obtain an equivalent linearly constrained nonlinear program. The regulatory constraint (12.10), however, cannot be linearized. For solution purposes the regulatory constraint is relaxed and its validity is tested ex post. Empirical results later on demonstrate that the regulatory constraint is not binding for the policies considered here nor for the generated scenarios of asset returns. However, there is no assurance that this will always be the case, and we may need to resort to a nonlinearly constrained optimization algorithm for solving this model.

Solving the nonlinear dynamic equations

We now solve analytically the nonlinear equations (12.5)–(12.9) and substitute in the objective function (12.12) to get a linearly constrained nonlinear program. At time $t = 0$, the liability is the pure premium L_0. At $t = 1$ (to simplify the notation in this section we drop the scenario superscript) we have

$$L_1 = L_0(1 - \Lambda_1)(1 + g + y_{+1}). \tag{12.15}$$

At $t = 2$ we use the value of L_1 from (12.15) to obtain

$$\begin{aligned}
L_2 &= L_1(1 - \Lambda_2)(1 + g + y_{+2}) \\
&= L_0(1 - \Lambda_2)(1 - \Lambda_1)(1 + g + y_{+1})(1 + g + y_{+2}).
\end{aligned} \tag{12.16}$$

Applying this process recursively for each t we obtain the final liability as

$$L_T = L_0 \prod_{t=1}^{T}(1 - \Lambda_t)(1 + g + y_{+t}). \tag{12.17}$$

For the equity dynamics we have that $E_0 = \rho L_0$. At $t = 1$

$$E_1 = \rho L_0(1 + r_{f1}) + y_{-1}L_0. \tag{12.18}$$

At $t = 2$ and substituting for E_1 and L_1 from (12.18) and (12.15) we obtain

$$\begin{aligned}
E_2 &= E_1(1 + r_{f2}) + y_{-2}L_1 \\
&= \rho L_0(1 + r_{f1})(1 + r_{f2}) + L_0 y_{-1}(1 + r_{f2}) \\
&\quad + L_0 y_{-2}(1 - \Lambda_1)(1 + g + y_{+1}).
\end{aligned} \tag{12.19}$$

At $t = 3$ we have

$$\begin{aligned}
E_3 &= E_2(1 + r_{f3}) + y_{-3}L_2 = \\
&= \rho L_0(1 + r_{f1})(1 + r_{f2})(1 + r_{f3}) + L_0 y_{-3}(1 + r_{f2})(1 + r_{f3}) \\
&\quad + L_0\, y_{-3}(1 + r_{f3})(1 - \Lambda_1)(1 + g + y_{-1}) \\
&\quad + L_0\, y_{-3}(1 - \Lambda_2)(1 - \Lambda_1)(1 + g + y_{-1})(1 + g + y_{+2}).
\end{aligned} \tag{12.20}$$

Applying this process recursively for each t we obtain after some simple algebra

$$E_T = L_0\left\{\rho\prod_{t=1}^{T}(1 + r_{ft}) + \sum_{t=1}^{T}\left[y_{-t}\phi(t, T)\prod_{\tau=1}^{t-1}(1 - \Lambda_\tau)(1 + g + y_{+\tau})\right]\right\}, \tag{12.21}$$

where $\phi(t, T) = \prod_{\tau=t+1}^{T}(1 + r_{f\tau})$ is the future value of one unit of an investment in the short rates from t to T.

With the same arguments it is possible to show that

$$y_{At} = L_0\,\Lambda_t\,(1 + g + y_{+t})\prod_{\tau=1}^{t-1}(1 - \Lambda_\tau)(1 + g + y_{+\tau}). \tag{12.22}$$

For the asset dynamics we have that $A_0 = L_0(1 + \rho)$. At $t = 1$,

$$\begin{aligned}
A_1 &= A_0(1 + R_{p1}) + y_{-1}L_0 - y_{A1} \\
&= L_0(1 + \rho)(1 + R_{p1}) + y_{-1}L_0 - y_{A1}.
\end{aligned} \tag{12.23}$$

At $t = 2$ substituting L_1 from (12.15) we obtain

$$\begin{aligned}
A_2 &= A_1(1 + R_{p2}) + y_{-2}L_1 - y_{A2} \\
&= L_0(1 + \rho)(1 + R_{p1})(1 + R_{p2}) + y_{-1}L_0(1 + R_{p2}) \\
&\quad - y_{A1}(1 + R_{p2}) + y_{-2}L_1 - y_{A2}.
\end{aligned} \tag{12.24}$$

The value of the assets at maturity is given by $A_T =$

$$L_0(1 + \rho)\prod_{t=1}^{T}(1 + R_{pt})L_0\sum_{t=1}^{T}y_{-t}\prod_{\tau=t+1}^{T}(1 + R_{p\tau})\prod_{\tau=1}^{t-1}(1 + g + y_{+\tau})\prod_{\tau=1}^{t-1}(1 - \Lambda_\tau)$$

$$- \sum_{t=1}^{T}y_{At}\prod_{\tau=t+1}^{T}(1 + R_{p\tau}). \tag{12.25}$$

By substituting y_{At} with the expression in (12.22) we obtain

$$
\begin{aligned}
A_T &= L_0(1+\rho) \prod_{t=1}^{T}(1+R_{pt}) \\
&+ L_0 \sum_{t=1}^{T} y_{-t} \prod_{\tau=t+1}^{T}(1+R_{p\tau}) \prod_{\tau=1}^{t-1}(1+g+y_{+\tau})(1-\Lambda_\tau) \\
&- L_0 \sum_{t=1}^{T} \Lambda_t\,(1+g+y_{+t}) \prod_{\tau=t+1}^{T}(1+R_{p\tau}) \prod_{\tau=1}^{t-1}(1+g+y_{+\tau})(1-\Lambda_\tau).
\end{aligned}
\tag{12.26}
$$

Collecting terms we obtain

$$
\begin{aligned}
A_T &= L_0(1+\rho) \prod_{t=1}^{T}(1+R_{pt}) \\
&+ L_0 \sum_{t=1}^{T} \left[y_{-t} - \Lambda_t\,(1+g+y_{+t}) \right] \prod_{\tau=t+1}^{T}(1+R_{p\tau}) \prod_{\tau=1}^{t-1}(1+g+y_{+\tau})(1-\Lambda_\tau).
\end{aligned}
\tag{12.27}
$$

The linearly constrained model

Substituting the expressions obtained above in the objective function we obtain the following equivalent linearly constrained nonlinear program.

Model 12.4.1 Insurance policies with guarantees

$$
\begin{aligned}
\text{Maximize} \quad & \sum_{l\in\Omega} p^l\,\mathcal{U}\left(\left\{ (1+\rho) \prod_{t=1}^{T}(1+R_{pt}^l)+ \right.\right. \\
& + \sum_{t=1}^{T} \left[y_{-t}^l - \Lambda_t^l\,(1+g+y_{+t}^l) \right] \\
& \prod_{\tau=t+1}^{T}(1+R_{p\tau}^l) \prod_{\tau=1}^{t-1}(1+g+y_{+\tau})(1-\Lambda_\tau^l)+ \\
& \left. - \prod_{t=1}^{T}(1-\Lambda_t^l)(1+g+y_{+t}^l) \right\} \\
& \left. \Big/ \left[\rho \prod_{t=1}^{T}(1+r_{ft}^l) + \sum_{t=1}^{T} y_{-t}^l \phi(t,T) \prod_{\tau=1}^{t-1}(1-\Lambda_\tau^l)(1+g+y_{\tau}^{+l}) \right] \right)
\end{aligned}
\tag{12.28}
$$

$$
\text{s.t.} \quad \sum_{i\in U} x_i = 1,
\tag{12.29}
$$

$$
\beta R_{pt}^l - g = y_{+t}^l - y_{-t}^l, \qquad \text{for } t=1,2,\dots,T,\ \text{and for all } l\in\Omega,
\tag{12.30}
$$

$$
R_{pt}^l = \sum_{i\in U} x_i r_{ti}^l, \qquad \text{for } t=1,2,\dots,T,\ \text{and for all } l\in\Omega,
\tag{12.31}
$$

$$
x \in X.
\tag{12.32}
$$

The inverse of the utility function $\mathcal{U}^{-1}$ of the optimal objective value of this problem is the CEexROE.

12.4.5   Surrender option

The rate of abandon Λ_t^l is determined from both actuarial events (death) and economic considerations (surrendering the policy). The actuarial component is readily obtained from mortality tables. However, the lapse behavior of policyholders needs to be modeled taking into account the economic incentive to surrender the policy and invest in competing products. This aspect of the product is modeled here.

Modeling the lapse behavior serves as a sensitivity analysis of the model for studying errors introduced due to various sources of data uncertainty. For instance, in recent years many actuaries have pointed out that the aging of the population has introduced a modeling risk in the actuarial framework. The longevity risk affects the probability of survival for sectors of the population in their retirement years. Pension fund managers will then face higher liabilities than those planned. In contrast, life insurance products benefit from longevity risk since the payments due to death are reduced. The modeling of lapse undertaken here is but one example of the additional sources of uncertainty that could be incorporated in the model if data were available.

We discuss here two assumptions about policy lapse which can be embedded into the model.

Fixed lapse. Under this assumption the probability of surrendering the policy (Λ_t) is constant throughout the life of the contract. This assumption is quite realistic. For instance, an analysis of a panel of British households shows that the percentage of lapse is constant over the period 1994–1997 and it averages to 1.4%, while a rough estimate from limited data for Italian households indicate a modest lapse rate on the order of 2%.

Variable lapse Under this assumption the policyholders' decision to surrender their policies is affected by economic factors. For instance, in the analysis of mortgage-backed securities in Section 8.3.5 we discuss prepayment models that describe household propensity to finance their mortgage loans driven by market factors, such as the prevailing mortgage refinancing rates, and social factors such as age of the household and demographics. Similarly we can link the dynamics of Λ_t^l to economic variables. If we assume that lapse is driven by the minimum guarantee level g then the lapse probability is a function of the spread between g and the rate on other investments offered in the capital markets

$$\Lambda_t^l = F(r_{It}^l - g), \tag{12.33}$$

where r_{It}^l is a suitable benchmark of the return offered by competing products; this can be, for instance, the return on the 10-year government bond index. The surrender probability is now indexed by scenario as it depends on the competitors' rate r_{It}^l. We expect policyholders to surrender their policies when alternative investments provide higher return than the guarantee g.

Perhaps the most significant factor affecting lapse is the bonus policy followed by the company (see also the discussion in Section 8.3.3 on single-premium deferred annuities). If the insurance company's crediting rate is significantly lower than that of the competition then lapse rates will be high. In participating policies the credit rate is determined by the performance of the portfolio. Thus an integrative asset and liability management approach is essential in accurately capturing the lapse rates of these products.

Assuming that the competitors offer rates equal to the relevant market benchmark we express lapse rates in the form:

$$\Lambda_t^l = F(r_{It}^l - (g + y_{+t}^l)). \tag{12.34}$$

(Recall that $g + y_{+t}^l$ is the rate credited to policyholders and it reflects both the guarantee and the bonus policy.)

This formula embodies the complex games facing the insurer: large minimum guarantees subdue the effects of the competition but come at a high cost or low CEexROE. This will also be demonstrated in Section 12.5 where the model is validated.

A convenient general form for function $F(\cdot)$ governing the surrender behavior is given in Section 8.3.3, and we can model the lapse probability by

$$\Lambda_t^l = a + b \tan^{-1}[m(r_{It}^l - i_t^l - c) - n]. \tag{12.35}$$

The variable i_t^l is the company's credit rate which can be modeled as a constant (e.g., $i_t^l = g$ in equation 12.33) or as a variable determined by policy and market performance (e.g., $i_t^l = g + \epsilon_t^{+l}$ in equation 12.34), r_{It}^l is the rate offered by the competitors, and c is a measure of policyholders' inertia in exercising the surrender option. The parameters a, b, c, m, n are chosen to give lapse rates that fit historically observed data. For instance, the model should fit the lowest and highest lapse rates that have been observed under extremely favorable and unfavorable conditions, and the lapse rates observed when the insurance product was offering the same rates as the benchmark.

Figure 8.3 (Chapter 8) shows different lapse curves when varying the parameter to fit maximum and minimum values and different average lapse rates. Lapse rates will be, on the average, lower when there are large penalties for early surrender of the policy. The different curves shown in the figure could fit, for instance, the historically observed lapse rates of policies with different surrender charges. We observer that lapse rates may differ substantially when the company is offering a guaranteed rate which is less than the competitors' rate. This situation occurs when assets perform poorly with respect to the rest of the industry. Careful modeling of the lapse behavior is needed in these cases to avoid igniting a vicious circle which could lead to bankruptcy.

12.4.6 Model extensions

We now point out possible extensions of this model. Periodic premia can readily be incorporated into equation (12.9). Bonus policies based on averaging portfolio performance can also be included in the model by revising the liability equation (12.2) for $t = 1, 2, \ldots T$, and for all $l \in \Omega$ to include average portfolio performance over the history of, e.g., the last t_h periods, as follows:

$$L_t^l = (1 - \Lambda_t^l)L_{t-1}^l \left(1 + \max\left[\beta \sum_{\tau=t-t_h}^{t} R_{p\tau}^l, g\right]\right). \tag{12.36}$$

Guaranteed rates and bonus rates that are exogenously given functions of time, g_t and β_t, are easy to incorporate. Similarly, we can incorporate liabilities due to lapse, although a lapse model must first be built and calibrated as discussed above. Incorporating participation rates that are functions of the asset returns – as is the case with the UK insurance policies – complicates the model since the participation rate β_t becomes a variable. The split of bonus into reversionary bonus, which is guaranteed, and an investment reserve which is returned as a bonus at maturity, if nonnegative, introduces significant modifications to the model. These issues are discussed in Section 12.4.7.

The base model developed here funds shortfalls through equity. Extensions to deal with the funding of shortfalls through long- or short-term debt are given in Section 12.5.3. Furthermore, unlimited access to equity for funding shortfalls is assumed in the base model. We could do away with this assumption by imposing additional constraints, but this would complicate the model rendering it computationally intractable. The probability of insolvency is analyzed through post-optimality analysis (see Section 12.5.3). This analysis can be used to guide the debt structure in funding shortfalls using a combination of equity and debt.

12.4.7   Reversionary and terminal bonuses

Some policies use a smoothing mechanism to estimate bonuses, disbursing higher bonuses when market conditions are favorable, and decreasing bonuses when the insurer's portfolio is under-performing. Changes are autoregressive so that big swings are avoided, as those are viewed unfavorably by policyholders. The policies offered in the UK are the best-known example with these characteristics. The bonus philosophy of UK insurers is based on regulatory requirements that bonus distribution should accord with the policyholders' reasonable expectations of the company's behavior. To satisfy the policyholders' expectations UK insurers offer *reversionary bonuses* that, once announced, are subsequently guaranteed. In addition they deliver a *terminal bonus* that is a function of the excess asset value upon maturity.

To model these policies we introduce variable RB_t^l to denote the reversionary bonus disbursed at period t in scenario l. This variable evolves according to the autoregressive equation

$$RB_t^l = 0.5 RB_{t-1}^l + \Delta B_t^l, \tag{12.37}$$

where the constant 0.5 ensures that policyholders are not too unpleasantly surprised by downward swings of their bonuses, and ΔB_t^l is the change in the bonus. This may be positive or negative and is computed as follows

$$\Delta B_t^l = 0.5 \max\left[\frac{r_{It}^l - g}{1 + g}, 0\right] - 0.25 \max\left[\frac{L_t^l - A_t^l}{A_t^l}, 0\right]. \tag{12.38}$$

The first term on the right of this equation is positive whenever some benchmark return r_{It}^l exceeds the guarantee, otherwise it is zero. The benchmark return is taken in the UK to be the yield on long risk-free securities. The second term is positive whenever the asset value is less than the liability value, otherwise it is zero. With this formula the bonus rate is increased whenever the market rates increase, but is decreased whenever the insurer faces the prospect of insolvency.

The variable dynamics and constraints of policies with smoothed reversionary and terminal bonuses can now be formulated, for $t = 1, 2, \ldots T$, and for all $l \in \Omega$, building on the base model of Section 12.4.3.

The dynamics of the liability account are given by

$$L_t^l = (1 - \Lambda_t^l) L_{t-1}^l (1 + g)\left(1 + \max\left[RB_{t-1}^l, 0\right]\right). \tag{12.39}$$

Liability payments are exactly as in the base model

$$y_{At}^l = \Lambda_t^l L_{t-1}^l (1 + g + y_{+t}^l). \tag{12.40}$$

The asset dynamics take into account outflows due to actuarial events but, unlike the base model, there are no cash infusions. The asset value is allowed to go below the liability value and this will have an effect on the reversionary bonus.

$$A_t^l = A_{t-1}^l (1 + R_{pt}^l) - y_{At}^l. \tag{12.41}$$

The equity equation from the base model (12.8) is split into two equations: one that models the dynamics of shareholder equity that grows at the risk-free rate; and one that models shortfalls so that the total shortfall (if any) at maturity can be assessed. The shareholder equity follows the dynamics

$$E_t^l = E_{t-1}^l (1 + r_{ft}^l). \tag{12.42}$$

The lag of assets against the liabilities is given by

$$E_t'^l = \max\left[(1 + \rho) L_t^l - A_t^l, 0\right], \tag{12.43}$$

and whenever the lag increases the total shortfall, z_t^l, increases according to the dynamics

$$z_t^l = z_{t-1}^l (1 + r_{ft}^l) + \max \left[(E_t^{'l} - E_{t-1}^{'l}), 0 \right] . \qquad (12.44)$$

With these dynamics the terminal bonus paid to policyholders at maturity T is given by

$$TB_T^l = \gamma \max \left[A_T^l - L_T^l, 0 \right] , \qquad (12.45)$$

and the return on equity to shareholders is given by

$$\text{ROE}^l = \frac{A_T^l - L_T^l - TB_T^l}{E_T^l} . \qquad (12.46)$$

12.5   Model Testing and Validation

We now turn to the testing of the model. We start first with the application of the traditional portfolio diversification approach based on mean-variance optimization. We show that the standard application of mean-variance optimization fails to capture some important characteristics of the problem, and the mean-variance portfolios are not efficient when one accounts for the nonlinearity of the embedded options. We show that the integrated model based on scenario optimization adds value to the risk management process for these complex insurance products.

Second, we show that the model quantifies the trade-offs between the different goals of the insurance firm: providing the best products for its policyholders; providing the highest excess return to its shareholders; satisfying the guarantee at the lowest possible cost and with high probability. Some interesting insights are obtained on the structure of the optimal portfolios as the trade-offs vary across the spectrum.

Third, we analyze alternative debt structures whereby the cost of the guarantee is funded through equity or through debt with either long or short maturities.

Fourth, we study some additional features of the model: the effects of the choice of a utility function, the effects of using international asset classes and corporate bonds, and the effects of policy surrender options (lapse).

Finally, we will see from the empirical results that the Italian insurance industry operates at levels which are close to optimal but not quite so. There is room for improvement either by offering more competitive products or by generating higher excess returns for the benefit of the shareholders. How are the improvements possible? The answer is found in the comparison of the optimal portfolios generated by our model with benchmark portfolios. We will see that the benchmark portfolios generate trade-offs in the space of cost of guarantee versus net excess return on equity that are inefficient. The optimized portfolios lead to policies with the same cost but higher excess return on equity.

The basic asset classes considered in our study are 23 stock indexes of the Milano Stock Exchange, and three Salomon Brother indexes of Italian government bonds. Italian insurers are also allowed to invest up to 10% of the value of their portfolio in international assets. We report results with the inclusion of international asset classes: the Morgan Stanley stock indices for USA, UK and Japan, and the JP Morgan government bond indices for the same countries.

We employ a simple approach for generating scenarios using only the available data without any mathematical modeling, by bootstrapping a set of historical records. Each scenario is a sample of returns of the assets obtained by sampling returns that were observed in the past. Dates from the available historical records are selected randomly, and for each date in the sample we read the returns of all asset classes realized during the previous month. These samples are scenarios of monthly returns. To generate scenarios of returns for a long horizon – say 10 years – we sample 120 monthly returns from different points in time. The compounded return of the sampled series is one scenario of the 10-year return. The process is repeated to generate the desired number of scenarios for the 10-year period. With this approach the correlations among asset classes are preserved. Additional scenarios could also be included, although methods for generating them should be specified using one of the techniques of Chapter 9.

For the numerical experiments we bootstrap monthly records from the 10-year period January 1990 to February 2000. The monthly returns are compounded to yearly returns. For each asset class we generate 500 scenarios of returns during a 10-year horizon ($T = 120$ months). We consider an initial liability $L_0 = 1$ for a contract with participation rate $\beta = 85\%$ and equity to liability ratio $\rho = 4\%$. The model is tested for guarantees ranging from 1% to 15%.

In our experiments we set lapse probabilities to zero and the probability that a policyholder abandons the policy is the mortality rate that we obtain from the Italian mortality tables. For each model run we determine the net annualized after-tax CEexROE

$$(\sqrt[T]{\overline{\text{CEexROE}}} - 1)(1 - \kappa), \tag{12.47}$$

where κ is the tax rate set at 51%.

12.5.1   Integrative asset and liability management

In this section we compare the scenario optimization asset and liability management model with traditional asset allocation using mean-variance analysis. We demonstrate that the integrative approach adds value to the asset and liability management process.

Traditional approach using mean-variance asset allocation

Diversified portfolios of stocks and bonds for an Italian insurance firm are built using mean-variance optimization. Using the asset classes of the Italian stock and bond markets we obtain the efficient frontier of expected return versus standard deviation illustrated in Figure 12.3. Should an insurance firm offering a minimum guarantee product choose portfolios – based on its appetite for risk – from the set of efficient portfolios? On the same figure we plot each one of the efficient portfolios in the space of shareholder's reward (CEexROE) versus the firm's risk (cost of the guarantee). There is nothing efficient about efficient portfolios when we account for the liability created by the minimum guarantee policy. Portfolios from A to G are on the mean-variance frontier that lie on or below the capital market line. It is not surprising that they are not efficient in the CEexROE versus cost-of-guarantee space. However, the tangent portfolio G is also inefficient. More aggressive portfolios are needed in order to achieve the minimum guaranteed return and deliver excess return to the shareholder. And still this increasing appetite for higher but risky returns is not monotonic. As we move away from portfolio G towards the most risky portfolio B we see at first the cost of the guarantee declining and CEexROE improving. But as we approach B shareholder value erodes. For these very volatile portfolios the embedded option is deep in-the-money, and shareholders' money is used to compensate for the shortfalls without realizing any excess returns.

This analysis has shown that it is important to take an integrative view of the asset allocation problem of firms issuing products with guarantees. Accurately accounting for the cost of the guarantee is important, if the firm is to avoid unnecessary risk exposures and not destroy shareholder value. In a nutshell, the management of minimum guarantee products is a balancing act. Too much reliance on bonds and the guarantee is not met. Excessive reliance on stocks and shareholder value is destroyed.

Is it possible to incorporate the random liability in a mean-variance model, and develop efficient portfolios in the CEexROE versus cost-of-guarantee space? Unfortunately, the return of the liability depends on the return of the asset portfolio and this is not known without determining simultaneously the structure of the asset portfolio. The return of the liability is endogenous to the

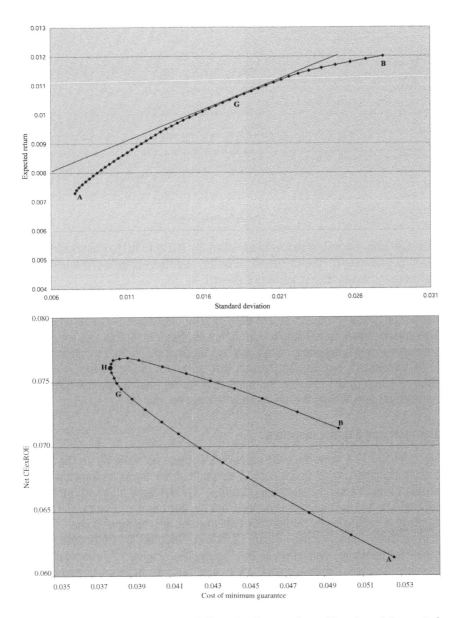

Figure 12.3: Mean-variance efficient portfolios of Italian stocks and bonds and the capital market line (top), and the corresponding certainty equivalent excess return of equity (CEexROE) to shareholders versus cost of the minimum guarantee for each portfolio (bottom).

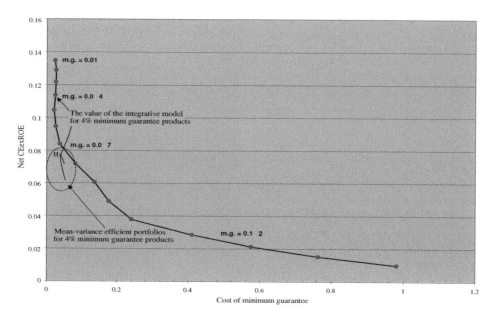

Figure 12.4: Certainty equivalent excess return of equity (CEexROE) to shareholders versus cost of the minimum guarantee for the integrated portfolios at different levels of minimum guarantee, and for the mean-variance efficient portfolios (insert).

portfolio selection model. Furthermore, the liability return has a floor – the minimum guarantee. This creates nonlinearities in the model, and highly asymmetric returns that are not conducive to mean-variance type of modeling. While semi-variance or other risk measures could be used to handle the asymmetric returns, the problem that the return of the liability is endogenous to the portfolio selection model remains. An integrative model, such as the one developed in this chapter, is essential in modeling the endogeneity of asset returns.

Integrative asset and liability modeling

The results in Figure 12.4 show the trade-off between upside potential versus the downside risk achieved when using the models in this book. Each point on this figure corresponds to an optimal asset portfolio for each level of minimum guarantee. On the same figure we plot the trade-off between CEexROE and cost of the guarantee from the portfolios of Figure 12.3. We see that even portfolio H is dominated by the portfolios obtained by an integrative model. The traditional approach of portfolio diversification – Figure 12.3 (top) – followed by a post-optimality analysis to incorporate the minimum guarantee liability and its cost – Figure 12.3 (bottom) – yields sub-optimal results. The integrative approach adds value, and the analysis carried out here with market data for a real policy shows that the added value can be substantial.

12.5.2   Analysis of the trade-offs

We now turn to the analysis of the trade-offs between the guaranteed rate of return offered to policyholders and the net CEexROE on shareholders' equity. This is shown in Figure 12.5, where the optimal asset allocation among the broad classes of bonds and stocks is also shown for the different guaranteed returns.

At first glance the portfolio structures appear puzzling. One expects that as the guarantee increases the amount of stock holdings should grow. However, we observe that for low guarantees (less than 7% for the market sectors we consider) the holdings in stock increase with lower

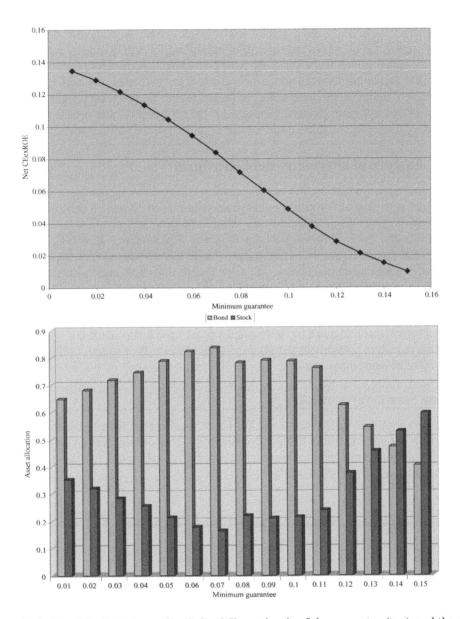

Figure 12.5: Net CEexROE (annualized) for different levels of the guarantee (top), and the corresponding broad asset allocations (bottom).

guarantees. For low g the embedded option is far out-of-the-money, even when the asset portfolio is mostly equity and very volatile. The asset allocation strategy maximizes CEexROE by taking higher risks in the equities market. A marginal increase of the shortfall cost allows higher CEexROE. This is further clarified in Figure 12.4, where we show the trade-off between the cost of the guarantee and the net annualized CEexROE. At values of g less than 7% the option embedded in the liability is out-of-the-money and any excess return is passed on to the shareholders, thus improving CEexROE. As the guarantee increases above 7% the option goes deeper into the money, the cost of the guarantee increases significantly and CEexROE erodes. Note from Figure 12.5 that higher values of the guarantee must be backed by aggressive portfolios with high equity content, but in this case the portfolio volatility is not translated into high CEexROE for the shareholders but into higher returns for the policyholders. However, for the guaranteed rates of 3 to 4% offered by Italian insurers it appears that the optimal portfolios consist of 20 to 25% in equities.

12.5.3   Analysis of alternative debt structures

So far we have assumed that the cost of the guarantee is covered by shareholders. It is possible, however, that such costs are charged to policyholders or funded by issuing debt. (Note that for mutual insurance firms the policyholders are the shareholders themselves, so the point of who pays for the cost is moot. However the issue of raising debt remains.) In either case there are advantages and disadvantages. In particular, if we let the policyholder assume the total cost, we run the risk of not being competitive, losing market share, and experiencing increased lapse. If we issue debt, we are liable for interest payments at the end of the planning horizon which could reduce our final return. Furthermore, companies face leverage restrictions. It may not be possible to cover all the cost of the guarantee by issuing debt because it will increase the leverage of the company beyond what is allowed by the regulators or accepted by the market.

Another important point in pursuing this question concerns the maturity of the issued debt. We start by considering long-term debt.

Long-term financing of shortfalls

To issue long-term debt we determine the amount of cash that we need to borrow in order to cover, with a certain probability, future expenditures due to shortfalls over all scenarios. If we indicate by α a confidence level we are searching for the α – percentile, O_G^α, such that the cost of the guarantee O_G^l in scenario l satisfies

$$\text{Prob}\left(O_G^l \geq O_G^\alpha | l \in \Omega\right) = \alpha. \tag{12.48}$$

The cost of the guarantee in scenario l is given by equation (12.14) as

$$O_G^l = \frac{E_T^l}{\prod_{t=1}^{T}(1 + r_{ft}^l)} - \rho L_0. \tag{12.49}$$

Note that O_G^α need not be raised through the issue of debt alone. It is just the reserves needed to fund shortfalls. Strategic considerations will subdivide O_G^α among policyholder charges; C_G, issue of debt or direct borrowing from money markets, D_G; and/or equity supplement, E_S. Thus, we have

$$O_G^\alpha = C_G + D_G + E_S. \tag{12.50}$$

Given the debt structure implied in (12.50) we determine the final income FI_T^l, for each scenario $l \in \Omega$, as

$$FI_T^l = A_T^l - L_T^l - D_G(1 + r_f + \delta)^T + (C_G - J_S)\prod_{t=1}^{T}(1 + r_{ft}^l), \tag{12.51}$$

Table 12.3: Net CEROE for different combinations of leverage and policyholder charges. The table is built for a guarantee $g = 4\%$ at a confidence level $\alpha = 1\%$, and the certainty equivalent is calculated using a logarithmic utility function.

Leverage levels	Policyholder charges									
	0	*0.01*	*0.02*	*0.03*	*0.04*	*0.05*	*0.06*	*0.07*	*0.08*	*0.09*
0	0.121125	0.124595	0.128295	0.132256	0.136515	0.141118	0.146123	0.151602	0.157650	0.164391
0.125	0.123946	0.127684	0.131656	0.135891	0.140430	0.145317	0.150612	0.156387	0.162740	0.169795
0.25	0.126654	0.130640	0.134860	0.139346	0.144137	0.149280	0.154834	0.160873	0.167495	0.174827
0.375	0.129260	0.133474	0.137923	0.142638	0.147659	0.153033	0.158821	0.165097	0.171960	0.179538
0.5	0.131770	0.136197	0.140857	0.145783	0.151014	0.156599	0.162599	0.169089	0.176169	0.183968
0.625	0.134193	0.138817	0.143673	0.148794	0.154219	0.159997	0.166190	0.172875	0.180151	0.188151
0.75	0.136533	0.141343	0.146381	0.151682	0.157285	0.163242	0.169612	0.176475	0.183932	0.192114
0.875	0.138798	0.143781	0.148989	0.154458	0.160227	0.166348	0.172882	0.179909	0.187530	0.195879
1	0.140991	0.146137	0.151505	0.157130	0.163053	0.169327	0.176013	0.183191	0.190964	0.199468
1.125	0.143118	0.148417	0.153935	0.159706	0.165774	0.172189	0.179016	0.186335	0.194250	0.202896
1.25	0.145182	0.150626	0.156285	0.162194	0.168396	0.174944	0.181903	0.189353	0.197399	0.206177
1.375	0.147188	0.152769	0.158560	0.164599	0.170928	0.177601	0.184682	0.192255	0.200423	
1.5	0.149138	0.154849	0.160766	0.166927	0.173375	0.180165	0.187362	0.195050	0.203333	
1.625	0.151037	0.156871	0.162907	0.169183	0.175744	0.182644	0.189950	0.197745		
1.75	0.152886	0.158837	0.164986	0.171371	0.178039	0.185044	0.192452	0.200349		
1.875	0.154688	0.160751	0.167007	0.173497	0.180265	0.187369	0.194875			
2	0.156446	0.162616	0.168974	0.175562	0.182427	0.189624	0.197222			
2.125		0.164433	0.170890	0.177572	0.184528	0.191814				
2.25		0.166207	0.172757	0.179529	0.186571	0.193942				
2.375		0.167938	0.174577	0.181435	0.188561					
2.5		0.169630	0.176354	0.183294	0.190499					
2.625			0.178089	0.185108						
2.75			0.179785	0.186879						
2.875			0.181443							
3			0.183064							
3.125										
3.25										
3.375										

where J_S are the fixed costs (in percentage of the initial liability) and δ is a spread over the risk-free rate so that $r_f + \delta$ is the borrowing interest rate. Debt structures for which $FI^l_T < 0$ for some scenario $l \in \Omega$ should be discarded as leading the firm into insolvency, even if the probability of such events is very low.

The net return on equity (ROE) corresponding to a given debt structure in each scenario is given by

$$ROE^l = \frac{FI^l_T(1 - \kappa)}{\rho L_0 + E_S}. \tag{12.52}$$

This is not the ex ante excess return on equity optimized with the base model, but the ex post realized total return on equity achieved when the structure of debt has also been specified, and the certainty equivalent of the random variable return on equity, given a utility function for the shareholders, is denoted by CEROE. This measure can be used to analyze the probability of insolvency when the cost of the guarantee is funded by shareholders instead of being charged, at least in part, to policyholders.

We report some results with the analysis described here. Tables are generated to study the trade-offs between leverage, policyholder charges, and shareholder returns. Table 12.3 summarizes data that assist the decision maker to take a position according to her strategic views and constraints. If no entries are displayed these choices cannot be implemented, either because some FI^l_T are negative (this occurs when charges to policyholders are very low and high debt levels yield a negative final income), or because the amount of money necessary to cover shortfalls is fully covered by the policyholder charges. This implies a negative debt level at maturity of the product.

For example, by choosing a leverage level equal to 0.5, the highest yearly net CEROE is 0.183. Note that, if the firm wishes to achieve higher performance level, the leverage should also increase. Also, observe the inverse relation between leverage and policyholder charges. The greater the amount we charge to the policyholder, the lower is the leverage required to achieve a given annualized net CEROE.

Table 12.4: The relation between net CEROE, policyholder charges and guarantee. The table is built with confidence level $\alpha = 1\%$ and leverage (debt-to-equity ratio) equal to 0.5.

Minimum guarantee

		0.01	0.02	0.03	0.04	0.05	0.06	0.07	0.08
	0	0.144564	0.139163	0.135832	0.131770	0.130433	0.120909	0.110348	0.099402
	0.01	0.148057	0.142648	0.139726	0.136197	0.136011	0.126397	0.115193	0.102442
	0.02	0.151703	0.146281	0.143803	0.140857	0.141965	0.132226	0.120278	0.105562
	0.03	0.155517	0.150077	0.148086	0.145783	0.148361	0.138457	0.125641	0.108770
Policyholder charges	**0.04**	0.159520	0.154056	0.152599	0.151014	0.155289	0.145166	0.131326	0.112075
	0.05	0.163732	0.158239	0.157375	0.156599	0.162863	0.152453	0.137390	0.115487
	0.06	0.168182	0.162651	0.162452	0.162599	0.171238	0.160450	0.143903	0.119017
	0.07	0.17290	0.167323	0.167876	0.169089	0.180626	0.169337	0.150957	0.122676
	0.08	0.177925	0.172291	0.173703	0.176169	0.191338	0.179370	0.158670	0.126479
	0.09	0.183304	0.177599	0.180007	0.183968		0.190924	0.167202	0.130443
	0.1	0.189093	0.183304	0.186880	0.192664			0.176778	0.134586

The model can generate similar tables to study the many interactions of endowments with guarantee. For example, we could be interested in investigating the effect of different guarantee levels on the policyholder charges and yearly returns. We first estimate, at a given confidence level α, the cost of the guarantee O_G^α, and then apportion this cost to policyholders (C_G in equation 12.50) and fund the rest through debt or equity surcharge. Depending on C_G we observe a change in the CEROE to shareholders. Table 12.4 shows this relationship. We observe the same behavior we had seen between the cost of the guarantee and net CEexROE in Figure 12.4. The model chooses more aggressive strategies for low g because it is then possible to achieve higher levels of CEexROE at little cost. Recall that we are working with percentiles and the impact of aggressive strategies is much more evident on the tails. When the guarantee is low at $g = 0.01$ a more aggressive portfolio is constructed and higher policyholder charges are needed to reach the highest return to shareholders, while for $g = 0.05$ the portfolios are more conservative and hence lower policyholder charges are required. These results highlight the trade-offs between the competing objectives of the policyholders and the shareholders as captured by the model.

The results in Table 12.3 should be examined taking into account a measure of risk associated with the CEROE of every combination of policyholder charges and leverage level. The probability that excess value per share will become negative – denoted by P_{EVS}^- and defined formally by equation (12.54) – is a measure of risk of the CEROE, and these probabilities corresponding to Table 12.3 are shown in Table 12.5. Observe that the upper-left entry has a P_{EVS}^- equal to 0.58. This means that there is a 58% chance that the present value of the final equity is less than the amount invested today by the shareholders, even though the net CEROE is acceptable (12%). This position is risky. The reason why this position is quite risky is due to the fact that we are asking our shareholders to fund the total α – percentile cost of the guarantee. No charges are passed on to policyholders.

Insolvency risks

So far we have analyzed alternative decisions based only on the net CEexROE and market constraints (policyholder charges, leverage, etc). Our analysis is missing a measure of risk of the ROE. It is not yet clear how alternative guarantees and debt allocations according to equation (12.50) affect the risk of ROE in equation (12.52). One could argue that the risk aversion of the decision maker is embedded in the utility function of the optimization model. This is true, but

Table 12.5: Relationship between the probability that excess value per share will fall below zero – the parameter P^-_{EVS} defined in equation (12.54) – leverage and policyholder charges. The table is built for a guarantee $g = 4\%$ and confidence level $\alpha = 1\%$.

Policyholder charges

Leverage Levels	0	0.01	0.02	0.03	0.04	0.05	0.06	0.07	0.08	0.09
0	0.580	0.522	0.462	0.400	0.344	0.278	0.208	0.148	0.096	0.042
0.125	0.534	0.478	0.416	0.366	0.302	0.242	0.172	0.112	0.072	0.020
0.25	0.508	0.444	0.394	0.338	0.274	0.212	0.150	0.100	0.060	0.012
0.375	0.476	0.416	0.368	0.306	0.252	0.188	0.134	0.092	0.042	0.012
0.5	0.444	0.396	0.346	0.284	0.226	0.162	0.118	0.076	0.032	0.006
0.625	0.418	0.374	0.322	0.266	0.212	0.152	0.106	0.068	0.022	0.004
0.75	0.404	0.366	0.304	0.258	0.198	0.144	0.098	0.056	0.016	0.002
0.875	0.400	0.354	0.286	0.234	0.184	0.136	0.092	0.050	0.012	0.002
1	0.378	0.330	0.280	0.224	0.162	0.124	0.088	0.040	0.012	0.002
1.125	0.370	0.318	0.266	0.216	0.156	0.114	0.078	0.036	0.008	0.002
1.25	0.364	0.310	0.264	0.208	0.146	0.108	0.074	0.032	0.008	0.002
1.375	0.356	0.296	0.254	0.200	0.146	0.104	0.070	0.026	0.004	
1.5	0.350	0.286	0.240	0.196	0.142	0.098	0.062	0.026	0.004	
1.625	0.332	0.282	0.234	0.188	0.136	0.096	0.060	0.020		
1.75	0.322	0.276	0.224	0.178	0.132	0.094	0.054	0.016		
1.875	0.316	0.266	0.220	0.162	0.126	0.092	0.052			
2	0.314	0.266	0.214	0.156	0.122	0.086	0.050			
2.125		0.264	0.214	0.150	0.118	0.084				
2.25		0.264	0.208	0.148	0.116	0.080				
2.375		0.260	0.202	0.146	0.112					
2.5		0.244	0.202	0.146	0.110					
2.625			0.198	0.146						
2.75			0.196	0.144						
2.875			0.196							
3			0.190							
3.125										
3.25										
3.375										

the utility function was used only to guide decisions on the asset side, and the estimation of net total CEROE from (12.52) does not incorporate risk aversion when choosing a debt structure. Furthermore, the utility function ensures the solvency of the fund by covering shortfalls with infusion of equity. However, under certain conditions no external sources of equity will be available. The analysis we carry out here compensates for these omissions. It considers the risk of insolvency when structuring the issue of debt, thus incorporating risk aversion in structuring the debt in addition to structuring the asset portfolio.

Define $\bar{R}_I$ as the expected excess return over the risk-free rate for this line of business and $\bar{r}_f$ as the expected risk-free rate. The rate at which we must discount the final income FI^l_G is given by $R_\mu = \bar{r}_f + \bar{R}_I$. For our shareholders FI^l_G represents the value of the equity at the end of the planning period and they are willing to stay in this business if the discounted value of this equity is not less than the initial capital invested. The shareholders will keep their shares if the *Excess Value per Share (EVS)* is greater than zero with a high probability. Recalling that the initial amount of equity is $\rho L_0 + E_S$ (E_S could be equal to zero), the *EVS* in each scenario is given by

$$EVS^l = \frac{FI^l_G (1 - \kappa)}{(1 + R_\mu)^T} - (\rho L_0 + E_S). \qquad (12.53)$$

The risk related to a specific debt allocation is given by the probability that EVS is less than zero, i.e., $P^-_{EVS} = \text{Prob}\,(EVS^l < 0 \mid l \in \Omega)$. This is the probability of insolvency and can be determined by calculating the EVS^l for each $l \in \Omega$, ordering from the lowest to the highest, and looking for the rank of the first EVS^l that is negative, i.e.,

$$P^-_{EVS} = \frac{\text{rank}\,(EVS^l < 0)}{N}. \qquad (12.54)$$

The EVS can be used to determine the amount of policyholder charges required to make P^-_{EVS} equal to a given confidence level. Recall that FI^l_G, and consequently EVS^l, are a function of C_G, E_S, and D_G. If we fix E_G then FI_G is a function of C_G (D_G is determined from equation 12.50). Through a linesearch we can determine C_G^* such that

$$\text{Prob}\left[EVS(C_G^*) < 0\right] = \alpha. \tag{12.55}$$

In our experiments we set $\bar{R}_I = 6\%$ and the probability of insolvency $\alpha = 1\%$. Figure 12.6 shows the results of the linesearch which solves equation (12.55) for different values of equity supplement E_S. We observe that for guarantees higher than 6% the CEROE increases. How is it possible that higher guarantees can yield higher returns? The puzzle is resolved if we note that the increase in returns is accompanied by a significant increase in policyholder charges. The increases in the policyholder charges fund the guarantee and preserve equity from falling below its present value.

In practice a significant increase in policyholder charges would be unacceptable, and would lead to increased lapses. This analysis can be used as a demarcation criterion between "good" and "bad" levels of the guarantee. For instance, the Italian insurance industry offers products with guarantees in the range 3% to 4%. The analysis shows that they could consider increasing the guarantee up to 6% without significant increase of charges to policyholders or reduction of CEROE. (One may justify the difference from the operating guarantee of 4% to the peak optimized value of 6% as the cost of running the business. If so this cost is high.) For guarantees above 6% we note a substantial increase in policyholder charges at a marginal improvement in CEROE, and this is clearly unacceptable to both policyholders and shareholders.

Short-term financing of shortfalls

To this point the analysis has determined the cost of the shortfall O_G^α and funded it through a combination of debt D_G, charges to policyholders C_G, and equity E_S. Now, let us fix policyholder charges and equity and let the debt fluctuate according to the shortfall O_G^l realized in each scenario. Thus we consider funding part of the shortfall through short-term financing. Instead of issuing a bond for a notional equal to D_G and maturity T, we will borrow money when a shortfall occurs. The debt for each scenario is given by

$$D_G^l = O_G^l - C_G - E_S. \tag{12.56}$$

We assume that it is possible to borrow money at a spread δ over the risk-free rate. The definition of the final income becomes

$$FI_T^l = A_T^l - L_T^l - D_G^l \prod_{t=1}^{T}(1 + r_{ft}^l + \delta) + (C_G - J_S)\prod_{t=1}^{T}(1 + r_{ft}^l). \tag{12.57}$$

We can apply the analysis of the previous section to determine policyholder charges C_G, and estimate the distribution of D_G^l, solving equation (12.55). We display in Figure 12.7 the C_G^* for different levels of the guarantee and for $\delta = 2\%$. Note that policyholder charges C_G^* are substantially lower than those obtained by solving (12.55) in the previous section as reported in Figure 12.6. This is expected, as short-term financing of the cost is a dynamic strategy, as opposed to the fixed strategy of issuing long-term debt. Since D_G^l is scenario dependent, it compensates for those scenarios with high shortfalls, while it is low or null for those scenarios with low or no shortfalls.

12.5.4   The view from the regulator's desk

We show in Figure 12.8 the distribution of the equity to liability ratio (cf. equation 12.10) for a guarantee of 5%. This figure shows that the minimum ratio of equity to liability is greater than

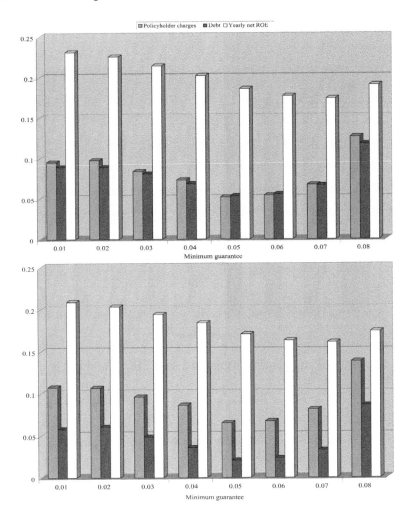

Figure 12.6: The levels of policyholder charge, debt, and net CEROE such that the probability of insolvency is $\mathrm{Prob}\,[EVS(C_G^*) < 0] = 1\%$, for equity supplement $E_S = 0$ (top), and $E_S = 0.02$ (bottom).

the regulatory requirement, and this observation holds true for different values of the guarantee as well. For the type of policies analyzed here using a logarithmic utility function, and for the bullish scenarios sampled from past years, the regulatory constraint is satisfied without explicitly including it in the model.

12.5.5   Additional model features

We study now some additional features of the model, namely the effects of the choice of a utility function, the effects of international diversification and investments in corporate bonds, and the effects of the policy surrender option.

Choice of utility function

The decision maker's risk aversion specifies a unique asset portfolio to back each guaranteed policy. Clearly increased risk aversion will lead to more conservative portfolios with higher

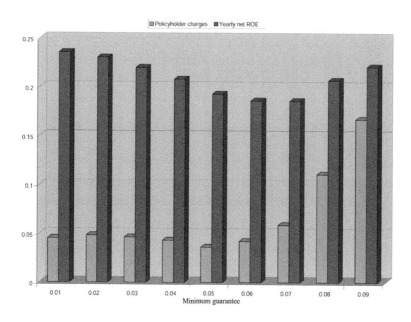

Figure 12.7: The levels of policyholder charges and net CEROE for different guarantees such that $\mathrm{Prob}\left[EVS(C_G^*) < 0\right] = 1\%$.

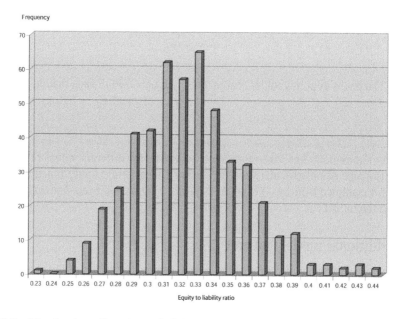

Figure 12.8: Distribution of equity-to-liability ratio at the end of the planning horizon for a guarantee of 5%.

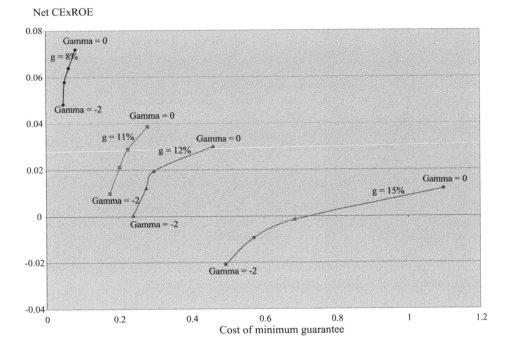

Figure 12.9: Trade-off of CEexROE against cost of the guarantee with varying risk aversion for target guarantees 8% (leftmost curve), 11%, 12%, and 15% (rightmost curve).

contents of fixed income. The result will be a simultaneous reduction in both the CEexROE to shareholders and the cost of shortfalls required to fund the policy. Figure 12.9 illustrates the trade-off as the risk aversion parameter γ of the utility function (12.13) varies from 0 (base case) to -2 (increased risk aversion) for five different target guarantees.

Note that for low target guarantees increased appetite for risk results in higher CEexROE for only a marginal increase in cost of the guarantee. For higher target guarantees (e.g., 15%) we note a substantial increase in the cost of the guarantee as the embedded option goes deep in-the-money when we increase the risk tolerance and invest in volatile assets. These results confirm our expectations on model performance and are consistent with the results of Figure 12.4. The model allows users to generate efficient trade-offs that are consistent with the contractual obligations and the firm's risk tolerance.

International diversification and credit risk exposures

We extended the analysis to incorporate other assets permitted by regulations such as corporate bonds and international sovereign debt. Italian insurers are allowed to invest up to 10% of the value of their portfolio in international assets. We run the base model for a guarantee of 4%, and allowing investments in the Morgan Stanley stock indices for USA, UK and Japan, and the JP Morgan government bond indices for the same countries. Figure 12.10 illustrates the trade-off of CEexROE against cost of the guarantee for international portfolios and portfolios with corporate bonds and for different levels of guarantee. The internationally diversified portfolio achieves CEexROE of 0.14 at a cost of the guarantee of 0.02. In contrast, we note that domestic investments in the Italian markets fund the guarantee at the same cost but yield a CEexROE of only 0.11. Similarly, investments in the US corporate bond market further improve the CEexROE to 0.16, but at an increase of the cost to 0.033.

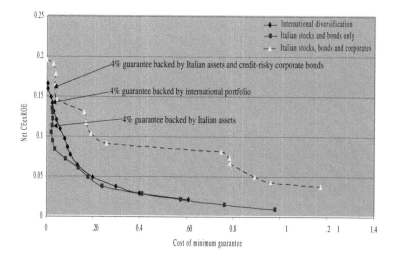

Figure 12.10: Trade-off of CEexROE against cost of the guarantee for internationally diversified portfolios, and portfolios with exposure to the corporate bond markets.

Impact of the surrender option

The testing of the model has so far used liabilities with only actuarial risk. Using the various assumptions on lapse behavior discussed in Section 12.4.5 we study the effect of the surrender option on the cost of the guarantee.

Figure 12.11 illustrates the effect of lapse on the cost of the guarantee for different levels of the minimum guarantee. It is worth noting that the difference between no lapse at all and fixed lapse is significant for high levels of the minimum guarantee ($g \geq 7\%$). This difference is less evident when lapse is modeled as in equation (12.35).

Figure 12.12 illustrates effects of lapse on the net CEexROE. Again, differences are more evident when we switch from no lapse to fixed lapse. It is worth commenting on the effect of lapse rates on the cost of the guarantee and the net CEexROE, over a range of minimum guarantees. Differences in the net CEexROE are observed for low minimum guarantees, say $g \leq 6\%$. In contrast, the alternative lapse assumptions yield substantially different costs for the guarantee for $g > 6\%$. This effect can be explained in view of the option embedded in the policy that the payment is the maximum between a fraction of the portfolio return and the guaranteed rate of return. For low levels of the minimum guarantee the option is almost always out-of-the-money and fixed lapse will depress the net CEexROE through a constant surrender of policies (see equation 12.6). For larger values of the minimum guarantee, the insurance company will benefit from lapses since, when promising large guarantees, it is more likely that the company will face occasional shortfalls, and in such cases any lapsed policies will relieve the company, in part, from shortfall.

12.5.6   Benchmarks of Italian insurance policies

In order to assess the effectiveness of the model in practice we compare the optimal portfolios with industry benchmarks. We take as benchmark a set of portfolios with a fixed broad asset allocation between bonds and stocks, and random allocation among specific assets. In order to be consistent with the usual fixed-mix strategies followed by the Italian industry we set the broad asset allocation between bonds and stocks to 90/10, 80/20, and 70/30. The results of this experiment are reported in Figure 12.13. Note that the optimized portfolios always dominate the benchmark portfolios in the space of cost-of-guarantee versus CEexROE. These results further

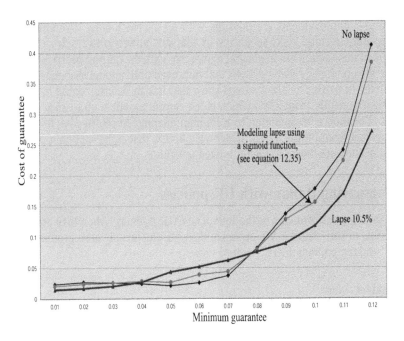

Figure 12.11: The effect of lapse on cost of the minimum guarantee.

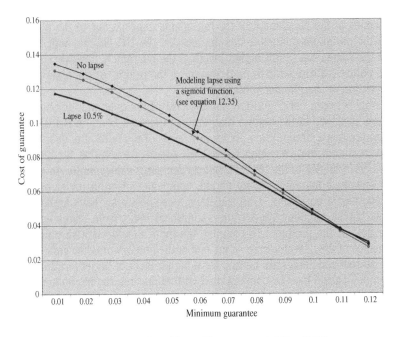

Figure 12.12: The effect of lapse on net CEexROE.

justify the integrative approach taken in this chapter, whereby the insurance policy is analyzed jointly with the asset allocation decision instead of being analyzed for an a priori fixed asset portfolio. Further improvements are possible with an internationally diversified portfolio and with some exposure to credit-risky securities, as analyzed in Section 12.5.5.

The results of this section are in general agreement with the current practices of Italian insurers. However, the optimized results suggest that improved policies and associated asset strategies are still possible. In particular, the findings show that Italian insurers could increase the equity exposure of their portfolio from 20%, which is the current practice, up to 25% to 30% – see the optimal asset allocation corresponding to minimum guaranteed return $g = 3\%$ in Figure 12.4. This is also evident from Figure 12.13, where we observe that some random portfolios from the 70/30 asset allocation are closer to the optimized portfolios.

12.5.7   Comparing Italian with UK policies

We now compare the performance of the Italian and UK policies, when they are both optimized using the models of this chapter. We optimize the performance of these products from both the shareholders' and the policyholders' point of view.

The shareholders' view

Figure 12.14 (top diagram) shows the annualized CEexROE, net of a flat tax rate, that shareholders receive for various levels of the minimum guarantee. Notice that the curve for the British policies begins below the curve for the Italian policies, but decreases at a much slower rate. In general, shareholders perform better with the Italian policies for low levels of the minimum guarantee, while they do better under the English policies for high levels of the minimum guarantee. This is due to the structure of the bonus policy in the UK case: the way we model the reversionary bonus forces the company – when solvent – to offer a total bonus that is at least as high as a benchmark rate to match the principle of PRE (We use the yield on long maturity UK government bonds as the benchmark of the reasonable expectations of the policyholders). For low levels of the minimum guarantee this implies that the UK policies will have much higher bonuses than the Italian ones. For higher levels of the guarantee, however, the more generous Italian bonus policy (with regards to participation in the returns of the asset portfolio) quickly results in an erosion of shareholder value.

The trade-off between net CEexROE and the cost of the guarantee for both the Italian and the UK policies is shown in the bottom diagram of Figure 12.14. The British policies and the Italian policies provide a similar trade-off for low levels of the minimum guarantee, both having relatively low cost and relatively high CEexROE. Again, we see that for higher levels of the guarantee, the performance of the Italian products decreases substantially. In order to meet high contractually specified guarantees every period, companies offering Italian-style policies must pursue very aggressive portfolios. Unfortunately, these portfolios have highly volatile returns, and this means that the company often requires additional equity from shareholders, which results in the higher cost of the product. In contrast, the more flexible British policies only finance underperformance of the guarantee rate at the end of the horizon or when solvency is threatened. In particular, British companies are aiming for a higher level of target terminal bonus, and low returns during one period may be compensated with higher returns in another (we observe that this relies on our assumption of a single insurance contract; it would be interesting to study the more realistic situation where numerous guarantee contracts are managed through a single asset portfolio, so that different terminal bonuses are paid at different times, and the company must worry about the "inherited estate" after the termination of one set of policies).

In general, we observe that the greater flexibility in both funding and structuring the bonus policy for minimum guarantee products in the UK results in better performance for shareholders.

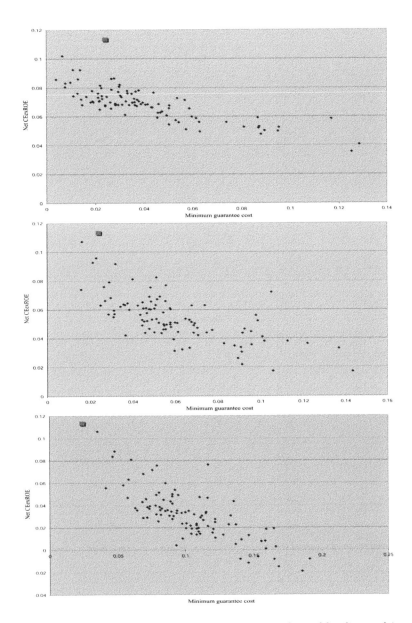

Figure 12.13: Performance of benchmark portfolios (points indicated by diamonds) against the optimized portfolio (point indicated by a square) for $g = 4\%$. The proportion of bonds to stocks for the benchmark portfolios is set at 90% to 10%, 80% to 20%, and 70% to 30%, respectively, from top to bottom.

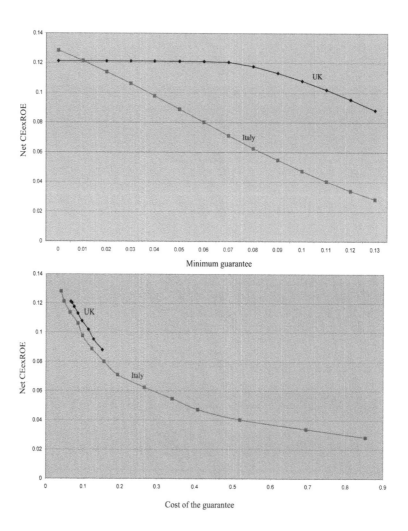

Figure 12.14: The shareholders' view of Italian and UK policies: (top) Rate of return on equity for different levels of guarantee to policyholders; (bottom) return versus cost frontiers.

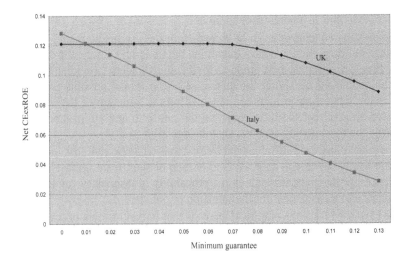

Figure 12.15: The policyholders' view of Italian and UK policies: expected return versus risk.

The policyholders' view

How do policyholders view the differences between the two policies, and in particular the bonus policies they offer? We assume that policyholders view these products as classic asset portfolios, and they expect to trade off risk and reward. In assessing the value of minimum guarantee policies to the policyholders, we take the classic approach to measuring these quantities. Reward to policyholders is measured by expected return, while risk is measured by the standard deviation of returns.

The expected rate of return against the standard deviation of returns to policyholders for different levels of the minimum guarantee is shown in Figure 12.15. We observe that UK policyholders face little trade-off between risk and return for different levels of the guarantee. Insurers uniformly pursue the portfolios that are in their best interests in the long run. The minimum guarantee to the policyholders is only a small fraction of the bonus. The policyholders' view is mainly based on the terminal bonus they receive, and this is close to the shareholders' view, which is based entirely on the leftover surplus on terminal bonus.

On the other hand, Italian policyholders face a rather extended frontier trading off risk and return. The rate of return for policyholders is monotonically increasing in the guarantee rate. The risk and return trade-offs faced by Italian policyholders are more complicated. At low levels of the guarantee, Italian insurers pursue more aggressive portfolios (as they are virtually assured of meeting the guarantee), which produce the higher variability seen at the low guarantee end of the Italian frontier. As the guarantee rate increases, Italian insurers invest in more conservative portfolios to ensure that they meet the higher guarantee – a task that is now nontrivial. The more conservative portfolios are reflected in the fact that for these levels of the guarantee Italian policyholders actually have less risk and higher return. For high levels of the guarantee, the only way for insurers to produce the returns needed to meet the guarantee is to invest in very aggressive portfolios. This results in the high return, high risk portion of the Italian frontier.

12.6   Postview

This chapter has, first, demonstrated that an integrative approach to the management of assets and liabilities for insurance products with guarantees and bonuses adds value. Asset structures generated with an integrative approach for specific insurance policies are efficient, as opposed to asset strategies developed in a nonintegrated model.

Several interesting conclusions can be drawn from the use of the model on data from the Italian insurance industry. First, we have quantified the trade-offs among the different targets of the insurance firm: providing the best products for its policyholders; providing the highest excess return to its shareholders; satisfying the guarantee at the lowest possible cost and with high probability. Some interesting insights are obtained on the structure of the optimal portfolios. Specifically, we observe that too little equity in the portfolio and the insurer cannot meet the guarantee, while too much equity destroys shareholder value.

Second, we have analyzed different debt structures whereby the cost of the guarantee is funded through equity or through debt with either long or short maturities. The effects of these choices on the cost of the guarantee and on the probability of insolvency can be quantified, thus providing guidance to management for the selection of policies.

Third, we have seen from the empirical analysis that Italian insurers operate at levels which are close to optimal but not quite so. There is room for improvement either by offering more competitive products or by generating higher excess returns for the benefit of the shareholders and/or the policyholders. The empirical analysis has also shed some light on the relative merits of the policies offered by Italian and UK insurers. The merits of each were assessed from the perspective of both the shareholders and the policyholders.

As a caveat we add that the increase in the equity exposure suggested from the use of this model should come with an increased sophistication in the technology used to manage these assets vis-à-vis the liabilities. In particular, the asset portfolios must be carefully fine tuned with models such as the one presented here.

Notes and References

The models in this chapter are based on the papers by Consiglio, Cocco and Zenios (2001, forthcoming). The modeling of the UK policies is from Consiglio, Saunders and Zenios (2006), and a comparison of the UK and Italian policies is given in Consiglio, Saunders and Zenios (2003).

The changing landscape for the demand in financial services is covered in the collection of papers compiled in Harker and Zenios (2000). The data on traded financial assets by Italian households are from ISVAP, the regulatory board of Italian insurers.

Contemporary products with guarantees are discussed in Hansen and Miltersen (2002), Ross (1989), and Chadburn (1997). Additional material is found in Kat (2001). Such products brought about a shift from actuarial to financial pricing of insurance liabilities, a topic addressed in Vanderhoof and Altman (1998), Embrechts (2000), Giraldi et al. (2000), and Babbel (2001).

The pricing of the option embedded in the early unit-linked maturity guarantee policies was addressed by Brennan and Schwartz (1976), and Boyle and Schwartz (1977). Pricing models for modern life insurance contracts are due to Grosen and Jørgensen (2000), and Jørgensen (2001). Hansen and Miltersen (2001) extend this model to the pricing of contracts with a smoothing surplus distribution mechanism of the form used by most Danish life-insurance companies and pension plans. Miltersen and Persson (1999) price multi-period guaranteed contracts linked either to a stock investment or the short-term interest rate. Bacinello (2001) develops pricing models that permit her to study the interplay between the volatility of the underlying asset portfolio, the participation level for determining bonuses, and the guaranteed rate, while Brennan and Schwartz (1979) consider the effects of "misspecification of the stochastic process" on the pricing. Boyle and Hardy (1997) analyze alternative reserving methods for satisfying the guarantee. More practical aspects of the problem are studied by Giraldi et al. (2000) and Siglienti (2000). The UK policies are discussed in Chadburn (1997), Berketi and Macdonald (1999), Smith (2000), Shelley, Arnold and Needleman (2002), and the report by Financial Services Authority (2001).

For modeling the lapse behavior of policyholders see the discussion in Section 8.3.3, which is based on the work of Asay, Bouyoucos and Marciano (1993).

The finding that excessive exposure to equities destroys shareholder value is consistent with the conclusion of Siglienti (2000). His simulations revealed a maximum desirable exposure to equities of 15%, which is lower than the range of 20 to 25% identified by the optimization model. This discrepancy could be, in part, due to the data of scenario returns used in the two studies. However, it may also be due to the fact that with the scenario model developed here the portfolio composition is optimized, something that was not done with the simulation analysis.

Portfolio optimization models for asset and liability management for insurance companies are the Yasuda Kasai model developed for the Frank Russel Company by Cariño and Ziemba (1998), the Towers Perrin model of Mulvey and Thorlacius (1998), the CALM model of Consigli and Dempster (1998), and the Gjensidige Liv model of Høyland (1998); see also the chapters in the two volumes by Zenios and Ziemba (2006, 2007). These models have been successful in several practical settings but their application does not cover participating policies with guarantees.

Chapter 13

Personal Financial Planning

With *Andrea Consiglio*[1] and *Flavio Cocco*[2]

13.1   Preview

In this chapter we develop a scenario optimization model for asset and liability management of individual investors. The model maximizes the upside potential of the portfolio vis-à-vis a target return, with limits on the downside risk. Post-optimality analysis using out-of-sample scenarios measures the probability of meeting the target for a given portfolio. It also allows us to estimate the required increase in the investor's initial endowment so that the probability of success is improved.

13.2   The Demand for Personal Financial Planning

The decline of the welfare state created demand on the part of consumers for more autonomy in the management of their financial assets, leading to a rapid change in their needs and desires. At the same time – on the supply side of financial services – the development of the worldwide web has created a rich channel for the distribution of customized financial services to satisfy the increased sophistication and diversity of the investor, be it a family household, a wealthy individual, or a couple of retirees.

Financial advisors and individual consumers can today rely on financial engineering tools to manage their financial assets. At the same time the worldwide web has provided an effective communication channel through which advances in financial engineering are made available to large networks of financial advisors and, through them, reach an increasing client base. In addition, the internet enables the most sophisticated segment of the client base to be reached directly, thus satisfying both client needs for more autonomy, and the desire of financial institutions to bypass the monopolistic control that financial advisors exert over clients.

While most of the advances in financial engineering discussed in the previous chapters are geared towards large institutions, the individual has not been ignored. In the inaugural issue of *Financial Services Review*, Harry M. Markowitz (1991a) published an essay comparing individual with institutional investing. He concluded that realistic game-of-life simulators would combine simulations of the family planning process – a complex and unwieldy process – with suitable models to optimize asset allocation for various approximations of this process.

In general, the simulation of the complex financial planning process is better left in the hands of the individual who, perhaps assisted by a financial advisor, carries out his or her own simulations in the form of "what if" analyses and scenario projections. The individual does not rely

---

[1]   Faculty of Economics, University of Palermo, Palermo, Italy.
[2]   Prometeia S.r.l., Bologna, Italy.

solely on the financial advisor, but also considers the demands of spouses and siblings, and the opinions of friends and relatives. Needless to say, this decision making process is not easily relinquished to a simulator. However, once some key parameters of the family plan are established – such as the target retirement age and required retirement income – the individual seeks professional advice on the best way to invest current assets in order to reach the agreed-upon targets. Expertise in market trends and availability of investment opportunities must be combined with the individual's investment style to produce a comprehensive portfolio. This portfolio should then be monitored for its ability to reach the targets on time: perhaps the targets were too ambitious and the savings too low, or the specific mutual fund selected underperformed against the broad market indices, or some changes in market trends seem likely to hasten or delay the achievement of our goals. In each case remedies may be suggested. Assets may be diverted away from poorly performing mutual funds; savings may be increased to reach the target for the children's college fund on time; a target may be revised.

In this chapter a system is developed that uses advances in financial engineering to optimize the financial planning process. It provides tools to support:

1. *Strategic asset allocation* with the creation of a well-diversified portfolio of broad asset classes in the global markets.

2. *Tactical asset allocation* with the recommendation of a portfolio of mutual funds – from those offered by the financial institution providing the financial planning advice – that best matches the strategic decisions.

3. *Monitoring and controlling* of the created portfolio, identifying risks of underperformance vis-á-vis the targets and allowing for portfolio revisions.

13.3   The Provision of Financial Services

The decline of the welfare state has led to an increased awareness among consumers that their well-being – current and future – and that of their families is more in their own hands and less in the hands of the state. This development has created a breed of consumers who demand "anytime-anywhere" delivery of quality financial services. At the same time, consumers now exhibit an increased sophistication in terms of the financial products they buy and the channels of service delivery they use. These trends are universal among developed economies.

The numbers are telling: In the 1980s almost 40% of US consumer financial assets were in bank deposits. Two decades later bank deposits account for less than 20% of consumers' financial assets, with mutual funds and insurance/pension funds absorbing the difference. Such trends seem to be global. For instance, the traded financial assets of Italian households more than doubled in the five-year period from 1997. The bulk of the increase was absorbed by mutual funds and asset management (see Table 12.1 in the preceding chapter).

The increase in traded financial assets comes with increased diversification. This trend towards diversification again was led by US investors, but has now spread worldwide. Figure 12.1 (Chapter 12) shows the strong growth of mutual funds and equity shares at the expense of liquid assets and bonds. Today more than one-third of the total revenues of the Italian banking industry are derived from asset management services.

These statistics were discussed in Chapter 12 in the context of insurance firms, and were used to explain the pressures on insurance industries to offer innovative financial products such as endowments with minimum guaranteed rates of return. An alternative approach to dealing with these pressures is to provide the consumer with the means to manage their own assets directly, by creating customized portfolios that satisfy individual needs. Thus, instead of offering attractive products (such as single-premium deferred annuities or endowments with guarantees), financial institutions may offer a flexible service. This is especially relevant as the changing attitudes

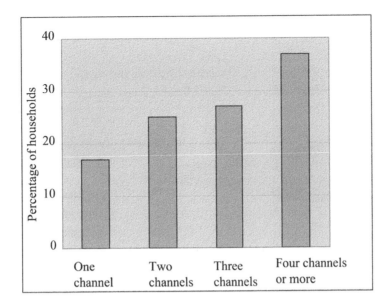

Figure 13.1: Percentage of US households using alternative delivery channels. (Source: Kennickell and Kwast 1997)

towards innovative products are coupled with a change in attitudes towards delivery channels. Data from a survey of households in the US show that modern consumers also demand access to more than one delivery channel. While a personal visit to a bank branch remains the predominant way of doing business, a significant percentage of US households use alternative channels such as the telephone, electronic transfer, ATM, PC-banking, etc. (see Figure 13.1).

Italian households follow this trend, although with a delay of some years. In 2000 only 16% of households could recognize on-line brands. Today this number has grown to more than 60%. Brand recognition has been followed by use of the new channels, as illustrated in Figure 13.2.

Technology and the internet are taking a larger role in the world of finance and investing. Innumerable companies operate on the internet, offering research, advice, brokerage operations, and other important financial data, just one click away. Browsing the web can lead anyone, anytime, to security prices, company and market news, and retirement plan consultants. Web sites are designed in a way that even financial novices are able to make decisions on which mutual fund to purchase; whether it is convenient to surrender their life insurance; or if they should place an order to sell or buy a given stock. The web investor is afforded the autonomy of deciding what is important and what is not, much as the institutional investor has been doing for years. The value added by the internet consists of spreading financial information, besides offering the possibility of immediate action on the basis of the news just downloaded. Of course, one must question the wisdom of quick reactions in dealing with problems of asset management, where a long-term perspective and cool-headedness are essential.

The market for direct distribution of financial products through the web is, however, a niche market. It is relatively modest in terms of the actual shares traded through the web compared to traditional channels. For instance, it is estimated that in Italy only 500,000 investors out of 12 million potential users rely on the web for trading. This is consistent with another significant change on the supply side of financial services: the changeover from product sales, pure and simple, to the active management of customers' financial planning expectations and needs. In this respect the internet has considerable potential as a facilitator. It is one more channel to be used in the management of existing relationships established with customers through the tra-

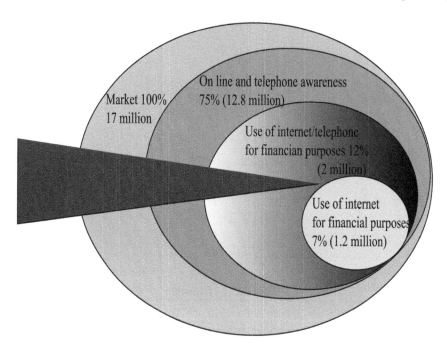

Figure 13.2: The use of new channels – on-line and telephone – by Italian households. (Source: *Household Savings Outlook*, Prometeia 2001).

ditional channels of banks, agencies, and advisors. Financial institutions endeavor to provide multichannel support, keeping up with the trends illustrated in Figure 13.1.

The shift towards multichannel distribution is due to both pull and push forces. The pull is coming from the changing demands of consumers and especially the younger generations. The push is coming from the suppliers of financial services who find in the web a rich medium that allows them to reach a wider client base.

The web is used not only to reach customers, but also as a valuable tool for the support of financial advisors. These are the internal clients of a financial service provider. Web-based services support financial advisors so they can better serve their clients. This leads not only to customer loyalty towards the advisor, but also creates disincentives for advisors in switching firms. In addition, web-based services provide an alternative channel of communication between the firm and the customer, so that the customer–firm relationship is not exclusively controlled by the network of financial advisors.

The last points should not be underestimated. Indeed, they are key considerations in the adoption of a scenario-based optimization system for private investors. Advisors are one of the most valuable assets to a financial service provider. The firm needs to serve them well, but must also work to loosen their tight grip on clients. Broker Stephen Sawtelle made front-page news in *The Wall Street Journal Europe* (August 29, 2001) when he left Wadell & Reed, instigating a clash for control of his 2,800 clients. Mr Sawtelle was eventually allowed to keep 2,600 of his clients, while an arbitration panel ruled that the firm owed $27.6 million in damages to its ex-broker. It is unlikely that Mr Sawtelle's departure could have been avoided even if Wadell & Reed had supported him through a web-based system – he was fired for "personality conflicts." However, the 2,800 clients would have been more autonomous in managing their assets directly, and the ensuing battle for their control would have been less disruptive.

The changes outlined above created the need for novel tools to bring together the evolving needs of both suppliers and consumers.

13.4 Web-Based Personal Financial Tools

Individuals have a variety of financial goals for which they must plan. A house, a car or other tangibles must be purchased, children's education financed, retirement planned, and health care and other insurance covered. All of these requirements face the typical family, but they appear with varying intensity at different stages of one's life-cycle. The young parents are concerned primarily with their children's education, newlyweds with purchasing a home, and middle-aged business executives with their retirement. Some personal asset allocation systems advocate an integrative approach to financial planning taking into account all of the above targets. Others focus on a single problem, namely that of retirement planning.

The integrative approach has significant advantages which have been elaborated throughout this book. However, for personal asset allocation the integrative approach could be unwieldy and, perhaps, inadvisable since several objections are raised on the part of end-users. First, the information requirements are very high, and users are reluctant to fully reveal their personal financial particulars to one investment advisor or a single financial institution. The silo approach to risk management – against which we have been arguing throughout this book – is alive and well in the world of personal financial planning. Individuals tend to segment their problems, rather than taking an integrative view which requires a certain level of sophistication. Furthermore, as mentioned above, the intensity of the various needs varies with time. A young couple will have great difficulty conceptualizing the issues surrounding children's college education, let alone retirement, when home ownership still remains unresolved. Of course it should be recognized that the silo approach could lead to sub-optimal results.

On the other side of the spectrum of personal financial advising we have specialized systems that focus on a single goal, such as retirement. The conceptual demands on the user are manageable, and the user receives expert advice on asset allocation decisions for a well-specified and significant problem.

The system of Personal Financial Tools we develop provides support for each one of the goals facing a typical family, but does so by segmenting the family's planning problem into distinct sub-goals. The user specifies the financial planning problem by indicating the time horizon of the project (T), the target goal (L_T), and the current asset availability (A_0). This information is sufficient for calculating the target return that the individual expects (g) (see Figure 13.3). The system will then assist the user in structuring an asset allocation consistent with this target return, and his or her appetite towards risk as revealed by answering an on-line questionnaire.

Personal Financial Tools provide three interactive modules that support the three steps of the financial planning process discussed in the introduction:

1. *Personal asset allocation.* This determines the strategic asset allocation decisions. That is, the asset allocation decisions based on sectors or broad market indices.

2. *Personal rating.* This provides a data warehouse of financial indicators and ratings of mutual funds to assist users in tactical asset location to specific investment vehicles such as a particular equity mutual fund.

3. *Personal risk analyzer.* This measures the portfolio risk and monitors the portfolio performance in achieving the target goals.

These three tools should form part of an integrated interactive system that will allow users to carry out game-of-life simulations, addressing both strategic and tactical issues. The personal risk analyzer provides a control module to ensure that the developed strategy and its execution will meet the targets.

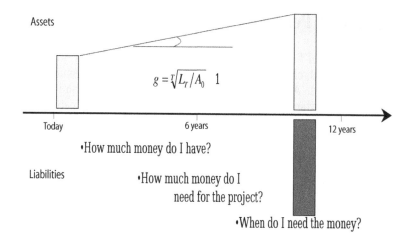

Figure 13.3: Specifying the requirements of a personal financial plan.

13.4.1   Strategic decisions: the Personal Asset Allocation tool

The first step in devising a strategic plan is to elicit the client's goals and preferences. As illustrated in Figure 13.3, users are asked to specify their targets, their planning horizon, and the availability of funds. The users must also reveal their attitude towards risk. This is a difficult issue to ascertain by direct questioning or with great precision. Typically, financial institutions will have an in-house questionnaire developed to assist the financial advisors in establishing the risk tolerance of clients. Through a short series of questions clients can be classified into one of five categories of risk-takers: *prudent*, *moderate*, *balanced*, *dynamic*, and *aggressive*. The risk tolerance of the customer is inferred through a questionnaire whose aims are to investigate the level of risk tolerance and identify the classes of instruments in which the individual is ready to invest.

Proprietary systems are used by various firms to solicit investors' risk preferences with typical questions such as: "What is your knowledge of financial markets?"; or questions relative to past investments such as: "In which assets have you invested so far, e.g., government bonds, stocks, a portfolio of stocks and bonds, short-term instruments like treasury bills, bank accounts, floating rate notes?"; and indirect questions that establish the customer's knowledge such as: "Which one of the following terms are you familiar with: Value-at-Risk, benchmark index, the difference between stocks and bonds?" The responses to such questions are then weighted to give each customer a weight from 0 to 100, and these weights are mapped into the five categories of risk-takers mentioned above.

The Personal Asset Allocation system uses a scenario optimization model to specify an asset allocation plan that meets the target using the available endowment, and which is consistent with the user's risk profile. The model takes a "target-first" view, i.e., the asset allocation is such that getting to the final target is the primary concern. Any surplus must be saved in order to back any subsequent shortfalls. The investor is averse to having a deficit vis-á-vis the target at the horizon, but is indifferent to upside potential that he or she is ready to forego for the sake of meeting the target.

13.4.2   Tactical decisions: the Personal Rating tool

Once the strategic asset allocation decisions are made the investor has to locate his or her assets in a specific portfolio. The Personal Rating tool provides a menu of mutual funds offered for sale by the institution, which are consistent with the broad asset categories in the client's strategic plan. The menu comes with ratings of the funds and other information relating to their past performance. The multitude of mutual funds creates push forces for financial institutions to provide Personal Rating tools to assist users in making their selection. For instance, the *Investment Funds* brochure of Union Bank of Switzerland offers more than 270 funds. With this diversity of products the support of the Personal Rating tool is invaluable.

There are also pull forces on the user side that demand a Personal Rating tool. The strategic asset allocation may be quite diversified, and as a result no single mutual fund may be available to satisfy the asset allocation specifications. The Personal Rating tool allows users to invest in a portfolio of mutual funds so that their strategic goals are met.

13.4.3   Control: the Personal Risk Analysis tool

The Personal Risk Analyzer provides the controls needed to complete the game-of-life simulations. The user can monitor the risk of his/her portfolio vis-à-vis the target at both the strategic and the tactical level. When both the strategic asset allocation and the tactical asset location perform as planned then the investor is on the way to meeting the goals within the specified time horizon. When the tactical portfolio fails, it is time to examine the performance of the individual managers and move away from underperformers. When the strategic portfolio fails, this indicates a general change in the prevailing economic conditions that threaten the success of the investor's plans. The user will then want to revisit the strategic plan, taking one of the actions outlined above: increasing the savings, trimming the targets, or accepting the fact that the goals will be met with some delay.

13.5   Model for Personal Financial Planning

We now return to the Personal Asset Allocation tool and develop the relevant model. Given an initial endowment A_0 and final target liability L_T, we denote by A_T the terminal assets that will fund the liability L_T. The target rate of return that will yield adequate assets at maturity is given by

$$g = \left(\frac{L_T}{A_0}\right)^{(1/T)} - 1. \tag{13.1}$$

The growth rate g is the target rate of return on the initial endowment.

Our objective is to deliver the final assets A_T to cover the liabilities. For this reason, we build our model in such a way that any deficit is always covered by cash infusion, i.e., increased savings on the part of the investor, and any surplus is set aside from the portfolio to back any future possible downside deviations from the target return. With this modeling construct the client can be advised if sufficient savings are available to meet the goals, if additional savings may be required or the goals reduced, or if more ambitious goals could be met with the current savings.

In order to take into account price appreciation, we adjust the target rate g by scenarios of inflation rates, I_t^l, so that the real target rate is given by

$$g_t^l = g + INFLOW_t^l. \tag{13.2}$$

The investor chooses a portfolio from the universe of available assets U, and the returns of such instruments, at period t, are denoted by r_{ti}^l, for each $i \in U$ and $l \in \Omega$, and the initial endowment A_0 is allocated to assets in nonnegative proportions x_i such that

$$\sum_{i=1}^{n} x_i = 1. \tag{13.3}$$

The dynamics of the portfolio value are given by

$$R_{pt}^l = \sum_{i=1}^n x_i r_{ti}^l, \text{ for } t = 1, 2, \ldots, T, \text{ and for all } l \in \Omega. \tag{13.4}$$

The liability is the target which must be matched in each period by the asset portfolio, in order to ensure that at the end of the planning period the final goal is fulfilled. The liability must grow at the rate given by g_t^l,

$$L_t^l = L_{t-1}^l (1 + g_t^l) \text{ for } t = 1, 2, \ldots, T, \text{ and for all } l \in \Omega, \tag{13.5}$$

where $L_0 = 1$.

In order to match assets and liabilities in each period we must infuse money every time a downside occurs. For the same reason, we reduce the current level of the portfolio value when an upside is experienced and create a separate account for surplus so that

$$A_t^l = L_t^l, \text{ for } t = 1, 2, \ldots, T, \text{ and for all } l \in \Omega. \tag{13.6}$$

Given that equality (13.6) holds, the downside risk is given by the amount of capital needed to cover the deficit as given by

$$d_t^l = \max \left[- \left(R_{pt}^l - g_t^l \right), 0 \right] L_{t-1}^l, \text{ for } t = 1, 2, \ldots, T, \text{ and for all } l \in \Omega. \tag{13.7}$$

Note that d_t^l depends only on the current mismatch between the portfolio rate of return and the target rate times the liability level at the previous period.

The same logic applies to the upside return given by the surplus definition:

$$u_t^l = \max \left[\left(R_{pt}^l - g_t^l \right), 0 \right] L_{t-1}^l, \text{ for } t = 1, 2, \ldots, T, \text{ and for all } l \in \Omega. \tag{13.8}$$

The dynamics of the total deficit and total surplus are defined, respectively, by

$$D_t^l = D_{t-1}^l (1 + f_{(t-1)t}^l) + d_t^l, \text{ for } t = 1, 2, \ldots, T, \text{ and for all } l \in \Omega,$$

$$U_t^l = U_{t-1}^l (1 + f_{(t-1)t}^l) + u_t^l, \text{ for } t = 1, 2, \ldots, T, \text{ and for all } l \in \Omega \tag{13.9}$$

$$\tag{13.10}$$

where $f_{(t-1)t}^l$ is the forward rate from $t - 1$ to t under scenario l.

In view of (13.6), the dynamics of the assets are given by

$$A_t^l = A_{t-1}^l (1 + R_{pt}^l) - u_t^l + d_t^l, \text{ for } t = 1, 2, \ldots, T, \text{ and for all } l \in \Omega. \tag{13.11}$$

The max operator in (13.7) and (13.8) introduces a discontinuity in the model. To circumvent this problem we introduce gap variables y_{+t}^l and y_{-t}^l to measure the portfolio excess return over the target rate and the shortfall below the target rate, respectively. Therefore, we have

$$R_{pt}^l - g_t^l = y_{+t}^l - y_{-t}^l, \text{ for } t = 1, 2, \ldots, T, \text{ and for all } l \in \Omega, \tag{13.12}$$

$$y_{+t}^l \geq 0, y_{-t}^l \geq 0, \text{ for } t = 1, 2, \ldots, T, \text{ and for all } l \in \Omega. \tag{13.13}$$

Only one of these variables can be nonzero for a given time and a given scenario. The dynamics for the deficit and surplus can be written as follows:

$$d_t^l = y_{-t}^l L_{t-1}^l, \text{ for } t = 1, 2, \ldots, T, \text{ and for all } l \in \Omega, \tag{13.14}$$

$$u_t^l = y_{+t}^l L_{t-1}^l, \text{ for } t = 1, 2, \ldots, T, \text{ and for all } l \in \Omega. \tag{13.15}$$

The optimal portfolio is chosen to maximize the expected value of the final surplus $\sum_{l \in \Omega} p^l U_T^l$ subject to targets on expected value of the final deficit, $\sum_{l \in \Omega} p^l D_T^l$. A parameter ω specifies the bound on downside risk; the lower this parameter the less risk our investor is willing to assume in order to meet the targets.

Note that all the constraints are linear. Before we formulate the linear programming model, we can simplify some of the equalities in order to reduce the size of the problem. In the next subsection we determine analytically expressions for U_T^l and D_T^l, and substitute the relations so obtained in the objective function to obtain a linear program. The resulting model is as follows:

Model 13.5.1 Personal financial planning

$$\text{Maximize} \quad \sum_{l \in \Omega} p^l \sum_{t=1}^{T} y_{+t}^l \Phi^l(t, T) \tag{13.16}$$

subject to

$$\sum_{l \in \Omega} p^l \sum_{t=1}^{T} y_{-t}^l \Phi^l(t, T) \leq \omega \tag{13.17}$$

$$\sum_{i=1}^{n} x_i = 1 \tag{13.18}$$

$$R_{pt}^l = \sum_{i=1}^{n} x_i r_{it}^l, \quad \text{for } t = 1, 2, \dots T, \, l \in \Omega. \tag{13.19}$$

$$R_{pt}^l - g_t^l = y_{+t}^l - y_{-t}^l, \text{ for } t = 1, 2, \dots T, \, l \in \Omega, \tag{13.20}$$

In the objective function we have used

$$\Phi^l(t, T) = \prod_{\tau=0}^{t-1} (1 + g_\tau^l) \prod_{\tau=t}^{T} (1 + r_{f\tau}^l), \tag{13.21}$$

derived below as equation (13.28), in order to simplify the model representation. We set also boundary conditions $g_0 = 0$ and $r_{fT} = 0$, so that the target rate of return is zero before the first time period and the risk-free rate is zero at the end of the horizon.

13.5.1   Solving the linear dynamic equations

The dynamic equation (13.9) which describes the evolution of the deficit can be solved analytically to obtain the value of D_T^l at the end of the planning horizon. To simplify the notation, in this section we drop the scenario superscript. It is easy to see that

$$L_t = \prod_{\tau=1}^{t} (1 + g_\tau), \tag{13.22}$$

where $L_0 = 1$.

At time $t = 0$, no deficit has occurred and $D_0 = 0$. At $t = 1$ we have

$$D_1 = D_0(1 + r_{f0}) + y_{-1} L_0. \tag{13.23}$$

At $t = 2$, we have $D_2 = D_1(1 + r_{f1}) + y_{-2}L_1$ and substituting for D_1 from (13.23) we obtain

$$D_2 = y_{-1}(1 + r_{f1}) + y_{-2}(1 + g_1). \tag{13.24}$$

Repeating for $t = 3$ we obtain

$$
\begin{aligned}
D_3 &= D_2(1 + r_{f2}) + y_{-3}L_2 \\
&= y_{-1}(1 + r_{f1})(1 + r_{f2}) + y_{-2}(1 + g_1)(1 + r_{f2}) + \\
&\quad + y_{-3}(1 + g_1)(1 + g_2).
\end{aligned} \tag{13.25}
$$

Repeating this process recursively for each t, we determine the expression for the final deficit

$$D_T = \sum_{t=1}^{T} y_{-t} \prod_{\tau=1}^{t-1}(1 + g_\tau) \prod_{\tau=t}^{T}(1 + r_{f\tau}). \tag{13.26}$$

Applying the same argument to the dynamics of the surplus, we obtain

$$U_T = \sum_{t=1}^{T} y_{+t} \prod_{\tau=1}^{t-1}(1 + g_\tau) \prod_{\tau=t}^{T}(1 + r_{f\tau}). \tag{13.27}$$

We also have the boundary conditions $g_0 = 0$ and $r_{fT} = 0$, so that target rate of return is zero before the first time period and the risk-free rate is zero at the end of the horizon.

To simplify the notation of the model we define, reintroducing the scenario index l:

$$\Phi^l(t, T) = \prod_{\tau=0}^{t-1}(1 + g_\tau^l) \prod_{\tau=t}^{T}(1 + r_{f\tau}^l). \tag{13.28}$$

13.5.2   Analysis of the model

Solving Model 13.5.1 we obtain an optimal portfolio, and estimate its upside potential and downside risk. Post-optimality analysis can be carried out to estimate quantities that are not readily available from the model, but that are important in a game-of-life simulation. In particular, we can estimate the probability that a given asset allocation will meet the target. We can also estimate the amount of additional capital required in order to improve this probability to an acceptable level $100\alpha\%$.

We first estimate the probability of success of a given allocation. We denote by Ω' an index set for out-of-sample scenarios of asset returns, that is, of scenarios that were not included in the sample indexed by Ω over which the allocation was optimized. Typically, many more scenarios N' can be generated in this set, that is, used in estimating simple quantities, than the number of scenarios N used in the optimization. We calculate now A_T^l and L_T^l for each $l \in \Omega'$ and define with $\Delta_T^l = A_T^l - L_T^l$ the asset and liability mismatch at the end of the horizon. We determine the present value of Δ_T^l using a discount factor $v^l(0, T)$. This factor could be scenario dependent, and later we discuss possible choices for the discount factor. The present value of the mismatch is then given by

$$\Delta_0^l = \Delta_T^l v^l(0, T). \tag{13.29}$$

The probability of success can be estimated from the empirical cumulative distribution function of the present value of the mismatch Δ_0^l. We first estimate the cumulative distribution function as:

$$F(h) = p^l \sum_{l \in \Omega'} \delta_{\{\Delta_0^l \leq h\}}, \tag{13.30}$$

where $\delta_{\{S\}}$ is the indicator function taking the value 1 when the expression S in its subscript is true, and 0 otherwise. The probability of success is then given by

$$P_s = 1 - F(0). \tag{13.31}$$

We can also use $F(h)$ to determine the percentile, Δ_0^*, at the confidence level α, such that

$$\text{Prob}\,(\Delta_0^l \leq \Delta_0^*) = \alpha, \tag{13.32}$$

or, equivalently,

$$1 - F(\Delta_0^*) = 1 - \alpha. \tag{13.33}$$

It follows that adding Δ_0^* to the initial endowment shifts the distribution of the final mismatch to the right. Thus, the probability of getting a final mismatch with present value less than zero will be less than $100(1 - \alpha)\%$. Δ_0^* is the amount of money which must be added to the initial endowment so that the probability that final asset value A_T exceeds the final liability L_T is at least $100(1 - \alpha)\%$.

The second point of the post-optimality analysis concerns the discount factor $v(0, T)$. How should we discount the final mismatch Δ_T^l? The answer depends on the instrument in which we will invest the amount Δ_0^* in order to improve the probability of success. If we invest Δ_0^* in the portfolio we have

$$v^l(0, T) = \frac{1}{\prod_{t=1}^{T}(1 + R_{pt}^l)}. \tag{13.34}$$

If at time t we choose a safer instrument such as a risk-free deposit with maturity τ and forward rates $f_{t\tau}^l$ we have

$$v^l(0, T) = \frac{1}{\prod_{t=1}^{T}(1 + f_{t\tau}^l)}. \tag{13.35}$$

By choosing the risky discount factor we reduce the amount of money to be infused, but then the investor is more exposed to adverse moves of the market. In contrast, by choosing the risk-free discount factor adverse scenarios will affect only the initial endowment. The supplementary funds are preserved to back future asset and liability mismatch.

The optimization model will specify an asset allocation decision which is consistent with the investor's risk preference and the projected scenarios. While a target-first view is taken there is no guarantee that the goals will be met under all circumstances. The goals maybe too ambitious, or the available endowment too low, or the prospective asset returns not high enough. The results of scenario optimization are analyzed to ascertain whether the goals are met.

13.6   Model Validation and Testing

We test here the model on a range of planning horizons, target returns, and risk tolerances. The set of asset classes are represented by benchmark indices as summarized in Table 13.1 and Figure 13.4.

Scenarios are generated by bootstrapping historical monthly records for the 13-year period from 1988 to 2001 (see Chapter 9). To generate scenarios of returns for a long horizon – say 10 years – we sample 120 monthly returns from different points in time. The compounded return of the sampled series is one scenario of the 10-year return. The process is repeated to generate the desired number of scenarios for the 10-year period.

Numerical experiments are carried out for target returns between 4% to 15% with increments of 1%, for time horizons ranging from 1 to 10 years with increments of one year. Limits on the downside risk ω are imposed in the range $[0, 10\gamma]$ where γ is a constant depending on the problem data, target return, and time horizon. $\omega = 0$ corresponds to very high risk aversion

Table 13.1: Benchmarks and corresponding asset classes.

DataStream Code	Asset Class
MSNAMR	Stocks North America
MSPACF	Stocks Pacific
MSEMKG	Stocks Emerging Countries
MSEMUI	Stocks EMU
MSEXEM	Stocks Ex-EMU
JPMUSU	Bonds North America
JPMJPU	Bonds Pacific
JAGALL	Bonds EMU
JPMUKU + SBSZEUE	Bonds Ex-EMU
JPMPTOT	Bonds Emerging Countries
JPEC3M	Cash

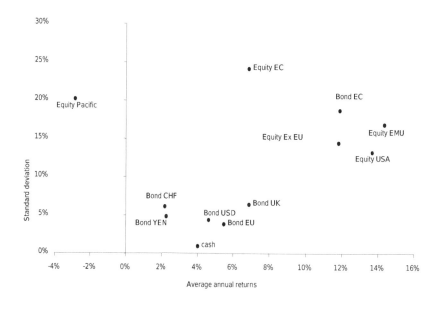

Figure 13.4: Performance of the benchmark asset classes during 1988–2000.

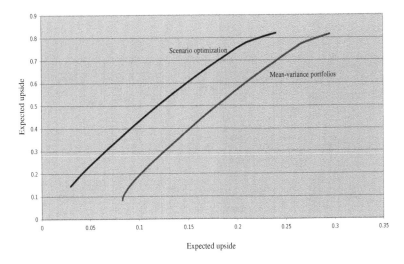

Figure 13.5: Expected upside and expected downside of mean-variance efficient portfolios, and of portfolios obtained with the scenario optimization model.

usually leading to an infeasible optimization model. For $\omega = 10\gamma$ we have high appetite for risk, and the constraint on downside risk is usually non-binding. In our experiments we group the risk aversion of the investor in three classes labeled *high*, *medium* and *low*, corresponding to values of ω in the range 0–3, 4–7, and 8–10, respectively.

For each asset class we generate 1,000 scenarios of returns during the target horizon. The target horizon is then discretized in quarterly, semiannual, or annual periods indicating the trading dates when the model equations apply. In order to maintain tractability of the model the discretization depends on the length of the horizon, with finer discretization being possible only for short horizons.

As a first step we compare the scenario-based model that integrates the asset allocation model developed in this chapter to meet the investor's target, with the classic approach of asset allocation based on the mean-variance analysis of Chapter 3. We generate an efficient frontier using mean-variance optimization, and then analyze the expected upside and the expected downside of the efficient portfolios vis-à-vis a nominal target return of 6%. The results are shown in Figure 13.5, together with the frontier of expected upside versus expected downside obtained with the scenario optimization model. We observe that the portfolios obtained with the scenario optimization model dominate those obtained with mean-variance analysis. Furthermore, the frontier obtained with the scenario optimization model is extended for lower downside risk than what is achieved with mean-variance analysis. These results are, of course, expected since the scenario optimization model takes an integrated view of the individual investor's problem. What is noteworthy is that the difference between the two sets of portfolios is substantial. Further improvements are possible when short sales are allowed and the efficient frontier is pushed significantly towards higher expected returns than those shown in the figure.

We then test the composition of the portfolio for different target rates of return. The asset allocations for different levels of target return are shown in Figure 13.6. We observe a transition to more risky portfolios as the target return increases. Even if investors do not change their risk aversion, their portfolio becomes riskier in order to achieve their goals. On the other hand, when investors keep their target return fixed and increase their risk aversion the portfolio composition will change, as expected, towards more conservative investments, as illustrated in Figure 13.7.

While each one of these observations, on its own, is rather obvious, together they reveal an important dilemma for the individual investor. Specifically, it is only with more appetite for risk

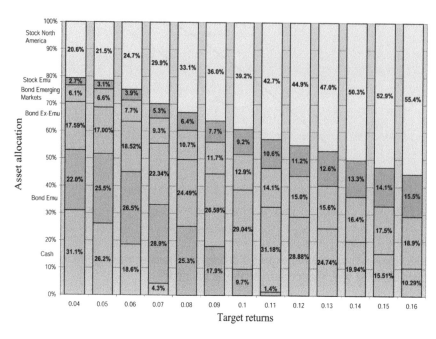

Figure 13.6: Asset allocations for time horizon of five years, and high risk aversion with increasing target nominal returns.

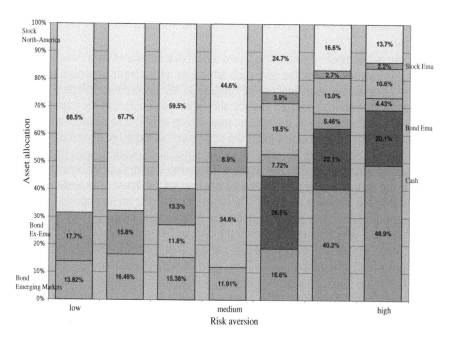

Figure 13.7: Asset allocations for time horizon of five years, target return 6%, and risk aversion ranging from low to high.

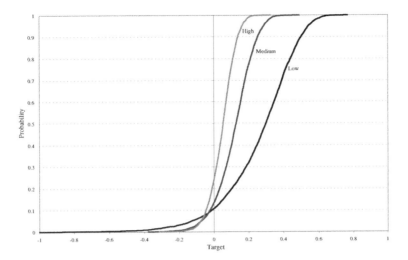

Figure 13.8: Empirical cumulative distribution function for time horizon 5 years, target return 6%, and different levels of risk aversion. When the cumulative function does not exceed the value 0, then the asset allocation does not meet the target, and the probability of success is given by one minus the intercept of the vertical axis at zero.

that higher targets can be reached. The probability of success will deteriorate if an investor keeps the target return constant and increases his risk aversion (see Figure 13.8). For high risk aversion the probability of success is about 75% and it increases to 90% for individuals ready to take more risks. However, note that the tail of the distribution is more pronounced towards the left for risk lovers, indicating higher losses in case of adverse scenarios.

Finally, in Figure 13.9 we show the asset allocations as we vary the individual's time horizons. As expected, with the increase in the time horizon we observe a gradual shift towards more risky investments, while the total exposure to cash and EMU bonds declines, and the difference is taken up by investments in the North American stock market indices, bonds from emerging markets, and non-EMU bonds.

13.6.1 Probability of success and how to improve it

The probability of success for different portfolios can be obtained as a by-product of the model results. Furthermore, this probability can be improved by a suitable increase in the initial endowment. To carry out this type of analysis we generate a set of out-of-sample scenarios (Ω'), which are different from the scenarios (Ω) used in the optimization model. (Note that since the out-of-sample scenarios are used for estimating simple quantities, such as percentile, we can utilize a much larger number of scenarios – 5,000 in our experiments – than the limited number of scenarios – typically 1,000 – used in the optimization model.) For each scenario we calculate the final mismatch Δ_T^l, and build the cumulative distribution function. The mismatch is discounted either at the rate of the risky portfolio or at the risk-free rate.

Figure 13.10 (top) illustrates the cumulative distributions and the probability of success for different target returns. The tails of these distributions are shown in the bottom diagram of the same figure, where we also show the amount of money – as a percentage of the initial investment – that must be infused to the endowment in order to back future shortfalls. For each target return two different amounts are calculated that will improve, respectively, the probability of success to 95% or 90%. For example, to achieve a confidence level of 95% for reaching a 6% target rate for five years, we must add 7% of the initial endowment. To have a 90% probability of success in

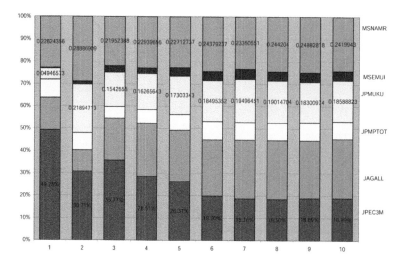

Figure 13.9: Asset allocations for target return 6%, different time horizons, and high risk aversion.

reaching 10% annual growth rate for the same horizon we must infuse an additional 21% of the initial capital.

Finally, we show the effect of different discount factors on the cumulative distribution curves $F(h)$. By discounting the final asset and liability mismatch at the rate of the asset portfolio we assume that the additional cash that will fund shortfalls is invested in the optimal portfolio. A safer strategy would be to invest the infused cash in a risk-free deposit. Figure 13.11 shows the tails of the distribution after sufficient cash is added to the initial endowment to improve the success rate to 95%. We observe that the shortfall when not meeting the target is larger when we invest the additional cash in the risky portfolio.

13.6.2   An apparatus to explain the equity premium puzzle

We now turn to an interesting feature of the model, which becomes apparent from a close examination of the model results. In particular, we observe that the model replicates investor behavior that gives rise to the equity premium puzzle and, more specifically, it shows conditions under which investors prefer more secure investments even for reasonable levels of risk aversion. From the results of Figure 13.12 we observe that as we decrease the discretization step, thus increasing the frequency with which individuals examine the performance of their portfolios vis-à-vis their goals, the asset allocation shifts towards secure investments. The investors of our model exhibit myopic loss aversion. This behavior of the model, or, to be more precise, the behavior of investors who use the model in determining their asset allocation, is also consistent with the prospect theory proposed in the literature as an explanation of the equity premium puzzle, since the model views upside potential differently from downside risk.

These are important points to bear in mind concerning the validity of the model as a normative tool for analysis. Not only does the model address constructively an important problem faced by individuals, but it does so in accordance with prevailing theories on how individuals behave. The model could be used to estimate the quantities of interest to economists studying the equity premium puzzle, such as the average frequency with which investors evaluate their portfolios and the investors' relative risk aversion, which results in the historically observed risk premium.

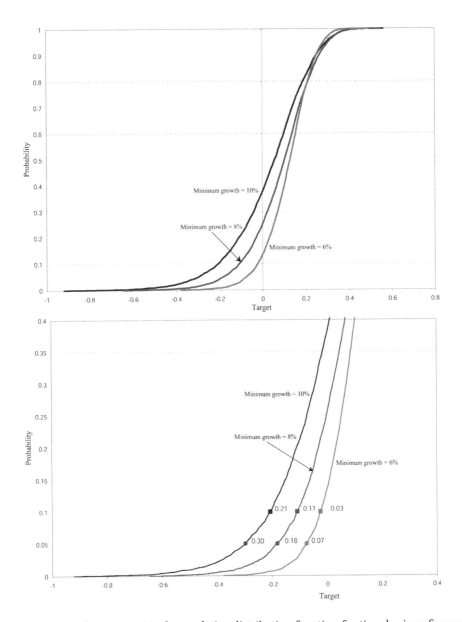

Figure 13.10: Top figure: empirical cumulative distribution function for time horizon five years, medium risk aversion and different target growth rates. Bottom figure: the distributions' tails of the top figure, with the labeled bullet points indicating the amount of cash infusion, in % of initial endowment, needed to improve the probability of success for the different target returns.

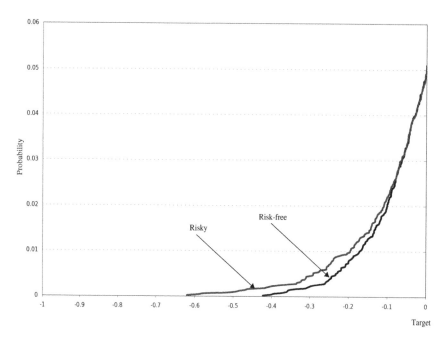

Figure 13.11: Detail of the distributions' tails of the asset/liability mismatch after cash is added
to the initial endowment and is invested either in the risky portfolio, or in a risk-free asset.

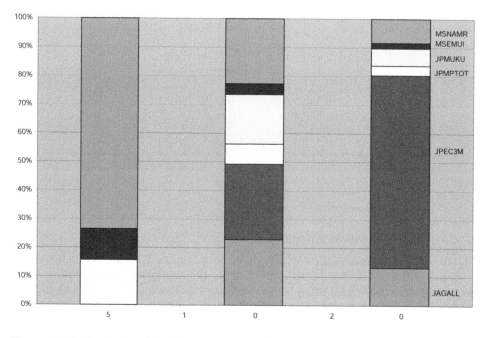

Figure 13.12: Asset allocations for target return 6%, time horizon five years, and high risk aversion as we decrease the discretization time step.

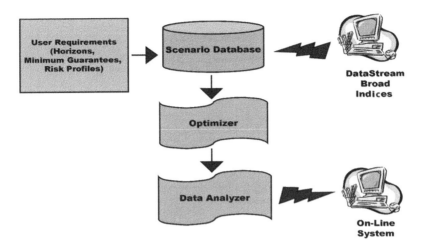

Figure 13.13: The off-line system: The optimization model is run periodically for several combinations of risk profiles, horizons, and target portfolio growth rates.

13.7   The Integrated Decision Support System

The three components of a personal financial planning system discussed in the previous sections – the strategic asset allocation model, the tactical asset allocation tool, and the control module for risk analysis – are integrated in a web-based system. The system is designed as a combination of an off-line module that runs the optimization, and an on-line module for product customization. The off-line module exploits the fact that large population segments are homogeneous, so that one could optimize for a range of planning horizons, financial targets, and risk preferences. Customization of a plan for an individual is then extrapolated from the pool of optimized plans.

The scenario optimization model is run off-line and the results are stored in a solution database (see Figure 13.13). The on-line system (Figure 13.14) interacts with the user and, for a given risk profile, horizon, and final goal, interpolates the optimal portfolio from the available solutions in the database.

The on-line system is interfaced through a set of web pages. The user's inquiry is first analyzed by an expert system that maps the risk profile to the appropriate risk aversion parameter, and the minimum growth rate is calculated. These data are passed on to the interpolation module that consults the off-line system through the database of solutions, and determines the strategic asset allocation that is closest to the user requirement. The broad asset allocation is then mapped to a set of mutual funds which can be purchased by the investor. A fund chooser takes care of this task by showing the user a set of mutual funds offered for sale by the institution, from the broad asset classes selected by the optimizer. A database of available funds is maintained by each institution providing the on-line service, and it reflects the institution's product portfolio.

13.7.1   The case of the Rossi family

Consider the case of the Rossi family. Mr Rossi, aged 55, and his wife have two children well into their own careers. Our couple have been accumulating a healthy retirement plan through a combination of private savings and a generous Italian social security system. With the prospec-

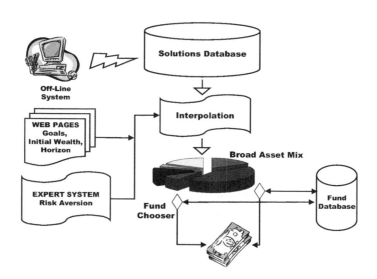

Figure 13.14: The on-line system: The user interacts through the web pages and the specific enquiry is mapped onto the solution database and matched with specific products from the fund database.

tive decline in the social security support by the state, the Rossi couple plan the purchase of a house in the Italian Alps. This would serve as their vacation home and eventually either as a retirement home or as an asset to be sold to finance "rainy days" at retirement.

The Rossis have available 50,000 EUR and expect to invest an additional 2,500 EUR per annum over the next decade to purchase a home of current value 100,000 EUR. They assume the standard inflation rate of 2% for housing and wish to invest in a balanced portfolio. They have a medium appetite for risky investments. Figure 13.15 illustrates the Rossis' web page and their cashflow specifications.

Running the system they are recommended a portfolio with a probability of success that is marginally over 55% (see Figure 13.16). The "success thermometer" points out that their plan amounts to flipping a coin, and hoping it lands heads so they can buy their house. This strategy is clearly unacceptable. Over a bottle of fine wine they discuss alternatives with their children. Delaying retirement by a couple of years is an option, but the analysis shows that the probability of meeting their goals after 12 years, instead of 10, improves only to 57%. This still sounds like flipping a coin. Increasing the annual savings to contribute to this project will increase significantly the probability of success. But our couple are reluctant to forego consumption over the next decade in order to enjoy a mountain home after retirement. Going for a more aggressive portfolio is another alternative. Developing a plan for a 12-year horizon, maintaining the 2,500 EUR per year contribution, and building a portfolio characterized as "aggressive" improves the probability of success to 80%. Since their essential retirement needs are covered – pension, health care and a fully paid house in the city – the Rossis are convinced, with some nudging from their younger children, that the proposed plan is sound.

Building the Rossis' portfolio now requires the assistance of the Personal Rating tool. The optimal asset allocation recommended by the system must be converted into specific funds. Another problem is raised here, since our couple is reluctant to place even a modest amount of money in "Obbligazioni paesi emergenti," that is government bonds in emerging markets. ("If I have not visited the country, I am not buying their government bonds," declares Mr Rossi.) The final portfolio composition is shown in Figure 13.17, indicating an overweight of US bonds and an underweight of bonds in emerging markets. The specific funds are also shown in this figure, where we note, for instance, that our couple has taken further liberties in splitting their cash assets among USD, the euro and Swiss francs.

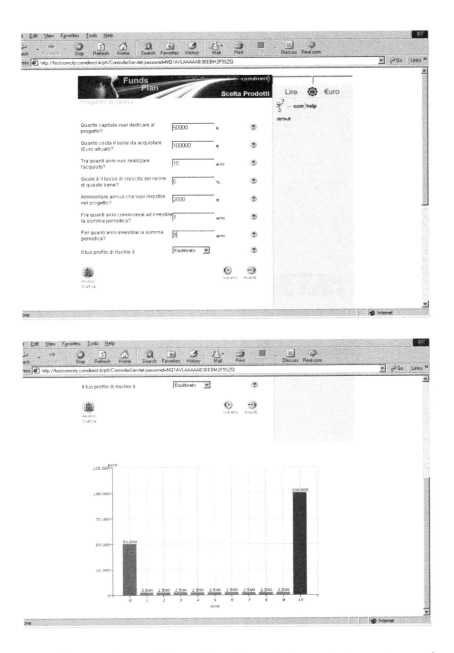

Figure 13.15: The Rossis' personal financial requirements for purchasing a retirement home at current market value 100,000 EUR.

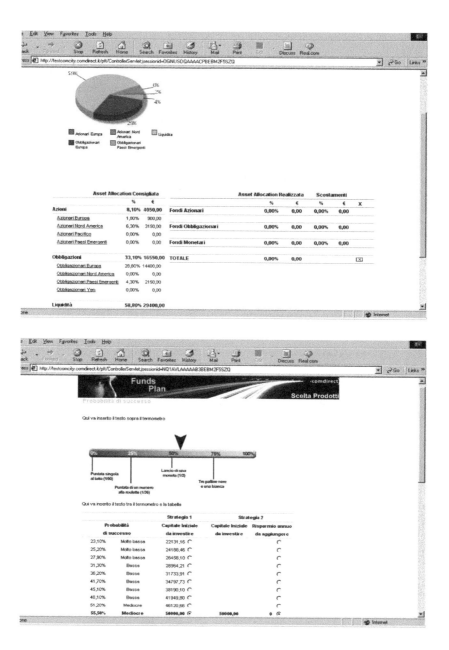

Figure 13.16: The Rossi's original portfolio and probability of success. Top screen: the proportional asset allocation as advised by the system (left) and as bought by our investors (right). Note that all entries on the right are zero; the investors have not yet decided to follow the advice and they have not bought anything. Bottom screen: the probability that the proposed plan from the top screen will succeed in meeting our investors' goals.

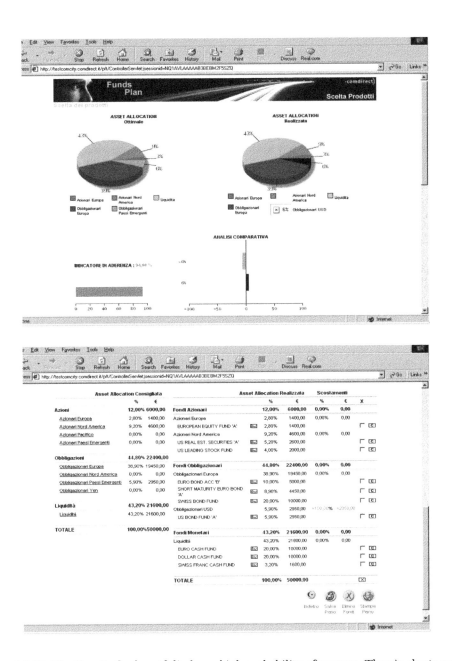

Figure 13.17: The Rossi's final portfolio has a high probability of success. The pie charts on the top screen illustrate the composition of the portfolio as advised by the system (left chart) and as purchased by the investors (right chart). The bottom screen gives the composition of the portfolio as advised by the system (left) and as purchased by the investors (right).

13.8 Postview

We have developed and tested a normative model for assisting individual investors in making asset allocation decisions to meet certain targets. The model improves on the classic mean-variance analysis for asset allocation, and it is consistent with prevailing positive theories on investor behavior. As such it can contribute to the needs of individual investors for asset and liability management, an area for which there is increasing demand on the part of consumers. Extensive empirical analysis provides some insights into the performance of the model.

An interesting extension of the model would be into a multi-stage, multi-period setting to account for investor targets that change with time, and whereby investors may change their asset mix as new information arrives. Such an extension is feasible using the techniques of stochastic programming. This approach may also be warranted given the fact that individuals do face multiple liabilities, and they do revise their portfolios as time goes by. On the other hand the conceptual demands imposed on the individual from a more integrative approach may be prohibitive.

Notes and References

The models in this chapter are based on the work of Consiglio, Cocco and Zenios (2007). The web-based integrated system is discussed in Consiglio, Cocco and Zenios (2004) and received the *EURO Excellence in Practice Award* in 2006.

A collection of recent literature on household finance can be found in Guiso, Haliassos and Japelli (2002). Optimization-based systems for retirement planing have reached some acclaim through the services provided by FinancialEngines.com of William Sharpe and associates. This line of development was taken a step further by the HOME Account Advisor™ of Berger and Mulvey (1998) to support additional needs of a household beyond retirement planning.

Consumer trends in asset management are discussed in Harker and Zenios (2000), and statistics on the use of alternative delivery channels for financial services are given in Kennickell and Kwast (1997); see also Harker and Zenios (2000, ch. 1), and Roth and Jackson (1995). The annual *Household Savings Outlook* survey carried out by Prometeia Calcolo in collaboration with Eurisko – a Milan based company conducting research on consumption, communications, and social transformation – provides data on consumer trends in Italy.

The literature on assessing risk preferences is vast, and is grounded on theoretical results found, for instance, in Kagel and Roth (1995), and Kahneman and Tversky (1979, 1981). For discussion on the equity premium puzzle see Mehra and Prescott (1985), and for myopic loss aversion see Benartzi and Thaler (1995).

Part IV

LIBRARY OF FINANCIAL OPTIMIZATION MODELS

To add a library to a house is to give that house a soul.

Cicero

Chapter 14

FINLIB: A Library of Financial Optimization Models

14.1   Preview

In this chapter we describe the library of financial optimization models, and suggest several projects that can be used as term assignments for studio designs by students.

14.2   FINLIB: Financial Optimization Library

The library of financial optimization models, called FINLIB, contains several of the models described in this book. It is available through the companion volume, *Practical Financial Optimization: A library of financial optimization models*, by Andrea Consiglio, Søren S. Nielsen and Stavros A. Zenios, Blackwell Publishers. The book starts with an introduction to the high-level modeling language GAMS – a *General Algebraic Modeling System* – that is used to develop optimization models. The bulk of the companion volume then describes several models drawn from the chapters of this book. The models in the FINLIB library range from simple cashflow matching models, to several variants of Markowitz mean-variance optimization, to advanced models for international asset allocation and currency hedging, corporate bond portfolio management, asset and liability modeling for insurers and for individual investors, and the management of indexed funds.

The companion volume comes with an executable version of the models in FINLIB. Each model is complete with sample market data. Interested readers may use the models of the library substituting their own data. More importantly, however, the models from the library can be used as the building blocks for more elaborate models to meet each reader's specific needs.

FINLIB is organized in directories corresponding to broad classes of models from this book. Each directory typically contains several variants of the models. Each directory corresponds to models that are described in a single section of the accompanying book, while models in each subdirectory are described in subsections.

The models of FINLIB are organized in the following directories.

EXAMPLE: Contains an example dedication model developed step-by-step to help users get started, and to become familiar with the key features of GAMS.

BASICS: Basic financial calculations using GAMS.

MEANVAR: Mean-variance portfolio optimization.

DEDICATION: Portfolio dedication.

IMMUNIZATION: Portfolio immunization.

CREDITIMMUN: Credit-risk immunization.

MAD: Mean absolute deviation portfolio optimization.

REGRET: Regret minimization.

CVAR: Optimizing Conditional Value-at-Risk.

PUT/CALL: Put/call efficient frontiers.

UTIL: Expected utility maximization

STOCHDED: Stochastic dedication models.

STOCHPROG: Stochastic programming models.

INDEX: Indexation models.

The following directories contain large-scale case studies of models. These models were developed in diverse real-world environments, and the setting presented here is indicative of production-quality models. However, they are not meant to be turnkey decision support tools for the applications they discuss. Instead, they can serve as points of departure for practicing financial engineers to develop their own solutions.

INTERNATIONAL: International portfolio management.

CORPORATES: Corporate bond portfolio management.

PROMETEIA: The PROMETEIA model for insurance with guarantees.

PAA: Personal Asset Allocation.

14.3   Studio Designs: Project Suggestions

Nothing hones the skills of a financial engineer like building a complete functional model to satisfy the needs of a particular enterprise, which is then put through the acid test of managing real portfolios. It is usually a long process from the first development of a model – closely related to the optimization models discussed in this book – to turning it over to the risk managers. And like students of architecture, whose education is not complete without many hours of studio work, so financial engineers should devote a considerable part of their training not only to studying and understanding financial optimization models, but also to implementing one or more of them. And they should do so in the context of real-world, large-scale applications.

The studio assignments should involve the interaction with an end-user in order to understand the specifics of the problem at hand, the requirements for a solution within the user's enterprise, and the available data. They should engage students in understanding the problem for which a model must be developed, collecting the data required for their model, implementing and debugging the model and, last but not least, testing and validating the model through backtesting, stress testing, or other "reality checks" that will gain the approval of the end-user.

The models in FINLIB can be used as the building blocks for the large-scale applications, so students can spend less time on the technical details that make a model work, and devote more attention to substantial issues that make a model useful as a decision support tool for enterprise-wide risk management.

14.3.1   Basics of modeling

A project that develops a better understanding of the material of each chapter, and familiarizes students with the studio implementation concepts, is to have the students run the FINLIB model that corresponds to each chapter. Students are asked to retrieve the model from FINLIB, to run it, and to write a short report that: (i) describes the model; (ii) illustrates the results of the model and discusses the intuition behind the model solutions; and (iii) criticizes the strengths and weaknesses of the model implemented in FINLIB, in relation to the material covered in the corresponding chapter.

14.3.2   Mean-variance analysis

Using time series of asset returns for a variety of asset classes – stocks in the domestic market, government bonds, corporate bonds of different credit rating classes, stocks or bonds in foreign markets – estimate means, variances and correlations and build mean-variance efficient portfolios. Show that adding asset classes (e.g., add corporate bonds to a stock portfolio) pushes out the efficient frontier towards higher expected returns for similar risks.

A statistical test must be run on the return data to verify whether they satisfy the normality assumptions that underlie the mean-variance models. Note that currency exchange rates must be used when dealing with assets in foreign markets, and this brings up the issue of currency hedging discussed in Chapter 10, and highlights the need for more sophisticated models.

Consider adding liabilities to the asset allocation model. This requires an end-user, such as a pension fund manager or the manager of an insurance portfolio, who will provide a stream of liabilities that are correlated with the underlying markets.

14.3.3   Portfolio models for fixed income

Portfolio dedication and immunization

Obtain a stream of deterministic liabilities that extend well into the future – such as the liabilities of a closed block of retirees of a pension fund, or the capacity expansion needs of a production plant, or the cashflow projections for building a university campus. Develop dedicated and immunized portfolios of fixed-income securities to match this liability stream. By adding increasingly more risky assets – from government bonds, to high quality credit-risk assets, to low credit rating assets – we may observe the cost reduction of the immunized portfolios, which entails, however, an increased risk of credit rating migration or default, two risk categories not captured by immunization strategies.

Factor immunization

For the liability stream obtained above develop factor immunized portfolios. To this end, data must be collected for the term structure of government bonds and – for enhanced performance and at the expense of increased model complexity – for corporate bonds.

14.3.4   Scenario optimization

Technical issues

Using the data collected for the studio on mean-variance analysis build scenario optimization models, such as mean absolute deviation and CVaR optimization. For asset classes with returns that are normally distributed – according to the statistical tests run above – compare the efficient frontiers of the mean-variance and mean absolute deviation optimization models to see that they are identical.

When using asset classes with non-normally distributed returns, compare the efficient frontiers obtained with the respective optimization model (e.g., mean-absolute deviation against expected return) with the trade-off curves computed with the alternative risk measures (e.g., CVaR against expected return). This will illustrate that there is nothing efficient about efficient frontiers when computed using inappropriate risk metrics.

Social security funds

The social security system in the USA and in most European countries is at risk of insolvency during the next few decades. This phenomenon is partly due to aging populations, whereby fewer actively contributing workers have to support an increasing number of retirees in what is known as a pay-as-you-go system. But it is also, in part, due to the conservative strategies followed in investing the surplus of the social security funds, so that the system has been unable to keep up either with inflation or with the aging population.

Collect data from the social security agency of your country, in particular the actuarial projections for the solvency of the fund, and develop scenario optimization models to propose more advanced portfolio strategies. This project can be used to show how policy parameters can be adjusted in the context of the optimization model to achieve the desired results. Policy parameters for social security fund management include: (i) extending the retirement age; (ii) increasing the contribution to the social security system; or (iii) investing part of the fund surplus in the financial markets.

14.3.5 Dynamic portfolio optimization

Extend any of the models developed and tested in the earlier studios to a multi-period setting using stochastic programming. Compare the results, showing in particular the added benefits obtained by allowing for portfolio rebalancing when using stochastic programming models. This project becomes particularly relevant when applied to financing long-term liabilities, such as a pension or a social security plan.

14.3.6 Index funds

Creating an indexed portfolio to track one of the standard stock indices, such as the S&P500, is a standard problem in portfolio optimization, and also one of little interest, especially as indexed funds are today widely available for most of the major markets.

The applications of indexation discussed in Section 7.7 provide good projects, and students can be asked to replicate and validate the results discussed in this section. The generation of scenarios from historical data for the needs of this project can use any of the methods discussed in Chapter 9.

14.3.7 Designing financial products

The development of the models in this section is likely to exceed the time availability for a term project. The implementation of a portfolio optimization model for fine-tuning the design parameters of any novel financial security involves: (i) the development of a simulation model to generate scenarios of holding period returns for a given setting of the security's parameters; (ii) the implementation of the design optimization model; and (iii) the solution of the model using global optimization techniques. This studio could make a good MSc thesis topic, and is suitable for a term project if the instructor has one or more of the three modules above readily available.

14.3.8   Scenario generation

The implementation of methods for scenario generation is an integral part of all of the above studios. Scenario generation, especially when Monte Carlo simulations are used, may take a significant amount of time and as a result will distract students from paying more attention to the development, testing, and validation of the optimization models. To the extent that instructors have scenario generation modules available, perhaps through other courses in mathematical finance, the studios on model building will focus more on the novelties of financial optimization, as opposed to some of the classic issues in security pricing and simulation.

14.3.9   Applications

Any of the models in Part III: Applications of this book would make suitable term projects if an end-user is available to work with students in fine-tuning the corresponding models from FINLIB for the user's unique environment, and applying it to the user's data. The project could focus on model testing and validation.

Notes and References

The models in FINLIB are described in Consiglio, Nielsen and Zenios (forthcoming), and are also available at //www.hermes.ucy.ac.cy/FINLIB. The high-level modeling language GAMS used for implementing the FINLIB models is described in Brooke, Kendrick and Meeraus (1992). However, the models can also be implemented in any other modeling language that is currently available, such as the AIMMS system of Bisschop and Entrikens (1993), and Bisschop and Roelofs (1996), AMPL of Fourer, Gay and Kernighan (2002), or CAMPS of Lucas and Mitra (1985).

Appendix A

Basics of Optimization

We give here some basic definitions on optimization, defining the optimality conditions for both linear and nonlinear programs. Readers of this book need not concern themselves with the details of solution algorithms for linear or nonlinear programs, as today robust and efficient software is widely available. The FINLIB library of Chapter 14 relieves readers of the burden of studying the technicalities of solution algorithms. However, the development of some models, and especially the analysis of some of their properties, relies on the optimality theory for optimization problems. This appendix provides adequate coverage, and additional material can be found in the textbooks by Luenberger (1984), and Nash and Sofer (1996).

A.1 Duality

There are many different ways to represent linear programs that are equivalent. Some formulations are more suitable for illustrating a property of the linear program, while others simplify the description of an algorithm. We give here what is commonly known as the "standard form" of linear programming using vector-matrix notation.

$$\text{Minimize} \quad c^\top x \tag{A.1}$$

$$\text{subject to} \quad Ax = b, \tag{A.2}$$

$$x \geq 0. \tag{A.3}$$

Here c and x are n-dimensional vectors of cost coefficients and decision variables, respectively; b is a vector of dimension m called the *resource vector*; and A is an $m \times n$ matrix called the *constraint matrix*.

Note that this is a minimization problem, which can be written as the following equivalent maximization problem by negating the objective function:

$$\text{Maximize} \quad -c^\top x \tag{A.4}$$

$$\text{subject to} \quad Ax = b, \tag{A.5}$$

$$x \geq 0. \tag{A.6}$$

It is possible to define the optimality conditions for the linear program in the standard form above. However, the so-called canonical formulation that we give next better reveals the symmetry between the *primal* linear program and the closely associated *dual* linear program. The following is the primal linear program in canonical form:

$$\text{Minimize} \quad c^\top x \tag{A.7}$$

$$\text{subject to} \quad Ax \geq b, \tag{A.8}$$

$$x \geq 0. \tag{A.9}$$

All parameters and variables are as defined above. The following is the corresponding dual linear program, where y is the vector of dual variables:

$$\text{Maximize} \quad b^\top y \tag{A.10}$$

$$\text{subject to} \quad A^\top y \leq c, \tag{A.11}$$

$$y \geq 0. \tag{A.12}$$

When the primal problem has n variables and m constraints, the dual problem has m variables and n constraints. That is, there is one dual variable for each primal constraint, and one dual constraint for each primal variable. The objective function coefficients (i.e., the cost vector) of the primal are the resource coefficients for the dual, and vice versa. The constraint matrix of the dual is the transpose of the constraint matrix of the primal. When the primal problem is formulated in standard form then the dual program becomes:

$$\text{Maximize} \quad b^\top y \tag{A.13}$$

$$\text{subject to} \quad A^\top y \leq c. \tag{A.14}$$

The dual variables are unrestricted.

A.2 Optimality Conditions

There are two major results relating the primal and the dual problem. The first (known as "weak duality") states that the primal objective values provide bounds for the dual objective values and vice versa. The second (known as "strong duality") states that the optimal objective values of the primal and the dual are equal, provided that they exist. Weak duality extends to nonlinear programs as well, while strong duality may not be valid for nonlinear programs. These two results are stated below without proof; the proofs can be found in the references.

Theorem A.2.1 Weak Duality. *Let x be a feasible point for the primal problem in standard form, and let y be a feasible point for the dual problem. Then*

$$c^\top x \geq b^\top y \tag{A.15}$$

Theorem A.2.2 Strong Duality. *Consider a pair of primal and dual linear programs. If one of the problems has an optimal solution, then so does the other and the objective values are equal.*

In an optimal solution some of the inequality constraints may hold with equality. These constraints are called "active." If a constraint holds with strict inequality at the optimal solution it is a non-binding constraint, and it can be removed from the formulation without changing the optimal solution.

It follows from strong duality that a unit change in the right-hand side b_j of the jth constraint will change the objective value by an amount equal to the dual price of this constraint y_j.

A.3 Lagrange Multipliers

It is possible to define dual problems for nonlinear programs, and in this case the dual variables are called Lagrange multipliers. We consider the following equality constrained nonlinear program:

$$\text{Minimize} \quad f(x) \tag{A.16}$$

$$\text{subject to} \quad Ax = b. \tag{A.17}$$

We assume that f is twice continuously differentiable and that the rows of the $m \times n$ constraint matrix are linearly independent. (This is a mild assumption, as otherwise linear dependence of the rows implies that some constraints are linear combinations of other constraints and can be eliminated without changing the problem.)

If we associate a dual variable λ_j for each row of the constraint set – these are also called *Lagrange multipliers* – then we can write the *Lagrangian function* in the form:

$$\Lambda(x, \lambda) = f(x) - \sum_{j=1}^{n} \lambda_j(a_j^\top - b_j) = f(x) - \lambda^\top(Ax - b), \tag{A.18}$$

where $a_j^\top$ denotes the jth row of A, transposed.

Taking derivatives of the Lagrangian with respect to both x and λ and searching for the values x^* and λ^* where these derivatives vanish we obtain a stationary point of the Lagrangian function, and it can be proved that this stationary point satisfies first-order optimality conditions for the nonlinear program.

That is, at optimality, we require

$$\nabla \Lambda(x^*, \lambda^*) = 0. \tag{A.19}$$

Hence we must solve the following system of $n + m$ equations in the $n + m$ uknowns x and λ to obtain a solution x^*, λ^*.

$$\nabla f(x) - A^\top \lambda = 0 \tag{A.20}$$

$$Ax = b. \tag{A.21}$$

The well-known Kuhn-Tucker optimality conditions for nonlinear programs which provide the foundation for nonlinear programming theory, generalize the first-order optimality conditions to necessary and sufficient conditions. The qualifications imposed by Kuhn-Tucker conditions in order for the first-order optimality conditions above to be necessary and sufficient hold true when the objective function is convex and twice continuously differentiable and some mild constraint qualifications apply. For the purposes of this book it suffices to work with the first-order optimality conditions given here.

Appendix B

Basics of Probability Theory

We give here some basic definitions on probability spaces. Additional background material on probability theory can be found, e.g., in Billingsley (1995) and – as applied to stochastic programming where the basics of probability theory are mainly needed in this book – in Kall (1976), and Wets (1989). A~denotes random variables which belong to some probability space as defined below.

B.1 Probability Spaces

Let Ξ be an arbitrary space or set of points. A σ-field for Ξ is a family Σ of subsets of Ξ such that Ξ itself, the complement with respect to Ξ of any set in Σ, and any union of countably many sets in Σ are all in Σ. The members of Σ are called *measurable* sets, or *events* in the language of probability theory. The set Ξ with the σ-field Σ is called a *measurable space* and is denoted by (Ξ, Σ).

Let Ξ be a (linear) vector space and Σ a σ-field. A *probability measure* P on (Ξ, Σ) is a real-valued function defined over the family Σ, which satisfies the following conditions: (i) $0 \le P(A) \le 1$ for $A \in \Sigma$; (ii) $P(\emptyset) = 0$ and $P(\Xi) = 1$; and (iii) if $\{A_l\}_{l=1}^{\infty}$ is a sequence of disjoint sets $A_l \in \Sigma$ and if $\cup_{l=1}^{\infty} A_l \in \Sigma$ then $P(\cup_{l=1}^{\infty} A_l) = \sum_{l=1}^{\infty} P(A_l)$. The triplet (Ξ, Σ, P) is called a *probability space*. The *support* of (Ξ, Σ, P) is the smallest subset of Ξ with probability 1. If the support is a countable set then the probability measure is said to be discrete. The term *scenario* is used for the elements of Ξ of a probability space with a discrete probability measure.

A property is said to hold P–*almost surely* – or *almost surely* abbreviated a.s. when P is understood from the context – if it holds on a subset $A \subseteq \Xi$ with $P(A) = 1$. The *expected value* of a random variable Q on (Ξ, Σ, P) is the Stieltjes integral of Q with respect to the measure P:

$$E[Q] \doteq \int Q dP = \int_{\Xi} Q(\tilde{\xi}) dP(\tilde{\xi}).$$

It is easy to see that $E[Q_1 + Q_2] = E[Q_1] + E[Q_2]$ and $E[\alpha Q_1] = \alpha E[Q_1]$ for constant α. The kth *moment* of Q is the expected value of Q^k, i.e., $E[Q^k] \doteq \int_{\Xi} Q^k(\tilde{\xi}) dP(\tilde{\xi})$. The *variance* of the random variable Q is defined as $\mathrm{Var}[Q] \doteq E[Q^2] - (E[Q])^2$.

Finally, we give a formal but restricted (to our needs) definition of a conditional expectation. Let (Ξ, Σ, P) be a probability space and suppose that $\mathcal{A}_1, \mathcal{A}_2, \ldots, \mathcal{A}_K$ is a finite partition of the set Ξ. From this partition we form a σ-field $\mathcal{A}$ which is a subfield of Σ. Then the *conditional expectation* of the random variable $Q(\omega)$ on (Ξ, Σ, P) given $\mathcal{A}$ at ω is denoted by $E[Q \mid \mathcal{A}]$ and defined as

$$E[\mathcal{Q} \mid \mathcal{A}] \doteq \frac{1}{P(\mathcal{A}_i)} \int_{\mathcal{A}_i} Q(\boldsymbol{\omega}) dP(\boldsymbol{\omega})$$

for $\boldsymbol{\omega} \in A_i$, assuming that $P(\mathcal{A}_i) > 0$.

Appendix C

Stochastic Processes

We give here a brief introduction to stochastic processes. Such processes do not appear explicitly in financial optimization models, however they are essential tools in asset pricing, and in the scenario generation methods that provide input data for the models. This chapter provides adequate coverage so that readers can follow the developments in the book when references are made to the use of stochastic processes. For additional material see the books by Bhat (1972), or Baxter and Rennie (2000).

A stochastic process is a family of random variables that are indexed by a parameter such as time or space. Modeling real-world phenomena as stochastic processes allows us to understand the behavior of the real-world situation. For example, we may want to study the behavior of a corporate security with respect to its credit rating. A corporate security may be in one of three possible states: it may have a high credit rating H, or be poorly rated P, or may go into default D. Analysis of firms' balance sheets will allow us to estimate the percentage of corporate securities that will remain in state H, or may be downgraded to P, or even go into default. The credit rating of the bond can be considered as a stochastic process which could be at one of the three states H, P, or D. Hence, this process is a discrete process. On the other hand, the number of corporate bonds that go into default is also a stochastic process, which takes a large number of possible values and hence can be modeled for all practical purposes using a stochastic process with a continuous state space.

Consider the random variable $\xi(t)$ indexed by the time parameters $t = 1, 2, \ldots, T$. For a given value of the time parameter t the stochastic process $\xi(t)$ is a simple random variable that takes values over some state space, and its probability distribution can be obtained as for any other random variable. The index of the random variable does not have to be time, and the space over which the index parameter varies does not have to be finite. However, for the financial applications this is usually the case.

For a set of parameters $t = 1, 2, \ldots, T$, the random variables $\xi(t), \xi(2), \ldots, \xi(\tau), \ldots \xi(T)$ will usually exhibit some type of dependence, so that the state of $\xi(\tau)$ may depend on the state of the process during the previous $\tau - 1$ periods. The simplest type of dependence is the first-order dependence known as "Markov dependence." This is formally defined as follows:

Definition C.0.1 Markov dependence. *The dependence exhibited by the process $\xi(t), t = 1, 2, \ldots, T$, is called Markov dependence if the conditional distribution of $\xi(t)$ for given values of $\xi(1), \xi(2), \ldots, \xi(\tau)$ depends only on $\xi(\tau)$ which is the most recent known value of the process.*

The stochastic process exhibiting this property is called a Markov process. For such processes, if the state is known for any specific value of the time parameter t, that information is sufficient to predict the behavior of the process beyond that point.

Depending on the nature of the state space and the parameter space we can classify Markov processes in the four types shown below in tabular form. Whenever the parameter space is discrete the Markov process is called a Markov chain.

Parameter space	State space	
Discrete	Markov chain with discrete state space	Markov chain with continuous state space
Continuous	Markov process with discrete state space	Markov process with discrete state space

We give below examples of some processes that have been referred to in the book.

C.1   The Poisson Process

This is a process with discrete state space and continuous parameter space. It models events that occur under the following postulates:

1. Events occurring in non-overlapping intervals of time are independent of each other.

2. There is a constant λ such that the probabilities of occurrence of events in a small interval of length Δt are given as follows:

   (a) Prob (No. of events occurring in $(t, t + \Delta t] = 0$)= $1 - \lambda\Delta t + o(\Delta t)$,

   (b) Prob (No. of events occurring in $(t, t + \Delta t] = 1$) = $\lambda\Delta t + o(\Delta t)$,

   (c) Prob (No. of events occurring in $(t, t + \Delta t] > 1$)= $o(\Delta t)$,

   where $o(\Delta t)$ is such that $o(\Delta t)/\Delta t \to 0$ as $\Delta t \to 0$.

Under these assumptions the process has the Markov property, and λ is the mean number of events per unit time.

If we let $\xi(t)$ be the number of events occurring in time $(0, t]$ then $\xi(t)$, for all $t = 1, 2, \ldots, T$, is a stochastic process with state space $0, 1, 2, \ldots$ and parameter space $t = 1, 2, \ldots, T$.

It can be shown that for a given t the random variable $\xi(t)$ has the Poisson distribution with mean λt:

$$\text{Prob } (\xi(t) = k) = \exp(-\lambda t)\frac{(\lambda t)^k}{k!}, k = 1, 2, \ldots. \tag{C.1}$$

The process $\xi(t)$, for all $t = 1, 2, \ldots, T$, is therefore called a Poisson process.

The number of telephone calls at a switchboard and the number of defaults of credit-risk assets can be modeled reasonably well as a Poisson process.

C.2   The Gaussian Process

This is a process $\xi(t)$ with continuous state and parameter spaces, and which has the following property: For an arbitrary set of n time points $\tau_1, \tau_2, \ldots, \tau_n$ the joint distribution of $\xi(\tau_k), k = 1, 2, \ldots, n$, is multivariate normal. If, furthermore, for any finite set $\{\tau_k\}, k = 1, 2, \ldots$, the random variables $\xi(\tau_k)$ are mutually independent and $\xi(t)$ is normally distributed for all t, then it is called a purely random Gaussian process.

A Gaussian stochastic process may be used to model the term structure of interest rates or credit spreads, leading to simple and elegant solutions, with the undesirable property, however, that the financial variable so modeled may take negative values.

C.3 The Wiener Process

This is a process $\xi(t)$ – also known as Brownian motion process – with continuous state and parameter spaces, with the following properties:

(i) The process $\xi(t)$, $t \geq 0$ has stationary independent increments. That is, for τ_1, τ_2 in the parameter space and $\tau_1 < \tau_2$, the distribution of $\xi(\tau_2) - \xi(\tau_1)$ is the same as the distribution of $\xi(\tau_2 + h) - \xi(\tau_1 + h)$ for any $h > 0$, and for non-overlapping time intervals (τ_1, τ_2) and (τ_3, τ_4) with $\tau_1 < \tau_2 < \tau_3 < \tau_4$, the random variables $\xi(\tau_2) - \xi(\tau_1)$ and $\xi(\tau_4) - \xi(\tau_3)$ are independent.

(ii) For any given time interval (τ_1, τ_2), $\xi(\tau_2) - \xi(\tau_1)$ is normally distributed with mean zero and variance $\sigma^2(\tau_2 - \tau_1)$.

If the mean of $\xi(\tau_2) - \xi(\tau_1)$ is $\mu(\tau_2 - \tau_1) \neq 0$ then we have a Wiener process with drift μ.

The classic example of a Wiener process is the model of the displacement of particles suspended in a fluid and moving under the successive random impacts of neighboring particles. This physical phenomenon was first observed by the botanist Robert Brown in 1827, and the theory for this phenomenon was developed by Norbert Wiener almost a century later. Wiener processes with drift can be used to model stock market prices.

C.4 Markov Chains

Markov processes with discrete parameter and state spaces are known as Markov chains. They are of particular interest in finance as they can be used to model the migration of corporate bonds among different credit rating categories and into default. We consider a K-state Markov chain $\xi(t)$, for all $t = 1, 2, \ldots T$, that takes values from the finite and discrete state space $\{\xi_0, \xi_1, \ldots \xi_{K-1}\}$. The transition probability matrix is the matrix

$$
P = \begin{pmatrix} P_{00} & P_{01} & \cdots & P_{0,K-1} \\ P_{10} & P_{11} & \cdots & P_{1,K-1} \\ \vdots & \vdots & & \vdots \\ P_{K-1,0} & P_{K-1,1} & \cdots & P_{K-1,K-1} \end{pmatrix}, \tag{C.2}
$$

where each P_{ij} denotes the probability that the stochastic process is at the jth state with value ξ_j at period τ, given that it was at the ith state with value ξ_i at the previous period $\tau - 1$. A state i is called an absorbing state if and only if $P_{ii} = 1$, in which case once the random variable $\xi(t)$ enters the ith state it will stay there. Absorbing states can be used to model default in credit-risk assets, if one assumes that once a corporation defaults it can not possibly return to the market at some later time.

Bibliography

Abken, P. A. and M. M. Shrikhande (Third Quarter, 1997). The role of currency derivatives in internationally diversified portfolios. *Federal Reserve Bank of Atlanta Economic Review*, 34–59.

Ahuja, R. K. and J. B. Orlin (2001). Inverse optimization. *Operations Research 49*, 771–783.

Allen, F. and D. Gale (1994). *Financial innovation and risk sharing*. Cambridge, MA: The MIT Press.

Altman, E. I., D. Cooke, and V. Kishore (1999). Report on defaults and returns on high-yield bonds: analysis through 1998 and default outlook for 1999-2000. In D. Shimko (Ed.), *Credit risk: models and management*, pp. 5–23. London, UK: Risk Books, Financial Engineering Ltd.

Andersson, F., H. Mausser, D. Rosen, and S. Uryasev (2001). Credit risk optimization with conditional Value-at-Risk criterion. *Mathematical Programming, Series B 89*, 273–291.

Artzner, P., F. Delbaen, J.-M. Eber, and D. Heath (1997, November). Thinking coherently. *RISK*, 68–71.

Artzner, P., F. Delbaen, J.-M. Eber, and D. Heath (1999). Coherent measures of risk. *Mathematical Finance 9*, 203–228.

Arvanites, A., J. Gregory, and J. P. Laurent (2001). Building models for credit spreads. *The Journal of Derivatives 6*(3), 27–43.

Asay, M. R., P. J. Bouyoucos, and A. M. Marciano (1993). An economic approach to valuation of single premium deferred annuities. In S. A. Zenios (Ed.), *Financial Optimization*, pp. 100–135. Cambridge, UK: Cambridge University Press.

Aziz, A. (1998a). Algo Academy Notes. Dynamically completed markets: pricing with contingent Arrow-Dubreu securities. *Algo Research Quarterly 1*(2), 59–70.

Aziz, A. (1998b). Algo Academy Notes. Valuation in complete markets: an optimization approach. *Algo Research Quarterly 1*(1), 47–54.

Aziz, A. (1999). Algo Academy Notes. Valuation in complete markets: incorporating state probabilities. *Algo Research Quarterly 2*(4), 49–60.

Aziz, A. (2000). Algo Academy Notes. Valuation in incomplete markets: incorporating state probabilities. *Algo Research Quarterly 3*(1), 75–85.

Babbel, D. F. (Fall 2001). Asset/liability management for insurers in the new era: Focus on value. *The Journal of Risk Finance 3*(1), 9–17.

Babbel, D. F. and C. B. Merrill (1998). Economic valuation models for insurers. *North American Actuarial Journal 2*(3), 1–17.

Babbel, D. F. and K. B. Staking (1991, May). It pays to practice ALM. *Best's Review 92*(1), 1–3.

Babbel, D. F. and S. A. Zenios (1992, July/August). Pitfalls in the analysis of option-adjusted spreads. *Financial Analysts Journal*, 65–69.

Bacinello, A. R. (2001). Fair pricing of life insurance participating policies with a minimum interest rate guaranteed. *Astin Bulletin 31*(2), 275–297.

Balduzzi, P. and A. Lynch (1999). Transaction costs and predictability: Some utility cost calculations. *Journal of Financial Economics 52*, 47–78.

Balduzzi, P. and A. Lynch (2000). Predictability and transaction costs: The impact on rebalancing rules and behavior. *Journal of Finance 55*, 2285–2309.

Bansal, R. (1997). An exploration of the forward premium puzzle in currency markets. *Review of Financial Studies 10*, 369–403.

Barberis, N. (2000). Investing for the long run when returns are predictable. *Journal of Finance 55*, 225–264.

Basel Committee on Banking Supervision (1996a). Overview of the amendment to the capital accord to incorporate market risks. Basel committee publications no. 23, Bank for International Settlement, Basel, Switzerland. http://www. bis. org/.

Basel Committee on Banking Supervision (1996b). Amendment to the capital accord to incorporate market risks. Basel committee publications no. 24, Bank for International Settlement, Basel, Switzerland. http://www. bis. org/. Modified in September 1997.

Basel Committee on Banking Supervision (2001, January). The new Basel capital accord. Consultative document, Bank for International Settlement, Basel, Switzerland.

Baxter, M. and A. Rennie (2000). *Financial calculus: an introduction to derivative pricing.* Cambridge, UK: Cambridge University Press.

Beale, E. M. L. (1955). On minimizing a convex function subject to linear inequalities. *Journal of the Royal Statistical Society 17*, 173–184.

Beltratti, A., A. Consiglio, and S. A. Zenios (1999). Scenario modeling for the management of international bond portfolios. *Annals of Operations Research 85*, 227–247.

Beltratti, A., A. Laurent, and S. A. Zenios (2004). Scenario modeling of selective hedging strategies. *Journal of Economic Dynamics and Control 28*, 955–974.

Benartzi, S. and R. H. Thaler (1995). Myopic loss aversion and the equity premium puzzle. *Quarterly Journal of Economics 110*, 73–92.

Benninga, S. (1989). *Numerical techniques in finance.* Cambridge, MA: The MIT Press.

Berger, A. J. and J. M. Mulvey (1998). The Home Account Advisor™: asset and liability management for individual investors. In W. T. Ziemba and J. M. Mulvey (Eds.), *Worldwide asset and liability modeling*, pp. 634–665. Cambridge, UK: Cambridge University Press.

Berketi, A. K. and A. S. Macdonald (1999). The effect of the nature of the liabilities on the solvency and maturity of a UK life office fund: a stochastic evaluation. *Insurance: Mathematics and Economics 24*, 117–138.

Bernstein, P. L. (1996). *Against the gods: the remarkable story of risk.* New York: John Wiley & Sons.

Bertocchi, M., R. Giacometti, and S. A. Zenios (2005). Risk factor analysis and portfolio immunization in the corporate bond market. *European Journal of Operational Research 161*, 358–363.

Bhat, U. N. (1972). *Elements of applied stochastic processes.* New York: John Wiley & Sons.

Billingsley, P. (1995). *Probability and measure.* New York: John Wiley & Sons.

Birge, J. R. and F. Louveaux (1997). *Introduction to stochastic programming.* Heidelberg: Springer.

Bisschop, J. and R. Entriken (1993). *AIMMS: the modeling system.* Haarlem, The Netherlands: Paragon Decision Technology B. V.

Bisschop, J. and M. Roelofs (1996). *AIMMS: the system reference (version 3).* Haarlem, The Netherlands: Paragon Decision Technology B. V.

Black, F. (1990). Equilibrium exchange rate hedging. *The Journal of Finance 45*, 899–908.

Black, F., E. Derman, and W. Toy (1990, January/February). A one-factor model of interest rates and its application to treasury bond options. *Financial Analysts Journal*, 33–39.

Black, F. and M. J. Scholes (1973). The pricing of options and corporate liabilities. *Journal of Political Economy 81*, 637–654.

Bodie, Z., A. Kane, and A. J. Marcus (1989). *Investments.* Boston: Irwin.

Bodnar, G. M., G. S. Hayt, and R. C. Marston (1998). 1998 Wharton survey of financial risk management by US non-financial firms. *Financial Management 27*(4), 70–91.

Boender, G. C. E. (1997). A hybrid simulation/optimisation scenario model for asset/liability management. *European Journal of Operational Research 99*, 126–135.

Bonett, D. G. and E. Seier (2003). Confidence intervals for mean absolute deviations. *The American Statistician 57*, 233–236.

Bos, R. J. (2000, September). Event study: quantifying the effect of being added to an S&P index. Technical report, Standard & Poor's Quantitative Services, New York.

Boyle, P. P. (1989, May/June). Valuing Canadian mortgage-backed securities. *Financial Analysts Journal*, 55–59.

Boyle, P. P. and M. R. Hardy (1997). Reserving for maturity guarantees: two approaches. *Insurance: Mathematics and Economics 21*, 113–127.

Boyle, P. P. and E. S. Schwartz (1977). Equilibrium prices of guarantees under equity-linked contracts. *The Journal of Risk and Insurance 44*, 639–660.

Bradley, S. P. and D. B. Crane (1972). A dynamic model for bond portfolio management. *Management Science 19*, 139–151.

Bradley, S. P., A. C. Hax, and T. L. Magnanti (1977). *Applied mathematical programming.* Reading, MA: Addison-Wesley.

Breiman, L. (1960). Investment policies for expanding business optimally in a long-run sense. *Naval Research Logistics Quarterly 7*, 647–651.

Breiman, L. (1961). Optimal gambling system for favorable games. In *Proceedings of the 4th Berkeley symposium on mathematics, statistics and probability*, pp. 63–68. Berkeley.

Brémaud, P. (1981). *Point processes and queues – martingale dynamics.* Heidelberg: Springer-Verlag.

Brennan, M. J. (1998). The role of learning in dynamic portfolio decisions. *European Economic Review 1*, 295–306.

Brennan, M. J. and E. S. Schwartz (1976). The pricing of equity-linked life insurance policies with an asset value guarantee. *Journal of Financial Economics 3*, 195–213.

Brennan, M. J. and E. S. Schwartz (1979). Alternative investment strategies for the issuers of equity-linked life insurance policies with an asset value guarantee. *Journal of Business 52*, 63–93.

Brennan, M. J. and E. S. Schwartz (1982). An equilibrium model of bond pricing and a test of the market efficiency. *Journal of Financial and Quantitative Analysis 17*, 301–329.

Brennan, M. J., E. S. Schwartz, and R. Lagnado (1997). Strategic asset allocation. *Journal of Economic Dynamics and Control 21*, 1377–1403.

Broadie, M. (1993). Computing efficient frontiers using estimated parameters. *Annals of Operations Research 45*, 21–58.

Brooke, A., D. Kendrick, and A. Meeraus (1992). *GAMS: a user's guide, release 2. 25*. Danvers, MA: The Scientific Press, Boyd and Fraser Publishing Company.

Bucay, N. and D. Rosen (1999). Credit risk of an interntional bond portfolio: a case study. *Algo Research Quarterly 2*(1), 9–29.

Bunn, D. W. and A. A. Salo (1993). Forecasting with scenarios. *European Journal of Operational Research 68*, 291–303.

Cagan, L. D., N. S. Carriero, and S. A. Zenios (1993, March/April). A computer network approach to pricing mortgage-backed securities. *Financial Analysts Journal*, 55–62.

Cairns, A. J. G. and G. Parker (1997). Stochastic pension fund modelling. *Insurance: Mathematics and Economics 21*, 43–79.

Cariño, D. R., D. H. Myers, and W. T. Ziemba (1998). Concepts, technical issues, and uses of the Russell-Yasuda Kasai financial planning model. *Operations Research 46*, 450–462.

Cariño, D. R. and W. T. Ziemba (1998). Formulation of the Russell-Yasuda Kasai financial planning model. *Operations Research 46*, 433–449.

Censor, Y. and S. A. Zenios (1997). *Parallel optimization: theory, algorithms, and applications*. Series on Numerical Mathematics and Scientific Computation. New York: Oxford University Press.

Chadburn, R. G. (1997). The use of capital, bonus policy and investment policy in the control of solvency for with-profits life insurance companies in the U.K. Technical report, City University, London.

Chopra, V. K. and W. T. Ziemba (1993, Winter). The effects of errors in means, variances, and covariances on optimal portfolio choice. *The Journal of Portfolio Management*, 6–11.

Christensen, P. E., F. J. Fabozzi, and A. LoFaso (1997). Bond immunization: an asset liability optimization strategy. In F. J. Fabozzi (Ed.), *The handbook of fixed income securities*, pp. 925–954. New York: McGraw-Hill.

Consigli, G. and M. A. H. Dempster (1998). The CALM stochastic programming model for dynamic asset and liability management. In W. T. Ziemba and J. M. Mulvey (Eds.), *Worldwide asset and liability modeling*, pp. 464–500. Cambridge, UK: Cambridge University Press.

Consiglio, A., F. Cocco, and S. A. Zenios (2001, Spring). The value of integrative risk management for insurance products with guarantees. *Journal of Risk Finance*, 1–11.

Consiglio, A., F. Cocco, and S. A. Zenios (2004). www. personal_asset_allocation. *Interfaces 34*(4), 287–302.

Consiglio, A., F. Cocco, and S. A. Zenios (2007). Scenario optimization asset and liability modeling for individual investors. *Annals of Operations Research 152*, 167–191.

Consiglio, A., F. Cocco, and S. A. Zenios (forthcoming). The PROMETEIA model for fund management with guarantees. In S. A. Zenios and W. T. Ziemba (Eds.), *Asset and Liability Management, Vol. 2, Applications*, Handbooks in Finance, pp. 663–705. Amsterdam: North-Holland.

Consiglio, A., S. S. Nielsen, and S. A. Zenios (forthcoming). *Practical financial optimization: a library of financial optimization models*. Oxford: Blackwell.

Consiglio, A. and S. A. Zenios (1997). Optimal design of callable bonds using tabu search. *Journal of Economic Dynamics and Control 21*, 1445–1470.

Consiglio, A. and S. A. Zenios (1999). Designing portfolios of financial products via integrated simulation and optimization models. *Operations Research 47*, 195–208.

Consiglio, A. and S. A. Zenios (2001a). Integrated simulation and optimization models for tracking international fixed income indices. *Mathematical Programming, Series B 89*, 311–339.

Consiglio, A. and S. A. Zenios (2001b). Model error in enterprise wide risk management: insurance policies with guarantees. In *Advances in operational risk: firm-wide issues for financial institutions*, pp. 199–216. London: Risk Books, Financial Engineering Ltd.

Consligio, A., D. Saunders, and S. A. Zenios (2003, Summer). Insurance league: Italy vs. UK. *Journal of Risk Finance*, 1–8.

Consligio, A., D. Saunders, and S. A. Zenios (2006). Asset and liability management for insurance products with minimum guarantees: The UK case. *Journal of Banking and Finance 30*, 645–667.

Constantinides, G. M. (1976). Stochastic cash management with fixed and proportional transaction costs. *Management Science 22*, 1320–1331.

Constantinides, G. M. (1979). Multiperiod consumption and investment behavior with convex transaction costs. *Management Science 25*, 1127–1137.

Constantinides, G. M. and A. G. Malliaris (1995). Portfolio theory. In R. Jarrow, M. Maksimovic, and W. T. Ziemba (Eds.), *Finance*, Volume 9 of *Handbooks in operations research and management science*, pp. 1–30. Amsterdam: North Holland.

Correnti, S. (1997, March-May). Integrated risk management for insurance and reinsurance companies—FIRM. *Global Reinsurance*, 81–83.

Crouhy, M., D. Galai, and R. Mark (2001). *Risk management*. New York: McGraw-Hill.

Crum, R. L., D. Klingman, and L. A. Tavis (1979). Implementation of large-scale financial planning methods: Solution efficient transformations. *The Journal of Finance and Quantitative Analysis 1*, 137–152.

Curley, C. and J. Guttentag (1974, Summer). The yield on insured residential mortgages. *Explorations in Economic Research*, 114–161.

Dahl, H. (1993). A flexible approach to interest-rate risk management. In S. A. Zenios (Ed.), *Financial optimization*, pp. 189–209. Cambridge, UK: Cambridge University Press.

Dahl, H., A. Meeraus, and S. A. Zenios (1993). Some financial optimization models: I. risk management. In S. A. Zenios (Ed.), *Financial optimization*, pp. 3–36. Cambridge, UK: Cambridge University Press.

Dantzig, G. B. (1955). Linear programming under uncertainty. *Management Science 1*, 197–206.

David, H. A. (1998). Early sample measures of variability. *Statistical Science 13*, 368–377.

D'Ecclesia, R. and S. A. Zenios (1994, September). Factor analysis and immunization in the Italian bond market. *The Journal of Fixed Income*, 51–58.

D'Ecclesia, R. and S. A. Zenios (2005). Demand for assets by heterogeneous agents. *European Journal of Operational Research 161*, 386–398.

Dembo, R. S. (1991). Scenario optimization. *Annals of Operations Research 30*, 63–80.

Dembo, R. S. (1993). Scenario immunization. In S. A. Zenios (Ed.), *Financial Optimization*, pp. 290–308. Cambridge, UK: Cambridge University Press.

Dembo, R. S., A. R. Aziz, D. Rosen, and M. Zerbs (2000). Mark to future: a framework for measuring risk and reward. Technical report, Algorithmics Inc., Toronto.

Dembo, R. S. and A. Freeman (1998). *Seeing tomorrow: weighing financial risk in everyday life*. New York: John Wiley & Sons.

Dembo, R. S. and A. J. King (1992). Tracking models and the optimal regret distribution in asset allocation. *Applied Stochastic Models and Data Analysis 8*, 151–157.

Dembo, R. S. and H. Mausser (2000). The put/call efficient frontier. *Algo Research Quarterly 31*(1), 13–25.

Dembo, R. S., R. L. Merkoulovitch, and D. Rosen (1998). Images from a portfolio. Research paper series 98–04, Algorithmics Inc., Toronto.

Dembo, R. S., J. M. Mulvey, and S. A. Zenios (1989). Large-scale nonlinear network models and their application. *Operations Research 37*, 353–372.

Dembo, R. S. and D. Rosen (2000). The practice of portfolio replication. *Algo Research Quarterly 3*(2), 11–22.

Dembo, R. S., D. Rosen, and D. Saunders (2000). Valuation in incomplete markets: an optimization approach. *Algo Research Quarterly 3*(2), 29–37.

Derivatives Policy Group (1995, March). Framework for voluntary oversight. Technical report, Derivatives Policy Group:the OTC derivative activities of securities firm affiliates to promote confidence and stability in financial markets, New York.

Derman, E. (2004). *My life as a quant: reflections on physics and finance*. Hoboken, NJ: John Wiley & Sons.

Dert, C. (1995). *Asset liability management for pension funds*. PhD thesis, Erasmus University, Rotterdam, Netherlands.

Doherty, N. A. (2000). *Integrated risk management*. New York: McGraw-Hill.

Duffie, D. and J. Pan (1997). An overview of value at risk. *The Journal of Derivatives 4*(3), 7–49.

Duffie, D. and K. Singleton (1993). Simulated moments estimation of markov models of asset prices. *Econometrica 61*, 929–952.

Duffie, D. and K. J. Singleton (1999). Modeling term structures of defaultable bonds. *Review of Financial Studies 12*, 687–720.

Duffie, D. and K. J. Singleton (2003). *Credit risk: pricing, measurement and management*. Princeton: Princeton University Press.

Dupačová, J. and M. Bertocchi (2001). From data to model and back to data: A bond portfolio management problem. *European Journal of Operational Research 134*, 261–278.

Dupačová, J., M. Bertocchi, and V. Morrigia (1998). Postoptimality of scenario based financial planning models with an application to bond portfolio management. In W. T. Ziemba and J. M. Mulvey (Eds.), *World wide asset and liability management*, pp. 263–285. Cambridge, UK: Cambridge University Press.

Dybvig, P. H. and S. A. Ross (1986). Tax clientele and asset pricing. *The Journal of Finance 41*, 751–771.

Elton, E. and M. Gruber (1991). *Modern portfolio theory and investment analysis* (4th ed.). New York: John Wiley & Sons.

Embrechts, P. (2000). Actuarial versus financial pricing of insurance. *The Journal of Risk Finance 1*(4), 17–26.

Fabozzi, F. J. (Ed.) (1989). *The handbook of mortgage-backed securities*. Chicago: Probus Publishing Company.

Fabozzi, F. J. (Ed.) (1997). *The handbook of fixed income securities* (5th ed.). New York: McGraw-Hill.

Fabozzi, F. J. and L. S. Goodman (Eds.) (2001). *Investing in collaterized debt obligations*. New York: John Wiley & Sons.

Filatov, V. S. and P. Rappoport (1992, July/August). Is complete hedging optimal for international bond portfolios? *Financial Analysts Journal*, 37–47.

Financial Services Authority (2001). A description and classification of with profits policies. http://www. fsa. gov. uk/pubs/other/with_profits. pdf.

Fishwick, E. (1994). High yield currency strategies. *New Zealand Investment Analyst*, 18–22.

Fong, H. G. and O. A. Vasicek (1984). A risk minimizing strategy for portfolio immunization. *The Journal of Finance 39*, 1541–1546.

Fourer, R., D. M. Gay, and B. W. Kernighan (2002). *AMPL: a modeling language for mathematical programming* (2nd ed.). Belmont, CA: Thomson Higher Education.

Gaivoronski, A. and G. Pflug (2005). Value at risk in portfolio optimization: properties and computational approach. *Journal of Risk 7*(2), 1–31.

Garbade, K. (1986). Modes of fluctuation in bond yields — an analysis of principal components. Technical report, Bankers Trust Company, Money Market Center, New York.

Garman, M. (1996). Improving on VaR. *RISK 9*(5), 61–63.

Garman, M. (1997). Taking VaR to pieces. *RISK 10*(10), 70–71.

Giraldi, C., G. Berti, J. Brunello, S. Buttarazzi, G. Cenciarelli, C. Daroda, and G. Stamegna (2000, April). Insurance optional. *RISK*, 87–90.

Glen, J. and P. Jorion (1993). Currency hedging for international portfolios. *Journal of Finance 48*, 1865–1886.

Glover, F. (1986). Future paths for integer programming and links to artificial intelligence. *Computers and Operations Research 13*, 533–549.

Glover, F. and M. Laguna (1997). *Tabu search*. Dordrecht, The Netherlands: Kluwer Academic Publishers.

Goldstein, A. B. and B. G. Markowitz (1982). SOFASIM: a dynamic insurance model with investment structure, policy benefits and taxes. *Journal of Finance 37*, 595–604.

Golub, B., M. Holmer, R. McKendall, I. Pohlman, and S. A. Zenios (1995). Stochastic programming models for money management. *European Journal of Operational Research 85*, 282–296.

Gondzio, J., R. Kouwenberg, and A. C. F. Vorst (2003). Hedging options under transaction costs and stochastic volatility. *Journal of Economic Dynamics and Control 27*, 1045–1068.

Grandville, de La, O. (2001). *Bond pricing and portfolio analysis*. Cambridge, MA: The MIT Press.

Granito, M. R. (1984). *Bond portfolio immunization*. Washington, DC: Lexington Books, Heath and Company.

Green, J. and J. B. Shoven (1986, February). The effects of interest rates on mortgage payments. *Journal of Money, Credit, and Banking*, 41–59.

Green, P. E. and A. M. Krieger (1991). Product design for target-market positioning. *Journal of Product Innovation Management 8*, 189–202.

Green, W. H. (1990). *Econometric Analysis*. New York: MacMillan.

Grinold, R. C. (1977). Finite horizon approximations of infinite horizon linear programs. *Mathematical Programming 12*, 1–17.

Grinold, R. C. (1983). Model building techniques for the correction of end effects in multistage convex programs. *Operations Research 31*(3), 407–431.

Grosen, A. and P. L. Jørgensen (2000). Fair valuation of life insurance liabilities: the impact of interest rate guarantees, surrender options, and bonus policies. *Insurance: Mathematics and Economics 26*, 37–57.

Grubel, H. (1968). Internationally diversified portfolios: welfare gains and capital flows. *American Economic Review 58*, 1299–1314.

Guiso, L., M. Haliassos, and T. Japelli (Eds.) (2002). *Household portfolios*. Cambridge, MA: The MIT Press.

Hakansson, N. H. (1970). Optimal investment and consumption strategies under risk for a class of utility functions. *Econometrica 38*, 587–607.

Hakansson, N. H. (1974). Convergence to isoelastic utility and policy in multiperiod portfolio choice. *Journal of Financial Economics 1*, 201–224.

Hakansson, N. H. and W. T. Ziemba (1995). Capital growth theory. In R. Jarrow, M. Maksimovic, and W. T. Ziemba (Eds.), *Finance*, Volume 9 of *Handbooks in Operations Research and Management Science*, pp. 65–86. Amsterdam: North Holland.

Hamilton, J. D. (1994). *Time series analysis*. Princeton: Princeton University Press.

Hansen, L. and J. Scheinkman (1995). Back to the future: Generating moment implications for continuous-time Markov processes. *Econometrica 63*, 767–804.

Hansen, M. and K. R. Miltersen (2002, September). Minimum rate of return guarantees: The Danish case. *Scandinavian Actuarial Journal 4*, 280–318.

Harker, P. T. and S. A. Zenios (Eds.) (2000). *Performance of financial institutions: efficiency, innovation, regulations*. Cambridge, UK: Cambridge University Press.

Harrison, J. M. and D. M. Kreps (1979). Martingales and arbitrage in multiperiod securities markets. *Journal of Economic Theory 20*, 381–408.

Hauser, J. R. and D. Clausing (1988, May-June). The house of quality. *Harvard Business Review*, 63–73.

Hayre, L. S. (1990, Summer). Understanding option-adjusted spreads and their use. *The Journal of Portfolio Management 16*, 68–71.

Heath, D., R. Jarrow, and A. Morton (1992). Bond pricing and the term structure of interest rates: A new methodology for contingent claim valuation. *Econometrica 60*, 77–105.

Heath, D. C. and P. L. Jackson (1994). Modeling the evolution of demand forecasts with application to safety stock analysis in production/distribution systems. *IIE Transactions 26*(3), 17–30.

Hiller, R. S. and J. Eckstein (1993). Stochastic dedication: Designing fixed income portfolios using massively parallel Benders decomposition. *Management Science 39*, 1422–1438.

Hillier, F. S. and G. J. Lieberman (2001). *Introduction to operations research* (7th ed.). New York: McGraw Hill.

Holmer, M. R. (1994). The asset/liability management system at Fannie Mae. *Interfaces 24*(3), 3–21.

Holmer, M. R. and S. A. Zenios (1995). The productivity of financial intermediation and the technology of financial product management. *Operations Research 43*, 970–982.

Hotelling, H. (1933). Analysis of a complex statistical variable into principal components. *Journal of Educational Psychology 24*, 417–441,489–520.

Høyland, K. (1998). *Asset liability management for a life insurance company: a stochastic programming approach*. PhD thesis, Norwegian University of Science and Technology, Trondheim, Norway.

Høyland, K., M. Kaut, and S. Wallace (2003). A heuristic for moment-matching scenario generation. *Computational Optimization and Applications 24*, 169–185.

Høyland, K. and S. Wallace (2007). Stochastic programming models for strategic and tactical asset allocation–a study from the Norwegian life insurance. In S. A. Zenios and W. T. Ziemba (Eds.), *Asset and Liability Management, Vol. 2, Applications*, Handbooks in Finance, pp. 592–625. Amsterdam: North-Holland.

Høyland, K. and S. W. Wallace (2001). Generating scenario trees for multi-stage problems. *Management Science 47*, 295–307.

Hull, J. (2000). *Options, futures and other derivatives* (4th ed.). Prentice-Hall.

Hull, J. and A. White (1990). Pricing interest rate derivative securities. *Review of Financial Studies 3*, 573–592.

Ingersoll, Jr., J. E. (1987). *Theory of Financial Decision Making*. Studies in Financial Economics. Totowa, NJ: Rowman & Littlefield.

Jacob, D. P., G. Lord, and J. A. Tilley (1987). A generalized framework for pricing contingent cash flows. *Financial Management*, Autumn, 5–14.

Jamshidian, F. and Y. Zhu (1997). Scenario simulation: theory and methodology. *Finance and Stochastics 1*, 43–67.

Jarrow, R. A. (1998, May/June). Current advances in the modeling of credit risk. *Derivatives*, 196–202.

Jarrow, R. A. and S. M. Turnbull (1995). Pricing derivatives and financial securities subject to credit risk. *Journal of Finance 50*, 53–85.

Jensen, M. C. (1969). Risk, the pricing of capital assets and the evaluation of investment portfolios. *Journal of Business 42*, 167–247.

Jobson, J. D. (1992). *Applied multivariate data analysis*, Volume 2, Categorical and multivariate methods. Heidelberg: Springer–Verlag.

Jobson, J. D. and B. Korkie (1981). Putting Markowitz theory to work. *The Journal of Portfolio Management 7*(4), 70–74.

Jobst, A. (2003). Collateralised loan obligations (CLO) - a primer. *The Securitisation Conduit 6*(1–4).

Jobst, N. J., G. Mitra, and S. A. Zenios (2006). Integrating market and credit risk: a simulation and optimisation perspective. *Journal of Banking and Finance 30*, 717–742.

Jobst, N. J. and S. A. Zenios (2001, Fall). The tail that wags the dog: integrating credit risk in asset portfolios. *Journal of Risk Finance*, 31–43.

Jobst, N. J. and S. A. Zenios (2003). Tracking corporate bond indices in an integrated market and credit risk environment. *Quantitative Finance 3*, 117–135.

Jobst, N. J. and S. A. Zenios (2005). On the simulation of interest rate and credit risk sensitive securities. *European Journal of Operational Research 161*, 298–324.

Jørgensen, P. L. (2001, Fall). Life insurance contracts with embedded options: Valuation, risk management and regulation. *Journal of Risk Finance*, 19–30.

Jorion, P. (1989, Summer). Asset allocation with hedged and unhedged foreign stocks and bonds. *The Journal of Portfolio Management*, 49–54.

Jorion, P. (1996). *Value at risk: the new benchmark for controlling market risk*. New York: Irwin Professional Publishing.

JP Morgan (1997). Creditmetrics: the benchmark for understanding credit risk. Technical document, JP Morgan, New York.

Judge, G. G., R. C. Hill, W. E. Griffiths, U. Lütkepohl, and T. C. Lee (1988). *The Theory and Practice of Econometrics*. New York: John Wiley & Sons.

Kaelhofer, S. (1996). *Managing default risk in portfolios of derivatives*. London: Risk Books, Financial Engineering Ltd.

Kagel, J. H. and A. E. Roth (Eds.) (1995). *The handbook of experimental economics*. Princeton: Princeton University Press.

Kahneman, K. and A. Tversky (1979). Prospect theory: an analysis of decision under risk. *Econometrica 47*, 263–291.

Kahneman, K. and A. Tversky (1981). The framing of decisions and the psychology of choice. *Science 211*, 453–458.

Kall, P. (1976). *Stochastic linear programming*. Berlin: Springer Verlag.

Kall, P. and S. W. Wallace (1994). *Stochastic programming*. New York: John Wiley & Sons.

Kallberg, J. G., R. W. White, and W. T. Ziemba (1982). Short-term financial planning under uncertainty. *Management Science 28*, 670–682.

Kallberg, J. G. and W. T. Ziemba (1981). Remarks on optimal portfolio selection. In G. Bamberg and O. Opitz (Eds.), *Methods of operations research*, pp. 507–520. Oelgeschlager, Gunn and Hain.

Kallberg, J. G. and W. T. Ziemba (1984). Mis-specification in portfolio selection problems. In G. Bamberg and K. Spreemann (Eds.), *Risk and capital*, pp. 74–87. Heidelberg: Springer-Verlag.

Kamakura Corporation (1998). *Asset and liability management: a synthesis of new methodologies*. London: Risk Publications, Kamakura Corporation.

Kang, P. and S. A. Zenios (1992). Complete prepayment models for mortgage backed securities. *Management Science 38*, 1665–1685.

Kaplanis, E. and S. M. Schaefer (1991). Exchange risk and international diversification in bond and equity markets. *Journal of Economics and Business 43*, 287–307.

Kat, H. M. (2001). *Structured equity derivatives: the definitive guide to exotic options and structured notes*. New York: John Wiley & Sons.

Keenan, C. (2000). *Historical default rates of corporate bond issuers, 1920–1999*. New York: Moody's Investors Service.

Kelly, Jr., J. L. (1956). A new interpretation of information rate. *Bell Systems Technical Journal 35*, 917–926.

Kendall, L. (1996). *A primer on securitization*. Cambridge, MA: The MIT Press.

Kennickell, A. B. and M. L. Kwast (1997). Who uses electronic banking? Results from the 1995 survey of consumer finances. Working paper, Division of Research and Statistics, Board of the Governors of the Federal Reserve System, Washington, DC.

Kenyon, C. M., S. Savage, and B. Ball (1999). Equivalence of linear deviations about the mean and mean absolute deviation about the mean objective functions. *Operations Research Letters 24*, 181–185.

Kiesel, R., W. Perraudin, and A. Taylor (2001). The structure of credit risk: spread volatility and ratings transitions. Working paper 1368–5562, Bank of England, San Fransisco, CA.

Kijima, M. (2000). A Gaussian term structure model of credit spreads and valuation of credit spread options. Technical report, Tokyo Metropolitan University.

Kijima, M., K. Komoribayashi, and E. Suzuki (2000). A multivariate Markov model for simulating correlated defaults. Technical report, Tokyo Metropolitan University.

Kijima, M. and Y. Muromachi (2000). Evaluation of credit risk of a portfolio with stochastic interest rate and default processes. Technical report, Tokyo Metropolitan University.

Kim, T. S. and E. Omberg (1996). Dynamic nonmyopic portfolio behavior. *Review of Financial Studies 9*, 141–161.

Kingsland, L. (1982). Projecting the financial condition of a pension plan using simulation analysis. *Journal of Finance 37*, 577–584.

Kirkpatrick, S., C. D. Gelatt, and M. P. Vecchi (1983). Optimization by simulated annealing. *Science 220*, 671–680.

Klaassen, P. (1997). Discretized reality and spurious profits in stochastic programming models for asset/liability management. *European Journal of Operational Research 101*, 374–392.

Klaassen, P. (1998). Financial asset-pricing theory and stochastic programming models for asset-liability management: a synthesis. *Management Science 44*, 31–48.

Klaassen, P. (2002). A comment on "Generating scenario trees for multistage problems" by K. Høyland and S. Wallace. *Management Science 48*, 1512–1516.

Konno, H. and H. Yamazaki (1991). Mean absolute deviation portfolio optimization model and its applications to Tokyo stock market. *Management Science 37*, 519–531.

Koskosides, Y. and A. Duarte (1997, Winter). A scenario-based approach for active asset allocation. *The Journal of Portfolio Management*, 74–85.

Kouwenberg, R. (2001). Scenario generation and stochastic programming models for asset liability management. *European Journal of Operational Research 134*, 279–292.

Kouwenberg, R. and S. A. Zenios (2006). Stochastic programming for asset and liabiity management. In S. A. Zenios and W. T. Ziemba (Eds.), *Asset and liability management, Vol. 1, Theory and methodology*, Handbooks in Finance, pp. 253–303. Amsterdam: North-Holland.

Kusy, M. I. and W. T. Ziemba (1986). A bank asset and liability management model. *Operations Research 34*, 356–376.

Lakonishok, J., A. Shleifer, and R. V. Vishny (1992). The structure and performance of the money management industry. *Brookings Papers on Economic Activity*, 339–391.

Lam, J. (1999a). Enterprise-wide risk management: staying ahead of the convergence curve. *Journal of Lending & Credit Risk Management 81*(10), 16–20.

Lam, J. C. (1999b). Integrated risk management. In *Derivative credit risk: Further advances in measurement and management*. London: Risk Books, Financial Engineering Ltd.

Lando, D. (1998). On Cox processes and credit risky securities. *Review of Derivatives Research 2*, 99–120.

Lando, D. (2004). *Credit risk modeling: theory and applications*. Princeton: Princeton University Press.

Leland, H. E. (1999, January/February). Beyond mean-variance: performance measurement in a non-symmetrical world. *Financial Analysts Journal 55*, 27–36.

Lintner, J. (1965). The valuation of risky assets and the selection of risky investments in stock portfolios and capital budgets. *Review of Economics and Statistics 47*, 13–37.

Litterman, R. (1996, December). Hot spots and hedges. *The Journal of Portfolio Management*, 52–75.

Litterman, R. and T. Iben (1991, Spring). Corporate bond valuation and the term structure of credit spreads. *The Journal of Portfolio Management*, 52–64.

Litterman, R., J. Scheinkman, and L. Weiss (1988, September). Common factors affecting bond returns. Technical report, Goldman, Sachs & Co., Financial Strategies Group, New York.

Liu, J. (1999). Portfolio selection in stochastic environments. Working paper, Stanford University, Stanford, CA.

Lo, A. W. (1999, January/February). The three P's of total risk management. *Financial Analysts Journal*, 51–57.

Lore, M. and L. Borodovsky (Eds.) (2000). *The professional's handbook of financial risk management*. Oxford, UK: Buttenworth Heinemann.

Lucas, C. and G. Mitra (1985). CAMPS: preliminary user's guide. Working paper, Department of Mathematics and Statistics, Brunel University, London.

Luenberger, D. G. (1984). *Linear and Nonlinear Programming* (2nd ed.). Reading, Massachusetts: Addison-Wesley.

Luenberger, D. G. (1998). *Investment science*. New York: Oxford University Press.

Macaulay, F. R. (1938). Some theoretical problems suggested by the movement of interest rates, bond yield, and stock prices in the United States since 1856. Technical report, National Bureau of Economic Research, New York.

Maloney, K. M. and J. B. Yawitz (1986, Spring). Interest rate risk, immunization, and duration. *The Journal of Portfolio Management*, 41–48.

Maranas, C. D., I. P. Androulakis, C. A. Floudas, A. J. Berger, and J. M. Mulvey (1997). Solving long-term financial planning problems via global optimization. *Journal of of Economic Dynamics and Control 21*, 1405–1425.

Markowitz, H. M. (1952). Portfolio selection. *Journal of Finance 7*, 77–91.

Markowitz, H. M. (1991a). Individual versus institutional investing. *Financial Services Review 1*, 1–8.

Markowitz, H. M. (1991b). *Portfolio Selection: Efficient Diversification of Investments* (2nd ed.). Oxford: Blackwell.

Markowitz, H. M. and E. van Dijk (2006). Risk-return analysis. In S. A. Zenios and W. T. Ziemba (Eds.), *Asset and Liability Management, Vol. 1, Theory and methodology*, Handbooks in Finance, pp. 139–198. Amsterdam: North-Holland.

Mausser, H. and D. Rosen (1999). Efficient risk/return frontiers for credit risk. *Algo Research Quarterly 2*(4), 35–48.

McLean, L. C., W. T. Ziemba, and G. Blazenko (1992). Growth versus security in dynamic investment analysis. *Management Science 38*, 1562–1585.

Mehra, R. and E. C. Prescott (1985). The equity premium: a puzzle. *Journal of Monetary Economics 15*, 145–162.

Merton, R. C. (1969). Lifetime portfolio selection under uncertainty: the continuous-time case. *Review of Economics and Statistics 51*, 247–257.

Merton, R. C. (1973). Theory of rational option pricing. *Bell Journal of Economics and Management Science 4*, 141–183.

Merton, R. C. (1974). On the pricing of corporate debt: the risk structure of interest rate. *Journal of Finance 2*, 449–470.

Merton, R. C. (1988). On the application of the continuous–time theory of finance to financial intermediation and insurance. Technical report, Geneva Association Lecture, Centre Hec–Isa, France.

Merton, R. C. (1990). *Continuous-time finance*. Cambridge, MA: Blackwell.

Miccolis, J. and S. Shah (2000). Enterprise risk management: An analytic approach. Monograph, Tillinghast–Towers Perrin, New York.

Michaud, R. (1989, January/February). The Markowitz optimization enigma: is 'optimized' optimal? *Financial Analysts Journal*, 31–42.

Michaud, R. O. (1998). *Efficient asset management*. Boston: Harvard Business School Press.

Michaud, R. O., G. L. Bergstrom, R. D. Frashure, and B. K. Wolahan (1996, Fall). Twenty years of international equity investing. *The Journal of Portfolio Management*, 9–22.

Miller, L., E. P. Krawitt, and M. P. Wands (1992). Mortgage-backed securities indexation. In F. J. Fabozzi (Ed.), *The handbook of mortgage backed securities*, pp. 53–76. Chicago: Probus Publishing Company.

Miller, M. H. (1986). Financial innovation: The last twenty years and the next. *Journal of Financial and Quantitative Analysis 21*, 459–471.

Miltersen, K. R. and S. Persson (1999). Pricing rate of return guarantees in a Heath–Jarrow–Morton framework. *Insurance: Mathematics and Economics 25*, 307–325.

Mossavar-Rahmani, S. (1997). Indexing fixed income assets. In F. J. Fabozzi (Ed.), *The handbook of fixed income securities* (5 ed.)., pp. 913–924. New York: McGraw-Hill.

Mossin, J. (1966). Equilibrium in a capital asset market. *Econometrica 34*, 768–783.

Mossin, J. (1968). Optimal multiperiod portfolio policies. *Journal of Business 4*, 215–229.

Mulvey, J. M. (1989). A surplus optimization perspective. *Investment Management Review 3*, 31–39.

Mulvey, J. M. (1993). Incorporating transaction costs in models for asset allocation. In S. A. Zenios (Ed.), *Financial Optimization*, pp. 243–259. Cambridge, UK: Cambridge University Press.

Mulvey, J. M. (1996). Generating scenarios for the Towers Perrin investment system. *Interfaces 26*, 1–15.

Mulvey, J. M., J. Armstrong, and E. Rothberg (Eds.) (1995, June). *TIRM: total integrative risk management*. RISK. (Special supplement).

Mulvey, J. M., G. Gould, and C. Morgan (2000). An asset and liability management system for Towers Perrin–Tillinghast. *Interfaces 30*(1), 96–114.

Mulvey, J. M. and A. E. Thorlacius (1998). The Towers Perrin global capital market scenario generation system. In W. T. Ziemba and J. M. Mulvey (Eds.), *World Wide Asset and Liability Management*, pp. 286–312. Cambridge, UK: Cambridge University Press.

Mulvey, J. M., R. J. Vanderbei, and S. A. Zenios (1995). Robust optimization of large scale systems. *Operations Research 43*, 264–281.

Mulvey, J. M. and H. Vladimirou (1989). Stochastic network optimization models for investment planning. *Annals of Operations Research 20*, 187–217.

Mulvey, J. M. and H. Vladimirou (1992). Stochastic network programming for financial planning problems. *Management Science 38*, 1643–1664.

Mulvey, J. M. and S. A. Zenios (1994a). Capturing the correlations of fixed-income instruments. *Management Science 40*, 1329–1342.

Mulvey, J. M. and S. A. Zenios (1994b, January/February). Diversifying fixed-income portfolios: modeling dynamic effects. *Financial Analysts Journal*, 30–38.

Naik, V. (1995). Finite state securities market models and arbitrage. In *Handbooks in OR&MS*, pp. 31–64. Amsterdam: Elsevier Science.

Nash, S. G. and A. Sofer (1996). *Linear and nonlinear programming.* New York: McGraw-Hill.

Navratil, F. J. (1985). The estimation of mortgage prepayment rates. *Journal of Financial Research 8*(2), 107–117.

Nielsen, S. S. (1997). Importance sampling in lattice pricing models. In R. S. Barr, R. V. Helgason, and J. L. Kennington (Eds.), *Interfaces in computer science and operations research*, pp. 281–296. Norwell, MA: Kluwer Academic Publishers.

Nielsen, S. S. and E. I. Ronn (1997). The valuation of default risk in corporate bonds and interest rate swaps. In P. Boyle, G. Pennacchi, and P. Ritchken (Eds.), *Advances in futures and options research*, Volume 9, pp. 175–196. JAI Press.

Nielsen, S. S. and S. A. Zenios (1996). A stochastic programming model for funding single premium deferred annuities. *Mathematical Programming 75*, 177–200.

Palmquist, J., S. Uryasev, and P. Krokhmal (1999). Portfolio optimization with conditional Value-at-Risk objective and constraints. Research report no. 99-14, Center for Applied Optimization, University of Florida, Gainesville.

Perold, A. F. (1984). Large-scale portfolio optimization. *Management Science 30*, 1143–1160.

Perold, A. F. and E. Schulman (1988, May/June). The free lunch in currency hedging: implications for investment policy and performance standards. *Financial Analysts Journal 44*, 45–50.

Perold, A. F. and W. F. Sharpe (1988, January/February). Dynamic strategies for asset allocation. *Financial Analysts Journal*, 16–27.

Peters, H. F. (1979). *Termination distributios of FHA insured residential mortgages.* PhD thesis, The Wharton School, University of Pennsylvania.

Pflug, G. C. (2000). Some remarks on the Value-at-Risk and the Conditional Value-at-Risk. In S. Uryasev (Ed.), *Probabilistic constrained optimization: methodology and applications*, pp. 272 – 281. Norwell, MA: Kluwer Acacemic Publishers.

Pflug, G. C. and A. Świetanowski (1998). Optimal scenario tree generation for multiperiod financial optimization. Technical report AURORA TR1998-22, Vienna University.

Pierides, Y. (1996, Summer). Legal disputes about complex interest rate derivatives. *The Journal of Portfolio Management*, 114–118.

Pierides, Y. and S. A. Zenios (1998). Measuring the risk of using the wrong model: a new approach. In *Operational Risk and Financial Institutions*, pp. 173–179. London: Financial Engineering Ltd.

Platt, R. B. (Ed.) (1986). *Controlling interest rate risk.* Wiley Professional Series in Banking and Finance. New York: John Wiley & Sons.

Pogue, J. A. (1970). An extension of the Markowitz portfolio selection model to include variable transaction costs, short sales, leverage policies, and taxes. *Journal of Finance 25*, 1005–1028.

Prisman, E. Z. (1986). Valuation of risky assets in arbitrage free economies with frictions. *The Journal of Finance 41*, 545–556.

Prometeia S.r.l. (2001). Household savings outlook. Technical report, Prometeia S. r. l., Bologna, IT.

Reddington, F. M. (1952). Review of the principles of life-office valuations. *Journal of the Institute of Actuaries 78*, 286–340.

Reitano, R. R. (1992, Spring). Non-parallel yield curve shifts and immunization. *The Journal of Portfolio Management*, 36–43.

Richard, S. F. and R. Roll (1989, Spring). Prepayments on fixed-rate mortgage-backed securities. *The Journal of Portfolio Management*, 73–82.

RISK Books (1998). *Operational risk and financial institutions*. London: Financial Engineering Ltd.

RISK Books (2001). *Advances in operational risk: firm-wide issues for financial institutions*. London: Risk Waters Group.

Rochet, J. C. and J. Tirole (1996). Interbank lending and systemic risk. *Journal of Money, Credit and Banking 28*, 733–762.

Rockafellar, R. T. and S. Uryasev (2000). Optimization of conditional Value-at-Risk. *The Journal of Risk 2*(3), 21–41.

Rosen, D. and S. A. Zenios (2006). Enterprise-wide asset and liability management: Issues, institutions, and models. In S. A. Zenios and W. T. Ziemba (Eds.), *Asset and liability management. Vol. 1. Theory and methodology*, Handbooks in Finance, pp. 1–23. Amsterdam: North Holland.

Ross, S. (1976). Risk, return and arbitrage. In I. Friend and J. Bicksler (Eds.), *Risk and return in finance*, pp. 189–218. Cambridge, MA: Balinger.

Ross, S. (1989). Institutional markets, financial marketing and financial innovation. *The Journal of Finance 44*, 541–556.

Roth, A. V. and W. E. Jackson, III (1995). Strategic determinants of service quality and performance: evidence from the banking industry. *Management Science 41*, 1720–1733.

Rudolf, M. and W. T. Ziemba (1998). Intertemporal surplus management. Working paper, University of British Columbia, Vancouver.

Samuelson, P. A. (1971). The "fallacy" of maximizing the geometric mean in long sequences of investing or gambling. *Proceedings of the National Academy of Sciences 68*, 2493–2496.

Samuelson, P. A. (1977). St. Petersburg paradoxes: defanged, dissected, and historically described. *Journal of Economic Literature XV*, 24–55.

Santomero, A. (1997). Commercial bank risk management: an analysis of the process. *Journal of Financial Services Research 12*, 83–115.

Santomero, A. M. and D. F. Babbel (1997). Financial risk management by insurers: an analysis of the process. *The Journal of Risk and Insurance 64*, 231–270.

Saunders, A. (1999). *Credit risk measurement: new approaches to value at risk and other paradigms*. New York: John Wiley & Sons.

Saunders, D. (2001). *Some mathematical problems in the theory of incomplete markets*. PhD thesis, University of Toronto, Toronto.

Schönbucher, P. (2000). *Credit risk modeling and credit derivatives*. PhD thesis, Rheinische Friedrich-Wilhelms-Universität, Bonn.

Schönbucher, P. (2003). *Credit derivatives pricing models: model, pricing and implementation*. Wiley Finance. New York: John Wiley & Sons.

Schönbucher, P. and D. Schubert (2001). Copula-dependent default risk in intensity models. Technical report, Department of Statistics, University of Bonn.

Seix, C. and R. Akhoury (1986, Spring). Bond indexation: The optimal quantitative approach. *The Journal of Portfolio Management*, 50–53.

Sharpe, W. F. (1963). A simplified model for portfolio selection. *Management Science 9*, 277–293.

Sharpe, W. F. (1964). Capital asset prices: a theory of market equilibrium under conditions of risk. *Journal of Finance 19*, 425–442.

Sharpe, W. F. (1966). Mutual fund performance. *Journal of Business 39*, 119–138.

Sharpe, W. F. (1975, Winter). Adjusting for risk in portfolio performance measurement. *The Journal of Portfolio Management*, 29–34.

Sharpe, W. F. (1994, Fall). The Sharpe ratio. *The Journal of Portfolio Management*, 49–58.

Sharpe, W. F., G. J. Alexander, and J. V. Bailey (1998). *Investments* (6th ed.). Englewood Cliffs, NJ: Prentice-Hall.

Sharpe, W. F. and L. G. Tint (1990, Winter). Liabilities—a new approach. *The Journal of Portfolio Management*, 5–10.

Shelley, M., M. Arnold, and P. D. Needleman (2002). A review of policyholders' reasonable expectations. Presented to the Institute of Actuaries, February 25, 2002. http://www. actuaries. org. uk/sessional/sm0202_report. html.

Shtilman, M. S. and S. A. Zenios (1993). Constructing optimal samples from a binomial lattice. *Journal of Information and Optimization Sciences 14*, 1–23.

Siglienti, S. (2000). Consequences of the reduction of interest rates on insurance. *The Geneva Papers on Risk and Insurance 25*(1), 63–77.

Sims, C. A. (1980). Macroeconomics and reality. *Econometrica 48*, 1–48.

Smith, A. (2000). Investment strategy and valuation of with-profits products. Available at http://www. actuaries. org. uk/library/proceedings/investment/2000conf/ASmith2. pdf.

Solnik, B. (1996). *International investments* (3rd ed.). Boston: Addison-Wesley.

Solnik, B., C. Bourcelle, and Y. L. Fur (1996, September/October). The free lunch in currency hedging: implications for investment policy and performance standards. *Financial Analysts Journal*, 17–34.

Speranza, M. G. (1993). Linear programming models for portfolio optimization. *Finance 14*, 107–123.

Stulz, R. (1996). Rethinking risk management. *Journal of Applied Corporate Finance 9*, 8–24.

Stulz, R. (2003). *Risk management and derivatives*. Cincinnati: Southwestern College Publishing.

Stulz, R. and R. Apostolik (Eds.) (2004). *Readings for the financial risk manager*. New York: John Wiley & Sons.

Sykes, D. (1989, April). Valuing debt securities under uncertainty: The option adjusted spread model. Mortgage products special report, Bear Stearns, New York.

Tillinghast–Towers Perrin (2001). September 11, 2001: implications for the insurance industry. Working paper, Tillinghast–Towers Perrin, New York.

Topaloglou, N., H. Vladimirou, and S. A. Zenios (2002). CVaR models with selective hedging for international asset allocation. *Journal of Banking and Finance 26*, 1535–1561.

Topaloglou, N., H. Vladimirou, and S. A. Zenios (2004). Risk management for international investment portfolios using forward contracts and options. Working paper, HERMES European Center of Excellence on Computational Finance and Economics, School of Economics and Management, University of Cyprus, Nicosia.

Tufano, P. (1989). Financial innovation and firstmover advantages. *Journal of Financial Economics 25*, 213–240.

Uryasev, S. (2000a, February). Conditional Value-at-Risk: optimization algorithms and applications. *Financial Engineering News 14*.

Uryasev, S. (2000b). Introduction to the theory of probabilistic functions and percentiles (Value-at-Risk). Research report no. 2000-7, Center for Applied Optimization, University of Florida, Gainesville.

Vanderhoof, I. T. and E. I. Altman (Eds.) (1998). *The fair value of insurance liabilities.* Norwell, MA: Kluwer Academic Publishers.

Vassiadou-Zeniou, C. and S. A. Zenios (1996). Robust optimization models for managing callable bond portfolios. *European Journal of Operational Research 91*, 264–273.

von Neumann, J. and O. Morgenstern (1953). *Theory of games and economic behavior.* Princeton: Princeton University Press.

Wets, R. J. B. (1974). Stochastic programs with fixed resources: the equivalent deterministic problem. *SIAM Review 16*, 309–339.

Wets, R. J. B. (1989). Stochastic programming. In G. L. Nemhauser, A. H. G. Rinnooy Kan, and M. J. Todd (Eds.), *Handbooks in Operations Research and Management Science*, Volume 1, pp. 573–629. Amsterdam: North-Holland.

Wilkie, A. D. (1995). More on a stochastic model for actuarial use. *British Actuarial Journal 1*, 777–964.

Williams, J. (1936). Speculation and carryover. *Quarterly Journal of Economics 50*, 436–455.

Wilson, T. (1997a). Portfolio credit risk I. *RISK 10*(9), 111–117.

Wilson, T. (1997b). Portfolio credit risk II. *RISK 10*(10), 56–61.

Wind, Y. (1987). Financial services: increasing your marketing productivity and profitability. *The Journal of Services Marketing 1*, 5–18.

Winklevoss, H. E. (1982). PLASM: pension liability and asset simulation model. *Journal of Finance 37*, 585–594.

Worzel, K. J., C. Vassiadou-Zeniou, and S. A. Zenios (1994, March-April). Integrated simulation and optimization models for tracking fixed-income indices. *Operations Research 42*, 223–233.

Xia, Y. (2000). Learning about predictability: the effects of parameter uncertainty on dynamic asset allocation. *Journal of Finance 56*, 585–594.

Zenios, S. A. (1991). Massively parallel computations for financial modeling under uncertainty. In J. Mesirov (Ed.), *Very large scale computing in the 21-st century*, pp. 273–294. Philadelphia: Society for Industrial and Applied Mathematics.

Zenios, S. A. (Ed.) (1993a). *Financial optimization.* Cambridge, UK: Cambridge University Press.

Zenios, S. A. (1993b). A model for portfolio management with mortgage-backed securities. *Annals of Operations Research 43*, 337–356.

Zenios, S. A. (1993c). Parallel Monte Carlo simulation of mortgage backed securities. In S. A. Zenios (Ed.), *Financial optimization*, pp. 325–343. Cambridge, UK: Cambridge University Press.

Zenios, S. A. (1995). Asset/liability management under uncertainty for fixed-income securities. *Annals of Operations Research 59*, 77–98. (Reprinted in *World wide asset and liability modeling*, W. T. Ziemba and J. M. Mulvey (eds.), Cambridge, UK, Cambridge University Press, 1998.).

Zenios, S. A. and P. Kang (1993). Mean-absolute deviation portfolio optimization for mortgage backed securities. *Annals of Operations Research 45*, 433–450.

Zenios, S. A. and W. T. Ziemba (1992). Theme issue on financial modeling. *Management Science 38*.

Zenios, S. A. and W. T. Ziemba (Eds.) (2006). *Asset and liability management. Vol. 1, Theory and methodology*. Handbooks in Finance. Amsterdam: North-Holland.

Zenios, S. A. and W. T. Ziemba (Eds.) (forthcoming). *Asset and liability management. Vol. 2, Applications*. Handbooks in Finance. Amsterdam: North-Holland.

Ziemba, W. T. (2005). The symmetric downside-risk Sharpe ratio. *The Journal of Portfolio Management*, 108–122.

Ziemba, W. T. and J. M. Mulvey (Eds.) (1998). *Worldwide asset and liability modeling*. Cambridge, UK: Cambridge University Press.

Ziemba, W. T. and R. G. Vickson (Eds.) (1975). *Stochastic optimization models in finance*. Academic Press.

Ziobrowski, B. J. and A. J. Ziobrowski (1995). Exchange rate risk and internationally diversified portfolios. *Journal of International Money and Finance 14*, 65–81.

Zipkin, P. (1989). The structure of structured bond portfolios. Technical report, Columbia University, Graduate School of Business, New York.

Index

Bold-faced page numbers indicate definitions.

Printed and bound by CPI Group (UK) Ltd, Croydon, CR0 4YY

16/04/2025